PENNSYLVANIA COLLEGE OF TECHNOLOGY LIBR

5 0608 01054960 7

D0161658

most current ed.
GH
9/2012

Prime-Time Religion

An Encyclopedia of Religious Broadcasting

by
J. Gordon Melton
Phillip Charles Lucas
Jon R. Stone

ORYX PRESS
1997

LIBRARY

Pennsylvania College
of Technology

One College Avenue
Williamsport, PA 17701-5799

SEP 0 1 1998

*The rare Arabian oryx is believed to have inspired the myth of the unicorn. This desert
antelope became virtually extinct in the early 1960s. At that time several groups of
international conservationists arranged to have 9 animals sent to the Phoenix Zoo
to be the nucleus of a captive breeding herd. Today the oryx population
is over 1,000 and over 500 have been returned to the Middle East.*

© 1997 by Oryx Press
4041 North Central at Indian School Road
Phoenix, Arizona 85012-3397

All rights reserved. No part of this publication may be reproduced or transmitted
in any form or by any means, electronic or mechanical, including
photocopying, recording, or by any information storage and
retrieval system, without permission in writing
from The Oryx Press.

Published simultaneously in Canada
Printed and bound in the United States of America

∞ The paper used in this publication meets the minimum requirements of
the American National Standard for Information Sciences—Permanence
of Paper for Printed Library Materials, ANSI Z39.48-1984.

Library of Congress Cataloging-in-Publication Data

Melton, J. Gordon
    Prime-time religion : an encyclopedia of religious broadcasting /
by J. Gordon Melton, Phillip Charles Lucas, Jon R. Stone.
        p. cm.
    Includes bibliographical references and index.
    ISBN 0-89774-902-2
    1. Religious broadcasting—Christianity—Encyclopedias.
2. Religious broadcasting—Islam—Encyclopedias.   3. Religious
broadcasting—Encyclopedias.   I. Lucas, Phillip Charles.
II. Stone, Jon R., 1959–   . III. Title.
    BV656.M45   1996
    269'.26'03—dc21   96-39495
                                                          CIP

To the brothers Stone and Lucas:

Richard L. Stone and David E. Stone;

Kevin Lucas, David Lucas, John Lucas,
Daniel Lucas, Michael Lucas, and Tim Lucas

Contents

Preface

Prime-Time Religion: An Encyclopedia of Religious Broadcasting is an authoritative guide to the fascinating world of religious radio and television. The encyclopedia's 396 entries detail the origins of religious broadcasting in America: the pioneer preachers, the most successful programs and personalities, and the many broadcasting companies, organizations, and ministries that have used electronic media to promote their religious worldviews. *Prime-Time Religion* also highlights missionary television and radio production and distribution outside the United States, and profiles a cross section of programs, stations, and personalities of foreign origin.

Unlike many fields of endeavor, religious broadcasting's origin can be precisely pinpointed to January 2, 1921, and this encyclopedia covers the entire period of its existence—from 1921 to the present. While evangelical Christians have, as a group, dominated the airwaves, they are by no means the only religious believers to have promoted their message over radio and television. This encyclopedia includes entries, therefore, that cover mainline Christian broadcasters and non-Christian personalities such as the African American Muslim leader W. Deen Muhammad, and Rosicrucian imperator H. Spencer Lewis. Also not forgotten are the important contributions of women broadcasters (e.g., Terry Cole-Whittaker, Elizabeth Clare Prophet, Marilyn Hickey, Alma White, Augusta Stetson, Rexella Van Impe, Beverly LaHaye, Kathryn Kuhlman, and Aimee Semple McPherson) and African

American ministers (e.g., John Washington Goodgame, Lightfoot Solomon Michaux, T. D. Jakes, and Frederick Price).

The number of people who have developed broadcast ministries is staggering and grows daily. In addition, while programs such as *The 700 Club* and personalities such as Oral Roberts and Jerry Falwell are now well known, other shows and people that were equally famous in their time have been forgotten over the years. Few today remember such important national radio stars as Methodist minister "Fighting Bob" Shuler (1920s), Catholic radical Charles Coughlin (1930s), or holiness preacher Lightfoot Solomon Michaux (1940s and 1950s). Given these facts, it became important early in the compilation of this volume to devise some criteria for inclusion. We decided to limit entries to programs, persons, and organizations that fit one or more of the following categories: (1) personalities of historical importance (the pioneers), (2) shows and ministries that have had more than local impact (national and international shows), (3) ministries that are exemplary of some important facet or dimension of religious broadcasting ministries, or (4) shows and ministries that have had success over a period of years (long-standing broadcasts). We also included major international and foreign-based personalities and ministries, particularly those in English-speaking countries with long-standing ties to the United States. The entries on Islamic religious broadcasting are included because Islam is one of the three Abrahamic religious traditions—Judaism and Christianity are the other two—and is growing by leaps and bounds in the United States. Islam, like Christianity, is highly missionary-minded and thus motivated to explore the potential of radio and television to spread its message. Hindus and Buddhists have shown very little interest in using radio or television to promote their religions.

Each entry attempts to present the pertinent facts in a succinct fashion concerning the person, show, or organization under discussion. Entries listed under a particular person sometimes include substantive information describing their shows, and entries listed under a program sometimes include biographical information concerning the show's founder or host. In general, however, entries on personalities concentrate on biographical details while entries on particular shows focus on information concerning the show's history, range of distribution, and format. Following each entry is a list of source materials for those interested in pursuing further reading and research on the topic.

Prime-Time Religion was compiled from a broad survey of the available primary and secondary sources on religious broadcasting. This includes the extensive files originally collected by the Institute for the Study of American Religion in Evanston, Illinois. In 1985, these files were moved and became the American Religions Collection housed at the Davidson Library of the University of California at Santa Barbara. The collection contains a wide variety of books, periodicals, and ephemera from the various broadcast ministries and is open daily for use by scholars and researchers. The current work also benefits from the files of the Trinity Foundation in Dallas, Texas, as well as a wide array of source materials collected independently by the authors. Photographs were generously supplied courtesy of the National Religious Broadcasters, the Billy Graham Center Museum, Fuller Theological Seminary, Gary Monroe, and the individual ministries indicated. Unfortunately, we were not able to get photographs of all the individuals profiled in the text.

There are eight appendices, the first three of which list the founders, presiding chairmen, and hall of fame inductees of the National Religious Broadcasters. The fourth and fifth appendices describe, respectively, the Blease Amendment to the Dill Radio Control Bill of 1926 and "sustaining time," the free airtime allotted to religious broadcasters by commercial radio and television networks. The sixth appendix lists Christian colleges and universities with broadcasting programs of study. The seventh is a timeline of selected historic highlights in the history of religious broadcasting up to the present time with an emphasis on "firsts." The eighth is a select bibliography of sources and works for further research, which is not intended to be an exhaustive list, but rather an overview of the scope and diversity of these programs across the United States.

We considered a ninth appendix that would have shown the distribution of programs and ministries by denomination or faith tradition. However, we quickly realized that such a listing would be impracticable and misleading. While some denominations do support specific programs as indicated in the index and specific entries, the majority of broadcast ministries are independent operations that have no denominational or sectarian affiliation. Most are run by independent, entrepreneurial broadcasters who have changed their denominational affiliation a number of times during their lives. The denominations that are most represented in this work, however, are Baptist (including Southern, Northern, American, and various independents), Pentecostal, Roman Catholic, Presbyterian, Lutheran, and Methodist, all of which have been at the forefront of religious broadcasting. To a great extent, this is because churches with large memberships have substantial resources to commit to electronic avenues of evangelization.

This encyclopedia is, of course, a first effort. Experience in compiling reference works has taught us that the initial explorations of a territory will necessarily overlook some topics and facts of interest that should have been included. The authors would appreciate readers bringing such oversights to their attention. Moreover, although the authors have made every effort to find and verify relevant information for each entry, occasionally such information, e.g., birth dates and places, was either unattainable or unverifiable. The authors would welcome readers' assistance in filling in these blanks and in correcting any factual errors that may inadvertently have been included in an entry. All such correspondence should be addressed to Phillip Lucas, Department of Religious Studies, Stetson University, Box 8350, DeLand, Florida, 32720.

ACKNOWLEDGMENTS

This encyclopedia could not have been completed without the kind assistance of numerous organizations and persons. In particular, we wish to thank the National Religious Broadcasters, who graciously allowed us to reproduce some of their archival photos and who were consistently helpful in finding other information. We also wish to thank the staff of the Trinity Foundation for sending us archival material on a number of broadcasting ministries. The Institute for the Study of American Religion provided us with files from their extensive collection, and the librarians at Vanderbilt University, the University of North Carolina at Chapel Hill, Biola University, the Billy Graham Center Archives at Wheaton College, Stetson University, and the University of California at Santa Barbara provided us with valuable assistance.

We also wish to thank the following people for their assistance and support: Garth Weber, Leslie Crenna, and Anne Thompson at the Oryx Press; Curtis and Lois Stone for their inspiration and encouragement; Ben Haden for his invaluable assistance and generous spirit; Clyde Narramore and his staff; Frederick Price and his staff at *Ever Increasing Faith*; Dennis Finnian; Eugene Lubot, Gary Maris, and the Professional Development Committee at Stetson University; Murray Steinman of Church Universal and Triumphant; Clyde Fant; Ruth Helen Blighton; Hank Hanegraaff; Paul Finkenbinder and his staff; Michael Guido and his staff; Joseph Jeter of *Have Christ, Will Travel*; David Breese and his staff; David Benson of *Russia for Christ*; Mark Boorman of Encounter Ministries; Ted Slutz; photographer Gary Monroe; Donna Webb of *Faith for Today*; and the staffs of Reinhard Bonnke Ministries, Joyce Meyer Ministries, Hal Lindsey Ministries, Lamb & Lion Ministries, Benny Hinn Ministries, Ligonier Ministries, Take Heed Ministries, Living Way Ministries, John Ankerberg, Bill Bright, David Hocking, *Bible Study Hour,* Far East Broadcasting Company, *Grace to You, It Is Written,* Cottonwood Christian Center, *Focus on the Family, Insight for Living,* Key Communications, International Lutheran Laymen's League, Jews for Jesus, Jewish Voice Broadcasts, Hineni, Institute for Creation Research, Roloff Evangelistic Enterprises, *Jack Van Impe Presents!, Voice of Prophecy,* and many more individuals too numerous to name. We owe our greatest debt and deepest affections to Irene Timme.

Introduction

J. Gordon Melton

Anyone who studies contemporary American religion must sooner or later deal with the reality and power of religious broadcasting. Most of my colleagues in religious studies have been slowly and reluctantly forced to consider it, if for no other reason than its obvious presence on the political landscape. For a long time scholars felt justified in ignoring religious broadcasting because of what they perceived to be a naive and anti-intellectual message. The growing number, quality, and influence of these programs, however, have forced scholars to put aside these personal biases and come to grips with a truly amazing American and international phenomenon.

Having grown up in a liberal Protestant denomination and having attended many church gatherings, I also heard numerous denunciations of "those radio preachers," who reportedly diverted financial resources away from vital congregational ministries. Religious radio merely entertained, it was charged, without delivering the pastoral assistance that listeners really needed.

During the years I served a parish, my experience proved quite the opposite. The parishioners who listened to or watched religious programs were among the most active congregational members, generously supporting the church with both their time and financial resources. They just happened to be among the people who wanted to fill some of their leisure hours with spiritual matters rather than the common fare of music radio or prime-time entertainment. My ministerial colleagues, serving in a denomination on a downward membership spiral, were searching, or so it seemed, for anyone to blame for shrinking congregations and decreased giving.

By attempting to marginalize religious broadcasting—and thus dismissing it—or by defining it as competition rather than supplement, we were simply blind to what was happening around us. Rather than grasping the potential of television, we concentrated on the pain created by religious broadcasting's challenge to previously dominant religious patterns that were fast becoming obsolete.

Then, in the late 1980s, two major scandals forced those who had ignored the steady expansion of religious broadcasting and its growing political clout to confront the world of television ministries. Suddenly, Jim and Tammy Faye Bakker and Jimmy Swaggart, already superstars in the Pentecostal world, became as recognizable as the president of the United States, and the news media turned its attention to analyzing the world of religious broadcasting. Secular news reporters allowed wish-fulfillment to replace in-depth analysis and predicted the end of televised religion. They were wrong. Religious broadcasting merely paused a second, took a deep breath, then kept right on expanding.

Given the size and impact of religious broadcasting—certainly as important as, for example, the development of the camp meetings in the nineteenth century or the rise of specialized urban ministries in this century—documentation on the topic is relatively scarce and systematic studies few. *Prime-Time Religion: An Encyclopedia of Religious Broadcasting* attempts to fill this information vacuum by providing the first comprehensive scholarly coverage of this important sector of religious endeavor—its origins, the key personalities whose entrepreneurial spirit made it happen, and the programs and organizations it has developed over the past 75 years.

BEGINNINGS IN RADIO

Religious radio programming is as old as radio itself. The first religious broadcast occurred on the two-month-old Westinghouse station, KDKA, in Pittsburgh, Pennsylvania. The station, the first to receive a commercial operating license, went on the air just in time to cover the November 1920 presidential election. Shortly thereafter, the fledgling station informally arranged to air the evening vespers service of the local Calvary Episcopal Church. The senior pastor, believing that radio was merely a passing fad, assigned his associate pastor, Lewis B. Whittemore, the task of leading the service.[1] On January 2, 1921, the service was broadcast, and it was a hit. The response was so favorable that the broadcast soon turned into a weekly program. Others saw and learned, and religious broadcasting quickly caught on around the country.

Ministers throughout the nation followed the lead of Whittemore and KDKA. In 1922, pastor and evangelist Paul Rader accepted an invitation to speak over a make-shift station in Chicago. The experience was so positive that Rader asked to use various Chicago stations for religious programming during the hours they were not regularly broadcasting. Radio station WBBM gave him 14 hours over a string of successive Sundays. In 1925, Rader initiated a daily show, *The Breakfast Brigade*, over station WHT. He then moved to acquire his own station, WJBT. Within a short time, other churches followed Rader's lead and acquired their own stations. The Moody Bible Institute launched its

station, WMBI, in 1925. By 1927, some 50 religious stations were on the air.

For the first five years after its birth, the world of radio, including religious radio, was chaotic; anyone could enter the fray. Evangelical Christians, who took the lead in exploiting the new medium, were by no means the only ones participating. In Kansas City, for example, the Unity School of Christianity, a New Thought organization, began broadcasting in 1922 over WOQ, the oldest of the licensed stations in the Midwest. Two years later, Unity bought the station, and it emerged as the focus of an expansive radio ministry. In September 1927, H. Spencer Lewis erected radio station WJBB in Tampa, Florida, as a teaching outreach of the esoteric Rosicrucian order he headed.

This first phase of radio broadcasting came to an end in 1927, however, when the newly established Federal Radio Commission (FRC) issued new regulations for licensed radio stations. The new regulations had the immediate effect of closing down many radio stations, including more than half of the religious ones. In time, however, the regulations created a second phenomenon. With the spread of radio, different ministers went beyond the mere acceptance of free time offered by stations and began buying time—a practice that would forever change religious broadcasting.

MATURATION

The marriage of religion and radio occurred in the midst of an acrimonious period of rising tensions between fundamentalists and modernists in most of the large Protestant denominations. The battle between the emerging modernist project of interfaith accommodation, a greater focus on society at large, and a liberal interpretation of biblical doctrine, and the separatism and biblical literalism of fundamentalists was to be largely fought over the airwaves.

By the end of the 1920s, a new wave of liberal Protestants was firmly in control of the American Baptist, Methodist Episcopal, Con-

---

[1] Some historical figures, stations and programs mentioned in the introduction do not have their own entries due to the incomplete nature of the information available.

gregational, and Presbyterian churches as well as the Federal Council of Churches. These mainline denominations wanted to control religious broadcasts and keep out independent fundamentalists and radicals such as Charles Coughlin, whose views they scorned. When the FRC was changed to the Federal Communications Commission (FCC) by the Communications Act of 1934, the newly formed FCC and the leadership of mainline religious denominations urged the NBC and CBS radio networks—established in 1926 and 1927, respectively—to adopt a policy of refusing to sell airtime to religious groups. Accordingly, the networks allocated "sustaining time" to religious groups at no cost, but limited its allotment to representatives of mainline Protestant, Catholic, and Jewish organizations. (See Appendix E: Sustaining Time.)

Although this policy served to shut out the voices of Fundamentalism from the national airwaves, individual preachers and musicians (overwhelmingly conservative in perspective) were still able to purchase time on numerous independent stations. By the late 1930s, they could also purchase airtime from the Mutual Broadcasting System. At the beginning of the 1940s, Mutual was receiving 25 percent of its income from religious broadcast ministries.

Charles Fuller, possibly the most successful of the early pioneers of religious broadcasting, led the way for evangelical Christians. He signed his original contract with Mutual in 1937 to air the *Old Fashioned Revival Hour* on 14 stations. That well-produced and appealing broadcast steadily grew in popularity, and the number of stations carrying it finally peaked at 456 in 1942. However, Fuller's success and the presence of religious broadcasts of lesser quality raised the concerns of mainline denominations, who found a public advocate in the Institute of Education by Radio (IER), a respected panel of academic experts. Although the IER had no statutory authority, its recommendations held considerable weight with the Federal Council of Churches and the big radio networks. In 1941, the IER formed a committee to study religious broadcasting and make recommenda-

tions for its further regulation. The committee came out in opposition to selling time to religious organizations, a policy recommendation that had its greatest impact on Mutual.

Fuller immediately saw the future implications of the committee's recommendation. Over the next two years, while Mutual deliberated on how best to implement the new policies, Fuller shifted his programming from Mutual's stations to independents. At the same time, the perceived attack on Fuller mobilized evangelical leaders. This tumultuous state of affairs became a crucial factor in the organization of the National Association of Evangelicals (NAE), which, after its formation, began receiving a percentage of the sustaining time allotted to religious organizations. The NAE organized the National Religious Broadcasters (NRB) as its electronic media arm in 1944. (See Appendices A, B, and C.) Over the next several decades, most religious broadcasting would shift to those independent radio stations that ignored the IER's policy suggestions.

TELEVISION

The establishment of the NAE came none too soon. The new National Council of Churches of Christ in the USA (NCC), which superseded the Federal Council of Churches, was established in 1950. The NCC recognized that television was about to make a cultural impact analogous to that made by radio in the 1920s. As one of its first actions, the council formally requested that the major networks refuse to sell television time to religious groups. Moreover, they encouraged the networks to accept the guidance of the council's own Broadcast and Film Commission in arranging any religious programming. The NCC, like the Federal Council of Churches before it, wanted to limit television access to those groups or individual preachers approved of by its member denominations. This attempt at religious censorship by the nation's mainline denominations would ultimately fail, however, because of commercial television's increasing appetite for programming revenues.

Even though network religious telecasts would be extremely limited over the next 20 years, the 1950s proved to be an era of religious television pioneering. A young preacher from an old evangelistic family, Rex Humbard, led the way. Having settled in Akron, Ohio, he began to televise the church services of his Calvary Temple in 1953 on an independent television station there. When a new church sanctuary was built in 1956, it included the first church-based television facilities for what would become one of the longest running religious television shows in history. In 1954, Humbard's colleague, Oral Roberts, entered the television fray. Roberts filmed his healing crusades and divided his weekly show between his forceful preaching and scenes of people reportedly being healed as a result of his prayers during the tent meetings. The famed evangelist broadcast his program on nationally syndicated television but was denied network time because of the controversial nature of his healing ministry.

As Humbard and Roberts were beginning their long-standing television presence in the early 1950s, their work was being overshadowed by the work of a Roman Catholic bishop. Since 1930, Fulton J. Sheen had been heard on *The Catholic Hour*, the national radio outreach of the Roman Catholic Church. He left his radio audience of over 4 million in 1950 to become the auxiliary bishop of New York and director of the Society for the Propagation of the Faith, the church's evangelistic arm. In 1952, he went on television with *Life Is Worth Living*. This show, which would run for six years, was noteworthy for its attraction of both Catholic and Protestant listeners who were drawn to Sheen's effective oratorical style and nonsectarian message.

The decade's other major pioneering television ministry began in 1957 with the first airing of the Billy Graham Crusade. These broadcasts aired live in prime time, showcased the evangelical community's leading light, and always attracted a large audience. Forty years later, Graham's crusades still command a large prime-time audience.

During the 1960s, religious television expanded in a manner similar to the expansion of religious radio in the 1930s. In 1959, the first Christian television station, WYAH in Portsmouth, Virginia, was purchased by a young minister-to-be, Pat Robertson. He was ordained in 1961, and in October of that year the first broadcast of the Christian Broadcasting Network (CBN)—then little more than Robertson's dream—was made. The station grew slowly and gained a significant audience only after Jim and Tammy Faye Bakker came to work at the station in 1965, and after Robertson launched a talk show, *The 700 Club*, in 1966. When other stations began to establish affiliations with CBN, it emerged as a genuine network. By the beginning of the 1980s, CBN had taken off nationally.

Through the 1970s and early 1980s, while the number of stations multiplied and cable television appeared in community after community, religious television grew steadily and enjoyed a period largely free of significant criticism. Most critics who said anything about religious programming limited their comments to one word, "boring." Talking heads speaking a message these critics did not wish to hear seemed a morass of bad television. In this atmosphere of critical indifference, evangelical leaders strategized about their next move. As religious programming gradually increased its paid airtime, its variety and quality steadily improved. Not only did two additional networks develop—the Trinity Broadcasting Network and LeSea Broadcasting—but weekend religious programming flourished on independent stations.

Religious broadcasters also began to address the fact that a good portion of their audience was composed of persons with disabilities. By the 1980s, many religious television programs were being close captioned for the hearing impaired and radio adapted for the visually impaired. Moreover, a number of programs appeared in syndication that were specifically designed for handicapped listeners. Among the best known of these shows were *Worship for Shut-Ins*, produced by the Lutheran Media Ministry, Fort Wayne, Indiana; *Bible Study for the*

Libya's Voice of Islam, have emerged, however. The former station is devoted solely to the teaching and recitation of the Qur'an and the latter to the propagation of the Islamic message in Africa.

Although Christians continue to dominate the religious airwaves, both Jews and Muslims have made increasing efforts over the past 20 years to provide teaching, inspiration, and worship for their followers through radio and television programming. Buddhists, Hindus, and Sikhs, on the other hand, have shown little interest in religious broadcasting up to the present time—particularly in the United States. This does not mean that Hindus never see religion-centered programming in India, however. A perennial favorite on Indian national television is the dramatization of Hinduism's most revered scripture, the Bhagavad Gita.

CONCLUSION

Religious broadcasting has been a powerful influence, especially in American religious life, since the founding generation of radio preachers in the 1920s and 1930s. That influence has only grown stronger and more pervasive with the rise of Christian television and radio networks over the past 20 years. Moreover, satellite technology and short-wave radio transmitters have fulfilled the fondest dreams of evangelical Christians who see broadcasting media as God's chosen instrument for spreading the gospel to every continent, people, and nation on earth. This encyclopedia answers the pressing need for a comprehensive historical guide to the complex and under-studied phenomenon of religious broadcasting.

A

ADIB EDEN EVANGELISTIC MISSIONARY SOCIETY
established: 1967

Headquartered in Miami, Florida, the Adib Eden Evangelistic Missionary Society or Sociedad Evangélica Misionera de Adib Eden (SEMAE) is a Protestant evangelical Spanish-language mission founded in 1967 and directed by evangelist Adib Eden. SEMAE distributes literature and sponsors a number of broadcast programs in Costa Rica, El Salvador, and Spain.

ADVENTURE PALS
see: Christian Children's Association

AGAPE EUROPE
established: 1967

Agape Europe is an international, interdenominational Christian mission organization that helps distribute Christian television programming to stations around the world. It also works with students, churches, athletes, diplomats, artists, and media specialists to spread the Christian gospel through conferences, books, brochures, video, and film. The organization has national ministries in Austria, Finland, France, Germany, Greece, Great Britain, Italy, the Netherlands, Norway, Portugal, Spain, Sweden, and Switzerland. Agape Europe began in 1967 as the European ministry of Campus Crusade for Christ, a US-based evangelical outreach to college students.

ALL ABOARD FOR ADVENTURE
see: Everett C. Parker

A. A. ALLEN
born: March 27, 1911, Sulfur Rock, Arkansas
died: June 11, 1970, San Francisco, California

Asa Alonzo Allen, Jr., was a Pentecostal healing evangelist who followed the example of Oral Roberts and built a successful television and radio ministry between 1951 and 1970. The ministry, Miracle Life Fellowship, was taken over by a close associate, Don Stewart, at Allen's untimely death at age 59.

Allen was born in the small Arkansas town of Sulfur Rock and grew up in a family of alcoholics. His father left the farm when Allen was three to find employment at a stave mill in nearby Batesville. Allen liked to tell stories of the hunger, squalor, and privation he endured during his childhood. A jug of moonshine was always nearby, and his parents chuckled as even their children drank from it and stumbled around the house. When his mother moved in with another abusive alcoholic, Allen made abortive attempts to run away from home.

During the eighth grade, the future evangelist, tired of the humiliation of coming to school in bare feet, dropped out. He spent his teen years drifting in what he later described as the "swirling rapids of sin." Summing up this period of his life, Allen recounted,

> If we had had a coat of arms, the beer bucket and the gin bottle would rightly have been emblazoned upon it. Drunkenness was a family trait. My mother had gone through one divorce and was destined for another. I had a loveless father in Arkansas, a loveless stepfather at home. . . . I had four wild sisters and I was an ex-bum, a drinking, carousing, smoking, stealing sinner.

Allen was helping his mother run a dance hall roadhouse in 1934 when he accepted a friend's invitation to attend a revival at a local Methodist church. During the revival's second night Allen knelt at the altar and accepted the minister's call for repentance and conversion. Two weeks later, he withdrew from the Methodist church in order to join the Pentecostal Assemblies of God. The exact reason for this change of denominations is unclear, but it likely had to do with the more powerful "conviction and knowledge of the Bible" that Allen found in the Pentecostal Church. In later years, Allen would claim that the stricter Assemblies community had saved him from a life of alcoholism.

Feeling a strong call to the ministry, Allen found work on a Colorado ranch and attempted unsuccessfully to enroll in a Bible school. He next decided to hit the road as a traveling revival preacher. It was a harsh life of desperate poverty and long hours spent preaching to small crowds in backwoods communities. After several years of limited success in these ventures, Allen began to pursue a more focused healing ministry. In prayer one day, he had an experience that showed him the 13 requirements God demanded for a successful healing ministry. The most important of these was complete faith in the Bible's promises, which would empower a person to accomplish all that Jesus had done and more.

Allen's evangelistic revivals began to attract larger crowds, but he was still unhappy with the progress of his career. After an unsuccessful pastorate at an Assemblies church in Corpus Christi, Texas, Allen visited an Oral Roberts healing service in Fort Worth and felt a call to a tent healing ministry. He convinced the well-known Dallas healer Jack Coe to sell him his old tent on credit and established A. A. Allen Revivals, Inc., in 1951. His first revival took place in Yakima, Washington, on July 4, 1951.

Within a few years, Allen's reputation as a healer and preacher spread throughout the country. As thousands sang and prayed with him, Allen paced across the healing platform like a caged cat, full of prophetic fire and judgment. Pointing, waving, screaming, and whispering, he delivered his dramatic sermons in a distinctive rapid-fire baritone voice. He coaxed, wrestled, and feinted with his wheelchair patients, and laid a gentle hand on those brought to him on stretchers. Sometimes he set up long lines of sinners along which he would move, slapping each person on the forehead. Those "slain in the Lord" would tumble to the ground and remain in ecstatic, death-like trances for hours. Often Allen would work through the night, casting out the demons he believed were the cause of most illnesses.

Allen established his headquarters in Dallas in 1953 and began to organize a multifaceted ministry that included healing crusades, the monthly publication of *Miracle Magazine*, and a new radio program called *The Allen Revival Hour*. The program, which was later renamed *Miracle Ministry Broadcast*, soon aired daily on 35 radio stations around the country.

People were drawn to Allen's crusades both by his "down home" approach and by the spectacular success of his healings. Clips of these tent healings became the basis of a regular television series, which was broadcast over four channels. Like the early telecasts of Oral Roberts's healing crusades, these dramatic shows had a powerful impact on viewing audiences. Allen promoted the new telecasts in newspaper ads that read,

> See! Hear! Actual miracles happening before your eyes! Cancer, tumors, goiters disappear. Crutches, braces, wheelchairs, stretchers discarded. Crossed eyes straightened. Caught by the camera as they occurred in the healing line before thousands of witnesses.

After an arrest on drunken driving charges and a subsequent loss of ministerial credentials from the Assemblies of God, Allen bounced back in 1956. He founded the Miracle Revival Fellowship and was given 1,280 acres in southern Arizona on which to build a new spiritual community, Miracle Valley. This community expanded over the next 10 years to include a Bible college, radio and television facilities, a publishing house, and a healing pool.

Allen's sensationalism, immodesty, and abrasive manner scared away many television station managers and assured that his telecasts would never draw a large national audience. Nevertheless, his radio program maintained a core of loyal listeners and stations. By 1965, *The Allen Revival Hour* was heard throughout the United States on 70 stations and in foreign countries such as the Philippines and England. In the latter country, Allen was forced to broadcast over a pirate station, Radio City London, because no legal station would air his programs. The radio ministry in England generated a heavy volume of favorable mail from listeners and encouraged Allen to initiate a large revival crusade in the United Kingdom and Finland. Although the revivals drew large crowds, Allen found Europeans to be spiritually cold and "bound in religious rituals and tradition." Allen's successful crusades in the Philippines in the late 1960s generated more enthusiasm and less criticism from the press.

In some ways, Allen's ministry was progressive for its time. Both at his revivals and at his Miracle Valley Bible College, for instance, African Americans and whites mixed on equal terms. Other ministry practices were not as admirable. For example, Allen hired "goon squads" to physically prevent journalists and photographers from reporting on his tent revivals. He also refused to minister to persons at his revivals who had not paid first. In spite of his questionable fundraising practices, Allen was never convicted of misappropriating ministry funds. He also survived an IRS audit in 1963, which allowed him to retain his tax exempt status.

Allen began to preach a health and prosperity message in the mid-1960s which would soon be adopted by evangelists like Kenneth Hagin and Kenneth Copeland. This "faith formula" assured contributors to his ministry that they would receive a blessing of prosperity for their support.

Allen's ministry continued to grow in the late 1960s, particularly among African Americans. By 1970, A. A. Allen Miracle Revivals, Inc., employed 175 people and sent out more than 55 million publications annually. *Miracle Magazine* alone boasted a circulation of 350,000. The independent-minded Allen pointedly kept himself apart from major evangelists such as Billy Graham, claiming that these religious leaders had corrupted themselves by associating with politicians.

In June 1970, rumors began to spread that Allen was in poor health. A prerecorded message was broadcast assuring his radio audience that these rumors were unfounded. Allen died alone in a San Francisco hotel room of "acute alcoholism and fatty infiltration of the liver" the same week this message was broadcast. In the wake of Allen's passing, Don Stewart took over the ministry, renaming it the Don Stewart Association and relocating to Phoenix, Arizona. The longtime Allen associate was subsequently accused of embezzlement by the ministry's board of directors but then was acquitted. Stewart set about modifying the ministry, eschewing Allen's more combative and vindictive style for what he termed a "compassion explosion." Stewart also tried to orient the ministry's revivals more in the direction of teens and young adults.

In spite of his obvious shortcomings, Allen is remembered today as one of the most influential healing evangelists of his era.

See also Oral Roberts

SOURCES

Allen, Asa Alonzo. *Born to Lose, Bound to Win.* Garden City, NJ: Doubleday, 1970.

———. *My Cross.* Miracle Valley, AZ: A. A. Allen Revivals, n.d.

———. *Power to Get Wealth: How You Can Have It!* Miracle Valley, AZ: A. A. Allen Revivals, 1963.

———. *The Price of God's Miracle Working Power.* Lamar, CO: A. A. Allen Revivals, 1950.

————. *The Riches of the Gentiles Are Yours.* Miracle Valley, AZ: A. A. Allen Revivals, 1965.

————. *Witchcraft, Wizards, and Witches.* Miracle Valley, AZ: A. A. Allen Revivals, 1968.

Erickson, Hal. *Religious Radio and Television in the United States, 1921–1991.* Jefferson, NC: McFarland, 1992.

Harrell, David Edwin, Jr. *All Things Are Possible.* Bloomington: Indiana University Press, 1975.

Hedgepath, William. "He Feels, He Heals, and He Turns You On to God." *Look* 33 (October 1969): 23–31.

Morris, James. *The Preachers.* New York: St. Martin's Press, 1973.

Randi, James. *The Faith Healers.* New York: Prometheus, 1987.

Stewart, Don. *Man from Miracle Valley.* Long Beach, CA: Great Horizons, 1971.

CHARLES L. ALLEN

born: June 24, 1913, Newborn, Georgia

Charles Livingston Allen has been a familiar fixture on religious radio and television since the late 1940s. He is also a popular author of books on Christian living and an honored minister within the Methodist Church.

Allen grew up in Georgia, the son of John Robert Allen and Lulu Franklin. After attending Young Harris Junior College and Wofford College, he entered Emory University in Atlanta, where he received his bachelor of divinity degree in 1937. Allen's ministerial career began in 1933, when he was provisionally accepted into the North Georgia Conference of the former Methodist Episcopal Church South. Midway through his Emory studies, he was granted full connection with the North Georgia Conference. Upon graduation, Allen was ordained a church elder and began the first of several temporary assignments. His first full-time pastorate was at a church in Acworth, Georgia.

In typical Methodist fashion, Allen was transferred to several other conference churches over the next 10 years. At pastorates in Douglasville and Thomas, Georgia, he began to build a reputation as a preacher. He also founded the homiletic periodical *Pulpit Preaching.* Based on his growing profile within Methodist circles, Allen

was asked to take over preaching duties at the prominent Grace Methodist Church of Atlanta. It was at Grace Methodist that Allen gained national stature. He not only convinced a local radio station to air his Sunday worship service, but he also started a column for *The Atlanta Journal* and published a series of popular books. The best loved of these include *Roads to Radiant Living* (1951), *God's Psychiatry* (1953), *The Touch of the Master's Hand* (1956), *The Twenty-third Psalm: An Interpretation* (1961), *Life More Abundant* (1968), and *The Secret of Abundant Living* (1968).

Allen's success in Atlanta led to his being called to pastor the American Methodist's largest and most prestigious congregation, First Methodist Church of Houston, Texas. Using this pastorate as a base, Allen continued his prolific output of books and radio programs. He added a weekly television show, *Charles Allen*, which has continued to air into the early 1990s. In 1981, Allen was recognized as Minister of the Year by the Religious Heritage Association. Having retired from his Houston pastorate in 1983, Allen continues to travel, publish, and host his weekly television show.

SOURCES

Allen, Charles L. *Healing Words.* Old Tappan, NJ: Fleming H. Revell, 1961.

————. *Prayer Changes Things.* Old Tappan, NJ: Fleming H. Revell, 1964.

————. *What I Have Lived By: An Autobiography.* Old Tappan, NJ: Fleming H. Revell, 1976.

Howell, Clinton H., ed. *Prominent Personalities in Methodism.* Birmingham, AL: Lowrey Press, 1945.

Who's Who in the Methodist Church. Nashville: Abingdon Press, 1966.

THE AMERICAN INDIAN HOUR

The American Indian Hour is a syndicated radio program of the American Indian Liberation Crusade (founded in 1952). The program is hosted by crusade president Howard Hedrick, and has been broadcast regularly since the 1970s. Its main purpose is to raise awareness concerning the physical and spiritual needs of Native Americans. The ministry also raises support for missionary work, Bible schools and camps, and emergency relief. *The American Indian Hour* provides useful news and information about Native American concerns to its nearly 4,000 supporters.

SOURCES

Erickson, Hal. *Religious Radio and Television in the United States, 1921–1991*. Jefferson, NC: McFarland, 1992.

AMERICAN RELIGIOUS TOWN HALL
first aired: 1956

One of the first religious television shows to openly debate contemporary theological and social issues was James Pike's *American Religious Town Hall*. The show was aired Sunday afternoons on the ABC-TV network from March 4, 1956, through April 6, 1957. Pike went on to host an interview documentary program, *The Dean Pike Show*, in 1957. *American Religious Town Hall* was revived in 1970 by Bishop A. A. Leisky of Dallas, Texas. The show appeared weekly in paid-time syndication and was still on the air in 1990 with its moderator, Robert Leisky. Although the telecast provided a welcome airing of controversial viewpoints, it never reached the level of heated debate found on such popular weekly half-hour programs as *The John Ankerberg Show*.

See also James A. Pike

SOURCES

Day, Beth. "The Joyful Dean." *Reader's Digest* 72 (February 1958): 140–45.

Erickson, Hal. *Religious Radio and Television in the United States, 1921–1991*. Jefferson, NC: McFarland, 1992.

AMG INTERNATIONAL
established: 1942

An international, interdenominational Christian organization founded in 1942 and directed by Otto Anderson, AMG International provides support for evangelistic mission work in a number of countries, including Greece, India, Indonesia, the Philippines, Haiti, Guatemala, Cyprus, Sri Lanka, Thailand, and Colombia. The main work of AMG is assisting in the founding of hospitals, schools, orphanages, and relief centers. Headquartered in Chattanooga, Tennessee, AMG's outreach includes a radio broadcast ministry that produces eight programs in the United States and Canada.

SOURCES

Melton, J. Gordon. *Directory of Religious Organizations in the United States*. 3d ed. Detroit: Gale Research, 1993.

BOB ANDERSON
see: Exposing the Lie

ANGELICA, MOTHER
see: Mother Angelica

ERNEST ANGLEY
born: 1921, Gastonia, North Carolina

The televangelist Ernest Angley is best known for the dramatic exorcisms and healings that allegedly take place during his televised evangelical crusades.

Angley is the son of devout Baptist textile workers from the mill town of Gastonia, North Carolina. At the age of seven Angley claims to have experienced a vision of God while he lay in bed at his family farmhouse. God reportedly showed him a myriad of stars and declared that the young boy would win a like number of souls for Christ. This early vision was confirmed when Angley had a powerful conversion experience at 18 and decided to join the Pentecostal Church.

To prepare for a preaching ministry, Angley left North Carolina to study in Cleveland, Tennessee, at the Church of God Bible Training School (now Lee College). Upon graduation, Angley and his wife, Esther Lee "Angel" Sykes, traveled throughout the South as Church of God evangelists. By 1952 Angley had decided to center his message around spiritual healing. He established the independent Healing Stripes Evangelistic Association and moved to Akron, Ohio. The association took its name from Isaiah's messianic oracle (53:5), which said, "by his stripes we are healed."

Dividing his time between work in Akron's rubber industry and evangelism, Angley began to develop a sizable following. In 1957, he built a large worship tabernacle and, in 1958, integrated his various evangelical outreaches under the church's new name, Grace Cathedral. Angley pursued his preaching ministry in Akron until the death of his wife in 1970.

Angley began to conduct revivalist crusades throughout the United States and inaugurated a weekly television program focused on his healing gifts, *The Ernest Angley Television Hour.* Between 1970 and 1980, the typical program included musical performances by the Grace Cathedral Singing Men, a sermon by the white-suited Angley, and videotaped instances of charismatic healing from one of the evangelist's Miracle and Salvation crusades with a backdrop of a galaxy of stars set within a deep blue wall.

Journalist Jim Auchmutey of the *Atlanta Constitution* described one of these healing events:

> For the next three hours, Ernest Angley "healed," squealed and ranted in the name of God. A line of the afflicted formed at one side of the stage, and the faith healer attended to them, usually one at a time, laying hands upon their foreheads, casting out "foul demons" and "loosing" them from Satan. Many were so overcome by Angley's cathartic commands that they collapsed to the floor, "slain in the spirit," and rose stunned, sometimes murmuring gibberish—"speaking in tongues." The multitude applauded frequently, urged on by Angley: "Give God a big hand, everybody!"

Those unable to attend these crusades were invited to put their hands on their television screens while Angley placed his hand before the camera. In a commanding voice, Angley called the demons out of his listeners and cried, "Heal! Heal! HEEEEEAL-aaa!" The evangelist claimed to be able to see demons coming out of the bodies of believers and on several occasions claimed to see angels and God himself. His estimated television audience by 1980 was 314,600.

Although Angley's healing ministry has been generally well received, the death of crusade participants on two occasions has stirred up controversy. The first of these events occurred in North Carolina when a woman died from heart failure seconds after receiving Angley's healing prayer for her weak heart. The second death, which took place during a crusade in Germany in 1984, resulted in Angley's brief imprisonment. This experience led to the writing of his popular book, *Cell 15* (1984).

Even though Angley's preaching style has been parodied by comedians such as Robin Williams, the faith healer has managed to maintain a faithful audience for his crusades and television show. Angley has also been given a clean bill of health by James Randi, the self-ordained debunker of faith healers. Randi has pronounced Angley's ministry to be free of the insincerity and questionable financial transactions that have plagued other healing ministries.

SOURCES

Angley, Ernest W. *Cell 15*. Akron, OH: Winston Press, 1984.

———. *Faith in God Heals the Sick*. Akron, OH: Winston Press, 1983.

———. *Miracles Are Real—I Got One!* Greensburg, PA: Manna Christian Outreach, 1975.

———. *Raptured*. Old Tappan, NJ: Fleming H. Revell, 1950.

Auchmutey, Jim. "Ernest Angley's Miracle Crusade." *Atlanta Constitution*, June 21, 1980.

Burgess, Stanley M., Gary B. McGee, and Patrick H. Alexander, eds. *Dictionary of Pentecostal and Charismatic Movements.* Grand Rapids, MI: Zondervan, 1988.

Hadden, Jeffrey K., and Charles E. Swann. *Prime Time Preachers: The Rising Power of Televangelism.* Menlo Park, CA: Addison-Wesley, 1981.

Simms, Patsy. *Can Somebody Shout Amen!* New York: St. Martin's Press, 1988.

JOHN ANKERBERG

born: December 10, 1945, Chicago, Illinois

Courtesy: National Religious Broadcasters

John Ankerberg is the president and founder of the John Ankerberg Theological Research Institute and the producer and host of *The John Ankerberg Show.* The weekly half-hour program airs debates between conservative Christians and proponents of various non-Christian teachings. Over the past 13 years, Ankerberg's programs have been seen on the Christian Broadcasting Network, Trinity Broadcasting Network, Praise the Lord Network, National Christian Network, and The Family Channel. By 1995, *The John Ankerberg Show* was airing via cable and 58 independent stations in 39,000 cities throughout the United States. The minis-try estimates that its potential viewing audience is 185 million people in all 50 states.

Ankerberg is the son of Floyd Ankerberg, a well-known minister who became Billy Graham's successor as the staff evangelist for Youth for Christ. During the summers of his youth, John traveled the evangelistic circuit with his father. He showed early promise as an evangelist when, during his years at Mount Prospect High School in Illinois, he organized a Youth for Christ Bible club that numbered over 400 teens.

Ankerberg earned a bachelor of arts degree with high academic honors from the University of Illinois (Chicago Circle Campus) in 1972. The following year he completed a master of arts in church history and the history of Christian thought and a master of divinity degree at Trinity Evangelical Divinity School in Deerfield, Illinois. At both campuses, Ankerberg lectured, debated, and traveled to over 78 colleges and universities. In the Chicago area, he supervised InterVarsity Fellowship's Chicago Evangelism Project, which set up Christian coffee houses on the north side of Chicago at the height of the 1960s counterculture.

Upon graduating with high academic honors from Trinity in 1973, Ankerberg became a founding member of the Willow Creek Community Church in Bartlett, Illinois, one of Chicago's northwest suburbs. The young team of evangelists of which he was a part developed a strategy to draw people who were turned off by conventional churches. In three years, Willow Creek increased its membership from 100 to 3,000 adult members. The church has continued to grow and has been amazingly successful in training ministers and lay leaders to create user-friendly "seeker services" in Protestant churches around the country. Ankerberg left the Willow Creek ministry and became a full-time evangelist in 1976. His crusades took him to major cities throughout Asia, Europe, South America, and Africa. In 1991, Ankerberg completed his education with a doctor of ministry degree at Luther Rice Seminary in Jacksonville, Florida.

Ankerberg's first foray into televangelism came as a result of his cooperation with Youth for Christ's Al Metsker. Metsker set up a television station in Kansas City and offered Ankerberg a time slot for a new program in 1982. Dubbed *Roundtable*, the show featured Ankerberg seated at a high table fielding questions from a circle of Christians. Ankerberg's idea was to create an open discussion format similar to that used by Phil Donahue except that the discussion would always include the evangelical Christian perspective.

In 1983, *Roundtable* was renamed *The John Ankerberg Show*. Soon, Ankerberg began bringing in leading non-Christian spokespersons to debate controversial topics with prominent conservative Christian thinkers. Ankerberg promoted his non-Christian guests in conventional show-business fashion and gave them time to represent their positions in a comprehensive manner. Ankerberg claimed that this format, though unique in Christian broadcasting at the time, replicated the spirit of the Apostle Paul's debates with the pagan philosophers of Athens. Although few participants changed their views as a result of the debates, the show did make for some entertaining theater.

Over the years, Ankerberg's programs have tended to focus on four major themes: world religions and cults, social issues, prophecy, and the New Age movement. The programs on world religions and cults have featured apologists for the Baha'i faith, the Association for Research and Enlightenment, Eckankar, the Mormons, Silva Mind Control, Roman Catholicism, Seventh-Day Adventism, the Unification Church of Sun Myung Moon, Unity, Islam, Garner Ted Armstrong of the Church of God International, astrologers, and former members of the Jehovah's Witnesses and the Freemasons.

The major social issues discussed on the program have included abortion, national economic policy, the decline of moral values in public schools, Christianity and politics, AIDS and homosexuality, and the dangers of rock music. Ankerberg has consistently aired programs that examine the intricacies of biblical prophecy and the application of biblical prophecy to current world events. He is a staunch enemy of the New

Age movement and regularly asks such new-age opponents as Constance Cumbey, Dave Hunt, and Brooks Alexander to discuss the dangers the movement represents to conservative Christians.

Ankerberg is the author of 39 books, including *Bowing at Strange Altars: The Masonic Lodge and the Christian Conscience; The Coming Darkness* (an exposé of modern occultism); *The Myth of Safe Sex; One World: Bible Prophecy and the New World Order; Protestants and Catholics: Do They Now Agree?; Rock Music's Powerful Messages*; and *Thieves of Innocence: Protecting Our Children from New Age Teachings and Occult Practices*.

The purpose of Ankerberg's ministry, according to his promotional literature, is "to present evidence to the public to demonstrate that Christianity is true so that they will embrace it for themselves and share it effectively with others." His programs are designed to appeal to a "thinking audience" of both Christians and non-Christians. Ankerberg believes that the informal debates and discussions that occur on his show allow non-Christians to hear their views presented fairly and at the same time to hear the Christian response to these views. The show also furnishes an opportunity for Christians to hear about other world views and to learn about how they can respond to the challenges they face from non-Christian belief systems. Some Ankerberg programs even give documentary-style presentations of major social issues and the historic Christian response to these issues.

During the Jim Bakker and Jimmy Swaggart scandals of the late 1980s, Ankerberg played a reluctant part in publicly exposing allegations of Bakker's "homosexual behavior." Ankerberg had heard rumors at a National Religious Broadcasters (NRB) annual meeting of Bakker's $265,000 payoff to Jessica Hahn, and arranged to see documentation of its details with Paul Roper, the California business consultant who had helped negotiate the deal. Ankerberg was willing to handle the matter in private according to scriptural principles. After Bakker made his story public in the *Charlotte Observer*, Ankerberg publicly defended Swaggart, a long-time friend, from allegations that Swaggart was orchestrating a hostile takeover of Bakker's ministry. He then received information concerning Bakker's alleged homosexual behavior, which he privately passed to Assemblies of God leaders. Ankerberg broke his silence only when Tammy Faye Bakker publicly demanded that he produce evidence of the allegations.

Ankerberg's ministry is supported entirely by the contributions of individuals. In its public appeals for funds, the ministry indicates exactly what the money is needed for and how it will be spent. A board of directors meets on a regular basis to approve the ministry's transactions and to review financial statements. Moreover, the ministry's finances are audited by an independent accounting firm each year.

The John Ankerberg Show's corporate producer, the Ankerberg Theological Research Institute, was, as of 1995, a full member in good standing of the Evangelical Council for Financial Responsibility. This council of evangelical, nonprofit ministries expects its members to abide by the highest standards of financial accountability and disclosure to government agencies and donors. Ankerberg was also involved in the development of EFICOM (the Ethics and Financial Integrity Commission) of the National Religious Broadcasters. EFICOM came into being to develop principles to insure the fiscal integrity of religious broadcasting ministries.

The NRB awarded Ankerberg its 1984 Genesis award for "excellence in concept and production of a Christian television program and ministry in its beginning years." In 1992, Ankerberg garnered NRB's prestigious Television Producer of the Year award. The Ankerberg ministry's current headquarters is in Chattanooga, Tennessee.

Ankerberg serves on the board of directors of NRB and the board of reference of the Christian Film and Television Commission. He is an ordained Baptist minister.

SOURCES

Ankerberg, John F. *One World: Bible Prophecy and the New World Order*. Chicago: Moody Press, 1990.

———. *Protestants & Catholics: Do They Now Agree?* Eugene, OR: Harvest House, 1995.

The Ankerberg Theological Research Institute. Resource List, 1995.

Bruce, Steve. *Pray TV: Televangelism in America*. London: Routledge, 1990.

"Introducing the John Ankerberg Show." 1995 leaflet detailing Ankerberg's ministry.

"Video Debates: An Ankerberg Specialty." *Christianity Today*, January 22, 1982.

See also Jim Bakker; Jimmy Swaggart

ANOTHER LIFE
first aired: June 1, 1981

Another Life was part of the Christian Broadcasting Network's (CBN) early-1980s attempt to produce programming that appealed to secular audiences.

When the daytime drama series was first proposed in 1980, it was called *The Inner Light*—an obvious attempt to resonate with audiences of CBS's long-running soap opera, *Guiding Light*. Bob Aaron, a former programming executive for NBC, was hired as the show's executive producer. CBN brought Roy Winslow—famous for *Search for Tomorrow* and *The Secret Storm*—out of retirement to be story consultant for the program. *Another Life* premiered on CBN and in commercial syndication on June 1, 1981.

The show mimicked the soap opera genre, focusing on the trials and victories of the Davidson family, who lived in the fictional town of Kingsley. The Davidson family consisted of a widowed nurse (played by Mary Jean Feton) and her two children (played by Jeanette Larson and Darrel Campbell). Other characters included an ace reporter, a gangster, a politician, and a business tycoon. The plot lines were fairly standard daytime drama fare: political intrigue, infidelity, illness, kidnapping, and substance abuse.

Unfortunately, several factors conspired to make the show a pale reflection of secular soap operas. To begin, CBN's Virginia Beach studios did not have the technical polish of Hollywood's soap opera factories. In addition, the show's imperative to resolve plot lines "through the application of Judeo-Christian values" failed to allow for the gradual, steady buildup that is the secret of longevity in daytime drama. Moreover, CBN's impatient desire to transmit a religious message before the story line could begin to build tension made it difficult to sustain suspense or to develop the characters beyond stereotypes. Finally, in its attempt to impart Christian doctrine into everyday dialogue, the show ended up sounding stilted, dogmatic, and preachy.

The program was dropped from most of its commercial syndication outlets by early 1982. It limped along on CBN and a few independent UHF stations until October 5, 1984, when the last episode was aired. Reruns of *Another Life* were still appearing on religious cable outlets in the early 1990s.

See also Christian Broadcasting Network

SOURCES

Erickson, Hal. *Religious Radio and Television in the United States, 1921–1991*. Jefferson, NC: McFarland, 1992.

Hoover, Stewart M. *Mass Media Religion: The Social Sources of the Electronic Church*. Newbury Park, CA: Sage, 1988.

APOSTOLATE FOR FAMILY CONSECRATION
established: 1975

An independent Catholic organization founded in 1975, the Apostolate for Family Consecration (AFC) devotes its energies to bringing the family closer to God. Its main focus is on building strong neighborhoods and God-centered town communities. AFC's main outreach is through the promotion of its video and audiocassette materials. The ministry also produces several weekly television and other broadcast programs that are carried on the Eternal Word Television Network and distributed by UNDA-USA. Headquartered in Bloomingdale, Ohio,

and directed by Jerome Coniker, AFC boasts a membership of some 26,000 people.

SOURCES

Melton, J. Gordon. *Directory of Religious Organizations in the United States*. 3d ed. Detroit: Gale Research, 1993.

ARAB WORLD MINISTRIES
established: 1952

An interdenominational missionary organization founded in 1952, Arab World Ministries (AWM) broadcasts religious programming over the radio to a number of countries in North Africa, the Middle East, and Europe. The ministry also distributes Christian literature and Bible correspondence courses and establishes churches throughout Arab countries and Arab communities worldwide. AWM is headquartered in the Philadelphia suburb of Upper Darby.

BEN ARMSTRONG
born: October 18, 1923, Newark, New Jersey

Courtesy: National Religious Broadcasters

Benjamin Armstrong was the executive director of the National Religious Broadcasters (NRB) during a period of rapid growth in the religious broadcasting industry. His tenure, which ran from 1978 to 1989, saw the advocacy organization attain a preeminent position in Christian broadcasting circles.

Armstrong is the son of Benjamin Leighton Armstrong and Margaret Denison. He earned his bachelor of science degree from New York University (NYU) in 1948 and was ordained the following year by the United Presbyterian Church. In 1950, Armstrong earned a master of arts degree from NYU, and five years later he received a master of divinity degree from Union Theological School. He pastored churches in New York and New Jersey prior to joining Trans World Radio, a popular short-wave religious service, in 1958. After working with Trans World's founder Paul Freed (his brother-in-law) as director of radio, Armstrong was appointed executive secretary of the NRB in 1967. That same year he earned his doctorate from NYU.

Armstrong is best known for his enthusiastic promotion of what he dubbed the "electric church," during the 1970s. He believed that the "awesome technology of broadcasting" was a "major miracle of modern times," which was returning the church to its earliest roots. Religious broadcasting did this by breaking down the walls of tradition that had imprisoned pristine Christianity for two millennia. As articulated in Armstrong's book *The Electric Church*, this church was

> a revolutionary new form of the worshipping, witnessing church that existed twenty centuries ago. . . . Members of the church gathered in homes, shared the Scriptures, prayed together, praised God. . . . They were on fire for the Lord, and their lives had been changed by Him. As a result, they changed the world.

For Armstrong the electric church was being used in the Last Days to "revitalize the older forms of churches," empowering them to keep up with the challenges of the twentieth century. He went so far as to suggest that the angel of prophecy in the Book of Revelation could be identified with communications satellites. Like this angel, satellite technology "preach[es] unto them that dwell in the earth, and to every nation, and kindred, and tongue, and people."

Armstrong was succeeded as executive director of NRB in 1989 by his one-time Trans World Radio coworker, E. Brandt Gustavson.

See also National Religious Broadcasters; Trans World Radio

SOURCES

Armstrong, Ben. *The Electric Church*. Nashville: Thomas Nelson, 1979.

Schultze, Quentin J. *Televangelism and American Culture: The Business of Popular Religion*. Grand Rapids, MI: Baker Book House, 1991.

Ward, Mark, Sr. *Air of Salvation: The Story of Christian Broadcasting*. Manassas, VA: National Religious Broadcasters, 1994.

GARNER TED ARMSTRONG

born: February 9, 1930, Portland, Oregon

Garner Ted Armstrong is one of the best-known voices in religious television. The son of Worldwide Church of God founder Herbert W. Armstrong and Loma Dillon, the younger Armstrong was reared in Eugene, Oregon, the church's headquarters from 1934 to the mid-1940s. When the ministry, at the time called the Radio Church of God, moved its headquarters to Pasadena, California, Armstrong decided to enlist in the navy. His enlistment was, in part, a rebellion against the church's peculiar teachings, which promoted Sabbatarianism (observance of the Sabbath on Saturday), the celebration of ancient Jewish festivals, and the unique apostleship of the senior Armstrong.

After his four years of navy duty, Armstrong enrolled in the church's university, Ambassador College, and married Shirley Hammer. It was during his student years that Armstrong experienced a conversion to his father's religious teachings and was accepted by the Radio Church of God for baptism.

Following his ministerial ordination in 1955, Armstrong became a regular speaker on his father's radio program, *The World Tomorrow*, and a frequent contributor to *The Plain Truth*, the ministry's widely circulated news magazine. By 1958, the younger Armstrong had emerged as Herbert W. Armstrong's heir apparent. He became the vice president of both Ambassador College and the Radio Church of God and increasingly assumed the role of the church's public spokesperson. In 1968, the elder Armstrong changed the name of the ministry to the Worldwide Church of God.

The younger Armstrong's role as spokesperson for the newly named church was confirmed when he became the anchor of a televised version of *The World Tomorrow*, which was inaugurated in 1960. The show gradually built up a national audience that peaked at 750,000 in 1972, the year the program began daily telecasts. *The World Tomorrow* mimicked secular news programs and included discussions of biblical prophecies and their fulfillment in a factual manner. The shows included special reports from field correspondents and Armstrong's editorial comments.

During the early 1970s, Garner Ted Armstrong began to resent his father's rigid authoritarianism, overspending, and belief that women would always be subservient to men. At the same time, Al Carrozzo, the director of the church's Counseling and Guidance Office, accused the younger Armstrong of numerous instances of sexual impropriety. These charges led to Armstrong's removal from *The World Tomorrow* telecasts. After a few weeks during which no explanation was given for his absence, viewers of the program clamored for his reinstatement. Unwilling to jeopardize his $50 million-per-year operation, the elder Armstrong brought his son back. However, within a short time the rebellious younger Armstrong was again taken off the air. The turmoil in the ministry was resolved only when Armstrong left his father's church in 1978 and created his own organizations, the Church of God, International, and the Garner Ted Armstrong Evangelistic Association. Based in Tyler, Texas, these new ministries also inaugurated a radio program, *The Garner Ted Armstrong Program*, which was broadcast from San Antonio, Texas.

Armstrong has been able to attract a loyal following of former members of his father's Worldwide Church of God. His church has established a growing presence both in the United States and in such Worldwide Church of God strongholds as Jamaica, Australia, South Africa, and Europe. The radio ministry has expanded into a highly rated television series, *The Garner Ted Armstrong Program*, which is broadcast across North America on Saturday and Sunday mornings. The show's format features Armstrong and other Church of God, International ministers in a roundtable discussion of current events in the light of biblical prophecy. Armstrong has rebuilt his broadcasting audience by adhering to a busy schedule of public appearances and lectures.

Armstrong has also continued to author books and articles. The most popular of these are *The Real Jesus* (1977) and *Europe and America in Prophecy* (n.d.). The latter work elaborates on the teaching of British Israelism, which claims that the modern Anglo-Saxon peoples are literal descendants of the lost tribes of Israel. Armstrong's ministry publishes two periodicals, numerous doctrinal pamphlets, Bible-study lessons, and audiotapes. Like the Worldwide Church of God, the Church of God, International distributes these publications free of charge to all who request them.

The church's doctrines are similar to those of its parent body. The main innovations have come in church polity, with the younger Armstrong's ministry advocating a less hierarchical and autocratic governing structure. Following Herbert W. Armstrong's death in 1986, no attempt was made by the Worldwide Church of God to bring Garner Ted Armstrong back into the fold. The Church of God, International reported 2,158 members in 88 congregations worldwide in 1986.

See also Herbert W. Armstrong

SOURCES

Armstrong, Garner Ted. *The Answer to Unanswered Prayer.* Tyler, TX: Church of God, International, 1989.

———. *Constitution and Bylaws.* Tyler, TX: Church of God, International, 1979.

———. *Europe and America in Prophecy.* Tyler, TX: Church of God, International, n.d.

————. *The Real Jesus.* Mission, TX: Sheed Andrews and McMeel, 1977.

————. *Sunday—Saturday . . .Which?* Tyler, TX: Church of God, International, 1982.

————. *Where Is the True Church?* Tyler, TX: Church of God, International, 1982.

————. *Work of the Watchman.* Tyler, TX: Church of God, International, 1979.

Erickson, Hal. *Religious Radio and Television in the United States, 1921–1991.* Jefferson, NC: McFarland, 1992.

Hopkins, Joseph. *The Armstrong Empire: A Look at the Worldwide Church of God.* Grand Rapids, MI: Eerdmans, 1974.

Robinson, David. *Herbert Armstrong's Tangled Web.* Tulsa, OK: Hadden, 1980.

HERBERT W. ARMSTRONG
born: July 31, 1892, Des Moines, Iowa
died: January 16, 1986, Pasadena, California

Herbert W. Armstrong was an influential pioneer of religious radio and television. During his fifty years in religious broadcasting he was instrumental in bringing such unconventional ideas as observance of the Sabbath on Saturday and British Israelism—a notion that identified the 10 lost tribes of Israel with the modern Anglo-Saxon peoples—to radio and television audiences around the world.

Armstrong grew up in Des Moines, Iowa, the son of two Quakers, Horace and Eva Armstrong. After dropping out of high school during his sophomore year, the young Armstrong took a job in the advertising department of the local newspaper. In 1915, he moved to Chicago and started his own advertising company.

After this enterprise failed in the early 1920s, Armstrong relocated to Salem, Oregon. While there his wife (the former Loma Dillon) came under the influence of Ira Runcorn, a teacher in the Oregon Conference of the Church of God. The church was a strong proponent of Sabbath (Saturday) worship and Adventism. Within a short time, Loma Armstrong became convinced of the validity of Sabbath worship and brought her husband into fellowship with the church. Herbert Armstrong began a thorough study of the Bible in order to disprove his wife's unconventional beliefs but ended up accepting them as true.

He continued his scriptural studies and, in time, came to believe that God was revealing the Bible's secrets to him. Armstrong delivered his first homily in the church in 1928. By 1931, he had been ordained as a minister in the Oregon Conference of the Church of God and become an avid believer in British-Israelism. Although this belief was never officially promoted by the Church of God, many of its ministers accepted it as true. During this period, Armstrong was asked to write articles for a Church of God periodical, the *Bible Advocate*. He also began to preach the biblical imperative to observe ancient Jewish religious festivals.

After holding a series of evangelistic meetings at a schoolhouse near Eugene, Oregon, in 1934, Armstrong inaugurated an independent radio program called the *Radio Church of God* over a local station. He also established a thriving congregation of the same name, and began publishing a mimeographed newsletter. This newsletter would, in time, become the widely distributed magazine *The Plain Truth*. After two years, the radio program changed its name to *The World Tomorrow* and began expanding its broadcast outreach to other stations. *The World Tomorrow* became a nationally broadcast program in 1944, airing six nights a week in early prime time.

During this period, the young broadcaster joined in a schismatic group of Church of God members who were attempting to observe the biblical Jewish feasts and install a more authoritarian form of church leadership. This group, called the Church of God (Seventh-Day), established its headquarters in Salem, Virginia, and called on Armstrong to be one of its 70 elders.

By 1937, the church had abandoned its observance of ancient Jewish festivals and renounced British-Israelism. These actions led Armstrong to leave the new church and dedicate his efforts solely to the Radio Church of God ministry. He proclaimed himself as God's chosen messenger and apostle in the endtimes and assumed a position of absolute authority within the organization he had founded. In numerous writings and broadcasts, Armstrong contended that his church was a restoration of the Philadelphia church described in the Book of Revelation. As such, it had a special role to play in the unfolding events of the latter days.

The scope of Armstrong's ministry began to change dramatically when he relocated his church's headquarters to Pasadena, California, after World War II. The evangelist began a series of worldwide speaking tours, opened a publishing house, and expanded his radio ministry to large, regional stations. One of these was a 100,000-watt Mexican station that was eager to take on the paid programming US stations were avoiding at the time. Armstrong raised funds by promising his listeners prosperity on earth and a place in heaven if they supported the Radio Church of God. Those who did not contribute were told that were he forced to resign due to insufficient funds, they would incur divine disfavor and bear the responsibility for his resignation.

On October 8, 1947, Armstrong launched Ambassador College with the intention of training students as missionaries for his religious system. The seminary evolved into a bona fide institution of higher learning and ordained its first graduates in 1952.

The church's ministry spread to Europe in the early 1950s, finding an especially receptive audience in England. By 1953, Radio Luxembourg, one of the few powerful commercial stations in Europe, was broadcasting *The World Tomorrow* throughout the continent.

Within four years, Armstrong's weekly radio audience had grown to almost 5 million people, and *The Plain Truth* was being read by an estimated 175,000 subscribers. Armstrong urged his growing body of followers to reject the traditional Christian doctrine of the Trinity, avoid conventional medical care, and prepare themselves for the Second Coming of Christ in 1972.

The 1960s were a period of prodigious growth for Armstrong's ministry. His son, Garner Ted Armstrong, began hosting a televised version of *The World Tomorrow* in March 1968, and *The Plain Truth* claimed a worldwide circulation of over a million. The ministry's mass media outreach adopted a deliberate strategy of downplaying overt indoctrination and fundraising, preferring to wait until a person had expressed a genuine interest in the teachings before introducing him or her to the church's religious beliefs and system of tithing. The ministry continued to spread around the world, opening new centers in Australia, New Zealand, South Africa, and the Caribbean. In 1968, Armstrong changed the church's name to Worldwide Church of God.

The early 1970s witnessed the movement's continued rapid growth and expansion. By 1972, *The World Tomorrow* had begun daily telecasts, and *The Plain Truth* reported an international circulation of 2 million. The television program would build up an estimated audience of 750,000 people during the decade.

By the late 1970s, however, a series of internal conflicts, scandals, and lawsuits threatened to destroy Armstrong's church. The conflicts centered on the proper dating for the feast of Pentecost and the church's controversial ban on divorce and remarriage for its members. These conflicts were exacerbated by accusations of sexual impropriety against the younger Armstrong, who was also having marital problems. After being taken off the air and reinstated several times, Garner Ted Armstrong broke with his father in 1978 and was denied fellowship by the church. The former heir apparent soon established the Church of God, International and the Garner Ted Armstrong Evangelistic Association in Tyler, Texas, and began new radio and television programs. His schismatic church has attracted a small band of former Worldwide Church of God members and continues to teach the latter church's doctrines, although within a less autocratic structure. Other splinter groups also broke off from the main church during this period. One such faction began publishing *The Ambassador Report*, which kept track of the continuing feuding within the Worldwide Church of God.

Then, in 1978, a major lawsuit was initiated by former members who alleged that Herbert Armstrong and church treasurer Stanley Rader had misappropriated $80 million of organizational funds for personal use. The suit led to the church being placed in receivership for seven weeks in early 1979 by the attorney general of California, George Deukmejian. This highly controversial action was made possible by a new California state law that allowed the state to treat religious groups as public trusts. Deukmejian obtained a court order placing a dissident member in charge of the church and attaching its financial records pending trial. Although this state of affairs was quickly brought to an end when a number of mainstream religious organizations successfully lobbied to have the law changed, the ministry was effectively shut down for a period of months and reportedly lost millions of dollars in contributions.

Following the tribulations of the late 1970s and early 1980s, Armstrong was able to reestablish the Worldwide Church of God as a stable and growing organization. His followers began to believe that he had been resurrected from the dead after his recovery from a heart attack and that he would live to see the return of Christ. This speculation came to an end when Armstrong died in 1986 at the age of 93. Within a short time Joseph W. Tkach had replaced Armstrong as pastor general of the church, publisher of *The Plain Truth*, executive producer of *The World Tomorrow*, and chancellor of Ambassador College. Tkach also took over as president of the church's cultural and humanitarian outreach, the Ambassador International Cultural Foundation.

The format of *The World Tomorrow* resembles the Public Broadcasting System's *The News Hour with Jim Lehrer*. The program has four alternating hosts who weave news footage and interviews in with church commentary on subjects such as AIDS, the environmental crisis, and the breakdown of the family. In 1989, the half-hour show ranked second only to Robert Schuller's *Hour of Power* telecast in Arbitron's ranking of religious programs. Its audience size was estimated at 1.4 million.

Although *The World Tomorrow* has declined in popularity over the last seven years, it maintains its place as one of the longest-running religious telecasts in the world. The show is currently broadcast in Canada, the United States, Australia, New Zealand, the Caribbean, and Asia. In Europe the show is aired on Sky Channel and Radio Luxembourg. Both *The Plain Truth* and *The World Tomorrow* continue to be wholly supported by church members, and the ministry continues its practice of distributing all printed literature free of charge.

The Worldwide Church of God congregation has been largely successful in maintaining a low profile over its 60-year history. Its 519 congregations in the United States and Canada meet in rented buildings, eschew advertising, and do not list their telephone numbers. The church's services are held for members only, and most new members are drawn by the ministry's magazine and broadcasting outreach. In 1986, the church reported nearly 80,000 members and many more adherents.

SOURCES

Armstrong, Herbert W. *Autobiography.* 2 vols. Pasadena: Worldwide Church of God, 1986–87.

———. *Incredible Human Potential.* Pasadena: Worldwide Church of God, 1978.

———. *The Missing Dimension in Sex.* Pasadena: Worldwide Church of God, 1964.

———. *The Seven Laws of Success.* Pasadena: Worldwide Church of God, 1981.

———. *This Is the Worldwide Church of God.* Pasadena: Ambassador College Press, 1971.

———. *Tomorrow . . .What Will It Be Like?* New York: Everest House, 1979.

———. *The United States and Britain in Prophecy.* Pasadena: Worldwide Church of God, 1980.

———. *The Wonderful World Tomorrow.* Pasadena: Worldwide Church of God, 1979.

Bruce, Steve. *Pray TV: Televangelism in America.* New York: Routledge, 1990.

Erickson, Hal. *Religious Radio and Television in the United States, 1921–1991.* Jefferson, NC: McFarland, 1992.

Hadden, Jeffrey K., and Charles E. Swann. *Prime Time Preachers.* Menlo Park, CA: Addison-Wesley, 1981.

Hopkins, Joseph. *The Armstrong Empire: A Look at the Worldwide Church of God.* Grand Rapids, MI: Eerdmans, 1974.

Lippy, Charles H., ed. *Twentieth-Century Shapers of American Popular Religion.* Westport, CT: Greenwood Press, 1989.

McNair, Marion J. *Armstrongism: Religion . . . or Rip-off.* Orlando, FL: Pacific Charters, 1977.

Rader, Stanley R. *Against the Gates of Hell.* New York: Everest House, 1980.

Richardson, James T. "Changing Times: Religion, Economics and the Law in Contemporary America." *Sociological Analysis* (December, 1988).

Robinson, David. *Herbert Armstrong's Tangled Web.* Tulsa, OK: Hadden, 1980.

THE ART OF LIVING
see: Norman Vincent Peale

KAY ARTHUR
born: 1933

Kay Arthur is the host of *How Can I Live?*, radio and television Bible-study programs with the same name that answer questions about the Word of God. The one-hour weekly television program and 15-minute daily radio show are produced by Precept Ministries of Chattanooga, Tennessee, which Arthur co-founded with her husband Jack in August 1970. The program is conducted before a live audience in a format similar to that of a business seminar. Each week the radio program includes a one-day, question-and-answer session. The expository Bible-teaching program was airing on more than 100 radio and television stations in 1995.

Arthur's listeners are primarily women, although she counts businessmen, truck drivers, and traveling salesmen as part of her audience. As she once remarked, "God has caused me to be vulnerable, to share where I've come from, to share my past, to share my conflicts; and that causes women to relate."

Arthur dedicated her life to Christ in 1964 and soon accompanied her husband on an evangelical mission to Guadalajara, Mexico. The couple's stay in Mexico was cut short by her husband's health problems, but missionary outreach has continued to be a part of Precept Ministries. The organization currently supports offices in Korea, Hong Kong, Australia, Guate-

mala, and Mexico. Arthur's Bible-study materials have been translated into 16 languages and are employed in 87 countries.

Arthur is also an award-winning author, having published more than 20 books. The books, Bible studies, and broadcast ministries are all vehicles through which Arthur accomplishes her primary calling, the teaching of God's word. As she remarked to Karen Hawkins of *Religious Broadcasting* magazine, "My career is the Word of God and teaching people how to study the Word of God and what the Word of God has to say."

SOURCES

Hawkins, Karen M. "Kay Arthur: Woman of the Word." *Religious Broadcasting* (February, 1996).

ASSOCIATION OF CATHOLIC TV AND RADIO SYNDICATORS
established: 1975

Founded in 1975, the Association of Catholic TV and Radio Syndicators (ACTRS) represents about 60 major Roman Catholic radio and television producers and similar media organizations affiliated with UNDA-USA, the American branch of UNDA. The ACTRS is located in Los Angeles and is currently directed by Mary Jane Hopkins.

See also UNDA-USA

ASSOCIATION OF REGIONAL RELIGIOUS COMMUNICATORS
established: 1960

Founded in 1960 and located in Seattle, Washington, the Association of Regional Religious Communicators (ARRC) is an ecumenical, interfaith broadcasting organization which represents a membership of some 65 broadcasters and their ministries in the United States and Canada. The ARRC produces radio and television programs and assists members in establishing ecumenical contacts with various denominations. The ministry also takes an active interest in broadcast regulation and legislation.

SOURCES

Melton, J. Gordon. *Directory of Religious Organizations in the United States.* 3d ed. Detroit: Gale Research, 1993.

WILLIAM WARD AYER

born: 1892, Shediac, New Brunswick, Canada
died: 1985, St. Petersburg, Florida

William Ward Ayer was an influential figure in Christian fundamentalism during the middle years of the twentieth century. He was also a popular radio preacher whose program, *Marching Truth*, was a long-running staple of evangelical Christian broadcasting.

Ayer's early life was troubled and unstable. Following the death of his mother in 1897, he ran away from home at the age of five and wandered around Northeast Canada and the United States. Ayer attended a Billy Sunday revival service in Boston in 1916, which resulted in his conversion to Christ. After his graduation from the Moody Bible Institute in 1919, Ayer pastored Baptist churches in Mason City and Atlanta, Illinois, and Valparaiso and Gary, Indiana. He also served as minister to the nondenominational Philpott Tabernacle of Hamilton, Ontario, between 1932 and 1936. Ayer came into national prominence as a fundamentalist spokesperson when he assumed the pulpit of Calvary Baptist Church in New York City. Between 1936 and 1949 (when his tenure ended), the church's membership increased from 400 to 1,600 members. Ayer also published books and started *Calvary Pulpit* magazine.

During the 1940s, Ayer began a weekly radio ministry on New York station WHN, later WMGM. By 1947 the show, *Marching Truth*, had an estimated audience of 250,000 people. In a radio poll taken that year to determine "New York's number one citizen," Ayer placed third behind Francis J. Spellman and Eleanor Roosevelt. When the National Religious Broadcasters (NRB) was founded in 1944 to promote the cause of evangelical Christian broadcasting, Ayer was chosen as its founding chairman. He also helped to draft NRB's code of ethics. A strong advocate of conservative Christian unity, Ayer attempted to bring warring evangelical factions together to form a united front against liberal revisionism.

Ayer served as a trustee of Bob Jones University and Eastern Baptist University and received a doctor of divinity degree from the former institution in 1937. During this time, he became a controversial figure because of his adamant stand against Soviet atheism and his outspoken condemnation of the Roman Catholic Church as a foe of religious freedom. Among Ayer's written works were *Questions Jesus Answered* (1941) and *God's Answer to Man's Doubts* (1943).

After his resignation from Calvary Baptist Church in 1949, Ayer worked tirelessly to promote evangelicalism around the world and to sponsor Bible conferences. He also continued an independent radio ministry until his death in 1985. Ayer was inducted into the NRB Hall of Fame in 1978.

See also National Religious Broadcasters

SOURCES

Armstrong, Ben. *The Electric Church.* Nashville: Thomas Nelson, 1979.

Erickson, Hal. *Religious Radio and Television in the United States, 1921–1991.* Jefferson, NC: McFarland, 1992.

Larson, M G. *God's Man in Manhattan: The Biography of Dr. William Ward Ayer.* Grand Rapids, MI: Zondervan, 1950.

Ward, Mark, Sr. *Air of Salvation: The Story of Christian Broadcasting.* Manassas, VA: National Religious Broadcasters, 1994.

B

BACK HOME HOUR
see: Oswald Smith

THE BACK TO GOD HOUR
first aired: 1939

The Back to God Hour began as a broadcasting outreach of the Christian Reformed Church. During its first six seasons, the show aired only intermittently throughout the year and failed to build an established audience. However by 1947, the program was being broadcast nationwide over the Mutual Broadcasting System. Peter Eldersveld, the program's popular speaker, had replaced Harry Schultze because he looked, sounded, and thought like Walter Maier of *The Lutheran Hour* and because his addresses expressed the high quality of biblical scholarship and personal commitment that had long been a hallmark of the Reformed tradition. Between 1954 and 1956, the Christian Reformed Church's broadcast ministry expanded into two 13-week television series. Though the programs were well produced, they could not compete with other religious television programming in terms of broadcasting style and audience and were subsequently dropped. By 1965, the year of Eldersveld's death, the radio show was being broadcast internationally in three languages and had moved into national syndication across the United States. It was estimated that 3 million listeners heard the program weekly over 300 stations.

The Back to God Hour's commitment to the clear articulation of an educated biblical perspective was carried on by Eldersveld's successor on the program, Joel Nederhood. Nederhood, who had joined the program's staff in 1960 as a protégé of Eldersveld, carried forward Eldersveld's format of half-hour preaching programs. In 1977, the church began a new television ministry that sought to uphold the radio ministry's high standards of technical excellence and Bible-centered teaching. During the same year, the radio program was given an Award of Merit by the National Religious Broadcasters.

The Back to God Hour does not solicit donations on the air yet receives a number of generous donations from listeners and from members of the Christian Reformed Church. Indeed, each member of the small denomination is regularly assessed an amount of money for support of the radio ministry. By 1979, *The Back to God Hour* was being aired on 300 radio stations throughout the United States and Canada.

Nederhood began a new weekly television program, *Faith 20*, in 1980. The show was taped at Back to God Hour Incorporated's home base in Palos Hills, Illinois. *Faith 20* uses a magazine format that includes a telephone consultation service and a financial advice service. The program had become a daily paid-time series by 1981.

SOURCES

Armstrong, Ben. *The Electric Church*. Nashville: Thomas Nelson, 1979.

Ellens, J. Harold. *Models of Religious Broadcasting.* Grand Rapids, MI: Eerdmans, 1974.

BACK TO THE BIBLE MINISTRIES

see: Teen Quest

JIM BAKKER

born: January 2, 1940, Muskegon Heights, Michigan

Courtesy: National Religious Broadcasters

Jim Bakker and Tammy Faye Messner (formerly Bakker) were pioneers of religious television, having been present at the birth of the three most prominent religious television networks of the 1960s and 1970s: the Christian Broadcasting Network, Trinity Broadcasting Network, and PTL Network. The Bakkers's rapid rise to prominence was followed by an equally precipitous fall from grace when, in the late 1980s, they were unable to weather a barrage of personal and professional scandals.

Jim Bakker was reared in the Assemblies of God Church by Ralaigh and Furnia Bakker, both of whom came from Dutch ancestry. Ralaigh Bakker, a factory worker, had left the Dutch Reformed Church as a young man and joined the Pentecostalist movement. His son, Jim, slowly overcame the extreme shyness and feelings of inferiority that plagued him as a child and worked as a disc jockey at local dances in high school. Following a 1958 car accident in which Bakker nearly ran over a young boy in his church's parking lot, Bakker began a spiritual search that led him to enter ministerial training at North Central College (Assemblies of God) in Minneapolis, Minnesota.

While there he met another student, the future Tammy Faye Bakker. The couple became inseparable and, by 1961, had made the decision to marry. Since entering into marriage while still a student was against school policy, the newlyweds left the college and began their careers as itinerant evangelists. A short time later, Jim Bakker managed to gain ministerial credentials in the Assemblies of God.

The couple's entry into religious television occurred under the auspices of Pat Robertson, who hired the couple to bring their puppet show to his fledgling Christian Broadcasting Network (CBN) in 1965. During a fundraising appeal one evening, Bakker spoke directly into the camera and told the audience: "Our entire purpose has been to serve the Lord Jesus Christ through radio and television. But we've fallen short. We need $10,000 a month to stay on the air, and we're far short of that. Frankly, we're on the verge of bankruptcy and just don't have the money to pay our bills." Bakker's voice then broke and he began to cry. As Robertson recounted in his autobiography,

> The cameraman in the studio held steady, his camera focused on Jim's face as the tears rolled down and splattered on the concrete floor. . . . Immediately the phones in the studio started ringing until all ten lines were jammed. . . . By 2:30 AM, we had raised $105,000.

Robertson recognized that Bakker's captivating and charismatic personality would come across well on television and, after preliminary discussions concerning format and content, named Bakker to host a new religious talk show, *The 700 Club.* The program premiered on November 28, 1966. Bakker had first conceived the idea of a religious talk show after tuning into Johnny Carson's *Tonight Show* during the days of its early success.

The Bakkers continued to work with CBN until 1973, when Jim Bakker felt guided to move on to a new ministry. After a short stint helping Paul Crouch get his Trinity Broadcasting Network off the ground in Santa Ana, California, the Bakkers relocated to North Carolina with the intention of founding their own television ministry.

Jim Bakker's first job after the move began in November 1974, when he became the daily host of an already existing talk show on Charlotte station WRET-TV. The show was soon renamed *The PTL Club* (PTL meant both "Praise the Lord" and "People that Love" according to Bakker) and became the cornerstone of Bakker's new Christian broadcasting network, the PTL Network. By 1980, the program was being aired on over 200 stations nationwide and reported an audience of 668,000.

During the mid-1970s, Jim Bakker took over and redecorated a former furniture showroom, which became the station's main studio. In 1976, Bakker bought a 25-acre parcel on Park Road in Charlotte. Though initially planned as a religious retreat facility, the land was eventually developed and named Heritage Village, a Christian vacation center modeled after Disneyland and other theme parks. The acreage was also used to house the PTL corporation's Heritage Schools, facilities that provided Christian-based education from kindergarten through college.

The PTL Club moved to a modern multimillion-dollar television studio in the Heritage Village complex during the late 1970s. The new building was modeled after the Bruton Episcopal Church in the colonial settlement of Williamsburg, Virginia. Soon over 200,000 "partners" were making a pilgrimage to Charlotte for the express purpose of participating in a live telecast. The complex built "total living" facilities to accommodate these visitors.

The PTL Club's format borrowed from secular programs like *The Tonight Show* and a variety of other entertainment shows. It was filmed before a live audience consisting of tourists and guests at Heritage Village. The audience was warmed up before the program with a round of inspirational songs and coached as to the proper times to applaud during the broadcast. Some audience members were even recruited as volunteers to staff the show's telephone banks.

The taping of the two-hour program would begin with the introduction of Jim, sidekick Henry Harrison, and Tammy Faye, who was cohost and often hosted the program when Jim was away on business. Harrison was a veteran religious broadcaster who had been nicknamed "Uncle Henry" while assisting the Bakkers on their puppet show for CBN. The program then proceeded with a parade of guests and singers. Jim Bakker typically interviewed his guests about their own "faith walk" and exclaimed "Glory!" and "Praise God!" as they shared their stories of miraculous healings and success in the face of hardships. During periods of financial difficulty, Bakker would preach short sermons, regularly breaking into tears as he detailed the dangers confronting his ministry. Like *The 700 Club*, *The PTL Club* encouraged listeners to attend local churches. It also established follow-up systems with local ministers and sent materials to new members emphasizing the importance of regular church attendance.

Although he was a practicing Pentecostal, Bakker usually downplayed glossolalia (speaking in tongues) and faith healing on *The PTL Club*. Instead he preached a gospel of health and wealth that affirmed God's desire to bless true believers with both spiritual and material prosperity. As Bakker himself stated, "We preach prosperity. We preach abundant life. Christ wished above all things that we prosper." This message was a skillful blending of the optimism, materialism, and revivalism that had long been a mainstay of American evangelical culture. Bakker's message also included the traditional Pentecostal emphasis on the Second Coming of Christ. As the evangelist once proclaimed, "I believe Jesus Christ will be coming very soon. I believe with all my heart that it will be within our generation. The Bible tells us to go out into the highways and hedges and compel people to come in to His feast."

As for television itself, Bakker clearly expressed his vision of the medium's role in the final days:

[Television is] the greatest influence in the world today. We have a better product than soap or automobiles. We have eternal life. I believe in what I'm preaching. I believe in it one million percent, with every fiber of my being. That's why I use the most effective means of communication known today. Our goal is to reach every human being on earth and teach them that peace comes only through knowing Christ. I believe Christian television will be the tool that ushers in the triumphant return of Jesus Christ.

In 1978, Bakker purchased a new parcel of land near Fort Mill, South Carolina. This 2,000-acre compound became the home of Heritage USA, a huge campground and vacation complex. Funds for this new venture were raised on the air, with Bakker pitching timeshares in the complex's residential facilities for large donations. Bakker's empire now included a television station in Canton, Ohio, and around-the-clock Christian programming transmitted via satellite to cable systems nationwide. The ministry had also expanded overseas with *Club PTL* for Spanish-speaking audiences. This show and others like it in Brazil, Nigeria, and South Korea used indigenous hosts, guests, and music, and resembled Bakker's program mainly in its basic message of God's love and redemption in Christ.

Bakker became one of the pioneers of direct-mail solicitation using computerized lists of people who contacted his ministry for any reason. In a typical four-month period, those on the list received monthly letters pitching different fundraising schemes—from keeping the phone lines running, to receiving the *PTL Devotional Guide* for a gift of $15, to helping fund the construction of the Heritage USA "barn."

During the 1980s, Jim and Tammy Faye became prosperous television superstars with a large and loyal following. Their daily program's name was changed to reflect this state of affairs: *The PTL Club* became *The Jim and Tammy Show*. By 1986, the couple had built an impressive media and recreational empire. This empire featured a state-of-the-art television studio in a large, barn-shaped building; a two-story "upper room" modeled after the supposed site of the Last Supper; a seminar and conference center; a modern shopping mall called "Main Street"; a recreational park complete with water slide, swimming pools, and tennis courts; a 504-room luxury hotel; an outdoor amphitheater; restaurants; and youth facilities. Bakker also raised funds for new projects, including a home for unwed mothers, a facility for handicapped children, outreach centers in cities around the United States, and various foreign missions. These fundraising appeals often spoke of the PTL corporation's spiritual battle against the demonic forces that were attempting to destroy its ministry. By contributing money, ordinary viewers were made to feel that they were delivering a heroic blow against the evil enemies of Jim and Tammy—viz., the *Charlotte Observer*, which regularly printed investigative articles critical of the ministry, and the Federal Communications Commission, which was examining Bakker's fundraising practices.

The Bakker empire began to crumble in the spring of 1987 when details of illicit sexual relations between Jim Bakker and a church secretary in 1980 began to leak out within the evangelist community. Prominent evangelists demanded action which prompted Jim Bakker to publicly admit to his misconduct. Bakker was forced to resign from the board of Heritage USA. Within a short time, the details of the scandal began to filter into the national media. The secretary, Jessica Hahn, claimed she had been paid a substantial sum of money by Bakker's lawyer to keep the incident quiet. She subsequently agreed to be interviewed and photographed by *Penthouse Magazine*. The interview contained highly damaging allegations concerning both Bakker and other television evangelists. Soon other stories of illicit sexual encounters began to surface, some of which implicated Bakker in homosexual activities.

Bakker also came under fire for his opulent lifestyle and alleged misappropriation of ministry funds. Funds raised by *The PTL Club* were used to furnish the Bakkers with a tenfold increase in salary between 1982 and 1987, to a reported $1.5 million annually. The couple's expense accounts included such luxuries as a Mercedes-Benz, a Rolls-Royce, houses and apartments around the country, and a 55-foot houseboat. This questionable use of funds raised ostensibly for new building projects landed Bakker's ministry in deep debt and proved to be the factor that attracted the attention of United States criminal justice authorities.

At the height of the scandal, fellow tele-vangelist Jerry Falwell took over the PTL cor-poration and attempted to resuscitate the fal-tering ministry. This action did not meet with universal approval since Falwell's Baptist the-ology was considered suspect among many of Bakker's charismatic faithful. Falwell's task was made especially difficult by the constant barrage of allegations against Bakker and his co-workers permeating the national news me-dia. In response to the ministry's dire financial straits, Falwell made dramatic appeals for viewer donations. After weeks of pleading and cajoling, enough monies were received to stave off bankruptcy, and the staid, business-suited Baptist minister followed through on his prom-ise to ride the company's giant water slide. In the meantime, Jim Bakker was defrocked by the Assemblies of God for sexual misconduct. Eventually, despite a series of efforts to salvage the PTL corporation, it was sold to cover its debts.

The Bakkers retained a small number of loyal followers and with their support attempted to begin a new ministry. Jim Bakker received min-isterial credentials from several independent Pentecostal organizations and, in 1989, inau-gurated a new television program, *Jim and Tammy*, in Charlotte. The show relocated within several months to Orlando, Florida, and Bakker assumed the pastorship of a new congregation, the New Covenant Church of Orlando. It was at this point that federal authorities placed Jim Bakker on trial for financial improprieties. Bakker was found guilty and was sentenced to 45 years in federal prison. The term was later reduced to eight years.

Amazingly, some loyalists have continued to donate money to Bakker's cause and to discount the media's stories about his criminal activi-ties. Tammy Faye obtained a divorce and re-married in October, 1993. Jim has been released from prison and now resides in the Charlotte area. He is currently active in a ministry for fallen religious professionals.

See also *The 700 Club*; Trinity Broadcasting Network

SOURCES

Armstrong, Ben. *The Electric Church*. Nashville: Thomas Nelson, 1979.

Bakker, Jim. *Eight Keys to Success*. Charlotte, NC: PTL Television Network, 1980.

———. *God Answers Prayer*. Charlotte, NC: PTL Television Network, 1979.

———. *You Can Make It!* Charlotte, NC: PTL Enterprises, 1983.

Bakker, Jim, with Robert Paul Lamb. *Move That Mountain*. Plainfield, TX: Logos International, 1976.

———. *Run to the Roar*. Harrison, AR: New Leaf Press, 1980.

Barnhart, Joe E. *Jim and Tammy: Charismatic Intrigue Inside PTL*. Buffalo, NY: Prometheus, 1988.

Hadden, Jeffrey K., and Charles E. Swann. *Prime Time Preachers: The Rising Power of Televangelism*. Menlo Park, CA: Addison-Wesley, 1981.

Schultze, Quentin J. *Televangelism and American Culture*. Grand Rapids, MI: Baker Book House, 1991.

Shepard, Charles E. *Forgiven: The Rise and Fall of Jim Bakker and the PTL Ministry*. New York: Atlantic Monthly Press, 1989.

Stewart, John. *Holy War*. Enid, OK: Fireside Publishing and Communications, 1987.

Ward, Mark, Sr. *Air of Salvation: The Story of Christian Broadcasting*. Manassas, VA: National Religious Broadcasters, 1994.

TAMMY FAYE BAKKER
see: Tammy Faye Messner

THE BAPTIST HOUR
first aired: 1941

The Baptist Hour was the first religious radio program to be developed by the Radio Com-mittee of the Southern Baptist Convention, now called the Radio and Television Commission. The committee had been established in 1938 by Samuel Franklin Lowe, the pastor of Euclid Avenue Baptist Church in Atlanta, Georgia. Under his guidance, *The Baptist Hour* premiered on January 5, 1941. The show featured a sermon and music format and was an immediate success. The principal speaker at this early stage was the pastor of the First Baptist Church of Shreveport, Louisiana, Dr. M. E. Dodd. By the show's eighth season in 1949–1950, it had become a full worship service and was being broadcast nationwide over the ABC radio network.

The Baptist Hour flourished in syndication for the next 40 years and retained its format as a modified worship service with segments of modern and traditional Christian music. It has continued to be a popular radio ministry into the 1990s, broadcasting over 450 stations nationwide. A Spanish language version, dubbed *La Hora Bautista*, has been broadcast to the Caribbean and South America since the 1950s. The program has also developed a television version, which is hosted by Edwin Young. Like other ministries of the Baptist Radio and Television Commission, these broadcasting outreaches are funded fully by the Southern Baptist Convention's unified budget. This allows the shows to air without tedious fundraising appeals.

See also Southern Baptist Convention, Radio and Television Commission

SOURCES

Baker, Robert A. *The Southern Baptist Convention and Its People, 1607–1972.* Nashville: Broadman Press, 1972.

Baptist Advance. Forest Park, IL: Roger Williams Press, 1964.

Erickson, Hal. *Religious Radio and Television in the United States, 1921–1991.* Jefferson, NC: McFarland, 1992.

McBeth, Leon H. *The Baptist Heritage.* Nashville: Broadman Press, 1987.

BAPTIST INTERNATIONAL MISSIONS
established: 1960

Founded in 1960 and currently directed by Don Sisk from its headquarters in Chattanooga, Tennessee, the Baptist International Missions, Inc. (BIM), has as its primary mission the production and distribution of radio and television programs aimed at evangelism and church growth. BIM's worldwide ministry supports over 1,000 missionaries in 50 countries and includes outreach programs to disabled persons and to members of the armed services.

SOURCES

The Directory of Religious Organizations in the United States. 2d ed. Falls Church, VA: McGrath, 1982.

DONALD GREY BARNHOUSE
born: March 28, 1895, Watsonville, California
died: November 5, 1960, Philadelphia, Pennsylvania

Courtesy: *Bible Study Hour*

Donald Grey Barnhouse was one of the early pioneers of religious radio programming in

America. For nearly 40 years, he preached his strict Presbyterian Fundamentalism over the national radio waves and educated a generation of young people in orthodox scriptural exegesis.

Barnhouse was reared in Northern California by his pious Methodist parents, Theodore Barnhouse and Jane Ann Carmichael. The future preacher showed an early interest in religious activities, joining the Christian Endeavor Society, a national Christian youth fellowship, while still a teen. It was through the Christian Endeavor Society that Barnhouse met Tom Haney, the society's local field representative. Haney facilitated a born-again experience for Barnhouse, during which he accepted Christ as his personal Savior and dedicated his life to spreading the gospel.

Upon graduation from high school at age 17, Barnhouse enrolled at the Bible Institute of Los Angeles (Biola). While studying with such fundamentalist luminaries as the dispensationalist Reuben A. Torrey, Barnhouse developed his trademark conservative theological views and joined the more doctrinally rigorous Presbyterian Church.

After two years at Biola, Barnhouse transferred briefly to the University of Chicago before deciding to continue his theological training at Princeton Theological Seminary. These studies were interrupted in 1917, however, by a two-year period of service in the Army Signal Corps during World War I. After being discharged from the army, the young student gained ministerial ordination in the Presbyterian Church. Barnhouse then signed up for missionary duty with the Belgian Gospel Mission and set out for Brussels, Belgium. After two years of missionary work, Barnhouse was asked to pastor a French Reformed church in Fessinieres, France. During his time in the French Alps, he pastored another church in Mure d'Isere, enrolled as a graduate student at the University of Grenoble, and married Ruth Tiffany.

After his return from Europe, Barnhouse assumed the pastorship of Philadelphia's Grace Presbyterian Church and earned his master of theology degree from Eastern Baptist Theological Seminary. By 1927, he was settled in as pastor of Philadelphia's Tenth Avenue Presbyterian Church, an appointment he would hold for the rest of his career.

Barnhouse had begun his radio career while still a student at Biola in the early 1920s. In 1927, the young minister convinced the leaders of Tenth Avenue Presbyterian to install broadcasting equipment in the church's pulpit. Although he barely covered his costs during his first year of local broadcasts, Barnhouse persevered. The following year, he signed a $40,000 contract with the CBS radio network, becoming the first Presbyterian minister to preach on a weekly national radio program. The program flourished during the 1930s and 1940s, despite the rapidly changing parameters of radio broadcasting and the challenges posed by the Great Depression and World War II. Barnhouse was also active as an author and publisher during this period, launching the independent evangelical magazine *Revelation* in 1931 (renamed *Eternity* in 1950) and publishing the first of his long list of books, *His Own Received Him Not* (1933), two years later. Barnhouse also created a series of Bible-study materials at this time.

During World War II, Barnhouse's Philadelphia congregation granted him six months each year for national and international evangelical work. Following the war, Barnhouse began planning a new radio show that would make the Bible relevant to the daily lives of his listeners. The *Bible Study Hour* was the fruit of these labors. The show's inaugural broadcast was in 1949. Against the advice of communications experts, the half-hour program consisted of a verse-by-verse interpretation of Paul's Epistle to the Romans. Much to the surprise of church leaders, this format proved immensely popular, especially with young adults. The program's success was attributable to Barnhouse's ability to explain the Scripture in plain, uncomplicated language. The popular radio preacher spent nearly 10 years worth of programming—455 broadcasts—with this intensive exposition of Romans. The nationally syndicated program was picked up by the NBC radio network in 1956.

Barnhouse also inaugurated a 15-minute weekly television program called *Man to Man* during the mid-1950s. This forum for Barnhouse's compact sermons became a regular fixture of America's Sunday morning religious viewing. Barnhouse's style was always that of an incisive Bible teacher, rather than a flashy evangelist. He was especially skeptical of Christian faith healers and others who offered instant solutions. The respected evangelist spoke in a personal, intimate style that challenged each listener to think about important questions of faith and morality. His favorite question was "If you die tonight and stand before the gates of heaven, what reason could you give for being allowed to enter in and enjoy eternal life?" Although his audience numbered in the millions, he spoke as if he were talking to each listener personally.

Barnhouse was intimately involved in the fundamentalist-modernist controversies at Princeton Theological Seminary during the 1930s and 1940s. In spite of his clear sympathies with the conservative cause, he decided not to align himself with the new Westminister Theological Seminary in Philadelphia, preferring instead to remain loyal to the Presbyterian Church. Barnhouse's willingness to maintain fellowship with opposing factions led to a straining of his relations with both independent fundamentalists and liberals during the 1950s. Fundamentalists were particularly disturbed when Barnhouse accepted an offer to speak before the liberal National Council of Churches, calling him a traitor to the Christian cause.

The independent-minded evangelist underwent a profound spiritual transformation in later life and decided to eschew narrow theological polemics. Instead, he placed a greater emphasis on loving relationships among fellow Christians.

Following Barnhouse's death, *Bible Study Hour* was taken over by James Montgomery Boice, another pastor of Tenth Avenue Presbyterian Church in Philadelphia. Boice essentially continued where Barnhouse left off—with an exposition of Romans. By 1979, the program was still being broadcast over 300 stations nationwide. Barnhouse's recorded sermons on Romans were also being broadcast over 50 stations in a separate program format. These shows' consistently high quality of biblical exposition attracted a significant audience of college-educated listeners. For his respected work on *Bible Study Hour*, Donald Grey Barnhouse was posthumously inducted into the National Religious Broadcasters Hall of Fame in 1978.

See also *Bible Study Hour*

SOURCES

Ben Armstrong. *The Electric Church.* Nashville: Thomas Nelson, 1979.

Barnhouse, Donald Grey. *God's Methods for Holy Living.* London: Pickering & Inglis, n.d.

———. *Guaranteed Deposits.* Philadelphia: Revelation Publications, 1949.

———. *His Own Received Him Not.* Philadelphia: Revelation Publications, 1933.

———. *Life by the Son.* Philadelphia: Revelation Publications, 1939.

———. *Teaching the Word of Truth.* Philadelphia: Revelation Publications, n.d.

Barnhouse, Margaret N. *That Man Barnhouse.* Wheaton, IL: Tyndale House, 1985.

Erickson, Hal. *Religious Radio and Television in the United States, 1921–1991.* Jefferson, NC: McFarland, 1992.

Hopkins, Paul A. "What Made the Man?" *Eternity* 12, 3 (March 1961).

Reid, Daniel G., Robert D. Linder, Bruce L. Shelley, and Harry S. Stout. *Dictionary of Christianity in America.* Downers Grove, IL: InterVarsity Press, 1990.

Russell, C. A. "Donald Grey Barnhouse: Fundamentalist Who Changed." *Journal of Presbyterian History* 59 (1981): 33-57.

BELIEVER'S VOICE OF VICTORY
see: Kenneth Copeland

DAVID BENSON

born: September 18, 1929, Los Angeles, California

Founder and director of Russia for Christ Ministries, David V. Benson has worked as a missionary to Russia and its former Communist satellites for nearly 40 years. His ministry has included both the distribution of Bibles and the hosting of a religious radio program.

Educated at Wheaton College, UCLA, Harvard, and Fuller Theological Seminary, Benson began producing Russian-language broadcasts from the Hollywood Presbyterian Church in California in the mid-1950s. By 1958, he had organized Russia for Christ, Inc., and begun traveling regularly behind the Iron Curtain as a translator in order to make contact with Russian-speaking evangelicals. While in the Soviet Union, Benson would hand out Bibles and offer encouragement to the churches he visited. He was ordained as a minister in 1967 by the conservative Congregational Christian Conference.

Much of Russia for Christ's activities are done through radio broadcasts to the former Soviet Union and the Slavic regions in Eastern Europe. While its signature 30-minute radio program, *Christ's Warrior*, typically features a Bible reading, Russia for Christ also produces radio dramatizations of Bible stories.

Although the Iron Curtain has fallen, Benson and his colleagues still receive a measure of resistance from the authorities. Especially hostile are officials of the Russian Orthodox Church, which was established over 1,000 years ago and is seeking to reestablish its monopoly over Russia's Christians. Benson is the author of four books, including *Christianity, Communism, and Survival!* (1967) and *Miracle in Moscow* (1973).

See also Russia for Christ Ministries

SOURCES

Benson, David V. *Christianity, Communism and Survival!* Glendale, CA: Regal Books, 1967.

————. *Miracle in Moscow.* Santa Barbara, CA: Miracle Publications, 1973.

The Directory of Religious Organizations in the United States. 2d ed. Falls Church, VA: McGrath, 1982.

Melton, J. Gordon. *Directory of Religious Organizations in the United States.* 3d ed. Detroit: Gale Research, 1993.

EUGENE BERTERMANN

born: 1914, Bittern Lake, Alberta, Canada
died: 1983

Eugene Bertermann, minister and administrator of the Lutheran Church, Missouri Synod, was raised in the home of a Lutheran minister. At the age of 15, Bertermann began his studies at Concordia College, St. Louis, where he studied for eight years before completing a bachelor's degree in 1937. The following year, Bertermann earned a master's degree and, in 1940, a doctorate from Washington University in St. Louis. In 1940, he was ordained a minister of the Lutheran Church, Missouri Synod.

While in college, Bertermann received a scholarship from the Lutheran Laymen's League (LLL) and worked for Walter Maier of *The Lutheran Hour*. After his graduation in 1937, he remained with the LLL for an additional 24 years, serving as its business manager. Though not a founder of the National Religious Broadcasters (NRB), Bertermann was heavily involved in its affairs and served as its president from 1957 until 1975.

From 1959 to 1967, Bertermann was also executive director of the Lutheran Church's television department. In 1964, he helped organize the Lutheran Bible Translators (LBT), a missionary organization. From 1967 to 1971, he resumed his duties with the LLL. Between 1971 and 1978, Bertermann worked for the Far East Broadcasting Company. He was also one of the executive planners of Key '73, an ecumenical evangelistic drive to bring religious revival to America. In 1978, Bertermann began a five-year tenure as associate director of LBT, a position he held until his death in 1983. In 1984, for his many years of service as president of the NRB and for his lifelong career in broadcast admin-

istration, Bertermann was inducted into the National Religious Broadcasters Hall of Fame.

See also National Religious Broadcasters

SOURCES

Billy Graham Center Archives, Wheaton College, Wheaton, Illinois.

Hadden, Jeffrey K., and Charles E. Swann. *Prime Time Preachers: The Rising Power of Televangelism.* Reading, MA: Addison-Wesley, 1981.

Ward, Mark, Sr. *Air of Salvation: The Story of Christian Broadcasting.* Grand Rapids, MI: Baker Book House, 1994.

THE BIBLE ANSWERMAN

Courtesy: Christian Research Institute

WALTER MARTIN

Originally hosted by Dr. Walter Martin (1929–1989), a once Mormon bishop turned evangelical Christian, *The Bible Answerman* has aired live over the radio since the 1970s. Sponsored by the Christian Research Institute (CRI) and headquartered in San Juan Capistrano, California, *The Bible Answerman* features a call-in, question-and-answer format focusing on such issues as the creation-evolution debate, the resurrection of Christ, new religious movements, and occult group activities. The show is now

hosted by CRI director Hendrik "Hank" Hanegraaff.

See also Christian Research Institute

SOURCES

The Directory of Religious Organizations in the United States. 2d ed. Falls Church, VA: McGrath, 1982.

Erickson, Hal. *Religious Radio and Television in the United States, 1921–1991.* Jefferson, NC: McFarland, 1992.

BIBLE CHRISTIAN UNION
established: 1904

Founded in 1904 and headquartered in Hatfield, Pennsylvania, the Bible Christian Union (BCU) is an interdenominational evangelical Christian mission agency that organizes churches and trains church leaders throughout Western Europe and North America. In addition to operating in Britain, Ireland, France, Germany, Greece, Italy, the Netherlands, Sweden, Portugal, Spain, the United States, and Canada, the BCU runs a radio service that broadcasts religious programming to Christians living in the former Soviet Union. Its program, *The Russian Radio Bible Institute*, has aired since the 1970s.

SOURCES

Melton, J. Gordon. *Directory of Religious Organizations in the United States.* 3d ed. Detroit: Gale Research, 1993.

BIBLE STUDY HOUR
first aired: 1949

Originally hosted by Donald Grey Barnhouse from 1949 until his death in 1960, the *Bible Study Hour* radio program has remained on the air under the direction of James Montgomery Boice, its host since 1969. Minister of the Tenth Presbyterian Church of Philadelphia and longtime president of Evangelical Ministries (formerly the Evangelical Foundation), Boice has continued the strict expository preaching style of Barnhouse.

On each week's program, a section of Scripture is interpreted, line-by-line, in simple, nontheological language. The program also uses the Scripture lesson to give practial Christian answers to pressing contemporary questions.

From 1960 until 1969, *Bible Study Hour* featured a number of hosts, including Reginald Thomas and, from 1965 to 1967, Ben Haden, who, at the time, was minister of the Key Biscayne Presbyterian Church near Miami, Florida. Periodically, Evangelical Ministries has rebroadcast programs of *Bible Study Hour* recorded while Barnhouse was its host. For his efforts on *Bible Study Hour* between 1949 and 1960, Barnhouse was inducted, posthumously, into the National Religious Broadcasters Hall of Fame in 1978.

See also Donald Grey Barnhouse; James Montgomery Boice

SOURCES

Melton, J. Gordon. *Directory of Religious Organizations in the United States.* 3d ed. Detroit: Gale Research, 1993.

BIBLE TRUTH RADIO CRUSADE
see: W. S. McBirnie

BILLY GRAHAM EVANGELISTIC ASSOCIATION
established: 1950

The Billy Graham Evangelistic Association (BGEA) is a nonprofit religious ministry that sponsors Billy Graham's preaching crusades and subsequent telecasts of those events. The association also sponsors the Billy Graham Evangelistic Training Center (the "Cove") in Asheville, North Carolina; a weekly radio broadcast, *Hour of Decision*; feature films from World Wide Pictures; and the monthly *Decision* magazine. In 1995, the ministry generated $88 million as well as raising $72 million in private donations. More than 500 people are employed at BGEA's Minneapolis headquarters, while 52 full-time employees work at the Cove.

BGEA is one of the top four evangelical nonprofits in the United States, trailing only Campus Crusade for Christ, the Christian Broadcasting Network, and Focus on the Family in size and income. A hallmark of the ministry is its financial integrity. Graham makes only $135,000 a year in salary and housing allowances, and places all royalties from his books in a trust that supports ministry operations. BGEA's strict standards of financial accountability have become a benchmark of honesty and integrity for other televangelists. In fact, the association's business manager was instrumental in the formation of the Evangelical Council for Financial Accountability. BGEA sends out a copy of its yearly audit to all who request it.

Graham founded BGEA in 1950, shortly after becoming convinced that God wanted him to begin a radio broadcast ministry. The first broadcast of *Hour of Decision* took place on Sunday, November 5, 1950. It featured the sermons of Graham's Atlanta crusade and was heard over 150 ABC-affiliated radio stations. Within weeks, the program had garnered an audience of over 20 million people. By 1978, 900 radio stations were broadcasting the program worldwide. The series has remained popular into the 1990s and celebrated its 45th anniversary in 1995. According to published figures, the show is now broadcast over 664 stations in the United States and Canada and 366 stations around the world.

In addition to the radio broadcasts, Graham's large televised crusades, which use electronic amplification and modern theatrical lighting, have been a mainstay of BGEA's ministry since 1957. These mass events are often staged in sports arenas and stadiums. BGEA's largest crusade to date occurred in March 1995 in San Juan, Puerto Rico's Hiram Bithorn Stadium. Under the careful technical supervision of Bob Williams, BGEA's director of international ministries, Susan Cherian, managing producer,

Roger Flessing, television director, and Mike Southworth, satellite services manager, BGEA planned, produced, promoted, and transmitted the Graham crusade around the globe via 30 satellites to 3,000 different venues. Audiences in 29 time zones, living in 185 countries, heard the broadcast translated into 117 languages.

In November of 1995, BGEA's 32-member board of directors voted unanimously to install Franklin Graham, Billy Graham's son, as first vice chair. This new position places him in direct succession to his father as BGEA's chair and chief executive officer should the senior Graham ever become incapacitated. The younger Graham has served as a director of BGEA since 1979 and has also begun to preach eight to ten small crusades a year, some with his father. Franklin Graham continues to serve as the leader of both Samaritan's Purse and World Medical Mission, nonprofit Christian relief organizations that specialize in providing relief to victims of war and famine in such countries as Rwanda and Bosnia. Like World Vision, the humanitarian aid organization founded by Robert Pierce, Samaritan's Purse broadcasts regular television fundraising specials that feature the many forms of outreach the ministry supports. Both Samaritan's Purse and World Medical Mission are headquartered in Boone, North Carolina.

See also Billy Graham; Franklin Graham

SOURCES

Cooke, Phil. "Star Tech." *Religious Broadcasting* (June 1995).

Frady, Marshall. *Billy Graham: A Parable in American Righteousness*. Boston: Little, Brown, 1979.

Kennedy, John W. "The Son Also Rises." *Christianity Today*, December 11, 1995.

Lippy, Charles H. *Twentieth-Century Shapers of American Popular Religion*. New York: Greenwood Press, 1989.

Pollock, John. *Billy Graham: The Authorized Biography*. New York: McGraw-Hill, 1966.

Samaritan's Purse. Promotional brochures, 1995.

THE BIOLA HOUR

The Bible Institute of Los Angeles (Biola) began broadcasting *The BIOLA Hour* in the early days of radio from Biola's location in downtown Los Angeles. The early program featured such well-known former students and radio pioneers as Donald Grey Barnhouse and famed evangelist Charles Fuller, who also served on Biola's board of directors in the late 1920s and early 1930s.

The BIOLA Hour's host between 1979 and 1989 was David Hocking, who left the ministry to begin a new program, *Solid Rocks Radio*. Hocking's first daily Bible-study program, *Sounds of Grace*, began airing on Long Beach, California, radio station KGER in 1974. His weekly *BIOLA Hour* Bible-study program was broadcast from La Mirada, California. Though Biola University discontinued production of *The BIOLA Hour* sometime in 1992 or 1993, the program still airs occasionally through syndication.

See also David Hocking

SOURCES

Melton, J. Gordon. *Directory of Religious Organizations in the United States*. 3d ed. Detroit: Gale Research, 1993.

BLACK BUFFALO POW WOW
first aired: 1972

An early entry into the children's religious television arena was *Black Buffalo Pow Wow*, a weekly kids' show that featured quizzes, contests, sing-alongs, conservative Christian social commentary, and the ebullient Ray Wilson as "Black Buffalo." Wilson's keyboard-playing wife, Priscilla, played the role of "Mrs. Music" on the program and the children were called braves and princesses. The show was taped in Hemet, California, using a large reservation teepee as a backdrop. Each episode was set in the imaginary land of the "singing waters." *Black Buffalo Pow Wow* appeared in syndication on UHF channels in the mid-1970s and was being aired on cable outlets and more than 20 television stations by the early 1990s.

SOURCES

Erickson, Hal. *Religious Radio and Television in the United States, 1921–1991*. Jefferson, NC: McFarland, 1992.

JAMES MONTGOMERY BOICE
born: 1938

Courtesy: *Bible Study Hour*

Minister of the Tenth Presbyterian Church of Philadelphia since 1969, James Montgomery Boice hosts the *Bible Study Hour*, a popular radio program that first aired in 1949 under the direction of Donald Grey Barnhouse. Barnhouse, who died in 1960, left the radio broadcast and his umbrella organization, the Evangelical Foundation (later Evangelical Ministries) in able hands. To maintain continuity with *Bible Study Hour*'s listeners while it searched for a permanent replacement for Barnhouse, the Evangelical Foundation re-

broadcast many of Barnhouse's best lessons. After brief stints by evangelists Reginald Thomas and Ben Haden, the broadcast and directorship of the broadcast ministry were finally passed to Boice.

A minister and scholar by training, Boice has continued Barnhouse's erudite expository teaching style. He has also authored a number of learned books on theology as well as Bible commentaries. These include a four-volume commentary on the New Testament Book of Romans and a four-volume study on the foundations of the Christian faith.

See also Donald Grey Barnhouse; *Bible Study Hour*

SOURCES

Melton, J. Gordon. *Directory of Religious Organizations in the United States*. 3d ed. Detroit: Gale Research, 1993.

REINHARD BONNKE
born: April 19, 1940, Königsberg, Germany

Reinhard Bonnke is the founder of Christ for All Nations, an international missionary organization that sponsors Bonnke's major evangelistic crusades around the world. Edited tapes of these crusades appeared sporadically on the Trinity Broadcasting Network (TBN) during the 1980s and early 1990s. Beginning on June 18, 1995, Bonnke's program, *Reinhard Bonnke Ministries*, became a weekly feature of TBN's programming schedule. As of late 1995, the half-hour mixture of crusade footage and Bonnke's personal messages was airing on Sunday mornings and Tuesday evenings.

Reinhard Bonnke attended college at the Bible College of Wales, in Swansea, United Kingdom. He was ordained in March of 1964 by the German Pentecostal Church and, later that same year, married Anni Sülzle.

In May of 1967, Bonnke began his work in Africa as a missionary pastor of a congregation of 40 people. On December 6, 1974, he founded his Christ for All Nations ministry in Frankfurt, Germany. The ministry has produced a range of videos and audio-cassettes recorded at Bonnke's African crusades and Fire Conferences. It also publishes *Revival Report*, which gives a detailed accounting of the ministry's successes. Christ for All Nations is a registered charity and raises funds through the donations of supporters around the world. It attempts to articulate the biblical and Christ-centered message of the cross in a relevant and nonsectarian manner.

Between 1990 and 1994, the Bonnke evangelistic team held 57 large crusades around the globe and claimed over 17 million participants. Of that number, 3,621,000 were reported to have declared their desire to follow Christ. In 1995, Bonnke held 13 major crusades and attended 77 conferences and meetings in such countries as Benin, Ethiopia, Austria, Indonesia, India, Senegal, Mali, Guinea Bissau, and Wales.

The American branch of Bonnke's ministry, Reinhard Bonnke Ministries, Inc., has also begun work designing a 20-page evangelistic booklet they hope to mail to all 112 million households in the United States and Canada in September 1997. This missionary effort follows a similar mailing to 24 million homes in the United Kingdom and 40 million households in Liechtenstein, Austria, Switzerland, and Germany. The ministry reported receiving 103,000 decision-for-Christ cards in England and Germany after the first mailing. The English version of the booklet, entitled *From Minus to Plus: The Epic of Christ's Cross*, featured full-color photographs and a simple message of salvation. The hope was that families would keep the booklet lying around the home because of its attractive appearance. The mass mailing in North America comes in response to a vision Bonnke had in 1992 during which God reportedly told him to blanket the continent with the "message of the Cross."

To assist in the North American mass mailing, which will cost an estimated $67 million, the Bonnke ministry in Sacramento, California, is hoping to enlist the support of 50,000 local churches, a practice he has used before with success. The Foursquare Gospel televangelist, Jack Hayford , a member of Bonnke's board of trustees and pastor of the 7,000-member Church on the Way in Van Nuys, California, has become one of the first high-profile Christian leaders to involve his congregation in the mass-mailing effort.

Meanwhile, Bonnke continues to conduct crusades in the Third World especially in Muslim-dominated countries with minority Christian populations, such as Mali and Chad. Bonnke is also the author of a number of inspirational and evangelistic books and pamphlets.

SOURCES

Biographical materials, Reinhard Bonnke Ministries, 1995.

"Evangelist Reinhard Bonnke Targets 285 Million People," *Christianity Today*, December 11, 1995.

PAT BOONE
born: June 1, 1934, Jacksonville, Florida

The popular singer and religious broadcasting celebrity, Charles Eugene "Pat" Boone, was raised as a member of the independent Churches of Christ. He made his breakthrough in the recording industry with the 1955 hit song, "Two Hearts." The song also made him an instant teen idol. In 1958, the same year he starred in the movie *Bernadine*, Boone authored an advice book for teens, *'Twixt Twelve and Twenty*. Handsome, talented, and warmly religious, Boone appeared regularly on radio and television programs during the 1950s and 1960s, singing devotional style songs and sharing his evangelical faith.

Through the influence of his wife, Shirley, Boone became associated with the Church of the Foursquare Gospel in the late 1960s. In 1969, while attending the Church on the Way in Van Nuys, California, he received the charismatic baptism of the Holy Spirit. Soon after, he began to appear on Pentecostal programs.

Boone's close association with David Wilkerson, a street-gang evangelist and Pentecostal preacher in New York City, led to Boone's starring role in the 1972 movie, *The Cross and the Switchblade*. The film was based on Wilkerson's ministry among New York gang members.

Ever popular among youth, Boone continued to make guest appearances on both secular and Christian television shows during the 1970s, even hosting his own family holiday specials. His autobiography, *A New Song*, was published in 1970. Boone also wrote *A Miracle a Day Keeps the Devil Away*, which was published in 1974.

At the height of his popularity as a celebrity representative of American evangelical faith, Boone spoke at the 1976 National Religious Broadcasters' A Prayer for the Nation convention in Washington, DC. That year had been dubbed the Year of the Evangelical and a great many celebrities had been "coming out" all year, declaring their faith in Jesus. Boone's address was on the subject of "morality in the media."

In the late 1970s, Boone's talented daughter, Debbie, became a singing star with her award-winning recording of "You Light Up My Life," a love song with subtle religious nuances.

In 1982 Boone inaugurated the worldwide Pat Boone Radio Network. The network continues to add new stations and to air Boone's one-hour contemporary Christian music program, *The Pat Boone Show*.

In addition, Boone continues to be a popular guest on religious television talk shows and currently hosts a Saturday evening half-hour music program, *Gospel America*, on Paul and Jan Crouch's Trinity Broadcasting Network.

See also David Wilkerson

SOURCES

Burgess, Stanley M., and Gary B. McGee, eds. *Dictionary of Pentecostal and Charismatic Movements*. Grand Rapids, MI: Zondervan, 1988.

Ward, Mark, Sr. *Air of Salvation: The Story of Christian Broadcasting*. Grand Rapids, MI: Baker Book House, 1994.

JUAN BOONSTRA
born: 1926, Argentina
died: March 24, 1995

For 26 years, Juan Boonstra was the voice of the Spanish-language broadcasting outreach of the Christian Reformed Church. The broadcast, entitled *La Hora de la Reforma* ("The Reform Hour"), began in 1964. Boonstra was the host of the program until his retirement in 1991. The popular radio personality died in 1995, at the age of 69.

BOTT RADIO NETWORK
established: November 12, 1962

The Bott Radio Network is a conservative Christian broadcast service that embraces as its first priority the preaching and teaching of God's Word. The service provides its audience with news, current events, and a discussion of controversial contemporary issues from a biblical viewpoint. The network's stated goal is to "help people grow in the Lord, and then to apply their Christian faith" in daily, private, and community service. Pastor Bob Phillips hosts a daily 26-minute Bible-teaching program. Dick Bott was the network's president as of June, 1995. The network's affiliates include: KCCV-AM and KCCV-FM, Kansas City, KCVW-FM, Wichita, KCVT-FM, Topeka, Kansas; KAYX-FM, Richmond, Virginia; KSIV-FM and AM, St. Louis; WCRV-AM, Memphis; KQCV-AM and KNTL-FM, Oklahoma City; WFCV-AM, Fort Wayne, Indiana; KLCV-FM, Lincoln, Nebraska; and KCIV-FM, Fresno and Modesto, California.

ROBERT BOWMAN
born: 1915, Los Angeles, California

Founder and president emeritus of the Far East Broadcasting Company (FEBC), Robert H. Bowman grew up in Los Angeles in a nominally pious family. At age 18, Bowman enrolled for study at the Southern California Bible College (SCBC), where he met and married Eleanor Guthrie. The couple would later have two sons.

In 1934, during his first year of college, Bowman joined Paul Myers's ("First Mate Bob") original *Haven of Rest* quartet as a baritone. The program first aired over KMPC radio, Los Angeles, and subsequently moved to KNX, a CBS-affiliate station. In Myers's absence, Bowman would host the broadcast, earning him the nickname "Second Mate Bobby." Bowman remained with the *Haven of Rest* quartet nearly 10 years after he and Eleanor had graduated from SCBC in 1936.

In the 1940s, Bowman, who was being groomed to take over the *Haven of Rest* radio ministry following Myers's retirement, suddenly began to envision using radio to preach the gospel to the peoples of Asia. In December 1945, Bowman and John Broger, a navy veteran, sometime actor, and college friend, joined with minister William J. Roberts to form the Far East Broadcasting Company (FEBC). To help raise money for their missionary venture, Bowman and Broger produced a number of radio programs in association with the Moody Bible Institute, entitled *The Call of the Orient*.

In 1947, Bowman and Broger chose Manila, capital of the Philippines, as the location of their first radio station. After raising initial funding, Broger, his wife, and a number of missionary associates traveled to Manila to set up the broadcast station. From their new compound in the Philippines, dubbed Christian Radio City Manila, Broger and his associates began their first broadcasts over radio station DZAS in June 1948, opening with the hymn "All Hail the Power of Jesus' Name." The Broger family was the first to manage the station, with the Bowmans arriving in the Philippines to relieve them in 1949. The Bowman and Broger 18-month rotations continued until 1954 when Broger resigned his position with FEBC and became director of armed forces information and education for the US Pentagon.

During these early years of the broadcast ministry, Communist-backed rebels posed safety problems for FEBC missionaries.

Though the FEBC was politically neutral, its strategic location in the Cold War struggle for Asia's allegiance also led to broadcast frequency problems.

In 1960, FEBC began to erect additional radio transmitters in Japan and elsewhere in the Philippines. By 1995, FEBC had erected over 30 such transmitters throughout Asia and the West. Using these transmitters, FEBC currently broadcasts the gospel in 145 languages worldwide.

In the early 1990s, Bowman began to expand broadcast coverage into the Middle East and into Muslim areas of Asia and West Africa. Though now retired, Bowman remains a vital part of FEBC, serving as president emeritus from its international headquarters in La Mirada, California.

See also Far East Broadcasting Company

SOURCES

Bowman, Eleanor (with Susan F. Titus). *Eyes Beyond the Horizon.* Nashville: Thomas Nelson, 1991.

Ward, Mark, Sr. *Air of Salvation: The Story of Christian Broadcasting.* Grand Rapids, MI: Baker Book House, 1994.

MYRON BOYD
born: July 19, 1909, Shelbyville, Illinois
died: 1978, Greenville, Illinois

Host of the *Light and Life Hour* from 1944 until his retirement in 1965, Myron Boyd had been in broadcasting for nearly a decade before he came to national prominence as a radio minister.

Boyd was the son of Edward Pliny Boyd and Greta Pierce and grew up in a pious Methodist environment. In 1932, he graduated from Seattle Pacific College, was ordained to the ministry, and married Ruth Eleanor Putnam. Following pastorships at churches in Tonasket and Wenatchee, Washington, between 1932 and 1938, Boyd was called as pastor of First Free Methodist Church, Seattle, in 1939. During this period, Boyd became the speaker for a popular regional radio program, *Gospel Clinic*. In 1944,

Courtesy: National Religious Broadcasters

after enjoying success with *Gospel Clinic*, he was tapped as host of *Light and Life Hour*, which broadcast from its headquarters in Winona Lake, Indiana. As the program expanded, so also did Boyd's involvement with the ministry. The show's format featured discussions of selected Bible topics, emphasizing practical scriptural principles that listeners could apply to their everyday lives.

Boyd was among the 150 religious broadcasters who attended a special session of the National Association of Evangelicals during its annual meeting in April 1944. It was at this meeting that plans for an association of religious broadcasters were discussed. The discussions resulted in the formation of the National Religious Broadcasters (NRB) later that year, with Boyd becoming a charter member.

In 1947, Boyd resigned his position at First Free Methodist of Seattle in order to devote his full energies to the broadcast ministry. In 1965, the popular radio preacher left the program to become a bishop in the Free Methodist Church of North America. He retired in 1976 and died at the age of 70 in 1978.

Boyd's work on the *Light and Life Hour* earned him NRB's Churchill award for outstanding achievement in 1947–1948, an honor he shared with Thomas Zimmerman of *Sermons in Song*. Boyd was also the recipient of a cita-

tion and trophy from the NRB in 1955 for the best all-around religious broadcast for five years.

Light and Life Hour continued after Boyd's retirement and was being carried over 200 stations nationwide well into the 1980s.

See also *Light and Life Hour*; National Religious Broadcasters

SOURCES

Ward, Mark, Sr. *Air of Salvation: The Story of Christian Broadcasting.* Grand Rapids, MI: Baker Book House, 1994.

JOHN L. BRANHAM
born: 1913, Texas

Along with such figures as Lightfoot Solomon Michaux and John Washington Goodgame, John L. Branham was one of the early African American stars of religious broadcasting.

Branham was the son of the prominent Baptist preacher, J. H. Branham. He grew up in Chicago, Illinois, and attended Morehouse College in Atlanta, Georgia, which would later become the alma mater of other noted African Americans such as Dr. Martin Luther King, Jr. Branham's first ministerial post was at St. Paul Baptist Church, a small, struggling congregation in Los Angeles, California. Branham built the church into a respectable congregation within a short time after his arrival. He also met and married Ethel Branham, a local social worker.

John Branham's entry into religious radio began with a Sunday evening program, *Echoes of Eden*. The show was broadcast over radio station KFWB in Los Angeles and overseas via the Armed Forces Network. Branham's gifts as an orator made *Echoes of Eden* immensely popular. The program's estimated audience grew to over 1 million people. Using his large radio following as a base of support, Branham inaugurated a fundraising drive to build a new church complex. The complex was completed in 1951 at an estimated cost of $550,000. It included such innovations as a barbecue pit, a snack bar, powder rooms, and an elevator controlled pulpit, as well as a parking lot with a capacity for 300 automobiles. The church's main auditorium seated 750 congregants and was completely soundproof. The composition of Branham's integrated congregation, whose slogan became "love for everybody," was nearly 75 percent African American and 25 percent white.

Branham survived a string of scandals during the 1950s. In one episode, he was shot under awkward circumstances by an "ex-bookie queen" named Hazel Simpson. Although a grand jury ruled the incident an accident, Branham and his church were subjected to embarrassing public questions. In a second episode, Branham was charged by a church usher with seducing his 21-year-old daughter. The young woman had been working at the time as Branham's personal secretary. The incident exploded into public view when eight black-market records containing sexually oriented conversations allegedly involving Branham and his secretary hit the streets during 1955. Both Branham and the secretary denied that the voices on the records were theirs. In three stormy church votes, Branham was overwhelmingly supported by his congregation, and the incident was declared closed.

SOURCES

"Branham Denies Voice on Questionable Records." *Ebony*, March, 1955.

"Top Radio Ministers." *Ebony*, July, 1949.

WILLIAM BRANHAM

born: April 6, 1909, Burkesville, Kentucky
died: December 24, 1965, Amarillo, Texas

The "Holy Ghost" Baptist minister and faith healer William M. Branham was instrumental in starting the postwar healing revival in Pentecostalism. Born in Kentucky to poor parents, Branham heard the voice of God, first at age three and then again at the age of seven,

calling him to a prophetic healing ministry. After an experience of personal healing at the age of 24, Branham began an independent Baptist tent ministry in Jefferson, Indiana, preaching to crowds as large as 3,000. He married Hope Brumback a year later in 1934.

Though moving toward Pentecostal-holiness style revival and a Oneness theology of God (as opposed to the Trinity), Branham did not openly associate with churches that held these beliefs. As he continued to report visions and promptings by the Spirit, however, his relations became increasingly strained with more mainstream fundamentalist Baptists. In 1937, Branham reported receiving a series of visions in which he saw the rise of Mussolini, Hitler, and Communism; the menace of technology; the decline of morality among women in the United States; and, last of all, the final destruction of America. Later, during a baptismal service in the Ohio River, Branham claims to have seen a bright light and heard a voice proclaim that just as John the Baptist's ministry heralded the first coming of Christ, Branham's would herald the Second Coming.

Branham's healing ministry began in 1946 after a visitation from an angel who promised him the powers of discernment and healing. Soon after that event, he put his new powers to the test by healing the daughter of a fellow pastor.

Branham's ministry increased and his fame as a healer spread throughout Pentecostal circles in the United States. In 1947, Jack Moore, founder and copastor of Life Tabernacle Church, Shreveport, Louisiana, and Gordon Lindsay, a minister of the Assemblies of God, joined Branham's ministry. From 1946 to 1955, when Branham was sued by the IRS for tax evasion, Branham's fame and success as a faith healer were matched only by that of Oral Roberts. *The Voice of Healing* news magazine, published by Lindsay, his wife Anna, and Moore in 1948, helped spread Branham's fame among more mainstream Pentecostals. The Branham team also pioneered the airing of revival meetings and healing sessions over radio in the 1950s.

In later years, the evangelist claimed that he himself was the prophetic angel spoken of in the third and tenth chapters of the Book of Revelation. When he died after a fatal car accident in 1965, many of his followers expected him to be resurrected, believing him to be divine. (A published 1950 photograph of Branham with a halo over his head, "the pillar of fire," did little to diminish this belief.) Indeed, to some, his sermons were regarded as divinely inspired and were revered as Scripture.

See also Gordon Lindsay

SOURCES

Billy Graham Center Archives, Wheaton College, Wheaton, IL.

Branham, William. *An Exposition of the Seven Church Ages*. Jeffersonville, IN: Branham Campaigns, n.d.

———. *The Revelation of the Seven Seals*. Tucson, AZ: Spoken Word Publications, 1967.

Burgess, Stanley M., and Gary B. McGee, eds. *Dictionary of Pentecostal and Charismatic Movements*. Grand Rapids, MI: Zondervan, 1988.

Melton, J. Gordon. *Religious Leaders of America*. Detroit: Gale Research, 1991.

Stone, Jon R. *A Guide to the End of the World: Popular Eschatology in America*. New York: Garland, 1993.

BREAKFAST BRIGADE
see: Paul Rader

BREAKTHROUGH
see: Rod Parsley

DAVID BREESE
born: October 14, 1926, Chicago, Illinois

David W. Breese is the engaging producer and host of the daily radio broadcast, *Pause for Good News*, and the weekly syndicated radio and television program, *Dave Breese Reports*.

Courtesy: Christian Destiny Ministries

Breese, who has been a fixture on Christian radio and television since the mid-1970s, is also the respected director of Christian Destiny Ministries.

Educated at Judson College in Elgin, Illinois, and Northern Baptist Theological Seminary in Lombard, Illinois, Breese began his ministry in the 1950s working as an evangelist for Youth for Christ (YFC), a teen ministry organization founded in 1944 by Torrey Johnson and Billy Graham. He was ordained as an independent fundamentalist minister in 1951. After nearly 12 years with YFC, Breese set out on his own, founding Christian Destiny Ministries in 1963. From 1963 to 1978, Breese spoke at conferences and rallies throughout the United States and periodically appeared as a guest on various radio and television programs.

In 1978, Breese began producing a radio program. The new 30-minute broadcast, *Dave Breese Reports*, was originally carried locally over radio station WABS, Washington, DC. A short time later, the show was produced for radio and television and broadcast in conjunction with television station KYFC-TV in Kansas City. In 1984, Breese moved Christian Destiny Ministries to its present facilities in Hillsboro, Kansas. Currently, *Dave Breese Reports* is carried over Christian stations from coast to coast and reaches an estimated audience of 1 million.

Breese's endtimes evangelistic ministry continued to grow during the late 1980s. In 1987, he added *The King Is Coming* to the list of programs he hosts. The half-hour Bible-teaching show, which uses films and maps to argue the validity of biblical prophecy, is produced by the World Prophetic Ministry of Colton, California. Carried initially over about 30 channels, it now airs Sundays over 300 channels worldwide via the Trinity Broadcasting Network.

In addition to his busy broadcast schedule, Breese finds time to write. He has authored numerous books and pamphlets, mostly on apocalyptic themes. His many titles include: *Discover Your Destiny*; *Know the Mark of the Cults*; *Living in These Last Days*; *The Rapture of the Church*; and *The Religion of the Last Days*.

SOURCES

Breese, Dave. *The Exciting Plan of God for Your Life.* Wheaton, IL: Christian Destiny, 1978.

———. *The Five Horsemen.* Lincoln, NE: Back to the Bible Broadcast, 1975.

———. *What's Ahead?* Lincoln, NE: Back to the Bible Broadcast, 1974.

Melton, J. Gordon. *Directory of Religious Organizations in the United States.* 3d ed. Detroit: Gale Research, 1993.

Stone, Jon R. *A Guide to the End of the World: Popular Eschatology in America.* New York: Garland, 1993.

BILL BRIGHT

born: October 19, 1921, Coweta, Oklahoma

William "Bill" Rohl Bright, the founder and head of Campus Crusade for Christ International, is one of the world's foremost Christian evangelists. Although his ministry has always preferred the more personalized activities of live rallies, small campus study groups, and direct witnessing, Bright has made frequent television appearances on the programs of fellow evan-

Courtesy: Campus Crusade for Christ International

gelists and hosted several television shows including *Training in Practical Christian Living* and *Keys to Dynamic Living with Bill Bright*. Campus Crusade has also been involved in a number of religious broadcasting initiatives, including television programs such as *Athletes in Action*.

Bright's earliest religious influences came from his mother, a pious Methodist woman who received Christ as a teen. Bright's own fervent religiosity, however, would not develop until he had experimented with the secular worlds of business and entrepreneurship. Upon graduation from Northeastern State College in Oklahoma, the future evangelist taught for a short time and then moved to Southern California, where he established a food marketing company, Bright's California Confections. The business sold its specialty items through department stores and exclusive shops. Driven by Bright's bold and aggressive salesmanship, the company quickly became successful.

During this period Bright met Dawson Trotman, the founder of the Navigators, an international evangelistic group, and Dan Fuller, the son of radio preacher Charles Fuller. Through their influence, Bright began attending Hollywood Presbyterian Church. The church's blending of evangelical witness and refined socializing appealed to the handsome newcomer, as did the opportunity to rub shoulders with Hollywood's wealthy and influential conservative subculture.

It was through the efforts of the church's charismatic director of Christian education, Henrietta Mears, that Bright dedicated his life to Christ in 1945. Mears was a highly successful evangelist who used Bible-study fellowships, missionary witnessing teams, and prominent celebrities as her primary proselytizing methods. Bright's future evangelistic enterprise would owe a large debt to Mears.

After enrolling in Princeton Theological Seminary in 1946, Bright was forced to return to Southern California to deal with business matters. He decided to finish his theological degree at Fuller Theological Seminary, which he entered in 1947. Bright married Vonette Zachary, a hometown sweetheart from Oklahoma, the following year. The couple's two sons, Zachary and Bradley, would later devote their lives to Bright's evangelical activities.

While studying for a Greek exam one night during his final year at Fuller, Bright had an "intoxicating experience" of God's presence and a vision of his future mission. As he recounted in a subsequent interview, "I received his commission to go into all the world and make disciples of all nations—to help fulfill the great commission."

Fired with a renewed zeal to preach the gospel, Bright dropped out of the seminary, sold his business, and rented a house within a block of the University of California at Los Angeles. He established a board of directors for his new evangelistic enterprise, Campus Crusade for Christ. The ministry brought over 250 students to Christ within its first few months of operation. Over the next 10 years, Bright's crusade spread to other college campuses, first along the West Coast, then gradually throughout the United States.

Campus Crusade for Christ's growth rode the crest of a postwar religious revival which saw the retreat of secularism and the rise of such evangelical mega-stars as Billy Graham, Oral Roberts, and Billy James Hargis. Bright, however, avoided traditional Fundamentalism's extreme attacks on all aspects of modern culture. He agreed with Graham, who argued, "Fundamentalism has failed miserably with the big stick approach, now it is time to take the big love approach." Bright's enterprise would retain historical evangelicalism's belief in biblical inerrancy, vicarious atonement, and personal conversion to Christ, while also finding a way to accommodate the larger American ethos of material prosperity and technological progress.

Bright's student groups followed a proven formula for proselytizing on college campuses. As spelled out in Bright's how-to booklet, "Have You Heard of the Four Spiritual Laws?," this formula presented Christian teachings as four rational and empirically testable facts: (1) God loves all persons and has a special plan for their lives; (2) human sinfulness creates alienation and separation from God; (3) God has provided his son Jesus as the sole remedy for this sinfulness; and (4) each person must accept Christ as Lord and Savior to avail themselves of God's grace and forgiveness. The booklet concluded by inviting readers to receive Christ into their hearts at that very moment, and provided a sample prayer to that end.

Campus Crusade's bright and energetic staff typically follow a four-pronged attack when proselytizing a campus. The first phase, penetration, attempts to find local leaders who are "teachable" and zealous for God. During the subsequent phases—concentration, saturation, and continuation—missionaries are encouraged to be a witness to at least 15 people every week, until an entire campus has received the teaching of the Four Spiritual Laws.

Bright's enterprise tends to attract young, conservative-minded students who are comfortable with the crusade's rigid authority structure, aggressive tactics, and continual calls for renewal and training. Most advanced training takes place at the ministry's well-appointed headquarters at Arrowhead Springs in the San Bernadino Mountains of Southern California. In addition to hosting annual training seminars, the facility houses the ministry's Lay Institute for Evangelism, International Christian Graduate University, and Executive Seminars.

Bright formed Athletes in Action during the mid-1960s to enlist championship athletes in personal witnessing for Christ. He also developed a ministry called Berkeley Blitz in the late 1960s, which adapted to the revolutionary tenor of the times by defending student dissent and using such phrases as "revolution now." Bright employed popular folk and country singers such as Paul Stookey and Johnny Cash to adapt his message to the folk-rock musical styles of the late 1960s and early 1970s. Finally, he held massive public Explo rallies for high school and college students in the early 1970s that mixed evangelical revivalism and staunch patriotism with the ambiance of a rock festival. In each of these outreaches, Bright displayed his uncanny ability to speak to youth in a language and style they could understand.

In spite of his willingness to appropriate contemporary trends and styles, Bright has remained a firm supporter of conservative middle-class American values. His Executive Seminars call on business and entertainment luminaries such as H. Ross Perot and Dale Evans to counter critics of the "American way of life" and to promote the Protestant work ethic, strict personal morality, entrepreneurial initiative, and free-market capitalism.

During the 1980s and early 1990s, Bright expanded his ministry's outreach to over 150 foreign countries. With the help of a budget that reached $120 million in 1987, he has successfully communicated his simple message to persons of widely divergent cultural and ethnic backgrounds. Explo '85, for example, made use of sophisticated telecommunications equipment to link over 94 sites around the world. The estimated 300,000 attendees of the event received intensive training in the Four Spiritual Laws.

In addition to appearing on the television programs of other well-known preachers, Bright has hosted two television series, *Training in Practical Christian Living* and *Keys to Dynamic Living with Bill Bright*, at his San Bernadino headquarters. The former program is a series of five-minute taped messages and the latter a half-hour special featuring persons who have turned their lives around with the help of Christ. *Keys to Dynamic Living*, which began broadcasting in 1994, has been featured on Paul Crouch's Trinity Broadcasting Network. Bright's staff at Campus Crusade have produced, among other radio and television specials, the popular television series *Athletes in Action* and the film *Jesus*, which Bright claims has been seen by over 270 million people in 104 languages worldwide.

Critics of Bright's ministry have found three general areas of concern. The first is what they allege to be Bright's rigid, patriarchal, and authoritarian management style. Women are absent from leadership positions in Campus Crusade for Christ, and dissent or questioning of executive decisions is discouraged. Bright's running of Campus Crusade may be authoritarian, but it is also efficient. He keeps administrative and fundraising expenses to under 10 percent of earnings, and expects all staff members (including himself) to raise their own support for their relatively modest fixed salaries.

A second line of criticism comes from outsiders who claim that Bright has relied too heavily on wealthy businessmen and their sophisticated methods of management. Bright has been unrepentant about his cultivation of conservative business leaders, however, stating, "They lead more people to Christ, they give more generously of their funds, and are less 'worldly' than some I know who really don't have anything."

A final area of criticism comes from church leaders and denominational campus pastors who claim that Bright's organization only pays lip service to the needs of local churches and that his volunteers preach a theologically simplistic "seventy-seven word crash course in Christianity" deceptively disguised as a "religious survey."

Bright has sought to bolster the intellectual credentials of his ministry by repeatedly reminding readers through his monthly magazine *Worldwide Challenge* that he "did graduate work at Princeton and Fuller Theological Seminaries" and that he has been awarded several honorary degrees from colleges in Korea and the United States. These honorary degrees include a doctor of laws, doctor of letters, and a doctor of divinity. Bright still, however, falls under the sweep of historian Nathan Hatch's judgment that modern conservative evangelicals have eschewed a serious intellectual life in their relentless pursuit of conversions. "Small wonder," Hatch observes, "that evangelical thinking which once was razor-sharp and genuinely profound, now seems dull, rusty, even banal."

Bright was awarded the Templeton prize for Progress in Religion in May of 1996. The prize carries an award of $1 million.

SOURCES

Bright, Bill. *Come Help Change Our World.* San Bernadino, CA: Campus Crusade, 1979.

———. *Have You Heard of the Four Spiritual Laws?* San Bernadino, CA: Campus Crusade, 1965.

———. *Revolution Now.* San Bernadino, CA: Campus Crusade, 1969.

———. *Transferable Concepts Series.* 9 vols. San Bernadino, CA: Campus Crusade, 1981.

Chandler, Russell. "Campus Crusade at 30," *Christianity Today*, January 22, 1982.

"Door Interview: Bill Bright." *Wittenberg Door*, (February-March 1977).

Flake, Carol. *Redemptorama: Culture, Politics, and the New Evangelicalism.* New York: Penguin, 1985.

Lippy, Charles H., ed. *Twentieth-Century Shapers of American Popular Religion.* Westport, CT: Greenwood Press, 1989.

Marsden, George M. *Evangelicalism and Modern America.* Grand Rapids, MI: Eerdmans, 1984.

Quebedeaux, Richard. *I Found It! The Story of Bill Bright and Campus Crusade.* San Francisco: Harper & Row, 1979.

Reid, Daniel G., et al., eds. *Dictionary of Christianity in America.* Downers Grove, IL: InterVarsity Press, 1990.

Taylor, J. Randolph. "Here's Bright America." *Christian Century* 93 (1976).

Wallis, Jim, and Wes Michaelson. "The Plan to Save America." *Sojourners* 5 (1976).

JOHN BROGAN

see: Far East Broadcasting Company

HUNTLEY BROWN

born: October 16, 1963, Brownstone, Jamaica

Huntley Brown is an acclaimed accompanist and soloist who works as the resident pianist on Chicago's public supported religious television station, WCFC-TV. Brown can be heard daily on WCFC's talk and interview show *Among Friends*, hosted by Jerry Rose.

Brown was born into a Christian home on the island of Jamaica. He learned piano at an early age by imitating his two brothers, who were taking lessons. Brown's father, an accordion and piano player, took note of his young son's dedication to music, and gave him rudimentary piano instruction. Brown attended Iona Christian High School in Ocho Rios, Jamaica, and took additional piano lessons from Paul Tucker, a family friend. During this period, Brown perfected his technique by imitating the records he heard of Oscar Peterson, Vladimir Horowitz, and his friend, Monty Alexander. Upon graduation from high school, Brown became a rising star on the Jamaica hotel circuit. The night club scene conflicted with his Christian commitment, however, and he decided to quit his popular band and follow God's guidance wherever it might lead.

Brown came to the United States in 1984. He enrolled in Judson College near Chicago and studied music and Christian doctrine. During this time he gained an international reputation as the chief accompanist and soloist for the Judson College Choir. The choir toured Europe, Mexico, Haiti, and Jamaica, as well as the United States. A new phase of his life came when Brown began to play at Willow Creek Church in Barrington, Illinois, a Chicago suburb. As Willow Creek grew into one of the nation's most successful independent churches, Brown gained increased attention. He began performing more and more as a soloist around the country. Following his graduation from Judson in 1988, Brown enrolled in a graduate program in piano performance at Northern Illinois University. He took his master's degree, and, in June of 1992, married Annette Chestnut, a college friend. Chestnut was a native of the Caribbean island of Barbados and a certified public accountant. She would soon become her husband's business manager.

In addition to his television work at WCFC-TV, Brown has become a deacon and regular pianist at the First Baptist Church of Big Rock, Illinois. He has also joined the Billy Graham Association. This affiliation takes him around the world as a pianist at evangelistic conferences and crusades. In 1995, Brown was a featured performer at the National Religious Broadcasters annual convention in Nashville, Tennessee.

SOURCES

"Casting Call for NRB 95." *Religious Broadcasting* (February 1995).

R. R. BROWN

born: 1885, Dagus Mines, Pennsylvania
died: 1964, Omaha, Nebraska

Robert R. Brown is best known as the host of *Radio Chapel Service*, a broadcasting ministry that lasted from 1923 to 1977. He was inducted into the Religious Broadcasters Hall of Fame for his role in airing the first nondenominational religious service over American radio.

Brown received his ministerial training at Nyack College in Nyack, New York (formerly the Missionary Training Institute) and pastored churches of the Christian and Missionary Alliance (CMA) in Chicago and Beaver Falls, Pennsylvania, during his early career. In 1923, he became the pastor of the Omaha Gospel Tabernacle in Omaha, Nebraska. In April of that year, Omaha's new radio station, WOW, asked Brown to preach on its first Sunday of operation. WOW would become the fabled training ground for

such media celebrities as Johnny Carson. Although Brown never intended to create a broadcasting ministry, his mind was changed when a man informed him that he had accepted Christ as a result of Brown's first radio sermon. Brown is reported to have exclaimed, "Hallelujah! Unction can be transmitted!" Within a year, *Radio Chapel Service* had become a weekly nondenominational program on WOW with Brown as its host.

Preaching over the radio airwaves took some getting used to for the young minister, and he continued for a time to shout at the microphone and gesture as if he were talking to a church congregation. By the 1930s, the "Billy Sunday of the air" was preaching to a Midwest radio audience of nearly 500,000. In addition to his radio ministry, Brown served as a board member of the CMA between 1925 and 1960 and established the Bible and Missionary Conference Center in Okoboji Lakes, Iowa, during the 1930s.

Brown was a pioneer in treating his radio audience as a new kind of church community. He invited his listeners to become members of the World Radio Congregation. This innovative "church of the airwaves," established by Brown, sent interested listeners official membership cards and raised money for humanitarian relief.

Brown continued to preach on *Radio Chapel Service* until his death in 1964. His duties on the program were assumed by his son, Robert, who also directed a weekly television series from Omaha Gospel Tabernacle during *Radio Chapel Service*'s fiftieth anniversary season. The ministry finally came to an end in 1977.

See also *Radio Chapel Service*

SOURCES

Armstrong, Ben. *The Electric Church*. Nashville: Thomas Nelson, 1979.

Erickson, Hal. *Religious Radio and Television in the United States, 1921–1991*, NC: McFarland, 1992.

Ward, Mark, Sr. *Air of Salvation: The Story of Christian Broadcasting*. Manassas, VA: National Religious Broadcasters, 1994.

STEVE BRUCE
born: 1954

Steve Bruce, reader in sociology at the Queen's University of Belfast, Northern Ireland, is a respected scholarly commentator on the American Christian Right and on televangelism in Europe and the United States. Bruce has travelled widely within America's conservative Christian subculture and has published such well-received studies of this religious community as *The Rise and Fall of the New Christian Right* (1988), *A House Divided* (1990) and *PrayTV: Televangelism in America.*

Pray TV is an excellent sociological analysis of modern religious broadcasting. It provides a British perspective that both illuminates the unique dimensions of American religious culture and offers apt European comparisons. In his assessment of religious broadcasting's influence on American society, Bruce cuts through the inflated claims of evangelicals and suggests that televangelism's primary function is to raise the morale of believers and to bankroll America's conservative subculture. Bruce disputes the findings of Jeffrey Hadden and Anson Shupe in their *Televangelism: Power and Politics on God's Frontier* (1988) and contends that televangelism is unlikely to spearhead any effective political mobilization of American conservatives. He argues that television ministries are only marginally successful at attracting unbelievers, and that religious conservatives are seriously divided by religion, education, and ethnic background. The book concludes that televangelism may actually pose a threat to the distinctive content of conservative Christianity, because it tends to blunt controversy and aim for the broadest possible appeal.

SOURCES

Bruce, Steve. *Pray TV: Televangelism in America.* New York: Routledge, 1990.

C. W. BURPO

Charles W. Burpo is a prominent example of the right-wing religious commentators that flooded the airwaves of America during the height of the Cold War. Always concerned with reaching the largest possible audience, Burpo worked hard to offer his supporters a wide range of services. These services included a radio communion rite, a faith-healing ministry attested to by "Doctor Burpo" himself, a literal exegesis of the Bible, and a spicy potpourri of apocalyptic millennialism, New Thought philosophy, and right-wing political commentary. Burpo's controversial radio ministry reached its peak of influence between 1950 and 1970.

Burpo spent his youth in the dusty rural areas of southern Oklahoma. He went to school in the oil field town of Madill and chopped cotton for $1 a day to help support his large family. After auditing a theology correspondence course with a school in St. Louis, Missouri, Burpo gained his ministerial credentials in 1934 from the Church of the Nazarene in the Western Oklahoma District. After serving as a minister in Guthrie, Oklahoma, and Beaumont, Texas, Burpo surrendered his preaching credentials and disappeared mysteriously from the Nazarene's assembly roll. He struck out on his own as an itinerant evangelist and gained new ministerial credentials from the International Ministerial Foundation in Fresno, California. In the early 1940s, Burpo drew large crowds to his independent evangelistic crusades in Los Angeles's stately Angelus Temple. The church had been built by the famed healing evangelist, Aimee Semple McPherson, and now served as the headquarters of the International Church of the Foursquare Gospel.

Burpo next took his crusade to the Midwest. He gained public notoriety when, during a service in Peoria, Illinois, he prayed for a great miracle that would be remembered for many years. During the day a woman had approached him and said, "I heard you on the radio this morning and I believe that God has given you the power to send the Word." The woman then asked Burpo to heal her pregnant daughter in Florida who was suffering from heart trouble and rheumatoid arthritis. Burpo asked his audience to stand with him and pray for a miracle. A week later a letter arrived claiming that the daughter had been miraculously healed. Burpo invited her to attend the revival and bear witness to what "Brother Burpo" and God had done.

The healing evangelist got his start in radio when a woman from Indianapolis left him $2,925 in her will. Using this money, Burpo taped a sermon in his small house trailer in Southern California and bought enough time to broadcast both the sermon and an appeal for financial support over radio station KBYE in Oklahoma City. The date of this first program was December 8, 1953.

Following in the steps of Oral Roberts and Jack Coe, Burpo mixed faith healing and Fundamentalism in his new radio ministry. Unlike Roberts and Coe, however, Burpo was modest in his claims, preferring to mention only specific instances when his prayers had helped bring about a miraculous healing. In fact, Burpo often spoke more of his own miraculous recoveries from illness than of those of his followers. During one of his initial broadcasts, for example, he claimed that he had been healed of diabetes and cancer by using his own "Aesculapian healing wand."

Burpo's *Bible Institute of the Air*, as his program was called, quickly spread to other gospel stations in large cities throughout the country. As he later recalled,

> We began to tell the great listening friends on KBYE that we had a desire to enlarge our program and we wanted them to help us, and they did. We spread from there to KFMJ in Tulsa, Oklahoma, then to KGRC in Miami, Oklahoma, and to a small 500-watt station in Newton, Kansas.

From this small regional expansion Burpo's radio ministry grew to include KFAX, San Francisco's 50,000-watt listening audience (which extended to Canada), a powerful San Diego station, and stations in Pennsylvania, Ohio, Alabama, and Washington, DC. When, in the early 1960s, Burpo's programs began airing over XERF, the 250,000-watt Mexican mega-station, the evangelist had achieved his goal of making himself heard in all parts of the continental United States. This expansion was made possible, in part, by a small group of right-wing supporters who asked that Burpo mix their extremist political views with his religious message. In the face of criticism from some listeners who preferred a straight religious message, Burpo responded that his political commentary was necessary to save America from its many internal and external enemies.

Burpo's broadcasting style fell somewhat below professional standards, and he often befuddled and amused his listeners with a mishmash of misinformation, fumbled lines, borrowed material, incorrect references, and the open discussion of his family problems. Nevertheless, Burpo's relaxed, casual, and gossipy microphone manner and his daily exclamation that "God loves you, and I do too!" helped him maintain a large and loyal following during his broadcasting career.

Brother Burpo also enjoyed holding rallies in cities where he had large radio audiences and could meet individual listeners. In appearance, he was of medium height and build, sported a thin, Prussian-style mustache, wore large, horn-rim glasses, and was always dressed in expensive-looking suits. As one commentator remarked, "He could pass for the local school superintendent or perhaps the owner of a small-town hardware store or funeral home."

Burpo's wife Margaret was rarely heard on his program. She was, however, often mentioned on the air, advising him on various matters, prompting him to alert listeners to her approaching birthday, or simply receiving his praise and flattery. While it was unclear how much real authority she exercised over his ministry, she did serve as an officer in his corporation from its earliest days and drew a salary. The Burpos had four children, three of whom became active supporters of the family ministry. Their daughter Virginia helped edit the ministry's monthly newsletter, *Bible Institute News*, and also assumed an active role in radio programming.

Bible Institute of the Air, Inc., moved from Oklahoma City to Mesa, Arizona (a Phoenix suburb), in 1963. The move took place shortly after a broadcast that gave Burpo national notoriety. In the midst of right-wing rumors of impending national catastrophe, including reports that the United Nations was beginning its takeover of America with the help of the United States Army, Burpo read from a report by conservative congressman James B. Utt:

> Now hear this and listen well! By the time this Washington Report reaches you, there will be under way one of the most fantastic and, to me, frightening military maneuvers ever to be held in the United States. It is called "Exercise Water Moccasin III." . . . We do not know whether African troops will be involved or not, but we do know that there is a large contingent of bare-foot Africans that have been moved into Cuba for training.

The military exercises mentioned in the report had been announced by the army as the last of three training maneuvers that were to be conducted in rural Georgia. The US forces would be joined by members of the United Nations who had been invited to participate. In response to Burpo's irresponsible rumor-mongering, Republican Senator Thomas H. Kuchel addressed the Senate floor and denounced the radio preacher by name along with other right-wing alarmists. Concluding his comments, Kuchel declared, "They are anything but patriotic. Indeed, a good case can be made that they are unpatriotic, and downright un-American. For they are doing a devil's work far better than Communists themselves could do."

Burpo ran into trouble with his right-wing allies, the John Birch Society, in 1964, when he welcomed Kilsoo Haan of the Sino-Korean Peoples League as a guest commentator on his show. The broadcasts featuring Haan proved so popular that Burpo rushed a paperback of the program's most interesting segments to press in 1965. The volume, entitled *The Impending Storm*, was distributed throughout the country

and to every member of Congress. It included interesting "facts" such as that the Russian Air Force had 150 nuclear-powered bombers capable of flying at speeds of 2,500 miles per hour and at a height of 85,000 feet. Moreover, the book alleged that these aircraft could remain airborne for 90 days and were capable of neutralizing all American radio and radar detection systems. In response to the radio programs and subsequent book, John Birch Society President Robert Welch fired off a letter to his section and chapter leaders warning "no really informed anti-Communist with careful judgment would touch Kilsoo Haan with a ten-foot pole." Burpo responded by telling his radio audience that "Mr. Welch is wrong by all standards" and that "Mr. Haan is a true American."

Burpo also became the butt of jokes when he reported as fact a facetious Russell Baker column revealing the "true identities" of notorious black militants. The director of the Institute for American Democracy, Charles R. Baker, was the first to notice "Burpo's Blooper," as the episode would later be dubbed, and to share it in his news bulletin with the nation.

Burpo was a skilled fundraiser, regularly pleading with his audience for contributions to fund new equipment and further expansion of his ministry. In his fundraising letters to "prayer partners" and "co-workers," Burpo would often reveal grim "truths" that were not fit for radio broadcasting audiences. He regularly teased his supporters with snippets of information that he could only share with them in full during his personal visits at rallies. *Bible Institute of the Air*'s annual income increased between 1963 and 1972 from $212,000 to $557,263. While this is a relatively insignificant amount of money compared to today's most popular televangelism ministries, it demonstrated Burpo's continuing appeal and fundraising acumen.

After losing a zoning battle with his neighbors, Burpo began to raise donations for a new headquarters complex. The $65,000 facility was completed in early 1968 and included a ranch-style building, 4,500 feet of floor space, a beautiful outdoor property landscaped with palm trees and cacti, and a small chapel. Over the next few years, Burpo and his wife would acquire a nearby ranch, where they could relax from the rigors of the studio and care for their menagerie of dogs, goats, donkeys, horses, and ponies.

Burpo continued to sound a cry of alarm for America's future over such issues as gun registration, Communist infiltration, and the floundering American military involvement in Vietnam. His *Bible Institute News* trumpeted these warnings in such headlines as "The Worst Is Yet to Come . . . Unless," "America Is Lost, Unless," "America Is Tottering," and "Pray or Perish." Yet Burpo never gave up hope that disaster could be averted through prayer and vigilance. In a September 1968 issue of the *News*, he wrote, "The fact of the matter is, this nation is dying. It is sick unto death. . . . The world hangs over an abyss, fearful to contemplate, and it hangs by a thread that only divine grace and mercy keeps from breaking!"

Burpo also issued warnings about the survival of his ministry. In a *News* item from 1970, he wrote,

There are forces in this government that do not want nonprofit organizations such as ours to continue the hard-hitting messages that we are bringing. This is why we are under heavy surveillance. Every word that I utter on the radio is monitored, and they are searching for something to use against me in trying to get our nonprofit corporation canceled.

On the occasion of his ministry's seventeenth anniversary, in December of 1970, Burpo announced that his messages were being aired on 65 daily half-hour radio programs, including several on FM stations. However, during the early 1970s, the ministry was dogged by IRS investigations, the Burpo family's poor health, and the defection of Burpo's beloved son Chet. C. W. Burpo apparently is no longer broadcasting.

SOURCES

Erickson, Hal. *Religious Radio and Television in the United States, 1921–1991*. Jefferson, NC: McFarland, 1992.

Morris, James. *The Preachers*. New York: St. Martin's Press, 1973.

C

E. HOWARD CADLE

born: August 25, 1884, Fredericksburg, Indiana
died: December 20, 1942

E. Howard Cadle began broadcasting *The Nation's Family Prayer Period* on Cincinnati radio station WLW in 1932. The program aired for 15 minutes Mondays through Saturdays and half an hour on Sundays. Until its "superpower" license was revoked in 1939, WLW's 500,000-watt signal blanketed much of America. As a result, Cadle and his staff described *The Nation's Family Prayer Period* as the nation's first daily radio broadcast and the most-listened-to religious radio program in America. A publicist for WLW estimated Cadle's weekly audience at 30 million people in 1939, though the accuracy of that claim is impossible to verify.

Cadle began his evangelistic career in Indianapolis, where he built the 10,000-seat Cadle Tabernacle in 1921. Over the course of the next two years, he hosted some of the era's best known evangelists, including Bob Jones, Aimee Semple McPherson, Gypsy Smith, and Billy Sunday. A dispute between Cadle and the Tabernacle's board caused him to lose control of the building in 1923, and he spent the next eight years involved in a variety of pursuits—politics, land speculation, and itinerant evangelism among them. In 1931, Cadle gathered enough support to buy the Tabernacle from the bank that had taken possession of it. Almost immediately, he began broadcasting on a local Indianapolis station and, within a few months, moved back to WLW.

Cadle made the story of his conversion experience a hallmark of his career. As told in his autobiography, *How I Came Back*, he lived a life of gambling and drunkenness before converting to Christianity in 1914. He repeated the story often, both in his personal appearances and on his radio program. Cadle continued to hold both a Sunday morning and evening service in the Tabernacle throughout his career, making the Tabernacle's 1,400-person choir another hallmark of his ministry. He promoted it as the largest permanently established choir in the world. In a brief article in 1939, *Time* magazine described it as "something to hear."

Cadle was remarkable for both the breadth of his business interests and for the entrepreneurial methods he used in reaching and expanding his radio audience. At the height of his radio evangelism, he owned a sawmill, an apple orchard, and a farm west of Indianapolis. In 1937, he began a program he called the Mountain Church Work, installing radio receivers in small Appalachian churches that were too small or too poor to have a full-time pastor. The members of these churches—located in rural parts of Indiana, Kentucky, Ohio, Tennessee, Virginia, and West Virginia—met in their buildings on Sunday mornings and listened to the Cadle Tabernacle broadcast on WLW. Cadle thus became the vicarious pastor for more than 600 "mountain churches" before his death from Bright's disease on December 20, 1942. The Tabernacle ministries continued under the direction of Cadle's widow and a succession of pastors, expanding in 1952 into television broadcasting. *The Nation's Family Prayer Period* never attained the prominence it had achieved under Cadle, however, and the ministry slowly declined. The Tabernacle was razed in 1968. The Cadle Chapel, a scaled-back version of the ministry, kept an office in Indianapolis and produced a syndicated radio program until 1991.

Ted Slutz
Indiana University, Indianapolis

SAMUEL PARKES CADMAN

born: December 18, 1864, Wellington,
Shropshire, England
died: July 12, 1936, Plattsburg, New York

The noted Congregational radio preacher Samuel Parkes Cadman grew up in the poor coal-mining region of England bordering on Wales. The son of lay minister Samuel Cadman and Betsy Parkes, the younger Cadman was steeped in the Bible and the pious works of John Bunyan. At 16, Cadman had a powerful conversion experience and decided to seek training as a Methodist lay minister. By 1884, he had received his license to preach within the Wesleyan branch of the Methodist Church. In 1889, Cadman received a degree in theology and classics at Wesleyan College in Richmond, London (later Richmond College), and married Lillian Esther Wooding. Soon thereafter, he traveled to America where he accepted calls to serve churches in Millbrook, New York City, and Yonkers, New York. He became pastor of New York's Metropolitan Tabernacle in 1895.

By the late 1890s, Cadman had become an ordained Congregationalist minister. In 1900, Cadman became the minister of Central Congregational Church in Brooklyn, a position he held until his death in 1936. During his long tenure at Central Church, the congregation grew to became one of the most prominent churches in the country. Not long after his pastorate began, Cadman distinguished himself as one of the leading representatives of the liberal wing of evangelicalism. He gave a sympathetic hearing to Darwinism, accepted the assumptions of continental biblical scholarship, and stressed the tenets of the social gospel. Among his many

books documenting these positions, *Charles Darwin and Other English Thinkers* (1911), *Imagination and Religion* (1926), and *The Parables of Jesus* (1931) were the best known.

Cadman's interest in ecumenical concerns began in the 1890s when he became active in the Open and Institutional Church League. This interest came to full blossom when he was elected president of the Federal Council of Churches (FCC), a position in which he served from 1924 to 1928. From 1928 until his death, Cadman took to the airwaves, reaching a national audience as speaker for the FCC over its Sunday afternoon NBC radio program, *National Radio Pulpit*, the first studio broadcast religious program in America. This program, which included guest spots by nationally known ministers such as Harry Emerson Fosdick and Ralph W. Sockman, featured inspirational messages by Cadman and music by various ensembles.

SOURCES

Cadman, S. Parkes. *Christianity and the State*. New York: Macmillan, 1924.

Melton, J. Gordon. *Religious Leaders of America*. Detroit: Gale Research, 1991.

Reid, Daniel G., Robert D. Linder, Bruce L. Shelley, and Harry S. Stout, eds. *Dictionary of Christianity in America*. Downers Grove, IL: InterVarsity Press, 1990.

Ward, Mark, Sr. *Air of Salvation: The Story of Christian Broadcasting*. Grand Rapids, MI: Baker Book House, 1994

CALVARY EVANGELISTIC MISSION

established: 1953

Founded in 1953, Calvary Evangelistic Mission (CEM) is a missionary organization that works to spread the Christian gospel to the Spanish West Indies through radio evangelistic programs, missionary training, and correspondence courses. Operating over radio stations WIVV in the Lesser Antilles and WBMJ in San Juan, Puerto Rico, CEM broadcasts two main programs in English and Spanish, *Cruzada con*

Luis Palau or *Luis Palau Crusade* and *Kids Are Christians Too*. The mission's headquarters are in San Juan, Puerto Rico.

HAROLD CAMPING
born: 1921

Courtesy: National Religious Broadcasters

Harold L. Camping is the general manager and president of Family Radio and its network of 40 stations and 12 substations. Begun in 1958 by Camping and amateur radio missionary Richard Palmquist, Family Radio is a non-affiliated, listener-supported radio broadcast network that features Christian music, Bible study, and Camping's national radio call-in program, *Open Forum*.

Camping worked as a civil engineer and builder during early adulthood and made enough money to retire and devote himself to a religious broadcasting ministry. His initial vision was to broadcast the gospel to San Francisco, California, and its vicinity. Unlike most Christian radio ministries, which are content to produce Christian programs for syndication, Camping and his associates decided to pour their resources into the founding of a Christian radio station. The result was Family Radio, which became one of the first listener-sponsored Christian radio stations in the world.

The first broadcast of station KEAR-FM, San Francisco, California, aired at precisely noon on February 4, 1959, with the program *The Sound of the New Life*. Positive audience response encouraged Camping to continue the venture. Listener contributions grew to exceed expenses by the end of the station's second year. Camping used the surplus funds to buy stations KEBR in Sacramento and KECR in El Cajon, near San Diego. Over the next three decades, Family Radio acquired 37 additional stations, which broadcast in 10 languages throughout the world.

Camping became a focus of controversy when he began telling his listeners that the end of the world would occur in September 1994. Camping based his prediction on a self-devised dating system that fit biblical events into a broader plan of salvation history. At a press conference in October 1994 in front of Camping's Oakland Family Radio headquarters, two ministers called on Camping's listeners to halt their financial support of the ministry. They also demanded that Camping resign from his position at the radio network. Camping resisted the firestorm of controversy surrounding his unfulfilled prediction and continues to maintain a high profile in radio, appearing daily on *Open Forum*.

SOURCES

Camping, Harold. *The Fig Tree: An Analysis of the Future of Israel*. Oakland, CA: Family Stations, 1983.

———. *When Is the Rapture?* Oakland, CA: Family Stations, 1979.

Melton, J. Gordon. *Directory of Religious Organizations in the United States*. 3d ed. Detroit: Gale Research, 1993.

Seaver, Dan. "End-of-World Predictions Draw Sharp Denunciations." *Oakland Tribune*, October 28, 1994.

Ward, Mark, Sr. *Air of Salvation: The Story of Christian Broadcasting*. Grand Rapids, MI: Baker Book House, 1994.

CAMPUS CRUSADE FOR CHRIST
see: Bill Bright

CASE IN CONTROVERSY
first aired: 1995

Case in Controversy is a radio program that provides information on how Christians can legally witness in public forums. The show is aired over the USA Radio Network. It discusses problems that Christians have faced in expressing their beliefs in such places as school, work, or on the street. The show is hosted by Jay Sekulow, the chief counsel for the American Center for Law and Justice (ACLJ), a legal affairs outreach designed by Pat Robertson to serve as a counterforce to the American Civil Liberties Union. In addition to this radio program, Sekulow hosts a weekly 30-minute program on the Trinity Broadcasting Network (TBN) that focuses on legal issues.

Sekulow has become a popular guest on religious news and talk programs because of his effective representation of the Christian Right's legal positions before the United States Supreme Court. ACLJ's lawyers, many of whom were trained at Robertson's Regent University, work within a $9 million annual budget to argue the conservative Christian viewpoint in important Supreme Court cases. Sekulow is a frequent guest on the Christian Broadcasting Network's *The 700 Club*, and a popular speaker at various evangelical Christian conventions. He also works as a substitute cohost on *Praise the Lord*, the flagship broadcast of TBN.

SOURCES

Kennedy, John W. "Redeeming the Wasteland?" *Christianity Today* (October 1995).

THE CATHOLIC HOUR
first aired: 1930

The Catholic Hour began in 1930 as a Catholic-sponsored "sustaining time" entry into the nascent field of religious radio. The half-hour program was aired on the NBC radio network and produced by the National Council of Catholic Men. The show's popular host and principal speaker between 1930 and 1952 was the charismatic Bishop Fulton J. Sheen. Like other sustaining-time broadcasts, *The Catholic Hour* eschewed on-air proselytizing and embraced as its mission the affirmation of human dignity.

The Catholic Hour was adapted for television in 1951 and aired until 1953 as part of a new ecumenical program named *Frontiers of Faith*. *Frontiers of Faith* featured teachings from the Catholic, Protestant, and Jewish faiths in three rotating segments. The Catholic Church produced 16 of these segments a year during the series' three-year history. In 1953, the three segments were separated and *The Catholic Hour* was restored to its previous title. The Jewish segment was formerly and subsequently named *The Eternal Light;* the Protestant segment retained the name *Frontiers of Faith* after the 1953 breakup.

During most of its television life span, *The Catholic Hour* featured dramatic readings, debate sessions, musical pieces, experimental plays, and short operas performed by Catholic university students. However in 1969, the show again changed its name as well as its format. The new program, titled *Guideline*, sought to avoid the art-oriented approach of its predecessor and instead focused on pressing social and ethical issues. This program was sponsored by Bishop Sheen's Catholic Office for Radio and Television.

When NBC-TV canceled its Sunday "sustaining time"—reportedly because of the show's increasingly radical commentary on contemporary society—*Guideline* survived as a radio program. This weekly radio broadcast ministry was produced by Joseph Fenton under the auspices of the National Council of Catholic Men. The most recent statistics indicate that the show was being aired over 100 radio stations around the United States by the late 1980s.

See also Fulton J. Sheen; *The Eternal Light*

SOURCES

Bruce, Steve. *Pray TV: Televangelism in America*. New York: Routledge, 1990.

Erickson, Hal. *Religious Radio and Television in the United States, 1921–1991*. Jefferson, NC: McFarland, 1992.

Hadden, Jeffrey K., and Charles E. Swann. *Prime Time Preachers: The Rising Power of Televangelism*. Menlo Park, CA: Addison-Wesley, 1981.

MORRIS CERULLO

born: October 2, 1931, Passaic, New Jersey

Morris Cerullo emerged during the mid-1990s as one of the most powerful televangelists and faith healers in the world. Better known in the Third World than in the United States, Cerullo is a flamboyant and charismatic preacher who runs international healing crusades, a daily television show, and Bible-training courses. He also owns the Inspirational Network, a 24-hour religious television station, and trains missionaries at his San Diego–based School of Ministry.

Cerullo was born to an Italian father and a Jewish mother. After his mother's death when he was two, he and his siblings were placed in foster care because of his father's alcoholism. Cerullo moved to the Daughters of Miriam Orphanage in Clifton, New Jersey, when he was eight. This strict Jewish Orthodox institution provided a comprehensive religious background for Cerullo and taught him Hebrew. Cerullo was introduced to Christianity at the age of 14 by Helen Kerr, a member of the Pentecostal Assemblies of God, who worked at the orphanage. When it was discovered that Kerr had given Cerullo a New Testament, she lost her job. A short time later Cerullo ran away and was taken in by Kerr's brother in Paterson, New Jersey.

After receiving the baptism of the Holy Spirit at an Assemblies of God church service, Cerullo spoke in tongues and prophesied that he was being called by God to a special work. He began preaching publicly in New Jersey at the age of 15. He also began to believe that God wanted him to minister to all nations and particularly to the Jews. His hope was that he could preach Christ to every Jew on earth in preparation for the Second Coming.

Cerullo attended Northeastern Bible College in Essex Fells, New Jersey, and was ordained by the Assemblies of God in 1952. He married Theresa Le Pari in 1951 and started his own independent ministry in 1956. Patterning himself after itinerant preachers like William Marrion Branham and Oral Roberts, Cerullo focused his efforts on becoming a faith healer. For the next few years Cerullo made the circuit of evangelical conferences, preaching, teaching, and healing. He also pastored a New Hampshire Assemblies of God church (1952–1953) and South Bend, Indiana's Calvary Temple (1959). Moreover, in the early 1960s Cerullo began publishing a monthly periodical entitled *Deeper Life*.

During this time, Cerullo's ministry flourished, and the young evangelist decided to create World Evangelism, a global evangelical ministry, in 1961. The headquarters for World Evangelism was established in San Diego, California. It was at this juncture that Cerullo began to devote almost 80 percent of his time to foreign missionary outreach. He believed that to properly spread the gospel abroad, it was necessary to work with and through indigenous church leaders. As a result, World Evangelism began to promote ministerial training around the world.

During the 1970s, Cerullo began to focus his efforts on evangelizing North America and, to that end, conducted healing crusades in over 60 cities. A typical Cerullo healing crusade included dramatic healings with immediate testimonials of their validity; anointings with sacred oil; singing, jumping, and clapping; organ music; and a concluding altar call.

In 1975, he created a television series called *Helpline*. This program preached an assertive gospel of victory over adversity to prisoners, the homeless, and the emotionally isolated. Cerullo was assisted in this program by his son, David Cerullo. During the 1980s, Cerullo ceased production of *Helpline* and began broadcasting another daily television program, *Victory with Morris Cerullo*.

As part of his continuing outreach to worldwide Jewry, Cerullo launched a radio broadcast from a station in Cyprus that could be heard in Israel. He also established and promoted the Messianic Bible Correspondence Course, which claimed to have enrolled 25,000 Israelis by the decade's end. World Evangelism received a copy of Israel's entire voter registration list during the 1970s, and the ministry has used the list to send a number of mass-mailings of missionary literature.

Cerullo has also authored over 20 books and conducted preaching tours around the world. One of the books, *Two Men from Eden*, was translated into every language spoken by a substantial Jewish population and mailed to almost every Jewish household in North America.

In 1990, a federal bankruptcy judge approved Cerullo's $7 million bid for the remains of Jim Bakker's PTL empire. Disagreements between Cerullo and a group of Malaysian investors ended up in court in 1991, however, and the relationship was severed. Both of the suits against Cerullo were ultimately settled in his favor, and the evangelist decided to pull out of the PTL corporation, selling his share to his former business partners. He did, however, retain ownership of the PTL (television) Network, renaming it the Inspirational Network.

Cerullo has spent much of the 1990s building up the 24-hour Inspirational Network. By 1991, the network claimed to have 6.4 million viewers. Cerullo also received a license from England's Independent Television Commission (ITC) in 1992 to start a 24-hour religious television channel, the European Family Christian Network. He then signed an agreement to use the Astra satellite, which beams its broadcasting signal to most of Britain's 3 million satellite dishes.

In June of 1991, the ITC took the weekly miracle-healing episode of *Victory with Morris Cerullo* off England's Super Channel. The regulators said that the program violated British standards that state, "Religious programs must not contain claims by or about living individuals or groups, suggesting that they have special powers or abilities, which are incapable of being substantiated." For the next six months the miracle-healing programs were replaced by

Cerullo's preaching programs. The ITC finally agreed that the healing programs could be reinstated as long as they included a written disclaimer that attributed the "special power" to God and not to Cerullo.

The evangelist's huge London healing crusades during the 1990s continue to receive a great deal of critical press treatment.

See also Inspirational Network

SOURCES

Cerullo, Morris. *The Backside of Satan*. Carol Stream, IL: Creation House, 1973.

———. *A Guide to Total Health and Prosperity*. San Diego: World Evangelism, 1977.

———. *The Miracle Book*. San Diego: World Evangelism, 1984.

———. *My Story*. San Diego: World Evangelism, 1965.

———. *Revelation Healing Power*. San Diego: World Evangelism, 1979.

———. *Victory Miracle Living, It's Harvest Time*. San Diego: World Evangelism, 1982.

Erickson, Hal. *Religious Radio and Television in the United States, 1921–1991*. Jefferson, NC: McFarland, 1992.

"Miracle-Healing Show Banned from British TV." *San Francisco Chronicle*, August 14, 1991.

Ostling, Richard N. "A New Preacher for PTL." *Time*, June 11, 1990.

SINGLETON ROBERT CHAMBERS

Singleton Robert Chambers was a popular African American radio evangelist cut from the mold of Lightfoot Solomon Michaux. He began his career as a preacher at the age of 13 and eventually took over the leadership of the Evangelist Temple, an affiliate of the Church of God in Christ. This Kansas City, Kansas, ministry gave Chambers an institutional base for his foray into radio preaching in 1933. Chambers eventually broadcast his two weekly radio programs over stations in Kansas City and Little Rock, Arkansas. It was claimed that almost two-thirds of his 200,000 listeners were non-blacks.

Chambers also gained a reputation as a faith healer, and it was alleged that many of the 14,000 people he healed received their ministrations during a telephone prayer session.

SOURCES

"Top Radio Ministers." *Ebony* 4 (July 1949): 56–61.

CHANGED LIVES
first aired: 1968

Airing on radio since 1968 and on television since 1971, *Changed Lives* is a weekly program hosted by Presbyterian minister and conference speaker Ben Haden, director of the Ben Haden Evangelical Association. The show runs 30 minutes every Sunday afternoon and features a Bible message on contemporary issues of universal human concern. Broadcast throughout the United States and overseas from Haden's ministry headquarters in Chattanooga, Tennessee, *Changed Lives*'s emphasis is both evangelistic and informative. The show demonstrates the modern relevance of Christ's teachings in a sincere and compassionate manner.

See also Ben Haden

SOURCES

Erickson, Hal. *Religious Radio and Television in the United States, 1921–1991*. Jefferson, NC: McFarland, 1992.

Melton, J. Gordon. *Directory of Religious Organizations in the United States*. 3d ed. Detroit: Gale Research, 1993.

CHAPEL OF THE AIR
first aired: 1939

Chapel of the Air began as the weekly radio outreach of John D. Jess, the pastor of a modest local church in Decatur, Illinois. The program was directed to regular churchgoers, who provided most of the show's financial support. *Chapel*'s format was simple. After an opening

Courtesy: National Religious Broadcasters

JOHN D. JESS

hymn, Jess delivered a pious message using standard homiletic discourse. In time, however, Jess became concerned that this format was, in effect, preaching to the converted while ignoring "the millions who need the gospel."

In 1964, he decided to revamp the program and make it more accessible to skeptics and the unconverted. Gone were the church hymns and conventional sermons. The show now began with an opening question that was focused on a contemporary topic of interest. Jess then delivered a carefully reasoned commentary on this question that combined traditional scriptural wisdom with a sophisticated grasp of the issue being discussed. This new approach expanded his listening audience to include secular-minded professors, businessmen, and college students, in addition to regular churchgoers.

By the late 1970s, *Chapel of the Air* was being heard daily over 250 stations. Jess began cohosting the program with his nephew David Mains in 1977. He continued with his commentaries on contemporary issues designed to attract the unchurched, while Mains directed his message to committed Christians in need of support and encouragement. Mains assumed Jess's responsibilities when his uncle retired. *Chapel of the Air* is still being aired over more than 250 radio stations. The broadcast is now headquartered in Wheaton, Illinois.

SOURCES

Armstrong, Ben. *The Electric Church.* Nashville: Thomas Nelson, 1979.

Erickson, Hal. *Religious Radio and Television in the United States, 1921–1991.* Jefferson, NC: McFarland, 1992.

CHILDREN'S BIBLE HOUR
first aired: November 1942

The longest running children's program on religious radio today is *Children's Bible Hour (CBH).* The program, which began in 1942 on a Grand Rapids, Michigan, radio station, is currently aired over 600 stations nationwide and in 100 countries around the world.

CBH was the brainchild of David Otis Fuller, who was struck by a young girl's observation that there were gospel broadcasts for adults and young people, but none for children. The show, which started as an hour-long live broadcast before a large studio audience, was hosted by "Uncle Mel" Johnson, who also served as the program's director. "Uncle Charlie" Vander Meer, *CBH*'s host since 1972, joined the broadcast as a 9-year-old child. Vander Meer read letters from listeners, presented a weekly object lesson called "Charlie's Scrapbook," and, in time, became the show's junior emcee.

CBH's technical production changed during the 1950s, when it began taping each live broadcast—including music and stories for children—for later transmission. By the 1990s, each musical segment and story was being prerecorded separately and mixed together at broadcast time. The music on *CBH* includes contemporary and traditional Sunday School songs, which are recorded in the ministry's studio and use solos, duets, and trios of children aged 5 to 15.

In May 1965, a 15-minute weekly and daily program called *Storytime* was added, featuring stories taken from the longer weekly broadcast of *CBH*. *Keys for Kids*, a four-and-a-half–minute program that airs six times per week, was added in September 1984. This program is based on the popular "Keys for Kids" devotional booklets. The audio and print formats of *Keys for Kids* were made available on the World Wide Web in 1995. In addition, *CBH* recently added a new segment called "Kids' Talk." This feature gathers a group of children around the studio microphone and airs their views on such topics as sibling rivalry, earning money, and sharing the gospel with friends.

SOURCES

"Children's Bible Hour Online Ministries." World Wide Web site. http://www.gospel.net/cbh (1995).

Vander Meer, Charlie. "Cheering for Children's Bible Hour." *Religious Broadcasting* (May 1996).

CHILDREN'S MEDIA PRODUCTIONS
established: 1980

Children's Media Productions (CMP) is an interdenominational Protestant ministry that produces various audio and video programs for use on television and radio. CMP also distributes Christian films and home videos with the aim of providing family-oriented entertainment that teaches biblical values and reinforces Christian morals. CMP is currently producing a series of television programs for distribution in Europe and a number of English speaking countries in Africa and Asia. Its ministry headquarters are located in Pasadena, California.

SOURCES

Melton, J. Gordon. *Directory of Religious Organizations in the United States.* 3d ed. Detroit: Gale Research, 1993.

CHINESE CHRISTIAN MISSION
established: 1961

An interdenominational evangelical organization founded in 1961 and located in Petaluma, California, the Chinese Christian Mission (CCM) specifically seeks to evangelize the Chinese peoples and to support Christian churches in Communist China and throughout the world. CCM broadcasts a radio program that airs weekly in China entitled *Pastoring on the Air*.

SOURCES

The Directory of Religious Organizations in the United States, 2d ed. Falls Church, VA: McGrath, 1982.

CHINESE OVERSEAS CHRISTIAN MISSION
established: 1959

Founded in 1959 and headquartered in Fairfax, Virginia, the Chinese Overseas Christian Mission (COCM) is an interdenominational Protestant missionary organization that works to spread the Christian message to Communist China and Chinese people in the United States. A member of the Evangelical Council for Financial Accountability, the COCM channels its evangelistic efforts through various broadcast and print media. Its work focuses on radio broadcasts into China, campus ministry to Chinese students in American colleges, and personal contact with the Chinese business and professional community in and around Washington, DC. Two of its better known programs, *Farmers' Time* and *Seminary of the Air*, air daily in China.

SOURCES

Melton, J. Gordon. *Directory of Religious Organizations in the United States.* 3d ed. Detroit: Gale Research, 1993.

PAUL CHO
born: February 14, 1936, Kyung Nam, Korea

Paul Yonggi Cho is the pastor of the largest Pentecostal church in the world, the Full Gospel Central Church of Seoul, Korea. He has also been a driving force behind the church's television ministry, which began in Korea and Japan

Courtesy: National Religious Broadcasters

and spread to the United States during the early 1980s. The Cho program was carried in Los Angeles, New York, and several other cities with large Asian populations. Cho was able to cobble together his Korean studio with the help of Jim Bakker. Bakker, whose *PTL Club* broadcast often featured Cho as a guest, at one time promised to install the Korean evangelist as the host of an Asian version of the program.

Cho is the son of Doo Chun and Bok Sun (Kim). He earned degrees from the Full Gospel Bible Institute in 1958 and the Department of Law at the National College of Korea in 1968. Following his ordination by the Korean Assemblies of God in 1960, Cho quickly rose in the ranks, assuming the post of general superintendent of the Korean Assemblies of God in 1966. During the same year, Cho became the chairman of the board of directors of the Full Gospel Bible College of Seoul.

Central Church began in 1958 as a primitive structure built with army tent remnants. The church joined the Assemblies of God in 1962 and, within 10 years, was building a 10,000-seat sanctuary for its members. To accommodate the rapidly growing ranks of the faithful, the church held seven services on Sunday and two on Wednesday evenings. By 1982, the church had added overflow auditoriums to seat an additional 10,000 members. During the mid-

1980s, seating capacity for another 20,000 congregants was added.

The phenomenal growth of Cho's congregation has been attributed to the system of home cell groups, which are led by lay leaders. Each leader of a cell group guides from 10 to 15 members in weekly Bible study, worship, and evangelism. By the early 1980s, Cho was in charge of 12 ordained ministers, 260 licensed ministers, and 15,000 lay leaders. A number of his former students have gone on to become pastors of their own Assemblies of God churches in South Korea. The membership of Central Church is now more than 200,000.

In addition to his broadcasting and ecclesiastical ministries, Cho has also published a number of books. Among his best-known works are *The Great Power of Faith* (1965), *The Communion of the Holy Spirit* (1968), *Beyond the Adversity* (1969), *Morning Meditation* (1969), *Life with Joy* (1975), and *The Key to Church Growth* (1976).

SOURCES

"Big Trouble at the World's Largest Church," *Christianity Today*. (January 1982).

THE CHOICE IS YOURS
see: Sarah Utterbach

CHOSEN PEOPLE MINISTRIES
established: 1986

Founded in New York City in 1894 as the Williamsburg Mission, Chosen People Ministries (CPM) directs its evangelistic work exclusively toward Jews both in the United States and abroad. CPM makes effective (albeit notorious) use of street corner evangelistic methods as well as more up-to-date techniques of radio and television programming.

The Williamsburg Mission was started by Leopold Cohn, a Hungarian Jewish immigrant who converted to Christianity soon after his arrival in New York in 1892. After theological study in Scotland, Cohn returned to New York as a missionary working in the Jewish community. He received his initial support from the American Baptist Home Mission Society. Around this time, Cohn began to publish the newsletter *Chosen People*. This news and information periodical was designed to raise Christian interest in Jewish missions located in the United States and abroad, particularly in Israel.

In 1924, due to an expanding ministry, Cohn renamed his organization the American Board of Missions to the Jews (ABMJ). After his death in 1937, Cohn was succeeded by his son, Joseph Cohn, who expanded the board's missionary work and reputation within the evangelical world. In 1973, the San Francisco branch of the ABMJ, led by Moishe Rosen, separated from the national organization to form Jews for Jesus. The original Cohn mission was then renamed Chosen People Ministries in 1986 and is now headquartered in Charlotte, North Carolina.

Chosen People Ministries currently produces radio spots and television programs for broadcast over non-commercial Christian networks. It produces the daily radio spot *Through Jewish Eyes*, which ranges from 10 seconds to 2 minutes in length, mostly dealing with news-related issues in the Middle East. CPM also produces a 15-minute radio program that typically features either an interview or teaching on Jewish feasts and rituals connected with Jesus as the Messiah.

For television, CPM produces seasonal specials on the messianic significance of major Jewish festivals, most recently "Messiah in the Passover," "Messiah in Pentecost," and "Messiah in the Day of Atonement." CPM distributes these and other programs both nationally to Christian networks as well as internationally to networks in Russia, Argentina, and Ukraine.

Currently, CPM's most popular program is *Shalom Jerusalem*, which has aired in the former Soviet Union and was released into national syndication in the summer of 1996. In 1996, CPM created a Web site on the Internet as a means of expanding its ministry to reach more Jews interested in the Messiah.

SOURCES

Melton, J. Gordon. *Directory of Religious Organizations in the United States.* 3d ed. Detroit: Gale Research, 1993.

Rausch, David A. *Messianic Judaism: Its History, Theology, and Polity.* New York: Edwin Mellen Press, 1982.

Reid, Daniel G., Robert D. Linder, Bruce L. Shelley, and Harry S. Stout, eds. *Dictionary of Christianity in America.* Downers Grove, IL: InterVarsity Press, 1990.

Stone, Jon R. "Messianic Judaism: A Redefinition of the Boundary between Christian and Jew?" In *Research in the Social Scientific Study of Religion 3.* Greenwich, CT: JAI Press, 1991.

CHRIST FOR ALL NATIONS
see: Reinhard Bonnke

CHRIST FOR EVERYONE
see: John Zoller

CHRIST IN PROPHECY
first aired: 1980

Hosted by David R. Reagan and Dennis Pollock of Lamb & Lion Ministries, *Christ in Prophecy* is a news commentary program that airs daily over more than 70 radio stations nationwide. Broadcast since 1980 on prerecorded tape, *Christ in Prophecy* presents analysis of current national and international events from a biblical perspective. The purpose of the program is to proclaim the imminent return of Christ to believers and unbelievers.

Pollock taught on radio and television programs for a number of years before joining Reagan at Lamb & Lion in 1993. The pair also records and distributes tapes on various religious themes, including biblical prophecy, new religious movements, Christian living, and church renewal. *Christ in Prophecy* is produced from Lamb & Lion headquarters in McKinney, Texas, 20 miles north of Dallas.

See also Lamb & Lion Ministries

SOURCES

Melton, J. Gordon. *Directory of Religious Organizations in the United States.* 3d ed. Detroit: Gale Research, 1993.

Reagan, David R. *Trusting God.* 2d ed. McKinney, Texas: Lamb & Lion Ministries, 1994.

CHRIST TRUTH MINISTRIES
established: 1949

Founded in 1949 by Dan Gilbert under the name *Prisoners Bible Broadcast*, Christ Truth Ministries (CTM) is an evangelical Protestant ministry whose main mission is the conversion of individuals in federal and state prisons. The ministry began when Gilbert, a pro-American, anti-Communist radio evangelist, began receiving letters from prison inmates asking for Bibles. After sharing this need with his listeners, Gilbert received sufficient donations to establish a radio ministry devoted exclusively to reaching inmates with the gospel.

Under Gilbert's charismatic leadership the ministry expanded, reaching nearly 1,000 prisons by 1960. Following Gilbert's sudden death in 1962, *Prisoners Bible Broadcast* was directed first by Chaplain Ray Hoekstra and then briefly by W. S. "Stuart" McBirnie. During Chaplain Ray's tenure, *Prisoners Bible Broadcast* changed its name to *Christ Truth Radio Crusade.* The outreach retained this title until the late 1970s, when financial concerns led to a redefinition of the ministry away from radio broadcasting. Christ Truth Ministries now expends most of its energies distributing correspondence course materials and copies of the New Testament and the Bible to interested prison inmates. Currently, CTM is headquartered in Upland, California, an eastern suburb of Los Angeles, and is directed by Carl F. Davis.

See also Dan Gilbert

SOURCES

Melton, J. Gordon. *Directory of Religious Organizations in the United States.* 3d ed. Detroit: Gale Research, 1993.

Roy, Ralph Lord. *Apostles of Discord.* Boston: Beacon Press, 1953.

CHRISTIAN AMATEUR RADIO FELLOWSHIP
established: 1966

The Christian Amateur Radio Fellowship (CARF) is a communications service of the Christian Church/Churches of Christ that seeks to equip and educate Christian missionaries and their support units in the production and use of evangelistic radio.

Founded in 1966 and headquartered in Holland, Michigan, CARF also provides free communications and education services to various church, college, and missionary organizations, including information on licensing and effective broadcasting methods. Much of its focus is on amateur radio use by missionaries in Oceania, Latin America, and parts of Africa. CARF reports a membership of nearly 200 missionaries and other supporters.

SOURCES

Melton, J. Gordon. *Directory of Religious Organizations in the United States.* 3d ed. Detroit: Gale Research, 1993.

CHRISTIAN BROADCASTING NETWORK
established: 1959

The Christian Broadcasting Network (CBN) is one of the world's largest religious television ministries, reaching 75 countries and enjoying annual revenues of over $189 million. The network's mission is "to prepare the United States of America, the nations of the Middle East, the Far East, South America and other nations of the world for the coming of Jesus Christ and the establishment of the Kingdom of God on earth." The ministry seeks to accomplish its mission "through the strategic use of mass communications, especially radio, television and film." It also distributes videos, books, and audiocassettes, and trains believers to relate biblical principles to all areas of their lives.

CBN is the brainchild of Pat Robertson, a former Southern Baptist pastor. As documented in Robertson's autobiography, *Shout It from the Housetops* (1972), the network began with the young pastor's 1959 purchase of a bankrupt UHF station in Portsmouth, Virginia, for $37,000. The network's first broadcast, which didn't air until October, 1961, on WYAH-TV (from Yahweh, a Hebrew name for God), barely had the power to blanket the city of Portsmouth. During the early 1960s, CBN was only able to air live programming from 7 to 10 PM daily. Gradually, as donations from local supporters increased, the broadcast day expanded—from 5 PM to midnight. Robertson refused commercial advertisements and often used free travelogue films to fill in blank spots.

CBN's flagship program, *The 700 Club*, received its name from a 1963 fundraising campaign that sought to raise the $7,000 per month needed to operate the station. Robertson asked his audience for 700 people willing to contribute $10 per month. The campaign, which featured a number of guests who stopped by to sing and give religious testimonials, was successful in providing the necessary operating funds. In 1965, a *The 700 Club* telethon generated a sudden outpouring of spiritual revival that led to a more stable financial foundation for the ministry. It was also at this telethon that Jim and Tammy Faye Bakker, who had been recently employed by the station, became active participants in the CBN ministry.

After a successful 1966 follow-up telethon, *The 700 Club* evolved into a daily 90-minute broadcast that copied the telethon format of prayer, ministry, and telephone response. The talk show featured Robertson discussing contemporary issues with a broad assortment of evangelical authors and musical performers. The show's first cohosts were the Bakkers. During the program, Robertson and his guests would pray for those calling into the program and exorcise demons from the sick and infirm. The talk-show format proved as successful on secular stations as on religious networks. Within six years, *The 700 Club* was in national syndication in a restructured format and length. Two years later, the show had earned the National Religious Broadcasters Award of Merit for Excellence in Station Operation.

In part due to *The 700 Club*'s success, CBN was operating television stations in Dallas, Atlanta, and Portsmouth, and FM radio stations in Norfolk, Virginia, and in Albany, Syracuse, Ithaca-Elmira, Rochester, and Buffalo, New York, by the mid-1970s. CBN was also a pioneer in the operation of satellite earth stations during this time. Uplinks were made to the Westar and RCA Satcom satellites, and a chain of 60 earth stations nationwide was created. Moreover, by the late 1970s, *The 700 Club* had 7,000 volunteer prayer counselors working 24 hours a day around the country. The telephone centers created a referral system that helped new converts find churches in their local areas. The network's operating budget for 1978 was nearly $40 million.

In 1980, Robertson retooled *The 700 Club* into its present talk show and news magazine format after consulting with market research specialists. The new format copied such morning network programs as *Good Morning America* and *The Today Show*. Robertson renamed his channel CBN Cable Network in 1981 and began adding family programs such as *Gentle Ben* and *Father Knows Best* to his religious lineup. When Robertson is periodically criticized for these shows' secular format, he responds that viewers want wholesome entertainment rather than preachy rhetoric. He once elaborated, "Only a masochist would want to watch religious shows all day long."

During the mid-1980s, Robertson sold many of his network's broadcast holdings in order to concentrate on the development of programming and the operation of his satellite channel. By the late 1980s, CBN's television signal was reaching over 190 different stations worldwide, and the network's annual budget had grown to $200 million.

CBN now sends out *The 700 Club* to 7 million viewers weekly and distributes Christian programming in over 75 countries worldwide. The network owns US Media Corporation and its subsidiary, Broadcast Equities, Inc. These companies operate Standard News, a radio news network with 272 stations under contract; Zapnews, a fax news service to 315 broadcasting stations; and NorthStar Entertainment, which produces and distributes family-oriented television programs and feature films.

The 700 Club is now seen by 2.2 million people each day and is available over 327 stations in the United States—fully 92 percent of the nation's homes. Also, it is rebroadcast over two other Christian networks, the Trinity Broadcasting Network and Family-Net. Aired before a live studio audience (each member of which must pass through a metal detector), *The 700 Club* begins with 30 minutes of news followed by 30 minutes of ministry profiles and features. The profiles feature both celebrities and ordinary Christians sharing stories about their conversions, healings, and marriage reconciliations. The program's cohosts are Ben Kinchlow, a longtime sidekick of Robertson, and the former Miss America Terry Meeuwsen.

CBN continues to operate a 24-hour counseling center that is staffed by over 200 volunteer and paid employees. In 1994, the center logged 1.78 million calls for problems ranging from drug addiction to marital discord. Telethons are conducted for three weeks out of every year, but the network's major source of revenue comes from direct-mail fundraising.

The network is still trying to plan for the eventual loss of its 66-year-old chairman. In 1988, when Robertson resigned from CBN to enter politics, the ministry's revenues dropped by one half, then recovered when Robertson returned. Although "there is no official plan to de-Robertsonize CBN," according to *The 700 Club*'s executive producer, Norman Mintle, the dangers of charismatic leadership in Christian broadcasting may be brought home to CBN dramatically if strategies aren't in place when Robertson eventually retires.

See also Pat Robertson

SOURCES

Armstrong, Ben. *The Electric Church.* Nashville: Thomas Nelson, 1979.

"Christian Broadcasting Network." World Wide Web site. http://the700club.org/cbn/cbn.html (December 1995).

Clark, Kenneth R. "The $70 Miracle Names CBN." *Chicago Tribune*, July 26, 1985.

Fineman, Howard. "God and the Grass Roots." *Newsweek*, November 8, 1993.

Harrell, David Edwin Jr. *Pat Robertson: A Personal, Religious, and Political Portrait.* San Francisco: Harper & Row, 1987.

Hoover, Stewart. *Mass Media Religion.* Newbury Park, CA: Sage, 1986.

Kennedy, John W. "Redeeming the Wasteland?" *Christianity Today*, October 2, 1995.

Morken, Hubert. *Pat Robertson: Religion and Politics in Simple Terms.* Old Tappan, NJ: Fleming H. Revell, 1987.

Robertson, Pat. *Shout It from the Housetops.* South Plainfield, NJ: Logos International, 1972.

CHRISTIAN CHILDREN'S ASSOCIATION
established: 1968

Founded in 1968 and located in Toms River, New Jersey, the Christian Children's Association (CCA) is a nondenominational Christian ministry that seeks to reach children with the gospel by conducting church rallies, offering Bible correspondence courses, and broadcasting weekly radio and television programs that air throughout the world. The ministry produces over 20 radio programs and nearly 12 cable television productions.

CCA's major radio and television program, *Adventure Pals*, is a weekly broadcast created by CCA president Jean Donaldson. The program presents real life issues such as divorce, drug abuse, peer pressure, and other moral concerns of children ages seven to 14 through the use of entertaining music, dramas, and puppet shows.

SOURCES

The Directory of Religious Organizations in the United States. 2d ed. Falls Church, VA: McGrath, 1982.

CHRISTIAN DESTINY MINISTRIES
see: David Breese

CHRISTIAN RESEARCH INSTITUTE
established: 1960

The Christian Research Institute (CRI) is an international nonprofit organization. The institute's chief aim is to counter the threat of religious cults and to counteract the secularizing effects of modern culture. The ministry produces or sponsors a number of radio programs that air throughout the United States and Canada.

Located in San Juan Capistrano, California, CRI disseminates information primarily about new religious movements and other types of religious and secular groups that CRI members and researchers believe threaten evangelical faith and traditional values. The organization produces *CRI Perspective*, a brief radio commentary by Henrik "Hank" Hanegraaff, its current director. It also produced, until 1989, *The Bible Answerman*, a live call-in radio program hosted by the late Dr. Walter Martin (1929–1989), a recognized authority on secular ideology, New Age thought, and cult movements. CRI also produced a daily 30-minute program, *Dateline Eternity*, which featured an expository Bible message.

See also *The Bible Answerman*

SOURCES

The Directory of Religious Organizations in the United States. 2d ed. Falls Church, VA: McGrath, 1982.

Melton, J. Gordon. *Directory of Religious Organizations in the United States.* 3d ed. Detroit: Gale Research, 1993.

CHRISTIAN TELEVISION MISSION
established: 1956

Founded in 1956 and headquartered in Springfield, Missouri, Christian Television Mission (CTM) is an independent evangelical Protestant organization made up of churches and individuals interested in producing Christian programs for television.

CTM began in the early 1950s, when the *Vernon Brothers Quartet* television program that aired over KOAM-TV, Pittsburg, Kansas, expanded its outreach and moved its base of operation to Springfield, Missouri. In addition to conducting revivals and crusades, the *Vernon Brothers Quartet* incorporated as CTM and produced a weekly television series called *Homestead USA*. To keep its supporters informed, CTM publishes a bimonthly information and programming magazine, *Christian TV News*.

SOURCES

The Directory of Religious Organizations in the United States. 2d ed. Falls Church, VA: McGrath, 1982.

Melton, J. Gordon. *Directory of Religious Organizations in the United States.* 3d ed. Detroit: Gale Research, 1993.

THE CHRISTIAN'S HOUR
see: James DeForest Murch

THE CHRISTOPHERS
established: 1945

Since 1945, the Christophers—a Catholic movement dedicated to moral and social uplift in government, eduation, labor-management relations, literature, and entertainment—have been spreading an ecumenically-oriented motivational message of positive social action and moral living through various media, including radio, television, pamphlets, and newspaper columns. The ministry's optimistic and life-affirming philosophy is best captured in its oft-quoted inspirational dictum: "It is better to light one candle than curse the darkness."

In 1952, the Christophers began producing the *Christopher Program,* hosted by Father James Keller. The 15-minute program featured the inspirational words and heroic life stories of some of Hollywood's leading Catholic and non-Catholic stars, such as Bing Crosby and Eddie Cantor. The broadcast originated from New York City and aired throughout the 1950s and 1960s over commercial television stations in many major US cities. By the late 1960s, the program was carried over the air by 225 stations nationwide. During this period, Father Keller began taping a daily 90-second inspirational spot entitled *Thought for Today,* which aired with modest success over a number of radio stations.

In 1969, *Christopher Program* changed its name and format, becoming *Christopher Closeup.* Hosted by the Reverend Richard Armstrong and Jeanne Glynn, this new half-hour broadcast switched its focus to public affairs and adopted a programming format similar to that of *60 Minutes.* Currently, this program airs over more than 100 commercial stations nationwide. The Christophers also produce a radio version of *Christopher Closeup.*

Building on the clear success of these ventures, the ministry began producing a brief one-minute inspirational program called *The Word Is* that resembled the testimonial style of the *Christopher Program* of the 1950s and 1960s. The Christophers also broadcast a number of programs over the Armed Forces Radio-TV Service and over a variety of Christian networks. The Christopher's radio and television programs now appear on more than 3,000 stations around the world.

SOURCES

Bluem, A. William. *Religious Television Programs: A Study of Relevance.* New York: Hastings House, 1969.

The Directory of Religious Organizations in the United States. 2d ed. Falls Church, VA: McGrath, 1982.

"CHURCH MAN"
established: 1992

The "Church Man" is the radio pseudonym of the Reverend George Exoo, a Harvard Divinity School graduate who has been evaluating Pittsburgh-area church services since late 1992 on WQED-FM. Exoo goes to churches, mosques, synagogues, and meeting houses to review, among other things, their choirs, sermons, architecture, and after-service food. His purpose, he claims, is to help churches improve and grow by showing what the average church-shopper might encounter at a random religious service. Exoo and his aide, WQED engineer Tom Ammons, express a preference for clear, inspiring sermons, and ministers who express warmth and care. The Church Man is now regularly invited by local churches to attend their services in hopes that they'll receive favorable publicity and constructive advice.

Exoo's critiques can be biting. Of the music at Mount Ararat Baptist Church, he observed, "Alas, the organ is a muddy old Hammond, which should, I believe, be retired to a friendly cocktail lounge." Of the preacher at the Covenant Church of Pittsburgh, he commented, "He promised to cast his sermon in four points, but ended up after 75 minutes discussing only three. The first claimed nearly an hour. Two and three were unrelated." This innovative program comes, fittingly, from Pittsburgh, home to the world's oldest broadcaster of religious radio programs, station KDKA.

SOURCES

"Critic Rates Worship Services." *Daytona Beach News-Journal*, March 5, 1994.

CHURCH OF CHRIST, SCIENTIST

Christian Scientists have been involved in publishing and broadcasting ministries since their founder, Mary Baker Eddy, started the *Journal of Christian Science* in 1883. Augusta Stetson, a disciple of Eddy's, used radio during the 1920s in an attempt to resuscitate her failing independent ministry in New York City. When the medium of television emerged during the 1950s, Christian Scientists produced the weekly *How Christian Science Heals*. This filmed, 15-minute program was widely distributed during the 1950s and 1960s and featured the testimonies of persons who had received spiritual healing through Christian Science.

The church developed a week-day television program, *Daily Bible Lesson*, during the late 1980s. This show was usually broadcast during the early morning hours. Another broadcast outreach, *The Christian Science Monitor Report*, featured a more secular and commercial news format. This show continues to air into the mid-1990s. Monitor Radio also produced a daily news program during the 1980s and 1990s that could be heard on National Public Radio broadcasting outlets.

At present, the Church of Christ, Scientist, produces and broadcasts a number of shortwave radio, public radio, and cable television programs under the direction of its publishing society, located at the "Mother Church" in Boston, Massachusetts. These programs include: *The World Service of the Christian Science Monitor* (radio), *The Herald of Christian Science* (radio), and *World Monitor* (television). Much to the church's chagrin, financial hardships in the early 1990s have forced a scaling back of these services, including its cable service, The Monitor Channel.

SOURCES

Erickson, Hal. *Religious Radio and Television in the United States, 1921–1991*. Jefferson, NC: McFarland, 1992.

Melton, J. Gordon. *Directory of Religious Organizations in the United States*. 3d ed. Detroit: Gale Research, 1993.

CHURCH OF THE AIR
see: Essek William Kenyon

THE CHURCH OF THE AIR
see: Paul Finkenbinder

CHURCH ON FIRE

Church on Fire is a recent addition to the ranks of Pentecostal praise and preaching television programs. The program features the fiery sermons of its host, Pastor Jentezen Franklin, who is the founder of Free Chapel Worship Center, an integrated Pentecostal congregation in Gainesville, Georgia.

Franklin's *Church on Fire* attempts to build the Kingdom of God and battle Satan "in a war for the souls of men and women." The ministry's activist program claims to be "charging at the gates of Hell" by building an army of disciples in every city Franklin visits. Like Gideon of Old Testament fame, Franklin believes he needs 300 believers to battle the forces of darkness in a particular locale. *Church on Fire* is strongly apocalyptic in orientation and markets such independently produced videos as *The Day after the Rapture.*

CJOS-FM, CANADA
established: 1995

The Canadian Radio-Television and Telecommunications Commission has granted only three licenses since its policy change in June of 1993 that allowed the licensing of religious radio stations. Two of these stations, one of which has a Catholic format, the other a multi-faith approach, are in Quebec. The third station, CJOS-FM, Caronport, Saskatchewan, is Canada's first evangelical radio station.

The FM outreach is designed to meet the local needs of Caronport, which is home to Briercrest Bible College and Briercrest Biblical Seminary. The college is the largest evangelical school in Canada. Don Millar, with 22 years of previous broadcasting experience in secular radio, was appointed as CJOS-FM's general manager. Millar graduated from Briercrest in April of 1995 and decided to remain in Caronport to help set up the station and develop its curricula. The station made its first live broadcast in September, 1995.

TERRY COLE-WHITTAKER
born: 1939

Terry Cole-Whittaker is an excellent example of a New Age religious television personality. The charismatic Southern California native extolled wealth, joy, and personal fulfillment during her six years on television (between 1979 and 1985) and defied most attempts to categorize her in religious terms.

Cole-Whittaker was ordained in 1975 by the Church of Religious Science, a New Thought church. New Thought, a movement that began in the late nineteenth century, emphasized the power of positive thinking and is generally considered a precursor to New Age thought. After her ordination, Cole-Whittaker quickly turned her quiet La Jolla (San Diego) church into a nationally known center of New Age motivational religion. Her first television program, dubbed *With Love, Reverend Terry*, began in January 1979. The show provided a congenial showcase for Cole-Whittaker's motivational speaking skills and flair for the dramatic, and was an immediate hit. The blonde, trim minister cajoled her audiences like Joan Rivers and favored quips, pokes, and puns over long, serious lectures. To take just one example, on the question of abortion Cole-Whittaker once quipped, "People want to know what my stand on abortion is. I think the Pope should have the choice of whether he wants an abortion or not! I want that man to have everything he wants, bless him."

During the early 1980s, Cole-Whittaker became a national celebrity, appearing on the Phil Donahue and Merv Griffin shows, on numerous radio programs, and in dozens of print interviews. She took advantage of each of these occasions to promote both her ministry and her two best-selling books, *New Age Positive Thinking* (1980) and *What You Think of Me Is None of My Business* (1979). Celebrities such as Lily Tomlin, Clint Eastwood, Gavin MacLeod, and Linda Gray flocked to hear her presentations and publicly expressed their admiration for her. Cole-Whittaker's popularity peaked around 1983 when her television program was being aired in 15 markets. Although the show was most popular in the West, it also was broadcast over New York superstation WOR-TV. With her fourth husband, Leonardo, Cole-Whittaker inaugurated a brief radio ministry that featured a program in Spanish. The radio ministry collapsed after the couple's divorce in 1984.

Cole-Whittaker's message wove together elements from Ernest Holmes's *Science of Mind* teachings, "est," humanistic psychology, Gnosticism, Eastern philosophy, and *A Course in Miracles*, a primer in spiritual thinking by Helen Schucman. The teachings emphasized the need to be freed from guilt over sex, power, and money. Cole-Whittaker's God was a loving, non-judging, Universal Spirit whose grace was available for the asking. As she said on numerous programs, "Prosperity and happiness are your divine right." This eclectic New Age message of personal happiness and self-empowerment made Cole-Whittaker the target of attacks by Christian fundamentalists. These attacks coupled with spiraling financial debts and the intrusions of tabloids and strangers into her personal life took their toll on the irrepressible minister. By March of 1985, she had decided to discontinue her religious broadcasts and to take time off for personal introspection.

Cole-Whittaker returned to television for a brief period during the late 1980s, sending out her programs on stations in Los Angeles, San Diego, and San Francisco. In time these programs were also taken off the air, and the minister turned her energies to Adventures in Enlightenment, a foundation that promotes Cole-Whittaker's speaking engagements, workshops, publications, and cassette tapes. Cole-Whittaker now devotes most of her time to this ministry and to conducting spiritual retreats in such exotic locales as Big Sur, New Zealand, and Fiji. Her teachings and methods are paradigmatic examples of the eclectic, tolerant, individualistic, and mystical style of indigenous California religion.

SOURCES

Cole-Whittaker, Terry. *New Age Positive Thinking*. San Francisco: New Dimensions Foundation, 1980.

———. *What You Think of Me Is None of My Business*. La Jolla, CA: Oak Tree Publications, 1979.

Peterson, Richard G. "Electric Sisters." In *The God Pumpers*, edited by Marshall Fishwick and Ray B. Browne. Bowling Green, KY: Bowling Green State University Popular Press, 1987.

COMMISSION OF PRESS, RADIO, AND TELEVISION
see: Lutheran Church in America

BAYLESS CONLEY
see: Cottonwood Christian Center

ROBERT COOK
born: 1912, Cleveland, Ohio
died: 1991

Host of the radio ministry *The King's Hour* from 1962 until his death in 1991, Robert Cook grew up in Ohio and was educated at the Moody Bible Institute, Wheaton College, and Eastern Baptist Seminary. In 1935, Cook was ordained a minister of the Northern Baptist Church and served in churches in Philadelphia and Chicago.

In 1948, Cook succeeded Torrey Johnson as president of Youth for Christ International (YFC), an organization that, at the time, sponsored evangelistic rallies for high school and college students. While president of YFC, Cook shifted the ministry's focus to on-campus high school Bible clubs. In 1957, Cook became vice president of Scripture Press.

In 1962, he was named president of The King's College of Briarcliff, New York, which had been founded in 1938 by YFC cofounder Percy Crawford. Crawford was also host of the *Young People's Church of the Air*. It was during Cook's tenure as president of The King's College that he began his radio ministry.

Beginning in 1962, Cook hosted the college's signature program, *The King's Hour*. Though retiring as president of The King's College in 1985, Cook remained host of the weekly show until his death in 1991. From 1985 until 1988, Cook also served as president of the National Religious Broadcasters.

See also Torrey Johnson; National Religious Broadcasters

SOURCES

Reid, Daniel G., Robert D. Linder, Bruce L. Shelley, and Harry S. Stout, eds. *Dictionary of Christianity in America*. Downers Grove, IL: InterVarsity Press, 1990.

Ward, Mark, Sr. *Air of Salvation: The Story of Christian Broadcasting*. Grand Rapids, MI: Baker Book House, 1994.

KENNETH COPELAND
born: 1937, West Texas

Kenneth Copeland and his wife Gloria are two of the more enduring presences on religious television over the past 15 years. The Kenneth Copeland Ministries now broadcasts its "health and wealth" theology via satellite hook-up around the world and reportedly operates with no debt, a rarity for television ministries.

Kenneth Copeland was born in West Texas and converted to Christianity with his wife in 1962. Drawn to the Pentecostal ministry of Oral Roberts, the couple moved from their home in Fort Worth to Tulsa, Oklahoma, in 1967. Copeland enrolled in Oral Roberts University and began ministerial training. During this period Roberts hired Copeland as a pilot and the young minister had a firsthand opportunity to witness Robert's healing work as he flew the evangelist to crusades around the country.

Before he graduated from ministerial training, Copeland came under the influence of the independent Pentecostal evangelist Kenneth Hagin. He began attending Hagin's seminars and soon decided to drop out of Oral Roberts University. Within a year Copeland had moved back to Fort Worth and become a full-time minister.

The first meetings of his newly formed Kenneth Copeland Ministries, Inc., took place in homes in the Fort Worth area. Aided by Copeland's charismatic preaching style and talent as a gospel singer, the new enterprise grew rapidly. A magazine, *Believer's Voice of Victory*, was inaugurated in 1973, and by the mid-1980s, it had a circulation of over 700,000. In 1976, Copeland created a religious radio show, and a television program, *Believer's Voice of Victory*, was added to his ministry in 1979. The show's national audience jumped from 240,000 viewers in 1980 to 550,000 by 1986. This program now airs around the world on satellite hookups, local religious television stations, and religious cable channels. In Europe the show is sent out over European Broadcasting Network's New World Channel.

Copeland, like his mentors Essek William Kenyon and Kenneth Hagin, has been criticized for preaching a "health and wealth" theology. This message emphasizes the role of faith in Christian living and asserts God's desire that every Christian enjoy both spiritual and material prosperity. Copeland continually exhorts his listeners to "claim" God's promises of health and wealth through dynamic, confident prayer. By stating in faith what they desire from God and trusting completely in God's promises, Copeland believes that abundance will appear in all dimensions of his viewers' lives. He also claims that contributions to his ministry will bring a financial return to the donor: "Do you want a hundredfold return on your money? Give and let God multiply it back to you." This synthesis of American evangelicalism, materialism, and positive thinking has proven to be highly attractive to young, upwardly mobile, conservative Christians. In many congregations, Copeland's teaching that God's goal for all believers is financial prosperity has replaced the traditional biblical warnings concerning the love of money and the war between God and mammon.

Criticism of his prosperity gospel compelled Copeland to reconsider the tenor of his message during 1985. However, he soon claimed that the Lord had given him "release to preach it once again . . . with a greater anointing and a greater zeal than ever before." "And this time," he asserted, "I am preaching prosperity through the persecution and the criticism. I am at liberty to do what I know best, and that is to teach the abundant life in Christ." Copeland was soon appealing, both on the air and through personalized letters to subscribers, for contributions to help him build a new ministry center. Using this center as a base, he promised to deliver his prosperity message throughout the world.

Like other Pentecostals, Copeland is a dynamic, entertaining television preacher. He strides up and down the stage as he delivers his message and frequently draws laughs and whistles from his audience. Copeland takes special pleasure in criticizing the staid, dry churches of the Christian mainstream. For him, an authentic church is alive with charismatic gifts: spiritual healing, speaking in tongues, and miracles. On one broadcast, Copeland shared his faith in the laying on of hands by describing how he had used this power to help him buy an airplane: "I walked all the way around it, putting my hands on it. I'm talking to this airplane, and I said, 'I'm speaking to you in the name of Jesus. And I demand any kind of corrosion or malfunction to get out of you right now—in the name of Jesus—you're not going to have that!'" At the end of each broadcast, Copeland looks into the camera and exclaims, "Jesus is Lord! Amen!"

Copeland's annual healing revivals are used to authenticate his television message. These crusades are well attended, and at the close of each evening, numerous healings are reported. Copeland also promotes his ministry through the distribution of numerous books, tapes, and records.

See also A. A. Allen

SOURCES

Barron, Bruce. *The Health and Wealth Gospel.* Downers Grove, IL: InterVarsity Press, 1987.

Bruce, Steve. *Pray TV: Televangelism in America.* New York: Routledge, 1990.

Burgess, Stanley M., Gary B. McGee, and Patrick H. Alexander, eds. *Dictionary of Pentecostal and Charismatic Movements.* Grand Rapids, MI: Zondervan, 1988.

Copeland, Gloria. *God's Will for You.* Fort Worth, TX: Kenneth Copeland, 1972.

———. *God's Will Is Prosperity.* Fort Worth, TX: Kenneth Copeland, 1978.

Copeland, Kenneth. "I've Received My Instructions. Our Calling Is Made Clear." *Believer's Voice of Victory* (January, 1985).

———. *The Laws of Prosperity.* Fort Worth, TX: Kenneth Copeland, 1974.

———. *Walking in the Realm of the Miraculous.* Fort Worth, TX: Kenneth Copeland, 1979.

Hadden, Jeffrey K., and Charles E. Swann. *Prime Time Preachers.* Menlo Park, CA: Addison-Wesley, 1981.

Schultze, Quentin J. *Televangelism and American Culture.* Grand Rapids, MI: Baker Book House, 1991.

THE CORAL RIDGE HOUR
see: D. James Kennedy

COTTONWOOD CHRISTIAN CENTER
established: 1982

The television ministry of the Cottonwood Christian Center in Los Alamitos, California, near South Los Angeles, began through the vision of its minister, Bayless Conley. Conley, a onetime hippie, converted in 1975. He lived as a street evangelist until enrolling for courses in 1979 at a charismatic Christian Bible college. After two years of study, he took a position as assistant minister with a small church in Beaumont, California. After a year, he and his wife,

Janet, began a weekly Bible study group in Los Alamitos with the intention of starting their own church. Beginning with fewer than 10 people, the study group grew to the size of a large house church. When he officially began the Cottonwood Christian Center, Conley had seen his congregation grow to 65 regular participants.

In 1985, Conley began recording his sermons and lessons in a local studio for broadcast over public access television. Within a few years, he had purchased his own equipment and was producing live recordings of his Sunday services for broadcast in the Los Angeles basin. In 1992, he moved his program, *Cottonwood Christian Center*, to the Fox Channel and, later, to KCAL-TV, Los Angeles, which still carries his program. Services of the Cottonwood Christian Center are also broadcast via satellite from the Netherlands to 22 countries throughout Europe.

At present, the center has an average weekly attendance of about 2,000 people. In addition to its television production facilities, Cottonwood Christian Center also houses a two-year Bible college. As an independent charismatic Christian church, the Center espouses the baptism of the Holy Spirit and a ministry of signs and wonders. Though interpreting the Bible from an apocalyptic endtimes perspective, Conley's messages also emphasize spiritual devotion to more day-to-day practical concerns such as marriage, work, and family life.

SOURCES

Conley, Bayless. *Cast Down But Not Destroyed*. Los Alamitos, CA: Cottonwood Christian Center, 1991.

CHARLES COUGHLIN

born: October 25, 1891, Hamilton, Ontario, Canada
died: October 27, 1979, Birmingham, Michigan

Charles Edward Coughlin was one of the dominant personalities in religious radio during the 1930s. He was also one of radio's most controversial figures because of his political and social views, which included anti-Semitism, anti-communism, anti-unionism, isolationism, and support for the Nazi party.

Coughlin was reared in Ontario by a Great Lakes seaman and attended St. Michael's College, University of Toronto, where he received his doctorate in philosophy in 1911. Following his ordination into the Roman Catholic priesthood in 1916, Coughlin lectured in philosophy and English at Assumption College in Sandwich, Ontario, and pastored churches in Detroit, Kalamazoo, and North Branch, Michigan. In 1926, the young priest was sent to establish a new parish at Royal Oak, Michigan. He named it the Shrine of the Little Flower after the recently canonized Therese Martin, popularly known as the Little Flower of Jesus. Coughlin developed a strong personal devotion to the saint and remained as pastor at the shrine until his retirement in 1966.

It was also in 1926 that the Ku Klux Klan, trying to frighten the young priest, burned a cross in front of his church. In response to this traumatic event, Coughlin was given a chance to defend Roman Catholicism on Detroit radio station WJR. This broadcast developed into an effective and respected radio ministry that focused on religious teachings and issues. The programs were sponsored by the Radio League of the Little Flower and broadcast on Sunday afternoons. Coughlin's radio ministry attracted little attention until he ventured beyond religious topics and began promoting his political and social views. Soon the CBS radio network picked up the program and his audience expanded to almost 40 million listeners.

Coughlin's more secular pronouncements began with blistering indictments of world Communism and gradually expanded to include attacks on Jews, Franklin D. Roosevelt's New Deal (although Coughlin had supported Roosevelt in the 1932 presidential campaign), unions, and United States involvement in foreign conflicts. Coughlin founded the National Union for Social Justice (NUSJ) in 1934 to promote his radical social views and began printing the magazine *Social Justice* in 1936. The NUSJ's program included such radical reforms as the abolition of the private banking system, the nationalization of key resources, and the establishment of a central bank to control prices. Coughlin's movement organized and supported the presidential campaign of William Lemke in 1936. Although Coughlin predicted that he would deliver 9 million votes for his candidate, Lemke garnered no more than 900,000. Deeply disappointed, Coughlin discontinued the efforts of the NUSJ and took a temporary leave from his radio program.

In the years leading up to World War II, Coughlin reconstituted the NUSJ as a "Christian Front" divided into gang-like platoons, which would raise funds for political organizations. He warned his audiences of a British-Jewish-Rooseveltian conspiracy that was drawing the United States into military entanglements around the world. Even after the Japanese attack on Pearl Harbor, Coughlin adamantly opposed the entry of the United States into World War II. By 1942, his views had become a national embarrassment. Roman Catholic authorities intervened and pressured him to quit his weekly radio program. He was also denied mailing privileges for *Social Justice* because of the magazine's purported violation of the Espionage Act of 1917.

From 1942 to 1966, Coughlin continued to serve as a pastor but never again gained a national radio audience for his strident political views. He did, however, continue to write anti-Communist tracts and was a vocal opponent of the Second Vatican Council. Coughlin died in obscurity in 1979 and is mainly remembered as a fiery right-wing religious broadcaster whose radical political views were out of step with American public opinion during World War II.

The commentator Wallace Stegner wrote, concerning Coughlin's popularity, "It would be well to consider how vague, misty, uninformed, contradictory, and insincere his program was, and yet how it won the unstinting belief of hundreds of thousands, even millions. It would be well to remember that even a people like the Americans, supposedly politically mature . . . can be brought to the point where millions of them will beg to be led."

SOURCES

Brinkley, Alan. *Voices of Protest.* New York: Vintage Books, 1983.

Coughlin, Charles E. *Bishops Versus Popes.* Bloomfield Hills, MI: Helmet and Sword, 1969.

———. *By the Sweat of Thy Brow.* Detroit: Radio League of the Little Flower, 1931.

———. *Eight Lectures on Labor, Capital, and Justice.* Royal Oak, MI: Radio League of the Little Flower, 1934.

———. *The New Deal in Money.* Royal Oak, MI: Radio League of the Little Flower, 1933.

Hadden, Jeffrey K., and Charles E. Swann. *Prime Time Preachers: The Rising Power of Televangelism.* Menlo Park, CA: Addison-Wesley, 1981.

Marcus, Sheldon. *Father Coughlin: The Tumultuous Life of the Priest of the Little Flower.* Boston: Little, Brown, 1973.

Mugglebee, Ruth. *Father Coughlin of the Shrine of the Little Flower.* Boston: L. C. Page, 1933.

Roy, Ralph Lord. *Apostles of Discord: A Study of Organized Bigotry and Disruption on the Fringes of Protestantism.* Boston: Beacon Press, 1953.

Tull, Charles J. *Father Coughlin and the New Deal.* Syracuse, NY: Syracuse University Press, 1965.

Ward, Louis B. *Father Charles E. Coughlin: An Authorized Biography.* Detroit: Tower Publications, 1933.

LOIS CRAWFORD
born: 1892, Boone, Iowa
died: 1986, Boone, Iowa

Lois Crawford gained her entry into religious broadcasting through her father, who created radio station KFGQ in 1927 as an evangelical outreach for his Boone, Iowa, Bible college. The station was the first religious radio ministry west of the Mississippi River and used a modest 10-watt transmitter. Crawford learned the technical dimensions of radio broadcasting and was the first American woman to be granted a first class radio telephone license. Crawford was ordained into the Congregational church in 1923 by her father. In time, she would succeed him as pastor of Boone Biblical Church and as president of Boone Biblical Ministries.

Soon after the conversion of a hard-bitten miner during a KFGQ broadcast, Crawford decided to become one of the first American women radio evangelists. One of Crawford's former students sent funds to upgrade the station's equipment, and an engineer at radio station WOI in Ames, Iowa, helped her with wiring diagrams and spare parts. During the 1920s and 1930s, Crawford hosted Bible programs, ran the station, and produced the programming.

After her father's passing in 1936, Crawford served as president of KFGQ-AM and FM. She continued in this capacity until her death in 1986. During her long career, Crawford also supervised a Christian day school, the Bible college, a retirement home, a youth camp, and a religious bookstore. In 1977, this well-respected broadcaster became the first woman to be inducted into the National Religious Broadcasters Hall of Fame.

SOURCES

Armstrong, Ben. *The Electric Church*. Nashville: Thomas Nelson, 1979.

Ward, Mark, Sr. *Air of Salvation: The Story of Christian Broadcasting*. Manassas, VA: National Religious Broadcasters, 1994.

PERCY CRAWFORD

born: 1902, Minnedosa, Manitoba, Canada
died: 1960, Pennsylvania

Percy Crawford, a respected evangelical youth minister, educator, and preacher, was also a pioneer broadcaster in FM-radio evangelism and religious television.

After experiencing a conversion to Christ as a young adult at the Church of the Open Door, Los Angeles, California, Crawford spent much of the next 10 years studying at various colleges around the country. He attended the Bible Institute of Los Angeles (Biola), the University of California at Los Angeles, Wheaton College (from which he earned a bachelor's degree in 1929), Westminster Theological Seminary (from which he earned a bachelor of theology degree in 1932), and the University of Pennsylvania. After receiving a master of arts from the latter school, he went on to earn a doctor of divinity degree from Bob Jones University in 1940. During this period, Crawford married an accomplished musician and vocalist, Ruth Duvall.

Crawford found himself drawn to youth ministry early in his career. In 1930, he inaugurated Saturday night evangelical rallies that would later develop into the Youth for Christ movement. He also inaugurated a national radio ministry, *Young People's Church of the Air*, which would ultimately be broadcast on more than 600 radio stations.

Crawford was one of the first fundamentalists to recognize the potential of television for spreading the gospel. In 1950, he began *Youth on the March*, a live television program that featured vivacious young musicians and speakers in an entertainment format. This popular show became the launching pad for a number of today's top executives in religious broadcasting. The program's national Sunday-evening audience was estimated to number in the millions. It aired on ABC-TV and DuMont television networks until April 1953.

Crawford's work as an educator began with his founding of the Pinebrook Bible Conference in Stroudsburg, Pennsylvania, and his establishment of The King's College in Briarcliff Manor, New York, in 1938. After launching the Crawford Broadcasting Company in Flourtown, Pennsylvania, Crawford purchased six FM radio stations and one television station. This latter station, WPCA, Philadelphia, featured a wide array of programming and operated as a local network affiliate.

Crawford died while still very much involved with religious broadcasting.

SOURCES

Armstrong, Ben. *The Electric Church*. Nashville: Thomas Nelson, 1979.

Reid, Daniel G., et al., eds. *Dictionary of Christianity in America*. Downers Grove, IL: InterVarsity Press, 1990.

Ward, Mark, Sr. *Air of Salvation: The Story of Christian Broadcasting*. Manassas, VA: National Religious Broadcasters, 1994.

W. A. CRISWELL
born: December 19, 1909, Eldorado, Oklahoma

Courtesy: National Religious Broadcasters

Wallie Amos Criswell is best known as the pastor of the largest Baptist congregation in the United States, the First Baptist Church of Dallas, and as an influential conservative voice in the Southern Baptist Convention. However, Criswell is also a prolific author and much-loved radio and television preacher who has made a significant impact on religious broadcasting.

Criswell was reared in pious and modest circumstances in rural Oklahoma and Texas. He developed an early love of Scripture and was converted to Christianity at the age of 10 by revivalist preacher John Hicks. When he turned 12, Criswell pledged himself to the Christian ministry in a ceremony at his local Baptist church. The music director at the church, John R. Rice, would go on to edit the noted fundamentalist newsletter, *Sword of the Lord*. Criswell enrolled as an undergraduate at Baylor University in Waco, Texas. His mother left the family homestead in Texline and moved to Waco to provide him with financial and emo-

tional support during his student years. The would-be-minister gained local prominence as a gifted preacher. He took every opportunity to refine his craft, preaching in jails, public squares, and area churches. Local legend has it that Criswell's voice could be heard from a distance of five miles on a clear Texas evening. His mother's attentions proved beneficial, and Criswell graduated magna cum laude from Baylor in 1931.

The young man decided to earn his ministerial credentials at Southern Baptist Theological Seminary in Louisville, Kentucky. While at Southern, Criswell worked with respected Baptist academics such as A. T. Robertson and John R. Sampey. He again distinguished himself as a scholar and preacher and earned a master of theology degree in 1934 and a doctorate in 1937. Like many ministerial students, Criswell worked as a student pastor to earn extra money. While serving at a church in Mt. Washington, Kentucky, he met and married the congregation's piano player, Betty Mae Harris. She bore the couple's only child, Mabel Ann, in 1939.

Upon graduation, Criswell accepted a call to pastor the First Baptist Church of Chickasha, Oklahoma. He helped the church grow significantly and was dubbed the "holy roller preacher with a Ph.D." Criswell parlayed his success in Chickasha into a higher profile pastorship at the First Baptist Church of Muskogee. During his three-year stint there, Criswell began to change his preaching style. Instead of the topical sermons he had been taught to deliver, he started preaching Scripture in an expository manner. To this day, Criswell's congregants bring their Bibles and notebooks and carefully jot down his interpretations of particular passages.

By the time Criswell was asked to take over the prestigious pastorship of First Baptist Church of Dallas (following the death of George W. Truett in 1944), the young minister had perfected his homiletic style. He preached with passion, intensity, poetry, and flair. His sermons were delivered without notes and combined scriptural exegesis, storytelling, sentiment, history, and humor. The homilies were usually at least 45 minutes in length and followed avidly by his audience. Criswell proved a worthy successor to the much loved Truett and would pastor the huge congregation into the 1990s, where he still serves as pastor emeritus.

By 1946, the new pastor was ready for a fresh homiletic challenge. He inaugurated a 17-year radio broadcast of sermons on every verse in the Bible. Speeding through the Old Testament in three years, he focused most of his attention—fully 10 years—on Acts of the Apostles, the Epistles, and the Book of Revelation. By 1958, his steadily growing church had increased its annual contributions 300 percent, to $1,303,000.

Criswell was a pioneer in religious television during the 1950s, producing several filmed, syndicated programs. The rising Baptist star also inaugurated his own radio syndication enterprise during this time.

Criswell has maintained a focus on evangelism throughout his career. At the end of each sermon, he initiates the traditional Baptist altar call with the words, "In a moment we shall stand and sing our appeal and while we sing it, a family you, a couple you, or just one, somebody you, to give your heart to the Lord, to put your life in the fellowship of the church, to answer God's call, upon the first note of the first stanza come." As a result of his untiring efforts in this direction, the church has grown into the largest single Baptist congregation in the country, with over 26,000 members. Most of the church's members come from the prosperous suburbs of Dallas. Others are modern celebrities such as evangelist Billy Graham and radio commentator Paul Harvey. Perhaps the church's most prominent member was H. L. Hunt, the Texas oil billionaire, who was a strong supporter of Criswell's ministry until Hunt's death.

Criswell's congregation building extended beyond evangelism and preaching, however. He also provided a wide array of services for members, including 15 nursery schools for the children of adults attending Sunday school classes, a Christian day school for grades K-12, Criswell Bible College, and the Graduate School of the Bible for aspiring ministers. During the 1980s, the church evolved into a more family-oriented

congregation with a wide range of facilities for children and young adults. These included gymnasiums, a roller skating rink, a weight training room, bowling alleys, and racquetball courts. The congregation's extensive music ministry was another means of engendering member commitment. It now includes over 23 choirs, a 50-piece orchestra, and a youth chapel chorus that gives performances throughout the world.

Criswell began his successful publishing career shortly after his move to Dallas. His first book, the somewhat pedantic *The Church Library Reinforcing the Work of the Denomination* (1947), was followed by such fundamentalist apologetics as *These Issues We Must Face* (1953), *Did Man Just Happen?* (1957), *Five Great Questions of the Bible* (1958), *In Defense of the Faith* (1967), *Why I Preach That the Bible Is Literally True* (1969), and *Christ and the Contemporary Crisis* (1972). While many of Criswell's books are simply collections of his sermons on particular books of Scripture, others are sharp polemics against liberal religious views. His most substantial work, the five-volume set entitled *Great Doctrines of the Bible*, appeared in 1985.

The expansion of his television and radio ministry in 1970 extended Criswell's influence throughout the southwestern United States. These programs consisted of broadcasts seen in color of his Sunday morning sermons at First Baptist in Dallas. The church purchased its own broadcasting equipment and, in 1989, was given a radio license by the Federal Communications Commission to operate its own 100,000-watt radio station, KCBI. The current pastor of First Baptist, Dr. O. S. Hawkins, delivers weekly services over KCBI, and Criswell hosts a half-hour call-in show every Wednesday on the church station. Criswell is currently pastor emeritus and occasionally delivers a locally broadcast Sunday sermon. Tapes of Criswell's past sermons are now sent out to interested listeners around the world.

The most controversial dimension of Criswell's career has been his leadership of the conservative forces within the Southern Baptist Convention. A fervent anti-Catholic during the early part of his life, he once spearheaded a coalition of Protestant ministers who opposed the election of John F. Kennedy. Criswell's anti-Catholic views changed somewhat during the early 1970s, and the famed preacher accepted the offer of an audience with Pope Paul VI in 1971.

Criswell was also a staunch and outspoken opponent of racial integration during the 1950s. In a speech before the South Carolina legislature in 1956, the conservative churchman reportedly condemned integration as "a thing of idiocy and foolishness." However, his views on this issue also underwent a shift during the late 1960s. Shortly before his election to the presidency of the Southern Baptist Convention in 1968, Criswell delivered a homily entitled, "The Church of the Open Door," and convinced his church's leaders to allow all races to attend services. He has forcefully condemned racism since this time, although his book *Criswell Study Bible* continues to interpret 9 Genesis as a divine curse on the people of Africa.

Criswell was instrumental in the growing conservative dominance of the Southern Baptist Convention during the 1960s and 1970s. He strongly affirmed biblical inerrancy and supported the founding of private Christian schools where children could pray and be taught creation science. At least in part due to his influence, the fundamentalist faction has gradually taken over the major committees, seminaries, and denominational boards of the convention during the 1980s and 1990s.

During his rise to national prominence as president of the Southern Baptist Convention, Criswell became a favorite of Republican presidents like Richard Nixon and Gerald Ford. He was often invited to briefings at the White House and was alleged to have gushed that Richard Nixon was "personally one of the finest men you could ever meet." Ford appeared at First Baptist of Dallas during the 1976 presidential campaign and was given Criswell's personal endorsement. Criswell was also one of the first Baptist leaders to join the New Christian Right supporters of Ronald Reagan during the 1980 presidential campaign. At the important national affairs briefing held in Dallas in August, 1980,

Criswell welcomed Reagan on behalf of 30 million evangelicals. Like many conservatives, he strongly supported the free enterprise system and a powerful American defense establishment. He was also highly critical of social welfare and of anything that smacked of the Christian social gospel of the late nineteenth century.

Criswell's interest in national political matters stemmed from his interpretation of apocalyptic biblical prophecies. Like other fundamentalist churchmen, he predicted the imminent onset of the battle of Armageddon. Criswell believed that this apocalyptic battle would be fought in the Middle East with Israel and the United States on one side, and the Soviet Union and the Arab nations on the other. Because of his vocal support for the State of Israel, he was awarded the prestigious Israel Humanitarian Award by Prime Minister Menachem Begin in 1978.

Criswell has been a lifelong advocate of the doctrine of biblical inerrancy. In his view, the Scripture contains no errors in its original manuscripts and has been inspired by God in every word. His literal interpretation of Scripture extends to church governance, in which dimension he believes the Bible supports autocratic rule by the pastor. Criswell's opinion on this matter was well summarized in his 1986 comments, "A laity-led, layman-led, deacon-led church will be a weak church anywhere on God's earth. The pastor is the ruler of the church. There is no other thing than that in the Bible." Although he has been criticized by moderates as lacking in intellectual depth, his ministry has provided an unambiguous message of certainty and conviction to those who struggle with an insecure and skeptical era.

SOURCES

Criswell, W. A. *The Bible for Today's World.* Grand Rapids, MI: Zondervan, 1965.

———. *Christ and the Contemporary Crisis.* Dallas: Crescendo, 1972.

———. *The Church Library Reinforcing the Work of the Denomination.* Nashville: Baptist Sunday School Board, 1947.

———. *The Criswell Study Bible.* Nashville: Thomas Nelson, 1979.

———. *Did Man Just Happen?* Grand Rapids, MI: Zondervan, 1957.

———. *Expository Sermons on Revelations: Five Volumes in One.* 5 vols. Grand Rapids, MI: Zondervan, 1962–66.

———. *Five Great Questions of the Bible.* Grand Rapids, MI: Zondervan, 1958.

———. *Great Doctrines of the Bible.* 5 vols. Grand Rapids, MI: Zondervan, 1982–85.

———. *In Defense of the Faith.* Grand Rapids, MI: Zondervan, 1967.

———. *Look Up, Brother!* Nashville: Broadman, 1970.

———.*These Issues We Must Face.* Grand Rapids, MI: Zondervan, 1953.

———. *What to Do until Jesus Comes Back.* Nashville: Broadman, 1975.

———. *Why I Preach That the Bible Is Literally True.* Nashville: Broadman, 1969.

Gill, Ed. *Through the Years: A History of the First Baptist Church Muskogee, Oklahoma, 1890–1965.* Muskogee, OK: Hoffman, n.d.

Hadden, Jeffrey K., and Charles E. Swann. *Prime Time Preachers: The Rising Power of Televangelism.* Menlo Park, CA: Addison-Wesley, 1981.

Hill, Samuel S., ed. *Encyclopedia of Religion in the South.* Macon, GA: Mercer University Press, 1984.

Keith, Billy. *W. A. Criswell: The Authorized Biography.* Old Tappan, NJ: Fleming H. Revell, 1973.

Lippy, Charles H., ed. *Twentieth-Century Shapers of American Popular Religion.* Westport, CT: Greenwood Press, 1989.

McBeth, H. Leon. *The First Baptist Church of Dallas: Centennial History (1868–1968).* Grand Rapids, MI: Zondervan, 1968.

Russell, C. Allyn. "W. A. Criswell: A Case Study in Fundamentalism." *Review and Expositor.* (Winter, 1984).

Towns, James E., ed. *The Social Conscience of W. A. Criswell.* Dallas: Crescendo, 1977.

CROSSROADS
first aired: 1955

Airing on ABC-TV from October 1955 to September 1957, *Crossroads* was a nonsectarian television drama that featured the true-life stories of clergymen and laymen—Protestant, Catholic, and Jewish—whose faith sustained them or helped others through difficult times. Not to be confused with the program of the same name created by David Mainse, *Crossroads* was created by a New York rabbi who, along with a Catholic priest and a Protestant minister, supervised the content of the half-hour show. Its cast included well-known character actors and actresses such as Pat O'Brien and Vincent Price, as well as television stars such as Chuck Connors. After a long run in syndication, *Crossroads* was rerun on a number of occasions and later became part of a 1960 series entitled *Way of Life*.

SOURCES

Erickson, Hal. *Religious Radio and Television in the United States, 1921–1991.* Jefferson, NC: McFarland, 1992.

CROSSROADS CHRISTIAN COMMUNICATIONS

Located in Toronto, Canada, Crossroads Christian Communications grew out of the early broadcast ministry of Canadian Pentecostal minister and Christian television personality David R. Mainse.

In 1962, while serving a pastorate in Pembroke, Ontario, Mainse began a television program entitled *Crossroads* (not to be confused with the nonsectarian television drama of the same name). The program ran successfully during the 1960s and 1970s, eventually airing over 150 stations in Canada and the northeastern United States. As a result of the show's success, Mainse founded Crossroads Christian Communications and located his broadcast production headquarters in Toronto. Mainse's *Crossroads* program eventually became *100 Huntley Street*, the address of his ministry broadcast organization. A Canadian version of Pat Robertson's *The 700 Club*, *100 Huntley Street* soon gained a large North American audience, receiving the 1984 Award of Merit from the National Religious Broadcasters.

Under the continuing direction of Mainse, Crossroads Christian Communications produces programs for broadcast over nearly 30 cable and satellite stations in Canada and the United States.

See also *100 Huntley Street*; David Mainse

SOURCES

Burgess, Stanley M., and Gary B. McGee, eds. *Dictionary of Pentecostal and Charismatic Movements*. Grand Rapids, MI: Zondervan, 1988.

PAUL CROUCH

born: March 30, 1934, St. Joseph, Missouri

Paul Crouch is among the most prominent religious broadcasters in the history of the electronic church. His Trinity Broadcasting Network (TBN) is carried on over 1,315 cable systems and is estimated to reach over 16 million households daily. Trinity and its subsidiaries own more than 100 stations nationwide and exercise control over a dozen other stations through loans from Trinity or Crouch family members. An additional 100 stations carry TBN's programming. TBN itself owns television stations in Tustin, California; Phoenix; Oklahoma City; Pembroke Park, Fort Pierce, and Jacksonville, Florida; Richmond and Greenwood, Indiana; Fishkill, New York; Federal Way, Washington; Westminster, Colorado; Louisville, Ohio; Irving, Harlingen, Orange, and Houston, Texas; Decatur, Georgia; Portland, Oregon; Nevis, West Indies; Castries, Saint Lucia; Milan, Italy; Athens, Greece; Bisho, Ciskei, and Umata, Transkei (South Africa); San José, Costa Rica; and Nueva San Salvador, El Salvador. TBN broadcasts on superpower short-wave radio station KTBN, and on Radio Paradise, a 50,000 watt nondirectional AM radio station located in St. Kitts, West Indies.

Paul Crouch was the son of the first two Assemblies of God missionaries to Egypt, Andrew Franklin and Sarah Swingle Crouch, and lived throughout the Middle East as a child. Later, Crouch followed his parents into the ministry and earned his ministerial credentials at Central Bible College in Springfield, Missouri. During this time, while attending a camp meeting run by the famed Assemblies of God evangelist Edgar Bethany, Crouch met his future wife, Janice Wendell Bethany, Bethany's daughter. After their marriage in 1958, Paul Crouch was called to a small church in Bruce, South Dakota. He decided against accepting the commission, however, because one member of the congregation had voted against him. Instead, the Crouches moved to Rapid City where Paul accepted his brother's offer of an assistant pastorate.

To make ends meet, the young minister found a moonlighting job at a radio station. Using the skills he learned there, he was hired by a television station and within three months had become program director. Crouch learned every aspect of television broadcasting during this period and soon was managing an Assemblies of God film studio in Burbank, California. From that position he jumped to KHOF, a Christian television station in the area.

TBN emerged in 1973, following an evening church service at which both Crouches reported being "slain in the Spirit." During this same service the church's pastor, Syvelle Phillips, prophesied that "a new television ministry is coming to birth." The Crouches believed that they were to be the founders of this new ministry and started looking around for a television station to buy. Paul Crouch called the owner of a new station that had flopped after only several months and struck a deal to purchase the station. He received the backing of a group of Christian businessmen who furnished studio facilities in an industrial complex rent-free for three months. The group also agreed to let Crouch sign a $250,000 lease agreement with no collateral. During this period, Crouch gave up his preaching credential from the Assemblies of God to dedicate himself fully to broadcasting and to retain his independence.

When the new station's transmitter was being tested, it turned out that the Whittier Hills were somehow blocking the signal between Anaheim and Mount Wilson. On Monday, May

28, 1973, however, TBN's engineers solved the transmission difficulties and the all-Christian station began live broadcasting. With these problems surmounted, a new challenge loomed. The station was completely dependent on listener contributions and available funds were exhausted after the first three days of broadcasting. Syvelle Phillips hosted an emergency fundraising broadcast the next evening that brought in pledges and gifts of more than $50,000. Some people reportedly drove to the station to drop off their money before the end of the broadcast.

TBN remained on the air and soon attracted the aid of Jim and Tammy Faye Bakker. Although at first the collaboration went smoothly, the two men began to have intense disagreements. As Crouch himself remembered in his booklet *The Miracle Birth of Trinity Broadcasting Network,*

> Jim and I, who had worked together beautifully in the early formative days of the ministry, began to grow farther apart in the concept and goals of the ministry. As a result of the confusion and dissension which followed, God began to lift His blessing and we began to suffer serious financial needs. We learned another important spiritual lesson. Where there is contention and strife, the Holy Spirit is grieved, and God cannot bless and prosper in this condition. As a result of all this, Jim and I both lost our spiritual direction for a time.

The "serious financial needs" were also the result of a fire at the TBN transmitter in August 1973. Because the network could not broadcast, financial support stopped, and the station's owner began negotiations with another buyer. Crouch moved quickly and found another station for sale, Channel 40. Thanks to generous credit terms, he was able to sign a purchase agreement with the station. TBN now had four times more broadcasting power and double its earlier population coverage.

Finally, on August 2, 1974, TBN received its official broadcasting license from the Federal Communications Commission (FCC) and was on its way. By May of 1977, the network had become the country's first 24-hour Christian television station. It then began to buy television stations in large metropolitan areas with the intention of converting them to full-time Christian stations. In June 1983, Channel 20 in Seattle became the seventh full time TBN station.

The network next began to feed its programming to independent translator stations and to over 200 cable systems nationwide. This expanded outreach was made possible by RCA's new communications satellite, which fed signals to the exploding cable television industry. The satellite costs in those early days were a bargain by today's standards—only $34,000 per month. Crouch reported that he had seen a vision just before RCA came selling space on its transponder:

> The lights went out, and it was as though I was several thousand miles in outer space, looking down on the earth. Then, a great light came into being right over the center of the United States, and I could see beams of light going out and hitting the major metropolitan areas of America. Then, as those secondary lights lit up, I could see little pencil threads of light emanating from them, and forming little dots of light until the whole country became like a blaze, a network of light all over. I was fascinated, enthralled, enraptured by it! I asked the Lord, "What is it?" And I heard one word: "satellite."

Crouch also showed his pioneering spirit by purchasing a mobile satellite transmitter that the ministry dubbed "The Holy Beamer." The transmitter was built by a firm that hoped to market the mobile units housed on 18-wheel trucks. Since they viewed TBN as a test client, they sold the $1 million unit for $600,000. TBN used the mobile transmitter to cover such live events as Billy Graham crusades, Full Gospel Business Men's Conventions, and Kenneth Copeland camp meetings.

TBN's programming is diverse and of consistently high quality. At least nine hours are filled with live telecasts and reruns of the popular *Praise the Lord* show. This program features both talk show and variety show formats and includes interviews of Christians by Paul and Jan and cohosts such as singer Laverne Tripp and evangelist Dwight Thompson. Other programs carried on the network include *Calling Dr. Whitaker*, a half-hour show that features a Christian physician who relates the latest in medical science to Christian values; *Treasures Out of Darkness*, which features ex–drug addict Sonny Arguinzoni and those who have been "saved" by his inner-city ministries; *Night Light*, an entertainment show hosted by Todd and Donna Fisher that features various Christian comedians and performers; *The Bible Bowl*, a quiz game show for Bible scholars; *One Way Game*, a Bible-based quiz program for high schoolers; and *Get in Shape*, a morning exercise show hosted by Pamela Cole.

TBN also broadcasts numerous teaching programs that feature such evangelical celebrities as Hal Lindsey, Lester Sumrall, Marilyn Hickey, and Father Joseph P. Manning. Most of these programs are produced at TBN's studios in Santa Ana, California, at little cost to the participants. The Crouches and Program Director Terry Hickey are committed to presenting programs by proven veteran ministers.

The network raises its funds mainly through twice-yearly telethons, and "special gift offers" and projects the rest of the year. By 1989, the network's market value stood at $500 million and was virtually free of debt. TBN also supports a volunteer prayer counselor ministry that provides over 100 phone counselors each evening. This ministry and the network's shows have led to the conversion, healing, and baptism of thousands who have reported their experiences in letters to the Crouches. These letters are on file at TBN in Santa Ana and serve as a kind of proof for the ministry's many supporters.

In 1989, TBN became the subject of an investigation by the National Religious Broadcaster's (NRB) Ethics Committee. The investigation stemmed from two formal complaints made against the network. The first of the complaints alleged that Crouch unethically took over control of an upstate New York television station. The second complaint came from Marvin L. Martin, the producer of *Praise the Lord* until 1981. Martin alleged that he had been fired because he demanded accountability from the Crouches, whom he accused of moral and financial improprieties. One specific accusation was that Paul Crouch had asked God to kill a man who had filed for an FCC license to take over Channel 40 in Orange County.

In a written response to the *Los Angeles Times*, Crouch acknowledged that

> I did pray for the wrath of God to fall on enemies of TBN who at the time were attempting to take the license of KTBN-Channel 40. This would have destroyed the entire ministry, which was just beginning to burst forth with growth. At the time we had four TV stations. Today, eight years later, we have 154. I probably did pray that God would kill anyone or anything that was attempting to destroy the ministry. My prayer has not changed.

On December 22, the NRB's executive committee decided that there was not sufficient documentation accompanying the complaints to warrant a termination of TBN's membership. Paul Crouch then announced in a January, 1990, newsletter that TBN was withdrawing from the NRB and

> every earthly man-made organization [because] lying [and] trumped-up charges were aimed at the very heart [of TBN]. . . . It was not a good year to be a TV evangelist! Of course, it was Satan's strategy to tar all TV ministries with the same brush. . . . Media reports were merciless. Many bought the lie and gave credibility to the enemies of TBN.

Crouch's withdrawal from NRB did not end TBN's legal entanglements. In 1992, the FCC began looking into allegations that Crouch tried to acquire more commercial television stations than the 12 he was allowed by law. This was reportedly done through a "sham front," National Minority TV, Inc., which allowed TBN to circumvent FCC rules and take advantage of minority representation loopholes. No charges have been brought by the FCC as of this writing. In Texas, parents of a teenage boy sued Crouch and another evangelist in an alleged sex-for-drugs scandal on TBN property. This matter was settled out of court.

Also during 1992, TBN expanded its outreach into Russia. The ministry began broadcasting its shows on Russian state television a few hours per week and is currently building a Channel 40 studio in Saint Petersburg that will carry the network's full complement of Christian programming. The station, 31 percent of which is owned by TBN, will be the first privately-owned television station in the former Soviet Union.

See also Trinity Broadcasting Network

SOURCES

Armstrong, Ben. *The Electric Church.* Nashville: Thomas Nelson, 1979.

"Broadcaster Quits Christian Group." *Los Angeles Times*, January, 1990.

Pinsky, Mark I. "Head of Religious Network Answers Allegations." *Los Angeles Times*, February 14, 1989.

Praise the Lord 19, no. 8 (August 1992).

Roberts, Dennis. "Trinity Broadcasting Network: The Dream Almost Didn't Happen." *Charisma* (June 1983) 18–25, 88–90.

"The T Stands for Troubled." *Newsweek,* March 30, 1992, 60.

D

DAVE BREESE REPORTS
first aired: 1978

Dave Breese Reports is a weekly syndicated radio and television news commentary, hosted by endtimes evangelist David Breese, that offers a prophetic interpretation of world events. The ministry is sponsored by Christian Destiny Ministries and originates from Hillsboro, Kansas. First produced from Christian Destiny's former headquarters in the Chicago suburb of Wheaton, Illinois, the program began life as a spin-off from Breese's brief association with the 1970s program, *Pause for Good News*. This earlier program was itself a 1972 spin-off from Theodore Epp's *Back to the Bible* broadcasts. Breese's program began airing nationally in the early 1980s. It currently can be heard over nearly 300 Christian radio and television stations nationwide.

See also David Breese

SOURCES

Breese, Dave. *The Exciting Plan of God for Your Life.* Wheaton, IL: Christian Destiny, 1978.

———. *What's Ahead?* Lincoln, NE: Back to the Bible Broadcast, 1974.

DAVEY AND GOLIATH
see: Lutheran Church in America, Commission of Press, Radio, and Television

DAY OF DISCOVERY
first aired: 1968

Day of Discovery has offered television viewers a half hour of clear, direct, and simple Bible teaching since it first came on the air in 1968. This television program grew out of the radio ministry of fundamentalist M. R. DeHaan, who broadcast the *Radio Bible Class* daily between 1941 and 1965, the year of his death. This popular radio program presented Bible lessons and discussions of the religious life in a quiet, sober, no-frills manner. Then in 1968, DeHaan's son, Richard, and Paul Van Gorder developed a similar format for television.

Day of Discovery typically opened with the image of a white bird flying into the blue sky while a chorus sang the program's uplifting theme song. Program host Al Sanders then welcomed viewers and previewed the teaching that Richard DeHaan or Paul Van Gorder would deliver later in the show. Religious songs presented by the *Day of Discovery* singers followed next. These tastefully presented musical segments were often videotaped with the peaceful and sunny Cypress Gardens of Florida as a backdrop. Each of the segments was conceived and directed by composer John W. Peterson, the program's music director. With the proper tone set, DeHaan or Van Gorder took center stage to deliver his Bible-centered message of faith and hope. On occasion, Sanders interviewed a young member of the *Discovery* singers or a special guest.

Sanders described the show's essence during an interview with Ben Armstrong of the National Religious Broadcasters:

> The heart of the program is the gospel message. Both DeHaan and Van Gorder work hard to make certain that the lesson for the day is always Christ-centered, clearly presented and related to today's needs. This is what reaches people with the truths of God and leads them to place their trust in Jesus Christ. Thousands have written to tell us that watching our telecast has brought them to their own day of discovery.

In 1978, *Day of Discovery* was recognized for excellence by the National Religious Broadcasters and given its Award of Merit. By 1980 the Sunday program had garnered a national audience, according to Arbitron, of 1,520,000 people. The show enjoyed its greatest popularity in the South, where 44 percent of its audience resided. In the Midwest, the broadcast drew 28 percent of its audience, while in the East and West the combined viewership amounted to 28 percent of its total audience.

Day of Discovery continued the *Radio Bible Class*'s practice of distributing a free copy of the day's Bible lesson to all who requested it. This distribution was part of a larger enterprise, The Radio Bible Class, Inc., which administered the radio and television ministries and published pamphlets, Bible lessons, and the popular daily inspirational guide *Our Daily Bread*. The umbrella organization was headed by Richard DeHaan and headquartered in Grand Rapids, Michigan. *Day of Discovery* and the *Radio Bible Class* were complemented by two other radio broadcasts: *On the Move* with M. R. DeHaan II, Richard DeHaan's son, and the daily devotional program *Our Daily Bread*. Each of these shows was aired on hundreds of radio and television stations around the world.

The Radio Bible Class Ministries have also continued the elder DeHaan's practice of the nonsolicitation of contributions, instead trusting that their needs would be taken care of by the freely-given offerings of grateful listeners. When offering Bible-study materials to viewers, the various programs offered them assurances that their names would not be given to other mailing lists. When the materials arrived, the respondents could return a card indicating their desire to receive more Bible teachings and devotional pamphlets. If they chose to do so, they were then given the opportunity to make a voluntary financial contribution to the ministry. The ministry's continued popularity and state-of-the-art broadcasting studios and printing plant bear witness to the effectiveness of the nonsolicitation strategy. As DeHaan explained,

> God has provided for every need. He honors the faithful teaching of His Word. For more than forty years, this has been a Bible-teaching ministry. We want everything we do to be focused upon Jesus Christ and the Word of God. Everything we have belongs to Him.

Without the charismatic hoopla and nonstop fundraising of many television ministries, *Day of Discovery* has retained its position as one of the top-10 syndicated religious telecasts in the United States throughout the 1980s and early 1990s. Perhaps DeHaan best expressed the secret of the show's success when he said,

> Our aim is to present helpful Bible messages in a forthright, nondenominational manner. We have two goals. First, that increasing numbers will be brought to Christ. And second, that believers will be strengthened in the faith through our television ministry.

See also Richard DeHaan

SOURCES

Adair, James R. *M. R. DeHaan: The Man and His Ministry*. Grand Rapids, MI: Zondervan, 1969.

Armstrong, Ben. *The Electric Church*. Nashville: Thomas Nelson, 1979.

Hadden, Jeffrey K., and Charles E. Swann. *Prime Time Preachers: The Rising Power of Televangelism*. Menlo Park, CA: Addison-Wesley, 1981.

Schultze, Quentin J. *Televangelism and American Culture: The Business of Popular Religion*. Grand Rapids, MI: Baker Book House, 1991.

M. R. DEHAAN

born: March 23, 1891, Zeeland, Michigan
died: December 13, 1965, Grand Rapids, Michigan

Martin Ralph DeHaan was one of the pioneers of religious radio and the founder of the long-running *Radio Bible Class* broadcast.

DeHaan was reared in the Dutch American subculture of western Michigan. His parents, Reitze DeHaan, a cobbler, and Johanna Rozema, were immigrants from the Netherlands. Following the tragic death of their younger son and the perceived lack of pastoral ministering from their local Christian Reformed Church, the DeHaan family decided to switch their church membership to the Reformed Church in America. Martin attended Hope University, a Reformed Church affiliate in Holland, Michigan, during his first year of college. After a year he decided to pursue a career in medicine and relocated to Chicago in order to enroll in the College of Medicine at the University of Illinois. His career at the university was highly successful and he graduated as class valedictorian in 1914. During this same period DeHaan met and married Priscilla Venhuizen. The couple moved back to western Michigan, and DeHaan began a rural family practice in Byron's Corner 14 miles from Zeeland.

DeHaan might have lived out his life in relative obscurity were it not for a near-fatal medical emergency in 1921 after he ingested some prescribed medicine. As he lay in recovery, DeHaan began to reexamine his life and, subsequently, experienced a religious conversion. At that moment, he made up his mind to enter the ministry. After selling his practice, he enrolled at Western Theological Seminary in Holland and began ministerial training. During this period DeHaan came under the influence of premillennialist ministers such as William McCarrell of the Independent Fundamental Churches of America, and he came to accept that Christ would soon return to set up his millennial kingdom on earth. An avid student of the premillenialist-oriented Scofield Reference Bible, he also came to the conclusion that infant baptism had no justifiable biblical foundation.

Upon graduation, DeHaan was called to pastor the Calvin Reformed Church of Grand Rapids, Michigan. Given his premillennialist beliefs and doubts concerning infant baptism, he soon came into conflict with the Reformed Church, which baptized infants and had little interest in millennialism. Within four years, DeHaan had left the Reformed Church and organized the independent fundamentalist Calvary Undenominational Church. DeHaan's nine-year tenure as the pastor of this congregation was marked by disputes with the membership over his desire to serve a larger audience. Following a serious heart attack in 1938, DeHaan resigned his pastorship and limited his activities to informal evening Bible classes.

His friend McCarrell urged him to turn these Bible classes into a radio ministry. DeHaan accepted this suggestion and began a radio program in Detroit. As his son Richard recalled,

> When my father stood before the microphone of a small Detroit station in 1938, little could he have envisioned the multifaceted, worldwide outreach that would grow from his Bible class broadcast. He was firmly convinced that the world needed a Bible-teaching ministry and dedicated himself to that purpose. He set the course the organization follows to this day.

By 1941, the show had garnered a significant audience and was renamed the *Radio Bible Class*. The daily program was unusual in that it never requested contributions by direct mail or on the air. Nevertheless, the contributions poured in and the broadcast was soon being aired on the Mutual Broadcasting System and ABC-TV. DeHaan also initiated the now common practices of providing printed copies of sermons to interested listeners and holding regular staff chapel services. As the ministry grew, it became the Radio Bible Class, Inc., newly headquartered in Grand Rapids. The organization expanded its outreach and distributed Bible lessons and sermon booklets around the world.

In 1946, DeHaan had another heart attack while on the air. Amazingly, he was able to complete the broadcast. During his recovery his son Richard took over the show. Richard DeHaan would go on to host his own religious television program, *Day of Discovery*, in 1968. The elder DeHaan continued his radio ministry until his death following a traffic accident in 1965. Throughout his 24 years of broadcasting, he set a standard in the industry for programming excellence and solid, Bible-based teaching. His many books on Bible interpretation, prophecy, and Christian doctrine bore witness to the serious and substantive quality of his teaching ministry.

The *Radio Bible Class* survived Martin DeHaan's passing and, in 1974, the show won the National Religious Broadcasters Award of Merit. By 1979, the popular program was being broadcast over 1,000 independent stations worldwide. Each month the ministry sends out millions of copies of *Our Daily Bread*, a daily devotional guide, to churches, hospitals, businesses, and schools. All the ministry's publications are provided on a "by request" basis only. Though still unsolicited, numerous gifts from individual contributors continue to fund the ministry's professional staff of pastoral counselors, broadcast technicians, clerical workers, and writers. The Radio Bible Class, Inc., has been able to avoid the scandals that have plagued other religious broadcasting organizations by focusing on its simple, biblical message, rather than on personal charisma and dramatic, flashy productions.

SOURCES

Adair, James R. *M. R. DeHaan: The Man and His Ministry*. Grand Rapids, MI: Zondervan, 1969.

Armstrong, Ben. *The Electric Church*. Nashville: Thomas Nelson, 1979.

DeHaan, M. R. *Daniel the Prophet*. Grand Rapids, MI: Zondervan, 1947.

———. *Dear Doctor: I Have a Problem*. Grand Rapids, MI: Zondervan, 1961.

———. *508 Answers to Bible Questions*. Grand Rapids, MI: Zondervan, 1952.

Hadden, Jeffrey K., and Charles E. Swann. *Prime Time Preachers: The Rising Power of Televangelism*. Menlo Park, CA: Addison-Wesley, 1981.

Schultze, Quentin J. *Televangelism and American Culture: The Business of Popular Religion*. Grand Rapids, MI: Baker Book House, 1991.

RICHARD DeHAAN
born: February 21, 1923, Holland, Michigan

Courtesy: National Religious Broadcasters

Richard DeHaan, M. R. DeHaan's son, grew up in an interdenominational atmosphere, attending Wheaton College and Calvin College, and pursuing advanced studies at Chicago's Northern Baptist Seminary.

When his father died in 1965, Richard took over his father's broadcast ministry, the Radio Bible Class, Inc. In 1968, he and Paul Van Gorder launched a new television program, *Day of Discovery*, which quickly became one of the 10 highest rated broadcasts in America. In 1987, it was ranked the fifth most watched religious program in the nation. As with *Radio Bible Class*, DeHaan asked his viewers for no donations, supporting the full cost of *Day of Discovery* from funds allocated by his larger ministry organization.

The Radio Bible Class, Inc.'s most popular program, *Radio Bible Class,* remains one of the most successful religious radio programs in broadcasting history. In 1983, Richard DeHaan was inducted into the National Religious Broadcasters Hall of Fame. DeHaan is, as of this writing, suffering from Parkison's disease and is no longer active in the Radio Bible Class ministry.

See also *Day of Discovery*

SOURCES

Billy Graham Center Archives, Wheaton College, Wheaton, IL.

Reid, Daniel G., Robert D. Linder, Bruce L. Shelley, and Harry S. Stout, eds. *Dictionary of Christianity in America.* Downers Grove, IL: InterVarsity Press, 1990.

Stone, Jon R. *A Guide to the End of the World: Popular Eschatology in America.* New York: Garland, 1993.

Ward, Mark, Sr. *Air of Salvation: The Story of Christian Broadcasting.* Grand Rapids, MI: Baker Book House, 1994.

JAMES DOBSON

born: April 21, 1936, Shreveport, Louisiana

Courtesy: National Religious Broadcasters

Christian radio psychologist James Dobson is the son of James C. Dobson, a Pentecostal minister. He graduated from Pasadena College with a bachelor of arts degree in 1958. During the mid-1960s, Dobson worked as a teacher and counselor in public schools in Hacienda and Covina, California, and as a psychologist and coordinator of pupil personnel services in the Charter Oak Unified School District of Covina. In 1967, he earned a doctorate in child development from the University of Southern California (USC). Dobson remained at USC as a professor of pediatrics in the School of Medicine and on staff at the Los Angeles Children's Hospital until 1980.

In 1970, he published his first major book, *Dare to Discipline,* which strongly criticized the permissiveness advocated by Dr. Benjamin Spock. Dobson's book was immensely popular among conservatives and became a banner around which fundamentalists rallied in their crusade against the liberal values fostered by the 1960s. Other best-selling books on the family, including *What Wives Wish Their Husbands Knew about Women* (1975), followed in rapid succession.

In 1977, Dobson launched a daily radio program, *Focus on the Family,* which aimed at countering liberal views of childrearing with conservative Christian values. Dobson's usual format has been to read questions sent in by listeners and to give his opinion on the subject or to interview individuals who support his conservative views. Though neither a theologian nor an ordained minister, Dobson freely offers his own interpretations of controversial biblical texts on parental authority, homosexuality, and women's roles in the church.

It was during the late 1970s that Dobson produced a popular five-part video lecture series bringing together his views on the family. Titled *Focus on the Family,* this series was enthusiastically received by conservative Christians and was repeatedly shown—and is still shown—in churches and at conferences throughout the United States. During the 1980s, Dobson began a number of magazines that expanded his work as a Christian child psychologist.

In 1988, Dobson created the Family Research Council, which produced additional programs, including a children's radio program entitled *Adventures in Odyssey*. So successful was the program that, by 1990, it was aired over 1,450 stations in the United States and abroad. It was about this time that Dobson moved his ministry to Colorado Springs, Colorado, from its original site in Arcadia, California. Presently, Dobson's program is heard worldwide over 4,000 stations. In spite of a 1990 heart attack, Dobson has continued to lead the fight for a conservative family values national agenda. His organization has a staff of over 1,000 workers, 50 ministries, six broadcast programs, eight magazines, a publishing house, and a video production studio.

In 1991, Dobson was inducted into the National Religious Broadcasters Hall of Fame. He has now published 13 best-selling books on marriage and the family.

See also *Focus on the Family*

SOURCES

Dobson, James. *Dare to Discipline*. Wheaton, IL: Tyndale House, 1970.

Erickson, Hal. *Religious Radio and Television in the United States, 1921–1991*. Jefferson, NC: McFarland, 1992.

Evory, Ann, ed. *Contemporary Authors*. Detroit: Gale Research, 1978.

Ward, Mark, Sr. *Air of Salvation: The Story of Christian Broadcasting*. Grand Rapids, MI: Baker Book House, 1994.

E

VIC ELIASON
born: 1936, Cook, Minnesota

Vic Eliason is the founder of Voice of Christian Youth (VCY), a Christian broadcasting ministry whose headquarters are located in Milwaukee, Wisconsin. The ministry owns four self-supporting radio stations, each of which carries VCY's conservative Christian programming via satellite. It also operates WVCY-TV Channel 30, a Milwaukee UHF channel that serves as VCY's keystone station.

Vic Eliason grew up in Cook, Minnesota, a lumber town located 100 miles north of Duluth. Eliason's father, Oscar, worked as a piano tuner and spent his free time as a lay preacher in a small, conservative Swedish Baptist church. The Eliason family lived simply and frugally. Both Eliason and his brother wore homemade shirts through high school, and their father drove a 1936 Ford until 1950. During high school, Eliason served as a photographer for the school yearbook, and as a projectionist, and he was a choir and school band participant. He was also a member of the Future Farmers of America.

After his graduation, Eliason decided to move to California and join the Navy. During a church service a short time later, Eliason experienced a call to the ministry, changed his mind about the Navy, and enrolled in the Open Bible College in Des Moines, Iowa. The college was an outreach of the Open Bible Standard Churches, a descendant of the Four Square Gospel movement of radio evangelist Aimee Semple McPherson.

Upon his graduation from college, Eliason worked with a Des Moines pastor for a year before receiving ordination as a nondenominational minister. In 1959, he and his wife, Freda, moved to Milwaukee, where they worked for several years with Youth for Christ, a national evangelistic organization. The group organized teen clubs near local high schools and held biweekly evangelical rallies at the city's YMCA.

In May of 1961, Eliason was given a half-hour of airtime on WBON-FM to broadcast a program he called the *Voice of Christian Youth*. Within a short time the ministry had expanded to a full broadcasting day. By 1970, Eliason had purchased WBON for $315,000 and renamed the station WVCY. Eight years later he moved the station to the former Spencerian Business College and inaugurated a successful K–12 Christian school. WVCY's programming consisted of nationally syndicated fundamentalist preachers, Christian music, and a locally produced radio talk show, *Crosstalk*. This latter program, which began in 1976, was aired daily from 2 until 3 PM.

In 1983, Eliason started WVCY-TV with donated equipment and volunteer labor. Later that year, the ministry added a live television broadcast on weeknights from 7 to 8 PM called *In Focus*. Until the beginning of 1990, the station subscribed to the Cable News Network (CNN) and filled its commercial slots with such conservative commentators as Tim LaHaye. In 1990, Eliason dropped CNN because of a series of profiles the network aired on rock stars. In 1988, Eliason's ministry reported more than $1.1 million in income and nearly $640,000 in revenues from syndicated shows that his stations air.

Eliason has gained notoriety through his public battles with such foes as the Roman Catholic Archdiocese, the conservative Elmbrook Church of Waukesha—reputed to be Wisconsin's largest Protestant church—United Press International, several public school systems, the Wisconsin legislature, and *The Milwaukee Journal*. He has aired a relentless barrage of criticism at Milwaukee's Roman Catholic Archbishop, Rembert Weakland, for his "liberal" positions on sex education in Catholic schools and homosexuality. Following a successful effort to kill a bill before the state legislature that would have prohibited discrimination against gays and others, Eliason created the Crosstalk Information Network. This service sends out a summary of legislative bills to subscribers for a $10 annual fee.

By the early 1990s, Eliason's small broadcasting empire was sending its programming via satellite to such states as Florida, Illinois, and Indiana. His network's radio stations include WVCX-FM, Tomah, Wisconsin; KVCY, Fort Scott, Kansas; and KVCX-FM, Gregory, South Dakota.

SOURCES

Rohde, Marie. "Commander & Servant." *The Milwaukee Journal* (July 1 1990).

ELISABETH ELLIOT
born: 1927, Brussels, Belgium

Elisabeth Elliot, the daughter of missionaries and a graduate of Wheaton College, first came to the attention of the Western world as the widow of one of five Christian missionaries killed by Aucan Indians in the jungles of Ecuador in January 1956. Her two books, *Through Gates of Splendor* (1957) and *The Savage My Kinsman* (1961), tell of her husband's faith and tragic death and give a dramatic account of her own ministry among the Aucan Indians. Since that time, Elliot has been a featured speaker at a number of Christian conferences and missionary gatherings.

In 1988, she began hosting *Gateway to Joy*, a program launched by Back to the Bible Ministries of Lincoln, Nebraska. A 15-minute radio show for women, *Gateway to Joy* focuses on issues such as motherhood, femininity, aging, and marriage. The program emphasizes traditional conservative Christian roles for contemporary evangelical women and is aired on stations in the US and Canada.

SOURCES

Billy Graham Center Archives, Wheaton College, Wheaton, Illinois.

Elliot, Elisabeth. *The Savage My Kinsman* (Picture Edition). New York: Harper, 1961.

———. *Shadow of the Almighty: The Life and Testament of Jim Elliot*. New York: Harper, 1958.

———. *Through Gates of Splendor*. New York: Harper, 1957.

ELWA, SUDAN
established: 1954

ELWA is Africa's oldest religious radio station. The Christian station's seven transmitters broadcast with over 230,000 watts of total power and include programs in nearly 50 languages, including Arabic, Berber, Fulfulde, Ibo, and Yoruba. The ministry is operated by the Sudan Interior Mission.

Ian Hay, the mission's general director, once explained how the ministry had made so many breakthroughs in evangelizing different ethnic groups:

ELWA's success comes from its indigenous nature. It is essentially an African voice. . . . Through our continuous training program, ELWA has trained more than 150 Africans who are involved in everything from technical services through programming, production, and counseling.

One of ELWA's most popular programs is Howard Jones's *Hour of Freedom*. Jones is a well-known religious broadcaster and associate evangelist with the Billy Graham Association. He has also been a director of the National Religious Broadcasters and a strong advocate for black speakers on African religious programs.

SOURCES

Armstrong, Ben. *The Electric Church.* Nashville: Thomas Nelson, 1979.

ENCOUNTER MINISTRIES
established: 1960

An evangelical Christian outreach organization founded in 1960 and headed by Stephen F. Olford, Encounter Ministries, Inc., aims at spreading the gospel message through a number of media, including conferences, seminars, ministerial workshops, literature distribution, missionary assistance, and radio broadcasts.

Originating from Memphis, Tennessee, Encounter Ministries' weekly half-hour radio broadcast, *Encounter*, features an expository sermon by Olford. The program is broadcast over 24 stations in the United States, Canada, and various parts of the world. *Encounter* also appears as a weekly cable telecast. A second radio ministry, *Encounter with Truth*, is a five-minute program that airs weekdays. Encounter Ministries is home to the Institute for Biblical Preaching, a training school for ordained and lay preachers.

See also Stephen Olford

SOURCES

The Directory of Religious Organizations in the United States. 2d ed. Falls Church, VA: McGrath, 1982.

Melton, J. Gordon. *Directory of Religious Organizations in the United States.* 3d ed. Detroit: Gale Research, 1993.

EPISCOPAL CHURCH IN AMERICA, EPISCOPAL RADIO-TV FOUNDATION
established: 1945

Founded as the communications division of the Episcopal Church in America, the Episcopal Radio-TV Foundation (ERTVF) produces and distributes radio and television programs, educational materials on video and audiocassette, and motion pictures. Among its many productions are a variety of television specials produced in conjunction with the British Broadcasting Company (BBC). The most notable of these have focused on the life and works of the British evangelical apologist and author, C. S. Lewis. ERTVF's best-known television production of Lewis's works was *The Lion, the Witch, and the Wardrobe*.

SOURCES

The Directory of Religious Organizations in the United States. 2d ed. Falls Church, VA: McGrath, 1982.

Melton, J. Gordon. *Directory of Religious Organizations in the United States.* 3d ed. Detroit: Gale Research, 1993.

THE ETERNAL LIGHT
first aired: 1944

Sponsored by the Jewish Theological Seminary in New York City, *The Eternal Light* was a radio drama narrated by Alexander Scourby. The program first aired in 1944 over radio station WEAF, New York City, and featured dramatized biblical and historical stories of Judaism and the Jewish people. It was heard nationally beginning in 1946 and continued to be broadcast over radio until 1951.

The Eternal Light was adapted for television in 1951 and aired until 1953 as part of a new ecumenical program named *Frontiers of Faith*.

Frontiers of Faith incorporated teachings from the Protestant, Catholic, and Jewish faiths in three rotating segments. In 1953, the three segments were separated and *The Eternal Light* was restored to its previous title. The Catholic segment was previously and subsequently named *The Catholic Hour*; the Protestant segment retained the name *Frontiers of Faith* after the 1953 breakup.

The Eternal Light's television run continued for nearly 20 years. Its nonsectarian style sought to explain Judaism to a non-Jewish world through song, dance, and drama. *The Eternal Light* went off the air in 1970.

See also *The Catholic Hour*

SOURCES

Erickson, Hal. *Religious Radio and Television in the United States, 1921–1991*. Jefferson, NC: McFarland, 1992.

ETERNAL WORD TELEVISION NETWORK
established: 1981

The Eternal Word Television Network (EWTN) is the largest religious television network in the United States, reaching 38 million households and collecting over $13 million in annual viewer contributions. The Roman Catholic ministry broadcasts 24-hours-a-day and features bishops, priests, nuns, and lay people talking about the Bible, church teachings, Marian devotions, and current events. On August 15, 1995, EWTN began 24-hour coverage to Europe, Africa, and South America. The network's programming is now transmitted to over 42 countries on the Galaxy 1R and Intelsat 332.5 satellites.

EWTN is the brainchild of Mother Angelica, a Franciscan nun who had made successful appearances on both Pat Robertson's *The 700 Club* and Jim and Tammy Faye Bakker's *The PTL Club* program during the late 1970s. Mother Angelica started EWTN in August of 1981 after the Birmingham, Alabama, television station where she taped her programs broadcast what she considered to be a blasphemous film. EWTN's first studio was in a converted garage at Our Lady of the Angels Monastery, which the 70-something nun founded in 1961 in response to a special healing she had received. EWTN was the first denominational cable-television service to receive a license from the Federal Communications Commission. Silvio Cardinal Oddi, Prefect of the Congregation for the Clergy, came from Rome to Birmingham to bless the new broadcasting outreach. By 1986, the station had moved into its current state-of-the-art broadcasting studio.

From an initial broadcasting day of four hours every evening, seven days a week, EWTN expanded to 24 hours of programming by 1990. The many programs carried by the network include *Pillars of Faith: The Catechism Explained*, *The Choices We Make* with Ralph Martin, *Joy of Music* with Diane Bish, *Martyrs* with Bob and Penny Lord, and the children's programs, *In the Beginning* and *Greatest Stories Ever Told*.

The network also carries syndicated religious series featuring Father Michael Manning, Father Michael Scanlan, Scott Hahn, Father Ken Roberts, and Father John Bertolucci; recitations of the rosary and other Catholic devotions; the Pope's weekly Angelus observance; Catholic news; and older programs such as Fulton Sheen's *Life Is Worth Living*. St. Joseph's Communications produces an hour of programming daily which features such teachers as Karl Keating and Patrick Madrid. Special programming is aired each month and includes such fare as *In Concert*, a music series that showcases the classical masses of Mozart, Bach, and Beethoven; *Franciscan University Focus*, a panel discussion of current church affairs produced by the Franciscan University of Steubenville, Ohio's communications arts department; *River of Light*, a program that highlights the history of Christianity in Spain, Portugal, and Mexico; public addresses by Pope John Paul II; and Spanish programming such as *Chavos Banda*, *Teresa de Jesús* (an eight-part miniseries), and *El Evangello según San Lucas: Las Parabolas* ("The Parables of the Gospel according to Saint Luke").

A majority of the network's programming is produced in-house, including the popular show, *Mother Angelica Live*. This program is taped before a studio audience Tuesday and Wednesday evenings and features Mother Angelica, dressed in the traditional nun's habit, holding forth, with a combination of humor and solemnity, on the state of the world and the problems facing the Catholic Church. The nun's television presence is homespun, practical, chatty, and friendly, yet with the "mildly intimidating manner of a maiden aunt who won't stand any nonsense," as one observer put it. Each program begins with Mother Angelica's trademark greeting, "Let's get on with it!"

The mainstream National Catholic Association for Broadcasters, after an initial attitude of ambivalence concerning the ministry, awarded Mother Angelica its prestigious Gabriel Award for Broadcasting Excellence. In 1992, EWTN launched WEWN, a privately owned, shortwave radio station that covers 90 percent of the globe with 24-hour Catholic radio programming.

See also Mother Angelica

SOURCES

Elvy, Peter. *Buying Time: The Foundations of the Electronic Church*. Mystic, CT: Twenty-Third Publications, 1987.

"Eternal Word Television Network." World Wide Web site. http://www.ewtn.com (December, 1995).

"Franciscan University Focus." World Wide Web site. http://esoptron.umd.edu/fusfolder/focus.html (December, 1995).

"Mother Angelica: Nun Better." *Christianity Today* (October 2, 1995).

THE EVANGELICAL ALLIANCE MISSION
established: 1890

The Evangelical Alliance Mission, or TEAM, was founded in 1890 as a society to unite Protestant missionaries. At present, its efforts extend into some 30 countries around the world.

While TEAM's main emphasis is evangelism and church planting, it also seeks to lend support for missionary endeavors, including medical aid, Bible translation, radio broadcasting, and the distribution of evangelistic literature. The ministry's facilities include three radio stations and five recording studios. In addition, TEAM acts as a liaison between missionaries and sponsoring churches, educating church leaders about the work of its member missions. The alliance's current headquarters are in Wheaton, Illinois.

SOURCES

The Directory of Religious Organizations in the United States. 2d ed. Falls Church, VA: McGrath, 1982.

Melton, J. Gordon. *Directory of Religious Organizations in the United States*. 3d ed. Detroit: Gale Research, 1993.

EVANGELICAL BROADCASTING CORPORATION
established: 1967

One of the most successful Christian broadcasting ministries in Europe is the Evangelical Broadcasting Corporation (EBC), a radio and television station in the Netherlands that airs each week 14 hours of programming on the national television channel and 67 hours of radio programming. The station offers a wide range of Christian-based news as well as educational, entertainment, and cultural programming. EBC's television division is headquartered in Hilversum and maintains a staff of 200. Since its inception in 1967, the ministry has played an important role in European religious broadcasting. It is linked with several North American broadcast networks and has cooperated with Luis Palau and Billy Graham on the coverage of their European tours. Three of EBC's initiatives—namely, Jan van den Bosch's documentary set, *Gifted Hands*; the series *Origins*; and the film *Shadowlands*—have won prestigious international awards. *Shadowlands*, based on C. S. Lewis's later life, was a cooperative venture between Gateway Films, the British Broadcasting Corporation, and EBC-TV.

EBC's technical and legal structures are unusual in that their operation is fully financed by the Dutch government. According to Dutch law, any group of citizens may receive broadcasting time if they meet certain requirements. The programs for EBC are produced by different nonprofit organizations representing a diverse array of religious and political views. Moreover, because it shares the technologically advanced facilities of the Netherlands Broadcasting Foundation, EBC is able to produce programming of a consistently high quality.

SOURCES

"Evangelical Broadcasting Corporation." World Wide Web site. http://www.omroep.nl/eo/foreign/whoweare.html (1995).

MIKE EVANS

born: June 30, 1947

Mike Evans is an Assemblies of God pastor and televangelist who has hosted a number of television and radio shows during his career. He is also the founder and president of Mike Evans Ministries International and the president of Evangelical-Israel Friendship Council, which has worked to have Jerusalem fully recognized as the capital of Israel by other countries.

During the 1970s, Evans gained prominence as one of several popular Second Coming prophets whose books were saturating the evangelical world. Evans helped found the Church on the Move in Euless, Texas, and began to travel around the world on evangelical crusades. During the late 1980s, Evans had a weekly television program that aired on the PTL cable network. Although he was mentioned as a possible replacement when PTL's Jim Bakker was mired in a sex scandal, Evans was unable to assume Bakker's mantle during PTL's dissolution. Evans's radio program, *Mike Evans Presents*, which originated from Euless, was being broadcast over 200 radio stations during the late 1980s.

Evans gained notoriety in late 1994 when he was forced by an angry mob to abandon an evangelical crusade in Cambodia. The crusade was the first by a Western evangelist to be allowed into Cambodia since the end of the Vietnam War. Evans's appearance had been widely publicized on government and private radio and television stations. According to published reports, the advertisements had promised that the blind would see and the lame would walk at Evans's five nightly sermons in Phnom Penh's national stadium. The crusade drew over 70,000 people to each of its first two mass prayer rallies. Thousands of those who attended were blind and infirm and came from remote areas. Many of these persons sold their belongings to make the trip to the capital.

On the third night of the rally, Cambodian officials informed Evans that Khmer Rouge extremists, who were engaged in a guerrilla war with the government, had secretly infiltrated the stadium and were planning to kill the evangelist and his crew with explosives. The officials canceled this third prayer rally and confined Evans and his assistants to their suites at the luxurious Hotel Cambodiana. Three hundred angry people then reportedly gathered at the hotel to demand compensation for Evans's failure to perform faith-healing miracles. The timely arrival of armed policemen prevented the stone-throwing crowd from storming the hotel. The crowd dispersed after hearing that Evans was no longer in the hotel, and Evans escaped to Thailand early the next morning.

Greg Mauro, the director of Mike Evans Ministries, explained that Evans had been caught in a political crossfire between the Khmer Rouge and the government: "The fact that the Khmer Rouge was successful in preventing the evening meeting was supposed to be a showpiece that the Cambodian government isn't stable and that government officials couldn't secure our lives." Evans added, "Personally, if I had traveled a long way to a crusade, in spite of the fact that there was no charge, I would wonder if the preacher was a swindler if he didn't show up. It breaks my heart to disappoint the people, but we were not permitted out of the hotel. . . . The matter was totally out of our hands." In spite of his difficulties, Evans declared the crusade a success in bringing the Christian message to Cambodia's largely Buddhist population.

See also Jim Bakker

SOURCES

Erickson, Hal. *Religious Radio and Television in the United States, 1921–1991*. Jefferson, NC: McFarland, 1992.

"Euless Evangelist Blames Cambodia Officials for Riot." *The Dallas Morning News*, November 29, 1994.

"Euless Evangelist Target of Riot in Cambodia." *The Dallas Morning News*, November 26, 1994.

Hoover, Stewart M. *Mass Media Religion: The Social Sources of the Electronic Church*. Newbury Park, CA: Sage, 1988.

RICHARD EVANS

born: March 23, 1906, Salt Lake City, Utah
died: November 1, 1971

Richard Louis Evans was, for over four decades, the voice accompanying the weekly Sunday-morning broadcast of the Mormon Tabernacle Choir over the CBS radio network.

Evans was born in Salt Lake City, Utah, the son of John Aldridge Evans and Florence Nelsen. Two accidents strongly affected his early life. Just 10 weeks after his birth, his father was killed in an accident. Then, when he was 11 years old and playing with some friends, an accident cost Evans his left eye. These traumatic events, however, did not hinder Evans from pursuing his goals. After graduating from high school, Evans enrolled at the University of Utah.

In 1925, he was called to a mission and left school to go to England for two years. While there he was assigned to write for the *Millennial Star*, the British periodical of the Church of Jesus Christ of Latter-day Saints, then under the editorship of James Talmage. In 1928, Evans researched and wrote a series of articles on the history of the Mormon Church in Britain (later revised and published as a book, *The History of Mormonism in Great Britain*). He completed his two year mission but decided to stay another year when he was offered a position as secretary of the European mission in France.

Upon his return to Salt Lake City, Evans continued his studies at the University of Utah. To support himself, he got a job as an announcer at KSL, the local radio station owned by the Mormon Church. In July of 1929, several months before he joined the KSL staff, the Mormon Tabernacle Choir had begun its weekly half-hour concerts. In the spring of 1930, Evans was assigned as the show's announcer. It was his job to announce the numbers performed by the choir and to bring a brief inspirational message. The message became the focus of intense activity at the end of each week as Evans wrote and edited and reedited the words which would be condensed into a two to three minute delivery. For many years, Evans worked on the wording of the familiar opening salutation of the broadcast, "Once more we welcome you within these walls [of the Tabernacle in Salt Lake City] with music and the spoken Word from the crossroads of the West."

Throughout his many years of broadcasting Evans was engaged in other tasks as well. During his early years at KSL, he attended university classes. He completed his bachelor's degree in English in 1931 and, a few years later, a master of economics degree. He began work on a doctorate but his busy schedule never allowed him to complete it. He was named the best announcer of 1933 by *Radio Engineering*, a trade publication. That same year he married Alice Ruth Thomley. Following the 1933 transfer of radio station KSL from NBC to CBS, Evans picked up additional duties as an announcer for various news events in the area.

In 1936, Evans received his next assignment from the church. He was called to become the managing editor of *Improvement Era*, the church's major periodical. The assignment took him away from full-time duties at the station, but he retained his role as the choir's announcer. Evans also continued to travel with the choir on its concert tours. He held this position with the *Improvement Era* for 14 years and then became senior editor for the next 21 years.

In addition to his duties at the *Improvement Era*, Evans was called as a member of the First Council of the Seventy, which has charge of the temporal affairs of the Mormon Church. He was the youngest general church authority to assume office in his generation. In 1953, Evans was called to the Quorum of the Twelve Apostles, the highest authority in the church.

Over the years, he had also become active in the Rotary Club. He was elected president of the Salt Lake City Rotary Club in 1943 and held increasingly higher regional and national offices. In 1966, Evans was elected president of Rotary International. His duties with the choir, the Mormon Church, and with Rotary required extensive travel. However, Evans always arranged his schedule to be back in Salt Lake City, or near a CBS affiliate radio studio, on Sunday morning in order to make the live broadcast. He missed very few shows in his more than 40 years of service.

Evans continued this hectic pace into the fall of 1971. Then, in the middle of October, he returned home exhausted from a church conference in Spokane, Washington, and died two weeks later. On the first anniversary of his death, Brigham Young University announced the establishment of the "Richard Evans Chair in Christian Understanding," in recognition of the value of Evans's efforts to work with people of different religious traditions without compromising his own faith.

SOURCES

Evans, Richard L., Jr. *Richard L. Evans—The Man and the Message*. Salt Lake City: Bookcraft, 1973.

EVER INCREASING FAITH
first aired: 1973

The weekly television ministry of the Reverend Frederick Price, *Ever Increasing Faith* first aired in April 1978 over the Trinity Broadcasting Network (TBN). The program was origi-

nally heard over radio in 1973, after Price founded the Crenshaw Christian Center in Inglewood, California. In an effort to reach an even larger African American population, Price moved his program to VHF station KTTV in Los Angeles within a month of his TBN debut. After the expansion to a larger viewer market, *Ever Increasing Faith* was seen in five major urban centers in the United States. Currently, the program airs over 125 television and 40 radio stations in the United States, the Caribbean, and Nigeria. It still can be viewed over KTTV, Los Angeles, every Sunday morning

Ever Increasing Faith is an hour-long program that features the lively expository preaching of Price, whose messages resemble the positive-thinking philosophy of Robert Schuller of the Crystal Cathedral—minus the clerical robes and stiff pulpit decorum. Indeed, during his sermons, Price is often seen pacing the auditorium, speaking personally to his parishioners, even shaking their hands or offering a kind word and a reassuring touch on the shoulder. At the end of every broadcast, he leads his congregation in an enthusiastic recitation of the Bible verse, "For we walk by faith and not by sight." Price's message, as well as his large congregation, are both ecumenical and interracial.

As Price's avenues of ministry have expanded, so too has the Crenshaw Christian Center. In 1981, the church bought Pepperdine College's old downtown campus and built a 10,000-seat facility on the 32-acre site. In 1984, the center moved again, this time to its present location on 79th and Vermont in South Central Los Angeles. Housed in the Faithdome, built in 1989, the church's current membership numbers around 15,000 people.

The Ever Increasing Faith Ministries now include a ministry training institute, a correspondence school program, a private Christian school, and numerous other social and Christian welfare programs. *Ever Increasing Faith* is among the top-10 rated Christian television programs in the nation today. Price remains the most successful African American evangelist in the history of religious broadcasting.

See also Frederick Price

SOURCES

Murphy, Larry G., J. Gordon Melton, and Gary L. Ward. *Encyclopedia of African American Religion*. New York: Garland, 1993.

EXPOSING THE LIE
first aired: 1984

Exposing the Lie is a 30-minute weekly television program produced by Robert "Bob" Anderson of Take Heed Ministries. The show attempts to warn evangelical Christians about the dangers of new religious movements and sects and to protect them from conversion to heterodox religious doctrines.

Currently headquartered in Murraysville, Pennsylvania, Take Heed Ministries is primarily an information network focused on Christian apologetics. Articles printed in its monthly newsletter tend to point out inconsistencies in the beliefs held by cult movements and sects. The aim is to show how far these groups deviate from orthodox Protestant beliefs, especially with reference to the triune nature of God and the divinity of Christ.

Founded in 1979, Take Heed Ministries began broadcasting on television in 1984 under the direction of the program's first host, Dave Hunt. Hunt is the author of the highly controversial cult exposé, *The Seduction of Christianity*. After Hunt's departure in 1986, Take Heed Ministries retained Tim LaHaye as its interim host for *Exposing the Lie* until December 1987. The program's current director and host, Bob Anderson, is a former television sportscaster and station manager. Anderson directs Take Heed Ministries' growing anti-cult activities and travels regularly throughout the region giving lectures, appearing on local radio and television shows, and holding conferences and Bible studies with interested churches. *Exposing the Lie* airs via satellite in the United States, Canada, and Mexico.

SOURCES

Anderson, Bob, et al. *Earth's Final Days: Essays in Apocalypse III*. Green Forest, AR: New Leaf Press, 1994.

Melton, J. Gordon. *Directory of Religious Organizations in the United States*. 3d ed. Detroit: Gale Research, 1993.

F

FAITH AND VALUES CHANNEL
established: 1988

The Faith and Values Channel (F&V) is a key conduit for the television outreach of such mainstream Protestant groups as the Methodists, the Presbyterians, and the Episcopalians. The New York-based network was created by the National Interfaith Coalition as a nonprofit consortium of 64 faith communities. Funding for the venture was provided by the wealthy, secular cable conglomerate, TCI. The channel airs Mormon, Jewish, and Islamic programs in addition to its predominantly Protestant lineup. Since 1992, the channel has also broadcast eight hours of programming a day from the Southern Baptist Convention's Fort Worth–based Radio and Television Commission (RTVC). This channel-sharing agreement has saved RTVC $1.7 million a year in satellite transponder and uplink fees.

In an effort to make the network more competitive with such rivals as Trinity Broadcasting Network and Christian Broadcasting Network, F&V has begun a major revamping of its program lineup. Many of its low-rated talking-head shows are being replaced with more creative formats. Among the new shows that began in late 1995 were *Inspiration, Please*, a breezy quiz show hosted by Christian standup comedian Robert G. Lee; *Keeping the Feast*, a combination of spirituality and good eating, starring the United Methodist minister Jeff Smith, also known as the "Frugal Gourmet"; *Our Generation*, a talk show hosted by Florence Henderson of *The Brady Bunch*; and *Our Show*, a magazine format program that "focuses on health, financial, and emotional issues of special concern to the 49-plus generation."

F&V's chief executive officer is Nelson Price, a United Methodist layman. The network's 24-hour programming package is now available in over 24 million cable households. The network doesn't participate in "on-air fund solicitation, proselytizing, and maligning of other faiths." While these standards are admirable, it remains to be seen whether the channel can compete with its more aggressive, innovative, and conservative rivals.

SOURCES

Kennedy, John W. "Redeeming the Wasteland?" *Christianity Today*, October 2, 1995.

FAITH THAT LIVES
see: Kenneth Hagin

FAITH THAT WORKS
see: Samuel Shoemaker

FAITH 20
see: The Back to God Hour

JERRY FALWELL

born: August 11, 1933, Lynchburg, Virginia

Courtesy: National Religious Broadcasters

Jerry Falwell is one of the major figures in the rise of conservative Christian broadcasting over the past 40 years. His political and religious leadership has galvanized America's Christian fundamentalists and made them a powerful force in the nation's social, economic, and political life. During the 1990s, Falwell's national influence has waned somewhat, but he continues to rule over a multimillion dollar evangelical empire that includes Liberty Baptist Fellowship, Liberty University, Lynchburg Baptist Theological Seminary, Liberty Federation, and a popular broadcasting ministry.

Jerry Falwell is a native of Lynchburg, Virginia, where he was reared by an alcoholic businessman and a staunchly fundamentalist mother. Both of his parents came from rural agricultural backgrounds and dropped out of school before completing their secondary education. Falwell's father, Carey Falwell, left his family's dairy business and became a successful manager of such enterprises as a dance hall, a trucking company, and an oil dealership. Falwell's mother attempted to instill firm Christian values in her children, but she was largely unsuccessful because of her husband's personal

disregard for religious matters. The elder Falwell's drinking problem was said to have stemmed from a violent dispute with his brother that ended in the brother's death and from his rebellion against his wife's family and their strong support of Prohibition. Carey Falwell died in 1948 of cirrhosis of the liver.

As a teenager, the younger Falwell tended to follow his father's example. Although he was a gifted athlete and student, he was also something of a hell-raiser. He stopped going to church with his mother and spent much of his time carousing with friends. After high school, Falwell enrolled in a mechanical engineering program at Lynchburg College. During this time he began listening to Charles Fuller's *Old Fashioned Revival Hour* on Sunday mornings. As he later recalled,

> My mother chose the program. She went to Sunday school and left the radio on, knowing full well that my twin brother and I would not get out of bed to turn it off. So Sunday morning after Sunday morning we heard that great opening theme and the refrain, "Jesus saves." I remember coming into a spiritual hunger. I began looking for a church that preached what I had been hearing Dr. Fuller preach.

In subsequent years, the *Old Fashioned Revival Hour* would serve as a model for Falwell's own broadcasting ministry.

Falwell found a preacher like Charles Fuller in Paul Donnelson, who had established the fundamentalist Park Avenue Baptist Church three years earlier. Within a short time, Falwell had joined the congregation, dedicated his life to Christ, bought his first Bible, and been "born again." He also met his future wife, Macel Pate, the church's piano player.

In reflecting upon his father's early death, Falwell became convinced that worldly achievements would only lead to pride and ruin unless they were grounded in a strong Christian faith. He decided to enter the ministry and set out for Bible Baptist College, a fundamentalist seminary in Springfield, Missouri. After his first year at school, he returned to Lynchburg. A year later he reenrolled at Bible Baptist College and completed his degree in 1956.

Although he had an opportunity to work in Macon, Georgia, Falwell decided to return to Lynchburg. During his absence, a new pastor had taken over the Park Avenue Church. A small group of 35 church members were dissatisfied with this change and asked Falwell to become their new pastor. Falwell agreed and preached his first sermon at the Thomas Road Baptist Church in June 1956. The church's first meeting place was an abandoned Donald Duck soft drink bottling factory.

Within a short time, the new church had inaugurated a daily radio ministry, *Deep Things of God*, featuring Falwell's preaching. The radio ministry proved successful and was soon expanded to include a half-hour, television broadcast of a studio worship service on Sunday evenings. At the end of the church's first year, its membership had grown to 850. Falwell later recounted the crucial importance of the broadcasting ministry to this phenomenal success:

> Between that local radio broadcast every day and that weekly telecast, Thomas Road Baptist Church came alive. There's no way to discount the fact that without the media we could not have made an entrance into the lives of that many people so quickly. Granted, some other things went into it, such as knocking on doors. When we knocked on doors and introduced ourselves, the people already knew us. We were welcome. The media became the tool for building the church.

Falwell's ministry continued to expand during the late 1950s and early 1960s. He organized a number of service programs, including the Elim Home for Alcoholics (built on a 165-acre farm in Appomattox County), a Christian academy, and a bus ministry that provided transportation to church for those who lived in the hinterlands around Lynchburg. In 1964, Falwell moved his congregation into a new 1000-seat sanctuary. He also continued to build his broadcasting enterprise; he greatly increased the number of radio outlets in 1966 and replaced the television studio worship service with a professional taping of Thomas Road's Sunday worship service. This improved program, dubbed the *Old-Time Gospel Hour*, gained syndication on a growing number of television stations, which in turn generated increased revenues.

Along with Baptist church-growth specialist Elmer Towns, Falwell developed a persuasive argument for his television ministry. Contending that television was "the most effective medium for reaching people" and for "accomplishing worldwide salvation," Falwell promoted what he termed "saturation evangelism." This strategy was designed to bring the Christian gospel "to every available person at every available time by every available means." If Christianity failed to make optimum use of television technology, it would "stand accountable at the judgment seat of Christ for its failure to utilize every means available to us to reach every creature." As he recounted later in his autobiography, "We were standing on the threshold of an incredible opportunity to preach Christ simultaneously to every television home in the country."

Falwell's ministry grew amidst the turbulent Civil Rights struggles of the mid-1960s. During this time, Falwell was a vocal critic of the clergy's involvement in political activities. On March 21, 1965, the same day that the march on Montgomery, Alabama, was being resumed after its violent interruption in Selma, Falwell preached a sermon condemning the hate and unrest being aroused by the demonstrators. In the sermon he declared "believing the Bible as I do, I would find it impossible to stop preaching the pure saving gospel of Jesus Christ, and begin doing anything else—including fighting Communism, or participating in Civil Rights reforms. Preachers are not called to be politicians but to be soul winners." Falwell's Lynchburg Christian Schools, which he inaugurated in 1967, began their first year of operation with what local newspapers referred to as a "white only" admissions policy.

Falwell's position on political activism was a reflection of Fundamentalism's traditional stance of separation from the world, as well as individual, rather than social, regeneration. In this perspective, the elect of God had to isolate themselves from the corruption of secular society so that they might maintain their purity and faith as they awaited the impending apocalypse. When Falwell repudiated this position in the 1970s, he claimed it was because such national crises as the rising divorce rate, the proliferation of pornography, drug abuse, the Vietnam debacle, and the legalization of abortion were beginning to threaten the enclaves of fundamentalist sanctity.

By 1970, Falwell's church had grown to 10,000 members and had built a new 3,200 seat sanctuary. This church was modeled on a design by Thomas Jefferson and incorporated sophisticated facilities for television and radio production. By 1978, the congregation's membership was 15,000, making it the largest Baptist church in the country after W. A. Criswell's First Baptist Church of Dallas, Texas.

The *Old-Time Gospel Hour* was being broadcast on 300 stations worldwide and the radio program on over 180 outlets. In 1977, *The Wall Street Journal* reported that the *Old-Time Gospel Hour*'s annual income had reached $32 million. Of this total, $8 million was spent on salaries for 700 employees, $14 million on the radio and television ministries, $3 million on gift items, and $3 million on printing, postage, and incidental expenses.

According to Arbitron, Falwell's weekly audience grew to almost 1.5 million people by 1980. This total placed him behind only Oral Roberts, Rex Humbard, Robert Schuller, Jimmy Swaggart, and Richard DeHaan on the list of the nation's top-10 religious television shows. His viewership had expanded beyond the South, with Los Angeles, Philadelphia, and Washington, DC, logging in as his top three markets outside Lynchburg and Roanoke. During this period, Falwell's television show and daily radio program were also being broadcast in Canada, the West Indies, Japan, and West Africa.

Falwell, however, was not content with a successful local church and international broadcasting ministry. He began construction of Liberty Baptist College in 1971 with the goal of "educating men and women to serve a world of people for whom Christ died." The college received its primary funding from Falwell's television audience, who sent both donations and their children to the new facility. By 1980, the college was enrolling 2,900 students per year. In 1972 and 1973, Falwell launched the Thomas Road Bible Institute and the Lynchburg Baptist Theological Seminary. This latter institution has struggled financially over the years but continues to graduate ministers who support Falwell's dream of establishing independent fundamentalist churches around the world. Falwell encourages his graduates to plant new churches by raising funds on the *Old-Time Gospel Hour* and by preaching at the new churches' first public worship services.

Liberty Baptist College became Liberty University in the early 1980s. By the end of the decade, the institution boasted 6,500 students and 33 buildings valued at $30 million. Falwell is proud that his university was the first independent, fundamentalist, locally affiliated liberal arts college in the United States to be accredited by the South Association of Colleges and Schools.

Falwell began to change his attitude concerning clergy involvement in national politics in the mid-1970s. In 1977, he was approached by Robert Billings, the founder of the National Christian Action Coalition (a lobbying organization for fundamentalist educators), about organizing an umbrella organization for conservatives, fundamentalists, anti-abortion advocates, and anti-ERA (Equal Rights Amendment) groups. Falwell had already entered the political fray during the nation's bicentennial celebration, barnstorming the country, holding patriotic rallies, and calling for a return to America's founding religious values. Although reluctant at first, Falwell finally agreed to organize what came to be known as the Moral Majority. The new organization was unveiled with a rally in front of the Virginia State Capitol in September 1979. Soon Falwell and a chorus of Liberty College students were traveling to rallies in all 50 state capitals. The new coalition's platform opposed the Equal Rights Amendment and supported aid for Israel, prayer in public schools, and a strong national defense.

Within nine months, Falwell had set up semi-autonomous Moral Majority organizations in every state in the country. He also broadcast "America, You're Too Young to Die," a television special, on over 215 stations nationwide in June 1980. A number of prominent senators, governors, and congressmen appeared on the program, and it became clear that the Moral Majority was becoming a potent national political force. Following up on the success of this program, Falwell sent out teams of Life Action Singers to stage multimedia patriotic extravaganzas and to drum up support for the Moral Majority.

Falwell also started a new daily radio show at this time, *Moral Majority Report*, which he billed as a Paul Harvey–like newscast. Offered at no charge, the show was picked up by 260 stations, most of them Christian, within six months. Most of these stations ran the broadcast for no charge, given that it did not directly solicit contributions. Falwell was able to use the rallies and radio program to build up a mailing list of over 480,000 by October 1980. Persons on the mailing list received copies of *Moral Majority Report*, the organization's news organ, and monthly solicitation letters. Each of these letters addressed issues ranging from pornography to homosexuality. The organization's success could be measured in its fundraising total of $3.2 million for its first year of operation.

Although opinions differ on how much the Moral Majority aided the election of Ronald Reagan in 1980, it is clear that Falwell's coalition mobilized a large population of conservative and fundamentalist Christians who had previously eschewed partisan politics. After Reagan's victory, Falwell claimed that his organization was responsible for the voter participation of 14 million Americans.

Throughout the 1980s, the Moral Majority busied itself with registering conservative voters, lobbying local and federal governments to pass its social agenda, rallying support for conservative politicians, establishing the Legal Defense Fund to battle the American Civil Liberties Union, and printing rebuttals of liberal initiatives in the nation's mass media. The coalition was successful in its push for congressional hearings on such issues as the "Star Wars" initiative and support for the Nicaraguan Contras.

Falwell dissolved the Moral Majority in the late 1980s and organized the Liberty Federation in its place. This successor organization showed a greater concern for international affairs and defense policy than for domestic issues. One of the likely reasons for this shift was the Moral Majority's inability to implement its conservative social agenda even while it enjoyed the support of a right-wing Republican president.

Falwell's foreign policy pronouncements tended to reflect his parochial background and lack of expertise in international affairs. While the people of the Philippines were overthrowing the Marcos dictatorship, for example, Falwell stated his conviction that the country already enjoyed substantial political freedoms. Falwell also supported the limited reforms of South Africa's Botha regime and advised the United States government against implementing economic sanctions. The television preacher brought down a hail of criticism upon himself when he suggested that the vocal South African critic Bishop Desmond Tutu was a "phony" who did not accurately represent the country's black majority. In the wake of this criticism, Falwell decided to step down from his position of leadership within the Liberty Federation and to withdraw from his involvement in partisan politics.

Falwell entered the public spotlight again in the late 1980s when he accepted Jim Bakker's offer to assume temporary control of his scandal-ridden PTL corporation. This move did not sit well with many of Bakker's supporters, who were uncomfortable with Falwell's previous denunciations of Pentecostalism and concerned that he would stack the board of directors with fundamentalists. The beleaguered evangelist defended his promise to maintain the show's Pentecostal nature by asserting the overriding importance of conservative Protestant solidarity in the face of secular critics. The mission of all religious television, he argued, was to attract nonbelievers. Proper instruction in Christian doctrine could be accomplished once the new believer began attending a local church.

As he strove determinedly to resuscitate the failing ministry, Falwell was attacked by both Jim and Tammy Faye Bakker on ABC's *Nightline* for having "stolen" their ministry away from them. Falwell retaliated by calling a national press conference. During the conference he presented evidence of Jim Bakker's "homosexual behavior" and of both Bakkers' egregious fiscal abuses. He then spent many weeks dancing, clapping, singing, and cajoling Bakker's audience for donations. In spite of his arduous efforts, the ministry was too deeply wounded by past mismanagement to survive in the long term. The corporation filed for bankruptcy, and when, in October 1987, the courts decided that PTL's creditors had the right to submit their own reorganization plan, Falwell resigned and returned to Lynchburg.

Throughout the triumphs and trials of the 1980s, the Thomas Road Baptist Church continued to flourish. By 1987, the Church boasted nearly 17,000 mainly white, working- and lower-middle-class members. The church has built up an impressive private school system that services children from kindergarten through college. Church members staff a 24-hour radio station, preach the gospel in local prisons, teach Sunday school, and perform corporal works of mercy. Liberty University reported an enrollment of 7,000 in the early 1990s and projected that the facility would grow to accommodate 50,000 students by the year 2000.

In recent years, however, Falwell has had to incorporate some innovations into the *Old-Time Gospel Hour* in order to resuscitate its flagging fortunes. One successful policy has been to turn his pulpit over to lay preachers who share their dramatic stories of Christ's redemptive work in their lives. This device utilizes the time-tested revivalist genre of the personal testimony. Another strategy has been to rebroadcast past programs that were especially successful in generating audience contributions.

Falwell's fundamentalist Baptist background has greatly influenced his preaching style. Unlike the more fiery and dramatic Pentecostal television preachers, Falwell delivers his sermons in a measured, sober, self-confident manner. Dressed in conservative business suits, Falwell projects dignity, success, conviction, and self-discipline. The *Old-Time Gospel Hour*, which is essentially a rebroadcast of Thomas Road Sunday services, features a musical selection that augments this image; the show favors traditional Protestant gospel hymns over more contemporary genres. The core of Falwell's message has consistently been the need for repentance from sin and a return to the "old-time religion" of an earlier era. He has steadfastly condemned secular humanism, homosexuality, abortion, the Equal Rights Amendment, pornography, sex education in public schools, and socialism, while staunchly advocating a strong national defense, support for the state of Israel, and a purging of immorality in the American mass media.

Falwell has also served to articulate a general popular anxiety concerning America's role on the world stage. He has warned that, like the Roman Empire of old, the United States will lose its influence in international affairs if it does not repent of its hedonism and immorality. Only a return to traditional biblical morality can avert a dangerous decline in America's fortunes and a catastrophe of apocalyptic proportions. Like many conservative Christians, Falwell has promoted a picture of America as a land chosen by God to carry out his providential plan of world evangelization.

A staunch Cold Warrior until the collapse of the Soviet Union, Falwell repeatedly dramatized the menace that Communism represented to the nation's freedom and prosperity. As he once declared,

> Communists know that in order to take over a country they must first see to it that a nation's military strength is weakened and that its morals are corrupted so that its people have no will to resist wrong. When people begin to accept perversion and immorality as ways of life, as is happening in the United States today, we must beware.

On the issue of women's rights, Falwell has relentlessly preached a traditionalist biblical perspective. He views the feminist movement as a dire threat to the American family and encourages women to submit themselves to the "Christ-like protection of their husbands." In one of his fundraising letters, Falwell denied that he was trying to deprive women of their rights, claiming, instead, that "our women have a constitutional right to be treated like ladies, mothers, and wives under our family laws." Nevertheless, his Moral Majority adamantly opposed the right of a woman to terminate a pregnancy, except in cases of incest or rape.

Like many conservatives, Falwell harbors a deep suspicion of governmental intrusion in the lives of ordinary citizens. He believes that state intervention in child abuse cases interferes with parental responsibilities and that welfare destroys personal initiative and weakens the Protestant work ethic. Uncontrolled governmental taxation, Falwell asserts, threatens the free enterprise system, which he teaches is mandated by Scripture. In this regard, he has been a vocal opponent of Bill Clinton's health care reforms, claiming that they would constitute a sellout to state-sponsored socialism.

In spite of his consistently conservative views, Falwell has, to a certain extent, risen above the most virulent prejudices of his rural upbringing. He now disavows segregation and supports equal opportunities for members of all races. He has also transcended his region's historic anti-Semitism and anti-Catholicism. Recognizing that Roman Catholics have long carried the banner in the struggle against abortion, he has welcomed Catholics into his conservative coalitions. Believing that the state of Israel plays a pivotal role in the events of the Final Days, he denounces anti-Semitism as demonic and un-Christian and freely acknowledges the Hebraic roots of Christianity. Falwell has also tried to mend fences with old antagonists. In November 1993, he visited Jim Bakker in federal prison in Jesup, Georgia, and the pair embraced and prayed together. Both men communicated through their spokespersons that they welcomed the opportunity to bury old wounds and to heal bitter feelings.

Since Clinton's election in 1992, Falwell has been at the forefront of efforts to portray the new president as an immoral, corrupt, and dangerous politician who will stop at nothing to assuage his lust for power. During television specials aired on religious broadcasting stations in the spring of 1994, he publicized Clinton's Whitewater dealings, Paula Jones's allegations of sexual harassment, and various conspiracy theories linking Clinton and his wife to drug smuggling and political murders. It appears that the downfall of the Clinton administration has become Falwell's crusade for the 1990s.

See also Jim Bakker

SOURCES

Armstrong, Ben. *The Electric Church.* Nashville: Thomas Nelson, 1979.

Bromley, David G., and Anson Shupe, eds. *New Christian Politics.* Macon, GA: Mercer University Press, 1984.

Bruce, Steve. *Pray TV: Televangelism in America.* New York: Routledge, 1990.

Cooper, John Charles. *Religious Pied Pipers: A Critique of Radical Right-Wing Religion.* Valley Forge, PA: Judson Press, 1981.

D'Souza, Dinesh. *Falwell Before the Millennium: A Critical Biography.* Chicago: Regnery Gateway, 1984.

Falwell, Jerry. *If I Should Die Before I Wake. . . .* Nashville: Thomas Nelson, 1986.

———. *Listen America!* Garden City, NJ: Doubleday, 1980.

———. *Strength for the Journey: An Autobiography of Jerry Falwell.* New York: Simon & Schuster, 1987.

"Feuding TV Evangelists Embrace, Pray Together." *Orlando Sentinel,* November, 1993.

Fitzgerald, Frances. *Cities on a Hill: A Journey through Contemporary American Cultures.* New York: Simon & Schuster, 1986.

Hadden, Jeffrey K., and Charles E. Swann. *Prime Time Preachers: The Rising Power of Televangelism.* Menlo Park, CA: Addison-Wesley, 1981.

Hill, Samuel S., and Dennis E. Owen. *The New Religious Political Right in America.* Nashville: Abingdon Press, 1982.

Jorstad, Erling. *The New Christian Right, 1981–1988: Prospects for the Post-Reagan Decade.* Lewiston, NY: Edwin Mellen Press, 1987.

Kater, John L. *Christians on the Right: The Moral Majority in Perspective.* New York: Seabury Press, 1982.

Lippy, Charles H., ed. *Twentieth-Century Shapers of American Popular Religion.* Westport, CT: Greenwood Press, 1989.

Liebman, Robert C., and Robert Wuthnow. *The New Christian Right: Mobilization and Legitimation.* New York: Aldine, 1983.

Pingry, Patricia. *Jerry Falwell: Man of Vision.* Milwaukee, WI: Ideals, 1980.

Schultze, Quentin J. *Televangelism and American Culture: The Business of Popular Religion.* Grand Rapids, MI: Baker Book House, 1991.

Shupe, Anson, and William A. Stacey. *Born Again Politics and the Moral Majority: What Social Surveys Really Show.* New York and Toronto: Edwin Mellen Press, 1982.

Simon, Merrill. *Jerry Falwell and the Jews.* Middle Village, NY: Jonathan David, 1984.

Strober, Gerald, and Ruth Tomczak. *Jerry Falwell: Aflame for God.* Nashville: Thomas Nelson, 1979.

THE FAMILY ALTAR PROGRAM
first aired: 1951

The Family Altar Program is a long-running radio ministry that airs daily on more than 100 stations in the United States, South Africa, and the Caribbean. The program was hosted from 1951 to 1982 by its founder, the late Lester Roloff. The show now features the recorded radio messages and taped sermons of Brother Roloff's nearly 40-year radio ministry. In addition to Roloff's preaching, *The Family Altar Program* features hymns and popular religious songs sung by Brother Roloff and his ministry's various choirs and music ensembles. The program originates from the Roloff Evangelistic Enterprises headquarters in Corpus Christi, Texas.

See also Lester Roloff

SOURCES

Melton, J. Gordon. *Directory of Religious Organizations in the United States.* 3d ed. Detroit: Gale Research, 1993.

FAMILY RADIO NETWORK
established: 1958

The Family Radio Network (FRN) is a noncommercial, nonprofit chain of independent religious radio stations that began in 1958 with the purchase of KEAR-FM in San Francisco, California. The stations in the chain have always relied on listener contributions to support their ministry, rather than on the chain's parent group, the Christian Reformed Church, or advertisers. The offerings on this network include daily Bible readings, religious music, advice on marriage and childrearing, prayer time, and various instructional programs, as well as the daily call-in show, *Open Forum*, which is hosted by the network's president and general manager, Harold Camping. In general, the program content on FRN tends to steer away from Christian Right (conservative) politics and to focus instead on fostering a revitalized Christian society in America.

By the mid-1960s, FRN had acquired KEBR in Sacramento and KECR in El Cajon, both in California. The network then expanded to the East Coast, purchasing WFME in Newark, New Jersey, in 1966. WFME's powerful 36,000-watt transmitter allowed the network to blanket the entire New York metropolitan area with evangelical programming.

Over the past 25 years, new stations have been bought in Camden, New Jersey, and Annapolis, Maryland. These stations have allowed FRN to broadcast Christian programming to both the Philadelphia and Washington, DC, metropolitan areas. Stations also have been added in Shenandoah, Iowa, and Long Beach, California. In addition to its domestic ministry, FRN owns a short-wave station which broadcasts Christian radio programming in seven languages to Europe and Latin America.

See also Harold Camping

SOURCES

Armstrong, Ben. *The Electric Church.* Nashville: Thomas Nelson, 1979.

FAR EAST BROADCASTING COMPANY
established: 1945

The Far East Broadcasting Company (FEBC) has become one of the largest international religious broadcasting organizations in the world, reaching out to over half of the world's population.

The FEBC is the brainchild of Robert Bowman, who once worked as "Second Mate Bobby," the baritone soloist on Paul Myers's *Haven of Rest* radio program. Inspired by the success of Myers's ministry in bringing souls to Christ, Bowman decided to establish a radio network that would bring the gospel to other areas of the world. Myers helped set up a meeting in 1938 between Bowman and John Broger, a producer and former classmate of Myers at Southern California Bible School. Their meeting did not result in any concrete plan, but the two continued to communicate during World War II.

Broger enlisted in the Navy and, in time, became a top communications expert. Shortly after returning to civilian life, in December of 1945, Broger and Bowman organized the Far East Broadcasting Company with $500 of their own money. Paul Myers assisted the fledgling company financially, providing the *Haven of Rest*'s list of contributors and offering to match whatever funds it was able to raise. Additional financial assistance came from William J. Roberts of the daily *Family Bible Hour* program. Roberts, FEBC's third partner, spearheaded efforts to garner contributions from Christians who supported missionary work in the Far East. Within a year, enough funds had been raised to send Broger to the Philippines, where he hoped to build the ministry's first radio station. Bowman and Roberts stayed in Los Angeles, where each continued to broadcast their respective radio programs.

Broger set up FEBC's first station in Manila, the capital of the Philippines. It broadcast over a humble 1,000-watt transmitter that covered only the Manila metropolitan area. The station's first broadcast, on June 4, 1948, began with the hymn "All Hail the Power of Jesus' Name."

Broger and his partners were undeterred by these modest beginnings. Already they were planning to operate two 10,000-watt transmitters from the Philippines that would include other countries in its broadcasting range. At the top of the list was mainland China, which had fallen into the hands of the Communists during 1948. This takeover had been accompanied by the closing of thousands of Chinese churches and the expulsion of 6,000 missionaries. Reflecting later upon this turn of events, Bowman observed,

> God in His great wisdom had caused a radio organization to be formed that would begin to broadcast the gospel message to the persecuted and isolated church. The voice of radio could still penetrate the land. We knew in the 1950s that the broadcasts even from our tiny 3,000-watt short-wave transmitter were getting through. Mail came to FEBC, Manila, from every major section of China.

The success and expansion of FEBC's broadcast outreach was more rapid than any of the three partners had expected. By 1958, the ministry was blanketing the Philippines' 7,000 islands with broadcasts from 11 stations. In addition, programs in 36 languages and dialects were being broadcast to Communist China and other Asian countries. FEBC's facilities grew to include two stations on Okinawa, an office on Formosa, recording studios in Hong Kong, and a new headquarters in Whittier, California. Between 1954 and 1958, letters to FEBC from its listeners totaled 200,000, including at least 40,000 from short-wave audiences in over 80 countries.

FEBC expanded its outreach still further during its second decade of operation with the purchase of KGEI, a powerful short-wave station, from *Voice of America*. This station began broadcasting religious programs to Latin America from its San Francisco studios. The ministry's facilities in the Far East also multiplied, allowing it to saturate Communist China with religious programming. In spite of highly effective jamming efforts by the Communist authorities, these broadcasts were believed to provide crucial support to the millions of Chinese Christians who were suffering persecution for their faith.

During its third decade of operation, FEBC added two stations in South Korea and a new AM broadcast facility on Saipan. This new installation went on the air in 1977 and replaced a smaller station on Okinawa after Okinawa was returned to Japanese control. By 1979, FEBC was operating 28 stations worldwide and broadcasting 300 hours daily in 72 languages and dialects. FEBC's American headquarters in La Mirada, California, housed offices, control rooms, recording studios, and an auditorium. The staff of broadcasters included a number of refugees from Communist controlled territories.

FEBC's ministry today encompasses almost 30 stations and transmits the gospel message to India, Australia, China, Eastern Europe, Asia, and Latin America. These stations offer programs in scores of languages and dialects.

See also Robert Bowman

SOURCES

Armstrong, Ben. *The Electric Church*. Nashville: Thomas Nelson, 1979.

Ward, Mark, Sr. *Air of Salvation: The Story of Christian Broadcasting*. Manassas, VA: National Religious Broadcasters, 1994.

FESTIVAL OF FAITH
see: Eugene Scott

PAUL FINKENBINDER
born: September 24, 1921, Santurce, Puerto Rico

Paul Finkenbinder, often referred to as the "Billy Graham of Latin America," has been evangelizing the Spanish-speaking world as a broadcast missionary since 1942. Known affectionately as "Hermano Pablo" (Brother Paul), Finkenbinder was born in Puerto Rico in 1921 to missionary parents Frank Finkenbinder and Aura Argetsinger. He grew up speaking Span-

Courtesy: National Religious Broadcasters

ish and only mastered English when he moved to the United States in 1936 to attend the Zion Bible Institute of Rhode Island. After graduating in 1941, Finkenbinder did postgraduate work at Central Bible College in Springfield, Missouri.

Finkenbinder began his mission work in New Mexico in 1942. A year later, he went as a missionary to the Central American nation of El Salvador. He remained in El Salvador 21 years and received his nickname, "Hermano Pablo," because "Finkenbinder" was too difficult for many Salvadorans to pronounce. Finkenbinder was ordained to the ministry of the Assemblies of God in 1948.

In 1955, Finkenbinder began broadcasting his radio program *The Church of the Air* (not to be confused with Essek William Kenyon's show of the same name). The following year, to attract more listeners, he changed the name of the program to *Un Mensaje a la Conciencia* ("Message to the Conscience"). He also changed the program's format. Although the refinements in the program gained him a larger audience, Finkenbinder continued to struggle financially for a number of years. It was not until 1967 that *Mensaje a la Conciencia* began to gain a wider audience, airing over 100 stations. Ten years later the program was being broadcast over 400 stations. Regular television broadcasts of *Mensaje* did not begin until about 1970.

In 1969, Finkenbinder moved his ministry headquarters permanently to Costa Mesa, California, where he has lived ever since. He was given a Distinguished Service citation from the National Religious Broadcasters in 1970. The following year he received an Oscar award for best Bible story from the National Evangelical Film Foundation for his film, *Elijah and Baal*.

Currently, Finkenbinder's radio and television programs air over more than 1,900 radio and 300 television stations in 27 countries throughout Central and South America. In 1993, the evangelist received an honorary doctorate from Southern California College in Costa Mesa.

See also *Mensaje a la Conciencia*

SOURCES

Melton, J. Gordon. *Directory of Religious Organizations in the United States.* 3d ed. Detroit: Gale Research, 1993.

DENNIS FINNAN
born: October 2, 1944, New York City

Dennis Finnan is the host of the eclectic national radio program, *The World, The Word & You Broadcast*. The program, whose motto is "Sowing the Winds, with God's Glorious Word," features such topics as twenty-first century prophecies, abortion, dinosaurs and DNA, the Promise Keeper movement, angels, Newton's laws, the discipline of fatherhood, Columbus, and cyber-Christianity. Transcripts of each program are available via a web page on the Internet.

The show began its broadcasting history on May 11, 1980, in Benton Harbor, Michigan. It now originates from the Saint Charles Bible Church in Saint Charles, Minnesota, and has a station coverage of 2 to 3 million potential listeners in Iowa, Minnesota, Wisconsin, Missouri, Arkansas, Wyoming, Nebraska, Colorado, and South Dakota. Finnan's radio ministry depends upon listeners, friends of the broadcast, and churches for financial support. Since its inception, the program has had all of its expenses met by this "faith giving" without any need for on-air solicitation of funds.

Finnan was working as an executive in an advertising company in Tampa, Florida, when he was "born again" as a result of a Christian radio ministry. He enrolled at the Moody Bible Institute and began a radio ministry in May of 1980 at the church where he was serving as pastor. Finnan now pastors the St. Charles Bible Church in St. Charles, Minnesota. The church is affiliated with the Independent Fundamental Churches of America. His program allows him to "declare the Word of God from the pulpit through the medium of radio."

SOURCES

"The World, the Word & You!" World Wide Web site. http://www.isl.net/wwyweb.html (June 1996).

FIRST EDITION

First Edition is a radio outreach program that features prominent Christian authors and musicians discussing their latest books and recordings. Hosted by Greg Cromartie, the 30-minute program airs Saturday afternoons on over 151 stations around the United States. The show reflects the growing popularity of Christian books and music in American culture and the growing marketing acumen of Christian publishers and recording companies. *First Edition* is distributed by the USA Satellite Network.

FOCUS ON THE FAMILY
first aired: 1977

One of the most popular Christian radio programs of all time is *Focus on the Family*, hosted by Christian psychologist James Dobson. Dobson, a protégé of pioneer Christian radio psychologist Clyde Narramore, adopted much of his question-and-answer format from

Narramore's long-running program *Psychology for Living*. In this ministry, Narramore responded to letters sent to him by his program listeners.

Originally syndicated nationally from Los Angeles, California, *Focus on the Family* currently broadcasts from Colorado Springs, Colorado, and is heard over nearly 1,500 radio stations nationwide. The program deals with topics as commonplace as breast-feeding and toilet-training and as controversial as corporal punishment, birth control, homosexuality, and abortion. In accord with many of his books on marriage and family life, Dobson's discussions of these and other issues are influenced by his conservative Christian beliefs.

Dobson's broadcasting ministry has expanded over the years to include a number of radio programs, production of audio- and videotapes, and a publishing department. Under the auspices of Dobson's Family Research Council, *Focus on the Family* offers a number of family advocacy services, sponsors Right-to-Life drives, and holds anti-pornography crusades. The ministry also has directed its resources toward an effort to return the public schools to a traditional educational and values-oriented framework.

In addition to its signature call-in program, Focus on the Family Ministries produces several other radio programs. *Adventures in Odyssey* is a daily 30-minute radio drama whose primary aim is to teach Christian family values to children. *Family News in Focus*, airing from 2 to 10 minutes daily, comments on the impact of current news stories on traditional family values. *Focus on the Family Commentary,* which grew out of Dobson's *Focus on the Family* program, is a 90-second daily spot hosted by Dobson that airs over major secular stations nationwide. In the program Dobson offers practical guidance on American family life. *James Dobson Family Commentary* is a 90-second spot hosted by Dobson in which he presents to the listener a "jewel of wisdom" on marriage and family life. Finally, *Weekend* is a one-hour weekly program that replays highlights from the previous week's broadcasts. *Weekend* follows a pattern similar to that of currently popular magazine digests.

A Spanish-language translation of *Focus on the Family*, entitled *Enfoque a la Familia*, airs daily over more than 600 stations in the United States and Latin America.

SOURCES

Melton, J. Gordon. *Directory of Religious Organizations in the United States.* 3d ed. Detroit: Gale Research, 1993.

Zetterman, Rolf. *Dr. Dobson: Turning Hearts toward Home.* Dallas Word Publishing, 1989.

HARRY EMERSON FOSDICK
born: May 24, 1878, Buffalo, New York
died: October 5, 1969, Bronxville, New York

The influential liberal Protestant minister Harry Emerson Fosdick was also a pioneer of religious radio broadcasting during the medium's founding era.

Fosdick was reared by devout Baptist parents in upstate New York. He attended Colgate University in Hamilton, New York, where he took his bachelor of arts degree in 1900. While a student at Colgate, Fosdick met liberal theologian William Newton Clarke, who became his mentor and spiritual godfather. In spite of serious religious doubts, Fosdick decided to study for the ministry. He enrolled first at Hamilton Theological Seminary and later at Union Theological Seminary in New York City. He graduated from Union in 1904 and was ordained to the ministry the same year.

He received his first call to the pastorate from the Montclair Baptist Church, where he remained until taking up teaching duties at Union Theological Seminary in 1915 as Jessup Professor of Practical Theology. In 1918, Fosdick served as a military chaplain in France. When the war ended, he took up duties as guest minister of the prestigious First Presbyterian Church of New York City. In this position, Fosdick rose to prominence as a liberal preacher.

In the early 1920s, Fosdick began speaking over the radio. In 1922, he launched a new radio program called *National Vespers*, which continued for the next several decades. Fosdick also became a frequent guest speaker on NBC's *National Radio Pulpit*.

From the very beginning of his tenure at First Presbyterian, Fosdick came to disdain the fundamentalists who were creating controversy within Baptist and Presbyterian churches. He gained national attention when he preached his famous sermon, "Shall the Fundamentalists Win?" As a result of his criticism of the fundamentalists and his highly liberal positions on central Christian doctrines, Fosdick became a target for censure. Though eventually forced to resign his pulpit in 1925 because of his views, he later became pastor of the Park Avenue Baptist Church and was subsequently installed as minister of John D. Rockefeller, Jr.'s newly erected interdenominational Riverside Church of New York City in 1931, a position he held until his retirement in 1946.

SOURCES

Ahlstrom, Sydney E. *A Religious History of the American People.* Vol. 2. Garden City, NJ: Image Books, 1975.

Fosdick, Harry Emerson. *The Living of These Days.* New York: Harper & Row, 1956.

Hutchison, William R. *The Modernist Impulse in American Protestantism.* New York: Oxford University Press, 1976.

Reid, Daniel G., Robert D. Linder, Bruce L. Shelley, and Harry S. Stout, eds. *Dictionary of Christianity in America.* Downers Grove, IL: InterVarsity Press, 1990.

Stone, Jon R. *On the Boundaries of American Evangelicalism: The New Evangelical Coalition, 1940-1965.* Albany: State University of New York Press, forthcoming.

FRANCISCAN UNIVERSITY FOCUS
first aired: 1993

In February of 1993, a monthly special called *Franciscan University Focus* began airing on the Eternal Word Television Network (EWTN). The program is a syndicated series produced by the faculty, staff, and students of the communication arts department of the Franciscan University of Steubenville, Ohio. It features a panel discussion on current teachings of and events in the Roman Catholic Church. Although the program asserts that it is "faithful to the teachings of the Magisterium" in Rome, it addresses difficult and controversial issues in an open manner.

The show's host and moderator is Father Michael Scanlan. Scanlan earned his bachelor's degree from Williams College in Williamstown, Massachusetts, and graduated from Harvard Law School in 1956. The following year, after serving as staff judge advocate for the United States Air Force, Scanlan entered the Franciscan Third Order Regular. Following training at the St. Francis Seminary in Loretto, Pennsylvania, Scanlan was ordained in 1964. After serving in several teaching and administrative posts at the College of Steubenville, he was chosen as the college's president in 1974. Scanlan is a popular speaker at national and international conferences and has authored such books as *Let the Fire Fall* (1986), *The Truth about Trouble* (1989), and *Rosary Companion* (1993).

Joining Scanlan on the program's panel are Dr. Scott Hahn, professor of biblical theology at Franciscan University, Father Giles Dimock, OP, chairman of the university's theology department, Dr. Regis Martin, professor of dogmatic and systematic theology, and Dr. Ronda Chervin, visiting professor of theology and philosophy. The panel has discussed a wide range of topics over the past three years, including youth and the Church, biblical fundamentalism, the role of Mary and women in the Church, the contemporary priesthood, euthanasia, bioethics, women and the priesthood, capital punishment and just war, the recent Beijing Women's Conference, and John Paul II's vision for families.

See also Michael Scanlon

SOURCES

"Franciscan University Focus." World Wide Web site, http://esoptron.umd.edu/fusfolder/focus.html (December, 1995).

PAUL FREED
born: 1918

Founder of the Voice of Tangiers Radio in 1954 and Trans World Radio (TWR) in 1960, Paul Freed was born into a missionary home and spent his youth in the Middle East. After serving as pastor of a church he founded in Greensboro, North Carolina, Freed became director of the local chapter of Youth for Christ International (YFC).

In 1948, Freed was encouraged by Torrey Johnson, founder of YFC, to consider missionary service. It was while attending a YFC rally in Switzerland that Freed learned of the spiritual needs of Spanish Protestants under the Franco regime. After soliciting financial help from patrons in the US, Freed established a radio ministry that broadcast to Spain from Morocco. This ministry was called the Voice of Tangiers.

In 1956, the Moroccan government, which had just recently regained control of Tangiers from Spain, began giving Freed and his ministry trouble. In 1959, they forced the Voice of Tangiers out of Morocco altogether. Later that same year, Freed bought a former Nazi broadcast center in Monaco with enough broadcasting power to reach all of Europe. With this new radio complex, Freed began Trans World Radio (TWR), one of the three largest Christian broadcast stations in the world.

Since that time, Freed's network of transmitters has continued to grow. In 1992, for example, Freed expanded his network into the old Soviet bloc, buying the large station, Radio Tirana, from the government of Albania, where Christianity had been outlawed for decades. With headquarters in Cary, North Carolina, Freed still directs the work of TWR, which has grown to include a network of high-powered transmitters that broadcast to 80 percent of the world's population in 100 languages.

See also Trans World Radio

SOURCES

Ward, Mark, Sr. *Air of Salvation: The Story of Christian Broadcasting*. Grand Rapids, MI: Baker Book House, 1994.

FRONTIERS OF FAITH
see: The Eternal Light; The Catholic Hour

FULL GOSPEL CENTRAL CHURCH
see: Paul Cho

CHARLES FULLER
born: April 25, 1887, Los Angeles, California
died: March 18, 1968

Courtesy: Fuller Theological Seminary

Charles E. Fuller was one of the first American ministers to realize the full potential of radio during the 1930s and 1940s for spreading the conservative Christian message. His *Old Fashioned Revival Hour* would eventually become one of the twentieth century's most respected and long-running religious radio programs.

Fuller was the youngest of three sons born into a devout Methodist family in Southern California. The future evangelist spent his childhood in his father's orange groves near Redlands. His father was successful enough as a farmer and businessman to become a strong financial supporter of Methodist foreign missions. Charles, however, showed little interest in religious matters as a young man. At his mother's insistence, he enrolled in Pomona College, where he showed promise as a football player, debater, and scientist. He graduated cum laude in chemistry in 1910. A year later he married Grace Payton, a high school sweetheart, and went to work for his father. After a killing freeze destroyed his father's orange groves, the younger Fuller and his wife moved to Placentia, California, where he managed a cooperative packing plant. Fuller proved to be a capable businessman and had soon accumulated substantial assets by leasing land to oil companies, selling agricultural real estate, and establishing a trucking firm. It was during this period that Fuller and his wife decided to join the Presbyterian Church.

In 1916, Fuller went to hear Paul Rader, the famed pastor of Chicago's Moody Church, preach at the Church of the Open Door in Los Angeles. Fuller, who had been plagued by a sense that something was lacking in his life, was inspired by the sermon and decided to dedicate his life to God's service. He began an intensive study of the Bible and soon organized a class of Bible students at the Placentia Presbyterian Church. Fuller also enrolled at Biola (the Bible Institute of Los Angeles, funded by fundamentalist oil millionaire Lyman Stewart) in preparation for his ordination into the ministry. While at Biola, Fuller studied fundamentalist eschatology and hermeneutics under such conservative Christian luminaries as Reuben A. Torrey, the institute's dean.

The Bible class Fuller had organized at Placentia Presbyterian soon found itself in conflict with the larger congregation because of his strict fundamentalist views. The rapidly expanding faction broke away from Placentia Presbyterian and organized itself into the independent

Calvary Church in 1925. Fuller, who had completed his training for the ministry at Biola in 1921, was called as the church's first pastor. He gained his ordination papers from a coalition of Baptist churches affiliated with the Baptist Bible Union. The congregation soon developed a reputation for excellence in Sunday school education and evangelistic crusades. Fuller himself was a popular speaker at these crusades, which took place up and down the West Coast. The evangelist also was hired as a trustee at Biola and later as the college's chairman of the board.

In October 1923, Fuller began what would become a lifelong commitment to radio evangelism when he broadcast his first religious program over a local commercial station. Within a year he was teaching Bible classes over Biola's privately owned radio station. Fuller's complete commitment to religious radio, however, did not occur until 1929. It was during that year, while preaching at a crusade in Indianapolis, that he was asked by the Defenders of the Christian Faith Convention to fill in on a local religious radio program. His sermon was a compact message on Mark 4:35–41, the story of Jesus's calming of the storm on the Sea of Galilee. The young evangelist was struck by the large number of positive calls and letters he received after this guest sermon and came to believe that God wanted him to begin his own regular radio ministry.

In February 1930, a Santa Ana educational station began carrying Calvary Church's Sunday morning worship service. The church next purchased time to broadcast a program of religious music that featured Calvary Church's youth choir and a phone-in show during which listeners could ask Fuller questions. The popularity of these programs had an immediate, positive impact on church attendance—soon the services were overflowing with congregants.

By September, the church's broadcasts had moved to the more sophisticated radio facilities of KGER, Long Beach, and were reaching over 15,000 listeners each week. In 1933, Fuller was forced to resign from his pastorship at Calvary Church because of financial disagreements with the church's leadership over his radio ministry. These leaders preferred to concentrate the church's resources on servicing their local community. Fuller's resignation came at the height of the Great Depression and the popular evangelist's personal financial resources were now exhausted. Nevertheless, he decided to continue broadcasting two weekly programs and to rely solely on the donations of his audience. His first independent broadcast, in March, occurred during the same week that President Franklin D. Roosevelt closed the nation's banks. To make matters worse, a large earthquake hit Long Beach the day before his first broadcast, and US Marines—sent in to prevent looting—almost stopped him from entering KGER's studio.

Fuller persevered and by May his programs were generating enough contributions to meet weekly expenses and to enable him to set aside a small amount for future expansion. At this point, Fuller organized a nonprofit corporation, Gospel Broadcasting Association, and devised plans for more programming. A new show on Saturday evenings was added in November and a fourth program began broadcasting in March of 1934 from 50,000-watt KNX in Hollywood. During the mid-1930s, Fuller judiciously expanded his radio ministry by entering into agreements with regional networks. In time, his programs were being carried up and down the West Coast and as far east as the Mississippi River. The programs were aired under such titles as *The Voice of Hollywood*, *The Prophetic Lamp Hour*, *Heart to Heart Hour*, *Sunday School Hour*, *Radio Bible Class* (not to be confused with M. R. DeHaan's program), and *Radio Revival Hour*. It was this show, a Sunday evening revival service performed before a live studio audience, that became Fuller's set format for the next 35 years. The show was renamed the *Old Fashioned Revival Hour* in 1937 when it was purchased for broadcast over the Mutual Broadcasting System.

The now successful radio evangelist introduced his first Mutual broadcast with the words,

Each Sunday by God's grace we have an hour to broadcast the old songs and the old gospel which is the power of God unto salvation. Our one message is Christ and Him crucified, and we endeavor by God's grace to beseech men and women to be reconciled to God in Christ Jesus.

In time the show would include familiar hymns and gospel songs sung by a professional choir and quartet. These singers were accompanied on piano by Rudy Atwood and on organ by George Broadbent.

The program was an immediate hit and within six weeks was being broadcast over 88 stations nationwide. The cost of this distribution was extremely high for the time, about $4,500 a week. Following a successful national appeal in 1939, the *Revival Hour* was able to purchase time on all of Mutual's 152 stations. This gave the program an estimated weekly audience of over 10 million listeners. As Mutual continued to expand its national network of stations, Fuller was pressured to accept the increased costs of programming or lose his prime-time Sunday evening slot. Fuller decided to meet this challenge, and his program was airing on 456 Mutual stations by 1942.

This expansion was made possible in part because of a promotional sheet, *Heart to Heart Talk*, that Fuller began publishing with the help of his wife. This periodical organized Fuller's national radio audience into a loose-knit group of supporters and financial contributors. Fuller also continued to conduct evangelistic revivals around the United States, which supplemented and complemented his radio ministry. His many millions of listeners were eager to see their radio preacher perform live. As a result, Fuller's appearance at Soldier's Field in Chicago for an Easter sunrise service in 1938 and at Carnegie Hall in New York City during the 1939 World's Fair were standing-room-only affairs. Fuller would often broadcast his services live from these revivals using Mutual's local affiliates.

Fuller's wife Grace was instrumental to the *Old Fashioned Revival Hour*'s huge popularity. On each program she read letters from people around the world who had been led to a closer relationship with God through Fuller's broadcasts. With her precise diction and lilting tones, Grace Fuller's voice was custom made for radio broadcasting. Charles Fuller's folksy mannerisms and friendly personality were also a key to the program's success. As he once re-marked, "If everything seems informal, just remember it's the *Old Fashioned Revival Hour*." Fuller always used simple language and con-crete images to make his homiletic points. To-gether, the Fullers projected the feeling of a loving yet well-disciplined home, run by a re-laxed, stable father and a kind, efficient mother. During the Depression and World War II, such a feeling served as a palliative to many troubled Americans.

Fuller continued his Sunday morning radio broadcasts on KGER and was joined in the stu-dio by loyal supporters before the evening *Re-vival Hour*. This group of fellow worshipers had, by 1939, grown so large that the Long Beach Municipal Auditorium was rented out to accom-modate them. The auditorium soon became the origination point for Fuller's Sunday morning program, *Pilgrim's Hour*, which began to be broadcast nationally in 1942. The cost of broad-casting the *Revival Hour* and *Pilgrim's Hour* over 1,000 stations across the country was nearly $35,000 a week, making Fuller's Gos-pel Broadcasting Association the network's highest paying customer. In 1943 alone, the association spent $1,556,130, almost all of it donated by small contributors from the listen-ing audience. Fuller was therefore the early pio-neer of today's multi-million-dollar television ministries.

Helped by its popular religious shows, the Mutual Broadcasting System built up a large national audience. Soon secular advertisers ea-ger for airtime began to pose a real threat to the system's religious programming. Slowly, Mu-tual gave in to pressures from militant church-men who disliked paid religious programs (be-cause of such controversial figures as Charles Coughlin) and from academic groups like the Institute of Education by Radio. The network moved to reschedule and limit its religious pro-gramming between 1943 and 1944.

Charles Fuller perceived the threat to his ra-dio ministry and enlisted the aid of J. Elwin Wright, a fellow radio evangelist and leader of the New England Fellowship of Evangelicals. Wright was instrumental in the formation of the National Association of Evangelicals (NAE), which took as one of its main tasks the protec-tion of religious broadcasting. He was also an effective advocate for conservative religious programming during the time he served as NAE's representative to the Institute of Educa-tion by Radio.

Perhaps because of Wright's efforts, the *Old Fashioned Revival Hour* and *Pilgrim's Hour* were allowed to continue for an additional two seasons on the Mutual network. Then, in Sep-tember 1944, Fuller was forced to scale back his broadcasts to one half-hour spot on Sunday mornings. He decided to produce a half-hour version of *Pilgrim's Hour* for this spot. By pre-paring the *Old Fashioned Revival Hour*'s lis-teners before the September cutback, Fuller was able to carry his huge audience over to the new stations he had lined up to broadcast the pro-gram in the fall. Within a few years the evange-list had built up a national listenership of nearly 20 million people. When the networks needed the program's revenues again in the late 1940s, Fuller worked out a deal with ABC's radio net-work. ABC broadcast the 60-minute *Old Fash-ioned Revival Hour* with a studio audience be-tween 1950 and 1957 on nearly 300 stations across the United States and Canada.

In spite of the growing popularity of televi-sion, Fuller's program maintained its huge au-dience and claimed to receive 400 letters a week attesting to conversions related to the show. This didn't mean the program was without critics. Some radical fundamentalists, for example, complained that the gospel of Christ would only be tainted by the "sinful" world of electronic broadcasting. To such critics Fuller responded "we haven't changed our message, just our me-dium."

ABC shifted its policy on religious radio broadcasting in 1958 and again Fuller was forced to scale back his broadcasts. The *Old Fashioned Revival Hour* became a half-hour program and the show's live broadcasts from the Long Beach Municipal Auditorium ended. In 1963, ABC decided to further limit its com-mercial religious programming, and Fuller found independent stations to broadcast the

Revival Hour. The show continued to boast a national audience of 20 million listeners up to the time of Fuller's retirement in 1967. Fuller's successor on radio was David Hubbard, who, by 1967, was the president of Fuller Theological Seminary mentioned below. The show has since changed its name to *The Joyful Sound.*

In addition to his radio work, Fuller was instrumental in the creation of Fuller Theological Seminary in 1947. The idea for the school had begun in the late 1930s with Fuller's dream of establishing a "Christ-centered, spirit-directed training school." Fuller's father set aside money to train foreign missionaries in the early 1940s and the fund was used to purchase land in Pasadena. Fuller then hired Harold Ockenga, the well-respected pastor of Boston's mission-oriented Park Street Church, to gather a suitable faculty. When Ockenga decided to commit the seminary to neo-evangelicalism, Fuller was faced with a quandary. Fuller himself was a staunch, old-school fundamentalist who wanted only to train missionaries for his foundation's evangelistic work overseas. Neo-evangelicals like Ockenga, on the other hand, sought to devise an intellectually credible defense of evangelical faith and to develop a more positive and sophisticated cultural and social agenda. They also hoped to do away with the strict separatism that had marginalized Fundamentalism between the 1920s and the early 1950s. Perhaps due to the influence of his son, Dan Fuller, who had studied at Princeton Seminary and with the Swiss theologian Karl Barth, Charles Fuller decided to maintain his support of the seminary despite his misgivings concerning its direction. Indeed, it is this respected evangelical seminary that has become Fuller's greatest contribution to American religion.

Charles Fuller is one of the pivotal figures in the history of evangelical religious broadcasting. Throughout his long and popular ministry, he took advantage of the phenomenal growth of the radio industry and used it to pursue his goal of seeing "the world evangelized in this generation." His influence was felt throughout the world, with his broadcasts being aired over short-wave bands and powerful AM stations from Europe to South America and the Far East. Fuller never deviated from his central message of personal salvation through the voluntary acceptance of Christ. His legacy can be found in a more accommodating and irenic Christian Fundamentalism as well as in such religious programs as Jerry Falwell's *Old-Time Gospel Hour.*

See also Appendix E: Sustaining Time

SOURCES

Armstrong, Ben. *The Electric Church.* Nashville: Thomas Nelson, 1979.

Fuller, Daniel P. *Give the Winds a Mighty Voice.* Waco, TX: Word Books, 1972.

Lippy, Charles H., ed. *Twentieth-Century Shapers of American Popular Religion.* Westport, CT: Greenwood Press, 1989.

Marsden, George M. *Reforming Fundamentalism: Fuller Seminary and the New Evangelicalism.* Grand Rapids, MI: Eerdmans, 1987.

Murch, James DeForest. *Cooperation without Compromise.* Grand Rapids, MI: Eerdmans, 1956.

Parker, Everett C., et al. *The Television-Radio Audience and Religion.* New York: Harper, 1955.

Saunders, Lowell Sperry. "The National Religious Broadcasters and the Availability of Commercial Radio Time." Ph.D. diss., University of Illinois, 1968.

Siedell, Barry. *Gospel Radio.* Lincoln, NE: Back to the Bible Broadcast, 1971.

Smith, Wilbur M. *A Voice for God: The Life of Charles E. Fuller, Originator of the Old Fashioned Revival Hour.* Boston: W. A. Wilde, 1949.

Wright, J. Elwin. *The Old Fashioned Revival Hour and the Broadcasters.* Boston: Fellowship Press, 1940.

FUNDAMENTAL BAPTIST MISSION OF TRINIDAD AND TOBAGO
established: 1921

The Fundamental Baptist Mission is a missionary organization that conducts evangelistic revival meetings, plants churches, distributes literature, and produces weekly radio broadcasts on the Caribbean islands of Trinidad and Tobago. While its parent group remains in Trinidad and Tobago, much of the ministry's support comes from its mainland operation offices in Hamilton, Ontario, and South Charleston, West Virginia.

SOURCES

Melton, J. Gordon. *Directory of Religious Organizations in the United States.* 3d ed. Detroit: Gale Research, 1993.

G

BILL GAITHER

born: March 28, 1936, Alexandria, Indiana

Bill Gaither is a famous Christian songwriter and performer who is now seen around the world on his weekly half-hour musical program on Trinity Broadcasting Network.

Gaither grew up in Alexandria, Indiana, and was encouraged in his musical aspirations by his mother, who recorded gospel quartets on the radio so that he could listen to them after school. Gaither started a gospel quartet after high school but folded the group when it became apparent there was little audience interest. Gaither then decided to pursue a career as a high school teacher and enrolled at Anderson College (now Anderson University), a Church of God–sponsored school in Anderson, Indiana. After receiving his English degree in 1959, Gaither entered the master's program at Ball State University. He earned his master's degree in guidance in 1961. It was during this period that Gaither published his first song, "I've Been to Calvary."

Gaither proved to be a successful high school teacher, spurring his students to complete their assignments with diligence and speed so there would be time for him to serenade them with his songs and guitar accompaniment. After transferring to his alma mater in Alexandria, Gaither met his future wife, Gloria Sickal. Sickal, the daughter of a minister from Michigan, had been hired as a substitute French teacher and was starting her job on the same day as Gaither. As Gaither now explains, "People say that opposites attract. In our case,

it was the likenesses that pulled us together. The draw was philosophical; it also helped that she was pretty."

Following his marriage to Gloria in 1962, Gaither continued to dabble in songwriting and singing. He, his brother, Danny, and his sister, Mary Ann, performed on the weekend church supper circuit. Gaither composed the group's new material, and his gift for theologically sound and understandable lyrics sparked a positive response from a growing legion of fans. Gaither's breakthrough single was the 1963 gospel hit, "He Touched Me." The song was nominated for a Grammy award and came to international attention when it was recorded by Elvis Presley, a longtime fan of gospel music.

Despite his deep attachment to teaching, Gaither left his high school job and formed the Bill Gaither Trio. The group had a string of popular contemporary-style gospel hits during the 1960s and performed in concerts around the country. Gaither sang and played piano and developed a homey, relaxed stage presence. His trademark sing-along style catalyzed audience participation throughout a concert.

Gaither has earned numerous accolades, including the Dove award for Songwriter of the Year in 1969 and 1972 through 1977, induction into the Gospel Music Association Hall of Fame in 1982, and appointment to Anderson University's board of trustees. The university also conferred an honorary doctor of music degree on him in 1973.

During the 1980s, the Gaithers' continued popularity helped them overcome criticism they were introducing elements of popular music into their gospel performances. Gaither created the New Gaither Vocal Band in 1981 and expanded the group's range of music styles throughout the decade. He also became president of Gaither Music Company, his music publishing business, and a distribution company, Alexandria House.

In 1995, Gaither was a featured performer at the National Religious Broadcasters national convention in Nashville, Tennessee. With his wife, Gaither continues to be a dominant force in contemporary gospel music.

Gaither's variety show on TBN, *Bill Gaither*, features musical performances by the Gaithers and their special guests.

SOURCES

Banas, Casey. "Bill and Gloria Gaither: They Sing the Way You Feel." *Christian Life*, August, 1978.

"Casting Call for NRB 95." *Religious Broadcasting*, February, 1995.

Gaither, Gloria. *Fully Alive*. Nashville: Thomas Nelson, 1984.

GATEWAY TO JOY

Hosted by the famed missionary to Ecuador and author, Elisabeth Elliot, *Gateway to Joy* is a 15-minute radio program that emphasizes conservative "family values" and traditional roles for the contemporary Christian woman. The show is one of two programs that were launched in the 1980s by the Back to the Bible Ministries of Lincoln, Nebraska, an evangelical organization that seeks to help Christians mature in their faith by applying biblical principles to their everyday lives.

See also Elisabeth Elliot

SOURCES

Melton, J. Gordon. *Directory of Religious Organizations in the United States*. 3d ed. Detroit: Gale Research, 1993.

DAN GILBERT
born: 1911
died: 1962

A vigorously pro-American Baptist minister and fiery communicator, Dan Gilbert was founder and host of *Prisoners Bible Broadcast* from 1949 until his untimely death in 1962.

Gilbert had appeared as a conference speaker for a number of years and was heard over radio throughout the 1940s. When he began receiving letters from prison inmates asking for Bibles, Gilbert relayed the need to his faithful listeners. From the donations sent to him by supporters, Gilbert began his radio broadcast ministry from Los Angeles in 1949, which reached federal and state prisoners throughout the region.

In addition to his radio ministry, Gilbert served for a time as secretary of the World Christian Fundamentals Association. He also worked to deliver Bibles to prisoners and to offer prison inmates correspondence courses. Moreover, Gilbert authored numerous books on anti-Communist and apocalyptic themes.

The evangelist's sudden death in 1962 did not end his radio ministry, however. Leadership of the broadcast ministry first passed to Chaplain Ray Hoekstra, who quickly renamed it *Christ Truth Radio Crusade*. In 1970, it passed to W. S. McBirnie, who remained its host until about 1974. After passing to a number of lesser-known hosts after 1974, the broadcast arm of Gilbert's ministry was abandoned, becoming simply a prison correspondence mission. In 1976, the prison outreach was renamed Christ Truth Ministries (CTM). Currently, CTM is directed from its headquarters in Upland, California, by Carl F. Davis.

See also Christ Truth Ministries

SOURCES

Billy Graham Center Archives, Wheaton College, Wheaton, Illinois.

Dollar, George W. *A History of Fundamentalism in America*. Greenville, SC: Bob Jones University Press, 1973.

The Directory of Religious Organizations in the United States. 2d ed. Falls Church, VA: McGrath, 1982.

Gilbert, Dan. *The Mark of the Beast.* Washington, DC: 1951.

———. *The Red Terror and Bible Prophecy.* Washington, DC: Christian Press Bureau, 1944.

Melton, J. Gordon. *Directory of Religious Organizations in the United States.* 3d ed. Detroit: Gale Research, 1993.

Roy, Ralph L. *Apostles of Discord.* Boston: Beacon Press, 1953.

Stone, Jon R. *A Guide to the End of the World: Popular Eschatology in America.* New York: Garland, 1993.

ANNE GIMINEZ

born: 1932

Anne Giminez is a Pentecostal evangelist and cofounder, with her husband John Giminez, of Rock Church, a 5,000-member church movement headquartered in Virginia Beach, Virginia. Giminez has also been a frequent guest on such religious television shows as *The 700 Club* and the cohost of *Rock Church*, which began airing in May of 1978. This television ministry features worship services at Rock Church and is designed to show the joy and spirit of the church's charismatic style of worship.

Giminez was born Anne E. Nethery in Corpus Christi, Texas. While working as an itinerant evangelist, she met and married John Giminez, a reformed drug addict from the Bronx. In taking this step, she had to contend with and overcome her parents' bigotry concerning Hispanic Americans and the advice of friends, who warned her against tainting herself by association with a former criminal.

The couple got their first break in broadcasting when they appeared on Pat Robertson's *The 700 Club* in 1968. John Giminez talked about his rescue from a life of heroin addiction, and Anne sang sacred hymns. The appearance went so well that the couple decided to continue their ministry by building a church in the Virginia Beach area. While looking for a suitable site, they stayed as guests in the home of Jim and Tammy Faye Bakker, who were employed by the Christian Broadcasting Network (CBN) at the time. The Giminezes found a white frame building a few blocks from CBN headquarters and began a ministry that would result in the establishment of more than 18 affiliated churches during the next 20 years. They also appeared as popular guests on subsequent airings of *The 700 Club*.

In its first few years, Rock Church was flooded by young people who were drawn to the Jesus Movement then sweeping the country. By 1971, the church had expanded to a five and one-half acre site on Kempsville Road. Within a short time, an education building had been added to the complex. During and perhaps because of the church's growth, Giminez had to contend with a number of conservative preachers who disapproved of her public preaching. One radio preacher went so far as to dub her "the witch of Kempsville." By May of 1977, the church had expanded to a 3,000-seat, round-shaped sanctuary that featured a 100-voice choir and orchestra.

With assistance from CBN's staff, Giminez and her husband began the television program *Rock Church* in 1978. The Rock Church ministry has since grown to include a Bible institute, a children's home in India, church-supported missionaries, and Rock Christian Academy. In 1986, the Giminezes launched the Rock Church Network, a 24-hour broadcasting ministry targeted at Hispanics.

Anne Giminez currently is seen on independent Christian television stations across the United States as the host of *Rock Church* on Sunday afternoons. The show's format features an animated and fiery sermon by Giminez to her church audience.

In addition to her ecclesiastical and broadcast duties, Giminez has always been a strong advocate of women. This conviction led her to publish *The Emerging Christian Woman* in the 1980s.

SOURCES

Hadden, Jeffrey K., and Anson Shupe. *Televangelism: Power and Politics on God's Frontier.* New York: Henry Holt, 1988.

Peterson, Richard G. "Electric Sisters." In *The God Pumpers*, edited by Marshall Fishwick and Ray B. Browne. Bowling Green, KY: Bowling Green State University Popular Press, 1987.

"GLOBAL MISSION"
aired: three-day event, March 1995

Billy Graham became the world's first electronic circuit rider when he broadcast his crusade from Hiram Bithorn Stadium in San Juan, Puerto Rico, via 30 satellites to 3,000 venues around the world. The three-day broadcast, called "Global Mission," enlisted the help of 47 interpreters in soundproof booths located at Robert Clemente Coliseum to transmit Graham's message to a total audience of 1 billion people in their native languages. The 47 on-site translators were aided by people in 29 time zones who assisted in translating the message into 117 languages in 185 countries. "Global Mission" was heard by an estimated 10 million people around the globe, including an average of 35,000 over three evenings in Puerto Rico. The Faith and Values Network and the Trinity Broadcasting Network carried the crusade live into North America on all three evenings.

See also Billy Graham; "Mission without Walls"

SOURCES
"Now!" *Religious Broadcasting*, June, 1995.

GLOBAL OUTREACH MISSION
established: 1943

Global Outreach Mission (GOM) is an evangelical Protestant organization whose mission is to spread the gospel around the world. Founded in 1943 as the European Evangelistic Crusade, GOM expanded its original work in Canada and France to include other French-speaking nations in Africa and the Caribbean. The ministry is currently headquartered in Buffalo, New York, and active in 26 French-speaking countries.

The main focus of GOM's ministry is the distribution of evangelistic literature, the planting of new churches, and the provision of medical and educational services. GOM also sponsors French-language radio ministries in Quebec (including production of Canada's *National Bible Hour*), France and other parts of Western Europe, and sections of Africa, the West Indies, and Bangladesh.

SOURCES
Melton, J. Gordon. *Directory of Religious Organizations in the United States.* 3d ed. Detroit: Gale Research, 1993.

RICK GODWIN

Televangelist Rick Godwin appears weekly on the Trinity Broadcasting Network with his program *Reaching Higher with Rick Godwin*. The show's format follows that of other evangelist teachers. Godwin is seated in a comfortable den setting and spends most of the program expounding his conservative evangelical interpretations of the Bible. Godwin is the founder of Eagle Ministries International (EMI), established in 1984, and The Eagle's Nest Christian Fellowship in San Antonio, Texas.

EMI is a team of pastors, ministers, teachers, and prophets who minister together to advance their vision of the Kingdom of God in the world. Each member of the team is based in a local church. According to Godwin, the purpose of EMI is to proclaim "God's desire for a strong, glorious church across the nation and around the world." The ministry accomplishes this purpose through two primary means. First, it organizes national and regional conferences in which EMI members work together and share in their areas of "gifting and anointing." Second, EMI goes into individual churches upon invitation and ministers to the needs of those congregations.

EMI is actively engaged in developing its own regional churches, starting new churches "that will have the ability to effectively affect their local areas for the Kingdom of God," and in providing oversight and guidance to ministers who seek to develop their own congregations. In addition, EMI tithes from its resources to support Compassion Ministries in Zimbabwe, Africa. Compassion Ministries, under the direction of its founders, Tom and Bonnie Deuschle, provides food and clothing aid to needy children and their families. They also organize children's schools with a strong biblical emphasis.

The various members of EMI's team are actively involved with nearly 40 different churches in the United States and abroad. Rick Godwin serves as EMI's team leader and is assisted by Andrew Shearman, Alan Vincent, Bob Nichols, Ron Corzine, Greg Manalli, and Charles Stock. The ministry also markets an extensive catalogue of books, cassettes, and videotapes.

Godwin summarizes EMI's sense of mission in promotional literature as follows:

> It is imperative that we understand that the greatest need of man today is to rediscover the Kingdom of God. . . . The Kingdom has been modified and diluted into a personal spiritual place of reward in heaven, thereby reducing the Kingdom and rendering it innocuous. . . . For the Church to be relevant in this generation, [therefore,] it must make the Kingdom the same priority that Jesus made it: supreme.

Some of Godwin's rhetoric resonates with the dominion theology of Rousas John Rushdoony, Greg Bahnsen, and Gary North. Dominion theology seeks to reconstruct American society along the lines explicitly set forth in the Law of Moses. Although Godwin does not openly espouse this theology, his call for a realization of the Kingdom of God in the modern world has similar implications for modern society. For example, he advocates the substitution of ancient Mosaic law for the US Constitution and the reinstatement of the death penalty for a host of offenses.

SOURCES

The Eagle's Nest Christian Fellowship. Promotional literature, 1994.

JOHN WASHINGTON GOODGAME

John Washington Goodgame began his adult life as a professional baseball player. After retiring from baseball and gaining ministerial credentials, he pastored the Sixth Avenue Baptist Church of Birmingham, Alabama. During his tenure as pastor, Goodgame decided to try his hand at radio evangelism. Station WVOK broadcast his hour-long Sunday radio programs throughout the 1940s and 1950s. It is estimated that his audience numbered around 750,000 at the height of his fame. Goodgame went on to serve in administrative positions in the National Baptist Convention, USA, including the Commission on Undergraduate Scholarships.

SOURCES

"Top Radio Ministers." *Ebony* 4 (July 1949): 56–61.

MARVIN GORMAN
born: 1933, Arkansas

Marvin Gorman was a popular televangelist and pastor of a 5,000-member Assemblies of God church in New Orleans, Louisiana, when he was summoned, in July of 1986, to a makeshift tribunal at Jimmy Swaggart's First Assembly headquarters in Baton Rouge. Swaggart confronted Gorman with rumors of his (Gorman's) adulteries. Swaggart then passed these rumors on to the Assemblies of God national hierarchy. Gorman was forced to resign his ministry immediately and was defrocked by the Assemblies a week later. Within a short time, Gorman's radio and television programs (including *Good News America* and *Marvin Gorman Presents*), which were being beamed into 400 American cities, had been canceled. Moreover, his congregation abandoned him, his schools were closed, and he was forced to file for bankruptcy. The former rising star in televangelism circles was reduced to preaching out of a swimming-pool supply warehouse to a small core of followers.

Two years after his public humiliation, Gorman retaliated by releasing photos of Swaggart coming out of a motel room following an alleged encounter with a prostitute. Gorman also filed a $90 million defamation suit against Swaggart's camp for spreading false rumors concerning Gorman's alleged infidelities, his siring of illegitimate children, the theft of church funds, and Mafia connections. Gorman's attorneys hinted that his television programs, which competed with Swaggart's, had been dropped from the PTL satellite network as a quid pro quo for Swaggart's silence about the network's payment of hush money to a woman who had had a sexual encounter with PTL President Jim Bakker. Following the suit's final settlement, Gorman received $185,000 of the requested $90 million.

With this money, Gorman made a cautious comeback. He now pastors a new congregation, the Temple of Praise, on Elysian Fields Avenue, the same New Orleans site where he established his first church in 1965. Moreover, he has been accepted into the World Bible Way Fellowship, a well-respected 2,000-member nondenominational fellowship that is headquartered in Irving, Texas. Gorman is also back on television and radio with a Sunday morning program on New Orleans UHF Channel 38 and a weekday radio program on WVOG. The preacher's services continue to be dynamic productions filled with altar calls, spiritual healings, exorcisms, songs, and glossolalia (speaking in tongues).

See also Jimmy Swaggart

SOURCES

"God and Money Part 9." *Time*, July 22, 1991.

"Survival and Revival." *New Orleans Times Picayune*, November 20, 1994.

GOSPEL BILL SHOW

One of Trinity Broadcasting Network's most popular children's programs is the *Gospel Bill Show*, which currently airs twice every Satur-

day. The half-hour musical show features the Old West adventures of a lawman, Gospel Bill, as he battles unsavory criminals. During the 1970s and 1980s, the program was produced by the Willie George Ministries of Broken Arrow, Oklahoma. Like other Trinity children's shows, *Gospel Bill* tries to instill in children such moral values as honesty, diligence, respect for others, and patriotic pride.

GOSPEL COMMUNICATIONS NETWORK
established: 1995

The Gospel Communications Network is a groundbreaking foray of Christian ministries into the fast-expanding world of the Internet. The network was launched in May of 1995 by Gospel Films and nine other Christian organizations. It makes a large range of materials available to Internet users, such as daily devotionals, multilanguage Bible translations, sermons, Bible lessons, and Christian cartoons. Such nationwide ministries as *Radio Bible Class*, *The Children's Bible Hour*, InterVarsity Christian Fellowship, and the International Bible Society are active participants in the network.

SOURCES

"Gospel Communications Network Online Christian Resources." World Wide Web site. http://www.gospelcom.net/ (1996).

GOSPEL SINGING JUBILEE
first aired: 1964

Gospel Singing Jubilee began as a gospel music program on local television stations in the South. Several national advertisers sponsored the program and received free advertising time in return for the show's free distribution. During its run in national syndication, *Gospel Singing Jubilee* aired in an average of 50 television markets. The star-studded showcase for gospel music stars became the highest-rated program of religious music in the industry, claiming 1 million viewers in February of 1980. Although an occasional testimony could be heard, the program was entertainment pure and simple for America's substantial gospel-music subculture. During the mid-1980s, *Gospel Singing Jubilee* was absorbed by the Nashville Network cable channel.

SOURCES

Bruce, Steve. *Pray TV: Televangelism in America.* New York: Routledge, 1990.

Hadden, Jeffrey K., and Charles E. Swann. *Prime Time Preachers: The Rising Power of Televangelism.* Menlo Park, CA: Addison-Wesley, 1981.

Hoover, Stewart M. *Mass Media Religion: The Social Sources of the Electronic Church.* Newbury Park, CA: Sage, 1988.

GRACE TO YOU
first aired: 1969

Hosted by fundamentalist preacher John MacArthur, Jr., *Grace to You* is a syndicated half-hour radio program that airs daily in the United States and throughout the world. Broadcasting since 1978, *Grace to You* began in 1969 as a modestly managed tape ministry at MacArthur's Los Angeles–based Grace Community Church. When church leaders learned that MacArthur's taped sermons were being played on the air at a small Christian station in Maryland, the idea for a radio program took shape. Soon, Grace Community Church was producing and distributing broadcast tapes throughout the United States. By 1980, *Grace to You* was one of the most popular radio-teaching programs in the nation, and John MacArthur was one of the top-10 radio preachers.

Similar to James Montgomery Boice's *The Bible Study Hour*, *Grace to You* features half-hour segments of expository Bible sermons by MacArthur. In each message, MacArthur progresses verse-by-verse through one passage or paragraph of the Bible at a time.

At present, *Grace to You* is heard over nearly 650 radio stations and serves an estimated daily audience of 2 million listeners. MacArthur's taped messages number almost 2,500 separate sermon titles with a circulation of more than 9 million tapes. In addition to his sermons, MacArthur has authored a number of popular books, many in translation. Some of his better selling titles include *God with Us, The Gospel according to Jesus, The Master's Plan for the Church*, and a number of others on prophecy and the endtimes. *Grace to You*'s production headquarters are located in Valencia, California, near The Master's College and Seminary (formerly Los Angeles Baptist College), where MacArthur is president.

SOURCES

MacArthur, Jr., John. *The Future of Israel.* Chicago: Moody Press, 1991.

———. *The Second Coming of the Lord Jesus Christ.* Panorama City, CA: Word of Grace Communication, 1981.

BILLY GRAHAM
born: November 7, 1918, Charlotte, North Carolina

Courtesy: National Religious Broadcasters

William "Billy" Frank Graham is probably the most highly respected and admired televangelist in modern history. His "crusades" have been personally witnessed by an estimated 100 million individuals. Countless others have heard his conservative evangelical message over radio and television. Along with Bishop Fulton J. Sheen and Oral Roberts, Graham was one of the first religious television superstars, a position he has retained during his 35 years of active television ministry.

Billy Graham was reared in a strict Presbyterian family in rural North Carolina. His father was William Franklin Graham, a dairy farmer, and his mother Morrow Coffey. At the age of 16, Graham attended an evangelistic revival under the direction of Mordecai F. Ham. The future evangelist experienced a conversion to Christ and two years later enrolled in classes at Bob Jones College in Cleveland, Tennessee. This stronghold of fundamentalist Christianity, would have a profound impact on Graham's religious worldview, though Graham would later eschew Jones's uncompromising separatism from mainline denominations. His stay at Bob Jones lasted only a year, and in 1937 Graham transferred to Florida Bible Institute in Tampa. It was during his time in Florida that the young Graham committed himself to a preaching ministry and joined the Southern Baptist Convention.

After graduation, Graham moved to Illinois and enrolled in Wheaton College. There he met Ruth Bell, the daughter of Presbyterian missionaries to China, and married her shortly after each graduated in 1943. Graham's first ministerial position was at a small church in Chicago. During this time the dynamic radio preacher Torrey M. Johnson persuaded Graham to take charge of his local religious radio show on WCFL, *Songs in the Night*. The young pastor recruited George Beverly Shea, an admired singer on WMBI, and the two began a long and fruitful association. Johnson convinced Graham to join the staff of his newly organized Youth for Christ movement in 1944 and to accompany him on two evangelistic trips to England in 1946–1947. At the end of Graham's last trip

abroad, the Baptist evangelist William Bell Riley asked him to take over his position as president of the Northwestern Bible College and Theological Seminary in Minneapolis, Minnesota. Graham accepted the offer and moved his family to Minneapolis. He retained this post for four years and made Minneapolis the headquarters of his emerging evangelistic enterprises.

Northwestern College was in the process of applying for a radio station license when Graham assumed the institution's leadership. Thanks to the efforts of George Wilson (who would later become executive vice president of Graham's evangelistic empire), station KTIS began broadcasting from the college during Graham's tenure. KTIS would go on to become the cornerstone of a nine-station network and a respected producer of religious radio and television programming.

It was during Graham's evangelistic campaign in Los Angeles in the summer of 1949 that William Randolph Hearst decided to feature the fiery young preacher in his newspapers. The planned two-week revival extended to two months, and over 350,000 men, women, teenagers, and children attended the event. Following this successful crusade, Graham became a highly sought after preacher. His belief in the Bible's true witness strengthened, and his crusades took on a new fire and conviction. Within a short time he was a nationally known figure, appearing on the covers of *Time*, *Newsweek*, and, later, *Life* magazines.

In 1950, Graham attended a pastors' conference in Ocean City, New Jersey. During the conference, he was approached by Theodore Elsner, the president of National Religious Broadcasters. Elsner was convinced that God had chosen Graham to fill the shoes of the recently deceased Walter Maier, the nationally-respected voice of *The Lutheran Hour*. Graham was intrigued about the possibility of having his own national radio program and met with Walter F. Bennett, a powerhouse in religious radio, and Fred Dienert (Elsner's son-in-law) at a subsequent Bible conference in Michigan to discuss the matter further. Bennett and Dienert offered to help Graham start his own radio ministry, but the young evangelist balked when he realized the time commitment that a weekly program would require.

Bennett and Dienert were undeterred by Graham's initial reticence and appeared two weeks later at his home in Montreat, North Carolina. They announced that for $92,000 they could arrange a 13-week nationally broadcast series on ABC radio. The programs would air at a peak listening hour on Sunday afternoons. Graham was completely intimidated by the financial commitment the proposal entailed and again balked. The two advertising men continued to pursue Graham, contacting him by telegram and telephone at a subsequent Portland, Oregon, crusade. They argued that, after an initial payment of $25,000 to get the program on the air, audience contributions would more than meet the show's $7,000 weekly cost. When the two men arrived at Graham's Portland hotel to discuss the matter further, the ambivalent evangelist refused to see them for a week.

In the meantime, a wealthy friend of Graham's called to offer him $2,000 to establish a radio fund. Graham finally agreed to meet with Bennett and Dienert and discussed the possibility of asking other wealthy donors to subsidize the radio ministry. Dienert in particular was against this idea and suggested instead that Graham tell his crusade audience that night about the proposed program. Graham asked the two men to pray with him. He ended the prayer by declaring, "I want You to give me a sign and I'm going to put out the fleece. The fleece is for $25,000 by midnight."

Bennett and Dienert attended the crusade that evening and were disappointed when Graham declined to mention the program before the offering was taken. Instead he waited until after the offering to discuss the broadcasting opportunity and invited anyone who was interested to meet with him when the service was over. The discouraged partners doubted many people would take Graham up on his offer and were flabbergasted when a large crowd later assembled outside the office door. A staff member passed around a shoe box that was quickly filled with cash and pledges scribbled on pro-grams and hymn sheets. At evening's end, $23,500 had been collected. Bennett and Dienert rejoiced and called it a miracle. But Graham was unconvinced. "No, it's not a miracle," he contended. "The devil could send $23,500. It's all or nothing." Just when it appeared that the radio ministry would never happen, associate evangelist Grady Wilson collected three letters from the hotel desk and brought them to Graham's suite. One letter was from another city pledging $1,000 for a radio program featuring Graham's sermons and the other two contained checks for $250.

Finally convinced that the program was God's will, Graham lost no time in founding the Billy Graham Evangelistic Association and beginning broadcasts of *Hour of Decision*. The program's first broadcast occurred on Sunday, November 5, 1950. It featured Graham's sermon at an Atlanta crusade and was heard over 150 ABC radio network stations. Within weeks the program had garnered an unprecedented audience of over 20 million people. After its first year more than 200,000 listeners had sent the association letters, which testified to the positive impact the broadcasts were having in their personal lives. By 1952, the show was drawing larger audiences than the Sunday news broadcasts, and by 1978, 900 radio stations around the world were airing the program. Although the number of stations carrying *Hour of Decision* decreased to 620 by 1988, the program ranks second only to *Lutheran Hour* in terms of national distribution.

Hour of Decision's format has remained the same since its inception. Graham or a guest preacher chooses an issue or event of contemporary concern and offers traditional biblical insight into the problem. The show emphasizes that only the Christian gospel can bring healing and resolution to humanity's present crises. Preparation for *Hour of Decision* became a major investment of time and resources for the Graham organization, with an average of two days being dedicated to the weekly addresses.

Graham resigned from the Northwestern College and Seminary in 1951 so that he could dedicate himself full-time to his evangelical ministries. He launched his daily "My Answer" newspaper column in 1952 and published his best-selling book, *Peace with God*, in 1953. A major breakthrough occurred in 1955 when Graham's crusade in England was broadcast countrywide on Good Friday. The acknowledged impact of this venture catapulted Graham to the international stage and created an opportunity to televise his Madison Square Garden crusade on ABC-TV beginning June 1, 1957. For 17 straight Saturdays the crusade was carried nationally, further solidifying Graham's reputation as the country's foremost evangelist. The pictures of a huge live audience responding to Graham's preaching gave evangelical broadcasting an immediacy and power it had never previously possessed. As Tedd Seelye wrote,

> When the average, moral, reputable American sees Dr. Graham in a studio telling him he needs to be "born again" his first impulse will be to discredit him as a religious fanatic. But if the viewer sees thousands of respectable, normal people listening and consenting . . . and then sees hundreds voluntarily get up and walk to the front in response to a low-pressure request, he'll begin to consider the message and situation with some sincere, honest interest. It's much easier to say a single speaker is wrong than to discredit the conviction and decision of thousands.

Graham's large televised crusades, which use electronic amplification and modern theatrical lighting, have become a mainstay of his evangelical ministry. Often staged in sports arenas and stadiums, these events have reached a worldwide audience estimated in the hundreds of millions. Each crusade produces thousands of personal decisions for Christ. Local ministers from many denominations regularly report a sharp rise in church attendance following the crusades.

The typical televised crusade opens with cameras panning a quickly filling athletic stadium. As crowds stream into the entrances, song leader Cliff Barrows directs his volunteer choir of several hundred in such revivalist standards as "How Great Thou Art." When the crowds have taken their seats, George Beverly Shea and other popular singers perform solos and give personal testimonies. When this "warm-up" is finished, Graham ascends the stage and begins to preach. His basic message of "Repent and be born again" has not changed in 40 years.

At the end of a typical crusade, Graham invites the audience to "come forward to Christ." Counselors and choir members immediately move forward, creating "an illusion of a spontaneous and mass response to the invitation." Each of these co-workers has been strategically assigned seating in a section of the stadium and instructed to come forward in a staggered sequence. Many in the audience are genuinely moved by this seemingly spontaneous response to Graham's message and join the crowds of individuals moving toward the center of the stadium from all directions. The televised impact of this seeming outpouring of charismatic power is enough to generate many thousands of letters to Graham after each crusade reporting personal conversions. In spite of the huge success of his televised crusades, Graham has never launched a weekly television show.

Graham tends not to address contemporary social ills in his crusades, insisting that he is called to be a New Testament evangelist rather than an Old Testament prophet. His personalized call for individual conversion to Jesus Christ has prompted criticism from critics who find his theology narrow and anachronistic. Graham ignores the criticisms and continues to create successful coalitions of local churches that handle logistical arrangements, supervise collections, and carry out follow-up activities. This policy of ecumenical cooperation during Graham's crusades led a number of fundamentalists to break with him in the late 1950s. They charged that the "decision cards" filled out during his altar calls were not being sent to conservative churches for follow-up ministering and that he was giving too much prominence to Protestant liberals. Graham was undeterred by these criticisms, agreeing with fellow evangelist Donald Grey Barnhouse that emphasis should be put on loving relationships among all Christians.

Graham became a major force in international evangelism during the late 1950s and early 1960s. He helped establish *Christianity Today* in 1956 and *Decision*, a magazine featuring Graham's own writings and news of his evangelical outreaches. *Christianity Today* has become a successful and influential evangelical periodical that attempts to live up to Graham's vision of it as "the finest journal in the Western world, comparable to what *Time* is in current events." In 1960, Graham convened the first of many important international congresses on evangelism in Montreaux, Switzerland. Other congresses followed in Berlin (1966) and Lausanne, Switzerland (1974). The most recent meeting, the International Conference of Itinerant Evangelists, was held in 1986 in Amsterdam, the Netherlands. In 1967, Graham founded the Billy Graham School of Evangelism in North Carolina to train ministers and lay workers in effective evangelical outreach.

The Graham association's strict standards of financial accountability have become a benchmark of honesty and integrity for other televangelistic enterprises. Graham's business manager was a leader in the formation of the Evangelical Council for Financial Accountability. This council was given an added impetus after Graham observed on national television that "there are some charlatans coming along and the public ought to be informed about them and warned against them." The Graham organization sends out a copy of its yearly audit to anyone who requests it.

Although he was embarrassed during the early 1970s when the Nixon administration used him as a pious smoke screen to cover its Watergate machinations, Graham emerged unscathed during the 1980 scandals that rocked televangelism. As one commentator wrote,

> Amid the scandals of the late 1980s, Graham stood like an honest and humble giant among seemingly hypocritical and arrogant broadcasters such as Bakker, Roberts, and Swaggart. If some religious broadcasters represented the stereotypical [Elmer] Gantry [Sinclair Lewis's archetypal sawdust trail charlatan], Graham's apparent moral rectitude symbolized the nation's longstanding appreciation of authentic piety and unpretentious religious devotion.

A lifelong anti-Communist, Graham nevertheless became a strong advocate for world peace and reconciliation between the former Soviet Union and the United States. He is one of the few American evangelists who was permitted to broadcast his religious crusades on Soviet television.

See also *Hour of Decision*; Billy Graham Evangelistic Association, "Global Mission"

SOURCES

Barnhart, Joe E. *The Billy Graham Religion.* Philadelphia: United Church Press, 1972.

Frady, Marshall. *Billy Graham: A Parable in American Righteousness.* Boston: Little, Brown, 1979.

Graham, Billy. *Peace with God.* Waco, TX: Word Books, 1953.

Hadden, Jeffrey K., and Charles E. Swann. *Prime Time Preachers: The Rising Power of Televangelism.* Menlo Park, CA: Addison-Wesley, 1981.

Hill, Samuel S., ed. *Encyclopedia of Religion in the South.* Macon, GA: Mercer University Press, 1984.

Inbody, Tyron, ed. *Changing Channels: The Church and the Television Revolution.* Dayton, OH: Whaleprints, 1990.

Lippy, Charles H. *Twentieth-Century Shapers of American Popular Religion.* New York: Greenwood Press, 1989.

Pollock, John. *Billy Graham: The Authorized Biography.* New York: McGraw-Hill, 1966.

Schultze, Quentin J. *American Evangelicals and the Mass Media.* Grand Rapids, MI: Zondervan, 1990.

———. *Televangelism and American Culture: The Business of Popular Religion.* Grand Rapids, MI: Baker Book House, 1991.

FRANKLIN GRAHAM
born: July 14, 1952, Montreat, North Carolina

Franklin Graham is the son and heir apparent of televangelist Billy Graham. By a unanimous vote of the 32-member board of directors of the Billy Graham Evangelistic Association (BGEA) on November 7, 1995, the younger Graham became BGEA's first vice chair. This position places him in direct succession to his father as BGEA's chair and chief executive officer.

BGEA is a nonprofit religious ministry that sponsors Billy Graham's preaching crusades and subsequent television broadcasts of those events. The association, which is one of the top four evangelical nonprofits in the United States, also sponsors the Billy Graham Evangelistic Training Center in Asheville, North Carolina; feature films from World Wide Pictures; the weekly radio broadcast *Hour of Decision*; and *Decision* magazine.

Franklin Graham was something of a rebel in his youth, gaining a reputation for chain smoking, hard drinking, and disciplinary problems. Following his expulsion from a technical college in Texas, he was converted to Christ in 1974. Within a short time he had become head of Samaritan's Purse (SP), a nonprofit Christian relief organization founded by Bob Pierce that provided relief to victims of famine and war around the world. Like another relief organization, World Vision, SP broadcasts regular television fundraising specials that feature various dimensions of the ministry's outreach. Graham continues to serve as SP's leader. The ministry currently has an annual budget of $22 million.

Graham also continues to serve as the head of World Medical Mission, a nonprofit Christian relief organization that specializes in providing humanitarian aid to such countries as Rwanda and Bosnia. Samaritan's Purse and World Medical Mission currently employ over 110 people combined, and are headquartered in Boone, North Carolina.

It was not until 1989 that Graham began to seriously consider a preaching ministry. John Wesley White, a part of BGEA's crusade team since the early 1960s, had convinced the younger Graham to speak at a rally in Canada in 1985, but the results were so humiliating that Graham vowed never to try again (no one came forward during the altar call). Four years later, again with White's encouragement, Graham agreed to devote 36 days a year to preaching. He now delivers sermons with his father's lilting voice, handsome appearance, and dynamic style.

Graham has limited his crusades to less-populated areas such as Bozeman, Montana, and Farmington, New Mexico. Eschewing the domed stadiums favored by his father, he typically appears in midsize gymnasiums and auditoriums. Beginning in October 1995, Graham began inviting his father to preach during his own four-day crusades. If the senior Graham's health holds up, the pair plan a crusade in New Zealand and Australia for late winter, 1996.

All four of Graham's siblings are also involved in evangelistic outreach. Gigi Tchividjian (50) works as an author and seminar speaker. Anne Graham Lotz (48) is a BGEA board member and founder of AnGeL Ministries in Raleigh, North Carolina. Ruth McIntyre (45) works for SP in Fort Defiance, Virginia, and Ned Graham (37) is president of East Gate Ministries, an outreach to missionaries in China, which is headquartered in Sumner, Washington.

Of his imminent succession to the leadership of BGEA, Graham says,

> I have not been asked to replace my father. If I had been asked to do that, I wouldn't, because I can't. But I have been asked to manage this organization and lead it. I'm committed to holding this organization together and keeping it in crusade evangelism.

It remains to be seen whether Franklin Graham will attain his father's mega-star status as a televangelist.

See also Billy Graham Evangelistic Association

SOURCES

Kennedy, John W. "The Son Also Rises." *Christianity Today*, December 11, 1995.

Samaritan's Purse. Promotional brochures, 1995.

HEBER GRANT

born: March 22, 1856, Salt Lake City, Utah Territory
died: May 14, 1945, Salt Lake City, Utah

The seventh president of the Church of Jesus Christ of Latter-day Saints, Heber Jeddy Grant was also a pioneer in the use of radio to propagate the Mormon religious message.

Grant grew up in the Utah Territory before statehood, the son of Jedediah Grant and Rachel Ivins. He was the first president of the church to be born in Utah and the first never to have known the Mormon prophet Joseph Smith. Grant's father, a Church Apostle, died eight days after Grant's birth. The future Mormon leader was raised by his mother during the church's period of consolidation and missionary expansion. Early childhood illnesses and an astigmatism interrupted Grant's normal educational and social development; he would work hard to overcome these disabilities throughout his youth.

In 1871, Grant found a job as an office boy and sold insurance on the side. In 1877, he married Lucy Stringham. In 1880, at the age of 24, Grant put together a business syndicate that purchased $350,000 worth of stock in Zion's Cooperative Mercantile Institution (ZCMI), the leading business corporation of the region. Business successes led to Grant's appointment to the presidency of the State Bank of Utah, and of the Home Fire Insurance Company, and to the incorporation of his own company, the Heber J. Grant Insurance Company.

In 1884, Grant married a second and a third wife, Hulda Winters and Emily Wells. His position in the church progressively improved from stake president in 1880, to Apostle in 1882, to president of the Quorum of the Twelve Apostles in 1916. In November 1918, upon the death of Mormon president Joseph F. Smith (b. 1838), son of the Mormon prophet Joseph Smith, Grant assumed leadership of the Church, a position he held until his death over a quarter of a century later.

During his long tenure as president, church membership almost doubled in size. A keen businessman, Grant saw to the further rationalization and bureaucratization of the Mormon Church as well as its adoption of modern technologies, including radio, to propagate its message. It was Grant himself who inaugurated the first radio broadcast in Utah, in 1922, atop the Deseret News Building in Salt Lake City.

Grant died having spent the last five years of his life as a semi-invalid nearly unable to discharge the duties of church president.

SOURCES

Alexander, Thomas G. *Mormonism in Transition: A History of the Latter-day Saints, 1890–1930.* Urbana, IL: University of Illinois Press, 1986.

Melton, J. Gordon. *Religious Leaders of America.* Detroit: Gale Research, 1991.

GREATER CHICAGO BROADCAST MINISTRIES

An ecumenical communications ministry, the Greater Chicago Broadcast Ministries assists local Protestant and Orthodox Christian groups in the production and broadcast of television programs over Chicago-based stations and cable networks. Its programs include *Different Drummers* (WBBM-TV), a contemporary-issues program that targets teens and young adults; *Heritage of Faith* (WGBO-TV), which features the more traditional format of religious music and inspirational message; *Sanctuary* (WLS-TV), a video journal program; and *Sunday Chronicles* (WMAQ-TV), a program that follows the popular audience-response talk show format.

SOURCES

Melton, J. Gordon. *Directory of Religious Organizations in the United States.* 3d ed. Detroit: Gale Research, 1993.

GREATER LOVE MINISTRIES
established: 1970

Headquartered in Falls Church, Virginia, Greater Love Ministries (GLM) is an independent Pentecostal organization that works to expose cult movements, the occult, and "false" religions, and to educate people concerning the dangers they pose to traditional Christian faith. Originally, GLM published books and tracts attacking Christian Science, Jehovah's Witnesses, Mormons, Asian religious ideas, and New Age spiritual practices (to name just a few). It also made wide use of radio broadcasting, its programs airing throughout the eastern seaboard and in Tennessee.

By the end of 1995, GLM had ended its radio broadcast ministry and planned to move its entire cult awareness information network to the Internet. The reason for this change was GLM's desire to reach people beyond traditional Christian networks. GLM is now expanding its efforts to non-Christians who may have questions about religion but are more likely to "surf the 'net" for answers than tune into a Christian radio station.

SOURCES

Melton, J. Gordon. *Directory of Religious Organizations in the United States.* 3d ed. Detroit: Gale Research, 1993.

THE GREATEST STORY EVER TOLD
first aired: 1947

Fulton Oursler's best-selling book, *The Greatest Story Ever Told*, became the basis for a half-hour weekly radio program of the same name during the late 1940s and early 1950s. The program, which was sponsored by Goodyear Tires, premiered on January 26, 1947, over the ABC radio network. Each episode was cowritten by Oursler (who also worked as *Reader's Digest*'s religion editor) and respected radio writer Harry Denker. The program attempted to make the teachings of Christ relevant to the challenges of modern life. Warren Parker was given the role of Jesus, marking the first time in national religious radio that anyone had ever been so honored (or courageous). The respected radio ministry ran until 1956 and was used by some denominations as a Bible-study aid.

SOURCES

Erickson, Hal. *Religious Radio and Television in the United States, 1921–1991.* Jefferson, NC: McFarland, 1992.

OLIVER GREENE
born: 1915

Oliver B. Greene has been heard nationwide on his radio program, *The Gospel Hour*, since the 1960s. In the two decades preceding this broadcasting outreach, the Baptist minister traveled the country as a tent revivalist. Greene has typically focused his broadcasts on prophecy and the imminent apocalypse.

SOURCES

Greene, Oliver B. *Bible Prophecy.* Greenville, SC: The Gospel Hour, Inc., 1970.

———. *The Second Coming of Jesus.* Greenville, SC: The Gospel Hour, Inc., 1971.

Stone, Jon R. *A Guide to the End of the World: Popular Eschatology in America.* New York: Garland, 1993.

GUIDO EVANGELISTIC ASSOCIATION
established: 1957

Founded by its director, the Reverend Michael Guido, the Guido Evangelistic Association is a nonprofit Christian organization located in Metter, Georgia, that aims to present the gospel to the world through newspaper, radio, and television. The ministry produces a variety of radio programs hosted by Guido, nicknamed "The Sower," including *A Seed from the Sower*, a one-minute radio spot that features a daily inspirational thought; *Seeds from the Sower*, a five-minute daily song and meditation program; *The Sower*, a 15-minute radio broadcast that has been airing nationally since 1958; and *The Sower 25*, a weekly program that features a half-hour sermon. All of these programs aim at presenting the gospel in the form of positive, inspirational, and life-affirming devotional thoughts.

Currently, the Guido Evangelistic Association also produces a one-minute television message, entitled *A Seed for the Garden of Your Heart,* which first aired in the late 1980s. One unique aspect of the Guido Evangelistic Association is that they receive enough contributions to continue broadcasting even though they don't make financial requests over the air.

SOURCES

Guido, Michael, and Audrey Guido. *Seeds from the Sower: The Michael and Audrey Guido Story.* Nashville: Thomas Nelson, 1990.

Melton, J. Gordon. *Directory of Religious Organizations in the United States.* 3d ed. Detroit: Gale Research, 1993.

E. BRANDT GUSTAVSON

born: June 2, 1936, Rockford, Illinois

Courtesy: National Religious Broadcasters

E. Brandt Gustavson has had a long and distinguished career in radio broadcasting and educational administration. After brief studies at Northwestern College in St. Paul, Minnesota, and Loyola University in Chicago, Gustavson began his religious broadcasting career in the 1950s on short-wave radio over the Trans World Radio service.

In 1960, he began his 20-year service with the Moody Bible Institute (MBI) as manager of its Cleveland radio station, WCRF. In 1967, he became director of MBI's broadcasting network and, from 1974 to 1986, served as vice president of the institute. From 1967 to 1968, Gustavson also served as station manager for the Billy Graham Evangelistic Association's Honolulu AM-FM radio complex, KAIM.

In 1982, while at Moody, Gustavson was appointed to a three-year term as chair of the National Religious Broadcasters. From 1986 to 1990, Gustavson returned to Trans World Radio, this time serving briefly as its executive vice president. During this period, he also served as a trustee for the Back to the Bible Broadcasts. In 1990, Gustavson was appointed executive director (now titled president) of National Religious Broadcasters, succeeding Ben Armstrong, and remains the president as of this writing.

See also National Religious Broadcasters

SOURCES

Ward, Mark, Sr. *Air of Salvation: The Story of Christian Broadcasting.* Grand Rapids., MI: Baker Book House, 1994.

Who's Who in Religion. 4th ed. Wilmette, IL: Marquis, 1993.

H

BEN HADEN
born: 1925, Fincastle, Virginia

Courtesy: *Changed Lives*

Host of *Changed Lives* since its radio debut in 1968, Ben Haden was born in Virginia, the only child of Benjamin and Anne Haden. As a boy, Haden was greatly impressed by the deep religious faith of his mother, who died of cancer while Haden was still young. Before finishing grade school, the boy lost his father as well. Haden attended a variety of churches during this early period of his life and was taught to respect several Protestant traditions.

After graduation from high school in Houston, Texas, in 1943, Haden attended the University of Texas, where he earned a bachelor's degree in 1947. In 1949, he was awarded a law degree from Washington and Lee College and became a member of the Virginia bar. The young lawyer took a job as a gasoline distributor the same year and married Charlyne Edwards in 1950. In 1951, he joined the CIA and served throughout the Korean War.

While living in Washington, DC, during the early 1950s, Charlyne Haden attended a Billy Graham crusade and was converted. When the Korean conflict ended, Ben Haden went into the newspaper business, becoming chief executive officer of the daily newspaper in Kingsport, Tennessee. In 1954, while working in journalism, Haden began attending the local Presbyterian church with his family. Impressed by the faith of an adult Sunday School teacher, he joined the church and decided to pursue a ministerial career.

To that end, Haden attended Columbia Theological Seminary in Decatur, Georgia, receiving a theology degree in 1963. He became minister of the Key Biscayne Presbyterian Church in Miami, Florida, that same year, and served there until 1967. During this period he was called to host the popular radio program *Bible Study Hour*. The position had been previously held by Donald Grey Barnhouse and, later, Reginald Thomas.

From 1965 to 1967, Haden traveled to Philadelphia to record his program. Scheduling conflicts and a call to pastor the First Presbyterian Church in Chattanooga, Tennessee, led to Haden's 1967 resignation from the show. The following year he began his own radio program, *Changed Lives*, broadcasting Sunday mornings over one station, WFLI, Knoxville, and gradually expanding the range of the half-hour program throughout the South.

Changed Lives features a conversational message on a topic of contemporary interest to both the churched and the unchurched. Haden aims his message primarily at men, believing that if he can capture their interest, he will win their wives and family to Christ as well. In 1970, Haden began broadcasting his program on cable television, using the same simple church-service format and informal style that was successful on radio. By the end of the decade, the weekly series was in national syndication. The program continues to be popular in the 1990s, holding fast to its song-and-sermon format.

SOURCES

Billy Graham Center Archives, Wheaton College, Wheaton, Illinois.

KENNETH HAGIN

born: August 20, 1917, McKinney, Texas

Courtesy: National Religious Broadcasters

Kenneth Erwin Hagin, Sr., was an itinerant healing evangelist in the 1950s who transformed his own experiences of spiritual healing into a popular broadcasting and publishing ministry during the 1960s and 1970s. By the 1980s, his

daily radio program *Faith Seminar of the Air* and his television show *Faith that Lives* were reaching millions of people with a message of the dynamic power of personal faith.

Hagin began life as a premature, less-than-two-pound baby who was given almost no chance of survival by the family doctor because of a congenital heart defect. Throughout his early years in rural east Texas, Hagin was forced, by his frail constitution, to live a lonely and bedridden existence. After his father deserted the family when he was six and his mother suffered a nervous breakdown, the sickly youth went to live with his stern grandparents. Hagin's condition suddenly took a turn for the worse during his fifteenth year. For 16 months he lay partially paralyzed in bed, wasting away to a body weight of 89 pounds. During this debilitating illness Hagin began reading the Bible and experienced a conversion to Christ. After contemplating Mark 11:24, "So I tell you, whatever you ask for in prayer, believe that you have received it, and it will be yours," he was gradually healed of his disability and resumed a normal life.

Hagin graduated from high school in McKinney and was called to minister at a Baptist church in nearby Roland. The fledgling preacher was reduced to memorizing verbatim the printed sermons of such homiletic masters as Charles Spurgeon since he lacked formal ministerial training. It was during his pastorship in Roland that Hagin first came into contact with Pentecostal teachers, who considered his recovery from illness an instance of divine healing. Within a short time, Hagin had decided to leave his own congregation and join the Assemblies of God (AOG). He underwent the baptism of the Holy Spirit, spoke in tongues, married a church member (Oretha Rooker), and gained AOG ministerial credentials. For the next 10 years, between 1937 and 1947, Hagin pastored small AOG congregations in east Texas. The young minister frequently ran into problems with church members because of his ignorance of biblical doctrines and his claims of special spiritual anointings. He gave up the settled ministry in 1947 and joined the growing ranks of traveling charismatic healers.

Moving in Pentecostal circles that included Oral Roberts, A. A. Allen, William Branham, and T. L. Osborn, Hagin distinguished himself more as a teacher with a folksy, amusing Texas style than as a spellbinding platform healer. He reported experiencing several "anointings" during this period, including one in which Jesus appeared to him and granted him a special gift of spiritual healing. This gift allowed him to see a fire jumping from one hand to another when a sick person before him was in need of an exorcism. Hagin also claimed that he had been given an anointing to prophesy, or speak on God's behalf to a congregation.

Hagin's career as an itinerant healer never reached beyond the small-town circuit in California and the Southwest. By the late 1950s, his ministry was accumulating greater and greater debts and drawing ever smaller audiences. At this point, Hagin decided to branch out into other evangelistic activities. He authored the first of many popular books, *Redeemed from Poverty, Sickness, and Death*, and became a regular guest speaker at meetings of the Full Gospel Businessmen's Fellowship. By 1962, he had withdrawn from membership in the Assemblies of God and formed his own independent organization, the Kenneth E. Hagin Evangelistic Association (later called Kenneth Hagin Ministries, Inc.). He next followed Oral Roberts's lead and moved his ministry to Tulsa, Oklahoma. In 1966, he gave the inaugural broadcast of his daily 15-minute radio program *Faith Seminar on the Air*. In time, this program would be carried on over 180 radio stations nationwide.

Hagin spent the next 10 years expanding his evangelistic empire. He created a monthly periodical, *Word of Faith*, in 1968, and began holding annual camp meetings in Tulsa during the early 1970s for his growing band of followers. During this same period, Hagin organized both the Rhema Bible Church and the Rhema Bible Training Center, a correspondence course and training facility. Participants in the center's two-year educational program lived on a $20 million, 80-acre campus outside Tulsa and studied Hagin's distinctive "Word of Faith" teachings.

These teachings claim that Christians have been granted the God-given power to pray for, and receive, the blessings of health, happiness, and prosperity. They also contend that the gift of divine healing is one of the blessings given to the human race (along with salvation and the forgiveness of sins) as the result of Christ's sacrificial atonement. In order to experience this healing, believers merely have to appropriate this blessing in full faith and to make a positive confession of their conviction. A third dimension of these teachings is the belief that "anointed" Christians have been given the authority to bind demonic forces in the holy name of Jesus.

These teachings, with their skillful blending of traditional Pentecostalism, New Thought mental hygienics, and biblical fundamentalism, quickly gained a mass following around the world. In 1987, the residential training center was enrolling about 2,000 students per year and the yearly old-fashioned camp meetings were attracting an average of 24,000 people. The correspondence course and the residential facility had trained a combined total of 16,000 students by the late 1980s. Among Hagin's more prominent students are the successful televangelists Kenneth Copeland and Fred Price.

It is estimated that the Hagin ministry sends out 4.2 million pieces of literature per year to a mailing list of over 400,000 and that the ministry's annual income from donations tops $14 million.

Aside from the 33 million copies of his 126 books that have been sold throughout the world, Hagin is perhaps best known as the voice of his weekly television program, *Faith that Lives*. Though not in the top-10 list of national religious television shows, the program has developed a loyal following and endured throughout the turmoil of the Jim Bakker–Jimmy Swaggart scandals in the 1980s.

Hagin is widely seen as the patriarch of the Faith movement, a distinction that has brought him both fame and criticism. He is credited with having brought Faith teachings into the mainstream of the charismatic movement and with having had an important influence on such Faith ministers as Copeland, Price, Jerry Savelle, Lester Sumrall, Robert Tilton, Ray Hicks, Marilyn Hickey, and Norvel Hayes.

The main criticisms of Hagin's Faith theology have come from fundamentalist Christian voices like the Christian Research Institute in San Juan Capistrano, California, Dave Hunt, Charles Farah, and the General Presbytery of the Assemblies of God. The main gist of these criticisms concern five alleged propositions of Hagin's teachings: 1) God is a kind of deistic creator figure who allows human beings to utilize spiritual laws for their personal benefit; 2) Christ himself had to be "born again" in hell before he could complete his divine mission; 3) spiritual revelation comes from within and can ignore the evidence of the physical senses; 4) salvation for humanity entails its gradual attainment of God-like powers; and 5) one can deny the physical manifestations of disease and reject conventional medicine.

Scholarly critiques of Hagin's doctrines maintain that his "name it, claim it" theology undercuts the doctrine of God's immutable sovereignty and makes a gratuitous presumption on divine grace. Instances of parents failing to get proper medical attention for their sick children and the children's subsequent deaths are also laid at Hagin's feet. A November 1980 meeting of the Society for Pentecostal Studies heard a paper describing Hagin's Faith teachings as "charismatic humanism" and "a burgeoning heresy." Dave Hunt and T. A. McMahon, in their book, *The Seduction of Christianity,* describe Faith teachings as a Christian-packaged version of the New Thought heresy. Other scholars have documented Hagin's alleged plagiarism of the writings of Essek William Kenyon and John A. MacMillan, particularly in such foundational Hagin books as *The Authority of the Believer.*

In spite of these criticisms, Hagin's ministry has continued to flourish into the 1990s. He has formed a loose coalition of Faith teaching ministers (many of whom are former students), the International Convention of Faith Churches and Ministers, and an evangelistic association, the Rhema Ministerial Association International.

Hagin also continues to preach, travel, and write. His Faith Library Publications publishes and distributes his many books. The aging evangelist has prepared for his eventual passing by making his son, Kenneth Hagin, Jr. his heir apparent at Kenneth Hagin Ministries, Inc.

See also A. A. Allen

SOURCES

Bruce, Steve. *Pray TV: Televangelism in America.* New York: Routledge, 1990.

Chappell, Paul G. "Kenneth Hagin, Sr." In *Twentieth-Century Shapers of American Popular Religion,* edited by Charles H. Lippy. Westport, CT: Greenwood Press, 1989.

Farah, Charles. "A Critical Analysis: The 'Roots and Fruits' of Faith-Formula Theology." *Society for Pentecostal Studies* (November, 1980).

———. *From the Pinnacle of the Temple.* Plainfield, TX: Logos International, 1979.

Hagin, Kenneth. *The Art of Intercession.* Tulsa, OK: Faith Library, 1981.

———. *Demons and How to Deal with Them.* Tulsa, OK: Faith Library, 1968.

———. *I Believe in Visions.* Old Tappan, NJ: Fleming H. Revell, 1972.

———. *Ministering to Your Family.* Tulsa, OK: Faith Library, 1986.

———. *The Ministry of a Prophet.* Tulsa, OK: 1960.

———. *The Real Faith.* Tulsa, OK: n.d.

———. *Redeemed from Poverty, Sickness, and Death.* Tulsa, OK: Faith Library, 1960.

———. *Seven Things You Should Know about Divine Healing.* Tulsa, OK: Faith Library, 1979.

———. *Understanding . . . Good Fight of Faith.* Tulsa, OK: Faith Library, 1987.

Hagin, Kenneth, Jr. *Kenneth E. Hagin's 50 Years in the Ministry: 1934–1984.* Tulsa, OK: Faith Library, 1984.

Hunt, Dave, and T. A. McMahon. *The Seduction of Christianity: Spiritual Discernment in the Last Days.* Eugene, OR: Harvest House, 1986.

McConnell, Daniel R. *A Different Gospel: The Cultic Nature of the Modern Faith Movement.* Peabody, MA: Hendrickson, 1988.

Matta, Judith A. *The Born-Again Jesus of the Word-Faith Teaching.* Fullerton, CA : Spirit of Truth, 1984.

H. R. HALL

The popular televangelist and faith healer Homer Richard Hall was born and raised in rural western North Carolina. He was greatly influenced by the dynamic faith of his widowed mother, a Baptist who converted to Pentecostalism and became a minister of the Church of God (Cleveland, Tennessee).

After receiving the baptism of the Holy Spirit at age 14, Hall began his own ministry, preaching on local street corners. Upon completion of high school, he enrolled in the Bible Training School of the Church of God of Prophecy (CGP). He spent additional time studying at the Atlanta Institute of Speech and Expression with the aim of becoming a lawyer until a bout with tuberculosis confined him to bed. Three months later, after a dramatic vision, Hall left his bed and launched a preaching career. At age 24, he was ordained to the Christian ministry by the CGP.

Hall served as CGP state overseer of Colorado until 1952, when he heard the voice of God calling him to preach deliverance. Resigning his position and his ordination in 1952, he pursued an evangelistic ministry independent of any denomination. For the remainder of his career, Hall preached mostly in small towns and rural regions of the country. In 1956, he founded the United Christian Ministerial Association (later United Christian Church and Ministerial Association) with the purpose of organizing other independent evangelists and unaffiliated churches. At the same time he inaugurated a news magazine, *The Healing Broadcast* (later *The Shield of Faith*), and launched a radio ministry that emphasized his message of spiritual healing. The radio broadcast was heard on numerous stations throughout the South. Hall also founded the United Christian Academy, a training center for ministers. By 1972, he had ordained more than 2,000 ministers.

During the 1960s, Hall identified with the concerns of the counterculture and began a ministry among street people and hippies. Though he cooperated with mainline Pentecostal and Holiness churches, he was never able to win their whole-hearted support. Hall began to back away from his radio program when he realized that the broadcast's distribution costs were placing unwanted limits on his live tent-revival ministry. He decreased the number of stations broadcasting his program from 100 to 15.

In the 1970s, Hall began a weekly television broadcast of his Sunday preaching and healing services. The broadcast continues to be syndicated to a select group of Southern cities. It features Hall's dramatic preaching and healing, as well as spirited musical interludes. Unlike some of his regional competitors, Hall's show has managed to retain the simple, primitive flavor of Appalachian Pentecostalism.

SOURCES

Burgess, Stanley M., and Gary B. McGee, eds. *Dictionary of Pentecostal and Charismatic Movements*. Grand Rapids, MI: Zondervan, 1988.

Erickson, Hal. *Religious Radio and Television in the United States, 1921–1991*. Jefferson, NC: McFarland, 1992.

Melton, J. Gordon. *Religious Leaders of America*. Detroit: Gale Research, 1991.

MORDECAI F. HAM
born: April 2, 1877, Scottsville, Kentucky
died: November 1, 1961, Pewell Valley, Kentucky

Independent Baptist minister and evangelist Mordecai F. Ham was the son of Tobias Ham and Ollie McElroy. The elder Ham was a Baptist minister, who claimed to be the seventh generation of a line of preachers descended from Roger Williams.

Mordecai Ham attended Ogden College in Bowling Green, Kentucky (later Western Kentucky University), after which time he moved to Chicago to pursue a career in business. From 1897 to 1900, Ham worked as a traveling salesman and then in a photo-enlarging firm before receiving a call to a preaching ministry. He married Bessie Simmons in July 1900 and returned to Bowling Green in 1901, where he was ordained to the Christian ministry and began his long career as an itinerant revivalist.

From 1901 until his wife's sudden death in 1905, Ham held continuous evangelistic meetings throughout the South. After a hiatus in the Holy Land, Ham returned to his work as a revivalist, meeting and marrying Annie Smith in 1908. An interruption of his evangelistic labors came when he accepted a call in 1927 from the First Baptist Church of Oklahoma City. He remained in this new position until 1929.

From 1929 to 1941, Ham conducted some 61 revival meetings in 15 states, converting an estimated 168,550 individuals to the gospel. Among his most famous converts was Billy Graham, who received the gospel during Ham's Charlotte, North Carolina, revival in 1934.

In order to gain publicity for his numerous evangelistic campaigns, Ham began a 20-year radio ministry in the early 1940s. The ministry bore fruit in numerous conversions and in an increasingly national profile for his evangelistic crusades.

Ham is best known for his strong attacks against evolution and Communism. He also ran afoul of liquor interests in the South, against whom he preached with relentless intensity. Ham received an honorary doctorate from Bob Jones University in 1935.

See also Billy Graham

SOURCES

Billy Graham Center Archives, Wheaton College, Wheaton, IL.

Reid, Daniel G., Robert D. Linder, Bruce L. Shelley, and Harry S. Stout, eds. *Dictionary of Christianity in America*. Downers Grove, IL: InterVarsity Press, 1990.

BILLY JAMES HARGIS
born: August 3, 1925, Texarkana, Texas

Billy James Hargis exemplifies a branch of religious broadcasting that, over the years, has combined American civil religion, fervent anti-Communism, and Fundamentalism into a potent brew of controversy and sectarian strife.

Reared in the "Dust Bowl" of north Texas during the worst years of the Depression, Hargis experienced a religious conversion and gained ministerial credentials from the Rose Hill Christian Church (independent) by the age of 18. For the next five years he pastored small churches in Oklahoma, Missouri, and Arkansas. He was fired from his first pastorate after admonishing the church's elders against attending movies and after accusing a local school principal of having a love affair with a teacher. During his pastorate in Arkansas, Hargis received a modicum of formal education at Ozark Bible College in Bentonville (1943–1944). He formed Christian Echoes National Ministry (later changed to Christian Crusade) in Tulsa, Oklahoma, in 1948.

The new ministry's stated mission was to do battle with "Communism and its godless allies." These "godless allies" and other enemies of America, in Hargis's view, included the American Civil Liberties Union, the National Association for the Advancement of Colored People, the United Nations, the national press, liberals, socialists, and the ecumenical National Council of Churches. When the World Council of Churches was formed in Amsterdam, Holland, in 1953, this body joined Hargis's "hit list" of Communist-front organizations. During the 1950s and 1960s, Hargis would add individual people to his list. Some of the more famous of these people included John and Robert Kennedy, Lyndon Johnson, Martin Luther King, Jr., and the Reuther brothers.

Hargis began a radio and television ministry in the 1950s and published *The Christian Crusade Newspaper*, a monthly periodical. His radio network broadcast a daily 15-minute program that gave Hargis a forum from which to attack the many "Communist-infiltrated" organizations he saw everywhere in the country.

These ventures into religious broadcasting were most popular during the pinnacle of the Cold War in the 1950s. However, even at the height of his popularity, Hargis never appealed to the huge audiences that Billy Graham, Robert Schuller, or Rex Humbard have been able to garner. His highly partisan religious-political message appealed only to radical fundamentalists and, in the end, began to alienate some Republican conservatives.

Hargis gained national attention in 1953 when he, together with the International Council of Christian Churches founder Carl McIntire, launched balloons carrying scriptural verses behind the Iron Curtain. He and McIntire also floated religious literature into Warsaw Pact countries from the East German border.

During the late 1950s and early 1960s, Hargis increased the number of stations carrying his radio and television programs and began a lucrative business selling medicines and vitamins (on radio and through direct advertising). By 1962, Hargis was being heard weekly over 200 radio stations in 46 states and seen on 12 television outlets serving 20 states. Also during this period, he became one of the early pioneers of direct-mail fundraising. As part of this initiative, he purchased and operated one of the first signature machines in this country. This made fundraising letters appear to be personally signed by Hargis.

After the election of John F. Kennedy and the rise of the counterculture in the 1960s, Hargis's hardball brand of religion began to lose favor. Because of his continued practice of attacking liberal political leaders on the air, his ministry lost its religious tax-exempt status in 1964. To adapt to new conditions, Hargis decided to withdraw from the Disciples of Christ denomination in 1966 and create an independent ministry in Tulsa, the Church of the Christian Crusade. As the country convulsed with violent demonstrations against the Vietnam War, Hargis held mass Christian Crusade rallies that featured retired military leaders such as General Edward Walker. These rallies succeeded in raising the funds necessary to keep Hargis's ministry alive during these lean times.

Hargis was also involved in the first test of the Federal Communications Commission's Fairness Doctrine (created in 1963). This doctrine stipulated that, when any broadcast program contained a personal attack on individuals or organizations, the station that carried the program was required to notify the attacked party of the broadcast within seven days and to offer airtime for a response. A Hargis broadcast in 1964 over radio station WGCB in Red Lion, Pennsylvania, pointedly attacked the author Fred J. Cook. When Cook became dissatisfied with his options of either paying for rebuttal time or proving that he was unable to pay, his complaint made it all the way to the Supreme Court. The Court, in this instance, affirmed the Fairness Doctrine in a decision handed down in 1967 and required that WGCB provide free airtime for Cook to rebut Hargis's charges.

In 1966, Hargis fulfilled a lifelong dream and inaugurated the conservative American Christian College in Tulsa. The school's avowed purpose was to teach "anti-Communist patriotic Americanism." In 1972, Hargis costarred with the college's coeducational glee club in the half-hour variety program, *Billy James Hargis and His All-American Kids.* The show was Hargis's first nationwide television outreach and added $100,000 to his monthly operating costs.

American Christian College flourished until 1974 when two students admitted to having had sexual relations with the evangelist. Hargis was forced by a coalition of leaders at the college to resign from his position. An attempt was made to avoid bad publicity by stating that Hargis had retired for health reasons. The evangelist attempted to regain the presidency of the college a year later but was unsuccessful. Without Hargis's fundraising skills, however, American Christian College was unable to attract the necessary operating funds and closed its doors in 1977.

Since the mid-1970s, Hargis has founded another ministry, the Billy James Hargis Evangelistic Association, and a charitable outreach, the Good Samaritan Children's Foundation. He has also conducted missionary work among the Native American population of the Southwest. Hargis's radio broadcasting outlets decreased to about 20 during the early 1980s. These stations were located, for the most part, in the South Central states.

During the early 1990s, Hargis operated his ministry from a farm in Neosho, Missouri. He publishes *Billy James Hargis' Christian Crusade* and continues to insist that "all I want to do is preach Christ and save America." Hargis has written over 16 books since 1960 through his Christian Crusade organization. The last of these books, *My Great Mistake* (1986), is his autobiography.

SOURCES

Bruce, Steve, *Pray TV: Televangelism in America.* New York: Routledge, 1990.

Dudman, Richard. *Men of the Far Right.* New York: Pyramid Books, 1962.

Foster, Arnold, and Benjamin Epstein. *Danger on the Right.* New York: Random House, 1964.

George, John, and Laird Wilcox. *Nazis, Communists, Klansmen, and Others on the Fringe: Political Extremism in America.* Buffalo: Prometheus, 1992.

Hadden, Jeffrey K., and Charles E. Swann. *Prime Time Preachers: The Rising Power of Televangelism.* Menlo Park, CA: Addison-Wesley, 1981.

Hargis, Billy James. *Communist America—Must It Be?* Tulsa, OK: Christian Crusade, 1960.

———. *The Cross and the Sickle—Super Church.* Tulsa, OK: Christian Crusade, 1982.

———. *Facts about Communism and the Churches.* Tulsa, OK: Christian Crusade, 1962.

———. *My Great Mistake.* Tulsa, OK: Christian Crusade, 1986.

———. *Riches and Prosperity through Christ.* Tulsa, OK: Christian Crusade, 1978.

———. *Thou Shalt Not Kill My Babies.* Tulsa, OK: Christian Crusade, 1977.

———. *Why I Fight for a Christian America.* Tulsa, OK: Christian Crusade, 1974.

Janson, Donald, and Bernard Eismann. *The Far Right.* New York: McGraw-Hill, 1963.

Nikitin, Vyacheslav. *The Ultras in the USA.* Moscow: Progress Publishers, 1971.

Penabaz, Fernando. *Crusading Preacher from the West.* Tulsa, OK: Christian Crusade, 1962.

Redekop, John Harold. *The American Far Right: A Case Study of Billy James Hargis and Christian Crusade.* Grand Rapids, MI: Eerdmans, 1968.

Schultze, Quentin J. *Televangelism and American Culture.* Grand Rapids, MI: Baker Book House, 1991.

BOB HARRINGTON
born: 1927

One of the most colorful personalities in religious broadcasting during the 1960s and 1970s was Bob Harrington, whose ministry in the infamous "Devil's Boot Camp" of New Orleans earned him the nickname the "Chaplain of Bourbon Street." His ministry was unique in that he felt called to preach to society's outcasts: prostitutes, alcoholics, gamblers, pimps, drug-abusers, and other pariahs. Harrington's style of dress featured bright red colors and flamboyant accessories. His ministry included popular radio and television programs in the New Orleans area, which eventually went into national syndication during the early 1970s. Harrington was a frequent guest on Jim Bakker's PTL network during its early history. His stock as a proponent of marital happiness began to fall, however, when his own marriage fell apart.

SOURCES

Erickson, Hal. *Religious Radio and Television in the United States, 1921–1991.* Jefferson, NC: McFarland, 1992.

RAY HARRISON
see: International Needs

HARVESTER HOUR
first aired: 1978

One of Trinity Broadcasting Network's (TBN) long-running programs is *Harvester Hour*, a popular television outreach of Earl Paulk Ministries of Decatur, Georgia. Paulk is a bishop in the International Communion of Charismatic Churches and head pastor of the Cathedral of the Holy Spirit (formerly the Gospel Harvesters' Church). The program was carried on many of TBN's local affiliates during the 1980s and continues to air weekly over the network as of this writing, even though Paulk's ministry struggled through a sex scandal that rocked his congregation in the early 1990s.

See also Earl Paulk

HAVE CHRIST, WILL TRAVEL MINISTRIES
established: 1965

Founded by the Reverend Joseph Jeter, Have Christ, Will Travel Ministries (HCWTM), located in Philadelphia, Pennsylvania, is an independent interdenominational organization that supports missions in Haiti, Liberia, and the Philippines. The ministry's main activities include church planting, Bible distribution, and Christian education. HCWTM's director, Reverend Jeter, regularly broadcasts over the radio, updating HCWTM projects for his listeners and presenting a brief inspirational message. The Reverend Jeter began the *Ambassador Radio Broadcast* in 1975, which now airs on Sunday mornings from 6 to 7AM over station WTMR-AM, Camden, New Jersey. The broadcast features Bible lessons and commentary aimed primarily at African Americans and African immigrants.

SOURCES

Melton, J. Gordon. *Directory of Religious Organizations in the United States.* 3d ed. Detroit: Gale Research, 1993.

HAVEN OF REST
see: Paul Myers

JACK HAYFORD
born: 1934

Jack W. Hayford has been a fixture of evangelical religious broadcasting since June 1977.

Courtesy: National Religious Broadcasters

He hosts a popular one-hour television program, *Living Way*, which is seen by millions of viewers each week on the Trinity Broadcasting Network (TBN). Hayford also hosts the *Living Way* week-day radio program, which is aired in over 40 states and on several international stations.

Hayford's base of operations is the Church on the Way in Van Nuys, California, where he serves as senior pastor. The church has 8,000 members, making it the largest congregation of the Church of the Foursquare Gospel in the United States. The Foursquare Gospel churches were founded during the 1920s by the charismatic evangelist Aimee Semple McPherson.

Hayford married Anna Marie Smith in 1954. Two years later he graduated with honors from LIFE Bible College of Los Angeles. Hayford's first ministerial position was at the Foursquare Church of Fort Wayne, Indiana, where he stayed from 1956 until 1960. Between 1960 and 1965 the Hayfords served as national youth directors for the International Church of the Foursquare Gospel.

While pursuing an advanced degree at Azusa Pacific University during the late 1960s, Hayford taught at his alma mater and was promoted to dean of students. He also received a temporary assignment as pastor to a struggling

Foursquare Gospel church in Van Nuys, California. The Church on the Way had only 18 members in 1969, the first year of Hayford's pastorate. The temporary assignment became permanent during the 1970s. Hayford was appointed president of LIFE Bible College in 1977. He served in this position until 1982, simultaneously pastoring at his Van Nuys congregation.

Hayford's television ministry began in 1977, when he inaugurated a half-hour weekly series, *Teach Us to Pray*, on TBN. His radio ministry got underway four years later with the weekday half-hour program, *FreeWay*, which was broadcast to members of his huge local congregation. In October 1987, Hayford changed the name of his television program to *Living Way* (to correspond with his radio program which he had since changed to *Living Way*) and expanded it to a one-hour format. TBN and several independent Christian television stations picked up the new show and made it a fixture of religious television during the late 1980s and early 1990s. As of 1995, the television program could be seen in all 50 states, Canada, and South Africa.

By 1989, Hayford's radio ministry had expanded to include The Church on the Way's Sunday morning service heard live throughout the West Coast. *Living Way* was being aired to a national radio audience on over 150 stations every weekday by 1995. During that same year, the church broadcast was being transmitted live on Sunday mornings around the country via satellite feed.

Living Way usually features the mild-mannered Hayford leading his congregation in a sober study of Scripture. Hayford projects the image of a pastor, teacher, and wise friend, and generally eschews the shouting, prancing, and rhetorical flourishes of Pentecostal-based healers and preachers.

In recent years, Hayford has spoken out against the drumbeat of criticism that has been directed toward religious broadcasters. In a 1993 *Ministries Today* article Hayford wrote, "I'm becoming sickened by the tireless, unforgiving assaults of some whose tactics for guard- ing from error have moved them from a loving concern for the truth to a virtual loss of honesty in handling it." He claimed that despite their faults, such televangelists as Robert Schuller, Oral Roberts, Kenneth Copeland, Frederick Price, Larry Lea, and Benny Hinn "are actually Christ-honoring, godly men whom I love in Christ!" He added that, indeed, "the preponderance of the ministry of these leaders is soundly Christian, thoroughly biblical and the source of great blessing in the United States and, in many cases, around the world." Hayford concluded his editorial by stating, "It's not as easy to damn as a heretic someone you've discovered by experience loves Jesus as much as you do." This call to Christian mercy seemed a welcome change from the judgmental attitudes so prevalent in conservative Christian circles.

During the 1980s and early 1990s, Hayford has also been active as an author, composer, and speaker at colleges, seminaries, and conferences. He was the plenary speaker at such venues as the Lausanne II Congress on World Evangelization in Manila, Philippines, in 1989; the National Religious Broadcasters national conventions in 1985, 1988, 1989, and 1995; the Gospel Music Association Convention in Nashville, Tennessee, in 1985; the National Association of Evangelicals Convention in Kansas City, Missouri, in 1986; and at the International Charismatic Congress held in Orlando, Florida, in 1995.

Hayford has composed over 500 gospel songs, hymns, and other musical works. The most popular of these songs is "Majesty." The long list of Hayford's published books includes *The Beauty of Spiritual Language*, *I'll Hold You in Heaven*, *Living and Praying in Jesus's Name*, *The Mary Miracle*, *The Power and Blessing*, *Rebuilding the Real You*, and *Ten Steps toward Saving America*. Living Way Ministries distributes over 60,000 audiocassettes of Hayford's sermons every year and estimates that over 1 million of these cassettes are in circulation around the world. The ministry markets these tapes as mini-albums, audio albums, and audio encyclopedias.

The Church on the Way considers itself to be an interdenominational fellowship. It accepts all those who claim to have been born again by faith in Christ. As a Foursquare Church, the congregation espouses such fundamental Christian teachings and practices as the Fall of Man, salvation through grace, baptism and the Lord's Supper, divine healing, evangelism, Heaven, Hell, the Second Coming, and the Last Judgment. The church proclaims Jesus Christ as savior, baptizer, healer, and coming king. During the mid-1990s, Church on the Way claimed a weekly attendance at its worship services of between 9,000 and 10,000 persons.

Hayford has made guest appearances on TBN, the Christian Broadcasting Network, *100 Huntley Street*, *Haven of Rest*, ABC's *PrimeTime*, and *The Merv Griffin Show*. Among his many honors are the Clergyman of the Year award (1985) and four Religion in Media Angel awards. As of 1995, Hayford was serving on the boards of the National Religious Broadcasters and the Lausanne Committee for World Evangelization. He has received honorary doctorates from LIFE Bible College (1977), Oral Roberts University (1984), and California Graduate School of Theology (1985).

SOURCES

"Because You Asked." Brochure published by Living Way Ministries, 1995.

Hayford, Jack. "To Avoid a Modern Inquisition." *Ministries Today*, September/October, 1993.

"The Living Way Ministries Resource Catalogue." Living Way Ministries, 1995.

Smith, Sarah E. "Casting Call for NRB 95." *Religious Broadcasting*, February, 1995.

HCJB, ECUADOR
established: 1931

HCJB, Ecuador, the short-wave radio station of the World Radio Missionary Fellowship, was the first religious radio station located outside the United States. Founded in 1931 by Clarence Jones and Reuben Larson in a converted sheep shed under the name HCJB World Radio, the fellowship now operates three short-wave transmitting stations in the western hemisphere and, over its 65 year history, has produced, broadcast and distributed worldwide radio and television programming in numerous foreign languages such as Russian, Spanish, and Quechua.

Clarence Jones was a musician and broadcaster who had helped Paul Rader's Chicago Gospel Tabernacle expand its radio ministry during the late 1920s. Reuben E. Larson was a graduate of the St. Paul Bible Institute in St. Paul, Minnesota, and a Christian and Missionary Alliance missionary to Ecuador who had been inspired by the founder of the World Radio Congregation, R. R. Brown, to use the power of radio to preach the gospel in foreign lands.

Jones and Larson met in 1929 and decided to explore the possibility of setting up a gospel radio ministry in Latin America. Through Larson's connections, the two men were invited by the president and congress of Ecuador to set up that nation's first radio station. With the help of an ex-CBS network engineer, Eric Williams, they set up a studio and 250-watt transmitter in a converted sheep shed just outside Quito, Ecuador.

The inaugural broadcast of radio station HCJB (signifying "Heralding Christ Jesus' Blessings" or "Hoy Christo Jesus Benedictos") took place on Christmas Day, 1931. During its first year of operation, programming was broadcast two hours a day in Spanish. After this first year, the "Voice of the Andes," as the station came to be called, began sending out programming in Quechua, an indigenous language spoken in Ecuador, Bolivia, and Peru by the descendants of the ancient Incas. The hours of broadcasting in Quechua have expanded over the years and, by 1979, 30 hours of programming in this language were being aired weekly. The station's principal tongue, however, has always been English.

The HCJB ministry has been amazingly successful among the Quechuas. It is reported that hundreds of small churches have been established in this mountainous region, despite the fact that oftentimes no missionaries are present. Native converts report that the voices received on their "magic boxes" are perceived as those of close friends. The station receives a steady stream of mail from these new believers requesting support and spiritual guidance. HCJB's evangelistic efforts have not always been well received, however. In 1956, a party of five Alliance missionaries associated with HCJB was killed by the Auca Indians in the Ecuadorian jungle.

HCJB greatly expanded its electronic outreach between 1940 and 1980. By the late 1980s, the station was broadcasting programs in 14 languages around the world, including 11 hours daily of Russian-language programming. Efforts to penetrate the Iron Curtain included the construction of a 500,000-watt short-wave transmitter. This international blanketing has borne fruit in a number of subsidiary ministries. One of the most famous of these is the station's coordinated radio program and correspondence course, *The Bible Institute of the Air*. This ministry trains future ministers and pastors in five languages through a series of college-level courses.

Expansion has also included the purchase of religious radio stations in Texas and Panama, the production of gospel programs for other religious networks around the world, the creation of religious television programs in Spanish, and the operation of hospitals and medical caravans in Ecuador. Under the leadership of its president Abe Van Der Puy, HCJB continues to provide high quality musical and educational programming, especially to the Spanish-speaking world.

HCJB began a television ministry called *Window of the Andes* during the 1970s. However, the station's limited signal area and the fact that few Ecuadorian citizens could afford television sets made this venture far less successful than HCJB's radio ministry. Clarence Jones's *Hour of Freedom* radio program, now hosted by his son Howard O. Jones, was still being broadcast in the 1980s, and Reuben Larson's *Grace Memorial Hour* was being transmitted over 120 stations in the early 1990s.

See also Clarence Jones

SOURCES

Armstrong, Ben. *The Electric Church*. Nashville: Thomas Nelson, 1979.

Ward, Mark, Sr. *Air of Salvation: The Story of Christian Broadcasting*. Manassas, VA: National Religious Broadcasters, 1994.

HEALING AND RESTORATION MINISTRY

Although it may seem the case, healing broadcast ministries are not always found within Pentecostal denominations or churches. *Healing and Restoration Ministry*, for example, a television and radio program of the 1960s and 1970s, came out of Father Edward McDonough's Boston Mission Church. McDonough was a charismatic Catholic who, in deference to his nervous superiors, was careful to point out that any healings taking place through his ministry were temporary and that "the greatest healing is a happy death."

SOURCES

Erickson, Hal. *Religious Radio and Television in the United States, 1921–1991*. Jefferson, NY: McFarland, 1992.

THE HEAVEN AND HOME HOUR

An early entry into radio evangelism was *The Heaven and Home Hour*, a 15-minute broadcast inaugurated by Clarence Erickson of Glendale, California, during the 1930s. This long-running program was still providing its listeners with common-sense advice, testimonies of faith, and interviews into the early 1990s. Erickson was succeeded as the show's host by such personalities as Russell Kilman and James Christenson.

SOURCES

Erickson, Hal. *Religious Radio and Television in the United States, 1921–1991*. Jefferson, NC: McFarland, 1992.

HEBREW CHRISTIAN FELLOWSHIP
established: 1944

The Hebrew Christian Fellowship (HCF) is the umbrella organization for a number of churches and individuals seeking to evangelize Jews. Moreover, it is one of five major Jewish Christian organizations in America that operate broadcast ministries. Founded in 1944, the independent evangelical association is located in the greater Philadelphia area and airs its programming in the United States and abroad. Recently, the fellowship has begun to cooperate with Christian stations that are beaming its message to countries in the former Soviet bloc. The ministry follows up its broadcasts by sending literature to interested individuals around the world. HCF also distributes Bibles, holds classes and seminars, and publishes the quarterly news magazine *Shalom*.

SOURCES

Rausch, David A. *Messianic Judaism: Its History, Theology, and Polity*. New York: Edwin Mellen Press, 1982.

Stone, Jon R. "Messianic Judaism: A Redefinition of the Boundary between Christian and Jew?" In *Research in the Social Scientific Study of Religion* 3. Greenwich, CT: JAI Press, 1991.

HERALDS OF HOPE
established: 1965

Founded by J. Otis Yoder and located in Breezewood, Pennsylvania, Heralds of Hope (HOH) is an independent Protestant ministry that seeks to spread the Christian message throughout the world using the media of radio, audiocassette, and pamphlet literature. The ministry produces two radio programs—the half-hour *The Voice of Hope* and the 15-minute

Hope for Today—each of which airs weekly. *The Voice of Hope* features unaccompanied singing, a Bible reading, and an expository Bible sermon. *Hope for Today*, which is broadcast over three Trans World Radio superstations, presents an expository lesson. Since much of HOH's ministry is aimed at evangelizing immigrant communities throughout the world, it broadcasts its programs in translation in Arabic, Hindi, Mandarin Chinese, and Spanish.

SOURCES

The Directory of Religious Organizations in the United States. 2d ed. Falls Church, VA: McGrath, 1982.

Melton, J. Gordon. *Directory of Religious Organizations in the United States*. 3d ed. Detroit: Gale Research, 1993.

MARILYN HICKEY
born: 1931, Dalhart, Texas

Courtesy: National Religious Broadcasters

Marilyn Seitzer Hickey is often called the "people's theologian" because of her ability to express the practical side of Christian teaching. Since she began Marilyn Hickey Ministries in 1976, she has become a globetrotting evangelist and the host of several popular radio and television programs.

Hickey is a native Texan who attended high school in Denver, Colorado. After earning a bachelor's degree in foreign languages from the University of Northern Colorado, Hickey taught high school and lived for many years in Pennsylvania with her pastor husband. Upon the couple's return to Denver, Hickey assisted her husband's ministry and devoted herself to an intensive study of the Bible. While deep in prayer one day, she experienced a calling from God to "cover the earth with His Word."

She began to organize Bible-study groups and to produce a Bible-teaching series on videotape. Hickey also created the Marilyn Hickey Training Center, a two-year comprehensive Bible institute that is located in her husband Wallace Hickey's Happy Church. During an interview in 1985, Marilyn Hickey explained the need for her institute as follows: "Many seminaries have poisoned their students with humanism and with every type of false doctrine and wrong teaching. We are not serving the poison of wrong doctrine; we are serving the life-giving Word of God."

The members of her Bible-study groups were the first to suggest to Hickey the idea of a radio ministry. Although her program was at first refused by a local station manager, the iron-willed, energetic teacher persevered. As she recalled, "There are testing times that we all have in which we really have to fight. I don't think we always need green lights—we need the leading of the Holy Spirit." By the late 1980s, Hickey's daily 15-minute radio shows were being aired on 178 stations across the United States and on seven foreign stations. The broadcasting entrepreneur was also, during the 1980s, producing a weekly half-hour television program over two cable networks, including the Trinity Broadcasting Network , and 20 stations. The names of Hickey's radio and television programs included *A Cry for Miracles*, *The Best Day of Your Life*, and *Today with Marilyn Hickey*.

Of her television ministry Hickey once explained, "With radio, it seemed as though I almost stumbled into it because of my Bible-study groups. But God really spoke clearly to me

about a television-teaching ministry. It became such a burning desire in my heart." In her eyes, the television program serves as a direct evangelical outreach to the unsaved, while the radio show is more of a daily "feeding" for committed Christians.

Hickey's overall ministry is known for its strong humanitarian thrust. She organized a "Fill the Ship" project that employed a 500-ton cargo ship to transport needed foodstuffs to impoverished countries in 1983, and, later that same year, she coordinated emergency shipments of powdered milk to the Philippines and bulgur wheat to Haiti. During the Cold War, Hickey was also active in smuggling Bibles into Russia and Poland and in providing religious books to such war-torn countries as Lebanon and Ethiopia. Since 1983, it is estimated that she has supplied over 72,000 Bibles to believers around the world. The dominant theme of her ministry, Hickey once asserted, could be found in Isaiah 11:9: "For the earth shall be full of the knowledge of the Lord as the waters cover the sea."

Hickey's style of Christianity has been characterized as of the "turned on charismatic" and the "be very happy in Christ" variety. Like many other Pentecostal Christians, Hickey exudes joy, optimism, and faith, emphasizing the empowerment of the Holy Spirit and a life of spiritual and material abundance. She circulates a monthly teaching magazine called *Outpouring* to over 100,000 followers and writes a monthly column for *Charisma* magazine. Hickey has also authored over 30 books and pamphlets on successful Bible teaching.

In the late 1980s, and into the early- and mid-1990s, Hickey has assumed a leading role in organizing and empowering Christian women. She does this not only by hosting the annual International Women's Convention but also by engaging in a demanding schedule of national teaching seminars and miracle crusades. In 1995, for example, Hickey preached at a historic evangelical crusade in heavily Muslim Pakistan. This crusade was believed to be the first ever led by a woman in Pakistan. According to Hickey,

I had been warned that nothing like this had ever been attempted before by a woman. . . . Eventually, an invitation to bring the gospel to Pakistan came. And even though no woman had ever publicly preached in that nation, I knew in my heart it was right, and that this was God's time for me to go.

As part of the crusade, Hickey held a five-day training session in Lahore for more than 1,200 pastors, Christian leaders, and workers.

When once asked whether she would like to slow down her frenetic pace of radio and television broadcasts, seminars, and miracle crusades, she responded, "I don't dare sit back and say, 'I see some good things, so this is it.' I see areas in our ministry that are very fruitful, but the world is dying and going to hell by the billions. So how can we stop now?" Hickey is a good example of the more prominent roles available to women in independent charismatic congregations.

SOURCES

Erickson, Hal. *Religious Radio and Television in the United States, 1921–1991.* Jefferson, NC: McFarland, 1992.

"Hickey Leads Crusade in Pakistan." *Charisma*, August, 1995.

Peterson, Richard G. "Electric Sisters." In *The God Pumpers*, edited by Marshall Fishwick and Ray B. Browne. Bowling Green, KY: Bowling Green State University Popular Press, 1987.

HINDUSTAN BIBLE INSTITUTE
established: 1950

The Hindustan Bible Institute (HBI) is an independent missions organization that runs training schools in Madras, India, and Sri Lanka. The ministry's evangelistic Christian activities include church planting, medical ministries, education and orphanage services, and construction projects. It broadcasts its program, *Voice of India*, over radio in India and Sri Lanka in six different languages and dialects. HBI also publishes *Voice of India*, a monthly news and devotional magazine.

SOURCES

Melton, J. Gordon. *Directory of Religious Organizations in the United States.* 3d ed. Detroit: Gale Research, 1993.

HINENI
established: 1973

Courtesy: Hineni

ESTHER JUNGREIS

Hineni (not to be confused with Hineni Ministries) is a Reform Jewish service organization located in New York City's Upper West Side. Founded in 1973 by the Rebbetzin Esther Jungreis (Rebbetzin signifying the wife of a rabbi), a Hungarian-born Holocaust survivor, Hineni seeks to educate Jews about their religious and cultural heritage. The ministry conducts classes on the Hebrew Bible and the Talmud and offers seminars and lectures on timely issues of interest to the Jewish community. It also maintains a Holocaust memorial center aimed at educating Jews on Jewish history.

Hineni has been broadcasting a weekly television program also called *Hineni* since 1982—the longest running national Jewish program in broadcast history. Hosted by Rebbetzin Jungreis, *Hineni* is carried by cable to some 8 million subscribers every Sunday afternoon and features a half-hour Scripture lesson. Hineni

also produces a number of video programs on the meaning and proper observance of Jewish holidays and publishes pamphlets and booklets on such subjects as intermarriage, women's issues, the family, Zionism, the meaning of the Holocaust, and the problems of Jewish assimilation into the larger Christian culture.

SOURCES

Melton, J. Gordon. *Directory of Religious Organizations in the United States.* 3d ed. Detroit: Gale Research, 1993.

HINENI MINISTRIES
see: Moishe Rosen

BENNY HINN
born: December 3, 1952, Jaffa, Israel

Courtesy: Benny Hinn Ministries

During the 1990s, Benedictus "Benny" Hinn has become one of the most prominent television healing evangelists in the world. His television shows include the Sunday worship services at his 7,000-member Orlando Christian Center, a half-hour program, *This Is Your Day*, which airs three times daily on Trinity Broadcasting Network (TBN), and excerpted segments from his monthly *Miracle Crusades.*

Hinn was born in Israel to a Greek father, Costandi Hinn, and an Armenian mother, Clemence Hinn. On the night before his birth, Hinn's mother had a dream in which she gave Jesus one of six beautiful roses in her hand. A short, slim man with dark hair had then appeared and covered her in a warm cloth. Hinn, who has five siblings, would later interpret this dream to be a prophecy of his eventual religious mission. During Hinn's childhood, his father served as the mayor of Jaffa, giving the family a measure of local prominence.

Although his parents were devout Greek Orthodox, Hinn's early education occurred within a Roman Catholic monastic context. As he would later reflect on his multicultural upbringing: "So here I was, born in Israel, but not Jewish. Raised in an Arabic culture, but not of Arabic origin. Attending a Catholic school, but raised as a Greek Orthodox." The future evangelist's facility for languages also was nurtured at this time. He spoke Arabic at home, studied French in school, and learned ancient Hebrew.

Very pious as a young boy, Hinn's first visionary experience took place when he was 11. As recounted in the autobiographical *Good Morning, Holy Spirit* (1990), Hinn felt "an incredible sensation that can only be described as 'electric.' It felt as if someone had plugged me into a wired socket." He then saw a white-robed man, whom he intuitively knew was Jesus, walk into his bedroom. The man looked at Hinn "with the most beautiful eyes. He smiled, and His arms were open wide. I could feel His presence." When he awoke from the vision, Hinn lay paralyzed for a time by the "intense, powerful feeling" that the experience had evoked. In later years, Hinn would interpret this vision as his call to the service of Christ.

In the wake of the political unrest caused by the Six Day War of 1967, the Hinn family moved to Toronto, Canada. Hinn's father quickly learned English and became a successful insurance salesman. Hinn attended a public high school and was introduced to charismatic Christianity by a co-worker at a hamburger stand. He began attending services at a local charismatic Anglican congregation and a short time later made a public confession of his acceptance of Christ. In spite of his father's strong opposition to his unusual religious proclivities, Hinn devoted himself to a study of scripture and participated in the local Jesus movement.

In 1973, Hinn accompanied a Free Methodist minister and several church members on a trip to Pittsburgh where they attended a Kathryn Kuhlman healing service. While singing hymns, Hinn experienced a powerful surge of religious ecstasy and heard a voice say, "My mercy is abundant on you." He then witnessed three hours of healings and healing testimonies. As he later recalled, "I thought, 'I want what Kathryn Kuhlman's got.' I wanted it with every atom and fiber within me." Kuhlman would become an important role model for Hinn's healing ministry.

The future evangelist did not begin preaching until 1974, when he experienced another vision in which he saw souls being led into a "roaring inferno of fire." He then heard a voice saying, "If you do not preach, everyone who falls will be your responsibility." Overcoming his fear of public speaking (he suffered from a severe stuttering problem since childhood), Hinn stood up before the Shilo fellowship at the Trinity Assembly of God in Oshawa, Ontario, on December 7, 1974, and began to preach. He remembered, "The instant I opened my mouth, I felt something touch my tongue and loosen it. It felt like a little numbness, and I began to proclaim God's Word with absolute fluency. . . . The stuttering was gone. All of it. And it has never returned." Hinn preached for the next five months in Pentecostal churches around Toronto and slowly began to gain a following. His entire family, including his father, were converted and became part of his new ministry.

In response to interior guidance, Hinn scheduled a series of weekly services on Monday nights in a high school auditorium. Within a short time the attendance at these meetings had mushroomed into the hundreds, and a larger facility was found. The tenor of these early gatherings was summed up in his *Good Morning, Holy Spirit*:

> The services were totally led by the Spirit, and I listened ever so closely to His voice. People were delivered from serious addictions. Families were reunited. We had "healing lines" and heard testimonies of miracles. . . . Then something happened. People began to receive miracles, deliverance, and healings right in their seats. No lines for "the laying on of hands." God began to do his work all across the auditorium—so freely that there was not time to hear all of the testimonies.

These mass healing phenomena would become hallmarks of Hinn's miracle crusades and a standard feature of his weekly broadcasts.

Hinn's rallies soon attracted national publicity in Canada. Newspapers like the *Toronto Star* and the *Toronto Globe and Mail* sent reporters to the crusades and featured case studies of persons who had experienced miraculous healings. The Canadian Broadcasting Corporation, independent Toronto station Channel 9, and Global-TV broadcast documentaries on Hinn's crusades, and his growing ministry began to air a prime-time television show on Sunday evenings. In 1978, the evangelist met Suzanne Harthern, the daughter of a Pentecostal minister based in Orlando, Florida. The following year the couple were married and Hinn began to establish an international ministry.

By 1983, the Hinns had relocated to Orlando and founded the independent, interdenominational Orlando Christian Center. Starting with a few hundred people, the church grew rapidly. By 1992, it had become a thriving megachurch situated on a 40-acre parcel of land and claiming over 7000 members. Hinn remained strongly committed to his congregation during his rise to international prominence. Most weeks he preached three times on Sunday and conducted a Wednesday evening Bible study. Although he had little time for a normal family life, Hinn and his wife had three children during this period.

Hinn's television ministry began during the mid-1980s with the broadcast of his church's

Sunday worship. The show was picked up by Paul Crouch's Trinity Broadcasting Network and soon became one of the network's most popular programs. The Sunday broadcast and the weekday *This Is Your Day* show now reach a reported audience of over 60 million homes in the United States and Canada. The weekly Sunday broadcast has been picked up by the Super Channel and reaches an estimated audience of over 100 million homes in Europe, Russia, and Israel. The main draw of the programs is their dramatic display of healing testimonials by people who attend Hinn's large crusades. These two-day events, which are free, regularly attract up to 40,000 people and provide Hinn with a growing international following.

Following the model of Kuhlman's meetings, Hinn rarely lays hands on individuals but rather waits for them to come forward and testify to their experiences of healing. After their testimony, Hinn demonstrates their recovery by such acts as running with cripples, applying pressure to formerly diseased parts of a person's anatomy, and whispering into a deaf person's ears and having that person repeat his words. He also touches the newly healed with his hands and watches as they fall backward into the arms of his assistants, a phenomenon known in Pentecostal circles as being "slain in the Spirit." Like other healing televangelists, Hinn has preached the healing power of prayer and regularly invites his broadcasting audience to place their hands on their television sets and pray fervently for a healing miracle. In addition, Hinn prays over the many thousands of letters sent to him and asks for healing for specific ailments that are revealed to him by the Spirit.

Hinn has become a successful author during the 1990s. His first book, *Good Morning, Holy Spirit*, was published by Thomas Nelson in October 1990. It rose quickly to the top-10 list of Christian booksellers and has reportedly sold over 1.5 million copies in the United States and 500,000 copies worldwide. Coauthored with close friend and freelance writer Neil Eskelin, the work is part autobiography and part sermon on the power of the Holy Spirit. Hinn emphasizes the need for more teaching about the third person of the Christian Trinity. Few books, he

claims, "have focused on just the Holy Spirit and His incredible power. So I wrote the book to introduce the Holy Spirit. It's that simple." Hinn has published two other popular books, *The Anointing* and *Lord, I Need a Miracle*.

Hinn's emphasis on the Holy Spirit and on the power of God to work miracles in the lives of ordinary Christians has not been received with universal acclaim in conservative Christian circles. Two anticult groups, the Irvine, California-based Christian Research Institute and the Watchman Fellowship, began to criticize Hinn's theology and lifestyle in 1990. Watchman spokesperson Bud Press called Hinn "one of the most prolific heretics of modern times." A November 1991 *Orlando Sentinel* feature publicized Hinn's opulent lifestyle. The article reported that Hinn's annual income was over $100,000, that he wore a diamond Rolex, drove a Jaguar, and lived in a $685,000 home. Hinn responded to the scrutiny of his personal finances in a *Publishers Weekly* article in February 1992: "I believe God wants all his children taken care of. There's a difference between taking care of and outright greed. Live in what you need to live in, and you're doing what He wants you to do." The televangelist defended his expensive home as necessary for security reasons.

In response to skeptics who voiced doubt concerning the claims of healings during his crusades, Hinn retained the services of five volunteer doctors who have worked to substantiate healing testimonies. He also hired a full-time staff person to interview and document those who have been healed while watching Hinn on television. Hinn answered succinctly those who had asked why every sick person was not healed at his crusades: "Look at me as a conduit. All I tell them is to pray for a miracle from God. It's up to the Lord to make that happen. I can't explain why some are healed and others are not. Only God has those answers."

The criticisms of Hinn's word-of-faith religious teachings and extravagant onstage theatrics came to a head in 1993. The Christian Research Institute's Hank Hanegraaff and televangelist James Robison contacted Hinn personally and warned him that his ministry would fail if he continued "in his slaughter of the innocent sheep." In the past Hinn had responded to such criticism by publicly wishing for a "Holy Ghost machine gun" to defeat his enemies. This time, however, Hinn was deeply shaken by Robison's rebuke and promised to change his ministry's emphasis. A short time later, Hinn appeared before his Orlando congregation and renounced the central elements of his faith message, including positive confession, the divine right-to-be-healed, and the "health and wealth" gospel. The teary-eyed audience heard Hinn proclaim,

> It's faith, faith, faith and no Jesus anywhere. We have to have faith in Jesus, the author and finisher of our faith. So, where do I stand on faith? Stop seeking faith and start seeking the Lord! The word-of-faith message is New Age and it doesn't work. I'm going to stop preaching healing and start preaching Jesus.

Hinn later blamed health-and-wealth preachers such as Kenneth Hagin and Kenneth Copeland for leading him away from the message of salvation. As for his healing ministry, Hinn reportedly told his congregation, "I once said if my daddy knew what I know, he wouldn't have died of cancer. [But] it was God's will to take my father home. I became so convinced I was right, God had to shake it out of me."

Although critics like Hanegraaff reminded audiences that Hinn has recanted his faith message in the past, only to return to it later, Hinn demonstrated his contrition by agreeing to edit out all references to word-of-faith teaching from subsequent editions of his books. In addition, he hired Dudley Hall, an associate of Robison, to help him avoid future doctrinal errors in his writing. As of 1996, Hinn's television shows continue to place a strong emphasis on dramatic healing testimonials. As he blesses the healed, however, Hinn makes a special point to do so "in the name of Jesus."

SOURCES

Bearden, Michelle. "Benny Hinn." *Publishers Weekly*, February 10, 1992, 42–44.

Benny Hinn Media Ministries. News Release, 1993.

Hinn, Benny. *Good Morning Holy Spirit*. Nashville: Thomas Nelson, 1990.

Perucci, Ferraiuolo. "Christian Leaders Admonish Him." *Christianity Today*, August 16, 1993, 38–39.

DAVID HOCKING
born: January 2, 1941, Long Beach, California

Courtesy: National Religious Broadcasters

The prominent conservative writer-preacher David Lee Hocking is the host of *Hope for Today*, a half-hour daily radio program that features a soft-rock soundtrack, audience questions and answers, and straightforward, scholarly, and practical biblical teaching. The program began in October 1995 and is currently carried over 35 radio stations with a potential listenership of 45 million people.

Hocking's radio ministry began in 1974 on station KGER, Long Beach, California, with the Bible-teaching program, *Sounds of Grace*. This ministry was an outreach of the First Brethren Church and aired over 10 stations in Southern California. Hocking went methodically through each book of the Bible, interpreting individual passages. He stopped his *Sounds of Grace* broadcast in 1979 to begin a 10-year run as host of *The BIOLA Hour*, a weekly Bible-study program broadcast from La Mirada, California. *The BIOLA Hour* was heard on radio stations along the West Coast of the United States.

Following disagreements with *The BIOLA Hour*'s board of directors in 1989, Hocking founded *Solid Rocks Radio*, another expository Bible-teaching program that featured an upbeat contemporary musical soundtrack. This show was heard nationally over 200 stations during its two years of broadcasting.

Hocking is the son of George Hocking and Ethel Leiss. His educational credentials include a bachelor's degree, magna cum laude, from Bob Jones University in 1961, a master of divinity degree, summa cum laude, from Grace Theological Seminary in 1964, a doctor of ministry degree from the California Graduate School of Theology in 1970, and a doctor of philosophy degree from Western Graduate School of Theology in 1976.

After his ordination into the National Fellowship of Brethren Churches in 1961, Hocking served as the national youth director of the Brethren churches in Winona Lake, Indiana, until 1964. He established Grace Brethren Church in Columbus, Ohio, in 1964, and served as its pastor until 1968, when he began his long pastorship of First Brethren Church of Long Beach.

In addition to his radio and television duties, Hocking has served as president of the Western Schools of Church Growth in Long Beach and the Bible Institute and Graduate School of Long Beach. He has a busy lecturing schedule, traveling to college and community groups around the country. Hocking is also the popular author of such books as *Spiritual Gifts* (1974), *How to Be Happy in Difficult Situations* (1975), *World's Greatest Church!* (1976), and *The Nature of God in Plain Language* (1984). Hocking joined the Calvary Chapel church movement in 1992 and continues to lecture and teach at local churches in Southern California.

SOURCES

Hocking, David L. *The Coming World Leader: Understanding the Book of Revelation.* Portland, OR: Multnomah Press, 1988.

RAY HOEKSTRA
born: 1913, Chicago

Chaplain Ray Hoekstra is the founder of the International Prison Ministry, which was established in 1970. Hoekstra got his start in evangelical prison broadcasting when he replaced Dan Gilbert, the late founder and host of *Prisoners Bible Broadcast* (later titled *Christ Truth Radio Crusade*), as the show's chaplain in 1962. Hoekstra served in that position until 1970, when he struck out on his own and started a successful radio program, *International Prison Broadcasts*, in Dallas, Texas. Broadcasting to prisoners in the United States, Mexico, the Caribbean, and the Philippines, the International Prison Ministry sends religious literature and Bibles to interested inmates. Hoekstra encouraged *The 700 Club* to begin its own prison ministry. He also claimed that his prison broadcasts resulted in the conversion of three jailed members of the Manson family. *International Prison Broadcasts* currently airs daily over the USA Radio Network.

See also International Prison Ministry

SOURCES

The Directory of Religious Organizations in the United States. 2d ed. Falls Church, VA: McGrath, 1982.

Melton, J. Gordon. *Directory of Religious Organizations in the United States.* 3d ed. Detroit: Gale Research, 1993.

DAVID HOFER
born: 1917, Dinuba, California

Raised in California's Central Valley near Fresno, radio evangelist David Hofer attended the Bible Institute of Los Angeles (Biola), graduating in 1936. He spent the next 10 years singing in a gospel quartet and attending Youth for Christ rallies.

During one of these rallies, Hofer was touched by prayers asking God for a Christian radio station in the San Joaquin Valley. In 1946, he and his brother, Egon, founded and began operating station KRDU from their childhood home of Dinuba. They managed expenses through the sale of commercial advertising and airtime to radio preachers, who were attracted to the idea that listeners would be drawn not only by their specific program but by the station's other religious programs as well.

KRDU celebrated its 50th year of successful operations in 1996. The 24-hour, 5,000-watt station covers the Fresno-Dinuba-Visalia broadcasting area with such popular programs as *The Back to God Hour*, *Radio Bible Class*, and *Unshackled*. David Hofer still serves as the station's president and his wife, Sylvia, serves as KRDU's secretary and treasurer.

Owing to the success of his broadcast ministry, Hofer was appointed to serve a three-year term as president of the National Religious Broadcasters, beginning in 1979. Hofer was also among the founders of the Hume Lake Christian Camps, located above Fresno in the foothills of the Sierra Nevada.

See also KRDU-AM, Dinuba, California; National Religious Broadcasters

SOURCES

Ward, Mark, Sr. *Air of Salvation: The Story of Christian Broadcasting.* Grand Rapids, MI: Baker Book House, 1994.

HOMESTEAD USA

see: Christian Television Mission

HOPE FOR TODAY

see: David Hocking

LA HORA DE LA REFORMA

see: Juan Boonstra

WILLIAM HOUGHTON

born: 1887, South Boston, Massachusetts
died: June 14, 1947, Los Angeles, California

William H. Houghton was an important leader in the early days of evangelical radio broadcasting, overseeing the Moody Bible Institute's radio station, WMBI, during the 1930s and hosting his own radio program, *Let's Go Back to the Bible*.

Houghton was born in South Boston to John Houghton and Carrie Grant. Houghton's father died while Houghton was still a child, forcing the family to move to nearby Lynn. In 1901, at age 14, Houghton was converted during a revival meeting in Lynn. He later joined the Cliftondale Pentecostal Church, a Wesleyan holiness group affiliated with the Church of the Nazarene.

At the prodding of a Nazarene minister in Brooklyn, Houghton decided to direct his life toward Christian ministry. In 1910, he enrolled at the Eastern Nazarene College of Rhode Island. Houghton remained there only six months before taking up evangelistic work at the invitation of Reuben A. Torrey, former dean of the Moody Bible Institute. Houghton married Adelaide Franks in 1914 and worked as a song leader for a number of evangelistic campaigns before receiving ordination in the Baptist Church in 1915. He served as a Baptist pastor in Canton, Pennsylvania (1915–1917), where his first wife died; New Bethlehem, Pennsylvania (1918–1922), where he met and married Elizabeth Andrews, his second wife; and Norristown, Pennsylvania (1922–1924).

In 1924, Houghton's interest in evangelism took him to Ireland for a campaign. He returned to the pastorate in 1925, serving as minister of the Baptist Tabernacle in Atlanta (1925–1930) and the Calvary Baptist Church (1930–1934), succeeding John Roach Straton. In 1934, Houghton was chosen to succeed James M. Gray as president of the Moody Bible Institute. Gray had served as Moody's dean and first president since 1904. Under Houghton's leadership, the Institute expanded its student enroll-ment, its ministry to the greater Chicago area, and its influence in fundamentalist circles. He also oversaw the expansion of Moody Bible Institute's radio station, WMBI, which had be-gun broadcasts in 1925. In 1938, Houghton be-gan his own radio program, *Let's Go Back to the Bible*.

As president of Moody Bible Institute, Houghton served as the unofficial host of the constitutional convention convened by evangeli-cal religious broadcasters during the second convention of the National Association of Evangelicals. This convention, which was held in the Moody Memorial Church in Chicago during September 1944, gave birth to National Religious Broadcasters. Houghton also is cred-ited with the birth of what later became the American Scientific Affiliation, a professional society of Christian scientists.

After months of ill health, Houghton died on June 14, 1947, while vacationing in Los Angeles.

See also WMBI, Chicago

SOURCES

Houghton, William H. *Let's Go Back to the Bible*. New York: Fleming H. Revell, 1939.

Melton, J. Gordon. *Religious Leaders of America*. Detroit: Gale Research, 1991.

Reid, Daniel G., Robert D. Linder, Bruce L. Shelley, and Harry S. Stout, eds. *Dictionary of Christian-ity in America*. Downers Grove, IL: InterVarsity Press, 1990.

Smith, Wilbur M. *A Watchman on the Walls: The Life Story of Will H. Houghton*. Grand Rapids, MI: Eerdmans, 1951.

Ward, Mark, Sr. *Air of Salvation: The Story of Christian Broadcasting*. Grand Rapids, MI: Baker Book House, 1994.

HOUR OF DECISION
first aired: 1950

Evangelist Billy Graham's most enduring broadcasting presence has been his weekly ra-dio series, *Hour of Decision*. The program pre-miered on the ABC radio network November 15, 1950. Graham's wife, Ruth, came up with the idea for the show's title after Graham made it clear he did not want the program named af-ter himself.

The young evangelist reportedly had a bad case of opening night jitters, but he delivered his sermon with characteristic aplomb. After a 13-week trial period, ABC renewed the show's contract and aired it over 150 ABC stations. The series has remained a popular staple of religious radio broadcasting, celebrating its 45th anni-versary in 1995. According to published fig-ures, the program is now broadcast over 664 stations in the United States and Canada and 366 stations around the world. Graham also hosted a filmed, weekly 15-minute *Hour of Decision* on ABC-TV between September 30, 1951, and February 21, 1954. Since that time, Graham's television appearances have been lim-ited, for the most part, to his special evangelis-tic crusades around the world.

See also Billy Graham

SOURCES

"Airwave News." *Religious Broadcasting*, December, 1995.

Erickson, Hal. *Religious Radio and Television in the United States, 1921–1991*. Jefferson, NC: McFarland, 1992.

Hoover, Stewart M. *Mass Media Religion: The Social Sources of the Electronic Church*. Newbury Park, CA: Sage, 1988.

HOUR OF POWER
see: Robert Schuller

HOUR OF ST. FRANCIS
first aired: 1959

Hour of St. Francis was the name of a respected half-hour drama series that ran for two seasons in 1959 and 1960. The series was the brainchild of four Franciscan priests, Fathers Hugh Noonan, Edward Henriques, Terence Cronin, and Carl Holtschneider. The four converted what had once been (during the early 1950s) a series of sermons filmed for television by producer William F. Broidy (of *Wild Bill Hickock* fame) into a half-hour filmed anthology. The sermon format had its roots in a 1946 radio program that had been started by the Los Angeles-based Noonan.

The entertainment-savvy priests directed, produced, and wrote the screenplays for the series, which starred such Hollywood notables as George Murphy, Ruth Hussey, Danny Thomas, Raymond Burr, and Jane Wyman. *Hour of St. Francis* was filmed in a makeshift studio located in a condemned Los Angeles schoolhouse.

SOURCES

Erickson, Hal. *Religious Radio and Television in the United States, 1921-1991.* Jefferson, NC: McFarland, 1992.

HOW CAN I LIVE?
see: Kay Arthur

DAVID HUBBARD
born: April 8, 1928, Stockton, California
died: June 7, 1996, Montecito, California

David A. Hubbard, the popular radio host of *The Joyful Sound*, was the son of missionary parents who had served briefly in Puerto Rico before accepting the call in the early 1920s to minister to a Methodist church near Oakland, California. Hubbard's parents came under the influence of the Foursquare Gospel preacher Aimee Semple McPherson and soon transformed their church into a Pentecostal meeting house.

After graduation from high school, Hubbard attended Westmont College in Santa Barbara, California, graduating in 1949. He immediately

Courtesy: Fuller Theological Seminary

enrolled in the Fuller Theological Seminary, earning a bachelor of divinity degree in 1952 and a master of theology in 1954. Hubbard was ordained into the Conservative Baptist Association in 1952. In 1957, he received a doctorate in Old Testament and Semitics from St. Andrews University in Scotland. Hubbard returned to Westmont College as professor of Old Testament the same year and served as chair of the Department of Biblical Studies and Philosophy from 1958–1963.

In 1963, following a search that had taken three turbulent years to complete, Charles Fuller invited Hubbard to be Fuller Theological Seminary's third president. His predecessors in the position had been Harold J. Ockenga (who served from 1947 to 1954 and 1959 to 1963) and E. J. Carnell (who served from 1954 to 1959). Hubbard's excellent academic credentials and conciliatory spirit saved the conservative evangelical seminary from near collapse. Under his 30-year leadership, the seminary expanded its student body and added several new programs, including a school of psychology and a school of world missions. Hubbard also became known for his influential role in smoothing off some of the rough edges in the American evangelical community without compromising biblical principles. He retired as president of the seminary in favor of Richard Mouw in 1993.

Hubbard began an additional career as a radio minister in 1967, when Charles Fuller retired from his popular radio program, *Old Fashioned Revival Hour*. Hubbard took charge of the international broadcast ministry and, in 1969, renamed it *The Joyful Sound*. He retained the preaching format of Fuller's earlier show and remained the chief speaker on the weekly program until 1980.

A prolific author, Hubbard published over 37 titles, including *With Bands of Love* (1968), *The Second Coming* (1984), and *Old Testament Survey* (with Frederick Bush and William LaSor, 1982). He resumed part-time teaching duties at Westmont following his retirement as president and was serving as general editor of the Word Biblical Commentary Series when he died from a heart attack in June 1996.

See also Charles Fuller

SOURCES

Billy Graham Center Archives, Wheaton College, Wheaton, Illinois.

Hubbard, David A. *The Second Coming: What Will Happen When Jesus Returns?* Downers Grove, IL: InterVarsity Press, 1984.

Marsden, George M. *Reforming Fundamentalism: Fuller Seminary and the New Evangelicalism.* Grand Rapids: Eerdmans, 1987.

Stone, Jon R. *A Guide to the End of the World: Popular Eschatology in America.* New York: Garland, 1993.

"Westmont Community Mourns Hubbard's Passing." *Santa Barbara News-Press*, June 11, 1996.

REX HUMBARD

born: Aug. 13, 1919, Little Rock, Arkansas

Rex Humbard is one of the most successful and respected television evangelists in the twentieth century. He and his family have constructed a television ministry that has taken them throughout the United States and the world.

Rex Humbard grew up in a traveling ministry headed by his parents Martha Bell Childers and Alpha E. Humbard, both Pentecostal evan-

Courtesy: National Religious Broadcasters

gelists. The elder Humbard encouraged his children's musical training and soon had them singing on a radio station in Little Rock, Arkansas, where he was pastoring an independent Pentecostal church. The music ministry expanded and, in 1939, the elder Humbard moved his family to Dallas to sing on a radio program with Virgil O. Stamps. It was in Dallas that Rex Humbard met the woman he would marry in 1942, Maude Aimee Jones. Ms. Jones was an experienced radio singer at the time, having performed before live audiences from the time she was five.

During the mid-1940s, Rex Humbard decided to become a Pentecostal minister. He received his ordination from the Gospel Tabernacle in Greenville, South Carolina, and his ministerial credentials from an organization of independent Pentecostal ministers, the International Ministerial Federation. In 1952, following a successful revival in Akron, Ohio, Humbard, his wife, and his brother-in-law, Wayne Jones, decided to retire from the family traveling ministry and founded a church in Akron, Ohio. They leased an old theater and incorporated in 1953 as Calvary Temple.

Television began to spread across the country in the early 1950s. Humbard perceived the potential power of this medium for evangelism and decided to broadcast Calvary Temple's Sunday services on a local Akron television station in 1953. The program was promoted as an outreach to the elderly, the sick, and all other persons who were unable to attend weekly worship services. As the ministry grew, Humbard decided to build a new church that would be specifically designed for radio and television broadcasts of its services. The 5,000-seat facility was begun in 1956 and named "The Cathedral of Tomorrow" at its dedication in 1958. The church would become home to over 15,000 worshippers, 10 pastors, a number of music ministries, and special church subgroups. It featured a sophisticated array of camera, sound, and lighting equipment and a large stage that accommodated television crews, an orchestra, and a choir.

Throughout his tenure as pastor of the Cathedral, Humbard received his salary by a special offering that was separate from the church's operating budget. The Cathedral's daily operation was the responsibility of a six-person board of trustees that included both Rex and Maude Humbard.

Humbard conceived of his task as "preaching the simple gospel." His sermons were peppered with familiar illustrations drawn from everyday life and delivered in a "down-home," folksy speaking style. The preacher's large family of sons, daughters, daughters-in-law, and grandchildren regularly took the stage with him and his wife, adding a sense of familial intimacy to his broadcasts. Humbard always eschewed political or doctrinal debates and preferred to proclaim boldly "the positive message of God's forgiveness and love." On one Sunday each year Humbard offered a communion service for his television audience. The audience was given instructions on the preparation of the elements one week before the service, and invited to join in the eucharistic celebration with his congregation.

By 1971, Humbard's weekly Sunday program *Cathedral of Tomorrow* was being broadcast over 650 television stations in North America and 700 radio stations. During the next decade the show expanded to an international audience that included Japan, Australia, the Philippines, Africa, and South America. His 1976 Christmas program became the first religious broadcast to be carried internationally by satellite.

Humbard also began holding televised rallies in major cities around the world. His 1977 rally in New York City reportedly created a huge traffic jam around Carnegie Hall when participants who were turned away crowded the surrounding streets and sidewalks. A series of 1978 rallies in São Paulo, Rio de Janeiro, and other large Brazilian cities drew over a half million people. Seventy percent of the television audience for these rallies was estimated to be 25 years or younger, and 80 percent of the live audience stood to pray for a religious rebirth in their lives. The Brazilian tour bore ecumenical fruits as well. At the beginning of his Rio de Janeiro rally, for example, over 150 pastors from different denominations attended a gala welcoming ceremony. At the tour's conclusion, the Brazilian pastors agreed to meet again in the future to form an alliance.

Benjamin Moraes, one of these clergypersons, discussed what made Humbard and his family so popular with believers from different denominations.

First, Humbard brought "cooperation to the cause of Jesus Christ among the churches." Second, his television programs were bringing "many new members into churches throughout Brazil," and thereby helping to strengthen all churches. Third, Humbard's ministry was manifesting Jesus Christ as Lord and Savior. This phenomenon was "changing minds and hearts of the people and making new persons out of them." The fourth reason for Humbard's popularity was that he spread "the sound doctrine of Jesus Christ" rather than doctrines that denied Christ's divinity. Finally, Moraes declared, "When so many families, both inside the churches and out, are being destroyed, [his] presentation with [his] wife and family is so wonderful. [His] family is an outstanding example of a Christian family."

The enormous success of Humbard's Brazilian tour resulted in requests from the Chilean government and Council of Pastors to come to Santiago for a similar series of rallies. His Chilean tour was another huge success. At a meeting with 600 pastors, Humbard addressed how their churches could benefit from his television ministry:

> Pastors are beginning to understand my role as their associate pastor. Through our ministry's weekly television programs, we are doing visitation work, door-to-door witnessing, and personal evangelism work—all of which is filling churches with new converts who are hungry to be fed and led in the Word. Because television reaches such a huge audience, it touches more homes in one week than many churches could contact in a year. Pastors are beginning to see that the Rex Humbard Ministry can be one of their most effective tools for building churches!

Humbard resigned the pastorate of the Cathedral of Tomorrow in 1983 and was succeeded by Wayne Jones, his brother-in-law. He continues to play a leadership role in Rex Humbard World Outreach Ministry and directs the Humbard Family Seminars, whose mission is to support and rebuild broken families. The Humbard television program has retained a significant audience share throughout the vicissitudes of the 1980s. It continues to feature a professional format that includes Humbard's sermons and music by his large family. Humbard has also been engaged in several writing projects, including revisions of his popular autobiography.

SOURCES

Armstrong, Ben. *The Electric Church.* Nashville: Thomas Nelson, 1979.

"Bridging the Barriers, Building New Hope." *The Answer* (October 1978), 21.

Humbard, A. E. *My Life Story (Just a Little Bit Different): From the Plowhandle to the Pulpit.* 1945.

Humbard, Maude Aimee. *Maude Aimee . . . I Look to the Hills.* Akron, OH: Rex Humbard Ministry, 1976.

Humbard, Rex. *How to Stay on Top When the Bottom Falls Out.* Akron, OH: Rex Humbard Foundation, 1981.

———. *Miracles in My Life: Rex Humbard's Own Story.* Rev. ed. Old Tappan, NJ: Fleming H. Revell, 1971.

———. *Put God on Main Street.* Akron: Cathedral of Tomorrow, 1970.

———. *The Third Dimension.* Old Tappan, NJ: Fleming H. Revell, 1972.

———. *Where Are the Dead?* Akron, OH: Rex Humbard World Outreach Ministry, 1977.

———. *Why I Believe Jesus Is Coming Soon.* Pasadena, CA: Compass Press, 1972

———. *Your Key to God's Bank.* Akron, OH: Rex Humbard Foundation, 1977.

"Rex Humbard TV Rallies in Brazil, Chile Set New Records." *Religious Broadcasting* (August/ September 1978), 41.

I

"I AM WITH YOU"
aired: four-part special, May 1963

"I Am with You" was another award-winning television special produced by Richard J. Walsh and Martin H. Work of the National Council of Catholic Men, in cooperation with Martin Hoade and Doris Ann of NBC-TV. The four-part program aired on the long-running religious series *The Catholic Hour* in 1963. The overall focus of the program was the 2,000-year history of the Catholic Church as seen through the lens of the great ecumenical councils. As Walsh explained, "Our purpose was to show that the Church itself is a living organism; that the history of the Church in its councils is the mystery of Christ in His Church." The title of the program came from Jesus's last words to his disciples in the Gospel of Matthew: "And remember, I am with you always, even to the end of the age."

Walsh hired Pulitzer Prize–winning cameraman Joe Vadala, who had worked at NBC and Universal Pictures for 33 years, to shoot the project. Vadala traveled 15,000 miles and visited 16 cities in Europe and the Middle East. The camera crew received special permission to film the final meeting of a Vatican II preparatory commission and shot more than 40,000 feet of film. Walsh chose Philip Scharper of the Catholic publisher Sheed and Ward to prepare a script for the program and commissioned Ralph Burns to compose and conduct a score. Proclaimed as "the most extensive religious-historical documentary ever filmed for television," the special aired on NBC's *The Catholic Hour* during the four Sundays of May 1963. Walsh dedicated "I Am with You" to His Holiness Pope John XXIII. The four programs were part of the long-standing tradition of production excellence for which *The Catholic Hour* was known.

See also *The Catholic Hour*

SOURCES

"I Am with You." *America*, May 4, 1963, 629.

IKE, REVEREND
see: Reverend Ike

IN THE SPIRIT
first aired: 1971

In the Spirit was the name of a weekly radio program hosted by Dr. Lex Hixon on WBAI-FM in New York City. The show, which aired from 1971 to 1984, featured interviews with representatives of the world's major religious traditions. Among the most famous of the program's guests were the Dalai Lama of Tibet and Mother Teresa of Calcutta.

Hixon was a native of Southern California who studied at Yale University and received his doctor of philosophy degree in comparative religion from Columbia University in 1976. During his academic career, Hixon lectured at the New School of Social Research in New York City. The scholar–radio personality died of cancer on November 1, 1995, in Riverdale in the Bronx. He was 53 at the time.

IN TOUCH
see: Charles Stanley

INSIGHT FOR LIVING
first aired: 1977

Insight for Living is the long-running, half-hour radio broadcast program of Chuck Swindoll, the former senior pastor of First Evangelical Free Church of Fullerton, California, and current president of Dallas Theological Seminary. The program features half-hour segments of Swindoll's Sunday morning or Sunday evening sermons, which typically blend expository Bible preaching with practical advice for Christian living. Airing initially over 27 stations nationwide in 1977, *Insight for Living* is currently heard over more than 1,000 stations worldwide in English, Spanish, Portuguese, Hindi, and Norwegian. The ministry's production headquarters are located in Anaheim, California, where it distributes audiocassettes, Bible-study guides, and a number of books and pamphlets written by Swindoll. The ministry also sponsors conferences for ministers and laypersons and oversees a counseling service.

See also Chuck Swindoll

INSPIRATIONAL NETWORK
established: 1990

In 1990, a federal bankruptcy judge approved evangelist Morris Cerullo's $7 million bid for the remains of Jim Bakker's PTL empire. Although he later sold much of his interest in this empire to other investors, Cerullo kept the PTL Network, which he renamed the Inspirational Network (INSP). During the 1990s, INSP has become one of the most successful religious broadcasting networks in the United States. The Charlotte, North Carolina–based ministry is headed by Cerullo's son, David Cerullo, who serves as INSP's president and chief executive officer.

INSP has been an industry leader in devising new strategies and approaches for religious broadcasting. Among these strategies are the development of alternatives to the religious program models of the past. These new models include the creation of a balanced lineup of shows that both entertain and engage audiences, and a network style that is not based on a flagship program or particular personality. In addition, INSP is seeking to turn to revenue based on sponsorship, fee-based interactive services, and advertising—rather than on viewer donations.

INSP is also taking the lead in the development of new genres of religious programming, including children's shows, music and concert specials, films, teaching and ministry series, and teen programs. These programs have included such specials as "Night of Joy from Walt Disney World"; "Cheyenne Country Live" with Bruce Carroll; the "True Love Waits National Celebration," created in cooperation with the Southern Baptist Sunday School Board and Youth for Christ; Bill and Gloria Gaither's annual New Year's Eve concert, *Jubilant*; and "The Cathedral's 30th Annual Reunion Concert." INSP has also created such popular programs as *Cheyenne Country with Steve Gatlin* (which was recently voted the International Country Gospel Music Association's top positive country show); *In the House*, an urban culture program hosted by Mike-E; the music-variety program *The Mark and Kathy Show*; and *Family Cinema with Grant Goodeve*.

In an effort to build alternative revenue sources that allow the network to finance new program development, INSP has created INSP-Direct, a direct-marketing venture that offers a broad array of proprietary consumer products, a roster of personalities, and turn-key packaging and promotion services. The products offered by INSP-Direct include exercise, diet, health, and beauty aids marketed under the trademark Accent Life.

INSP has also taken a leading role in developing alliances among Christian broadcasters. The network's syndication group provides free programming, sales resources, and promotional materials to over 40 Christian television stations, as well as producing programs in cooperation with Zomba Records, Youth for Christ, and Star Song Communications, among others. In order to overcome the secular resistance to Christian sounding names, INSP has begun to change its ministries' titles. In late 1995, for example, the network changed its corporate identity to Homecast, although the network itself has retained the name Inspirational Network.

See also Morris Cerullo

SOURCES

Cerullo, David. "A New Brand of Inspirational Television." Religious Broadcasting, December, 1995.

Ostling, Richard N. "A New Preacher for PTL." *Time*, June 11, 1990.

INSP-DIRECT
established: 1995

INSP-Direct is a multidimensional direct-marketing business established in 1995 by the Inspirational Network (INSP)—to offer new sources of revenue to Christian broadcasters dissatisfied with traditional fundraising models. Among the formats offered are short-form commercials ("spots"), long-form commercials ("infomercials"), entertainment programs with revenue-generating spots, a roster of personalities available for guest appearances on a station's flagship programs, and aftermarket support and materials. The personalities include speaker Neil Eskelen, nutrition expert Cheryl Townsley, and author Michael Pink.

INSP-Direct has developed both products and the resources to package and market them. The products include diet, exercise, health, and beauty aids marketed under the trademark Accent Life. The marketing resources are natural spin-offs from the network's teleproduction activities, including videos and audiotapes. Larry Sims, INSP-Direct's vice president, developed the Accent Life product line with special sensitivity to the needs of Christians. As he reflected,

> Our Accent Life brand provides a well-balanced package with products for spirit, soul, and body. Accent Life focuses on communicating a proper lifestyle as well as providing clear direction in daily life using biblical principles. These products benefit viewers while enabling them to contribute to the work of ministry outreach.

INSP-Direct is an intriguing example of how Christian broadcasters are adopting the methods, strategies, and technologies of the secular business and broadcasting worlds to further their evangelistic missions.

See also Inspirational Network

SOURCES

Cerullo, David. "A New Brand of Inspirational Television." *Religious Broadcasting*, December, 1995.

Roos, John. "INSP-Direct: Revenue for You." *Religious Broadcasting*, December, 1995.

INSTITUTE FOR CREATION RESEARCH
established: 1970

Founded in 1970 as the Creation-Science Research Center, the Institute for Creation Research (ICR) is an interdenominational, non-profit research and education institute that disseminates information to interested Christians on the creation-versus-evolution debate. The institute's director is the creation science apologist Henry Morris.

Located in El Cajon, California, ICR produces two main broadcast programs, a brief weekday radio spot called *Back to Genesis* and a 15-

minute weekly radio program entitled *Science, Scripture, and Salvation*. The institute also sponsors college campus debates between proponents of creationism and evolutionism. These events are seen as a way to evangelize curious students by presenting their evidence that refutes the theory of evolution.

See also Henry Morris

SOURCES

The Directory of Religious Organizations in the United States. 2d ed. Falls Church, VA: McGrath, 1982.

Melton, J. Gordon. *Directory of Religious Organizations in the United States.* 3d ed. Detroit: Gale Research, 1993.

INTERNATIONAL CHRISTIAN MEDIA
see: Marlin Maddoux

INTERNATIONAL LUTHERAN LAYMEN'S LEAGUE
established: 1917

The International Lutheran Laymen's League (ILLL) is the national auxiliary organization of the laity of the Lutheran Church (Missouri Synod). It got its start in broadcasting when, in 1929, it agreed to help sponsor Walter Maier's first radio ministry. In the depths of the Great Depression, the ILLL raised nearly $100,000 from its member churches, just enough to begin broadcast production of Maier's program, *The Lutheran Hour*, which first aired in October 1930 over the CBS radio network. It quickly became one of the most successful programs of its kind.

Since that time, the Laymen's League has sponsored a variety of radio and television programs and specials. In addition to *The Lutheran Hour*, its radio productions have included *Crosswalk*, a short-run program that went off the air in the early 1990s. ILLL's forays into television have included *This Is the Life*, a long-running program now in syndication that is pro-duced with funds generated by the success of *The Lutheran Hour*. With headquarters in St. Louis, Missouri, the International Lutheran Laymen's League boasts a membership of some 130,000 lay persons.

See also *The Lutheran Hour*

SOURCES

Hadden, Jeffrey K., and Anson Shupe. *Televangelism: Power and Politics on God's Frontier.* New York: Henry Holt, 1988.

Hadden, Jeffrey K., and Charles E. Swann. *Prime Time Preachers: The Rising Power of Televangelism.* Reading, MA: Addison-Wesley, 1981.

Melton, J. Gordon. *Directory of Religious Organizations in the United States.* 3d ed. Detroit: Gale Research, 1993.

Ward, Mark, Sr. *Air of Salvation: The Story of Christian Broadcasting.* Grand Rapids, MI: Baker Book House, 1994.

INTERNATIONAL MISSION RADIO ASSOCIATION
established: 1963

Originally founded in 1963 as the Catholic Mission Radio Association, the International Mission Radio Association (IMRA) is an interdenominational nonprofit organization of amateur short-wave radio operators who provide communications links among missionaries in 40 countries worldwide. In addition to operating a missionary short-wave network, IMRA loans out broadcast equipment, trains and licenses members, and assists in establishing short-wave stations. Directed by the Reverend Thomas Sable of the University of Scranton in Scranton, Pennsylvania, IMRA boasts a membership of nearly 1,000 radio volunteers.

SOURCES

Melton, J. Gordon. *Directory of Religious Organizations in the United States.* 3d ed. Detroit: Gale Research, 1993.

INTERNATIONAL NEEDS
established: 1974

International Needs, an evangelical missionary organization, was founded in 1974 by Ray Harrison. The mission of International Needs is to help establish closer ties between Christians in developed and developing nations worldwide and to encourage Christian service by nationals. In addition to evangelism, literature distribution, and church planting, International Needs sponsors medical and educational services in a number of its mission areas.

International Needs makes use of radio broadcast services to spread its message to a number of Asian countries including Japan, Thailand, and the Philippines. It uses television broadcast services in South Asia and the Middle East. Although its main headquarters are in Scranton, Pennsylvania, International Needs also maintains offices in Britain, Canada, Australia, and New Zealand.

SOURCES

Melton, J. Gordon. *Directory of Religious Organizations in the United States.* 3d ed. Detroit: Gale Research, 1993.

INTERNATIONAL PRISON MINISTRY
established: 1970

Begun by Chaplain Ray Hoekstra, International Prison Ministry is an independent evangelical organization in Dallas, Texas, that broadcasts evangelistically-charged messages of faith and encouragement to prison inmates in the United States, Mexico, the Caribbean, and the Philippines. It also sends religious literature and Bibles to interested inmates and publishes a bimonthly news magazine, *Prison Evangelism.* Hoekstra was the host of *Christ Truth Radio Crusade* (previously *Prisoners Bible Broadcast*) from 1962 to 1970. His program, *International Prison Broadcasts,* airs daily over the USA Radio Network.

See also Ray Hoekstra

SOURCES

Melton, J. Gordon. *Directory of Religious Organizations in the United States.* 3d ed. Detroit: Gale Research, 1993.

HARRY IRONSIDE
born: October 14, 1876, Toronto, Canada
died: January 15, 1951, Cambridge, New Zealand

The popular radio preacher and longtime pastor of the Moody Memorial Church, Harry A. Ironside, was the son of English immigrants John and Sophia Ironside. The couple settled in Toronto, Canada, and joined the Plymouth Brethren Church. John Ironside was an active street preacher before his sudden death when Harry was only three. After her husband's death, Sophia Ironside decided to move the family to Los Angeles.

In 1888, at age 12, Ironside attended an area revival held by Dwight Moody and decided to become an evangelist. Two years later, he had a religious experience that resulted in his full conversion. From 1890 to 1896, Ironside served in various positions with the Salvation Army. In 1892, he was commissioned an officer by the Salvation Army and earned the nickname "the boy preacher from Los Angeles." By 1895, however, Ironside was becoming disenchanted with the Salvation Army and Holiness doctrine. The following year, after moving to San Francisco, he decided to join a branch of the Plymouth Brethren Church. For the next 34 years, Ironside was a Bible-conference speaker and itinerant preacher.

In 1898, Ironside married Helen Schofield in San Francisco. The couple moved to Oakland two years later. While in Oakland, Ironside began collecting his expository messages into book form, publishing a number of works, such as *Notes on Esther* (1900), *Notes on Jeremiah* (1902), *Notes on the Minor Prophets* (1904) and *Notes on Proverbs* (1906). In 1914, he helped organize the Western Book and Tract Company, which published his books and those of the Brethren. Eventually, Ironside wrote over 40 such books (two dozen of which remain in print), each with a Scofield dispensational flavoring. (The Scofield dispensation is a complex form of eschatology once popular and still taught at the Dallas Theological Seminary.) By 1946, Ironside had sold nearly a million copies of his books.

In 1930, though not an ordained minister, Ironside was called as pastor of the Moody Memorial Church, a position he held until 1948. It was in Chicago that he began broadcasting his Sunday morning sermons over WMBI radio. These popular and successful broadcasts consisted of expository lessons which were later compiled and published in book form. Ironside also served as a visiting professor at Dallas Theological Seminary from 1925 to 1943.

Ironside died on January 15, 1951, in Cambridge, New Zealand, while on a preaching tour.

SOURCES

Billy Graham Center Archives, Wheaton College, Wheaton, Illinois.

Ironside, Harry A. *The Lamp of Prophecy: or, Signs of the Times.* Grand Rapids, MI: Zondervan, 1951.

Melton, J. Gordon. *Religious Leaders of America.* Detroit: Gale Research, 1991.

Sandeen, Ernest R. *The Roots of Fundamentalism.* Chicago: University of Chicago Press, 1970.

Stone, Jon R. *A Guide to the End of the World: Popular Eschatology in America.* New York: Garland, 1993.

ISLAMIC INFORMATION CENTER OF AMERICA

With the tremendous growth of Muslim populations in Europe and North America, Islamic communications centers have sprung up in such cities as London, New York, Paris, and Washington, DC. One such center is the Islamic Information Center of America (IICA), headquartered in Des Plaines, Illinois, and operated by both Americans and non-Americans. This nonprofit, tax-exempt organization provides information about Islam to the American mass media and to the general public.

The center's main objectives are to deliver the pure message of Islam as comprehensively as possible to the American populace and to assist American converts to Islam in their missionary efforts. IICA gives lectures about Islam in colleges and universities, distributes copies of the Qur'an with an approved translation, writes and publishes pamphlets about Islam, and uses television, radio, and newspapers to deliver the message of Islam. IICA speakers regularly appear in seminars, discussions, symposia, and radio and television programs.

As Islamic influence expands in the West, organizations such as the IICA will continue to utilize the latest technological advances in telecommunications to promote their sectarian versions of the message of Muhammad.

SOURCES

Boyd, Douglas A. *Broadcasting in the Arab World: A Survey of the Electronic Media in the Middle East.* Ames, IA: Iowa State University Press, 1993.

Hale, Julian. *Radio Power: Propaganda and International Broadcasting.* Philadelphia: Temple University Press, 1975.

Islamic Information Center of America. Promotional Brochure, 1995.

Kamalipour, Yahya, and Hamid Mowlana, eds. *Mass Media in the Middle East: A Comprehensive Handbook.* Westport, CT: Greenwood Press, 1994.

ISLAMIC STATES BROADCASTING ORGANIZATION
established: 1975

With the rise of satellite technology during the 1970s and 1980s, barriers to coordinated regional broadcasting in the Middle East have been surmounted. Three major satellite systems—the International Telecommunications Satellite Organization, PALAPA of Indonesia, and ARABSAT of the Middle East—now serve the needs of Southeast Asia, North Africa, and the Persian Gulf. Regional organizations such as the Islamic States Broadcasting Organization (ISBO), GulfVision, and the Arab States Broadcasting Union have assisted in technical cooperation and the exchange of programming between member countries.

ISBO, the largest of these regional organizations, was created in Jeddah, Saudi Arabia, in 1975 by the Sixth Islamic Conference of Foreign Ministers. It seeks to spread Islamic teachings, to expose people to the objectives of Islam, and to assist Islamic broadcasting institutions in the development of cooperative ventures. Between 1970 and 1990, the number of broadcasting transmitters has increased greatly in most Islamic countries, as has the distribution of radios and televisions.

SOURCES

Boyd, Douglas A. *Broadcasting in the Arab World: A Survey of the Electronic Media in the Middle East*. Ames, IA: Iowa State University Press, 1993.

Hale, Julian. *Radio Power: Propaganda and International Broadcasting*. Philadelphia: Temple University Press, 1975.

Kamalipour, Yahya, and Hamid Mowlana, eds. *Mass Media in the Middle East: A Comprehensive Handbook*. Westport, CT: Greenwood Press, 1994.

J

JACK VAN IMPE PRESENTS!
first aired: 1980

Jack Van Impe Presents! is a half-hour weekly news program that analyzes and interprets world events in the light of biblical prophecy. The show is cohosted by Jack and Rexella Van Impe and is broadcast in both the United States and abroad over the Inspirational Network, the 357 stations of the Trinity Broadcasting Network, Black Entertainment Television, Chicago's WGN Superstation, Cornerstone TV, and Christian Channel Europe. Jack Van Impe's greatest accomplishment has been to capitalize on the interest in biblical prophecy generated by books such as Hal Lindsey's *The Late Great Planet Earth* and to create a professional quality broadcasting ministry based on this fundamentalist interpretive framework.

See also Jack Van Impe; Rexella Van Impe

JESSE JACKSON
born: October 8, 1941, Greenville, South Carolina

Jesse L. Jackson represents a myriad of crossover media personalities, whose message of hope and emphasis on social redemption is at once religious and political. Jackson is not only a social activist, television host, and political commentator, therefore, but also a Baptist religious leader and preacher.

Born into poverty in Greenville, South Carolina, to Noah Robinson and Helen Burns, Jackson was later adopted in 1957 by his mother's first husband, Charles Jackson. A religious upbringing instilled in Jackson a strong sense of Christian morality and a desire to better himself through education and hard work. Upon graduation from Sterling High School in 1959, Jackson, a football star, received a scholarship to play at the University of Illinois. Barred from playing quarterback—the position he had played in high school—because of his race, Jackson transferred in 1961 to the North Carolina Agricultural and Technical College, where he became an honor student and president of the student body. He graduated in 1964 with a degree in sociology. During this time, Jackson became involved in a number of protests, including successful sit-in demonstrations at local theaters and restaurants. Though he had a distaste for the traditional black Baptist overemphasis on other-worldly concerns, Jackson was drawn to the ministry as an avenue of effective social activism by the example of Martin Luther King, Jr..

In 1965, Jackson entered the Chicago Theological Seminary, where he combined theological study with political action. That same year, Jackson participated in King's march on Selma, Alabama, and joined the Coordinating Council of Community Organizations. In 1966, before finishing his degree, Jackson left the seminary to work with King and the Southern Christian Leadership Conference (SCLC). The conference appointed him head of the Chicago branch of Operation Breadbasket, which worked with city businesses to promote jobs for urban blacks. In 1968, Jackson was ordained to the Christian ministry by the Progressive National Baptist Convention. The following year, he received an honorary degree from the Chicago Theological Seminary, one of over 30 honorary degrees that would be bestowed upon him over the next 25 years.

Following King's assassination in 1968, tensions between Ralph Abernathy, King's successor, and Jackson led to the young minister's withdrawal from the SCLC and his founding of operation PUSH (People United to Save Humanity, later People United to Serve Humanity) in 1971. In 1976, Jackson founded PUSH for Excellence, which aimed at building self-esteem among black youth. By the late 1970s, Jackson began to emerge as an international figure, speaking out against human rights violations in South Africa and the Middle East.

In 1983, Jackson launched his candidacy for the Democratic presidential nomination, built upon a strong grassroots movement he named the Rainbow Coalition (later the National Rainbow Coalition). Despite losing to Walter Mondale, Jackson attempted a second, and more successful, run at the White House in 1988, with a stronger base of support and the motto, "Keep Hope Alive." After losing to Michael Dukakis in the Democratic primary, Jackson made regular appearances as a political commentator on *Firing Line* and became the host of two short-lived radio and television talk shows, *Jesse Jackson* and *Frontline*, which dealt with religious and social issues.

Although he declined to run for president in 1992, Jackson has remained a forceful presence in American politics. At the conclusion of the O. J. Simpson trial in 1995, for example, Jackson appeared on television to help soothe racial tensions that Simpson's acquittal seemed to intensify. Jackson has been appearing regularly on television news programs to outline his positions on a number of social and political issues. Jackson also continues to host the weekly talk show he began in 1990 for CNN cable news service named *Both Sides*.

SOURCES

Melton, J. Gordon. *Religious Leaders of America.* Detroit: Gale Research, 1991.

Murphy, Larry G., J. Gordon Melton, and Gary L. Ward. *Encyclopedia of African American Religion.* New York: Garland, 1993.

Reid, Daniel G., Robert D. Linder, Bruce L. Shelley, and Harry S. Stout, eds. *Dictionary of Christianity in America.* Downers Grove, IL: InterVarsity Press, 1990.

MAHALIA JACKSON
born: October 26, 1911, New Orleans, Louisiana
died: January, 1972, Evergreen Park, Illinois

Perhaps the greatest gospel singer of the twentieth century, Mahalia Jackson was the daughter of John Jackson, a Baptist preacher, and Charity Clark. Mahalia was raised in a deeply pious religious environment filled with sacred music. As her social world expanded, she was exposed to both the blues and operatic music, which greatly influenced her own development as a singer.

At 13, Jackson left school to work as a maid and sang in the church choir every Sunday. In 1928, Jackson left her home in New Orleans to work in Chicago, where she joined the choir of the Greater Salem Baptist Church. It was not long before she was chosen as a church soloist, beginning her long and successful career in music. During the late 1920s and early 1930s, Jackson was a soloist in the 156-voice choir that accompanied Lightfoot Solomon Michaux's popular *Radio Church of God* program on WJSV, Washington, DC. When the CBS radio network purchased WJSV, Jackson's voice was heard on over 50 affiliated stations.

In 1934, Jackson recorded her first single with Decca Records, entitled "God Gonna Separate the Wheat from the Tares." The song garnered only local notice, but it provided clear evidence of her vocal gifts. Her first big break came in 1945 with the recording of "Move on Up a Little Higher" on Apollo Records. The song demonstrated her ability to move an audience with her unique blend of gospel and blues music and eventually brought her national attention by selling over 1 million copies. Within a short time, Jackson was offered contracts to sing in night clubs and similar venues throughout the United States. She turned these opportunities down, however, believing that these venues were inappropriate for gospel music.

Jackson debuted at New York's Carnegie Hall in 1951 and followed this triumphant performance with a European tour two years later. In 1954, she began her own radio program, *Mahalia*, which featured her gospel singing talents. The program aired weekly from September 1954 to February 1955. Jackson was also invited to the White House for a concert hosted by President Dwight D. Eisenhower and sang at the inauguration of John F. Kennedy in 1961. During the early 1960s, Jackson starred in a syndicated five-minute musical program distributed by TV Enterprises. She also was the special guest star on a splashy Oral Roberts television special in 1969.

Jackson became active in the Civil Rights movement, demonstrating her support by traveling to Montgomery, Alabama, during the 1955 bus boycott. She later appeared with Martin Luther King, Jr., during the March on Washington in August 1963, and sang at his funeral in April 1968.

After King's death, Jackson continued her strong commitment to Civil Rights but was increasingly plagued by failing health. She died of a heart attack in January 1972.

See also Lightfoot Solomon Michaux

SOURCES

Murphy, Larry G., J. Gordon Melton, and Gary L. Ward. *Encyclopedia of African American Religion*. New York: Garland, 1993.

T. D. JAKES
born: 1957, West Virginia

T. D. Jakes is the host of *Get Ready with T. D. Jakes,* a weekly television program that features the African American preacher's taped addresses to nationwide conferences and his weekly Temple of Faith Church Services. The program is a popular part of Trinity Broadcasting Network's weekly lineup.

Jakes grew up in West Virginia and spent much of his youth in hospitals, caring for his father, who died of kidney failure when Jakes was 10 years old. As a young Pentecostal minister, Jakes preached in the coal fields of West Virginia around potbelly stoves, in store fronts, and in small house churches. As his reputation as a preacher grew, Jakes began to attract a cross-denominational, cross-generational, and interracial following. During the 1980s, Jakes was elected the diocesan bishop of the Eastern Ohio-West Virginia jurisdiction of the Higher Ground Always Abounding Assemblies and pastor of the Temple of Faith Ministries in Charleston, West Virginia.

Jakes's growing popularity—he traveled almost 300 days in 1994 on the nationwide Christian circuit—is linked to his compassionate message of reconciliation, healing, and restoration in special meetings for each gender. Jakes's conferences for women, entitled Woman, Thou Art Loosed, drew 75,000 participants between 1993 and 1995. The events feature weeping, dancing in the aisles, speaking in tongues, and ecstatic dashing around the sanctuary. Jakes's sermons address topics that range from drug addiction, rape, incest, failure to attain personal goals, and low self-esteem. His book, *Woman, Thou Art Loosed,* is a bestseller in Christian bookstores.

SOURCES

Howard, Judith Lynn. "Healing Words." *Dallas Morning News,* June 10, 1995.

Ward, Ken. "Successful Books, TV Exposure Allow Kanawha Minister to Live in Style." *Charleston* (West Virginia) *Gazette*, April 5, 1995.

JACOB JAMBAZIAN
see: Radio AR Intercontinental, Armenia

JANET PARSHALL'S AMERICA
first aired: March 13, 1995

Janet Parshall is a conservative radio and television commentator, author, and advocate for family issues. Her latest radio show debuted on WAVA-FM in Arlington, Virginia, March 13, 1995. The show, called *Janet Parshall's America*, addresses public policy, current affairs, and lifestyle topics in a talk-show format. The program replaces an earlier program, *On the Mark*.

Along with such conservative Christian commentators as James Dobson, Wanda Franz, and Jay Sekulow, Parshall represents the growing number of conservative religious personalities thriving in national broadcasting forums geared toward the discussion of political, lifestyle, and legal issues. During the late 1980s and early 1990s, Parshall was the cohost on Vic Eliason's conservative radio talk show *Crosstalk*.

LEROY JENKINS
born: 1935, Fort Mill, South Carolina

Leroy Jenkins follows in the Pentecostal faith healing tradition of Oral Roberts, A. A. Allen, and Robert Schambach, in that he developed a television ministry from his healing services.

Jenkins grew up in Greenwood, South Carolina, the son of an alcoholic father. Although he later claimed to have seen visions and to have received a call to the ministry as a child, Jenkins did not attend church during his teen years. After marrying Ruby Garrett when he was 17, Jenkins moved to Atlanta and worked as an antiques dealer. During this time, he and his new wife joined the Presbyterian Church.

Jenkins's conversion to Pentecostal Christianity was precipitated by a Mother's Day, 1960, accident during which his arm was almost completely severed. Refusing to have the arm amputated, Jenkins attended a healing service led by A. A. Allen a few days later. After hearing a voice that said, "There is somebody up there

that loves you," his arm was reportedly healed miraculously. Inspired by this experience, Jenkins founded his own independent tent ministry.

Like Allen's ministry, Jenkins played to racially integrated audiences. He managed to garner support from both the Full Gospel and Pentecostal movements, and to withstand the attacks of the Ku Klux Klan for his inclusive services. Jenkins's first healing crusade outside the United States took place in Nassau, Bahamas, in 1963. The itinerant ministry slowly began to grow, and Jenkins established a headquarters for his Church of What's Happening Now in Delaware, Ohio.

Although Jenkins was frustrated in his attempts to start a television ministry during the 1960s, he finally succeeded in 1973. His new program, *Revival in America*, began to garner a substantial national audience by 1975. Jenkins's success was short-lived, however. Numerous allegations led to an increasing swirl of controversy. Jenkins was said to have bilked a wealthy Texas woman, who believed Jenkins was her son, out of thousands of dollars; taken credit for the deaths of certain enemies and claimed that the deaths were due to divine providence; abused alcohol and drugs; and declared that his ministry's four-man board was "the Father, the Son, the Holy Spirit, and Me." While some close associates were quitting the ministry because of Jenkins's reported arrogance and ego, others (such as Mae West, who offered him a role in an upcoming film) were insisting that he had changed his ways once and for all.

Perhaps in an attempt to escape these controversies, Jenkins moved his ministry back to his hometown of Greenwood, South Carolina, in 1977. There he founded the Spirit of Truth Church and continued his television ministry. When fires destroyed some highly-insured ministry property, the local press began to investigate Jenkins more carefully. In 1979, the evangelist was arrested and charged with two counts of conspiracy to commit arson, as well as conspiracy to injure a local newspaperman who had written articles about Jenkins's misadventures. Following his conviction and 12-year prison sentence, Jenkins lost his television ministry and its backlog of valuable videotapes. Jenkins's son, Danny, attempted to keep the ministry afloat during this turbulent period, but he eventually left his father's ministry and went to work for the controversial faith healer, W. V. Grant. A lawsuit to decide legal ownership of *Revival in America*'s videotapes resulted in an out-of-court settlement between Jenkins and his producer which avoided the public disclosure of the faith healer's finances.

Jenkins served only three years of his sentence at a prison in Ohio before gaining a work release decision in 1982. By the time of his official parole in 1985, he had resumed his healing ministry and set up a new headquarters in Anderson, South Carolina. Jenkins was also able to resume his broadcasting ministry, although his audience was greatly diminished and the programming quality of his shows was subpar.

Jenkins gained new notoriety in 1987 when he publicly offered to hire the embattled Jim Bakker to help him develop his television ministry. Some commentators saw the move as an attempt to make a national comeback using Bakker's broadcasting empire.

SOURCES

Burgess, Stanley M., Gary B. McGee, and Patrick H. Alexander, eds. *Dictionary of Pentecostal and Charismatic Movements*. Grand Rapids, MI: Regency Reference Library, Zondervan, 1988.

Erickson, Hal. *Religious Radio and Television in the United States, 1921–1991*. Jefferson, NC: McFarland, 1992.

Jenkins, Leroy. *God Gave Me a Miracle Arm*. Delaware, OH: Leroy Jenkins Evangelistic Association, 1963.

———. *How I Met the Master*. Delaware, OH: Leroy Jenkins Evangelistic Association, 1970.

———. *How You Can Receive Your Healing*. Delaware, OH: Leroy Jenkins Evangelistic Association, 1966.

Randi, James. *The Faith Healers*. Buffalo, NY: Prometheus, 1987.

JOHN JESS
see: Chapel of the Air

JEWISH VOICE BROADCASTS
established: 1967

Founded in 1967 by Messianic Jewish minister Louis Kaplan, Jewish Voice Broadcasts (JVB) is an evangelical Christian outreach to Jews. From its headquarters in Phoenix, Arizona, JVB broadcasts a 15-minute radio program and a weekly television program. JVB's daily radio spot features Jewish worship music and testimonies by Jews who have converted to Christianity. The television show, *Le Chayim* (To Life) is aired throughout Arizona and large parts of the United States over Christian networks via cable and satellite. *Le Chayim* presents the life stories of Messianic Jews as well as sermons by Messianic Jewish ministers. The show often runs in tandem with other Jewish Christian programs, such as Jewish evangelist Zola Levitt's telecast, *Zola Levitt Presents*.

In addition to these broadcast ministries, JVB publishes *Jewish Voice Prophetic Magazine*, a monthly periodical that features the testimonies of converted Jews, radio and television programming guides, news stories supportive of apocalyptic scenarios, and articles geared toward Jewish interests.

SOURCES

Kaplan, Louis. *My Life Story and the Story of Jewish Voice*. Phoenix, AZ: Jewish Voice Broadcasts, n.d.

Melton, J. Gordon. *Directory of Religious Organizations in the United States*. 3d ed. Detroit: Gale Research, 1993.

JEWS FOR JESUS
see: Moishe Rosen

SHERROD JOHNSON

born: November 24, 1899, Pine Tree Quarter,
North Carolina
died: February 22, 1961, Kingston, Jamaica

Sherrod C. Johnson was one of the early African American pioneers of radio evangelism. Born to a family of sharecroppers in North Carolina, Johnson eventually left his rural home and worked as a musician and building contractor. By 1919, he was living in Philadelphia and preaching his Pentecostal message to a small group of followers who met in his home.

In time, Johnson met Robert Clarence Lawson, who had founded the Church of Our Lord Jesus Christ of the Apostolic Faith, an independent Pentecostalist church. Johnson affiliated himself with Lawson and helped the church establish a periodical, a day nursery, a pastoral training school, and several businesses. Although Lawson followed the traditional Pentecostal prohibitions against divorce and remarriage, he did allow women to wear jewelry and makeup, and to dress in brightly colored clothing. This liberalism did not coincide with Johnson's highly conservative reading of Scripture. In 1930, the young preacher broke away from Lawson and founded his own derivative congregation, the Church of the Lord Jesus Christ of the Apostolic Faith. Johnson became the new church's apostle and overseer.

Johnson's new congregation held its meetings in a small storefront in Philadelphia and grew slowly during the early 1930s. Perhaps inspired by the successes of such radio evangelists as Lightfoot Solomon Michaux, Johnson decided to start a Sunday radio ministry from his church. His twice weekly broadcast, called *The Whole Truth*, first aired on Philadelphia's WIBC and Washington, DC's WOOK. Johnson's rigidly conservative message seemed to strike a responsive chord during the Depression era, and his program gained a large and loyal following. In time, the broadcast's popularity led to the establishment of about 100 congregations in 18 states and missions in Liberia, England, Honduras, Jamaica, Haiti, the Bahamas, Jordan, Portugal, and the Maldives. During this time,

Johnson also issued numerous tracts that carefully explained his teachings. Following the destruction of the Philadelphia church in 1958, a new denominational headquarters and church were built. This facility was expanded and became known as Apostolic Square in 1972. The complex provided housing for members and offices for various church administrators.

Johnson's unrelentingly conservative message condemned tobacco and alcohol consumption, movies and television, and the celebration of such "pagan" festivals as Christmas, Lent, and Easter. His views on the role and deportment of women were particularly strict. Women were to refrain from preaching and teaching and from adorning themselves in "worldly" fashions. In practical terms this meant they were to wear only opaque cotton stockings and plain, ankle-length dresses.

The Whole Truth was eventually carried on over 70 religious broadcasting outlets both nationally and internationally. Johnson, after completing his doctor of philosophy degree at Rutgers University, died while visiting a congregation of his in Kingston, Jamaica. S. McDowell Shelton succeeded "Bishop" Johnson as the Church of the Lord Jesus Christ of the Apostolic Faith's apostle and universal overseer.

SOURCES

Anderson, Arthus M., ed., *For the Defense of the Gospel*. New York: Church of Christ Publishing Co., 1972.

Dupree, Sherry Sherrod. *Biographical Dictionary of African-American, Holiness-Pentecostals, 1880–1990*. Washington, DC: Middle Atlantic Regional Press, 1990.

Johnson, Sherrod C. *The Christmas Spirit Is a False Spirit*. Philadelphia: Church of the Lord Jesus Christ of the Apostolic Faith, n.d.

———. *Church Yearbook and Radio History*. Philadelphia: Church of the Lord Jesus Christ of the Apostolic Faith, 1957.

———. *False Lent and Pagan Festivals*. Philadelphia: Church of the Lord Jesus Christ of the Apostolic Faith, n.d.

———. *Let Patience Have Her Perfect Work*. Philadel-

phia: Church of the Lord Jesus Christ of the
Apostolic Faith, 1964.

———. *21 Burning Subjects: Who Is This That Defies
and Challenges the Whole Religious World on
These Subjects?* Philadelphia: Church of the Lord
Jesus Christ of the Apostolic Faith, n.d.

"Top Radio Ministers." *Ebony* 4 (July 1949): 56–61.

TORREY JOHNSON
born: 1909

Founder of Youth for Christ International (YFC)
and mentor to Robert Cook, Paul Freed, and
Billy Graham, Torrey Johnson attended
Wheaton College and Northern Baptist Theological Seminary. He began his career in religious broadcasting not long after assuming duties as pastor of Chicago's Midwest Bible
Church in 1933, a position he held for 20 years.
His radio program, *Songs in the Night*, aired in
the 1930s and 1940s over WCFL, Chicago. It
later moved to WMBI, the radio station of the
Moody Bible Institute. Although Johnson had
passed his program on to Billy Graham in 1943,
he was still invited to attend the National Association of Evangelicals meeting in 1944 that led
to the founding of the National Religious Broadcasters (NRB). Johnson subsequently became
a charter member of the NRB.

When, as a result of the radio ministries and
youth work of Lloyd Bryant, Percy Crawford,
and Jack Wyrtzen, churches throughout the
United States began sponsoring youth rallies,
Johnson decided to hold his own national youth
rally in Chicago in 1944. The success of this
campaign led Johnson to consider establishing
a national Christian youth organization. The
next year, Johnson and other evangelical leaders met at Winona Lake, Indiana, to formalize
Youth for Christ International, electing Johnson
as its first president. The young Billy Graham
became a traveling representative for YFC and
conducted a number of youth rallies and crusades across the country.

In 1948, Johnson handed leadership of YFC
over to Robert Cook and returned to his full-
time pastoral ministry. Five years later, in 1953,
Johnson resigned his ministry with the Midwest

Bible Church to become an itinerant evangelist. He later headed the Bibletown Conference
Center in Boca Raton, Florida, where he ministered from 1968 to 1983. Still active, Johnson
continues to be in demand as a popular speaker
on the evangelical conference circuit.

See also Robert Cook; National Religious
Broadcasters

SOURCES

Reid, Daniel G., Robert D. Linder, Bruce L. Shelley,
and Harry S. Stout, eds. *Dictionary of Christianity in America.* Downers Grove, IL: InterVarsity
Press, 1990.

Ward, Mark, Sr. *Air of Salvation: The Story of
Christian Broadcasting.* Grand Rapids, MI: Baker
Book House, 1994.

BOB JONES, JR.
born: October, 1911, Rural Alabama

The fundamentalist evangelist and college president, Bob Jones, Jr., was a pioneering figure in
the use of electronic broadcasting for the spread
of the gospel.

The son of the famed evangelist Bob Jones,
Sr., Jones grew up in a charged religious atmosphere. After graduation from Bob Jones College and the University of Pittsburgh, Jones followed in the footsteps of his father, becoming
an independent fundamentalist preacher and
ardent crusader against modernism. In 1932, the
younger Jones joined his father as acting president of Bob Jones College. He succeeded his
father as president in 1947.

During his long tenure, Jones attempted to
make the college a center for Christian arts and
culture. The school's Art Gallery of Religious
Paintings gained an international reputation.
Jones also became a pioneer of quality Christian radio and television broadcasts, as well as
the use of film in missionary work. During the
1940s, he was a featured speaker over WKBW,
Buffalo, the broadcast station of Churchill Tabernacle.

Bob Jones University (BJU), as it was renamed in the late 1940s, has produced a number of syndicated radio programs over the past three decades, including a teaching program entitled *Bible Institute of the Air, Chapel Echoes, Miracles, Sunshine on the Soapsuds,* and *World of Truth.* These programs are aired over BJU campus radio station WMUU and in syndication elsewhere in the United States.

The evangelist's most famous controversy was his break with Billy Graham over the Graham Crusade's advocacy of ecumenical cooperation with nonfundamentalist churches. Jones retired as president in favor of his son, Bob Jones III, in 1971.

See also Bob Jones, Sr.

SOURCES

Dollar, George W. *A History of Fundamentalism in America.* Greenville, SC: Bob Jones University Press, 1973.

Reid, Daniel G., Robert D. Linder, Bruce L. Shelley, and Harry S. Stout, eds. *Dictionary of Christianity in America.* Downers Grove, IL: InterVarsity Press, 1990.

BOB JONES, SR.

born: October 30, 1883, Skipperville, Alabama
died: 1968

The famed evangelist Bob Jones, Sr., grew up in rural Alabama, the son of William Jones and Georgia Creel. At age 11, Jones had a conversion experience and, after showing signs of talent as a speaker, preached his first revival a short time later. At 15 he became licensed as a minister in the Alabama Conference of the Methodist Episcopal Church, South, and was given his own circuit. Shortly after this, Jones suffered the loss of both of his parents.

From 1900 to 1902, Jones attended Southern University in Birmingham, Alabama (now Birmingham-Southern College) and, not long after his graduation, married Bernice Sheffield. Following her death from tuberculosis less than a year later, Jones launched a career as a revivalist preacher, traveling from tent meeting to lecture halls holding evangelistic crusades. Within a short time his success rivaled that of evangelist Billy Sunday. In 1908, Jones married the former Mary Gaston Stollenwerck and settled in Birmingham, where he continued his work as an evangelist.

Jones's strong conviction that modern culture threatened orthodox Christian faith persuaded him to found a Christian college where a literalist interpretation of the Bible and its statutes would be taught and honored. This plan came to fruition in 1926 with the establishing of Bob Jones College in St. Andrews Bay, Florida. The college did not survive the Great Depression, however, and, in 1933, Jones was forced to move his operation, with the help of his son and acting president, Bob Jones, Jr., to Cleveland, Tennessee. The college prospered in its new setting until 1947, when the campus was sold to the Church of God, Cleveland, Tennessee (where it became Lee College).

Following the sale of the Cleveland campus, Jones and his son moved the college to Greenville, South Carolina, and renamed it Bob Jones University. The student body grew substantially over the next two decades, increasing to over 4,000 students by 1970. Jones's desire to remain separated from the sinful society around him would later create problems for his college, since this also included the racial segregation of students. A controversial Supreme Court ruling in 1983 forced Bob Jones University to integrate its student body and allow for interracial relationships.

During the 1940s and 1950s, Jones increasingly turned over the administration of his college to his son and spent much of his time traveling as an evangelist and revival speaker. Periodically he made appearances on radio and later television. For example, Jones was a featured guest speaker over the radio station of the Churchill Tabernacle, Buffalo, New York, during the 1930s and 1940s. He also began a broadcast ministry from his college and aired Bible lessons and sermons regularly over Bob Jones University radio station WMUU. Jones's interest in the medium of broadcasting led to his support for the founding of the National Religious Broadcasters (NRB) in April of 1944. Jones was among the 12 nationally recognized religious broadcasters assembled in Columbus, Ohio, who founded the NRB.

See also National Religious Broadcasters

SOURCES

Dollar, George W. *A History of Fundamentalism in America.* Greenville, SC: Bob Jones University Press, 1973.

Jones, Sr., Bob. *Heritage of Faith.* Greenville, SC: Bob Jones University Press, 1973.

Reid, Daniel G., Robert D. Linder, Bruce L. Shelley, and Harry S. Stout, eds. *Dictionary of Christianity in America.* Downers Grove, IL: InterVarsity Press, 1990.

Ward, Mark, Sr. *Air of Salvation: The Story of Christian Broadcasting.* Grand Rapids, MI: Baker Book House, 1994.

CLARENCE JONES
born: 1900, Sherrard, Illinois
died: 1986

Pioneer missionary radio broadcaster and co-founder, with Reuben Larson, of station HCJB, Ecuador, Clarence W. Jones grew up in Illinois and attended the Moody Bible Institute. He graduated from Moody in 1921 as valedictorian and class president. Jones then joined radio evangelist Paul Rader and served as his assistant with the Chicago Gospel Tabernacle and its local broadcast ministry, Where Jesus Blesses Thousands (WJBT). Jones, who had participated in Rader's first radio broadcast over station WHT in 1922, assisted Rader in making the move from a local to a national radio audience. During this period, Jones also helped found what later became known internationally as the AWANA program for youth.

In 1928, the young evangelist set off for South America to locate a site for a missionary broadcasting station. At first, his vision for a gospel broadcast center met with little success. Following a meeting with Reuben Larson in 1929,

however, his luck changed. Jones and Larson were able to obtain a broadcasting license from the Ecuadorian government to begin a radio station in Quito. It became Ecuador's first radio station. Larson moved to Quito the following year, and the pair began broadcasting from station HCJB on Christmas Day 1931.

In 1940, Christian builder and philanthropist R. G. La Tourneau donated the funds to erect a 10,000-watt transmitter, greatly expanding the range of the station's broadcasts. Today, HCJB is one of the three largest Christian broadcast centers in the world.

After his retirement in 1961, Jones devoted the remainder of his life to promoting radio missionary evangelism. Along with many other honors, Jones became the first individual inducted into the National Religious Broadcasters Hall of Fame in 1975. He died in 1986.

See also HCJB, Ecuador

SOURCES

Hill, George H. *Airwaves to the Soul: The Influence and Growth of Religious Broadcasting in America.* Saratoga, NY: R & E, 1983.

Ward, Mark, Sr. *Air of Salvation: The Story of Christian Broadcasting.* Grand Rapids, MI: Baker Book House, 1994.

JIM JONES
born: May 13, 1931, Lynn, Indiana
died: November 18, 1978, Jonestown, Guyana

Jim Jones is infamously known as the charismatic leader of the Peoples Temple and the man who led 914 men, women, and children to their deaths, then committed suicide, in the jungles of Guyana on November 18, 1978. What is not commonly known is that Jones could be heard on regular radio broadcasts over KFAX, a Northern California station, during the early 1970s.

Jones grew up in a Pentecostal environment in rural Indiana and often alluded to his father's membership in the Ku Klux Klan. After his parents divorced, he moved with his mother to

Richmond, Indiana, where he worked as an orderly at a local hospital. Following his marriage to a nurse, Marceline Baldwin, Jones moved to Indianapolis, where he developed his ideas on the two areas of concern that would mark his subsequent ministry: socialism and racial integration.

Jones founded the Community Unity Church, which would later become the Peoples Temple, in Indianapolis in 1954. The church was unusual in that it was an integrated body in a highly racist community. Jones, who had already made a name for himself in Pentecostal circles as a dynamic healer and prophet, was the church's pastor. By 1955, he had renamed the congregation the Peoples Temple Full Gospel Church and was attracting large crowds to Sunday faith-healing services. In later years, Jones would claim that the healing dramas of his early ministry were mainly a way to introduce people to his more important messages of apostolic socialism and racial equality.

Following a visit to Father Divine, the charismatic black minister of the Peace Mission Movement in Philadelphia, Jones returned to Indianapolis and began to organize community services such as soup kitchens and the distribution of free groceries and clothing. Jones's sincere efforts to promote interracial harmony were praised by the Indianapolis African American community and earned him the position of director of the Indianapolis Human Rights Commission in 1961.

In the early 1960s during the height of the Cold War, Jones had a vision of apocalyptic destruction. In the vision, the Midwest was destroyed during a nuclear war. Jones took the vision seriously and decided to move his congregation to Ukiah, California, in the Redwood Valley region north of San Francisco. This area was believed to be one of nine places on earth that would be safe during a global nuclear war.

By the early 1970s, Jones's ministry had expanded into Los Angeles and into the predominantly black Fillmore district of San Francisco. The city missions in Los Angeles and San Francisco bused members to Ukiah for Jones's dramatic healing services. During some of these services Jones claimed he had resurrected members from the dead. It was at this time that Jones began a regular radio ministry on San Francisco station KFAX. Jones also received several humanitarian awards in Northern California for his work with the poor and was appointed to the San Francisco Housing Authority.

In 1973, eight close aides defected from Jones's church, and a series of critical articles appeared in the *San Francisco Examiner*. Jones interpreted these events as the beginning of a great persecution against him and his church by the powers of darkness. Within a short time, he had begun making plans to move his congregation to the South American nation of Guyana. This Third World country on South America's northern coast was ruled by a socialist regime that was sympathetic to the socialism of the Peoples Temple.

By 1974, 15 of Jones's followers had negotiated a lease for 3,000 acres on Guyana's western border. They immediately began clearing the jungle for what would become the Peoples Temple Agricultural Project. Jones referred to Guyana in his sermons of this period as the "Promised Land." He also predicted that this was the land to which his people would make their exodus from the degradations and persecutions of American society. Jones himself, however, did not relocate to Guyana until July of 1977. His move occurred a few weeks before a *New West* magazine article appeared suggesting that the Peoples Temple should be investigated for financial fraud, the mistreatment of members, and questionable dealings in San Francisco politics.

In 1978, a group of ex-members calling themselves the Committee of Concerned Relatives published literature that likened Jonestown, as the new colony was called, to a concentration camp. In this so-called camp, armed guards were allegedly subjecting residents to torture, forced labor, and complete isolation from the world. This public attack on his utopian experiment had a powerful effect on Jones. He began talking seriously about mass suicide and held practice runs to test his members' loyalty.

Later that year, California congressman Leo Ryan initiated an official investigation of the

Guyana community. He and several others visited Jonestown on November 17 and heard from both supporters and detractors of the project. Ryan told the community that anyone who wanted to leave could return with him to the United States. Fourteen people took him up on this offer. Ryan and his entourage were on their way home when they were ambushed and killed by Jones's security forces. The next day, the entire community of 914 men, women, and children drank a deadly potion of Fla-Vor Aid laced with poison. Though some coercion was involved, the evidence indicated that most of the community supported the plan. After the mass suicide of his followers, Jones and a close aide shot themselves rather than face the repercussions of the Ryan murders.

SOURCES

Chidester, David S. *Salvation and Suicide: An Interpretation of Jim Jones, the Peoples Temple, and Jonestown.* Bloomington: Indiana University Press, 1988.

LARRY JONES
born: October 22, 1940, Scottsville, Kentucky

Larry Jones of Larry Jones International Ministries has earned a reputation for being a television preacher who makes sure the money he solicits for the poor actually gets to those for whom it was intended. From the debut of his weekly half-hour television program, *Larry Jones Crusade*, in the early 1980s, Jones has consistently offered videotaped vignettes from his many mission stations depicting those who are receiving his aid.

Jones is the founder and director of Feed the Children (FTC), an international, nonprofit Christian organization that provides food, clothing, medical supplies, and other necessities to people who are suffering because of natural disasters, war, and other calamities. According to the ministry's literature, FTC has provided various commodities through 10,833 individual feeding centers, food pantries, and distribution centers throughout the United States. It has also delivered food, medical assistance, and emergency supplies to 67 countries around the world. FTC's medical teams performed 38,400 examinations, filled 84,000 prescriptions, and completed 1,127 dental extractions in 1991 alone. Much of the food that FTC distributes comes from US government surpluses. According to *Money* magazine, FTC is the 16th most efficient charity in America, using almost 94 percent of its contributions for food, relief, medical care, and education.

Jones's television program focuses on the positive results that have been achieved by FTC's many ministries, rather than strident evangelizing. Jones is assisted by his wife, Frances, in running FTC's operations. In 1989, Jones's television show was ranked fifteenth among nationally syndicated religious programs according to Arbitron, with an estimated audience of 141,000 viewers per broadcast.

FTC is headquartered in Oklahoma City and has received the endorsement of such notables as George Bush, Garth Brooks, Marie Osmond, Thomas P. "Tip" O'Neill, Jr., televangelist E. V. Hill, The Oak Ridge Boys, and Peter C. Myers, the deputy secretary of the United States Department of Agriculture.

SOURCES

Erickson, Hal. *Religious Radio and Television in the United States, 1921–1991.* Jefferson, NC: McFarland, 1992.

Feed the Children. Promotional Literature, 1992.

JONI AND FRIENDS
first aired: 1982

Joni and Friends is a daily, 5-minute radio program that seeks to give hope and encouragement to people struggling with disabilities or adverse life situations. Hosted by Joni Erickson-Taeda—who was left completely paralyzed by a ski accident—the program is broadcast on over 700 outlets worldwide. Erickson-Taeda, who paints landscapes by holding a brush in her mouth, published the tragic tale of her accident and subsequent conversion to Christ in her 1970s autobiography titled simply *Joni*. The inspiring story also became the subject of a late-1970s movie, *The Other Side of the Mountain*. *Joni and Friends* began airing during the 1980s and has continued into the 1990s. Erickson-Taeda received the Maggie Sloan Crawford award of Olivet Nazarene University in April 1996. The award is given to honor and recognize women whose lives and accomplishments mark them as role models for young women.

JOY OF LIVING
see: Reverend Ike

A JOYFUL SOUND
see: David Hubbard

JUDGE RUTHERFORD
born: 1869, Morgan County, Missouri
died: January 8, 1942, San Diego, California

Joseph Franklin "Judge" Rutherford, best-known as the successor of Jehovah's Witnesses founder Charles Taze Russell, was born in Morgan County, Missouri, and raised in a Baptist family. In 1904, while practicing law, Rutherford met Russell and joined his Bible-study group. By 1906, Rutherford had formally joined the Watch Tower Bible and Tract Society (the name of the Jehovah's Witnesses before it adopted its more popular name in 1931).

Though mostly a loose collection of Bible-study associations when Rutherford took over leadership of the society after Russell's death in 1916, the group soon became a highly organized religious sect. Believing that the millennium had arrived in 1914—a date he arrived at using his own elaborate numerological system based on study of the Bible—Rutherford stood firmly against member participation in this-worldly concerns, including military service. For his defiant opposition to the draft, he was sentenced, in June 1918, to 20 years in federal prison. Released by the government after serving only a year of his sentence, Rutherford returned to his duties as head of the Watch Tower Society and focused his energies on the consolidation of its growing membership. During his 25-year tenure as president, Rutherford initiated a number of new methods of outreach, including radio broadcasts, tract distribution, and publication of the doctrinal writings of Russell and others.

By placing greater emphasis on evangelism, the membership of the Jehovah's Witnesses grew from 1,000 in 1918 to 30,000 by the time of Rutherford's death in 1942. Under the leadership of Rutherford's successors, Nathan Knorr and Fred Franz, the Jehovah's Witnesses had grown to roughly 3.5 million members by the beginning of the 1990s.

SOURCES

Ahlstrom, Sydney E. *A Religious History of the American People*. New Haven, CT: Yale University Press, 1972.

Hudson, Winthrop S. *Religion in America*. 4th ed. New York: Macmillan, 1987.

Melton, J. Gordon. *Encyclopedic Handbook of Cults in America*. Rev ed. New York: Garland, 1992.

Reid, Daniel G., Robert D. Linder, Bruce L. Shelley, and Harry S. Stout, eds. *Dictionary of Christianity in America*. Downers Grove, IL: InterVarsity Press, 1990.

K

KCBI, DALLAS
see: W. A. Criswell

KDKA, PITTSBURGH
established: 1920

Radio station KDKA, Pittsburgh, Pennsylvania, has a place of prominence in the history of religious broadcasting. It was across its airwaves, on January 2, 1921, that the first religious program in history was broadcast. KDKA was also the first full-fledged radio station in the country, having begun its operations on November 2, 1920. The station had received its commercial broadcasting license from the US Department of Commerce just in time to broadcast the results of the presidential election of 1920, won by Warren G. Harding. The November inaugural broadcast was transmitted from a primitive studio and was heard by a listening audience of no more than 1,000 private radio operators nationwide.

The January 1921 broadcast came about through the efforts of a Westinghouse engineer who was a member of the Calvary Episcopal Church choir. The church's junior associate pastor, the Reverend Lewis B. Whittemore, agreed to broadcast a normal Sunday evening vespers service, using a makeshift electronic hookup. Two KDKA engineers, dressed as choir members (one was a Roman Catholic and the other a Jew), assisted in the broadcast. In the

words of Gleason L. Archer, a radio historian, "The broadcast went over splendidly, making so favorable an impression on the radio audience that it became a regular Sunday feature of KDKA."

SOURCES

Archer, Gleason L. *History of Radio to 1926*. New York: The American Historical Society, 1938.

Armstrong, Ben. *The Electronic Church*. Nashville: Thomas Nelson, 1979.

PAUL KEENAN
born: June 13, 1946, Hamilton, Ontario, Canada

Father Paul A. Keenan is the host of two popular radio programs that air on the 50,000-watt radio stations WOR and WABC in New York City. The two programs, *As You Think* and *Religion on the Line*, have an audience range that includes most of the Eastern third of the country.

Keenan grew up in Kansas City, Missouri, where he attended Rockhurst College. Following his graduation magna cum laude in 1967, Keenan enrolled in the novitiate of the Society of Jesus in Florissant, Missouri. After studying Moral and Pastoral Theology at Saint Louis University, he was ordained into the Roman Catholic priesthood in 1977. During the 1970s, Keenan taught philosophy and theology at Rockhurst and philosophy at Saint Louis University. In 1983, Keenan earned his doctorate in philosophy from Fordham University, one of the premier Jesuit universities in the country. He then served as an associate pastor in various Catholic parishes in Manhattan, becoming assistant director for radio ministry in the office of communications of the Archdiocese of New York in 1993 and assistant director of the office of communications in 1994.

Keenan's broadcast career began in 1990, when he became a broadcaster for IN TOUCH Networks, a radio network for the blind and visually impaired. His work on *Religion on the Line* began in 1992, when he served as Catholic cohost of the WABC radio program during the summers. This interfaith radio ministry included a rabbi, a Protestant minister, and Keenan. Keenan became the show's permanent Catholic cohost in fall 1993. *Religion on the Line* is a current events, listener call-in program that claims an estimated audience of 250,000. The current cohosts are Keenan, Rabbi Joseph Potasnik of the New York Board of Rabbis, and Dr. Byron Shafer, who represents the Council of Churches of the City of New York.

Keenan began his tenure as host of the radio program *As You Think* when it aired on station WOR for the first time in August 1992. This program also has a listener call-in format and has a regular audience of 50,000. The show focuses on spirituality and features discussion and interviews with celebrities or experts in spirituality, the arts, business, and society. *As You Think* is a paid program, meaning that Keenan purchases time from the station and does most of the fundraising himself.

In addition to his two radio ministries, Keenan served as commentator for the television broadcast of the papal mass for World Youth Day in Denver on WNBC-TV in New York. He has also served as a commentator on the Faith and Values Network for Holy Week 1996 services from St. Patrick's Cathedral, and has hosted the radio broadcast of the Christmas midnight mass from St. Patrick's Cathedral for WOR Radio. During spring 1996, Keenan aired the series *The Spirituality of the Catholic Church* over Worldwide Catholic Radio, the radio outreach of Mother Angelica's Eternal Word Network in

Birmingham, Alabama. He has also begun to do two interactive "chat" events weekly on the commercial Internet service Prodigy. *As You Think* is a weekly chat room on spirituality and *Fr. Keenan Online* is a weekly forum on topics in religion and society.

D. JAMES KENNEDY
born: November 3, 1930, Augusta, Georgia

Courtesy: National Religious Broadcasters

D. James Kennedy is pastor of the 7,000-member Coral Ridge Presbyterian Church of Fort Lauderdale, Florida, and a leading Christian conservative spokesperson. Called the "most listened-to Presbyterian minister in the world," Kennedy hosts the weekly television show *The Coral Ridge Hour*; the daily 30-minute radio program *Truths That Transform*; and the daily three-minute radio commentary *The Kennedy Commentary*. He is also the founder and overseer of Coral Ridge Ministries, Westminster Academy, Knox Theological Seminary, Evangelism Explosion International, and station WAFG-FM, Ft. Lauderdale, Florida.

Kennedy was born in Georgia, grew up in Chicago, and moved, with his family, to Florida while still in high school. He was earning his living as an Arthur Murray dance instructor during the 1950s when he accidentally tuned his radio one night to Donald Grey Barnhouse's *The Bible Study Hour*. After hearing the program's opening question, "If you die tonight and stand before the gates of heaven, what reason could you give for being allowed to enter in and enjoy eternal life?" Kennedy became so intrigued that he listened to the rest of the broadcast and soon experienced a conversion to Christ. He enrolled a short time later in the Columbia Theological Seminary in Decatur, Georgia.

After graduating from Columbia in 1959, Kennedy became the pastor of Coral Ridge Presbyterian Church in Fort Lauderdale, Florida. At the time, the church had 17 members who met in the cafeteria of a Fort Lauderdale elementary school. In 1962, Kennedy developed a plan for teaching lay parishioners to evangelize in their local community. The new method, emphasizing personal witnessing and careful training, made every church member a force for preaching the "simple, primitive statement of the good news of the gospel." Through this dynamic outreach, dubbed "Evangelism Explosion," Coral Ridge became the fastest growing Presbyterian congregation in the United States for 15 years running. The methods of Evangelism Explosion spread to hundreds of American churches and branched out to such countries as England, South Africa, Australia, and West Germany in the late 1970s. The organization's goal was to have a presence in every country in the world by the beginning of 1996.

In 1981, Evangelism Explosion was shaken by the sudden firing of its executive vice president, Archie Parrish, at a November board meeting. Kennedy claimed that Parrish was fired because of his "continued unwillingness to submit to the direction and authority of the board of directors and president." In the wake of Parrish's firing, 13 staff members at Evangelism Explosion and one board member, theologian and author R. C. Sproul, resigned.

Kennedy's weekly television broadcast, *The Coral Ridge Hour*, followed the basic structure of a traditional Presbyterian worship service:

magisterial hymns sung by a large, robed choir; scriptural readings; and a formal, sedate homily delivered by Kennedy. Kennedy's intention from the outset was to draw in viewers who were uncomfortable with the more entertainment-oriented style of many religious television shows. As he explained, "We feel that many who might be turned off by other approaches will want to watch. . . . One of our aims is to avoid the stereotype that anyone who believes the Bible is obviously uneducated, narrow-minded, and backwoodsy." The show was successful in attracting people who preferred a professional scriptural exegesis and a more sophisticated intellectual and cultural content. Kennedy bolstered his own intellectual credentials during this period by earning a doctor of philosophy degree from New York University and a doctor of divinity degree from Trinity Evangelical Divinity School in Deerfield, Illinois.

Over time, *The Coral Ridge Hour* has broadened its appeal by adding magazine-style feature segments, interviews, faith testimonies, and organist Diane Bish's musical interludes. The show's Sunday morning broadcast on the Christian Broadcasting Network garnered a Nielsen rating of 540,000 viewers in November 1986. By 1989, the show claimed an audience of over 1 million and was the fourth-rated syndicated religious television program in the United States, according to Arbitron. The program had dropped to sixth in the Arbitron ratings by 1992, but it was still reaching 111 markets nationwide. By 1995, the show also claimed an international audience.

Kennedy's 30-minute daily radio broadcast, *Truths That Transform*, features his sermons on contemporary issues and discussions with experts from around the country. *Truths That Transform* and the daily three-minute commentary *The Kennedy Commentary* reach across denominational boundaries and feature Kennedy's common-sense presentation of the biblical perspective on gay rights, church and state separation, education, abortion, and the American Civil Librties Union (ACLU). Kennedy continues to be a much sought-after speaker. He has made guest appearances on

Larry King Live, CBS Nightwatch, Crossfire, MacNeil/Lehrer News Hour, Merv Griffin, and *Donahue.*

During the mid-1980s, Kennedy began to grapple with such controversial issues as abortion, school prayer, television violence, and creation science in his weekly sermons. The underlying theme of these new sermons was the Christian struggle against the growing tide of secular humanism in America. Kennedy used these emotion-laden issues in his fundraising appeals as well. He often sent viewers surveys that inquired about the moral health of the country. These direct-mail appeals also asked for contributions to help his ministry do battle with the forces seeking to separate America from its Christian heritage. In shifting his ministry's focus in this manner, Kennedy was choosing sides in the larger cultural war being waged in the country between the Religious Right and secular society.

Kennedy has also embraced conservative politics during the past decade. Shortly before the 1992 presidential election, he blasted the Democratic Party, complaining, "I find it absolutely appalling that in a nation founded by Christians we have people in one of our major political parties conspiring about how to get rid of Christians in this country." The day after President Bill Clinton's election, Kennedy declared, "I think a nation that would put a man like that in a position of leadership is just asking for the judgment of God."

Kennedy has been a long-standing proponent of private Christian education for the young. In 1971, he founded Westminster Academy in Fort Lauderdale, Florida, to provide first-class Christian-based learning for grade levels K–12. As of 1995, the nationally recognized school claimed an enrollment of 1,000 students and had gained accreditation from the Southern Association of Colleges and Schools. Kennedy founded Knox Theological Seminary in Fort Lauderdale in 1990 and opened a second campus in Colorado Springs, Colorado, in 1993. The seminary has also been offering classes in South Korea and Miami, Florida.

SOURCES

Armstrong, Ben. *The Electric Church.* Nashville: Thomas Nelson, 1979.

Bruce, Steve. *Pray TV: Televangelism in America.* New York: Routledge, 1990.

"Casting Call for NRB 95." *Religious Broadcasting,* February, 1995.

Clapp, Rodney. "Unhappy Shakeup at Evangelism Explosion Ministry." *Christianity Today,* January 22, 1982.

"Coral Ridge Ministries." *Impact Magazine,* September, 1992.

Erickson, Hal. *Religious Radio and Television in the United States, 1921–1991.* Jefferson, NC: McFarland, 1992.

Schultze, Quentin J. *Televangelism and American Culture: The Business of Popular Religion.* Grand Rapids, MI: Baker Book House, 1991.

ESSEK WILLIAM KENYON

born: April 24, 1867, Saratoga County, New York
died: March 19, 1948, Seattle, Washington

Essek William Kenyon was a popular radio preacher during the 1930s and 1940s in the Pacific Northwest. His combination of mainstream evangelical Christianity and New Thought philosophy influenced a generation of "Positive Confession" televangelists, including Kenneth E. Hagin, Kenneth Copeland, Robert Tilton, Frederick K. C. Price, and Charles Capps. Kenyon embodied the American religious ethos of conservative moralism, missionary zeal, and pragmatic self-empowerment.

Although Kenyon's father—a logger and school teacher—and mother instilled in him a love of knowledge, he never actually completed an educational degree. Following a conversion to Christ in his teens, he began his preaching career at a Methodist church in Amsterdam, New York, in 1886. In 1892, after dabbling in various college programs in New York state, Kenyon was accepted at Emerson College in Boston. Emerson specialized in the teaching of oratory but was strongly influenced by the New Thought metaphysics of its president, Charles Wesley Emerson. Ralph Waldo Trine, the best-selling author of such New Thought classics as *In Tune with the Infinite*, was also a member of the faculty at this time. Although Kenyon never finished his degree at Emerson, it is likely that his exposure to New Thought's mental hygienics influenced his presentation of the gospel message. By the late 1890s, Kenyon was preaching this message as a nonaligned Baptist itinerant evangelist throughout most of New England.

A new phase of Kenyon's life began in 1900, when John and Susan Marble donated a farm in Massachusetts to his ministry. Kenyon decided to open a Bible school, Bethel Bible Institute, on the property, and to model it after the hospices of the Episcopalian spiritual healer Charles Cullis. The school publicized its activities with a periodical, *Realities*, and was marginally successful in its first decade of operation, partially due to Kenyon's nationwide evangelical tours, which earned needed funds for the school. After his marriage to Alice Whitney in 1914, Kenyon turned to writing. His first major work, published in 1917, was *The Father and His Family*.

The exigencies of World War I led to a sharp drop in Bethel Institute's enrollment. Following the school's merger with Nichols Academy in Dudley, Massachusetts, Kenyon resigned as superintendent and organized a new evangelical ministry on the West Coast. This ministry included a pioneering radio outreach in the Los Angeles area that may have been inspired by Kenyon's friendship with the charismatic evangelist Aimee Semple McPherson. After brief pastorates at a Baptist congregation in Pasadena and an independent church in Los Angeles, Kenyon again moved, this time to Seattle, Washington. It was in Seattle that a second radio ministry, Kenyon's *Church of the Air*, began (not to be confused with Paul Finkenbinder's show of the same name). This morning radio program would become the main focus of Kenyon's pastorate at the New Covenant Baptist Church and occupy much of his final years.

Kenyon continued his vocation as an educator during his Seattle years, creating a systematic Bible-study correspondence course for ra-

dio listeners and a set of lessons called "Personal Evangelism." The former course was published in later years as *The Bible in the Light of Our Redemption*. Kenyon also disseminated his radio homilies through the Kenyon Gospel Publishing Society and published a periodical, *Kenyon's Herald of Life*. Other books published during the 1940s included his *The Two Kinds of Life* (1943), *In His Presence* (1944), *New Creation Realities: A Revelation of Redemption* (1945), and *What Happened from the Cross to the Throne* (1945). His most popular book was probably *The Wonderful Name of Jesus*, published in 1927. Kenyon's pithy and rambling writing style stressed the power of the spoken word, uttered in faith, and the superiority of "revelation knowledge" over sensory knowledge. Following Kenyon's death in 1948, his daughter took over his publishing ministry and released several of his unpublished manuscripts.

Although Kenyon has sometimes been criticized for the gnostic tendencies in his thought, systematic expositions of his theology in works such as *The Bible in the Light of Our Redemption* clearly demonstrate the essentially evangelical Christian thrust of his message. His emphasis on such issues as healing, faith, revelation knowledge, and the spiritual power of new creation believers, however, clearly demonstrates the influence of New Thought philosophy in his beliefs.

Kenyon's national influence has probably been greater in the years after his death, becoming especially noticeable with the rise of televangelists such as Kenneth Hagin and Robert Tilton, who espouse "Positive Confession," a teaching that centers around the idea that Christians can receive from God whatever they want if they pray for it with whole-hearted belief and vocal affirmation.

SOURCES

Kenyon, Essek William. *The Bible in the Light of our Redemption*. Old Tappan, NJ: Fleming H. Revell, 1969.

Matta, Judith A. *The Born Again Jesus of the Word-Faith Teaching*. Fullerton, CA: Spirit of Truth Ministry, 1987.

McConnell, D. R. *A Different Gospel*. Peabody, MA: Hendrickson, 1988.

Reid, Daniel G., et al., eds. *Dictionary of Christianity in America*. Downers Grove, IL: InterVarsity Press, 1990.

JAY KESLER
born: September 15, 1935, Barnes, Wisconsin

The prominent Youth for Christ International (YFC) leader Jay Kesler grew up in Wisconsin and graduated from Taylor University in Upland, Indiana, in 1958. He began his long career with Youth for Christ in 1955, becoming a crusade staff evangelist in 1959. Over the next decade and a half, Kesler rose steadily in YFC's ranks to become president of the ministry in 1973. During this period he also served as a member of the faculty of the Billy Graham School of Evangelism. In 1985, Kesler became president of Taylor University, where he has remained ever since.

During the 1970s, Kesler hosted a daily radio ministry known as *Family Forum*. The program featured a Bible-study format that presented the message of the gospel in easily understood and applicable concepts. In addition to his administrative duties, Kesler has found time to write practical books on adolescent and family concerns. He is the author of some 17 books for parents and youth, including *Let's Succeed with Our Teenagers* (1973), *Parents and Teenagers* (1984), *Being Holy, Being Human* (1988), and *Raising Responsible Kids* (1991).

SOURCES

Erickson, Hal. *Religious Radio and Television in the United States, 1921–1991*. Jefferson, NC: McFarland, 1992.

Who's Who in Religion. 4th ed. Wilmette, IL: Marquis, 1993.

KEY COMMUNICATIONS
established: 1978

An evangelical Protestant broadcasting ministry founded in 1978, Key Communications (KC) sends its programs via short-wave radio to Arabic-speaking regions of the Indian subcontinent and the Middle East. Operating from its ministry base in Portland, Oregon, KC broadcasts a series of prepared messages on Christian doctrine to Muslim-dominated regions, hoping for converts from Islam. KC also sends Christian literature to listeners who respond by mail to its broadcasts.

KEYS TO DYNAMIC LIVING
see: Bill Bright

KFSG, LOS ANGELES
see: Aimee Semple McPherson

BEN KINCHLOW
born: 1936, Uvalde, Texas

Courtesy: National Religious Broadcasters

Ben Kinchlow has become one of the best-known African Americans in televangelism due to his daily appearances as Pat Robertson's cohost on *The 700 Club*.

Kinchlow grew up in Texas, the son of a Methodist minister. After his graduation from St. Peter Claver's Academy in San Antonio in 1954, Kinchlow served 13 years in the US Air Force. His career included assignments in French Morocco, Labrador, Saudi Arabia, Okinawa (Japan), and Libya. The years of Kinchlow's military service were a time of his growing awareness of the racism that oppresses African Americans. Although he never officially joined the Black Muslims, Kinchlow became increasingly interested in the teachings of Malcolm X during this period. Also during this time, Kinchlow married Vivian Carolyn Jordan. The couple now has three sons and five grandchildren.

Following his discharge from the military, Kinchlow enrolled at Southwest Texas Junior College. He earned an associate's degree in business in 1971 and became a member of Phi Theta Kappa. The national honor society would present him its Most Distinguished Alumnus award in 1986. While at college, Kinchlow had several difficult confrontations over race with a white minister, John Corcoran. Ironically, it was through these confrontations that Kinchlow converted to Christianity in 1968.

Kinchlow created a successful ministry for teenage runaways called His Place in 1971 and later became the executive director of a drug and alcohol rehabilitation program, Christian Farms. He was ordained in the African Methodist Episcopal Church in 1971.

It was during his tenure at Christian Farms that Kinchlow met Pat Robertson, the founder and chief executive of the fledgling Christian Broadcasting Network (CBN). Robertson asked Kinchlow to direct a CBN counseling center in Dallas. A year later, Robertson invited Kinchlow to appear as a guest on *The 700 Club*, CBN's flagship program. The drug rehabilitation officer established such a favorable rapport with Robertson and *The 700 Club* audience on this and subsequent guest appearances that he was eventually offered the job of cohost. By 1982,

Kinchlow had risen to the position of vice president and director of domestic ministries. Three years later he became CBN's executive vice president for ministry and development. In this capacity, Kinchlow headed up "Operation Blessing," CBN's humanitarian outreach program. The ministry was distributing an estimated $45 million in aid by 1985.

Kinchlow took over as host of *The 700 Club* when Robertson left the show to campaign for the 1988 presidential nomination. Kinchlow, however, decided to retire from CBN in January of 1988, halfway through Robertson's presidential bid. After conducting a more private independent ministry for four years, he returned as cohost of the rejuvenated *The 700 Club* in April of 1992. In addition to his work with Robertson and Terry Meeuwsen on the daily *The 700 Club*, Kinchlow has taken over as host of *The 700 Club*'s international edition. As of 1995, the program was being aired in 45 countries around the world.

Kinchlow's role on *The 700 Club* is similar to that of sidekicks on secular talk shows. He laughs at Robertson's jokes, picks up the slack if he feels Robertson is about to lose his train of thought, and sets Robertson up with questions when he thinks the host has not expounded sufficiently on an important issue. Kinchlow has also been able to maintain viewer interest as guest host during Robertson's periodic absences from the show.

Among Kinchlow's written works are *Plain Bread* (1985) and *Making Noise . . . and Going Home*.

See also *The 700 Club*; Pat Robertson

SOURCES

"Casting Call for NRB 95." *Religious Broadcasting*, February, 1995.

Erickson, Hal. *Religious Radio and Television in the United States, 1921–1991*. Jefferson, NC: McFarland, 1992.

Hadden, Jeffrey K., and Anson Shupe. *Televangelism: Power and Politics on God's Frontier*. New York: Henry Holt, 1988.

Hadden, Jeffrey K., and Charles E. Swann. *Prime Time Preachers: The Rising Power of Televangelism.* Reading, MA: Addison-Wesley, 1981.

Harrell, David Edwin. *Pat Robertson.* San Francisco: Harper & Row, 1987.

Hazard, David. "Ben Kinchlow: Off Camera and Off-the-cuff." *Charisma*, March, 1986.

Kinchlow, Ben. *Plain Bread.* Waco, TX: Word Books, 1985.

"Kinchlow Leaves '700 Club.'" *Charisma and Christian Life*, March, 1988.

THE KING'S HOUR
see: Robert Cook

KINI-FM, ST. FRANCIS, SOUTH DAKOTA
established: 1978

KINI is a noncommercial FM radio station that provides religious and educational programming for the Rosebud Indian Reservation, South Dakota, and its surrounding areas. The broadcast originates from St. Francis, South Dakota. KINI is owned and operated by the Rosebud Educational Society (RES) of the St. Francis Indian Mission, a Catholic mission to the Rosebud Sioux founded by Jesuit priests in 1886.

Apart from its radio broadcasts, RES provides community support for the reservation's local inhabitants, and offers such social programs as schools, youth camps, drug and alcohol rehabilitation services, personal and spiritual counseling, and shelter services for abused and battered women. KINI's broadcasts reach several of South Dakota's major Indian reservations.

SOURCES

Melton, J. Gordon. *Directory of Religious Organizations in the United States.* 3d ed. Detroit: Gale Research, 1993.

KRDU-AM, DINUBA, CALIFORNIA
established: 1946

KRDU-AM in Dinuba, California, was one of the earliest Christian radio stations in the country. The idea for a station grew out of the meetings of a group of businessmen during the mid-1940s in the San Joaquin valley who believed that a Christian radio station would help ignite a local religious revival. Not long after this, Paul Pietsch, a revivalist, was speaking at a Youth for Christ rally in the valley town of Dinuba. At some point during his talk he challenged his listeners to build a Christian radio station. The challenge was accepted by two members of a performing quartet visiting from Biola University, who set to work on the project. The two applied for, and received, an FCC license in 1946 and began broadcasting "time-tested gospel programs" under the call letters KRDU.

KRDU and its program director David Hofer were given the National Religious Broadcasters (NRB) Award of Merit in 1976 because of the consistently high standards the station set for technical excellence, program selection, commercial management, and community service. This station's sale of airtime to independent program producers and advertisers pioneered a model that was to be adopted by many subsequent religious stations. The success of this mode of operation alerted investors to the profit potential of stations that offered a consistent format of quality religious programming.

KRDU-AM celebrated its 48th anniversary in 1994 as "the Christian Voice of Central California." The station is now operated and owned by Hofer, whose wife, Donna L. Hofer, is the station's general manager. Among KRDU's 1995 program offerings are *American Indian Hour, The Back to God Hour, Back to the Bible, Chapel of the Air, Focus on the Family, Haven of Rest, Hour of Decision, Lutheran Gospel Hour, Radio Bible Class, The Word Today*, and *Women of Worth*.

See also David Hofer

SOURCES

Armstrong, Ben. *The Electric Church*. Nashville: Thomas Nelson, 1979.

Ward, Mark, Sr. *Air of Salvation: The Story of Christian Broadcasting*. Manassas, VA: National Religious Broadcasters, 1994.

KTBN, SALT LAKE CITY
established: December 1990

KTBN is the worldwide short-wave radio ministry of the Trinity Broadcasting Network (TBN). Most of the station's programming mirrors TBN's television schedule. KTBN is transmitted from Salt Lake City, Utah, on a Harris SW-110B transmitter operating at 100,000 watts. The network's effective radiated power is estimated to be nearly 2,500,000 watts, allowing it to reach remote areas of the world not covered by TBN's satellite transmissions.

See also Trinity Broadcasting Network

KATHRYN KUHLMAN
born: May 9, 1907, near Concordia, Missouri
died: February 20, 1976, Tulsa, Oklahoma

Kathryn Kuhlman was the grand dame of American faith healing and religious broadcasting between 1947 and 1976. Through the auspices of the Kathryn Kuhlman Foundation, she broadcast her message of faith in the power of God to millions of listeners around the world on daily 30-minute radio programs. She also hosted a half-hour television show between 1966 and 1976 that was seen on over 65 stations at the peak of her fame.

Kuhlman was born on a farm in central Missouri and reared in the German-speaking community of Concordia, where her father, Joseph Adolph Kuhlman, was the mayor and leading citizen. Kuhlman's early religious training occurred within both the Baptist and Methodist traditions. Her father was a nominal Baptist who distrusted preachers and would sometimes cross the street to avoid talking to one. Kuhlman's mother, Emma Walkenhorst, was a Methodist who saw to it that young Kathryn accompanied her to services every Sunday.

In early adolescence, Kuhlman experienced an intense religious conversion and chose to become a member of her father's Baptist congregation. The young woman completed her formal schooling at the age of 16 and convinced her parents to allow her to work with her older sister and brother-in-law as an itinerant preacher. The Parrott Tent Revival, as the family troupe was called, traveled west to Oregon in the summer of 1923. There Kuhlman came under the influence of Charles S. Price, a Pentecostal healer who was holding large meetings in city auditoriums. Price's emphasis on the reality of God's healing power, rebirth in the Holy Spirit, and the need to reach out to non-Pentecostal Christians would all become part of Kuhlman's later independent ministry.

Kuhlman first preached in Boise, Idaho, when she was 21. For five years she and her assistant, Helen Gulliford, traveled the Northwest, calling themselves "God's Girls." Gulliford walked the aisles during Kuhlman's services and brought people forward who wished to testify about a personal healing. Kuhlman visited conventional healing services during this period and was both appalled at the chicanery she witnessed and deeply moved by the despairing faces of those who remained unhealed. As she recounted later, "I knew why the evangelist asked people to fill out those cards to get into the healing line. It was to get a mailing list, that's all. I used to sit there and watch this kind of thing and I wasn't satisfied it was real."

Although skeptical about the methods of other deliverance evangelists (evangelists who offered deliverance of the soul from sin and healing of the body from disease), Kuhlman maintained her faith in God's merciful healing power.

Kuhlman acquired the only ministerial credentials she would ever have from the Fundamental Ministerial Association (now called the Evangelical Church Alliance) in the early 1930s. Even in this instance, the young evangelist had to be convinced by a group of supporters that ordination would augment her credibility among those who were ambivalent about women preachers.

Kuhlman's first settled ministry evolved out of a six-month revival she held in 1933 in Denver, Colorado. The revival was so well received that Kuhlman was asked to stay and pastor a proposed new Kuhlman Revival Tabernacle. A converted paper warehouse was opened in 1934 and quickly attracted an enthusiastic and growing membership. By the following year, a new facility, called the Denver Revival Tabernacle, had been dedicated, and Kuhlman was hosting such evangelical luminaries as Phil Kerr and Raymond T. Richey. Her first foray into religious broadcasting also occurred during this period, when she agreed to broadcast the end of her services over a local radio station.

Kuhlman's successful Denver ministry came to an end as a result of a marital scandal. In 1937, the Texas evangelist Burroughs A. Waltrip held a revival at Kuhlman's tabernacle. Within a year, Waltrip had divorced his wife, left his children, and married Kuhlman. This chain of events led to the resignation of Helen Gulliford, the disintegration of the Denver Revival Tabernacle, and an eight-year period of itinerant preaching for the newly married couple. Dogged everywhere she went by the scandal, Kuhlman finally chose her religious calling over personal love and left Waltrip in Los Angeles in early 1944. She ended up in the small town of Franklin, Pennsylvania, where she pastored a small church, the Gospel Revival Tabernacle. During this pastorship, Kuhlman attended a healing revival conducted by a well-known evangelist. She was deeply troubled by the evangelist's implication that it was through his touch and prayer that healing virtue was transmitted. She also deplored the commercialism of the meeting and the reason given for why a person was not healed—that he or she lacked faith.

After searching the Scriptures, Kuhlman came to understand divine healing as both spiritual and physical in nature. She also experienced what she called her "baptism of the Holy Spirit" and started emphasizing the Holy Spirit in her sermons. Suddenly people in her congregation began reporting spontaneous healings of such diseases and conditions as cancer and blindness. All of these events took place without the traditional long healing lines or laying on of hands by a preacher.

Convinced that God was calling her to a special healing ministry, Kuhlman moved to Pittsburgh in 1947. By the following year she was conducting her "miracle services" in local auditoriums and churches. As her fame grew, Kuhlman organized a grueling weekly schedule for herself. The schedule included a Sunday healing service in Youngstown, Ohio, a Tuesday-evening Bible class at the First Presbyterian Church of Pittsburgh, and a Friday-morning healing service at Pittsburgh's Carnegie Auditorium. Kuhlman believed it was necessary to remain in Pittsburgh as much as possible in order to verify that the healings at her meetings were authentic and permanent.

It was during this period that Kuhlman began broadcasting a popular half-hour radio program from a hotel suite in Pittsburgh. These broadcasts included Kuhlman's sermons on the powerful working of the Holy Spirit in the lives of believers and testimonies from those who were healed at her services. In time these radio shows would be aired five days a week on over 60 stations around the world.

Kuhlman's growing fame did not always result in universal adulation, however. In Pittsburgh, for instance, local churchmen picketed her miracle services, claiming that she was siphoning off their membership. After conducting a healing service in Akron, Ohio, at the request of Rex Humbard, an ultraconservative Baptist minister attacked her for engaging in "faith healing" and for transgressing the Scripture's proscription of female preaching. Kuhlman was undeterred by these attacks, however, and defended her ministry in a direct and firm manner.

In 1957, Kuhlman created the Kathryn Kuhlman Foundation to handle the many contributions that poured into her ministry. In time, these funds were used to support a scholarship and student loan fund, grocery commissaries for the needy, drug rehabilitation projects, 22 foreign missions, and the radio ministry. Kuhlman kept her organization simple and solvent, thereby avoiding the financial crises that were plaguing other broadcasting ministries. The only way she solicited contributions was by allowing a single collection at her live miracle services. Kuhlman never sought to enrich herself through her ministry. Although contributions to the Kathryn Kuhlman Foundation totaled almost $2 million by 1972, Kuhlman's yearly salary remained at about $25,000.

The 1960s were a time of increasing national exposure and popularity for Kuhlman. Her book recounting her healing ministry, *I Believe in Miracles*, became a bestseller in 1962. By early 1966, she had been persuaded by evangelist Ralph Wilkerson to conduct monthly miracle services at the Los Angeles Shrine auditorium. The popularity of these services led, in turn, to the inauguration of a weekly half-hour television series, *I Believe in Miracles*. The programs were taped at CBS Television City in Los Angeles and aired on over 65 stations, including the superstation WOR-TV in New York City. A total of 490 of these broadcasts were taped and transmitted between 1966 and 1976. The programs showcased Kuhlman's inspirational sermons on the power of the Holy Spirit and made her an international celebrity with an ecumenical following.

Kuhlman was aware of the financial worries the television show engendered for her ministry, once remarking,

> The response is great, but we are unlike most other religious telecasts because we do not offer any giveaways. People write in only because they are hungry for the Lord. Financially, the telecasts do not pay for themselves. The greatest combination is television and radio . . . together they form a combination that is unbeatable.

To raise the money required to keep the television series on the air, Kuhlman began to conduct healing crusades throughout the country in the early 1970s and to publish more books.

A typical Kuhlman crusade began with hundreds of persons waiting for hours in line outside the auditorium where she was scheduled to appear. Like the cripples waiting at the Pool of Siloam in the Gospel, the sick persons coming to her miracle services did not want to risk missing their chance to be healed. The service itself began with gospel music and the appearance of Kuhlman. Often she spent a few minutes chatting casually with the audience before launching into her message of faith.

Author James Morris described one of Kuhlman's sermons in the following manner:

> While she spoke she constantly moved about the platform. Her sermon seemed to be built around an emotional tribute to the Holy Spirit. The full sleeves and the long, dazzling white dress billowed and wafted as she glided and turned. At first her voice seemed halting and slow, then more vibrant and mellow. Suddenly it was mixed with throaty sobs, and she was almost crying. Her audience was carried along on the tide of emotion, and many dabbed at their eyes, and more than a few wept openly and unashamedly.

Following her sermons, the healing "miracles" would begin. As if by some hidden telepathy, Kuhlman announced the cures as soon as she became aware of them. She then pointed to the person healed and watched as he or she was guided to the stage by her assistants. After congratulating the person, Kuhlman laid her hands on his head and watched him collapse into the arms of waiting ushers. This phenomenon was called "falling under the power of the Spirit" or being "slain in the Spirit." According to numerous reports, both believers and nonbelievers experienced healings at Kuhlman's services. When once asked to explain this phenomenon, she answered,

> When I was twenty years of age, I could have given you all the answers. My theology was straight and I was sure that if you followed certain rules, worked hard enough, obeyed all the commandments, and had yourself in a certain spiritual state, God would heal you. . . . Lo and behold, my theology came tumbling down and was crushed into a thousand pieces when one day a man who had just entered the auditorium during a miracle service stood silently against the back wall, and after not more than five minutes walked boldly to the stage and freely admitted, "My ear has just opened and I do not believe!"   . . . He never

recanted. . . . He had not been to church for more than twenty-five years and had put himself in the category of an atheist. It is possible for me to relate many cases where people have been healed who were amazed, who freely admitted that they did not expect to be healed. . . . Until we have a way of defining it, all that I can tell you is that these are mercy healings.

The evangelist's television program, which was produced by Billy Graham film assistant Dick Ross, featured the tall, slender Kuhlman greeting her audience with a radiant smile. She was described by one reporter as being "supercharged with electric confidence and all the natural chutzpah-gusto of a whole slew of cheerleaders." Kuhlman consistently disavowed her part in the miraculous healings that occurred during the program. On one occasion she exclaimed, "The Holy Spirit, people, oh, I'm so sold on the Holy Spirit. Don't you understand? Without the Holy Spirit I'm sunk, I haven't a crutch, I haven't anything to lean on." At another meeting she stated plainly, "I have nothing, nothing to do with these healings. I have only yielded my life to Him. Do not try to reach out and touch Kathryn Kuhlman. Reach up and touch Him."

The healing evangelist Oral Roberts became a staunch supporter of Kuhlman's ministry in 1971 and organized the granting of Oral Roberts University's first honorary doctorate to her in 1973. During the ceremony Roberts declared, "The one person in the world who epitomizes all we believe in is Kathryn Kuhlman."

From 1974 to 1976, Kuhlman grew steadily weaker because of an enlarged heart. However, rather than cut back on her schedule, she increased it. Her last healing service was conducted in Los Angeles in November 1975. A short time later, Kuhlman underwent a heart operation from which she never fully recovered. She died of complications from the surgery in Tulsa, Oklahoma, on February 20, 1976. Entry into her funeral plot at Forest Lawn Memorial Park in Glendale, California (the same cemetery in which Aimee Semple McPherson is buried), is by key only to ensure that the gravesite does not become a popular shrine.

Kathryn Kuhlman brought the phenomena of spiritual healing and being "slain in the Spirit" to an interdenominational, middle-class audience during the charismatic revival of the mid-twentieth century. Unlike many healing evangelists, she always made sure that a cross-section of denominational clergy were present on-stage during her services. Moreover, she invited doctors from respected medical schools like Stanford University and Johns Hopkins to attend her performances and to authenticate the healings that occurred there. Ms. Kuhlman was a remarkable spiritual leader and broadcasting personality who carried forward a long tradition of American women folk healers. Although the Kathryn Kuhlman Foundation did not outlive her, Kuhlman's style of healing has been carried forward by the Orlando-based Pentecostal evangelist Benny Hinn.

SOURCES

Buckingham, Jamie. *Daughter of Destiny: Kathryn Kuhlman, Her Story.* Plainfield, TX: Logos International, 1976.

Casdorph, H. Richard. *The Miracles.* Plainfield, TX: Logos International, 1976.

Erickson, Hal. *Religious Radio and Television in the United States, 1921–1991.* Jefferson, NC: McFarland, 1992.

Farr, Louise. "The Divine Ms. K." *MS,* July, 1975: 12–15.

Hosier, Helen Kooiman. *Kathryn Kuhlman: The Life She Led, the Legacy She Left.* Old Tappan, NJ: Fleming H. Revell, 1976.

"Kathryn Kuhlman." *Current Biography.* 1974: 227–229.

Kathryn Kuhlman Foundation. *From Medicine to Miracles.* Minneapolis: Bethany Fellowship, 1978.

Kuhlman, Kathryn. *God Can Do It Again.* Englewood Cliffs, NJ: Prentice-Hall, 1969.

———. *I Believe in Miracles.* Englewood Cliffs, NJ: Prentice-Hall, 1962.

———. *10,000 Miles for a Miracle.* Minneapolis: Dimension Books, 1974.

———. *Twilight and Dawn.* Minneapolis: Dimension Books, 1976.

Leisering, Katherine Jane. "An Historical and Critical Study of the Pittsburgh Preaching Career of Kathryn Kuhlman." Ph.D. diss., Ohio University, 1981.

Lippy, Charles H., ed. *Twentieth-Century Shapers of American Popular Religion.* Westport, CT: Greenwood Press, 1989.

Morris, James. "Kathryn Kuhlman." In *The Preachers.* New York: St. Martin's Press, 1973.

Peterson, Richard G. "Electric Sisters." In *The God Pumpers,* edited by Marshall Fishwick and Ray B. Browne. Bowling Green, KY: Bowling Green State University Popular Press, 1987.

Roberts, Oral. "A Tribute to Kathryn Kuhlman." *Abundant Life* (May 1976): 2-5.

Spraggett, Allen. *Kathryn Kuhlman: The Woman Who Believes in Miracles.* New York: World Publishing, 1970.

L

Courtesy: National Religious Broadcasters

Beverly LaHaye has become one of the most influential and admired conservative women in America. Working together with her husband, Tim LaHaye, LaHaye has worked tirelessly to discredit the secular humanism she believes has infiltrated the nation's educational, political, and religious institutions. The LaHayes have been broadcasting their moralist-activist message on television and radio since 1956.

Born Beverly Jean Ratcliffe, LaHaye grew up in a conservative family. She lost her father when she was a child, and the family relocated several times before her mother eventually remarried. Nevertheless, the experience of uncertainty and instability in the wake of her father's death had a decisive impact on LaHaye's future views concerning family life. It also gave her something in common with the man she would marry, Tim LaHaye. Tim and Beverly met in 1946 at Bob Jones University in Greenville, South Carolina. The school was a bastion of Christian Fundamentalism and racial segregation, and the LaHayes were both deeply indoctrinated in its conservative ideology. Beverly LaHaye dropped out of college after her marriage. She spent the next few years raising the couple's four children and supporting her husband in his work as pastor of a Baptist church in Pickens, South Carolina.

After Tim LaHaye's six-year stint as a pastor at a Baptist church in Minneapolis, Minnesota, the family moved to El Cajon, California, near San Diego, where Tim became the pastor of Scott Memorial Baptist Church. At this time the couple began broadcasting a 30-minute television program, *The LaHayes on Family Life*. The taped show promoted the LaHayes' highly conservative Christian vision of family life and was nationally syndicated between 1956 and 1959. The show was revitalized later and continues to be broadcast in the 1990s. The LaHayes' ministry also included the publication and distribution of books and articles on family life and, beginning in 1972, a lecture series entitled Family Life Seminars that took the couple around the country. In the 1970s and early 1980s, Beverly and her husband conducted nearly 465 family-life seminars in over 40 countries, during which time she continued to cohost a call-in radio talk show and a weekly television show.

In 1979, while watching a Barbara Walters interview with Betty Friedan, the founder of the National Organization for Women (NOW) and author of the feminist manifesto *The Feminine Mystique*, LaHaye became disturbed by Friedan's assumption that she spoke for all American women and by her statement that she hoped to make America a humanist nation. The interview galvanized LaHaye into action. She organized a small group of San Diego women who began holding educational meetings concerning NOW, the Equal Rights Amendment, and other feminist initiatives. Out of these meetings came Concerned Women for America (CWA), which was chartered in 1979 as a national body dedicated to bolstering the American family, organizing prayer networks, and upholding high moral values. CWA concerns itself with opposing gay rights, the Equal Rights Amendment, and abortion, and strongly supports prayer in public schools and governmental aid for private religious-based schools. The group included a diverse array of ethnic groups and ages and boasted active chapters in every state of the union by the late 1980s.

LaHaye's initiative was synchronous with the rising tide of the New Christian Right in national politics, and her new movement counted over 500,000 members by 1984. During that same year, CWA chose Washington, DC, for its first annual convention, which attracted over 2,000 attendees. By 1985, LaHaye was voted the fifth most admired conservative woman in the nation, narrowly trailing Nancy Reagan and Jean Kirkpatrick.

During the 1990s, the LaHayes have continued their torrid pace of publishing, lecturing, and producing radio and television programming. In addition to their own *The LaHayes on Family Life* and *Tim LaHaye's Capital Report* (a short news broadcast), the couple now makes frequent guest appearances on the programs of other Christian broadcasters.

In 1993, Beverly LaHaye began airing three hard-hitting radio programs of her own from a broadcasting studio just blocks from the White House in Washington, DC. The shows, *Beverly LaHaye Live*, *This Week with Beverly LaHaye*, and *The Beverly LaHaye Commentary*, cover current issues, personalities, and challenges that affect American families. *Beverly LaHaye Live* was awarded the National Religious Broadcasters Talk Show of the Year award in 1993.

The LaHayes' teachings on the family have been in the vanguard of the backlash against feminism and gay liberation in America during the 1980s and 1990s. For Beverly LaHaye, the ideal domestic situation is a traditional nuclear family headed by a father who works outside the house and a mother who remains at home with the children, even though she, herself, has spent most of her adult life traveling and pursuing an active career outside the home. LaHaye sees radical feminists and gays as agents of Satan who are leading the attack on the traditional family by encouraging mothers to work outside the home and by accepting alternative family structures. She often refers to Gloria Steinem's proclamation—that the children of America will be trained to believe in their own, as opposed to God's, potential by the beginning of the third millennium—as evidence of these attacks on the family.

LaHaye believes that secular humanism stems from the atheistic and egotistic desires of humanity and that its main task is to rid society of a God-centered focus. In looking back on the growth of secular humanist philosophy over the past 30 years, LaHaye asks, "Who are [secular humanists] after? They're after our young people." She reserves special condemnation for pornography, "the satanic, filthy lyrics in some rock music," and Planned Parenthood. Like her husband, however, she remains optimistic about the future. "As I travel around this country, I see more and more people waking up . . . willing to roll up their sleeves and do something about it. . . . I think God is going to use us to turn the tide from becoming a humanistic nation."

Whether the LaHayes' Christian fundamentalist worldview will become the norm in the twenty-first century remains to be seen, but Beverly LaHaye has certainly become a powerful voice in the nation's debate over its moral and religious future.

SOURCES

Bruce, Steve. *Pray TV: Televangelism in America.* London: Routledge, 1990.

Erickson, Hal. *Religious Radio and Television in the United States, 1921–1991.* Jefferson, NC: McFarland, 1992.

LaHaye, Beverly. *How to Develop Your Child's Temperament.* Old Tappan, NJ: Fleming H. Revell, 1977.

———. *I Am a Woman by God's Design.* Old Tappan, NJ: Fleming H. Revell, 1980.

———. *The Restless Woman.* Old Tappan, NJ: Fleming H. Revell, 1984.

———. *Spirit-Controlled Family Living.* Old Tappan, NJ: Fleming H. Revell, 1978.

———. *The Spirit-Controlled Woman.* Old Tappan, NJ: Fleming H. Revell, 1976.

Lippy, Charles H., ed. *Twentieth-Century Shapers of American Popular Religion.* Westport, CT: Greenwood Press, 1989.

Peterson, Richard G. "Electric Sisters." In *The God Pumpers*, edited by Marshall Fishwick and Ray B. Browne. Bowling Green, KY: Bowling Green State University Popular Press, 1987.

TIM LaHAYE

born: April 27, 1926, Detroit, Michigan

Courtesy: National Religious Broadcasters

Tim LaHaye has been an outspoken advocate of Christian fundamentalist values since his first nationwide television program, *The LaHayes on Family Life*, appeared in 1956. LaHaye's most significant contribution to the national fundamentalist resurgence of the 1970s and 1980s was his coining of the term "secular humanist" to describe any person who does not agree with his archconservative religious worldview.

LaHaye grew up in Detroit, Michigan, where his father, Francis T. LaHaye, worked as an electrician. The elder LaHaye died when Tim was nine years old, leaving him to care for his mother, Margaret Palmer LaHaye, and two younger siblings. Despite receiving help from relatives, Mrs. LaHaye was forced to work evenings to support her children. LaHaye's early religious training occurred in the conservative Baptist tradition. His family was active in local Baptist congregations, with his mother serving as a fellowship director and his uncle as a minister.

After serving in the US Air Force at the end of World War II, LaHaye enrolled in Bob Jones University in Greenville, South Carolina. The school's staunch conservatism and segregationism were both congruent with LaHaye's upbringing and influential in forming his subsequent philosophies. LaHaye met Beverly Jean Ratcliffe during his freshman year and the couple were married July 5, 1947.

Beverly LaHaye's upbringing was similar to that of Tim's in that her father had died during her childhood, and she had been forced to deal with the uncertainty and instability occasioned by the sudden loss of a father figure. This common loss and their shared conservative Christian values probably contributed to the couple's lifelong crusade to promote traditional father-dominated families as the norm for American society.

Shortly after her marriage, Beverly LaHaye quit school and became a housewife, bearing four children. She also supported her husband in his pastoral duties at a small Baptist church in rural South Carolina while he finished his bachelor of arts degree. Upon Tim's graduation, the LaHayes settled in Minneapolis, Minnesota, where Tim became pastor of a Baptist church. Six years later, in 1956, the family moved again, this time to El Cajon, California, near San Diego. LaHaye took over the pastoral duties at Scott Memorial Baptist Church, and would continue in this role for the next 25 years.

The LaHayes on Family Life began broadcasting during their first year in California. The half-hour taped program was nationally syndicated and continued promoting LaHaye's conservative Christian vision for the family until 1959. The LaHayes' ministry also included the publication and distribution of books and articles on family life and, beginning in 1972, a lecture series entitled Family Life Seminars that took the couple around the country.

LaHaye's teachings on the family have become a keystone in the backlash against feminism and gay liberation in America during the 1980s and 1990s. For LaHaye, the ideal is a traditional nuclear family headed by a father who works outside the house and a mother who remains at home with the children. Radical feminists and gays, therefore, are seen as demonic agents who are leading the attack on the traditional family by encouraging mothers to work at outside jobs and by accepting alternative family makeups.

LaHaye also has been a pioneer in private fundamentalist religious schooling, organizing the Christian High School of San Diego, the Christian Unified School System, and Christian Heritage College between 1965 and 1970. LaHaye was president of the college until 1976. To buttress his own educational credentials, LaHaye attended Western Conservative Baptist Seminary in Portland, Oregon, where he earned a doctorate of ministry degree in 1977.

LaHaye continued to publish books on family life and pop-Christian psychology throughout the 1960s and 1970s. One of his most popular works, entitled *Spirit-Controlled Temperament* and published in 1966, sold over 500,000 copies in 10 years. Other popular titles published during this period included *Transformed Temperaments* (1971), and *Sex Education Is for the Family* (1974). LaHaye also published self-guided Bible-study books such as *Revela-*

tion Illustrated and Made Plain (1973), and *How to Study the Bible for Yourself* (1976).

The LaHayes rode the crest of the new Christian Right's rise to power in the late 1970s, presenting their Family Life Seminar in numerous cities around the nation and in several foreign countries. However, it was the publication of his 1980 book *The Battle for the Mind* that firmly established LaHaye as a national conservative leader. The book laid out the main structure of his argument against secular humanism and was widely lauded in conservative political and religious circles. For LaHaye, secular humanism was a godless philosophy of individualism that was covertly seeking to de-Christianize America through such liberal organizations as the National Educational Association, the National Organization for Women, the Sex Information and Education Council of the United States, the United Nations, and the American Civil Liberties Union.

Secular humanism became the great rallying cry and enemy of Christian conservatives during the 1980s. It also became a convenient label with which to smear political candidates, religious leaders, educators, and entertainment executives who did not agree with the Christian fundamentalist vision for America. LaHaye followed up *The Battle for the Mind*'s phenomenal success with two new works which continued in the same vein, *The Battle for the Family* (1982) and *The Battle for the Public Schools* (1983).

LaHaye's eschatology has become extremely influential in right-wing circles and has recently been seen to be fully congruent with the eschatologies of various paramilitary militias, survivalists, and Christian Identity groups. In LaHaye's apocalyptic vision, such international organizations as the United Nations and the World Council of Churches are identified as the beast and the scarlet whore of the Book of Revelation. LaHaye also predicts a coming nuclear catastrophe during which all Christians will perish except those who have been raptured up to the heavens by God:

> The Rapture will be an event of such startling proportions that the entire world will be con-

scious of our leaving. There will be airplane, bus and train wrecks throughout the world. Who can imagine the chaos on the freeways when automobile drivers are sucked out of their cars?

The LaHayes began to take an interest in overt political action on a national level during the mid-1980s. Tim LaHaye, who had already worked to elect conservative candidates to public office with the Coalition for Religious Freedom in the 1970s, formed the American Coalition for Traditional Values (ACTV) in 1984, and relocated to Washington, DC, to run the new lobby's national offices. The membership in this organization included such prominent Christian personalities as the founder of Campus Crusade for Christ, Bill Bright, and televangelists James Kennedy, Charles Stanley, Jim Bakker, Jimmy Swaggart, Jerry Falwell, Rex Humbard, Robert Tilton, James Robison, and Kenneth Copeland; former Presidents of the Southern Baptist Convention Adrian Rogers and Jimmy Draper; General Superintendent of the Assemblies of God Thomas Zimmerman; and Director of the National Association of Evangelicals Bob Dugan. The ACTV was widely credited with helping Ronald Reagan gain his landslide presidential victory in 1984.

LaHaye's star became tarnished during the 1980s when it was revealed that his Coalition for Religious Freedom had allowed the Unification Church of Sun Myung Moon to underwrite the Pageant for Religious Freedom, a gala event attended by religious professionals from around the nation. The pageant grew out of the concern among many religious leaders that the government was overstepping its constitutional powers and intruding into the nation's religious communities. Much of this concern was related to the Internal Revenue Service's criminal prosecution of Sun Myung Moon on tax-evasion charges. A firestorm of protest broke out when the attendees of the event learned of the Unification Church's sponsorship. LaHaye, though disassociating himself from Unificationist doctrines, affirmed the mission of the gala.

LaHaye came under further criticism in 1986 when it became known that ACTV had accepted financial support from a top aide to Moon. The relationship between Moon and LaHaye had a certain logic, however, insofar as both men were zealous anti-Communists and vocal advocates of right-wing American causes. In fact, LaHaye is an uncharacteristic figure in late twentieth-century Christian Fundamentalism because he has often gone beyond classic fundamentalist separatism and embraced non-Protestant conservatives from the Mormon, Unificationist, Jewish, and Catholic traditions.

The embarrassment surrounding his Moon connections notwithstanding, LaHaye has continued to be a powerful national voice for religious conservatives. In addition to his syndicated television program, national seminars, publishing endeavors, and ACTV presidency, LaHaye became a staff member of the highly successful Prestonwood Baptist Church in north Dallas, Texas, in 1986. During the 1990s, the LaHayes have continued their torrid pace of publishing, lecturing, and producing radio and television programming. In addition to their own *The LaHayes on Family Life* and *Tim LaHaye's Capital Report* (a short news broadcast), the couple now makes frequent guest appearances on the programs of other Christian broadcasters.

SOURCES

Bruce, Steve. *Pray TV: Televangelism in America.* London: Routledge, 1990.

Erickson, Hal. *Religious Radio and Television in the United States, 1921–1991.* Jefferson, NC: McFarland, 1992.

LaHaye, Tim. *The Battle for the Family.* Old Tappan, NJ: Fleming H. Revell, 1982.

———. *The Battle for the Mind.* Old Tappan, NJ: Fleming H. Revell, 1980.

———. *The Battle for the Public Schools.* Old Tappan, NJ: Fleming H. Revell, 1983.

———. *The Beginning of the End.* Wheaton, IL: Tyndale House, 1972.

———. *The Hidden Censors.* Old Tappan, NJ: Fleming H. Revell, 1984.

———. *How to Study the Bible for Yourself.* Irvine, CA: Harvest House, 1976.

———. *Revelation Illustrated and Made Plain.* Grand Rapids, MI: Zondervan, 1973.

———. *Spirit-Controlled Temperament.* Wheaton, IL: Tyndale House, 1966.

———. *Ten Steps to Victory over Depression.* Grand Rapids, MI: Zondervan, 1974.

———. *Transformed Temperaments.* Wheaton, IL: Tyndale House, 1971.

———. *The Unhappy Gays.* Wheaton, IL: Tyndale House, 1978.

Lippy, Charles H., ed. *Twentieth-Century Shapers of American Popular Religion.* Westport, CT: Greenwood Press, 1989.

NORA LAM

born: September 4, 1932, Beijing, China

Courtesy: National Religious Broadcasters

Nora Lam has been a popular Christian evangelist since the early 1970s. Her ministry, Nora Lam Chinese Ministries International, is located in San Jose, California, and directs most of its efforts to supporting the underground Church in mainland China. Lam makes frequent speaking tours of US cities where she talks about the fate of China's people and what can be done to help them. Lam's infomercials, which feature guests such as Pat Boone and Carol Lawrence, are a staple of Christian television. These programs raise funds that support Lam's efforts to bring Bibles and the "good news" of the gospel to China. Lam is a frequent guest on Paul and Jan Crouch's Trinity Broadcasting Network (TBN) program *Praise the Lord.*

Lam's life story was chronicled in a feature film entitled *China Cry,* which was produced, to the tune of $7 million, by Paul Crouch. The lushly photographed and professionally edited drama, which opened in November 1990 in 135 theaters around the country, was based on Lam's autobiographical book of the same title. The film portrayed Lam's miraculous escape from Communist China and drew enthusiastic reviews from both secular and Christian film critics.

In one of the film's more dramatic sequences, the pregnant Lam is beaten repeatedly by her Chinese Red Army captors and finally taken before a firing squad. As the soldiers take aim and fire, a strange electrical storm seemingly diverts the bullets from their target. In her talks before churches and other groups, Lam declares that her life was spared by God. During one speaking engagement, she recounted,

> I was down on the ground and I heard every bullet come from the guns, and in two minutes the men from the firing squad came around and said, "What was that light that blinded everybody? And we saw every bullet come from the guns, but they went over you and around you, but none of them hit you."

After this narrow escape, Lam was put back in prison and told by God that her baby would not be born in China. She alleges that she carried the child for 12 months before being expelled from China and giving birth in Hong Kong in 1958. After arriving in Hong Kong, Lam divorced her first husband, married S. K. Sung, a respected evangelical leader in the Hong Kong Christian community, and emigrated to the United States.

Her career as an evangelist began in the early 1970s. She returned to China for the first time in 1983 and visited her homeland twice every year until 1992. In January 1992, Lam was refused an entry visa by Chinese authorities. She claimed that she had been labeled "the most dangerous evangelist in China" because of her language skills.

Lam became a center of controversy in 1990 when Southern California attorney and Christian radio talk-show host John Stewart was asked to endorse *China Cry*. Stewart decided that he should first investigate complaints he had heard about Lam's ministry. Based on numerous interviews with acquaintances of Lam, Stewart concluded that little in the film could be documented and that Lam's stories were not credible. He dubbed the film, "China Lie." In addition, it was revealed that the Assemblies of God had warned its ministers in 1977 that Lam was not endorsed by the denomination's Division of Foreign Missions and was not recommended as a speaker at church functions where presentations about missions were made. This vote of no confidence was reinforced in a 1989 ruling by the National Association of Evangelicals, which turned down Lam's application for membership.

Subsequent articles in *Christianity Today* and *Christian Research Journal* alleged that Lam's story of her divorce and subsequent remarriage with Sung was inaccurate. Lam claimed that she had been physically abused by her first husband but had never disclosed her suffering to her pastor. The pastor, she wrote, had become aware of the abuse through supernatural means and had subsequently encouraged her to leave her husband. Lam's pastor remembered these events differently. He alleged that Lam had discussed her abusive spousal relationship with him several times and that he had not counseled her to leave her husband. Moreover, Lam's claim that her relationship with Sung had blossomed long after her divorce was also contradicted by the pastor. He claimed that Lam ran away with an elder in his congregation (Sung) who left behind his first wife.

The articles also criticized Lam for alleged fundraising irregularities and deceptive evangelizing techniques. David Plymire of China Radio claimed that at one crusade the Chinese audience was asked to come forward to receive a free book. The American tourist audience, Plymire alleged, was told by an interpreter via headphones that "the people were responding to Lam's invitation to accept Christ." When confronted with these allegations, Lam's son,

Joseph, called his mother's critics "dart throwers" who were "motivated by jealousy and vendettas." He asserted that Lam had been caught in a crossfire between Stewart and Crouch. Stewart, he claimed, bore a grudge against Crouch.

In spite of the controversy, Lam's ministry continues to flourish. As of 1991, it was taking in an estimated $2.5 million annually. Lam continues to air her infomercials and to make speaking tours around the world. The evangelist's biographical entry in *Who's Who in Religion* states that she earned a bachelor of law from Soochow University in Shanghai in 1953 and was professor of law and history at Soochow between 1951 and 1958.

Ms. Lam has five children, some of whom work in her ministry. Her published works include *For Those Tears* (1973), *China Cry* (1980), *Bullet-Proof Believer* (1988), *God's Never Too Late* (1988), and *Asians for Bush* (1988).

See also Paul Crouch

SOURCES

"Critics Question Nora Lam's Story." *Christianity Today*, January 14, 1991.

Lam, Nora, and Cliff Dudley. *For Those Tears*. Carol Stream, IL: Creation House, 1972.

"Truthfulness of TBN's 'China Cry' Movie Called into Question." *Christian Research Journal*, Spring, 1991.

Who's Who in Religion. 4th ed. Wilmette, IL: Marquis, 1993.

LAMB & LION MINISTRIES
established: 1980

An independent evangelical Protestant organization founded in 1980 by David R. Reagan, Lamb & Lion Ministries seeks to proclaim the Second Coming of Christ to believers and unbelievers. Its radio program, *Christ in Prophecy*, airs daily over more than 70 stations nationwide. The broadcast emanates from Lamb & Lion Ministries' headquarters in McKinney, Texas, north of Dallas.

Other Lamb & Lion Ministries activities include distribution of audio- and videotapes; publication of books, pamphlets, and prophecy newsletters; and the presentation of lectures at various prophecy seminars and conferences. Reagan, a former college professor and administrator, also conducts a number of special church meetings and at least one Holy Land tour each year.

See also *Christ in Prophecy*

SOURCES

Melton, J. Gordon. *Directory of Religious Organizations in the United States.* 3d ed. Detroit: Gale Research, 1993.

Reagan, David R. *Trusting God.* Rev. ed. McKinney, TX: Lamb & Lion Ministries, 1994.

BOB LARSON
born: May 28, 1944, Westwood, California

Courtesy: National Religious Broadcasters

Bob Larson is the controversial evangelical author, lecturer, composer, film producer, former host of the radio show *Talk-Back with Bob Larson*, and the current host of *Bob Larson Live*.

The son of Earl Larson and Viola Baum, Larson grew up on a farm near Culbertson, Nebraska. During his years at Culbertson Public School, he had his own program at radio station KICK in nearby McCook and was a member of the basketball, football, and track teams. He was honored as the best all-around student, best athlete, and homecoming king during his senior year of high school. During high school, Larson also became interested in rock and roll and helped form a band, The Rebels, with two friends. The group, one of the first rock bands in southwest Nebraska, played at fairs and rodeos as well as in schools, churches, and pizza parlors. Larson was The Rebels' lead singer and gained a reputation for his brashness, ambition, arrogance, and intensity. The father of the band's drummer acted as the group's chaperone when it played to capacity audiences in such national venues as Atlantic City, New Jersey.

After high school, Larson enrolled in McCook Junior College and transferred to the University of Nebraska at Lincoln in September 1963. Following his freshman year of college, Larson returned home and reported that he had become a Christian. He also announced that God would no longer allow him to play rock music. "He was just like a born-again," a bandmate remembered. "He was so totally taken with it. It was like he was struck by lightning." Larson was persuaded to fulfill The Rebels' remaining bookings but was much more subdued in his final performances.

The future evangelist dropped out of college in 1964 and began lecturing on the college circuit about the spiritual dangers of the rock-and-roll lifestyle. A few years later, Larson met Kathryn J. Larson in Hamilton, Ontario. They were married on January 24, 1968. Soon after, he published his first book, *Rock and Roll: The Devil's Diversion*. The anti-rock diatribe gained him national attention, including a mention in a 1970 *Newsweek* article. Two similar books, *Rock and the Church*, and *Hippies, Hindus, and Rock and Roll*, appeared in 1971 and 1972, respectively.

In 1972, Larson created Bob Larson Crusades (later Bob Larson Ministries) in Denver, Colorado. Over the next eight years, he traveled to 70 countries as part of two worldwide evangelistic campaigns. Larson also lectured at over

2,000 colleges and universities, composed numerous songs, cut five albums, and produced Christian films. During the late 1970s, he became involved in a half-hour Christian television series. Larson also continued to publish such anti-rock and anti-Eastern religion books as *The Day the Music Died* (1973), *Hell on Earth* (1974), *The Guru* (1974), *Babylon Reborn* (1976), *Raising Children in the Rock Generation* (1979), and *Rock* (1980).

Larson became a vocal critic of so-called "cults" following the Jonestown mass suicide in 1978 and authored *Larson's Book of Cults* in 1982. This encyclopedic volume claimed to analyze "dozens of prominent cults from historical, sociological, and theological perspectives" and to detail precisely "how each cult deviates from Christian truth." It also claimed to trace "cultic roots in major world religious systems" and to "explain clearly major cult concepts such as enlightenment, reincarnation, and meditation." The book had gone through seven printings by 1985.

In 1983, Larson began *Talk-Back with Bob Larson*, a daily two-hour radio talk show. At the height of its popularity in 1992, the show was being carried via satellite from Denver on approximately 200 radio stations in Canada and the United States. *Talk-Back* was a fiery slugfest between Larson and the "supernatural forces of evil." On it he discussed "hot-button issues" such as satanic ritual abuse, abortion, and sexual morality. The show also gave Larson a forum for articulating the theological and moral teachings of evangelical Christianity. In a promotional tape for the program, Larson asked, "What do you want? Mr. Milquetoast? Hey, flip the dial. This is me, this is real, this is *Talk-Back*." The program helped Bob Larson Ministries (BLM) attract more than $5.6 million in donations and other moneys annually by the early 1990s.

Talk-Back became famous for Larson's riveting dialogues with rock stars, reformed sinners, and therapists, and for on-the-air exorcisms and healings. On one such occasion, a woman named Rebecca claimed to be possessed by a devil named "Keeper." Her voice alternated between that of a snarling animal and of an emotionally distraught woman. At the end of the exorcism, the woman expressed her trust in Jesus Christ. Background music then increased in volume and Larson intoned, "Keeper, you are bound. Stay right there and I'm going to come back to you in a minute. I have to go away." The demon and Rebecca were placed on hold while *Talk-Back* took a commercial break.

Larson dropped his strong opposition to rock music during the 1980s and began supporting Christian rock groups such as Petra and Tourniquet. At one Tourniquet performance, Larson jumped on the stage and jammed with the group for 10 minutes. Larson also counts among his friends such rock aficionados as Bob Guccione, Jr., the son of *Penthouse* founder Bob Guccione, Sr., and publisher of the alternative-rock periodical *Spin*.

Larson's abrasive, controversial style began to arouse strong criticisms during the early 1990s. In an article in Denver's *Westword* magazine in 1992, Larson's campaign against satanic ritual abuse (SRA) was questioned by psychologists, scholars, former co-workers, and victims he had interviewed. One such victim, a Boulder teenager who had shared her story with Larson's listeners, objected to his portrayal of her in his 1989 book, *Satanism: The Seduction of America's Youth*. According to the teen, she had asked Larson not to focus on the more gruesome aspects of her story but rather to emphasize her victorious struggle to survive and move on with her life. The book's account of the teen's abuse, however, contained graphic descriptions of incest, drug abuse, and human and animal sacrifice. The teen also complained that, in spite of her requests, she had been photographed and videotaped at a Satan Symposium in Denver. Moreover, Larson's ministry had used the story of her victimization as part of a gift package for donors. A final charge was that BLM had claimed a pivotal role in the teen's rehabilitation. In fact, according to the article, the teen had received no financial support from the ministry for her ongoing counseling.

Larson was also criticized in the article by Bob and Gretchen Passantino, the founders of Answers in Action, a nonprofit educational organization that provides information on new religions, cult movements, and occultism. The couple had helped Larson with his *Book of Cults* and later appeared as guests on *Talk-Back*. According to the Passantinos, Larson's approach to SRA was uncritical and lacking in tangible evidence. "When he got into satanic ritual abuse," Gretchen Passantino observed, "he got in way over his head as far as his ability to look critically at the information and the evidence." The Passantinos joined author Jon Trott in calling for a boycott of Larson's novel, *Dead Air*, which was published in 1991. According to the article, both the Passantinos and Trott labeled the book "Christian pornography."

Larson initially responded to the Passantinos' criticisms with claims that he had been unfairly treated. He also defended his crusade against SRA, stating that "there are major psychiatric programs and large inpatient treatment centers in hospitals all over the country which, for a decade, have been carrying on work in this area." In the end, however, Larson toned down his attacks on the Passantinos and concluded,

> The Passantinos would like to discredit people like me for whatever reason—that I'm some kind of gullible village idiot running around believing any crazy story anyone tells me. Nothing could be further from the truth. I'm as deeply concerned about getting to the truth as anyone else. . . . My attitude is, you're in pain, you've been a victim of what you believe to be abuse; I'm going to let you speak your pain, I'm going to listen to what you say—and when you get it out, then we can look at what can be proven and not proven, that which can be validated and that which is invalid, and we'll sort it out.

Another charge in the article came from a woman who had befriended Larson and his wife, Kathryn. At one social gathering, she claimed, Larson had asked her to call in to *Talk-Back* so that she could compliment him and exhort the listening audience to make contributions to his ministry. "He basically wanted me to pump him up on the air and tell him how wonderful he was and change the climate from

all the attacks." Larson conceded that on occasion he had asked previous callers to call in, but he denied that any pretense was made that such calls were spontaneous.

In 1991, Larson and his wife Kathryn were divorced. As part of the customary legal proceedings, Larson was required to disclose his financial condition. According to a copy of court transcripts, Larson earned $220,000 per year after taxes, including his salary from BLM, his expense, retirement, transportation, and housing allowances, his salary from International Broadcasting Network (which distributed *Talk-Back*), and his consulting fees from BLM's Canadian affiliate. Larson also received health and life insurance benefits, an athletic club membership, and $1,000 per month for recreational purposes. According to BLM's general counsel, these compensations were all above board. In addition, BLM had received a "seal of approval" from the Ethics and Financial Integrity Commission, the National Religious Broadcasters' watchdog organization for member ministries. The general counsel defended the $200,000 in bonuses Larson and his wife had received from BLM's board of directors between 1989 and 1990 on the grounds that the couple deserved compensation for "hardships suffered during the early years of the ministry."

A second critical article appeared in *World* magazine, an evangelical periodical whose stated mission is "to help Christians apply the Bible to their understanding of and response to everyday current events." In this piece, both current and former employees and associates of BLM described Larson as a "self-absorbed man who verbally and emotionally abuses employees and exaggerates the number of people he helps." Moreover, these informants claimed that Larson watches a computer screen to get a running amount of contributions even as he counsels callers on the air. The article reported that Larson's Compassion Connection Hope Line, which offered referrals to professional counseling and aid agencies, was open for only four hours on weekdays and was a toll call. His toll-free *Talk-Back* number was open for only two hours daily, while his toll-free Communicator Club line (reserved for donors) was open

50 hours a week. An ex-employee alleged that callers who needed counseling and could not afford the long-distance cost of the Compassion Connection were not allowed to get free help. "We weren't allowed to talk to them," she recalled, "because it was an 800 line. We would be reprimanded if we were caught counseling. It cost the ministry money."

The *World* article also disclosed Larson's use of "re-airs" when he was away from *Talk-Back*. The re-airs were composed by producers who reviewed past programs and combined the best callers on a particular topic into one show. Larson would record new "drop-in" breaks that gave the impression he was present for the broadcast. As one informant explained, "We make it sound as live as possible. When he does the drop-ins, we give him a tape and a listing of what the callers were before and after so he can blend his voice right in. It's become an art form. We're not trying to lie to the public, although the opening says, 'Live. *Talk-Back*.'" BLM responded that they provided a disclaimer at the end of each hour informing listeners that the show was prerecorded. One employee, however, admitted, "We kind of whisper it. We don't shout it throughout the program, because our donations go way down if people find out they're listening to a tape." In time, the article claimed, the re-airs began to generate more donations than the live show.

Larson defended himself in a subsequent article that appeared in the *Dallas/Fort Worth Heritage*. He explained that BLM's limitations on toll-free counseling came about as a result of harassing phone calls. "I'm sorry I can't make the Hope Line toll-free," he stated, "but if I did nobody would be able to get through for help. They'd shut it down with harassing calls." Apparently Larson was unconcerned about similar problems on his toll-free donor's line. Larson also asserted that liability issues made counseling over the phone a difficult undertaking. The people who operated the donor lines were not trained to counsel, nor were they tied into the computer that releases referral information. "It is not a counseling line," he acknowledged.

If they want to be led to the Lord, we'll lead them to the Lord. But many of the people who call are just looking for help, and we're trying to get them to network with a local person who can help. This is an effort above and beyond paying for our air time that we do in an effort to help the Christian community. We don't have to do it, and nobody else does it quite the way we do.

In the wake of these controversies, KKLA, a Christian radio station in Los Angeles, and WHLV in Hattiesburg, Mississippi, dropped Larson's program. By May 5, 1993, the number of stations carrying *Talk-Back* had decreased, and BLM's reported income had dropped 14 percent.

On June 9, 1995, Larson ended *Talk-Back* after 12 years on the airwaves. BLM reported that the 150 stations then carrying the talk show had agreed to air Larson's new one-hour program, *Bob Larson Live*. The format of the new show is a series of monologues by Larson on such pet topics as Satanism, cult movements, and rock-and-roll lyrics. Live callers are a thing of the past, although interviews with various guests occasionally occur. In response to critics who contended that the new show sought to eliminate embarrassing calls from listeners who were upset by rumors of Larson's adultery and of BLM's misrepresentation of its financial condition, Larson asserted, "The talk-show format doesn't lend itself to in-depth analysis of issues."

Bob Larson continues his "in-your-face" brand of religious radio and shows no signs of backing down or changing his style.

SOURCES

"Bob Larson 'Talks Back' about *World* Investigation." *The Dallas/Fort Worth Heritage*, May, 1993.

Contemporary Authors. New Revision Series, vol. 5. Detroit: Gale Research, 1984.

Grelen, Jay, and Doug LeBlanc. "This Is Me, This Is Real. " *World*, January 23, 1993.

Larson, Bob. *Larson's Book of Cults*. Wheaton, IL: Tyndale House Publishers, 1985.

Morgan, Timothy C. "Personnel Woes Persist at Larson Ministries." *Christianity Today*, September 13, 1993.

Roberts, Michael. "The Evil That Men Do." *Westword*, June 2, 1992.

REUBEN LARSON
see: HCJB, Ecuador

LARRY LEA
born: 1950, Texas

Courtesy: National Religious Broadcasters

Healing televangelist Larry Lea, the son of a wealthy Texas business leader, converted to Christianity in 1967 while confined in a psychiatric ward. Following his release, he attended Dallas Baptist College, graduating in 1972. After graduation, Lea worked as a youth minister at the Beverly Hills Baptist Church in Dallas and rose to prominence as the pastor of Church on the Rock in the Dallas suburb of Rockwall. When he started the charismatic-flavored congregation in 1980, he had 13 members. By 1992, the church boasted 8,000 members and was affiliated with over 70 churches around the country in an umbrella association led by Lea.

Lea stepped down from pastoral work at the Church on the Rock to devote himself to a television ministry, which featured a daily half-hour show. The program was broadcast every morning on Pat Robertson's Family Channel and on religious channels around the country. At its peak, it was estimated that Lea's "prayer warriors" (his term for his television audience) numbered around 300,000. Lea also became the dean of the Theological Seminary of Oral Roberts University in the late 1980s, and spent part of each week in Tulsa, Oklahoma, the university's home.

In November 1991, ABC-TV's weekly newsmagazine *PrimeTime Live* aired an exposé segment that highlighted the practices of three Dallas-based televangelists. The three were Robert Tilton, W. V. Grant, and Lea. The program raised questions concerning the veracity of Lea's televised funding appeals. Included in *PrimeTime's* allegations were charges that Lea had raised a large sum of money ostensibly to build a church in Auschwitz, Poland, but had, instead, given away only a small percentage of the money to a church founded two years earlier by native Poles. In another allegation, *PrimeTime* questioned Lea's statement that a house fire in Tulsa had left him on the verge of poverty. They pointed out that he still owned a fully furnished home on a 5.1-acre Dallas estate.

Lea responded by writing a letter to his supporters refuting *PrimeTime's* accusations. Tim Lavender, Lea's ministry spokesperson, claimed that information clarifying the questions raised by ABC had been sent to the network prior to the show's airing, but that none of the information had been used in the broadcast. Moreover, Diane Sawyer had allegedly given Lea a different set of questions than the ones she asked on the air, making it appear that Lea was being evasive during the show.

In the wake of the *PrimeTime* exposé, Lea decided to suspend his television ministry for "an indefinite period" beginning December 29, 1991. The purpose of the suspension, according to Lea and Lavender, was to reflect upon the ministry's priorities and to see whether a television ministry was the most effective way to spread the Christian gospel. (As of this writing, Lea has remained off the air.)

Lea, who was a prominent member of the National Religious Broadcasters—in 1990 he had given an address to the organization's national convention—emphasized during his live interview with Sawyer that his ministry had received the seal of approval from the NRB's Ethics and Financial Integrity Commission (EFICOM). However, following the *PrimeTime* exposé, NRB's executive committee disputed Lea's statement, claiming that Lea's ministry "has not been in compliance with the EFICOM requirements since February 1991 because it did not submit the required audited financial statements for 1989." The committee also alleged that Lea's ministry had failed repeatedly to respond to EFICOM's reminders concerning the situation.

Lea promised to open his ministry to proper NRB inspection, claiming in a letter to his supporters that he had asked for an examination of his financial affairs by EFICOM. Lea also promised to seek the counsel of "a group of pastors and spiritual leaders." These ministers would review the accusations against Lea and recommend any changes they believed would be appropriate in his life and ministry. The Lea episode has resurrected questions about the effectiveness of EFICOM's self-regulatory program, which was approved at NRB's 1988 convention. Records indicate that about 70 of the 810 NRB members (9 percent) are still not in compliance with any of EFICOM's categories of evaluation.

Lea has been the senior pastor at the San Diego Lighthouse Church since February, 1994. He has no radio or television program at present, however he is currently seen on a program aired in Israel and sponsored by Lighthouse International, the missionary outreach of Lea's church.

SOURCES

Burgess, Stanley M., Gary B. McGee, and Patrick H. Alexander, eds. *Dictionary of Pentecostal and Charismatic Movements.* Grand Rapids, MI: Zondervan, 1988.

Lawton, Kim. "Broadcasters Face Ethics Questions— Again." *Christianity Today*, January 13, 1992.

RICHARD LEE
born: 1946

Richard Lee, the senior pastor of metro-Atlanta's Rehoboth Baptist Church, is a rising star in religious broadcasting. Lee hosts Rehoboth's weekly radio and television program *There's Hope*. He has also been a guest on such national television programs as *CBS News with Dan Rather*, *CNN News*, *NBC News with Tom Brokaw*, *The 700 Club*, *Focus on the Family*, *Headline News*, *Sonya Live in L.A.*, and *USA Today Television*.

Lee earned an honors bachelor of arts degree at Mercer University, and master of divinity and doctor of ministry degrees from Luther Rice Seminary. Lee also received a doctor of laws degree from Liberty University.

His tenure as pastor of Rehoboth Baptist Church began in 1982. Since that time the church has become the second largest Baptist congregation in the state of Georgia. At the beginning of 1995, the church reported a membership of 9,000.

Lee has been an active member of the Southern Baptist Convention, serving on the convention's Resolutions Committee and Committee on Committees. The Atlanta preacher also was appointed as president of the Convention's Pastors' Conference in 1991. Lee's work as a board member and committee member has expanded over the past few years to include posts at RAPHA Health Care Foundation (president and chairman), Masters Academy (chairman), Liberty University (board member), National Religious Broadcasters (board member), and There's Hope Ministries (president and chairman). In 1995, Lee was a featured speaker at the National Religious Broadcasters' annual convention in Nashville, Tennessee.

There's Hope, hosted by Lee, has grown in stature over the past 10 years, receiving NRB's Television Program Producer of the Year award in 1988. As of early 1995, the program was being aired in Canada, the Caribbean, Mexico, and every state in the US.

In addition to his broadcast ministries, Lee has authored a number of popular books. Some of his best-known titles include *The Unfailing Promise*, *Angels of Deceit*, *There's Hope for the Hurting*, and *Miracles Still Happen*. Lee has also written editorials in such publications as *USA Today*, *Atlanta Journal*, *Los Angeles Times*, and *The London Times*. The evangelist resides in Atlanta with his wife, Judy.

SOURCES

"Casting Call for NRB 95." *Religious Broadcasting*, February, 1995.

LᴇSEA BROADCASTING
established: 1971, Indianapolis, Indiana

LeSea Broadcasting is the religious television network of Lester Sumrall, a prominent revivalist preacher.

During a successful career as both a traveling evangelist and pastor in the 1950s, Sumrall began planning a prime-time television ministry. His plans were stymied, however, by local programmers and advertisers in South Bend, Indiana, who refused to relinquish their prime-time broadcasting hours to religious programming. Sumrall was finally successful in establishing a radio ministry at a South Bend radio station in 1968. Three years later, he parlayed this success into the acquisition of a bankrupt Indianapolis UHF television station, WHBM-TV. The station, which was connected to several regional cable services, became the linchpin for LeSea Broadcasting, a network of religious ministries that, at the time, included stations in Miami, Florida; Honolulu, Hawaii; and South Bend.

In order to pay the network's bills, LeSea's stations were forced to run secular feature films, comedy shorts such as the *Three Stooges* and the *Little Rascals*, and network reruns along with Sumrall's daily lectures and sermons. By the 1980s, the stations were able to generate enough listener support to dedicate most of their airtime to religious programming. By 1989,

Sumrall's weekly hour-long talk show, *LeSEA Alive*, was appearing on six of his television stations and on the Inspirational Network. LeSea programming has continued to spread to independent stations around the United States, in large part due to Sumrall's marketing savvy. Among the network's most popular offerings are the daily *Lester Sumrall Teaching Series* and *LeSEA Alive*, and *The Renewed Mind*, a weekly program. Two other popular shows, *Light and Lively* and *Blackwood Brothers Show*, feature musical formats.

Sumrall has remained true to his conviction that religious television should avoid constant fundraising and crisis appeals on the air. LeSea Broadcasting holds periodic week-long telethons during which viewers are informed of its various ministries and instructed on how they can support these activities. Aside from this, the network eschews on-the-air fundraising.

SOURCES

Burgess, Stanley M., Gary B. McGee, and Patrick H. Alexander, eds. *Dictionary of Pentecostal and Charismatic Movements*. Grand Rapids, MI: Zondervan, 1988.

Erickson, Hal. *Religious Radio and Television in the United States, 1921–1991*. Jefferson: McFarland and Co., 1992.

Hadden, Jeffrey K., and Charles E. Swann. *Prime Time Preachers: The Rising Power of Televangelism*. Menlo Park, CA: Addison-Wesley, 1981.

"No Glitter for Lester." *Christianity Today*, February 3, 1989, 36.

LET GOD LOVE YOU
see: Lloyd Ogilvie

ZOLA LEVITT
born: December 3, 1938, Pittsburgh, Pennsylvania

Zola Levitt is a teacher, writer, and scholar who has become perhaps the best-known Evangelical Jewish (Christian) television personality of the late-twentieth century. His most recent pro-

Courtesy: National Religious Broadcasters

gram is entitled *Zola Levitt Presents*. In 1992, the half-hour show was being aired in 29 states; by 1996, it was being carried on 105 independent channels in 33 states and on the Family Network, the Trinity Broadcasting Network, and The Inspirational Network. The program offers Levitt's writings and music—including 45 book titles and 15 musical albums—for sale, with the proceeds helping to fund the ministry.

Levitt was raised in an Orthodox Jewish family in Pittsburgh, Pennsylvania. During the 1970s, he became part of the Evangelical Jewish movement and established a base of operations in the Dallas-Fort Worth area. The Evangelical Jewish movement attempts to persuade Jews to accept the messiahship of Jesus while at the same time allowing them to retain the beliefs and customs of their Jewish heritage. Jewish Christians are careful not to offend fellow Jews by the use of such "hot" phrases as "converted," "cross," and "Jesus." Rather they substitute words such as "completed," "tree," and "Yeshua." Levitt's first broadcasting outreach was in radio. His two radio talk shows, *The Heart of the Matter*, which aired in the Dallas area, and *Zola Levitt Live*, which aired nationally in syndication, became top-rated programs. He moved into television in 1978 at the request of Dallas television Channel 39.

During his television programs, the energetic, friendly Levitt includes mini-musicals, dra-

matic segments, and travelogues of the Holy Land filmed during the high holy days—Yom Kippur, Passover, and Rosh Hashana. When he first began taping the programs in Israel, his producer suggested that Levitt dress himself in flowing white robes to add period flavor to the broadcasts. Against his better judgment, Levitt complied, and the flowing robes have since become a trademark. Combined with his portly shape and untrimmed beard, Levitt looks every bit the part of ancient Hebrew prophet. Throughout his career, Levitt has exercised a greater appeal to Christians—who strongly endorse the idea of Jewish conversion—than to fellow Jews, many of whom consider him a crackpot.

Levitt's fundraising appeals are minimal by the standards of the industry, and by all accounts he lives a frugal lifestyle. In his early days as a television host, his co-workers reportedly had to fill in the holes in his suits with magic markers. When a viewer sent him money for a new suit, he gave the funds to his son. Levitt drives only used cars and has never earned more than a modest five-figure income. The evangelist also composes music and operates his own travel agency. The agency books tours to the Holy Land which employ Levitt as tour guide.

Levitt made a name for himself during the 1970s through political writings such as *The Cairo Connection*. This 1977 book predicted a coming peace between Israel and its traditional rivals. The volume specifically prophesied an Egyptian-Israeli truce a few months before the beginning of peace talks between Anwar Sadat and Menachem Begin.

Levitt became even better known following the breakup of his second marriage. During this time he became depressed and, in 1988, began seeing a psychiatrist. When the psychiatrist attempted to have him hospitalized and allegedly committed a breach of confidence, Levitt initiated a campaign to penalize him. Among other actions, Levitt filed a formal complaint against the psychiatrist with the Dallas County Medical Society. When the society essentially exonerated the doctor, Levitt sent a letter to various politicians asking that the psychiatrist be forced to discontinue his "unethical methods" and that the medical society be investigated for its failure to monitor professional misconduct. The complaint forced the Texas State Board of Medical Examiners to pursue an inquiry into Levitt's case. Afer an examination, the board exonerated the doctor of any wrongdoing.

Levitt was involved in further controversy during 1994 when two former employees filed sexual harassment lawsuits against him. The suits alleged that Levitt was guilty of "unwelcome sexual advances, requests for sexual favors," and "vulgar and abusive language." The plaintiffs both reported the incidents to officials of Zola Levitt Ministries, but were unable to bring about a cessation of the alleged harassment. Levitt's lawyer dismissed the claims as groundless and suggested that the two women were trying to extract money from the Levitt ministry. As of late 1995, the suits were still pending.

Levitt holds degrees in music from Duquesne and Indiana Universities and an honorary doctor of theology degree from Faith Bible College. Zola Levitt Ministries services The Institute of Jewish-Christian Studies, which teaches the Jewish roots of Christianity to its more than 3,000 enrolled students. The ministry also publishes *The Institute of Jewish-Christian Studies*. The ministry serves believers in the United States, Europe, Scandinavia, Africa, Australia, Israel, and the countries of the former Soviet Union. Levitt and his followers have sent hundreds of books to Israel and planted thousands of trees throughout that country.

SOURCES

Erickson, Hal. *Religious Radio and Television in the United States, 1921–1991*. Jefferson, NC: McFarland, 1992.

Hadden, Jeffrey K., and Charles E. Swann. *Prime Time Preachers: The Rising Power of Televangelism*. Reading, MA: Addison-Wesley, 1981.

"Second Harassment Suit Filed against Religious TV Host." *The Dallas Morning News*, January 28, 1995.

"Unholy Crusade." *Dallas Observer*, January 23, 1992.

"Zola Levitt Ministries Home Page." World Wide Web site. http://www.levitt.com/watiszlm.html (June 1996).

C. S. LEWIS

born: November 29, 1898, Belfast, Ireland
died: November 22, 1963, Cambridge, England

The British scholar, Christian apologist, and well-known children's author Clive Staples Lewis was the son of Albert James Lewis and Flora Augusta Hamilton. The death of Lewis's mother when he was nine deepened his already melancholic temperament and led indirectly to his renunciation of Christianity at the age of 14.

Lewis was educated at Malvern College and at University College, Oxford. Active service in World War I interrupted his studies in 1917. He was wounded in action in late 1917 and spent a considerable time in convalescence. Following his discharge in December 1918, Lewis returned to his studies at Oxford. He earned a double First in English and Literae Humaniores from University College in 1924. Upon graduation, Lewis was hired as a substitute lecturer at Oxford. He then served as a university fellow and tutor in English language and literature at Magdalen College, Oxford, from 1925 to 1954.

Lewis converted to Christianity from atheism in 1931. His conversion came as a result of his thinking through major philosophical issues. He concluded that Christianity made sense, and he subsequently converted. His writings from this point reflect this conviction. From 1938 to 1963, Lewis published nearly 40 books on religious themes, among which the most famous are *The Screwtape Letters*, *The Great Divorce*, and *Mere Christianity*.

During the middle years of World War II (1941–1944), Lewis was invited by the BBC to give a series of 15-minute inspirational radio talks on Christian doctrine, which he titled "Right and Wrong: A Clue to the Meaning of the Universe." From these talks and others, Lewis published such works as *Christian Behavior*, *Mere Christianity*, and *Beyond Personality*. This series of radio talks and subsequent lay-oriented books, such as *The Problem of Pain*, expanded his popularity as a writer and commentator on evangelical Christianity in

Britain and the United States. Lewis's Narnia series of fantasy stories for children continues to be popular.

Lewis moved to Cambridge in 1954 and served as professor of Medieval and Renaissance English until his death.

SOURCES

Beversluis, John. *C. S. Lewis and the Search for Rational Religion*. Grand Rapids, MI: Eerdmans, 1985.

Green, Roger Lancelyn, and Walter Hooper. *C. S. Lewis: A Biography*. London: Souvenir Press, 1988 [1974].

Lewis, C. S. *The Case for Christianity*. New York: Macmillan, 1943.

Walsh, Chad. *C. S. Lewis: Apostle to the Skeptics*. New York: Macmillan, 1949.

H. SPENCER LEWIS

born: November 25, 1883, Frenchtown, New Jersey
died: August 2, 1939, San Jose, California

Harvey Spencer Lewis was a pioneer of religious radio during the mid-1920s, broadcasting programs over radio stations KPO in San Francisco and WJBB in Tampa, Florida. These programs were somewhat unusual in that they promoted a version of Rosicrucian Christianity. This blend of Western occultism and traditional Christianity was a far cry from both the liberal and conservative Protestantism that would come to dominate the religious airwaves later in the century.

Lewis grew up in a Methodist household in New York City and worked as an artist and journalist for the *New York Herald*. His interest in occultism led him to found the New York Institute for Psychical Research in 1904. Although the institute supported a number of esoteric studies, its primary interest was in discovering the ancient teachings of the Rosicrucians. The Rosicrucians were a legendary secret society that had emerged into public view in Germany during the early seventeenth century with the publication of two tracts, the *Fama Fraternitatis* and the *Confessio Fraternitatis*. Rosicrucian

societies had subsequently been organized throughout Europe, and Lewis was interested in gaining entry into these mysterious groups. Through the intercession of May Banks-Stacey, a British Rosicrucian, Lewis was introduced to the Rosicrucian Grand Lodge of Toulouse, France. He traveled to France in 1909 and was given the lodge's final initiatory examination. After passing this test he received the papers and jewels authorizing him to make public negotiations for the establishment of a Rosicrucian branch order in America. He called his new branch the Ancient and Mystical Order Rosae Crucis (AMORC).

Following the organization of a Supreme American Council in 1915, Lewis received final approval from his French masters to establish lodges in every state of the union. In the same year, Lewis published the first issue of *The American Rosae Crucis*, a 15-cent "magazine of life's mysteries" that resembled in format and content the popular mystery magazines of the early 1900s. AMORC began to establish itself over the next two years as an influential part of America's occult underground. The order held its first national convention in Pittsburgh in 1917, where it approved a plan to create a correspondence course. Lewis would subsequently write this course and use it to spread his Rosicrucian teachings throughout the world.

In June of 1918, Lewis's lodge room was raided by New York City police as he taught an evening class. Lewis was arrested and charged with selling fraudulent bonds. The charges, which were later dropped, were based on a complaint by an ex-member who had bought a bond from Lewis and subsequently left the organization. The public humiliation of Lewis's arrest forced him to retrench. He moved AMORC's headquarters to San Francisco in 1919 and began working with his students primarily through correspondence-course lessons. During this period, Lewis withdrew from public meetings and retooled AMORC's Rosicrucian lineage. He tied AMORC more closely to a group of early American Rosicrucians who had left Europe in the late seventeenth century and settled outside Philadelphia. He also announced a new connection to "The Supreme Council of the Universe," the purported central directing body of more than 30 eminent secret orders, including the Essenes, the Oriental Theosophists, and the Knights of Jerusalem.

During the early 1920s, Lewis established a joint physics and photography laboratory at his San Francisco headquarters and began experimenting with vacuum tubes and other transmitting equipment. He built his own transformers, induction coils, and condensers. These experiments led to bona fide innovations in such areas as circuitry and the multifunctioning of vacuum tubes. Lewis claimed that the basic principles of Rosicrucianism had suggested the course of his research and that some of his ideas had come to him intuitively during deep meditation.

KPO was the first radio broadcasting station to be established in the San Francisco area. The station's owners, a large department store, asked if Lewis would be willing to give inspirational, but non-proslytizing, talks on the air on Sunday mornings. Lewis quickly realized the potential of radio to reach those who held no special creed and were disinclined to attend conventional churches. He decided to draft a proposal for a radio church program that would be nondogmatic and nonsectarian in tone. The program would include a musical interlude and a short lecture on general moral principles, the psychology of religion, or comparative religions. It would stress that spiritual ideas tended to be syncretic and eclectic rather than the exclusive possession of any one sect or denomination. The program would end with a question and answer session and a closing rite.

KPO accepted Lewis's proposal, and the show aired every Sunday morning for two years. Lewis alternated as host with another Rosicrucian teacher who was given his topic and outline by Lewis. The innovative new program was well received by the public and became the impetus for the establishment of the Pristine Church of the Rose Cross. Lewis served as the church's bishop until AMORC decided to dissolve the congregation and stress only the order's nonreligious and fraternal character.

AMORC's teachings claimed to prepare its students—through an intellectual study of the fundamental laws of esoteric science and the experimental development of the body's psychic centers—for cosmic initiation into the Great White Brotherhood. This Brotherhood was described in AMORC's literature as a group of men and women who had attained high spiritual development and worked behind the scenes to guide humanity's evolutionary growth. AMORC's basic teachings are similar to those of other proponents of the western occult tradition. First, it teaches that humans have an outer self and an inner self. Second, it claims that the inner self is a spiritual being, and that through the awakening of the inner self the Divine Intelligence can guide the disciple's life. Third, it teaches that a person's soul reincarnates as it evolves through eternity. Finally, AMORC proclaims that individuals can master their physical conditions through mental imaging, and draw health, wealth, and happiness to themselves.

Lewis published a number of books that elaborated AMORC's complex spiritual teachings. The best known of these works were *The Mystical Life of Jesus* (1929), *Self Mastery and Fate* (1929), *Mansions of the Soul* (1930), *The Secret Doctrines of Jesus* (1937), and *Mental Poisoning* (1937).

In 1925, Lewis moved AMORC's headquarters to Tampa, Florida, in response to a special appeal from that city's grand lodge. Lewis decided to inaugurate a Sunday night public lecture series that would include a brief Oriental ritual and the discussion of various psychological, mystical, and intellectual topics. The series drew its audience from both the local resident and tourist populations. Recalling his successful foray into religious radio in San Francisco, Lewis convinced his AMORC colleagues in Tampa to purchase a radio station. By September of 1927, Radio Station WJBB was on the air. This new ministry allowed AMORC to broadcast its own propaganda freely without the nonsectarian restrictions imposed by KPO. Lewis saw the station as a medium for education, public service, entertainment, and promotion.

The design of the new station's studios was in line with Lewis's esoteric interests. Oriental drapes, hangings, and pieces of art together with aromatic scents and soft lights created the ambience of an Eastern temple. Lewis personally ordered the proper electronic equipment and helped design the studio's acoustics and soundproofing. After identifying itself with its legal call letters, WJBB announced, "This program comes to you from the Oriental Studio of the Rosicrucian Order in Tampa, Florida."

In order to reach the largest possible audience, WJBB obtained the proper licenses and built equipment for short-wave transmissions. Soon the station was airing its programs throughout South America, North America, the Caribbean, Africa, and Europe. WJBB's diverse programming included drama, choral groups, philosophical and metaphysical discourses, addresses by public officials, and news. Among the station's innovations were a listener call-in program, morning birthday greetings to individual listeners, and simultaneous long- and short-wave broadcasts.

A popular children's program was inaugurated, called the *Mummy Club*. Children would send their names to WJBB and ask to be "initiated" into the club. On initiation nights candidates' names would be announced over the air and special sound effects were used to simulate the ordeals of the initiates. A deep voice representing the mummy would interrogate candidates, whose responses would be playfully and humorously mimicked by studio personnel.

In the end, Lewis's time in Tampa was cut short by a sudden real estate boom that made physical expansion in the area an impossibility. AMORC's "Imperator" returned to California in 1927 and established a new supreme grand lodge in San Jose. The complex would eventually grow to include an acclaimed Egyptological and science museum, the Rose-Croix University in America, a planetarium, a recording studio, the Rosicrucian Research Library, and a temple designed after the ancient Egyptian temple of Dendera. Rosicrucian Park, as this headquarters was called, has been a major tourist attraction in San Jose since the 1930s.

In spite of continual legal battles over the authenticity of the order's Rosicrucian credentials, AMORC thrived until Lewis's death in 1939. Under Ralph Lewis, Lewis's son, the order continued to grow, becoming an important purveyor of Western esotericism to ordinary Americans. Such groups as Scientology, the Mayan Order, Astara, Silva Mind Control, the Holy Order of MANS, and the Order of St. Germain can be viewed as direct or indirect offshoots of AMORC. In the late 1980s, the group claimed 250,000 active members in more than 100 countries. In terms of longevity, membership, financial holdings, and cultural influence, it is among the most successful secret societies in the world.

SOURCES

Clymer, R. Swinburne. *The Rosicrucian Fraternity in America*. Quakertown, PA: Philosophical Publishing, 1935.

Lewis, Harvey Spencer.. R*osicrucian Principles for the Home and Business*. San Jose, CA: Rosicrucian Press, 1929.

———. *Rosicrucian Questions and Answers*. San Jose, CA: Rosicrucian Press, 1929.

Lewis, Ralph M. *Cosmic Mission Fulfilled. 2d ed.* Kingsport, TN: Kingsport Press, 1977.

McIntosh, Christopher. *The Rosicrucians: The History and Mythology of an Occult Order*. Wellingborough, Great Britain: Crucible, 1987.

Melton, J. Gordon. *Biographical Dictionary of American Cult and Sect Leaders*. New York: Garland, 1986.

JOSHUA LIEBMAN
born: April 7, 1907, Hamilton, Ohio
died: June 9, 1948, Boston, Massachusetts

The religious radio host and Reform Jewish rabbi, Joshua Loth Liebman, was the son of Simon Liebman and Sabina Loth. As a youth, Liebman showed early signs of intellectual brilliance, entering high school at age 10 and graduating from the University of Cincinnati in 1926 while still in his teens. Liebman took up rabbinical study at Hebrew Union College and was ordained a rabbi in 1930. While still a student, he also became a lecturer in Greek. Upon graduation, Liebman accepted lectureships at Harvard, Columbia, and Jerusalem Universities over the course of a year. He finally took up residence as instructor in Bible and Medieval exegesis at his alma mater.

In 1934, Liebman moved to Chicago to serve as rabbi of the Kelilath Anshe Maarab Temple. In 1939, he received a doctorate from Hebrew Union, later moving to Boston to accept the position of rabbi of Temple Israel. Liebman remained in Boston for the rest of his active career. A strong congregation, at the time, of over 500 families, Temple Israel grew to 1,400 families under Liebman's leadership. He was also appointed to the faculty of Andover Newton Theological Seminary, the first rabbi to hold a regular faculty appointment at an American Protestant seminary.

Throughout the 1940s, Liebman hosted a Sunday morning radio program, during which he preached on topics of interest to both Jews and Christians. During this same period, he began to explore the relationship between religion and psychology, publishing his best-selling book *Peace of Mind* in 1946. The volume would go through more than 40 printings. In 1964, a sequel was published posthumously, edited by his wife. *Hope for Man*, as it was entitled, further elaborated Liebman's ideas concerning religion and psychology.

SOURCES

Liebman, Joshua. *Peace of Mind*. New York: Simon & Schuster, 1946.

Melton, J. Gordon. *Religious Leaders of America*. Detroit: Gale Research, 1991.

LIFE IN THE WORD
see: Joyce Meyer

LIFE TODAY
see: James Robison

LIGHT AND LIFE HOUR
first aired: 1944

Light and Life Hour was the first religious radio program launched by the Free Methodist Church. Its inaugural airing took place in 1944. Myron Boyd, who had gained valuable radio experience as the host of *Gospel Clinic* for 15 years—a Seattle, Washington, religious broadcast—was chosen as the show's host. Boyd became the guiding force behind *Light and Life Hour*'s rapid expansion into more than 70 countries. He was also a founding member of National Religious Broadcasters, serving as the organization's president in 1952.

When Boyd was elected presiding bishop for the Free Methodists, he was succeeded as the *Light and Life Hour*'s host by Robert F. Andrews. Boyd retired officially from the show in 1965 and died in 1978—at which time the popular program was being aired over 200 stations in the United States and 25 stations abroad.

See also Myron Boyd

SOURCES

Armstrong, Ben. *The Electric Church*. Nashville: Thomas Nelson, 1979.

Erickson, Hal. *Religious Radio and Television in the United States, 1921–1991*. Jefferson, NC: McFarland, 1992.

LIGONIER MINISTRIES
established: 1971, Orlando, Florida

Ligonier Ministries is a producer of Christian educational materials for lay persons which cover the areas of theology, Bible study, history, Christian ethics, and apologetics. The ministry was founded by R. C. Sproul, a professor of systematic theology at Reformed Theological Seminary in Orlando, Florida. Sproul started Ligonier in 1971 as a small study center in western Pennsylvania. By 1984, the ministry had moved to Orlando, where it now has a staff of 50 people. In addition to publishing and distributing Sproul's books and those of other conservative Christian pastors and theologians, Ligonier Ministries produces "Renewing Your Mind Online with R. C. Sproul," a daily radio program hosted by Sproul that airs on over 70 stations around the United States. It also sponsors "Renewing Your Mind Online with R. C. Sproul," a Gospel Communications Network website; various conferences and seminars featuring Sproul and other Christian scholars; and *Tabletalk*, an award-winning Bible-study publication.

According to Sproul, the ministry's purpose is "to awaken as many people as possible to the holiness of God by proclaiming, teaching, and defending God's holiness in all its fullness." Ligonier's website is a pioneer in making the resources and messages of Christian broadcasters available to the computer-literate public.

SOURCES

"Renewing Your Mind Online with R. C. Sproul." World Wide Web site. http://www.gospelcom.net/ligonier/ (1995).

GORDON LINDSAY

born: June 18, 1906
died: April 3, 1973, Dallas, Texas

The radio evangelist Gordon J. Lindsay was reared in an atmosphere charged with religious healing and millennial expectation. His parents were members of faith healer John Alexander Dowie's communitarian experiment in Zion City, Illinois. When the Zion City experiment failed, the Lindsay family moved to Finis E. Yoakum's Pisgah Grande community in California. When Yoakum's community collapsed, the family moved to Portland, Oregon. Lindsay was converted to Christ at the age of 14 during a meeting held by Pentecostal evangelist Charles Fox Parham in Portland. He received the baptism of the Holy Spirit and the gift of tongues not long afterwards.

Lindsay began a preaching ministry at the age of 18, holding revival meetings in the Assemblies of God and other Pentecostal churches.

He served as a pastor for small churches in Avenal and San Fernando, California, before returning to Portland in 1932. Lindsay married Freda Schimpf, a member of the Church of the Foursquare Gospel, in 1937.

During World War II, Lindsay pastored a church in Ashland, Oregon, but resigned this post in 1947—leaving the church in the care of his wife Freda—in order to manage the revival meetings of William Branham. In 1948, Lindsay, together with Jack and Anna Jeanne Moore, established *The Voice of Healing* magazine to help publicize the successes of Branham's meetings.

To capitalize on the growing healing movement, Lindsay also founded the Voice of Healing Fellowship, headquartered in Shreveport, Louisiana, to function as a loosely gathered association of healing evangelists. In Dallas in 1949, Lindsay's organization sponsored the first convention of faith healers, a forum which has been popular among Pentecostal evangelists ever since. Later, during the 1950s, Lindsay's organization began to broadcast revival meetings and healing sessions over the radio. The program, known as *The Voice of Healing*, was not well received by Lindsay's supporters, many of whom viewed radio as a tool of the devil. In 1956, Lindsay began the Winning the Nations Crusade, which sent evangelistic teams throughout the world. As his work began to focus on missions, Lindsay started sponsoring such foreign missions programs as the Native Church Crusade, founded in 1961.

In 1962, the Voice of Healing Fellowship changed its name to the Full Gospel Fellowship of Ministers and Churches. To reflect his growing interest in foreign missions, Lindsay changed the name of *The Voice of Healing* magazine to *World-Wide Revival* in 1968 (later the name would again be changed to *Christ for the Nations*). He opened a Bible-training school, Christ for the Nations Institute, in Dallas, Texas, in 1970.

Lindsay was a prolific writer and speaker throughout his career, authoring over 250 books and tracts. Many of these works treated the history of the faith healing movement. Following

Lindsay's sudden death, his wife Freda was appointed president of Christ for the Nations Institute. The couple's daughter Carole is also heavily involved in their worldwide evangelistic ministry.

see also William Branham

SOURCES

Billy Graham Center Archives, Wheaton College, Wheaton, IL.

Harrell, David Edwin, Jr. *All Things Are Possible.* Bloomington, IN: Indiana University Press, 1975.

Lindsay, Gordon. *Bible Days Are Here Again.* Shreveport, LA: 1949.

———. *The Gordon Lindsay Story.* Dallas: n.d.

Melton, J. Gordon. *Religious Leaders of America.* Detroit: Gale Research, 1991.

Reid, Daniel G., Robert D. Linder, Bruce L. Shelley, and Harry S. Stout, eds. *Dictionary of Christianity in America.* Downers Grove, IL: InterVarsity Press, 1990.

Stone, Jon R. *A Guide to the End of the World: Popular Eschatology in America.* New York: Garland, 1993.

HAL LINDSEY
born: 1930, Houston, Texas

Hal Lindsey is perhaps the most influential preacher of popular evangelical eschatology in the twentieth century. His best-selling books, including *The Late Great Planet Earth* (1970) and *The Rapture* (1983), have laid out a detailed vision of the world's final generation before the Last Judgment. Lindsey has also become a fixture in religious broadcasting, hosting a weekly call-in radio program, *Saturdays with Hal Lindsey*, and interpreting current events in the light of biblical prophecy on religious television shows.

Early in his life, Hal Lindsey grappled with a deep ambivalence concerning religion. As he recounted in a magazine interview, "Religion made me feel guilty, and so I just kissed it off." After studying business for two years at the University of Houston, Lindsey served in the United States Coast Guard then piloted a tugboat on the Mississippi River. He experienced a conversion to Christianity after going through a divorce and a bout of suicidal depression. After converting, he kept to himself, learned New Testament Greek, and began an intensive study of the Bible. After meeting some Christians who claimed that "the Bible was filled with errors" and "wasn't historical," Lindsey again began to doubt the truth of Scripture and the validity of Christianity.

A turning point in Lindsey's life occurred in 1956, when he heard a sermon on biblical prophecy by Jack Blackwell. Intrigued and excited by the possibility that the Bible's prophetic books accurately foretold current events, Lindsey rededicated himself to an intensive study of Scripture. In 36–38 Ezekiel, Lindsey discovered what he took to be a prophecy of Israel's reconstitution as a nation. He also found mention of a powerful enemy from the north which he identified as the Soviet Union. These two correlations of scriptural prophecy with modern geopolitical realities convinced Lindsey of the Bible's authenticity and, in time, became the foundations of his apocalyptic vision of the earth's future.

After finding other instances of contemporary history appearing to fulfill biblical prophecies, Lindsey decided to enroll at Dallas Theological Seminary. He specialized in the study of early Greek literature, Hebrew, and the New Testament. Lindsey graduated with a master's degree in theological studies in 1962, and he and his new wife Jan began to teach college students throughout North America as missionaries for Campus Crusade for Christ. Over the next 10 years, Lindsey served in such hot spots of student rebellion as UC Berkeley and San Francisco State University. His ministry with these students forced him to adapt conventional theological language to the argot of the youth counterculture. By the early 1970s, Lindsey and his wife had settled into a more permanent campus ministry at UCLA. They called the ministry the Jesus Christ Light and Power Company.

Lindsey's publishing career began in 1969 when he hired freelance religious writer Carole

C. Carlson to help him edit his sermon notes into a book-length manuscript. Carlson's credits included books coauthored with Billy Graham and Corrie ten Boom. The fruits of the Lindsey-Carlson collaboration were published in 1970 as *The Late Great Planet Earth*. The book became a surprise bestseller and by the late 1980s was reported to have sold over 20 million copies in 52 languages. The widespread circulation of this first book launched Lindsey's career as a major interpreter of evangelical Christian eschatology and dispensationalism.

It was in the wake of *The Late Great Planet Earth*'s phenomenal success that Lindsey launched his call-in radio show, *Saturdays with Hal Lindsey*. This weekly broadcast allowed Lindsey to comment on current events in the light of biblical prophecy. By the late 1980s, the program was being heard in over 100 radio markets in 200 US cities. Lindsey also parlayed his success as an author into a television ministry in the 1980s. His programs and guest appearances consisted of low-key discussions of specific geopolitical events and their relationship to the prophetic books of the Bible. Lindsey acted more as a teacher, interpreter, and discussion leader than as a preacher in these broadcasting formats.

Lindsey has continued his radio and television ministry during the 1990s. With cohost Cliff Ford, Lindsey hosts a live radio program called *Weekend Review*. This show is broadcast across the US on Saturdays at 12 noon PST. The program follows the format of earlier Lindsey shows and includes discussions of current events in the light of biblical prophecy. The show features interviews with such expert political analysts as John Gizzi and allows listeners to call in and ask questions on a toll-free line. As of late 1995, the show was being heard on 79 stations nationwide. Lindsey follows a similar news and commentary format on a weekly half-hour television program, *Hal Lindsey*, which airs Saturday evenings on Trinity Broadcasting Network.

Lindsey's central maxim in *The Late Great Planet Earth* is that the birth of the state of Israel in 1948 signaled the beginning of the apoca-

lyptic events prophesied in the Bible. In his eschatological scenario, the Arabs and Africans will align themselves against Israel, the (former) Soviet Union and Communist China will increase in power and threaten Israel's existence, a restored Roman Empire will arise within the European Common Market, there will be a growing movement to create a single planetary religion and government, and wars and natural disasters will increase in frequency and magnitude. During this apocalyptic unfolding, the Antichrist will emerge as the world's false messiah. After rebuilding the Jewish temple on Jerusalem's Temple Mount, this incarnation of evil will preside over a seven-year period of mounting planetary disasters that Lindsey calls the "Great Tribulation." These events will culminate in a final catastrophic battle near the town of Megiddo in Israel's Valley of Jezreel—the fabled Battle of Armageddon.

The only escape for the human individual in Lindsey's apocalyptic scenario is to accept Christ as one's personal savior and to be "raptured" out of the world before the "Tribulation" begins. The exact nature of the rapture remains somewhat unclear, but Lindsey posits the event as an "ultimate trip" during which the believer meets Christ in the air and is taken to heaven. Lindsey elaborated on his dispensational teachings and on several post-tribulation and midtribulation scenarios in a subsequent work, *The Rapture: Truth or Consequences*, published in 1983.

Following the success of their first book, Lindsey and Carlson collaborated on *Satan Is Alive and Well on Planet Earth* (1972), which also became a bestseller. This book traced the reputed increase of Satan's influence in the modern world and discussed, among other things, the rising popularity of occultism, the dilution of traditional Christian truths in mainstream churches, and the phenomenon of demon possession. During 1973, Lindsey published both *The Guilt Trip* and *There's a New World Coming*. The latter volume contained an extensive discussion of the Book of Revelation and an interpretation of the work's prophetic visions in terms of an impending nuclear holocaust. By the end of the 1970s, Lindsey had published four more books and become one of a select group of authors to have three of his works appear on the *New York Times'* bestseller list simultaneously. During the 1980s, Lindsey continued to write popular books, including *The 1980s: Countdown to Armageddon, The Promise*, and *Combat Faith*. This last work claims that the New Age movement is feeding on the disillusionment of the 1960s counterculture generation and emerging as a demonic substitute for authentic biblical religion.

Lindsey's apocalyptic visions have grown more detailed and horrific with each new book. He now associates the "seven bowls of wrath" of the Book of Revelation, for instance, with the Battle of Armageddon and a third world war. During the course of this final battle, Lindsey predicts that nuclear exchanges will cripple the former Soviet Union, Eastern Europe, and Israel. The emptying of the seventh bowl, he claims, symbolizes the firing of all remaining nuclear weapons in a great crescendo of destructive fury. Following this devastating nuclear war, Lindsey foresees the return of Christ to earth and the inauguration of a millennium of peace and prosperity for the Christian faithful.

Like most apocalypticists, Lindsey adopts a passive view of human agency and locates the ultimate responsibility for the final catastrophes of history in an all-powerful God. Not surprisingly, therefore, he has consistently criticized arms control treaties like SALT, contending that such human initiatives have only enabled the former Soviet Union and its satellites to fulfill more quickly their ordained role in history.

The key to Lindsey's phenomenal success as an author and broadcast personality is his ability to communicate complex religious ideas in a language accessible to modern, secular-minded people. His "passion for simplicity" has led him to eschew theological jargon and to relate the Bible's symbolic prophecies to contemporary events in business, politics, education, and science. Lindsey draws on a number of sources for his analysis of current affairs, including the news media and informants in the Defense Department and the US intelligence community. More than any other single religious broadcaster, he has capitalized on America's enduring popular interest in biblical apocalypticism. What he will do now that the Cold War has ended and the Palestinians and Israelis have negotiated a peace treaty remains to be seen.

SOURCES

Clark, Stephen. "The Last Days According to Hal Lindsey." *Christian Life* 43 (February 1982): 44–47.

Erickson, Hal. *Religious Radio and Television in the United States, 1921–1991*. Jefferson, NC: McFarland, 1992.

Fishwick, Marshall, and Ray B. Browne, eds. *The God Pumpers: Religion in the Electronic Age*. Bowling Green, KY: Bowling Green State University Popular Press, 1987.

Jeschke, Marlin L. "Pop Eschatology: Hal Lindsey and Evangelical Theology." In *Evangelicalism and Anabaptism,* edited by C. Norman Kraus. Scottsdale, AZ: Herald Press, 1979.

Lindsey, Hal. *Combat Faith*. New York: Bantam, 1986.

———. *The Guilt Trip*. With C. C. Carlson. Grand Rapids, MI: Zondervan, 1973.

———. *The Late Great Planet Earth*. With C. C. Carlson. Grand Rapids, MI: Zondervan, 1970.

———. *The Liberation of Planet Earth*. Grand Rapids, MI: Zondervan, 1974.

———. *The 1980's: Countdown to Armageddon*. New York: Bantam, 1980.

———. *The Promise*. Eugene, OR: Harvest House, 1974.

———. *The Rapture: Truth or Consequences*. New York: Bantam, 1983.

———. *Satan Is Alive and Well on Planet Earth*. With C. C. Carlson. Grand Rapids, MI: Zondervan, 1972.

———. *The Terminal Generation*. With C. C. Carlson. Old Tappan, NJ: Fleming H. Revell, 1976.

———. *There's a New World Coming*. Eugene, OR: Harvest House, 1973.

———. *There's a New World Coming*. Rev. ed. Santa Ana, CA: Vision House, 1984.

———. *The World's Final Hour: Evacuation or Extinction?* Grand Rapids, MI: Zondervan, 1976.

Lippy, Charles H., ed. *Twentieth-Century Shapers of American Popular Religion*. Westport, CT: Greenwood Press, 1989.

Nelson, J. W. "The Apocalyptic Vision in American Popular Culture." In *The Apocalyptic Vision in America: Interdisciplinary Essays on Myth and Culture,* edited by Lois P. Zamora. Bowling Green, KY: Bowling Green State University Popular Press, 1982.

Stone, Jon R. *A Guide to the End of the World: Popular Eschatology in America.* New York: Garland, 1993.

Weber, Timothy P. *Living in the Shadow of the Second Coming: American Premillennialism, 1875–1982.* Rev. and enl. Grand Rapids, MI: Zondervan, 1983.

Wilburn, Gary. "The Doomsday Chic." *Christianity Today* 22 (January 1978): 22–23.

LISTEN TO JESUS
see: Sarah Utterbach

LIVING WAY
see: Jack Hayford

LOVE SPECIAL
first aired: mid-1980s

A popular genre of religious television is the "song-and-praise" program, during which a musical host and guest performers sing both contemporary and traditional hymns and songs. One of the most durable of these programs during the 1980s and 1990s has been Nancy Harmon's *Love Special*, a half-hour weekly program of praise and inspirational music. The program is videotaped in Portland, Oregon, and broadcast around the world on Paul and Jan Crouch's Trinity Broadcasting Network (TBN). In late 1995, TBN aired the show on Tuesday afternoons from 12 to 12:30 PM EST.

LOVE WORTH FINDING
see: Adrian Rogers

LUTHERAN CHURCH IN AMERICA, COMMISSION OF PRESS, RADIO, AND TELEVISION
established: 1962

The Lutheran Church in America (LCA) was formed in 1962 when the United Lutheran Church in America, the Finnish Evangelical Lutheran Church, the American Evangelical Lutheran Church, and the Augustana Evangelical Lutheran Church merged into one body. The planners for the new organization, recognizing the communications-oriented culture that was rapidly emerging in America, created the Commission of Press, Radio, and Television (PRT) to communicate the church's message to the public. *Church World News*, a 15-minute newscast, was already in production at the time of the merger. By 1967, it was airing on 355 radio stations in the United States and Canada. The new church also decided to produce 12 segments annually for *The Protestant Hour*, a radio sermon program overseen by the National Council of Churches consisting of segments produced by five member denominations including the LCA.

The PRT also produced several television shows, the most popular of which was *Davey and Goliath*, an animated children's series. The show originally had been launched in 1961 by the United Lutheran Church in America. It became a hugely popular show during the mid-1960s, airing on 321 stations in 1965. The PRT added seasonal specials to the series and began dubbing it in foreign languages. Two other television shows were produced during the 1960s, *The Antkeeper* and *Stalked*. These programs were directed toward adult audiences and, though well-received, never gained the popularity of *Davey and Goliath*.

These broadcasting outreaches continued into the 1970s. By 1970 the Lutheran segments of *The Protestant Hour* were giving LCA ministers over 3,200 hours of preaching time annually. The American Lutheran Church and LCA also voted to combine their weekly newscasts in a new version of *Church World News*. By

1970, this radio news program was being aired on 484 stations around the world. *Davey and Goliath*, however, continued to be the most popular television program produced by the church. In the United States alone, the program audience was estimated at over 1,700,000 children each week. The show also had become a hit with audiences in South America, the Far East, New Zealand, Australia, and Europe. In all, the show's episodes were broadcast in seven different languages worldwide. After intensive negotiations with the Roman Catholic Board of Parish Education and Publication, PRT agreed to allow the show to be carried on closed circuit television in parochial schools in six large metropolitan areas. The commission also agreed to allow Catholics to use the program's characters in a film that introduced children to the rite of Communion.

During the 1970s, the PRT refined its administrative organization by creating the Office of Communications. This office attempted to identify the different audiences the church was trying to reach and to coordinate the various communications media within the church's agencies and synods. PRT's responsibilities essentially dealt with getting the church's message out to the general public. Communicating on a regular basis with radio and television reporters became an increasingly significant aspect of this work. Another important task of the commission entailed taking advantage of the opportunities presented by the advent of cable television and videotaping. PRT encouraged local congregations to create their own cable television ministries by sponsoring training workshops for synodal communications chairpersons and sending out media kits that were adaptable to local conditions.

During the 1980s, the Office of Communications was again reorganized, this time to devote more specialized attention to new telecommunications technologies. The PRT divided itself into a Department of News and Information Services and a Department of Telecommunications. The Department of Telecommunications began to make use of new technologies such as satellite transmissions to broadcast live events. One memorable transmission using the Westar V satellite occurred at a 1987 evangelism conference, "Together in Witness," in Denver. The transmission linked participants in Colorado with Lutherans gathered in Albuquerque, El Paso, Salt Lake City, and Casper, Wyoming.

In the 1980s, the Department of Telecommunications also attempted to compete for air time with the rapidly proliferating television evangelists. The challenge was articulated by the Office of Communications to the 1986 LCA convention:

> The radio and cable-TV ministries of mainline denominations have been rendered virtually invisible by the massive "paid time" broadcast efforts of fundamentalists and independent Christian programmers. The few moments of public and community service time the church bodies have relied upon are no longer available because of federal deregulation of the American broadcast industry.

Despite these new challenges, the department continued to produce biblically and theologically sophisticated programs like the Lutheran segments of *The Protestant Hour* and *Davey and Goliath*, which remained as popular as ever, even after 35 years. During 1986–1987, *Davey and Goliath* was aired on 29 broadcast stations, eight cable stations, five cable and satellite stations, and five Roman Catholic educational systems. *Church World News*, which had been renamed *Intersect: World and Religion*, was discontinued, however, after 35 years of radio broadcasts.

The department also created a series of 13 radio shows for a rapidly growing Spanish audience and continued its encouragement of local parish cable shows with guidelines and suggestions. A significant new series of broadcasts entitled *Lutherans in Person* was produced in 1980. This program featured interviews with such notable scholars and preachers as historian Roland Bainton and theologian Joseph Sittler. Another significant success was the film *The Joy of Bach*, which was produced as a cooperative venture by Lutheran Film Associates. This film premiered during Christmas 1979 on 300 Public Broadcasting Network stations and was rebroadcast during Bach's two hundredth birthday anniversary in 1985.

Some programming initiatives during the 1980s took a more evangelical thrust. The office inaugurated a series of spot announcements called *Welcome . . . The Doors Are Open* that were directed to such special audiences as minorities and single parents. These spots appeared in both English and Spanish in over 50 large television markets.

The PRT continues to produce and distribute various communications media and to help local congregations create their own television ministries. The Lutheran Church in America is now a member of the Evangelical Lutheran Church in America (established in 1988) along with the former American Lutheran Church and the Association of Evangelical Lutheran Churches.

SOURCES

Gilbert, W. Kent. *Commitment to Unity: A History of the Lutheran Church in America*. Philadelphia: Fortress Press, 1988.

THE LUTHERAN HOUR
first aired: October 2, 1930

The Lutheran Hour has been arguably the most popular radio program in the history of religious broadcasting. At its peak of fame in 1989, the show was heard around the world by a listening audience of over 20 million.

The first broadcast of *The Lutheran Hour* was sent out from the studios of WHK in Cleveland, Ohio, with the Cleveland Bach Chorus providing the show's music. Host Walter Maier dedicated this premier broadcast "to the fundamental conviction that there is a God." His closing statement offered encouragement to families caught in the throes of the Great Depression:

But in the crises of life and the pivotal hours of existence, only the Christian—having God and with Him the assurance that no one can successfully prevail against him—is able to carry the pressing burdens of sickness, death, financial reverses, family troubles, misfortunes of innumerable kinds and degrees, and yet to bear all this with the undaunted faith and Christian confidence that alone make life worth living and death worth dying.

The Lutheran Hour was an instant hit, generating more audience mail after eight weeks than the hugely popular comedy program *Amos 'n' Andy*. This massive listener response was also greater than the written responses garnered by all the radio programs sponsored by the FCC. Both lay persons and clergy from many denominations wrote to praise the show's clear presentation of traditional Christian doctrines and values. CBS estimated the program's weekly audience at over 5 million. Within a year, the show was able to pay for half of its $4,000 weekly broadcasting costs with listener contributions. By 1935, *The Lutheran Hour* was being produced at KFUO in St. Louis and had expanded its national outreach to include the stations of the Mutual Broadcasting System.

The format of *The Lutheran Hour* was simple. Using professional choirs, each show opened with a presentation of classical religious hymnody. Then Maier began his 19-minute homily using a forceful, evangelical preaching style. Every fourth program was directed at a teenage and preteen audience. Much of the show's popularity stemmed from Maier's forthright, uncompromising presentation of strict, Bible-based teachings. *The Lutheran Hour*, a favorite program among evangelical ministers, claimed to have received several thousand letters each year attesting to conversions that were facilitated by Maier's preaching.

After Maier's death in 1950, the popular program continued with the same format as before, except that Lawrence Archer and Armin Oldsen were the main preachers. Following a two-year hiatus in 1953 and 1954, the show returned with Oswald Hoffman as the principal speaker. Hoffman, a former student of Maier's Hebrew Scripture classes at Concordia, carried on his professorial "father's" tradition of classical Bible-based preaching. He would continue to serve the broadcasting ministry until his retirement in 1989. Dr. Dale Meyer replaced Hoffman in 1989, at a time when *The Lutheran Hour* was the most widely distributed weekly radio ministry in the United States.

The Lutheran Hour's executive producer until 1959 was Eugene R. Bertermann, an ordained minister with a doctorate in classics. Bertermann was given the National Religious Broadcasters Distinguished Service award in 1974, partly for his distinguished 18-year service as the NRB's president.

Funds generated by *The Lutheran Hour* have not only supported its broadcasts, but also the broadcasts of another Missouri Synod ministry, the very successful television program *This Is the Life*.

See also International Lutheran Laymen's League; Walter Maier

SOURCES

Armstrong, Ben. *The Electric Church*. Nashville: Thomas Nelson, 1979.

Erickson, Hal. *Religious Radio and Television in the United States, 1921–1991*. Jefferson, NC: McFarland, 1992.

Paul L. Maier. *A Man Spoke, A World Listened*. New York: McGraw-Hill, 1963.

LUTHERAN MISSION SOCIETIES
established: 1921

One of the few Lutheran mission stations in Alaska, the Lutheran Missionary Societies (LMS) operates from Anchorage, providing evangelistic and social services to various regions of Alaska. Originally founded in 1921 as the Federated Norwegian Lutheran Young People's Societies of America, the ministry changed its name in 1962, in part to reflect the greater diversity of Alaska's growing population. LMS broadcasts a number of radio programs from a station in Naknek, Alaska, near Kvichak Bay and the Aleutian Islands.

SOURCES

Melton, J. Gordon. *Directory of Religious Organizations in the United States*. 3d ed. Detroit: Gale Research, 1993.

M

JOHN MacARTHUR
see: Grace to You

CLARENCE MACARTNEY
born: September 18, 1879, Northwood, Ohio
died: February 19, 1957, Beaver Falls, Pennsylvania

Clarence E. Macartney was an important figure in the fundamentalist-modernist controversies of the 1920s and 1930s. He was also a tireless evangelist who experimented for a time with radio preaching during the early days of religious broadcasting.

Born the last of seven children to John Longfellow, a minister-professor, and Catherine Macartney, Clarence was descended from a long line of Scottish Covenanters (Reformed Presbyterians). At age 11, he experienced a quiet conversion and became a member of the Covenanter Church in Beaver Falls, Pennsylvania, where the family lived at the time. Owing to John Macartney's failing health, the family moved West in 1894 in search of a dryer climate, settling in California.

Clarence graduated from Redlands High School, in Redlands, California, and took preparatory courses at Pomona College before enrolling at the University of Denver. When his family moved East again, Macartney transferred to the University of Wisconsin, from which he graduated in 1901. He earned a master's degree from Princeton University in 1904 and finished additional studies at Princeton Theological Seminary in 1905. Macartney was then ordained as a minister in the Presbyterian Church USA.

A lifelong bachelor, Macartney served only three churches in a career that spanned nearly five decades: the First Presbyterian Church of Paterson, New Jersey (1905–1914), the Arch Street Presbyterian Church of Philadelphia (1914–1927), and the First Presbyterian Church of Pittsburgh (1927–1953). It was while pastoring the Arch Street Church that Macartney led the attack against Modernism in the Presbyterian Church. When Harry Emerson Fosdick preached his famous sermon in 1922, "Shall the Fundamentalists Win?," Macartney answered, "Shall Unbelief Win?" The fundamentalist partisan further responded to Fosdick's attack by petitioning the General Assembly to condemn Fosdick's opinions and by asking the New York Presbytery to censure Fosdick for his remarks.

In 1924, Macartney was elected moderator of the Presbyterian General Assembly. He used this position to continue the fundamentalist's fight against creeping Modernism in the Presbyterian Church, both at home and abroad. In 1925, Princeton Theological Seminary offered him the chair of apologetics but, in a defining moment, Macartney declined, asserting that he would rather preach than teach preaching. In 1929, he assisted J. Gresham Machen during the reorganization of Princeton Seminary but was unable to prevent the liberals from taking control. Although Macartney supported Machen's break with Princeton and his founding of Westminster Seminary in 1929, he refused to join Machen when Machen later broke with the Presbyterian Church USA to form the Orthodox Presbyterian Church in 1936. Macartney believed that it was crucial to maintain a fundamentalist presence in the more liberal denomination.

A preacher of grand eloquence and great pulpit presence, Clarence Macartney believed strongly that the central purpose of the sermon was evangelism. He therefore made his sermons the central focus of worship throughout his long ministry. It was to that end that Macartney experimented with various channels of communication, including newspapers, street preaching, and radio evangelism.

Macartney was a prolific writer, publishing over 57 books during his career. He was also a severe moralist, crusading against divorce, alcohol consumption, and birth control.

SOURCES

Macartney, Clarence E. *The Faith Once Delivered*. New York: Abingdon-Cokesbury Press, 1952.

Melton, J. Gordon. *Religious Leaders of America*. Detroit: Gale Research Inc., 1991.

Russell, C. Allyn. *Voices of American Fundamentalism*. Philadelphia: The Westminster Press, 1976.

MARLIN MADDOUX
born: Beaumont, Texas

Marlin Maddoux is the founder and president of International Christian Media and the USA Radio Network. He is also the host of *Point of View,* a live, two-hour, Christian talk show that airs on over 340 radio stations nationwide and around the world on several short-wave stations. Begun over local radio in 1975 in Dallas, Texas, *Point of View* gives a conservative Christian perspective on issues and current events that affect the family, schools, religious principles, and public policy. The program, which went national in 1983, also features guests that include media experts, educators, politicians, and best-selling authors.

Maddoux produces *Point of View* through his ministry organization, International Christian Media (ICM). ICM also enabled him to found the USA Radio Network in 1985. Maddoux's network is the first 24-hour Christian radio ministry supported completely by commercial advertisement. As of this writing, the fast-growing news radio network had more than 1,200 affiliated stations and was carried over the Armed Forces Radio Service. In 1994, the National Religious Broadcasters (NRB) gave USA Radio Network its Program Producer of the Year award.

Maddoux is a native Texan who ministered at churches in Austin and Dallas before pursuing a vocation in religious radio. His first local broadcasts emanated from a garage. Maddoux's broadcasting ministries have brought him numerous honors, including NRB's 1986 Award of Merit for Program Production and NRB's 1996 Talk Show of the Year award for *Point of View.*

Maddoux is a founding member—along with James Dobson, Bill Bright, Larry Burkett, and D. James Kennedy—of the Alliance Defense Fund, an organization that funds legal defenses of religious liberty. Over the past 10 years, Maddoux has been a frequent guest on such national television programs as *CBS Morning News,* ABC's *Nightline, The 700 Club*, and *Focus on the Family.* He is the author of several popular books, including *A Christian Agenda: Game Plan for a New Era, What Worries Parents Most, Free Speech or Propaganda?* and *The Selling of Gorbachev.* Maddoux lives near Dallas with his wife Mary. He has four grown children.

See also *Point of View*

SOURCES

Ward, Mark, Sr. *Air of Salvation: The Story of Christian Broadcasting*. Grand Rapids, MI: Baker Book House, 1994.

WALTER MAIER

born: October 4, 1893, Boston, Massachusetts
died: January 11, 1950, St. Louis, Missouri

Courtesy: National Religious Broadcasters

Walter A. Maier, professor of Old Testament Studies at Concordia Seminary (Lutheran Church, Missouri Synod), was the creator and host of *The Lutheran Hour*, arguably the most popular radio program in the history of religious broadcasting. Maier gained his first radio experience in 1922 when, as the executive secretary of the Walther League (a youth organization sponsored by the Missouri Synod), a Louisville, Kentucky, radio station carried his address to the league's national convention. By December 1924, Maier and an engineer at Concordia had set up a radio station on the seminary grounds and garnered financial support from the readers of the Walther League's newspaper. The call letters assigned to the station by the Federal Radio Commission were KFUO, which Maier interpreted as "Keep Forward Upward Onward."

Maier's duties on the new station included two weekly programs. He managed to prepare and present these programs while teaching Hebrew classes at Concordia and finishing his doctorate in Semitic studies from Harvard University. During this time, Maier became more and more convinced of radio's potential for spreading "authentic Christianity" to large audiences.

By 1928, he and the engineer who had helped him set up KFUO began to plan the format of a religious program that could be broadcast around the country on the major radio networks. The first radio network they approached, NBC, had already adopted a policy against selling airtime to religious groups. NBC had also worked out an arrangement with the Federal Council of Churches (FCC) by which it donated free airtime—called "sustaining time"—to the council's member churches. The Lutheran Church, Missouri Synod, however, was not a member of the FCC and was unable to participate in this arrangement.

The CBS radio network, on the other hand, was more flexible. Although it would only grant free sustaining time to interdenominational religious broadcasts, it decided to sell airtime to one additional religious program. The price, however, was steep. For one season of weekly half-hour program slots the bill would be a whopping $200,000! Maier appealed to the Missouri Synod's membership and received pledges of about $100,000 to get the program started. He had faith that the rest of the program's expenses would be met by his listening audience.

The first broadcast of *The Lutheran Hour* aired on October 2, 1930, over the CBS radio network. The program originated from the studios of WHK in Cleveland, Ohio, with the Cleveland Bach Chorus providing the show's music. Maier dedicated this premier broadcast "to the fundamental conviction that there is a God."

The program quickly gained a large audience and generated more fan mail after its first eight weeks than the popular comedy show *Amos 'n' Andy*. Much of *The Lutheran Hour*'s success was attributable to Maier, who was careful to present his weekly sermon in a manner that reached out to all mainstream Christian listeners. This nondenominational approach and Maier's low-key, winsome manner won him accolades from a broad cross-section of American Christians. Senior leaders of the Missouri Synod Lutherans, however, expressed concern that the program did not have a more denominational focus and mission. Maier was able to prevail against these denominational elders by articulating a solidly biblical perspective in his messages and attacking elements of the modernist theology that had come to dominate many mainstream Protestant denominations. Each weekly program featured a sermon punctuated by song, and every fourth show was geared toward a teenage and preteen audience.

Following CBS's reconsideration of its paid-time policy in 1935, *The Lutheran Hour* switched to the Mutual Broadcasting System. It also moved its production facilities to KFUO's studios in St. Louis. During the late 1930s, Maier began recording his programs for syndication and broadcasting the show around the world over short-wave radio. He took a courageous stand against the Nazis before World War II despite the Missouri Synod Lutherans' silence due to strong nationalistic feelings among its German-American membership. *The Luteran Hour* continued to grow in popularity, garnering an estimated audience of 20 million in 55 countries by the late 1940s.

By the time of his death in 1950, Maier was probably the most listened-to preacher in history. After 1950, the popular program continued with the same format as before, except that Lawrence Archer and Armin Oldsen were the main preachers. Following a two-year hiatus in 1953 and 1954, the show returned with Oswald Hoffman as the principal speaker. Hoffman, a former student of Maier's Hebrew Scripture classes at Concordia, carried on his professorial "father's" tradition of classical Bible-based preaching. He would continue to serve the broadcasting ministry until his retirement in 1989. Dr. Dale Meyer replaced Hoffman in 1989, at a time when *The Lutheran Hour* was the most widely-distributed weekly radio ministry in the United States. Maier was inducted posthumously into the National Religious Broadcasters (NRB) Hall of Fame at a special Pioneer's Night in 1975 along with Clarence Jones, John Zoller, and Charles Fuller. *The Lutheran Hour*'s executive producer until 1959 was Eugene Bertermann, an ordained minister with a doctorate in classics. Bertermann was given the NRB's Distinguished Service award

in 1974, partly for his distinguished 18-year service as the NRB's president.

Funds generated by *The Lutheran Hour* have not only supported its broadcasts, but also the broadcasts of another Missouri Synod ministry, the very successful television program *This Is the Life*.

SOURCES

Armstrong, Ben. *The Electric Church*. Nashville: Thomas Nelson, 1979.

Erickson, Hal. *Religious Radio and Television in the United States, 1921–1991*. Jefferson, NC: McFarland, 1992.

Paul L. Maier. *A Man Spoke, A World Listened*. New York: McGraw-Hill, 1963.

DAVID MAINSE
born: 1936, Campbell's Bay, Quebec, Canada

David R. Mainse, a minister of the Pentecostal Assemblies of Canada and longtime Christian radio and television host, grew up in the home of Pentecostal missionaries. After studies at Eastern Pentecostal Bible College, Mainse became a Pentecostal minister, periodically speaking over radio.

In 1962, while serving a church in Pembroke, Ontario, Mainse began a television ministry. His program, entitled *Crossroads*, was produced in Toronto by his media ministry organization, Crossroads Christian Communications. By 1976, Mainse had gained access to nearly 150 stations in much of Canada and the northeastern United States. By the 1980s, Mainse's broadcast had evolved into an hour-long program called *100 Huntley Street*. The program is a Canadian version of Pat Robertson's *The 700 Club*.

In 1984, the same year *100 Huntley Street* began reaching the United States through syndication, Mainse and his program received an Award of Merit from the National Religious Broadcasters. Currently, *100 Huntley Street* can be seen over Canada's Vision TV Network and Trinity Broadcasting Network as well as over two dozen additional stations in the United States. Mainse published the story of his broadcast ministry in his 1983 autobiography, *100 Huntley Street*.

See also Crossroads Christian Communications; *100 Huntley Street*

SOURCES

Burgess, Stanley M., and Gary B. McGee, eds. *Dictionary of Pentecostal and Charismatic Movements*. Grand Rapids, MI: Zondervan, 1988.

MAN'S HERITAGE
first aired: 1956

A syndicated program that aired in a series over television in 1956, *Man's Heritage* featured dramatic readings from the Bible by actor Raymond Massey (1896–1983).

MARCHING TRUTH
see: William Ward Ayer

THE MARK AND KATHY SHOW
first aired: September, 1995

The Mark and Kathy Show is an innovative hour-long music and variety program broadcast on David Cerullo's Inspirational Network (INSP). The show is cohosted by recording artist Kathy Troccoli and Christian personality Mark Lowry. Each program is taped in front of live audiences at INSP's $12 million production complex in Charlotte, North Carolina. The program, which made its debut in September of 1995, features audience interaction, comedy, music, and skits performed by the cohosts and by such guests as Fred Travalena, Clifton Davis, Yolanda Adams, Lee Greenwood, and the Gaither Vocal Band. Phil Cooke directs *The Mark and Kathy Show*, which airs Saturday evenings at 10 PM EST as part of the Inspirational Network's Saturday evening family entertain-

ment line-up. The program also airs on dozens of independent religious stations throughout the United States.

J. C. MASSEE
born: November 22, 1871, Marshallville, Georgia
died: February 25, 1965, Atlanta, Georgia

A Baptist evangelist whose ministry stretched over 70 years, Jasper Cortenus Massee led a moderate faction of conservatives during the fundamentalist crusade against Modernism in the Northern Baptist Church in the 1920s.

Massee was the youngest of 13 children born to Drewry Massee, a rural Georgia physician, and Susan Bryan. The younger Massee joined the local Southern Baptist congregation while still in his youth. In 1893, a year after his graduation from Mercer University, Massee was ordained to the Christian ministry by the Northern Baptist Convention and served as pastor in a number of churches in Ohio and throughout the South. He studied at Southern Baptist Theological Seminary in Louisville, Kentucky, from 1896 to 1897.

In 1920, he accepted the call to preach at Brooklyn's Baptist Temple before moving to Boston's Tremont Temple in 1922, where he was one of the first preachers in New England to broadcast his Sunday services over the radio, airing his messages on WNAC Boston.

Upon his arrival in Brooklyn in 1920, Massee was greeted by other New York conservatives, who were convening a conference on the Fundamentals of Our Baptist Faith. During this conference the Fundamentalist Federation was founded, and Massee was elected its president. Soon after his election, Massee became somewhat disturbed by the aggressive and negative behavior of his colleagues John Roach Straton and Cortland Myers, who were aggressively anti-liberal and spoke harshly against the leftward drift of the Baptist Church. Dissatisfied members of the federation founded the Baptist Bible Union in 1923, isolating Massee all the more from his fundamentalist colleagues. His attempts to serve as a moderating influence between liberals and fundamentalists in the Baptist Church failed, and he resigned as president of the federation in 1925. In 1926, Massee called for a six-month truce between fundamentalists and modernists in order to bring peace and reconciliation to the churches, a move that resulted in an easing of tensions within the Northern Baptist Convention.

After 1929, Massee became an evangelist and conference speaker, spending the remainder of his life preaching against moral decay, holding interdenominational revivals, and becoming a regular speaker at the Winona Lake, Indiana, Bible Conference.

SOURCES

Dollar, George W. *A History of Fundamentalism in America.* Greenville, SC: Bob Jones University Press, 1973.

Massee, J. C. *Revival Sermons.* New York: Fleming H. Revell, 1923.

———. *The Second Coming.* Philadelphia: Philadelphia School of the Bible, 1919.

Russell, C. Allyn. *Voices of American Fundamentalism.* Philadelphia: Westminster Press, 1976.

W. S. McBIRNIE
born: February 8, 1922, Toronto, Canada
died: 1994, Glendale, California

Author, academic administrator, and religious broadcaster, William Stuart McBirnie was the son of William McBirnie, a minister, and Betty Potter, a concert cellist. Ordained to the ministry of the Southern Baptist Convention at the age of 17, McBirnie earned a bachelor of arts degree from Kletzing College in 1944 and a bachelor of divinity degree from Bethel Seminary in 1945. He pastored Trinity Baptist Church in San Antonio, Texas, from 1949 to 1959. During the late 1940s and early 1950s, he attended Southwestern Baptist Theological Seminary, where he earned a master of religious education degree in 1948 and a doctor of religious education in 1953. McBirnie completed a doctor of divinity degree at Trinity Bible College in 1958, and a doctor of philosophy de-

gree at California Graduate School of Theology in 1973.

From 1961 to his death in 1994, McBirnie served as pastor of the United Community Church in Glendale, California. From 1970 to 1974, he headed the *Bible Truth Radio Crusade* ministry, which evangelized prison inmates from its headquarters in Upland, California. Beginning in the early 1970s, McBirnie also worked as professor of Middle Eastern studies at the California Graduate School of Theology, a dispensationalist college located in Pasadena, California. After moving to Pasadena, his role in broadcasting was mostly as a guest lecturer on radio. By 1989, McBirnie had become the graduate school's president.

McBirnie was a much traveled speaker and prophecy teacher, and a popular Christian radio commentator on the Second Coming of Christ. He received a number of honors and awards for his ministry successes and unyielding support of the State of Israel. Among these honors were three Angel awards for Religion in Media and the Pilgrims medal from the State of Israel. His many books included *The Coming Decline and Fall of the Soviet Union*, *The Antichrist* (1978), *Search for the Twelve Apostles*, and *Search for the Tomb of Christ*.

SOURCES

Billy Graham Center Archives, Wheaton College, Wheaton, IL.

McBirnie, W. S. *The Antichrist.* Dallas: Acclaimed Books, 1978.

Stone, Jon R. *A Guide to the End of the World: Popular Eschatology in America.* New York: Garland, 1993.

J. VERNON McGEE
born: 1904
died: 1988, Southern California

Born and raised in the South, John Vernon McGee decided as a young man to pursue a career in the ministry. He earned a bachelor of divinity degree from Columbia Theological

Seminary in Decatur, Georgia, and a graduate degree from Dallas Theological Seminary. In 1933, McGee was ordained as a minister in the Southern Presbyterian Church. After serving a number of Presbyterian pastorates throughout the South and the West, McGee was appointed pastor of the Church of the Open Door in Los Angeles in 1949. He served the church in this position until his retirement in 1970.

McGee began his long radio career in 1941 while serving a Presbyterian church in Pasadena, California. He called his weekly Bible-study program *The Open Bible Hour*. After moving to the Church of the Open Door in 1949, McGee continued his radio ministry and changed the program's name to its popularly known title *Thru the Bible*. McGee preached daily over the radio, finishing a complete *Thru the Bible* sermon series—from Genesis to Revelation, verse by verse—about once every five years. The radio teacher became well known for his deep Southern drawl and prophetically-oriented endtimes studies.

By the late 1980s, *Thru the Bible* was heard over more than 700 stations in a dozen languages worldwide. The first Spanish language broadcasts were heard in 1973 over Trans World Radio. The show was taped at McGee's Pasadena headquarters. Though he died in 1988, McGee's taped lessons are still broadcast over the airwaves. In 1989, the popular Bible teacher was inducted, posthumously, into the National Religious Broadcasters (NRB) Hall of Fame. In 1981, he was presented with the William Ward Ayer Distinguished Service award by NRB.

SOURCES

Billy Graham Center Archives, Wheaton College, Wheaton, Illinois.

McGee, J. Vernon. *The Best of J. Vernon McGee*. Vol. 1. Nashville: Thomas Nelson, 1988.

Stone, Jon R. *A Guide to the End of the World: Popular Eschatology in America*. New York: Garland, 1993.

Ward, Mark, Sr. *Air of Salvation: The Story of Christian Broadcasting*. Grand Rapids, MI: Baker Book House, 1994.

CARL McINTIRE
born: May 17, 1906, Ypsilanti, Michigan

Carl McIntire has been the patriarch of fundamentalist separatism in American Protestantism since the death of his mentor, J. Gresham Machen, in 1937. McIntire has also been a durable presence in religious radio, airing his far-right views on *The Twentieth Century Reformation Hour* continually since 1936. At the peak of its popularity in the late 1960s, McIntire's program was being broadcast over 635 radio stations.

Carl McIntire was born in Michigan and reared by his Scotch-Irish parents on the conservative plains of Oklahoma, where his father, Charles Curtis McIntire, served as a Presbyterian minister. After graduating from high school, the future evangelist enrolled at Southeastern State College in his hometown of Durant with plans to become a lawyer. He transferred to Park College in Kansas City, Missouri, to finish his bachelor of arts degree and worked as a janitor and traveling salesman to make ends meet. McIntire would look back at this period as crucial to his future vocation:

> Those years selling were better preparation for life than the seminary. I started out walking, then I bought me an old gray mare and rode her two summers, then a motorcycle, then an old car. It was a rough-and-tumble life, with all the hard knocks you could ask for, but I learned people, and I learned the value of a dollar, and I learned to respect the capitalist system.

While completing his bachelor of arts degree, McIntire changed his mind about becoming a lawyer. Following graduation from Park College, he married his college girlfriend and enrolled at Princeton Theological Seminary with the aim of becoming a minister.

While at Princeton, McIntire came under the influence of J. Gresham Machen, a respected New Testament scholar and fundamentalist who was engaged in a protracted struggle to purge liberals from the school's faculty, graduate school, and board of trustees. Machen was ultimately unsuccessful in convincing the Presbyterian Church USA's leadership to take these steps. Therefore, Machen resigned from Princeton in 1929 and founded Westminster Theological Seminary, just outside of Philadelphia. McIntire followed Machen to this bastion of "true" Christianity and, in time, joined his mentor's battles against both the Presbyterian Church leadership and the Federal Council of Churches.

In 1931, McIntire was ordained and called to pastor the Chelsea Presbyterian Church in Atlantic City, New Jersey. Two years later he moved to Collinswood, New Jersey, where he assumed at the local Presbyterian church what would become the longest pastorship in his career.

Both Machen and McIntire were ousted from the Presbyterian Church USA in 1936 for their unrelenting accusations against the denominational leadership (i.e., that the leadership was promoting Communism through its foreign missionaries) and for creating a rival board of foreign missions. Within the year they had founded the Presbyterian Church of America. They advertised this church as the only Presbyterian denomination that had remained faithful to the Westminster Confession. McIntire's Collinswood congregation followed him into the new denomination and would provide him with both financial and moral support in the coming decades.

McIntire and Machen began to disagree over a number of issues soon after the formation of their new denomination. These issues included the wording of the church constitution, premillennial dispensationalism, and the proper use of alcohol. Ultimately, the two conservative warriors broke ranks, and McIntire founded the Bible Presbyterian Church, a new sect and the new name of his church in Collinswood, and Faith Theological Seminary. Machen's followers reorganized themselves as the Orthodox Presbyterian Church. Over the next two decades McIntire's sectarian church would create Shelton College in Cape May, New Jersey, and Highlands College in Pasadena, California.

During 1936, McIntire started a weekly newspaper called *The Christian Beacon*, which featured news articles from other periodicals that supported McIntire's views and his own dia-

tribes against various "enemies." McIntire also founded the Christian Beacon Press. This company would publish most of McIntire's 12 books, including the first, *A Cloud of Witnesses*.

McIntire began broadcasting his church's Sunday worship services during the late 1930s. This program evolved into the well-known radio series *The Twentieth Century Reformation Hour* in 1955. Over the years, this half-hour program would provide a national forum for McIntire's vociferous mix of fundamentalist orthodoxy, anti-Communism, apocalyptic premillennialism, and laissez-faire capitalism. The show aired each morning coast to coast, Monday through Friday, and in its heyday during the late 1960s was heard over 635 radio stations. Although McIntire used a wide variety of communications media to spread his message—e.g., speeches, lectures, pamphlets, rallies, books, and newspapers—*The Twentieth Century Reformation Hour* became his most effective propaganda tool.

McIntire's program began with his trademark greeting, "Good morning! Good morning! Good morning! This is Dr. McIntire!" Eschewing scripts, he would then launch into whatever topic was occupying his mind at the moment. At times, McIntire would open his telephone lines and discuss contemporary issues with loyal followers throughout the country. He was not shy about asking for money, often soliciting a special donation of $1 million. With this dream contribution, he claimed, his program could be heard on 1,000 radio stations.

McIntire often invited his personal friend, Dr. Charles Richter, into the studio as a sidekick. Richter would sit near McIntire and exhort the preacher to rhetorical heights with a fervent "Amen" or "Praise the Lord." McIntire would also turn to "Amen Charlie," as Richter was called, at appropriate junctures in his delivery, and ask for his approval. A typical exchange might include: "Isn't that right, Charlie?" "That's right, Reverend Carl. Amen!" "Thank you, Amen Charlie!"

The list of enemies that McIntire denounced on his broadcasts was long and illustrious. It included, among others, Billy Graham, the Roman Catholic Church, Martin Luther King, Jr., and his family, Oral Roberts, protesters against the Vietnam War, the United Nations, the United Methodist Church, hippies, the US Post Office, feminists, UNICEF, medical care providers, income tax officials, the World Baptist Alliance, and the YMCA. Concerning the Catholic Church, McIntire once stated,

> As we enter the post-war world, without any doubt the greatest enemy of freedom and liberty that the world has to face today is the Roman Catholic system. Yes, we have Communism in Russia and all that is involved there, but if one had to choose between the two . . . one would be much better off in a communistic society than in a Roman Catholic Fascist set-up . . . America has to face the Roman Catholic terror. The sooner the Christian people of America wake up to this danger, the safer will be our land.

In his later years, McIntire would tone down his anti-Catholic rhetoric and find common ground with ultra-conservative Catholics on social and doctrinal issues.

McIntire's list of "friends" was similarly long and star-studded. It featured Billy James Hargis; the fundamentalist educator Bob Jones; the ultra-right Church League of America's Edgar Bundy; the conservative Texas billionaire H. L. Hunt; and the reactionary radio commentators Clarence Manion and Dan Smoot.

McIntire was the main force behind the formation of the American Council of Christian Churches (ACCC) in 1941. This para-church body served as a fundamentalist alternative to the ecumenically-oriented Federal Council of Churches (FCC). The new organization sought to promote "a united stand against religious modernism" and to awaken "Bible-loyal Protestants everywhere to a twentieth century reformation." McIntire was especially upset with the FCC's overtures toward Catholics and Jews and lambasted all ecumenism as a form of socialist internationalism. In one famous segment from *The Twentieth Century Reformation Hour*, he declared,

> Let the Baptists be Baptists. Let the Presbyterians be Presbyterians. Let the Lutherans be Lutherans. Let the Methodists be Methodists. Let us all be what we are, and in the strength of our individual convictions we shall be stronger Chris-

tians, and shall hold more tenaciously to the great Christian doctrines that unite the Lord's people.

McIntire soon felt compelled—by the alleged encroachment of Marxism into world Protestantism—to organize the International Council of Christian Churches. This rival to the World Council of Churches (WCC) held its first meeting to coincide with the WCC's conference in Amsterdam in 1948. McIntire's fear of Marxism was also evident in his speeches and writings. He advocated a first-strike use of the atomic bomb against what he considered to be the satanic power of the former Soviet Union. McIntire's relentless anti-Communism also led to his cooperation with Senator Joseph McCarthy's staff during the late 1940s and early 1950s. He was especially interested in supporting McCarthy's attempts to expose the ecumenical movement and the Revised Standard Version of the Bible as parts of the world Communist conspiracy.

McIntire remained a staunch anti-Communist throughout the middle decades of the twentieth century and openly supported Barry Goldwater in the 1964 presidential election. He condemned the Civil Rights movement as a Communist plot designed to take away the property rights of American citizens and spoke out against the United Nations–sponsored Year of the Child as a plot to incite "children to rebel against their parents."

McIntire's popularity began to fade during the 1970s and 1980s as New Christian Right leaders such as Pat Robertson and Jerry Falwell took up the banner of the conservative crusade. After his *Twentieth Century Reformation Hour* was canceled in the Philadelphia radio market in 1970, McIntire purchased radio station WXUR in Media, Pennsylvania. The Federal Communications Commission soon attempted to revoke the station's license, claiming that WXUR was violating the Fairness Doctrine by not airing opposing viewpoints. The commission also charged that the station was not operating in the best interests of the community and that it was misrepresenting the facts. After extended litigation, an appeals court allowed McIntire to keep his station's broadcasting license. The court let stand the charges of misrepresentation, however, and declared that WXUR was "an independent frolic" with "more bravado than brains."

McIntire lost his position on the board of the American Council of Christian Churches in 1969 and promptly formed the marginal American Christian Action Council. During the 1970s, Faith Theological Seminary steadily declined in both enrollment and financial viability. And in 1985, the Supreme Court upheld a decision of the New Jersey Department of Higher Education to withdraw state accreditation from Shelton College.

McIntire continues his reactionary diatribes on *The Twentieth Century Reformation Hour* but finds fewer and fewer listeners. Clearly the world has become an unfriendly place for career cold warriors.

SOURCES

Carl McIntire's 50 years, 1933–1983, as Pastor of the Congregation of the Bible Presbyterian Church of Collinswood, N.J. Collinswood, NJ: Bible Presbyterian Church, 1983.

Clabaugh, Gary K. *Thunder on the Right: The Protestant Fundamentalists*. Chicago: Nelson-Hall, 1974.

Dollar, George W. *A History of Fundamentalism in America*. Greenville, SC: Bob Jones University Press, 1973.

Harden, Margaret G. *A Brief History of the Bible Presbyterian Church and Its Agencies*. Collinswood, NJ: Bible Presbyterian Church, n.d.

Jorstad, Erling. *The Politics of Doomsday: Fundamentalists of the Far Right*. Nashville: Abingdon Press, 1970.

Liebman, Robert C., and Robert Wuthnow. *The New Christian Right: Mobilization and Legitimation*. New York: Aldine, 1983.

McIntire, Carl. *Author of Liberty*. Collinswood, NJ: Christian Beacon Press, 1946.

———. *The Death of a Church*. Collinswood, NJ: Christian Beacon Press, 1967.

———. *For Such a Time as This*. Collinswood, NJ: Christian Beacon Press, 1946.

———. *Modern Tower of Babel*. Collinswood, NJ: Christian Beacon Press, n.d.

———. *The New Bible, Revised Standard Version: Why Christians Should Not Accept It*. Collinswood, NJ: Christian Beacon Press, 1953.

———. *The Rise of the Tyrant*. Collinswood, NJ: Christian Beacon Press, 1945.

———. *Servants of Apostasy*. Collinswood, NJ: Christian Beacon Press, 1955.

———. *The Struggle for South America*. Collinswood, NJ: Christian Beacon Press, 1950.

———. *Twentieth Century Reformation*. Collinswood, NJ: Christian Beacon Press, 1944.

Morris, James. *The Preachers*. New York: St. Martin's Press, 1973.

Roy, Ralph Lord. *Apostles of Discord: A Study of Organized Bigotry and Disruption on the Fringes of Protestantism*. Boston: Beacon Press, 1953.

Sandeen, Ernest R. *The Roots of Fundamentalism: British and American Millenarianism, 1800–1930*. Chicago: University of Chicago Press, 1970.

AIMEE SEMPLE McPHERSON

born: October 9, 1890, near Ingersoll, Ontario, Canada
died: September 27, 1944, Oakland, California

Courtesy: National Religious Broadcasters

Aimee Semple McPherson was the first woman ever to broadcast a sermon over radio and the founder of the first radio station in America owned and operated by a religious organization, KFSG radio. During her long and controversial career, she embodied the figure of both the simple, itinerant revivalist of the nineteenth century and the more showy and sophisticated radio preacher of the 1920s and 1930s.

McPherson was the only child of Mildred and James Kennedy. Her father was a successful Ontario farmer and active member of the local Methodist church. Mildred Kennedy was an orphan who had been reared in the Salvation Army religious tradition. She was hired as a nurse for James Kennedy's first wife and married Kennedy after the woman's death. According to family legend, Mildred Kennedy dedicated her daughter "Beth" (Aimee's first name) to God's service when the child was only six weeks old.

McPherson, who attended Salvation Army services with her mother throughout her childhood, enjoyed marching her playmates in parades while leading them in rousing hymns. As a young student, she won awards for her oratory skills and was an enthusiastic participant in school plays. As she grew to maturity, however, McPherson turned away from the piety of the Salvation Army and joined her father's local Methodist congregation.

In 1907, McPherson attended a Pentecostal revival meeting with her father and experienced the baptism of the Holy Spirit. She also became enamored of the revival's preacher, Robert Semple, and attended the prayer meetings he was leading in the homes of local believers. Within a short time, McPherson decided that the Pentecostal "gifts" had a sound biblical foundation and that she would join the Pentecostal movement. By 1908, she had married Semple and started her career as an itinerant evangelist. The couple preached and healed in such Canadian and American cities as Toronto and Chicago. In 1909, McPherson was ordained a preacher at William Dunham's North Avenue Mission in Chicago. The mission was affiliated with the Full Gospel Assembly.

The next phase of McPherson's life began in 1910, when she and her husband traveled to Hong Kong to begin work as missionaries in China. The mission came to an abrupt end when McPherson's husband died of typhoid fever shortly after she had given birth to their daughter, Roberta. The young widow and mother managed to make her way back to the United States, where she eventually joined her mother at a Salvation Army mission in New York State. The loss of her husband took a heavy toll on McPherson, and she found that she had little zeal for religious work without him.

In 1912 another phase of McPherson's life began, when she married a Chicago grocery clerk named Harold McPherson. This second marriage proved to be an unhappy one for both parties. After the birth of their son, Rolf, in 1913, McPherson was required to undergo an operation that left her unable to bear more children. After three years of marital disharmony, McPherson took her two children and went to live with her parents in Canada. The future radio preacher continued to hold a lukewarm attitude toward religion until she was asked by Elizabeth Sharp, a local supporter of revivals, to lead a series of revival meetings in Mount Forest, Ontario. These meetings proved successful, and a reinspired McPherson decided to resume her career as a traveling evangelist.

Over the next three years, McPherson conducted tent revivals throughout the United States and Canada. She developed a reputation as a charismatic, compelling, and persuasive preacher, faith healer, and a guaranteed draw for local revivals. Harold McPherson was reunited with his increasingly famous wife and accompanied her on revival crusades. The reconciliation was short-lived, however, and the couple separated permanently in 1918. From this time onward, McPherson's mother managed the business and administrative details of her crusades. During these years, McPherson inaugurated some important dimensions of her later work. She began wearing a nurse's white dress and blue cape as her official costume; driving the "gospel auto," a battered old car with evangelistic slogans such as "Jesus Is Coming— Get Ready" painted on its sides; and publishing *The Bridal Call*, a movement periodical.

It was in the gospel auto that McPherson first came to Los Angeles in the fall of 1918. She held a successful crusade in the city and established the headquarters of a nascent evangelical organization. Though the young preacher continued to hold successful tent revivals around the world for the next five years, she began to see Los Angeles as her home and base of operations.

In 1922, McPherson organized the construction of Angelus Foursquare Temple, a 5,000-seat worship facility located next to Echo Park in Santa Monica. She claimed that the site, which was located at a busy crossing of streetcar lines in the fastest-growing part of the city, had been divinely revealed to her. The white, pie-shaped temple was financed by donations collected at various revival crusades. It cost a total of $1.5 million to build, and opened on January 1, 1923. Within a short time, the facility had become the center of a wide array of religious and social service activities for her estimated 50,000 followers.

After her ordination as a Baptist minister in 1923, McPherson organized the International Church of the Foursquare Gospel. Although she had never intended it, the church soon became a separate Protestant denomination, being officially recognized as such by the State of California, which endorsed the denomination's incorporation papers in 1927. By the time of McPherson's death in 1944, the new denomination was represented by over 400 churches in North America.

The idea of the "Foursquare Gospel" came from the Old Testament vision of Ezekiel. In McPherson's interpretation, the four figures in the vision—a man, a lion, an eagle, and an ox—each stood for a fundamental facet of Christ. The man represented Christ as the sole Savior of humankind. The lion signified his role as the mighty baptizer with the Holy Spirit. The eagle represented Christ as the coming king, and the ox symbolized Christ as the divine physician of the soul. This conception skillfully synthesized elements of evangelicalism, Pentecostalism, and millennialism that dominated the American Protestant landscape of the time.

The Angelus Temple showcased McPherson's increasingly sophisticated and performative religious services. Called "illustrated sermons," these dramaturgical extravaganzas took place on a large stage that adapted props from Hollywood film sets. One such prop was a proscenium arch that Charlie Chaplin helped design. There also were painted backdrops that

graphically represented the central themes of particular sermons. A remarkable example of such a backdrop depicted George Washington at Valley Forge. After mounting the stage dressed in a replica of Washington's uniform, McPherson solemnly inspected the troops while snow fell around her. Another prominent part of her worship extravaganzas was the music performed by a brass band, an orchestra, and a robed choir.

McPherson's mentor in this stagecraft was Thompson Eade, a former vaudeville performer who had undergone a miraculous recovery from shell shock at Angelus Temple. After enrolling in the church's newly instituted Bible college (the Lighthouse of International Foursquare Evangelism), Eade was asked by McPherson to help her with set design and stage management.

He was to play a prominent role in the production of programming on KFSG (Kalling Four Square Gospel), the nation's first radio station owned and operated by a religious institution. The 500-watt station, which was inaugurated in 1923, catapulted McPherson to national fame as a radio personality and evangelist. She was not only the first woman to gain a Federal Communications Commission broadcaster's license, but also the first woman to deliver a sermon over the air (in San Francisco, 1922).

KFSG broadcast the dramatic worship services at Angelus Temple beginning in 1924. Early in the station's history, these services were transmitted into tents that had been set up in nearby towns such as Huntington Park, Santa Ana, Pasadena, and Venice. The assembled congregations listened to the service via radio receiver. They, in turn, responded to McPherson's exhortations using a telephone that amplified their voices at KFSG and transmitted them to the Angelus Temple and to radio audiences around the country. On some broadcasts McPherson would ask the tent listeners, "Do you believe in the inspiration of the Scripture? In the virgin birth? In the Atonement?" Her Temple audience would cheer loudly when they heard the tent listeners answer "I do!" This declaration of faith in McPherson's version of the fundamentals of Christianity entitled the tent audience to full membership in the Angelus Temple.

McPherson was never a doctrinal hard-liner, however. Like many spiritual leaders in the tolerant, independent religious atmosphere of Southern California, she aimed at the broadest possible audience and tried to avoid doctrinal "quibbles and hairsplitting." She also emphasized positive thinking and hope for the future, once declaring,

> [W]ho cares about old Hell, friends? Why, we all know what Hell is. We've heard about it all our lives. A terrible place, where nobody wants to go. I think the less we hear about Hell, the better, don't you? Let's forget about Hell. Lift up your hearts. What we are interested in, yes Lord, is Heaven and how to get there!

McPherson's innovative use of radio sometimes led her into conflict with federal regulators. Herbert Hoover, for instance, who at the time (1927) held the post of Secretary of Commerce, criticized the evangelist for arbitrarily changing the frequency of her station (a common occurrence in the relatively unregulated milieu of early radio). In response to this criticism, McPherson sent him a telegram that read: "Please order your minions of Satan to leave my station alone. You cannot expect the Almighty to abide by your wavelength nonsense. When I offer my prayers to Him I must fit into His wave reception. Open this station at once."

McPherson's showy performances at the Angelus Temple also aroused the opposition of more conventional Protestant ministers in Southern California. "Fighting Bob" Shuler was perhaps the most vocal of McPherson's enemies. This pastor of Los Angeles' Trinity Methodist Church, whose radio station's audience was second only to that of KFSG, regularly launched personal attacks against McPherson. Shuler's opposition was blunted, however, by his increasingly bizarre antics. These included his well-publicized support for the Ku Klux Klan, his placing of a curse on the state of California after his unsuccessful senate bid in 1932, and his accusation during Al Smith's presidential campaign that Catholics were planning to murder Protestants in their beds.

McPherson's greatest fame came as the result of her mysterious disappearance from an Ocean Park beach in May 1926. The city of Los Angeles was in a tumult as authorities searched for her in vain and her followers held prayer vigils on the beach. When the evangelist was found wandering in the Arizona desert six weeks later, she claimed to have been kidnapped and to have made a daring escape from two drunken desperados, Jake and Mexicali Rose. The residents of Los Angeles gave McPherson a thunderous public welcome upon her return. The event was reportedly attended by at least 50,000 persons, including the mayor, the city council, and the fire department. The welcome soon soured, however, when reporters began noting irregularities in her story.

Within a short time, McPherson was accused of perpetrating a public hoax in order to cover up a sex scandal that involved a handsome radio station operator. The evangelist's considerable rhetorical abilities served her well during a series of court appearances about the matter over the next few years. Mounting a spirited defense, McPherson donned an "admiral-general" uniform, created a Fight the Devil fund for her legal representation, and successfully counter-attacked her enemies at every turn. In the end, the charges were dropped and McPherson's fame was greater than ever.

One service every week at Angelus Temple was dedicated to healing, during which a nonstop prayer vigil was held in the Temple's tower. In addition to this emphasis on prayer and healing, McPherson's ministry followed the example of the Salvation Army and organized missions to serve the local indigent population. These included a commissary that provided medical care, clothing, shelter, and an estimated 1.5 million free meals to the poor during the 1930s. The most notable dimension of this service work was that no one was subjected to a sermon while he or she ate, and no one was required to make a statement of belief before receiving help. The commissary became so well respected that the police department routinely sent indigents to the facility for care.

McPherson's International Church of the Foursquare Gospel continued to grow during the 1930s despite the evangelist's growing personal problems. McPherson struggled with alcoholism, entered into another unhappy marriage, suffered a nervous breakdown, and became estranged from her mother and daughter. Her radio audience also began to decrease. By 1939, however, McPherson was staging a comeback. The Angelus Temple's membership grew to 12,000, and the popular preacher traveled around the country, strengthening the churches in her denomination and laying plans for future expansion. McPherson also published a number of books, including several autobiographical accounts.

In March 1944, the Foursquare Church applied for an FCC television and FM license and purchased hilltop property suitable for a television transmitter. Before she could bring her illustrated sermons to television, however, McPherson died from a heart attack induced by an overdose of sleeping medication. On the anniversary of her fifty-fourth birthday, the famed radio preacher was buried in Los Angeles' Forest Lawn Cemetery. Her ornate funeral was estimated to have cost $40,000. McPherson's radio ministry continued, with her son, Rolf McPherson, as host until his retirement in 1988. The ministry did not continue after his retirement.

Aimee Semple McPherson was a bold innovator in religious broadcasting, evangelistic dramaturgy, and folk theology. She effectively combined the piety of her youth and New Thought gospel of positive thinking with a genuine concern for the poor. The denomination she founded has continued to grow and now counts over 1,800 churches and 200,000 members worldwide. McPherson belongs to a select group of powerful American women that includes such religious leaders as Phoebe Palmer, Amanda Berry Smith, Mary Baker Eddy, Kathryn Kuhlman, and Elizabeth Clare Prophet.

SOURCES

Bahr, Robert. *Least of All Saints: The Story of Aimee Semple McPherson*. Englewood Cliffs, NJ: Prentice-Hall, 1979.

Clark, David L. "Miracles for a Dime: From Chautauqua Tent to Radio Station with Sister Aimee." *California History* 57 (1978–79).

Cox, Raymond L. *The Verdict Is In*. Los Angeles: Research Publishers, 1983.

Mavity, Nancy Barr. *Sister Aimee*. New York: Doubleday, 1931.

McLoughlin, William G. "Aimee Semple McPherson: 'Your Sister in the King's Glad Service.'" *Journal of Popular Culture* 1 (1967).

McPherson, Aimee Semple. *Divine Healing Sermons*. Los Angeles: 1921.

———. *The Foursquare Gospel*. Comp. by Raymond L. Cox. Los Angeles: Foursquare Publications, 1969.

———. *Give Me My Own God*. New York: H. C. Kinsey, 1936.

———. *In the Service of the King*. New York: Boni and Liveright, 1927.

———. *The Second Coming of Christ*. Los Angeles: 1921.

———. *The Story of My Life*. Los Angeles: Echo Park Evangelistic Association, 1951.

———. *This Is That: Personal Experiences, Sermons and Writings*. Los Angeles: Bridal Call Publishing, 1919.

———. *This Is That: Personal Experiences, Sermons and Writings*. Rev. ed. Los Angeles: Echo Park Evangelistic Association, 1923.

Peterson, Richard G. "Electric Sisters." In *The God Pumpers*, edited by Marshall Fishwick and Ray B. Browne. Bowling Green, KY: Bowling Green State University Popular Press, 1987.

Scanzoni, Letha Dawson, and Susan Setta. "Women in Evangelical, Holiness and Pentecostal Traditions." In *Women and Religion in America*, edited by Rosemary Radford Ruether and Rosemary Skinner Keller. San Francisco: Harper & Row, 1986.

Thomas, Lately [pseud.] *The Vanishing Evangelist*. New York: Viking, 1959.

TERRY MEEUWSEN

Since June of 1993, former Miss America Terry Meeuwsen has been a permanent cohost of *The 700 Club*. The show is the flagship production of the Christian Broadcasting Network (CBN). Meeuwsen is a native of Wisconsin who attended St. Norbert College in De Pere. After moving to Los Angeles with hopes of becoming an actress and singer, Meeuwsen joined the New Christy Minstrels, a popular folk group of the 1960s. She toured with the group for two years, made seven recordings, and appeared on a number of television talk and variety shows. Following her crowning as Miss America in 1973, Meeuwsen spent a year touring and speaking before returning to her acting and singing career. The young performer joined a daily talk show, *A New Day*, at NBC's Milwaukee affiliate WTMJ-TV in 1978. Meeuwsen produced serious news documentaries for the station and served as a director of special projects until she left in 1986.

It was in the early 1980s that Meeuwsen began appearing on *The 700 Club* as a guest cohost. She also worked on a short-lived CBN morning show, *USAm*, in 1981. After a period in the mid-1980s, during which she devoted more time to her growing family, Meeuwsen was chosen as the show's permanent cohost with Pat Robertson in 1993. With the return of Ben Kinchlow at about the same time, the show now has a steady troika of attractive, articulate cohosts. In addition to being a skillful interviewer and reporter, Meeuwsen works well with children on CBN's *Summer Kids Club* television ministry.

See also *The 700 Club*; Pat Robertson

SOURCES

"Terry Meeuwsen." The Christian Broadcasting Network, publicity sheet, 1995.

MELODY MOUNTAIN
first aired: August, 1983

Melody Mountain is a weekly half-hour program of "down home gospel music" that is broadcast throughout the world on Paul and Jan Crouch's Trinity Broadcasting Network. The show's host is Betty Jean Robinson, a motherly figure who strolls through a studio set designed to simulate the inside of a simple mountain

home. The set includes a fireplace, a clock, a book shelf, couches, chairs, quilts, and homey knickknacks. Robinson sings old-time gospel favorites with country-and-western-style musical accompaniment. She also tells inspirational stories about her family and friends and asks her audience to worship the Lord with her in song. *Melody Mountain*'s musical format has become a standard feature of Christian programming schedules in the United States.

MENSAJE A LA CONCIENCIA
first aired: 1955

On the airwaves since July 1955, *Un Mensaje a la Conciencia* ("Message to the Conscience") is a Spanish-language evangelistic radio and television program that airs over 1,900 radio and 300 television stations in 27 countries throughout Central and South America. The program is hosted by Paul Finkenbinder ("Hermano Pablo" or Brother Paul). Since the mid-1960s, *Mensaje a la Conciencia* has been produced from Finkenbinder's ministry headquarters in Costa Mesa, California. Perhaps one of the best-known evangelical programs in the Western Hemisphere, *Mensaje* reaches an estimated 25 to 30 million people daily. The success of the program has earned Finkenbinder the unofficial title of the "Billy Graham of Latin America."

See also Paul Finkenbinder

SOURCES

The Directory of Religious Organizations in the United States. 2d ed. Falls Church, VA: McGrath, 1982.

Melton, J. Gordon. *Directory of Religious Organizations in the United States*. 3rd ed. Detroit: Gale Research, 1993.

TAMMY FAYE MESSNER
born: March 7, 1942, International Falls, Minnesota

Tammy Faye Messner and her former husband Jim Bakker were pioneers of religious televi-

Courtesy: National Religious Broadcasters

sion, having been present at the birth of the three most prominent religious television networks of the 1960s and 1970s: Christian Broadcasting Network, Trinity Broadcasting Network, and the PTL Network. The Bakkers's rapid rise to prominence was followed by an equally precipitous fall from grace when, in the late 1980s, they were unable to weather a barrage of personal and professional scandals.

Messner came from a broken family in northern Minnesota and as a teen had set her sights on missionary work. As a student at North Central College (Assemblies of God) in Minneapolis, Minnesota, she met another student, Jim Bakker. The couple decided to marry, but since entering into marriage while still a student was against school policy, the newlyweds left the college and began their careers as itinerant evangelists.

The Bakkers entered into religious television broadcasting under the auspices of Pat Robertson and the Christian Broadcasting Network, and were present during the founding of the Trinity Broadcasting Network. Jim Bakker moved on to found his own network, the PTL Network, and began his own show, *The PTL Club*, which Tammy Faye joined as cohost in the 1970s. She often hosted the program alone when Jim was occupied with other dimensions of his expanding ministry.

During the 1980s, Jim and Tammy Faye became prosperous television superstars with a large and loyal following. Their daily program's name was changed to reflect this state of affairs: *The PTL Club* became *The Jim and Tammy Show*. By 1986, the couple had built an impressive media and recreational empire.

After a scandal involving relations between her husband and a church secretary all but destroyed the couple's empire, and Jim was sentenced to 45 years in prison by federal authorities for financial improprieties, Tammy Faye Bakker obtained a divorce. She married Roe Messner, a wealthy Kansas developer and old family friend, in a private ceremony near her Palm Springs home in October 1993. Tammy Faye has continued to plan a comeback television ministry.

See also Jim Bakker

SOURCES

Bakker, Tammy, with Cliff Dudley. *I Gotta Be Me.* Charlotte, NC: PTL Club, 1978.

Barnhart, Joe E. *Jim and Tammy: Charismatic Intrigue Inside PTL.* Buffalo, NY: Prometheus, 1988.

JOYCE MEYER
born: 1942, St. Louis, Missouri

Joyce Meyer is a fast-rising star in religious broadcasting circles. Her *Life in the Word* radio program, which began in 1985, is currently being carried each weekday over 211 stations throughout the United States. The show has a teaching format and presents Meyer's practical application of biblical principles to everyday life. In the early 1990s, Meyer began her *Life in the Word* television ministry. By 1996, the half-hour program was being aired weekday mornings on BET Network, WGN Chicago, Trinity Broadcasting Network, LeSea Broadcasting, and the Inspirational Network, and on cable networks in Canada, Central and South America, and England. The program was also seen weekly on 94 local television stations in the United States.

According to Meyer's ministry literature, she came from an abusive background and was able to rise above the obstacles in her life through the practical application of biblical teachings and through "learning to receive God's grace to bring about change in her life." Her televised messages stress the experiential application of God's Word more than doctrinal correctness. They are filled with personal stories of triumph over adversity. The format of Meyer's television program mixes studio footage with a taped sermon or exegesis on a biblical passage. On stage, Meyer comes across as a down-to-earth, plain-speaking, savvy teacher and pastor who is clearly at ease before a large audience.

Meyer's husband, Dave Meyer, and their four children all work full-time in her Joyce Meyer Ministries. Dave oversees radio and television negotiations, ministry finances, travel schedules, and the marketing of his wife's books and tapes. The ministry is located in Fenton, Missouri, a suburb of St. Louis.

Joyce Meyer started her first Bible-study group in her home in 1976. In 1980, she was ordained and became a staff minister at Life Christian Center in St. Louis. It was at Life Christian Center that Meyer began her first weekly women's meetings. After five successful years of teaching and administering these Life in the Word Meetings, Meyer felt led to take her message on the road. She established Life in the Word, Inc., and began traveling throughout the United States, giving marriage and women's seminars to thousands of people. Meyer became known for her ability to draw examples from her own life experiences to facilitate emotional healing in others. Her ministry also markets her 12 popular books (published by Harrison House and Creation House) and hundreds of thousands of teaching tapes. A monthly 16-page magazine, *Life in the Word,* is sent to 177,000 subscribers in Canada and the United States.

Meyer believes her mission is establishing believers in God's Word. She observes, "Jesus died to set the captives free, and there are far too many Christians that have very little or no victory in their daily lives." Out of her own vic-tory over adversity, she feels qualified to help others "exchange ashes for beauty."

SOURCES

"Doctrine of Faith." *Life in the Word.* Fenton, MO: Joyce Meyer Ministries, 1995.

"Joyce Meyer Ministries." Introductory brochure, 1995.

Kerby, James H. "A Life in the Word." *Religious Broadcasting,* January, 1996.

LIGHTFOOT SOLOMON MICHAUX

born: November 7, 1884, Buckroe Beach, Virginia
died: October 20, 1968, Washington, DC

Lightfoot Solomon Michaux, an African American, was one of the early pioneers of radio evangelism. He began broadcasting his religious message in 1929 over a Newport News, Virginia, radio station.

Around the turn of the century, Michaux had become a successful seafood merchant in the Newport News area, marketing his products to local naval establishments. After his marriage to Mary Eliza Pauline in 1906, Michaux left the Baptist tradition, in which he had been raised, and joined the Church of Christ (Holiness) congregation of St. Timothy's. He served as the church's secretary-treasurer before deciding to begin his own church, which he called Everybody's Mission, in 1917. Michaux received his ministerial credentials under the auspices of the Church of Christ.

Following the success of his new church, Michaux was asked by C. P. Jones, the Church of God's founder, to relocate and create another congregation. Michaux decided to refuse this offer and, instead, he incorporated, as an independent church, the Gospel Spreading Tabernacle Building Association, on February 26, 1921. Between 1921 and 1928, Michaux ministered at two different congregations in Hampton and Newport News, Virginia. In 1922, he gained notoriety by conducting racially integrated baptismal services. After his arrest for these actions, he mounted a successful defense and was acquitted in court.

In 1928, Michaux decided to join several of his congregations in Washington, DC, and to change the name of his church to the Church of God and Gospel Spreading Association. Michaux's interest in radio evangelism led to the inaugraral broadcast of *Radio Church of God* on radio station WJSV in 1929. The show featured a 156-voice choir (which included among its members Mahalia Jackson and Clara Ward) and commenced with Michaux's signature theme song, "Happy Am I." Michaux's sermons mixed traditional holiness themes with the New Thought message of positive thinking. When CBS radio bought WJSV, the "Happy Am I" Evangelist, as Michaux was known, was picked up by 50 stations throughout the network. It is estimated that Michaux's Saturday evening radio audience in 1934 numbered 25 million nationwide, making him the most listened to African American of his time. His broadcasts were also carried on short-wave frequencies around the world. The radio ministry supported *Happy News*, the church's monthly periodical.

Michaux's radio ministry had a huge impact on his Washington, DC, church, which began to stage annual mass baptisms in the Potomac River and Griffith Stadium. These events were conducted in a festival-like atmosphere which included parades and gospel singing. His church also embraced a strong social welfare ministry. It supported numerous programs to find work for the unemployed, support orphanages, and provide food and shelter for the indigent. The church's Happy News Cafe became a popular, affordable eatery for the district's poor. Michaux also supported the Mayfair project, which provided low-cost apartments for 594 families in the late 1940s and became a model for privately owned housing developments for the underprivileged. The radio ministry also led to the formation of new African American congregations on the Eastern seaboard.

Michaux became an early supporter of Franklin Roosevelt and is credited with wooing a large proportion of African Americans to the Democratic party during the 1930s. Both Eleanor Roosevelt and Mamie Eisenhower supported Michaux's ministry, and President Eisenhower was made an honorary member of the Church of God and Gospel Spreading Association. Michaux's Depression-era message of faith and optimism, however, did not translate successfully into the cultural context following World War II, and Michaux's radio audience dwindled to only a few stations in cities where his church had congregations. This did not deter the popular minister, however, who became a pioneer in television evangelism in 1947, preaching his homilies from the nation's capital over WTTG-TV. The program was picked up by the DuMont Television Network for its Sunday lineup in October 1948, making Michaux one of the earliest African Americans featured on a regular television series. DuMont canceled the show on January 9, 1949.

Michaux, after reorganizing his congregations in 1964 as the Gospel Spreading Church, died of a heart attack in 1968. The pioneer radio evangelist remains a model for ministers committed to both spreading the gospel via the electronic church and serving the practical needs of disadvantaged Americans.

See also Mahalia Jackson; Clara Ward

SOURCES

"Biggest Baptism." *Ebony* 3 (February 1948): 35–39.

Green, Constance McLaughlin. *Washington.* 2 vols. Princeton, NJ: Princeton University Press, 1963.

Lark, Pauline, ed. *Sparks from the Anvil of Elder Michaux.* Washington, DC: Happy News, 1950.

Lewis, Roscoe. *The Negro in Virginia.* New York: Hastings House, 1940.

Michaux, Lightfoot Solomon. *Spiritual Happiness Making Songs.* Washington, DC: n.d.

"Top Radio Ministers." *Ebony* 4 (July 1949): 56–61.

Webb, Lillian Ashcraft. *About My Father's Business.* Westport, CT: Greenwood Press, 1981.

MIDDLE EAST MEDIA
established: 1975

Middle East Media (MEM) is an international organization of Arab Christians whose aim is to evangelize Muslims in the United States and abroad. The ministry distributes literature and produces video programs that attempt to convince Muslims of the validity of the claims of Christ and the relevance of His teachings to modern life. Founded in 1975, MEM also produces television programs that target Muslim youth. The organization's headquarters are in the north Seattle suburb of Lynwood, Washington.

SOURCES

Melton, J. Gordon. *Directory of Religious Organizations in the United States.* 3rd ed. Detroit: Gale Research, 1993.

MIDDLE EAST TELEVISION
established: 1995

American Christian broadcasters have long sought a means to transmit the gospel to audiences in the Middle East. During 1995, Middle East Television began offering these ministries program time on Sunday mornings. The broadcast service estimates that its viewership includes approximately 11 million people in Israel, Lebanon, Jordan, Syria, and Egypt. Of this number, 500,000 are cable households in Israel. For many evangelicals, the conversion of the Jews to Christianity is a necessary prerequisite to the Second Coming of Christ.

MISSION TO THE DEAF, INTERNATIONAL

Mission to the Deaf, International (MDI) is a nondenominational ministry to the deaf and hearing-impaired that sponsors Christian education, classes in sign language, and indoor and outdoor social activities. Known simply as Mission to the Deaf until 1985, MDI has expanded its ministry to include sponsorship of a weekly television program for the deaf, entitled *The Silent Ear.* Its ministry headquarters are in San Jose, California.

SOURCES

Melton, J. *Gordon. Directory of Religious Organizations in the United States.* 3rd ed. Detroit: Gale Research, 1993.

"MISSION WITHOUT WALLS"
aired: March 1995

"Mission without Walls" was a special one-hour television follow-up to Billy Graham's enormously successful "Global Mission" of March 1995. The show aired in the top 200 United States television markets during Easter week, 1995. This nationwide broadcast was part of a larger prime-time airing on the national television networks of 117 other countries. "Mission" featured a mixture of fast-moving documentary segments and was hosted by Grant Goodeve. The total audience for the program was estimated to be 1 billion, or fully one-fifth of the world's population. Two highlights of the broadcast were a performance by singer-songwriter Twila Paris of the crusade's theme song, "The Time Is Now," and a personal testimony by San Antonio Spurs basketball team center David Robinson. The program was also shown in a special Spanish-language version on the Telemundo Network.

See also Billy Graham Evangelistic Association; "Global Mission"

SOURCES

"Now!" *Religious Broadcasting*, June, 1995.

W. STANLEY MOONEYHAM
born: January 14, 1926, Houston, Mississippi
died: June 3, 1991, Los Angeles, California

Walter Stanley Mooneyham was best known as the president of World Vision International, a nondenominational Christian aid organization that supports evangelical Christian missions and provides basic medical and humanitarian assistance to the poor and orphaned worldwide. During Mooneyham's tenure as president,

World Vision produced and aired a number of successful television fundraising specials that dramatized the suffering of Third World peoples.

Mooneyham grew up in Mississippi, the son of Walter Scott Mooneyham and Mary Sullivan. Following his service in the United States Navy during World War II, he married La Verda M. Green. Mooneyham then attended Oklahoma Baptist University and graduated with a bachelor of science degree in 1950. He was ordained as a Baptist minister in 1947 and served as the pastor of First Free Will Baptist Church in Sulphur, Oklahoma, from 1949 to 1953, before becoming executive secretary of the National Association of Free Will Baptists. Mooneyham served in this capacity in the association's Nashville, Tennessee, headquarters from 1953 to 1959. He then took a position as director of information for the National Association of Evangelicals (NAE) in Wheaton, Illinois. As part of his duties, Mooneyham edited the periodical *United Evangelical Action* from 1959 to 1964. He became the interim executive director of NAE in 1964. During this same year, Mooneyham became a special assistant to evangelist Billy Graham. As vice president for international relations for Billy Graham, Mooneyham helped plan the 1966 World Congress on Evangelism in Berlin and the 1968 Asia–South Pacific Congress on Evangelism in Singapore.

In the wake of founder Bob Pierce's failing health, Mooneyham took over as president of World Vision in 1969. The humanitarian outreach of the agency had expanded to include Latin America as well as Asia during the 1960s, and now, under Mooneyham's leadership, World Vision began airing syndicated television specials in Canada and the United States. The fundraising programs, which were hosted by leading celebrities, generally aired late at night or on weekends. They included such titles as "Let the Children Live," "Women in Crisis," and "Children between Life and Death." The impact of these riveting documentaries was spectacular. By 1982, World Vision's budget had increased from $7 million to more than $158 million and its staff had more than tripled. The organization expanded its humanitarian outreach—especially to children—and continued to organize pastors' conferences and assist in world evangelism through its research department.

In the early 1970s, Mooneyham led a relief convoy into Cambodia and later gained permission to conduct the first public evangelistic campaign in that country. In 1978, the evangelist played a key role in rescue efforts that saved more than 100 Vietnamese boat people who had been stranded in the South China Sea. During this same year, Mooneyham and Ted W. Engstrom reorganized World Vision into an international partnership with one central office coordinating field and fundraising offices. The partnership's headquarters was located in Monrovia, California.

In 1979, Mooneyham cofounded the Evangelical Council for Financial Accountability (ECFA). This council promoted voluntary financial disclosure according to uniform standards among evangelical agencies. The impetus behind Mooneyham's efforts came from Senator Mark Hatfield, who reported to a group of evangelical leaders in 1977 that Congress would pass legislation regulating religious broadcasting if the industry did not take steps to regulate itself. One such bill had already been introduced by Congressman Charles Wilson of Texas. The bill would have required religious broadcasters to disclose financial information "at the point of solicitation."

To avoid further legislation, representatives from 32 evangelical groups met in Chicago in December 1977 to discuss ways the industry could become self-policing. Thomas Getman, Hatfield's chief legislative assistant, impressed upon the group that "legislation is not important; disclosure is." He admonished the representatives to create "a voluntary disclosure program . . . that will preclude the necessity of federal intervention into the philanthropic and religious sector." Mooneyham later acknowledged that the threat of governmental controls had galvanized evangelists into action. "There is no denying that this threat of governmental action was one of the stimuli." Among ECFA's 115 charter members were Jerry Falwell's Thomas Road Baptist Church and related ministries, the

Billy Graham Evangelistic Association, Bill Bright's Campus Crusade for Christ, and World Vision International. Falwell's ministry, however, was the only regular television ministry among ECFA's charter group.

Mooneyham stepped down as president of World Vision in 1982 and assumed the pastorship of Palm Desert Community Presbyterian Church in Palm Desert, California. The international presidency of World Vision passed to Tom Houston in 1984. In 1987, Robert Seiple and Don Scott took over the leadership of the organization's United States and Canadian offices, respectively. World Vision continues to air its television specials and to raise money for international humanitarian outreach. By the late 1980s, more than 500,000 children and families were being cared for in 4,500 projects worldwide. The organization employed over 4,000 staff in 60 offices.

Mooneyham served as pastor of Palm Desert Presbyterian and as chairman of the Global Aid Foundation (which aided Kurdish refugees) until his death of kidney failure at the age of 65. Mooneyham was survived by his second wife, Nancy, his first wife, and four children. In an obituary in *Christianity Today*, Seiple stated, "Stan's impact on World Vision was immeasurable. Much of our significant growth, especially through television, came under his leadership. Additionally, the energy he gave to the Vietnamese boat people through Operation Seasweep stands as one of the pillars of World Vision folklore."

Mooneyham was the author of numerous books, including *What Do You Say to a Hungry World?* (1978), *Come Walk the World* (1978), *China: A New Day* (1979), *Sea of Heartbreak* (1980), and *Dancing on the Strait and Narrow* (1989). He was awarded a doctor of laws degree by Seattle Pacific University in 1978.

SOURCES

Contemporary Authors. Vol. 6. New Revision Series. Detroit: Gale Research, 1982.

Erickson, Hal. *Religious Radio and Television in the United States, 1921–1991*. Jefferson, NC: McFarland, 1992.

Hadden, Jeffrey K. *Prime Time Preachers: The Rising Power of Televangelism*. Reading, MA: Addison-Wesley, 1981.

Mooneyham, Stanley. *China: A New Day*. Plainfield, TX: Logos International, 1979.

———. *Come Walk the World*. Waco, TX: Word Books, 1978.

———. *Dancing on the Strait and Narrow: A Gentle Call to a Radical Faith*. San Francisco: Harper & Row, 1989.

———. *Is There Life before Death?* Ventura, CA: Regal Books, 1985.

———. *Sea of Heartbreak*. Plainfield, TX: Logos International, 1980.

———. *Traveling Hopefully*. Waco, TX: Word Books, 1984.

———. *What Do You Say to a Hungry World?* Waco: Word Books, 1978.

Mooneyham W. Stanley, ed. *Christ Seeks Asia*. Hong Kong: Rock House, 1969.

———. *The Dynamics of Christian Unity: A Symposium on the Ecumenical Movement*. Grand Rapids, MI: Zondervan, 1963.

———. *One Race, One Gospel, One Task*. Minneapolis, MN: Worldwide Books, 1967.

Reid, Daniel G., et al., eds. *Dictionary of Christianity in America*. Downers Grove, IL: InterVarsity Press, 1990.

"Stan Mooneyham." *Christianity Today*, July 22, 1991.

MORMON TABERNACLE CHOIR
see: Richard Evans

MORNINGSTAR RADIO NETWORK
established: 1992

Morningstar Radio Network, based in Nashville, Tennessee, is a fast-growing Christian music source that offers two format choices to affiliated stations. The first format is reflected in the program *Today's Christian Music*, which features adult contemporary music by Christian artists. The second available format is *High Country*, which combines both Christian and "positive" country music. The network was being heard over 120 stations nationwide by May 1995. It provides its music via CD-quality satellite transmission and offers digital addressability, which allows local stations to reinforce their identity by using their call letters up to 13 times per hour.

HENRY MORRIS
born: October 6, 1918, Dallas, Texas

Creation Science apologist and director of the Institute for Creation Research, Henry Madison Morris, Jr., is the son of Henry Morris, Sr., and Ida Hunter. The younger Morris graduated from Rice University in 1939 with a degree in engineering. Following graduation he became an engineer with the Texas Highway Department and worked as a civil engineer in various positions before returning to Rice University in 1942 as an instructor of engineering. Morris held this position until 1946, when he moved to Minneapolis to take a position as instructor and, later, as assistant professor of engineering at the University of Minnesota. Less than a year after completing his doctorate in hydraulics at the University of Minnesota in 1950, Morris took a position as professor and head of the department of civil engineering at the University of Southwestern Louisiana, remaining there from 1951 to 1956. After a one-year sabbatical at Southern Illinois University, Morris was hired as professor of hydraulics at Virginia Polytechnic Institute, a position he held from 1957 to 1970.

Morris's apologetic interest in "creation science," a term he coined, took hold while he was a young engineer in the early 1940s. He wrote his first apologetic work, *That You Might Believe*, in 1946. There soon followed his two most popular apologetic works, *The Bible and Modern Science* (1951) and *The Genesis Flood* (1961), both of which are still in print. Other books written during this period include *The Twilight of Evolution* (1963), *Science, Scripture, and Salvation* (1965), and *Evolution and the Modern Christian* (1968). From 1967 to 1973, Morris served as president of the Creation Research Society, an apologetics organization of which he has been a member since 1963.

Gaining the notice of leaders within Protestant fundamentalist circles for his many books attacking evolution and modern science, Morris became a close associate of Tim LaHaye. In 1970, Morris and LaHaye founded Christian Heritage College (CHC) in San Diego, where Morris taught as professor of apologetics until 1980. He served a two-year term as president of CHC, relinquishing his duties in 1980 when he became president of the Institute for Creation Research (ICR) in El Cajon, California.

As president of ICR, Morris oversees its various research activities and educational services, the most important of which are its radio broadcasts. The two main programs of the ICR are *Back to Genesis*, a daily one-minute radio spot, and *Science, Scripture, and Salvation*, a weekly 15-minute program. Both programs are hosted by Morris and focus almost exclusively on the battle between creationism and evolution. Morris believes strongly in the inerrancy of the Bible and teaches that its record of a literal six-day creation can be demonstrated scientifically. This conviction has become an evangelistic tool which he has used with some measure of success.

Since 1970, Morris has authored a great many other apologetic books, including *Scientific Creationism* (1974), *The Battle for Creation* (1976), *The Scientific Case for Creation* (1977), and, more recently, *Biblical Creationism* (1993). All but the last of these works, which was published by Baker Books, were published by ICR's Creation-Life Publishers.

SOURCES

The Directory of Religious Organizations in the United States. 2d ed. Falls Church, VA: McGrath, 1982.

Melton, J. Gordon. *Directory of Religious Organizations in the United States.* 3d ed. Detroit: Gale Research, 1993.

Morris, Henry. *The Bible and Modern Science.* Chicago: Moody Press, 1951.

———. *Biblical Creationism.* Grand Rapids, MI: Baker Book House, 1993.

———. *The Genesis Record.* Grand Rapids, MI: Baker Book House, 1976.

MOTHER ANGELICA
born: 1923, Canton, Ohio

Courtesy: National Religious Broadcasters

The best-known personality in Catholic broadcasting today is Mother Angelica, a Franciscan nun who founded the Eternal Word Television Network (EWTN) in 1981. Her no-frills, straight-talking program, *Mother Angelica Live*, is broadcast to millions of avid Catholic and Protestant viewers around the world. EWTN is now the largest religious television network in the United States.

Mother Angelica began life as Rita Antoinette Rizzo. She was reared in poverty in a Canton, Ohio, slum and endured social ostracization because of her parents' divorce. The shy, lonely girl was forced to work full-time at the age of 11 and was plagued by severe abdominal pains. Her life began to change when, after being healed by the reputed stigmatist Rhoda Wise, she joined the Franciscan order in Cleveland. By 1946, "Sister Angelica" was back in Canton helping to found the Sancta Clara monastery. While scrubbing a floor, she suffered a severe leg injury. The young nun promised God that she would open a monastery in the deep South if her leg was healed. When she subsequently recovered from the injury, she followed through on her

pledge and founded Our Lady of the Angels Monastery in 1961 on the eastern flanks of Shades Crest mountain near Birmingham, Alabama.

The new convent struggled to survive in the inhospitable Protestant culture of 1960s Alabama. Despite mounting debts and a lack of local support, "Mother Angelica," as she was now called, and her small group of nuns hawked everything from fishing lures to peanuts to raise funds, eventually establishing themselves on a more secure financial footing. Her experiences in overcoming adversity led her to write several books advocating her peculiar brand of self-help and positive-thinking philosophy. To publish the books, the monastery was forced to purchase its own printing press because it had exhausted the funds set aside for outside printing. After mastering the press's operation, the sisters gradually increased their output of publications. By 1986, they were producing 20,000 items per day.

Mother Angelica's books made her a nationally recognized figure and led to her first foray into the world of religious television. This occurred in 1978 when she was interviewed on a Chicago UHF religious channel, WCFC-TV. Struck by the medium's potential for spreading her message, Mother Angelica decided to tape a series of talks and to air them on Pat Robertson's Christian Broadcasting Network. These first programs garnered favorable reviews and the diminutive nun soon became a regular guest on Jim Bakker's PTL network broadcasts. The novelty of having an old-fashioned Catholic nun appearing on an up-tempo Pentecostal telecast increased the network's viewership across both secular and sectarian lines.

In August 1981, after the Birmingham station where she taped her programs broadcast a film she considered blasphemous, Mother Angelica established the Eternal Word Television Network. As she recalled, "I told [them] I wouldn't do any more broadcasts at his station, that I'd build my own station." Undeterred at finding herself suddenly without broadcast facilities, the nun set up shop in the monastery's garage. This series of events led to the decision to create an independent television service.

EWTN was the first denominational cable-television service to receive a license from the Federal Communications Commission. Silvio Cardinal Oddi, Prefect of the Congregation for the Clergy, came from Rome to Birmingham to bless what he termed "the satellite dish through which the Eternal Word is projected from ocean to ocean." The station used secondhand equipment during its first years of operation but by 1986 had a state-of-the-art broadcasting studio. The service's programming was transmitted on the Westar III satellite until the mid-1980s, when it occupied a position on Satcom IIIR's Transponder 18.

From an initial broadcasting period of four hours every evening, seven days a week, EWTN expanded to 24 hours of daily programming by 1990. Sixty percent of the network's programming is produced in-house by a staff of 95, including the popular show *Mother Angelica Live*. This program features Mother Angelica's straightforward talks on matters of faith and morals and her probing interviews with special guests. The nun's television presence is down to earth, homespun, and friendly, yet with the "mildly intimidating manner of a maiden aunt who won't stand any nonsense," as one reviewer observed. She wears the brown habit and oversized crucifix of her religious order and makes no effort to disguise the leg brace that is the last vestige of an old spinal condition. Each show begins with her trademark greeting, "Let's get on with it!"

After the Catholic Church's initial ambivalence about supporting Mother Angelica's television outreach—probably related to her low opinion of some of the church's bishops and her pre-Vatican II sympathies—the mainstream National Catholic Association for Broadcasters awarded the nun its prestigious Gabriel award for broadcasting excellence.

Mother Angelica continues to build a huge international audience—often by advising viewers to pester cable companies with a stream of calls—and to deal successfully with the considerable financial and technological challenges of religious broadcasting in the 1990s. Her network was reaching an estimated 38 million households in 1995 and was taking in more than

$13 million in annual contributions. Eternal Word television is seen in 42 countries, including, since August 1995, 24-hour coverage in Central and South America, Africa, and Europe.

The story of Mother Angelica resonates with the classic American virtues of hard work, perseverance, personal initiative, and optimism.

See also Eternal Word Television Network

SOURCES

Elvy, Peter. *Buying Time: The Foundations of the Electronic Church.* Mystic, CT: Twenty-Third Publications, 1987.

Erickson, Hal. *Religious Radio and Television in the United States, 1921–1991.* Jefferson, NC: McFarland, 1992.

"Eternal Word Television Network." World Wide Web site. http://www.ewtn.com (December 1995).

"Mother Angelica: Nun Better." *Christianity Today,* October 2, 1995.

W. DEEN MUHAMMAD
born: October 30, 1933, Hamtrack, Michigan

Warith Deen Muhammad is the son of and successor to Elijah Muhammad, who built the Nation of Islam into a national religious organization serving African Americans. Muhammad is also a religious broadcaster of note, having hosted programs representing Muslim viewpoints to African Americans since 1975.

The Nation of Islam became well known in the 1960s for its sectarian form of Islamic teachings and its racially exclusive policies. Following Elijah Muhammad's death in 1975, Wallace (he'd later change his name to Warith) began to move the organization gradually toward Orthodox Islam. He changed the Nation's name to the World Community of Al-Islam in the West and then to the American Muslim Mission. These changes soon led to a break with Louis Farrakhan, a leading Muslim minister, who reorganized his following, restoring its name to the Nation of Islam, and assumed the program and beliefs that had been in place during Elijah Muhammad's lifetime.

Over the next few years, Wallace Muhammad asked members to reject any names with a slavery heritage (i.e., white Christian names) and to adopt in their place Muslim or African names. Muhammad himself changed his name from Wallace to Warith, though he is generally referred to as W. Deen Muhammad. In 1984, Muhammad demoted himself as leader, a precursor to his disbanding of the American Muslim Mission altogether in 1985. The disbanding of the mission was symbolic of the African American Muslim community's integration into the larger Orthodox Muslim world and of W. Deen Muhammad's position of leadership of note among American Muslim spokespersons. Muhammad's quiet style has disguised his importance as the leading minister among the largest segment of African American Muslims, especially in face of the continued controversy which surrounds Louis Farrakhan.

In reorganizing the Black Muslims, Muhammad established himself as the imam of a large mosque in Chicago. He continued to publish a weekly tabloid, *The Muslim Journal*, and took over the radio broadcasts for the Nation of Islam that had been hosted by Minister Farrakhan from 1965 to 1975.

The radio ministry, *Imam W. Deen Muhammad Speaks*, was airing on over 70 stations by the early 1980s, with the station and timing of the programs being arranged by believers in specific locales. The program was heard in Bermuda, Trinidad, and Belize in Central America in addition to stations in the United States. The show's format was similar to that of Christian radio programming, with a single speaker sharing his thoughts with the audience.

By 1995, the twentieth year of his leadership in the Muslim community, Muhammad's radio show was being heard on over 60 stations across the United States, primarily (though by no means exclusively) those stations targeting the African American community. Among these stations is WLAC in Nashville, whose broadcasting range covers 28 states.

Muhammad has recently begun to expand his broadcast ministry with a few television specials. The fall 1995 special "Imam W. Deen Muhammad and Guests" was aired by 23 cable stations and picked up by CTN of New Jersey, which fed it to an additional 34 cable stations.

SOURCES

Hill, George H. *Airwaves to the Soul: The Influence and Growth of Religious Broadcasting in America*. Saratoga, CA: R & E, 1983.

Murphy, Larry G., J. Gordon Melton, and Gary L. Ward. *Encyclopedia of African American Religion*. New York: Garland, 1993.

JAMES DeFOREST MURCH
born: 1886
died: 1973

A longtime editor of *United Evangelical Action*, the news magazine of the National Association of Evangelicals (NAE), and vehement opponent of the National Council of Churches, James DeForest Murch was among the founders and charter members of National Religious Broadcasters (NRB) in 1944.

Desiring to declare independence from the meddling of the Federal (later National) Council of Churches, Murch, who hosted the radio program *The Christian's Hour*, and his associates convened a special meeting of the NAE with the purpose of forming a self-monitoring association of religious broadcasters who would vow to follow a strict code of broadcast ethics. The guidelines of the newly formed National Religious Broadcasters included four statements: (1) that all broadcasts be nonprofit and for the purposes of spreading the gospel; (2) that the content of the programs be positive and constructive; (3) that the content and presentation of religious programs, including music, be consistent with federal, state, and local broadcast laws and standards; and (4) that appeals for money be for genuine ministry purposes and that receipts be issued to broadcast donors. Murch remained in close association with the NRB for the remainder of his life, serving a brief term as its president from 1956 to 1957.

Apart from his broadcast interests, Murch also was influential in developing the strength of the new evangelicalism during the 1950s and 1960s and giving it a strong anti-liberal voice. For instance, he strenuously opposed the founding of the World Council of Churches in 1948 on the grounds that it would result in a "superchurch," forcing independent Christian churches to conform to its dictates or perish. Moreover, Murch openly opposed the publication and use of the Revised Standard Version of the Bible in 1952, primarily because of its sponsorship by the National Council of Churches.

See also National Religious Broadcasters

SOURCES

Gasper, Louis. *The Fundamentalist Movement: 1930–1956*. Grand Rapids, MI: Baker Book House, 1981 [1963].

Murch, James DeForest. *Cooperation without Compromise: A History of the National Association of Evangelicals*. Grand Rapids, MI: Eerdmans, 1956.

Roy, Ralph L. *Apostles of Discord*. Boston: Beacon Press, 1953.

Ward, Mark, Sr. *Air of Salvation: The Story of Christian Broadcasting*. Grand Rapids, MI: Baker Book House, 1994.

MUSIC 'TIL DAWN
first aired: 1995

A recent arrival on late night religious radio is *Music 'Til Dawn*, broadcasting Christian hymns and inspirational songs available via satellite on Spacenet 3, Transponder 13. As of early 1995, the music program was airing daily between 11 PM and 5 AM CST. Each program is built around a particular devotional theme that brings out an aspect of the Christian path. *Music 'Til Dawn* is a production of VCY America, a Christian programming service that had its origins in a Milwaukee, Wisconsin, Youth for Christ ministry. The show is hosted by the Reverend Victor Eliason, a nondenominational evangelical broadcasting personality who is best known for his daily *Crosstalk* call-in program.

See also Vic Eliason

PAUL MYERS
born: 1896
died: 1973; Los Angeles, California

Paul Myers was the beloved "First Mate Bob" on the popular Sunday radio program *Haven of Rest* between 1934 and 1973.

Myers grew up as a radio performer and worked at the Hal Roach Studios in Hollywood as a musician. His talents could be heard in the background music for the studio's *Our Gang* and *Laurel and Hardy* comedies. Myers also became a celebrated radio orchestra leader during this period with his band of six men called the "Hal Roach Happy-Go-Luckies." During the 1920s, however, Myers succumbed to alcoholism and eventually found himself living on skid row, bereft of family and friends.

In February 1934, Myers was awakened from a drunken stupor near San Diego harbor by the sound of a ship's bell. Myers understood that the bell was sounding God's call to a life of Christian witness. He made his way to a dingy motel, began reading a Gideon Bible, and accepted Christ as his personal Savior. Within a month, Myers had resuscitated his career, made peace with his family, and begun hosting a new radio ministry, *Haven of Rest*, on Beverly Hills radio station KMPC. "First Mate Bob and the crew of the good ship Grace coming from the harbor called Haven of Rest" would soon become a national network broadcast. By the late 1970s, *Haven of Rest* was being heard 1,240 times a week on over 200 stations worldwide.

Haven of Rest was filled with shipboard imagery and motifs. It began with a ship's boatswain whistle and the tolling of eight bells. Next came a male quartet who sang, "I've anchored my soul in the haven of rest" with a pipe organ playing in the background. A friendly voice then exclaimed, "Ahoy, there, shipmate! Eight bells and all's well." Myers's listeners were referred to as "shipmates," and Myers himself was "First Mate Bob." In addition to Myers's sermons and songs, various "second mates" came aboard over the years as guest speakers. The half-hour show ended with the ringing of ship's bells and a whistle that called the shipmates back to shore. Finally, a voice intoned, "All's well."

Myers was instrumental in the founding of Bob Pierce's World Vision and Robert Bowman's Far East Broadcasting Company. Both men began their careers with Myers and were encouraged by him to inaugurate innovative international teaching and service ministries. Following his death January 28, 1973, Myers was inducted into the Religious Broadcasters Hall of Fame. *Haven of Rest* has continued broadcasting into the 1990s under the leadership of Ray Ortlund and host Carl Lawrence. The show has dropped its shipboard motif and adopted a conventional sermon format.

See also National Religious Broadcasters

SOURCES

Armstrong, Ben. *The Electric Church*. Nashville: Thomas Nelson, 1979.

Erickson, Hal. *Religious Radio and Television in the United States, 1921–1991*. Jefferson, NC: McFarland, 1992.

Ward, Mark, Sr. *Air of Salvation: The Story of Christian Broadcasting*. Manassas, VA: National Religious Broadcasters, 1994.

nguages. Moreover, the Narramore
Foundation still claims a membership
0,000 faithful supporters.

SOURCES

y of *Religious Organizations in the United*
2d ed. Falls Church, VA: McGrath, 1982.

ordon. *Directory of Religious Organiza-
the United States.* 3d ed. Detroit: Gale
ch, 1993.

Clyde M. *Why a Psychologist Believes the*
Rosemead, CA: Narramore Christian
tion, 1989.

NAL FEDERATION OF TEMPLE BROTHERHOODS
established: 1923

nal Federation of Temple Brother-
FTB), founded in New York City in
division of the Union of American
Congregations, whose aim is to ad-
interests of Reform Judaism and to
erfaith dialog and understanding.
FTB's community outreach activities
eships, study courses, and television
programs that highlight such aspects
life as holidays and ritual observances.
ints among its membership 75,000 lay
s. The ministry maintains close ties
ster" organization, the National Fed-
f Temple Sisterhoods (founded in
hich has a membership of 110,000

SOURCES

Gordon. *Directory of Religious Organiza-
in the United States.* 3d ed. Detroit: Gale
rch, 1993.

ATIONAL RADIO PULPIT

see: Samuel Parkes Cadman;
Ralph Washington Sockman

NATIONAL RELIGIOUS BROADCASTERS
established: 1944

The National Religious Broadcasters (NRB) is
an association of more than 800 organizations
that produce religious radio and television programming or operate stations that carry predominantly religious fare. The members of the
association produce an estimated 75 percent of
all religious broadcasting in the United States.
NRB's current headquarters are in Manassas,
Virginia. Its 1996 Executive Committee includes E. Brandt Gustavson (president),
Michael Glenn (vice president), Robert Straton
(chairman), Stuart Epperson (first vice chairman), Jon Campbell (second vice chairman),
Tom Rogeberg (secretary), Mike Trout (treasurer), and David Clark, Sue Bahner, Glenn
Plummer, Paul Ramseyer, and Jerry Rose
(members-at-large).

NRB emerged in the early 1940s out of the
growing rift between conservative evangelicals
and the Christian mainstream as represented by
the Federal Council of Churches. It was during
this period that conservative evangelicals, led
by the head of the New England Fellowship of
Evangelicals, J. Elwin Wright, decided to form
a national organization to promote the interests
of independent fundamentalists and conservative denominations. A major factor in the subsequent establishment of the National Association of Evangelicals (NAE) in 1942 was the
desire of ministers like Wright and Charles
Fuller to protect evangelical radio ministries,
which were clearly bringing people into the
pews of conservative churches.

The specific threat to conservative religious
programming came from the Institute of Education by Radio, which had been formed in 1941
by an independent group of academics to monitor religious radio ministries. Its recommendations held considerable weight with the Federal Council of Churches and the big radio networks. The institute's first set of recommendations had sharply criticized Fuller's *Old Fashioned Revival Hour* and made radio network

riety of l
Christian
of some 3

N

The Directo
    States
Melton, J. (
    tions
    Resea
Narramore
    Bible
    Foun

CLYDE M. NARRAMORE
born: 1916

Courtesy: Narramore Christian Foundation

One of the pioneers of Christian radio psychology, Clyde M. Narramore, who received his doctorate in psychology from Columbia University, got his start in radio work at the urging of M. R. DeHaan and Charles Fuller. Both of these popular radio preachers recognized the need for a licensed psychologist to speak professionally to the problems of Christian lay people.

During 1950 and 1951, Narramore and his wife bought their own recording equipment and began taping a radio program, later known as *Psychology for Living*, in their home in Pasadena, California. In 1958, Narramore decided

to expand his minis
programs and peri(
quit his position as
Angeles County Sul
formally establishe
Foundation. In addi
broadcasts, Narram(
nars and retreats. H(
distribute a number
various marriage a
Narramore added ar
vice to his ministry.

With the success of
Narramore founded
School of Psycholog
of the new school w
chologists for both re
In 1975, under the de
chologist Bruce Narr
American Psycholog
tation. The school w
versity in 1977.

The only Christian
the time, Narramore v
ing the 1960s and into
the rise of James D
1980s, Narramore's
television began to d
ing off of listener
Narramore's influenc(
ever. Indeed, includir
has been on the air alr
years, reading letters
tions of Christians and
out the United States. I
30 books, many transl

NATIO

The Nat
hoods (1
1923, is
Hebrew
vance th
foster ir
Among I
are lectu
and radi(
of Jewisł
NFTB cc
supporte
to its "s
eration
1913), v
women.

Melton, J
    tion
    Res(

executives nervous about carrying commercial religious programming.

Representatives of fundamentalist churches, conservative denominations, and evangelical radio ministries met in St. Louis in April 1942 and elected the popular radio preacher J. Harold Ockenga of Park Street Church in Boston as the first president of the NAE. At a second meeting, the association decided to create a committee that would research the plausibility of a distinct organization devoted solely to the promotion and protection of religious broadcasting. Over 150 radio ministries were invited to a meeting organized by this committee in April 1944 in Columbus, Ohio.

The participants at the meeting agreed that a special organization was needed to work with secular institutions to protect the rights of radio broadcasters. They selected a name for this organization, National Religious Broadcasters, and adopted a faith statement attesting to the divine inspiration of the Bible. The assembly also set about the task of drafting a constitution, a code of ethics, and a set of bylaws. William Ward Ayer, a popular New York City radio preacher and pastor of Calvary Baptist Church, was selected as temporary chairman and Dale Crowley was chosen to serve as temporary secretary.

By September 21, a committee headed by *Christian Hour*'s James DeForest Murch was ready to present a draft constitution to an NRB convention held at Moody Memorial Church in Chicago. The convention adopted the draft constitution and incorporated NRB as the "official broadcasting arm of the National Association of Evangelicals." There were 50 member organizations during this founding period. There are more than 800 today.

The constitution's foreword, a portion of which follows, clearly articulates the collective identity of NRB's member organizations:

> A corporation of doctrinally evangelical individuals concerned for the spread of the Gospel of our Lord and Savior Jesus Christ . . . banded together for the sake of strength which comes from numbers united in a common cause. Thus united, the religious broadcasters feel they can contribute to the improvement of religious broadcasts, better serve the interest of Christian people, and more effectively minister to the spiritual welfare of this nation.

The constitution's code of ethics was the brainchild of William Ward Ayer and Rosel Hyde, the chief counsel (at the time) of the Federal Communications Commission. The code obligated members to maintain the highest technical standards for their programming, to comply with all government regulations, and to conduct their financial affairs within strict canons of accountability. This code was a significant step in establishing subsequent religious broadcasting ministries on a sound financial and doctrinal foundation. It also led to a raising of technical standards throughout the industry and to greatly improved programming quality.

NRB's first executive committee reads like a who's who of conservative evangelicals. Among its members were James DeForest Murch; the president of Barrington College, Howard W. Ferrin; broadcaster Glenn V. Tingley of *Radio Revival* fame; Assemblies of God General Superintendent Thomas F. Zimmerman; *Light and Life Hour* speaker Myron F. Boyd; the founder of Youth for Christ, Torrey M. Johnson; *Haven of Rest*'s Paul Myers; Bob Jones University founder Bob Jones, Sr.; *Faith Gospel Broadcast*'s Charles Leaming; and John Zoller. The convention also selected William Ward Ayer as NRB's first president, Clinton H. Churchill of radio station WKBW, Buffalo, New York, as vice president, David J. Fant as treasurer, and Dale Crowley as secretary.

NRB continues to encourage high standards of financial accountability and technical production through awards, workshops, and periodicals. Among the winners of NRB's prestigious Award of Merit are Billy Graham (for his *Hour of Decision*), Charles Fuller (for the *Old Fashioned Revival Hour*), C. M. Ward (for *Revivaltime*), Oswald Hoffman (for his service to *The Lutheran Hour*), Pat Robertson (for his Christian Broadcasting Network), Richard DeHaan (for both *Radio Bible Class* and *Day of Discovery*)and Theodore Epp (for *Back to the Bible*).

Members of the NRB Hall of Fame, which was instituted in 1975, include William Ward Ayer, Donald Grey Barnhouse, Eugene Bertermann, Myron Boyd, R. R. Brown, Lois Crawford, Percy Crawford, Richard DeHaan, James Dobson, Theodore Epp, Jerry Falwell, Charles Fuller, Herman Gockel, Billy Graham, Rex Humbard, Clarence Jones, Walter Maier, J. Vernon McGee, Paul Myers, George Palmer, Bill Pearce, Paul Rader, Pat Robertson, Lester Roloff, Charles Stanley, C. M. Ward, Thomas Zimmerman, and John Zoller.

During the 1980s and 1990s, the NRB has become more involved in the politics of the Christian Religious Right. It relocated its head-quarters to the Washington, DC, area and hired Mark Gorman of Gorman Consulting to help develop a grassroots program to affect public broadcasting policy. The other participants in this new program are Stuart Epperson, chair of NRB's Public Policy Action Committee, and committee members Jerry Rose and Mike Trout. To gain an insider's expertise, NRB has hired Richard E. Wiley as its general counsel. Wiley is a former chairman of the Federal Communications Commission.

In early 1995, members of NRB's executive committee visited various senators in Washington, DC, and interviewed Republican presidential candidates Richard Lugar, Phil Gramm, and Pat Buchanan to get their views on issues affecting Christian broadcasting. The NRB also plans to sponsor a bipartisan dialogue in fall 1996, where presidential candidates and other Washington players could discuss a broad range of moral, ethical, and political issues that are of interest to the organization.

See also Appendices A, B, and C

SOURCES

Armstrong, Ben. *The Electric Church*. Nashville: Thomas Nelson, 1979.

Murch, James DeForest. *Cooperation without Compromise*. Grand Rapids, MI: Eerdmans, 1956.

National Religious Broadcasters. Constitution of National Religious Broadcasters. Morristown, NJ: National Religious Broadcasters.

Ward, Mark, Sr. *Air of Salvation: The Story of Christian Broadcasting*. Manassas, VA: National Religious Broadcasters, 1994.

NATIONAL UNION FOR SOCIAL JUSTICE
see: Charles Coughlin

NATIONAL VESPERS
see: Harry Emerson Fosdick

THE NATION'S FAMILY PRAYER PERIOD
see: E. Howard Cadle

NEW ENGLAND FELLOWSHIP RADIO MINISTRY
see: The Radio Ensemble

NEW LIFE LEAGUE
established: 1954

Founded in 1954, with headquarters in Waco, Texas, the New Life League (NLL) is an independent interdenominational missionary distribution organization with contacts in 16 countries throughout the world. Among NLL's ministry emphases are the distribution of religious literature and the establishment of new churches. The NLL also provides education, medical assistance, and social relief through its mission stations, and makes broad use of radio broadcasts for evangelism and teaching.

SOURCES

Melton, J. Gordon. *Directory of Religious Organizations in the United States*. 3d ed. Detroit: Gale Research, 1993.

NEWSTALK
first aired: 1973

Newstalk is a daily hour-long nondenominational radio program produced by Probe Ministries. The show seeks to present non-sectarian Christian views on current events and on pressing social and religious issues. Founded in 1973, with headquarters in the Dallas suburb of Richardson, Texas, Probe Ministries also produces a five-minute radio news update program, called *Probe,* which airs over some 200 stations nationwide. The ministry describes itself as a body of Christian scholars who promote a Christian world view by critiquing contemporary culture and presenting balanced, Bible-based information.

SOURCES

Melton, J. Gordon. *Directory of Religious Organizations in the United States.* 3d ed. Detroit: Gale Research, 1993.

NO COMPROMISE WITH STEVE CAMP
first aired: August 1995

In August of 1995, Grammy Award-winning songwriter Steve Camp became the first contemporary Christian artist to inaugurate his own nationally syndicated live call-in radio ministry. The program, *No Compromise with Steve Camp*, airs Sundays on the Salem Radio Network.

J. FRANK NORRIS
born: September 18, 1877, Dadeville, Alabama
died: August 8, 1952, Keystone Heights, Florida

J. Frank Norris was one of the first Baptist preachers to exploit radio's potential to reach large numbers of people with a religious message. The nature of that message, in Norris's case, was a radical Christian Fundamentalism that fervently defended the Bible's inerrancy and took no prisoners in its religious battles. Norris remained an influential radio preacher throughout his career and played a key role in the fundamentalist controversies that split American Protestantism during the first half of the twentieth century.

Norris was born in rural Alabama and reared in abject poverty by his sharecropper parents. After moving his family to Hubbard, Texas, in 1888, Norris's father became involved in a cattle rustling trial as a witness for the prosecution. The convicted thieves exacted their retribution by critically wounding Frank. The boy survived the incident but was confined to a wheelchair during his three years of recovery.

Norris experienced a conversion to Christ while still a teen and decided to enroll in Baylor University as a ministerial student. He refined his pastoral skills in the rural town of Mount Calm and impressed classmates with his self-confidence and ambition to "preach in the greatest church and pulpit in the world!" During his years at Baylor, Norris married Lillian Gaddy, with whom he would have four children.

After graduating from Baylor in 1903, Norris pursued an advanced ministerial degree at Southern Baptist Theological Seminary in Louisville, Kentucky. He graduated with a master's degree two years later and took up his first ministerial post at the faltering McKinney Avenue Baptist Church in Dallas. The energetic young pastor soon began attracting new members, and the church's membership rolls increased from 13 to over 1,000 within three years.

Norris began to make a reputation for himself within the Southern Baptist Convention when he helped B. H. Carroll establish Southwestern Baptist Seminary in Fort Worth, Texas, and bought the *Baptist Standard*, a leading denominational newspaper. Norris's editorship of the paper gave him an opportunity to articulate his ultra-conservative religious views to a wide audience for the first time. He gained public notoriety when he successfully campaigned to end racetrack betting at the Texas State Fair.

In 1909, Norris left the *Standard* and assumed the pastorship of Fort Worth's First Baptist Church. For two years the new pastor tried to accommodate himself to the values and expectations of First Baptist's well-heeled membership. By 1911, however, he abruptly changed his approach and began preaching controversial sermons that took the wealthy to task for their sins. Norris's new combativeness drew large numbers of working-class people to the church and infuriated the upper-crust board of trustees. Before they could fire him, however, Norris dismissed both the trustees and the church deacons, an act that precipitated a mass defection from the congregation.

The controversial pastor set up a tent revival during that same year and began preaching against alcohol, prostitution, and political corruption in Fort Worth's city center. After he began regularly castigating the city's mayor, Norris's tent was cut down by local fire officials. Norris also found himself ostracized by Fort Worth merchants and newspapers. When a fire destroyed his church, Norris lashed out at his critics, accusing them of responsibility for the church's destruction. His critics, for their part, initiated their own investigation of the fire and were able to gather enough evidence to indict Norris on arson charges. When the charges were dropped a month later due to insufficient evidence, Norris emerged from the incident more confident than ever in his fundamentalist crusade.

Over the next 20 years, Norris continued to insert himself into denominational and political controversies. Unhappy with Norris's virulent criticism of other Baptists in the *Baptist Standard*, the Pastors Conference of Fort Worth expelled him from its ranks in 1914. By 1924, the county and state conventions had followed suit, going so far as to disfellowship his entire congregation. Norris began another newspaper, the *Fence Rail* (later called the *Searchlight* and the *Fundamentalist*), in 1917. Although the publication was an embarrassment to denominational leaders because of Norris's tactless and vituperative attacks on his enemies, it quickly garnered a readership of 80,000 and was enormously popular among rank-and-file fundamentalists.

During the early 1920s, Norris became embroiled in a major controversy at Baylor University. The fervent fundamentalist had learned that certain professors on the faculty were teaching the theory of evolution. Rejecting the consensus opinion among Baptist leaders that the matter should be handled as quietly as possible, Norris publicly took the denomination to task for its tardiness in addressing the issue. In the end, he was successful in forcing eight professors to resign.

Norris entered the new field of religious broadcasting in 1924, when he purchased station KFQB and began broadcasting his own sermons and commentaries. Though his programs were transmitted over a relatively limited number of radio stations—about 25—this media exposure made Norris a force to be reckoned with in conservative Protestant circles.

In 1926, Norris, who had become a particularly bitter opponent of Fort Worth's Roman Catholic mayor, M. C. Meacham, going so far as accusing him of rampant misappropriation of city monies, was charged with murder after a supporter of Meacham's was found shot in Norris's study. After the trial venue was changed to Austin, a jury acquitted Norris, claiming he had acted in justifiable self-defense. He was welcomed back to Fort Worth by an enthusiastic throng of 8,000 supporters.

In the 1930s, the difficulties continued for Norris. The magnificent Fort Worth church that had been built on the burned ruins of the congregation's earlier structure itself succumbed to fire in 1929. The rebuilding of the church became an extended ordeal in the wake of the depressed economic conditions nationwide. Norris also reluctantly admitted that his efforts to take over the Southern Baptist Convention had failed. His Fort Worth congregation formally withdrew from the convention in 1930. Undaunted, Norris organized an itinerant Bible school, the Premillennial Baptist Missionary Fellowship, and began to attract other congregations around the country to his fundamentalist views. One such congregation, the Temple Baptist Church of Detroit, hired Norris as its pastor in 1934. Over the next 14 years, Norris commuted between Fort Worth and Detroit by plane and served both congregations at once. He built large memberships in both churches—15,000 in Forth Worth and 10,000 in Detroit—and won the congregations over to his radically conservative political, social, and religious views.

By 1938, Norris had built a large enough national constituency to establish the World Fundamental Baptist Missionary Fellowship (WFBMF). The fellowship committed itself to education, the battle against modernism, and the evangelization of the world. The following year Norris helped organize the organization's flagship seminary, the Baptist Bible Institute, in Fort Worth. He would serve as the seminary's president until 1950. The namesake of the John Birch Society, John Birch, was a graduate of this college.

Norris's influence began to wane in the 1940s, as his bullying style of leadership alienated more and more of the WFBMF's leaders. A large group of the fellowship's pastors broke away from Norris's iron-handed grip and created the Baptist Bible Fellowship. They organized the Baptist Bible College in Springfield, Missouri, and spent the next few years fending off Norris's vicious campaign to discredit them. Norris regrouped with his remaining supporters and renamed his organization the World Baptist Fellowship.

A vocal critic of politicians who did not share his hatred of Communism, Norris took Franklin Roosevelt to task for his appeasement of Stalin at Yalta and scorned Harry Truman for his policy of containment. Following protracted battles with other fundamentalist leaders throughout the 1940s, Norris was dismissed from his pastorate in Detroit and began to decline in health. He died on the morning of August 8, 1952, while attending a youth rally in Florida. The *Fort Worth Star-Telegram* provided a fitting epitaph for Norris in its obituary later that month:

> The new generation may not fully recognize in the death of Rev. J. Frank Norris the passing of an unusual personality and the close of a life in which strife and storm and the exercise of dynamic leadership played the dominant chords. . . . He possessed ambition, and brilliance, and the ability to gather others to his will. The force of his personality was tremendous. . . . He built in beliefs, in numbers, and in stone. The monuments remain.

To those who espoused his views, Norris was a champion of the truth and the "lion of Fundamentalism"; to those of a more moderate theological bent, he was the "religious Joseph McCarthy of his generation."

SOURCES

Entzminger, Louis. *The J. Frank Norris I Have Known for Thirty-Four Years*. Fort Worth, TX: n. d.

Falls, Royce. *A Biography of J. Frank Norris, 1877–1952*. Euless, TX: 1975.

Hughes, Charles Evans, and J. Frank Norris, eds. *New Dealism Exposed: Communism in Baptist Circles, Red Hot Messages*. Fort Worth, TX: Fundamentalist, n. d.

Lippy, Charles H., ed. *Twentieth-Century Shapers of American Popular Religion*. Westport, CT: Greenwood Press, 1989.

Morris, Clovis Gwin. "He Changed Things: The Life and Thought of J. Frank Norris." Ph.D. diss., Texas Tech University, 1973.

Norris, J. Frank. *Infidelity among Southern Baptists Endorsed by Highest Officials: Exposed by J. Frank Norris*. Fort Worth, TX: Bible Baptist Seminary, 1946.

———. *Inside History of First Baptist Church, Fort Worth*. Fort Worth, TX: n. d.

———. "Inside the Cup; or, My 21 Years in Fort Worth." Fort Worth, TX: *Fundamentalist*, 1932.

Norris Papers 1927–1952. Fort Worth, TX: Southwestern Baptist Seminary, n. d.

Pitts, William L., ed. *Texas Baptist History: The Journal of the Texas Baptist Historical Society*. Vol. 1, no. 1. Waco, TX: Baylor University Press, 1981.

Russell, C. Allyn. *Voices of American Fundamentalism: Seven Biographical Studies*. Philadelphia: Westminster Press, 1976.

Tatum, E. Ray. *Conquest or Failure? Biography of J. Frank Norris*. Dallas: Baptist Historical Foundation, 1966.

Toulouse, Mark G. "A Case Study in Schism: J. Frank Norris and the Southern Baptist Convention." *Foundations* 21 (January-March 1981): 32-53.

O

HAROLD OCKENGA
born: July 6, 1905, Chicago, Illinois
died: February 8, 1985, Hamilton, Massachusetts

Courtesy: National Religious Broadcasters

Harold John Ockenga was one of the pioneers of religious broadcasting and a seminal figure in the Reformed Protestant neo-evangelical movement of the 1940s.

The son of Herman Ockenga and Angelina Tetzlaff, Ockenga received his bachelor of theology degree from the Westminster Theological Seminary, Philadelphia, Pennsylvania, in 1930. This school was organized by the conservative Presbyterian theologian J. Gresham Machen, who left Princeton Theological Seminary and the Presbyterian Church USA to form

the fundamentalist Orthodox Presbyterian Church in the early 1930s. Ockenga's first position after graduation was as assistant minister of First Presbyterian Church in Pittsburgh, Pennsylvania. A year later he was ordained as the pastor of Pittsburgh's Breeze Point Presbyterian Church.

Ockenga's star really began to rise, however, after his appointment as pastor of Boston's Park Street Church in 1936. He preached four times a week, inaugurated a popular radio ministry, and began to publish a series of books that brought him a national audience. The works included *These Religious Affections* (1937), *Our Protestant Heritage* (1938), *Have You Met These Women?* (1940), *Everyone that Believeth* (1942), and *The Comfort of God* (1944). Ockenga's fame as a preacher, author, and radio evangelist led to his selection as the first president of the National Association of Evangelicals (NAE) in 1942. This organization was set up in 1941 to serve as an alternative to the Federal Council of Churches. Fundamentalist Christians of the time were dissatisfied with the Federal Council, believing it had lost its evangelical fervor and become too accommodated to the modern world. Out of the NAE would emerge the National Religious Broadcasters, which was incorporated in Chicago on September 21, 1944 as the official broadcasting arm of the National Association of Evangelicals. Ockenga served as NAE's president from 1942 to 1944.

In the late 1940s, Ockenga spearheaded a movement within fundamentalist circles to present Fundamentalism in a warmer and more humane light to the larger Christian world. He called this movement "Neo-Evangelicalism." Neo-Evangelicalism championed the theological rigor of conservative Protestantism but was open to cooperation with liberal Protestants on social initiatives as long as such cooperation did not compromise Neo-Evangelicalism's strict orthodoxy. Ockenga's new approach was articulated in three books, *Our Evangelical Faith* (1946), *The Spirit of the Living God* (1947), and *Faithful in Christ Jesus* (1948).

When the popular radio evangelist Charles Fuller decided to create Fuller Theological Seminary in Pasadena, California, in 1947, he called upon Ockenga to be the seminary's first president. Ockenga hired a first-rate faculty and turned Fuller Theological Seminary into a showcase of Neo-Evangelical thought. Between terms as the seminary's president (1947–54; 1959–63) Ockenga assumed the chairmanship of the neo-evangelical magazine *Christianity Today* in 1956. Upon his retirement from Park Street Church in 1969, the tireless evangelical was chosen as president of Gordon-Conwell Theological Seminary in Hamilton, Massachusetts, and Gordon College, in Wenham, Massachusetts.

See also Charles Fuller

SOURCES

Armstrong, Ben. *The Electric Church*. Nashville: Thomas Nelson, 1979.

Frame, Randy. "Modern Evangelicalism Mourns the Loss of One of Its Founding Fathers." *Christianity Today* 29, no. 5 (March 1985): 34–36.

Ockenga, Harold J. *Faithful in Jesus Christ*. New York: Fleming H. Revell, 1948.

———. *Our Evangelical Faith*. New York: Fleming H. Revell, 1946.

———. *Our Protestant Heritage*. Grand Rapids, MI: Zondervan, 1938.

———. *The Spirit of the Living God*. New York: Fleming H. Revell, 1947.

———. *These Religious Affections*. Grand Rapids, MI: Zondervan, 1937.

LLOYD OGILVIE
born: September 2, 1930, Kenosha, Wisconsin

Lloyd John Ogilvie was a prominent Presbyterian televangelist and radio broadcaster during the 1970s, 1980s, and early 1990s. His radio and television program, called *Let God Love You*, consisted of Presbyterian preaching and teaching.

Ogilvie was the son of Varde Ogilvie and Katherine Jacobson. He earned a bachelor of arts degree from Lake Forest College, Lake Forest, Illinois, in 1952, and a bachelor of divinity degree from Northwestern University in 1956. In 1974, he was awarded a doctor of humanities degree from the University of Redlands, California. The following year he accepted a doctor of humane letters degree from Moravian Theological Seminary in Bethlehem, Pennsylvania.

Ogilvie rose to prominence as the senior pastor of the First Presbyterian Church of Hollywood, California, which provided him a base of operations. Like D. James Kennedy, Ogilvie was a pastor first, and a televangelist second. His duties as pastor to his congregation always took precedence over his broadcasting ministry and grounded his programs in the realities of community life.

On January 24, 1995, Ogilvie was unanimously elected by the United States Senate to serve as the institution's 61st chaplain. He was chosen from a candidate pool of 200 by a search committee headed by Senator Mark Hatfield of Oregon, a leading Christian evangelical. Ogilvie's television ministry had just celebrated its 17th anniversary and his daily radio broadcast its 10th anniversary when he closed both programs to concentrate on his new chaplaincy.

Ogilvie is also a respected inspirational author, having published such popular works as *Let God Love You* (1974), *Life without Limits* (1975), *Cup of Wonder* (1976), and *Loved and Forgiven* (1977).

SOURCES

"Prayer Warrior." *Religious Broadcasting*, May, 1995.

OLD FASHIONED REVIVAL HOUR
see: Charles Fuller

OLD-TIME GOSPEL HOUR
see: Jerry Falwell

STEPHEN OLFORD
born: March 29, 1918, Kalene Hill, Northern Rhodesia

Courtesy: Encounter Ministries

Founder of Encounter Ministries, an evangelistic radio ministry emanating from Memphis, Tennessee, Stephen F. Olford was reared in the missionary home of his parents, Frederick and Bessie Olford. As a young man, Olford decided that he would follow in his parents' footsteps and join the ministry. After studies at Oxford and St. Luke's College, London, where he earned a diploma in theology in 1937, Olford attended a missionary training institute until the beginning of World War II in 1939. From 1939 until the end of the war in 1945, Olford served in the British army as a chaplain.

Olford's ministerial career did not take full shape until 1953, when he was ordained a Baptist minister and called to serve the Duke Street Baptist Church in Richmond, Surrey, England. After serving with distinction for six years, he came to the United States in 1959 to begin a fruitful 15-year pastorate at New York's famed Calvary Baptist Church. It was in Calvary's pulpit that John Roach Straton had preached against modernism a generation earlier.

While pastor of Calvary Baptist Church, Olford began a radio ministry in 1970 that featured his Sunday sermons. As a result, his audience and fame expanded slowly over time. He served as minister of the Calvary Baptist congregation until 1973, when he decided to dedicate his entire energies to religious broadcasting.

In 1973, Olford founded Encounter Ministries to advance biblical preaching. The ministry produced his program *Encounter,* which features a finely polished expository sermon preached by Olford. He served continually as *Encounter*'s host until the early 1990s, when he was succeeded by his son, David Olford. Encounter Ministries' radio broadcasts are heard over more than 20 stations nationally and are carried over stations in Britain, Canada, Central and South America, the South Pacific, West Africa, and the West Indies. Olford's *Encounter* program is also broadcast weekly over HCJB, Ecuador.

See also *Encounter*; Encounter Ministries

SOURCES

Melton, J. Gordon. *Directory of Religious Organizations in the United States.* 3d ed. Detroit: Gale Research, 1993.

Phillips, John. *Only One Life: The Biography of Stephen F. Olford.* Neptune, NJ: Loizeaux Brothers, 1995.

100 HUNTLEY STREET

Produced by Crossroads Christian Communications and hosted by Canadian Pentecostal minister David Mainse, *100 Huntley Street* is was a spin-off program of Mainse's 1960s and 1970s *Crossroads* television show.

Patterned after Pat Robertson's famed *The 700 Club*, the program features a talk-show format with informational stories and interviews of Christian celebrities. In 1984, the program was awarded the National Religious Broadcasters Award of Merit. At present, *100 Huntley Street* is seen over nearly 30 stations via cable and satellite in much of Canada and the United States.

See also David Mainse; Crossroads Christian Communications

SOURCES

Burgess, Stanley M., and Gary B. McGee, eds. *Dictionary of Pentecostal and Charismatic Movements*. Grand Rapids, MI: Zondervan, 1988.

ORAL ROBERTS AND YOU
see: Oral Roberts

OVERSEAS RADIO & TELEVISION
established: 1960

The Overseas Radio & Television (ORT) ministry is an independent interdenominational missionary organization whose mission is to spread the Christian gospel on the island of Taiwan. Founded in 1960, ORT produces a number of evangelistic programs for broadcast over radio and television as well as audiotapes and videos for international distribution. ORT's headquarters are in Seattle, Washington.

SOURCES

Melton, J. Gordon. *Directory of Religious Organizations in the United States.* 3d ed. Detroit: Gale Research, 1993.

P

PACIFIC GARDEN MISSION
established: 1877

Originally established by Sarah Dunn Clarke and her husband as Clarke's Mission, the Pacific Garden Mission (PGM) began as a one-room shelter for the "down-and-out" amid the noise and depravity of saloons, gambling halls, and brothels in downtown Chicago. In 1880, the Clarkes moved their mission to the Pacific Beer Garden and, at the suggestion of evangelist Dwight L. Moody, renamed it the Pacific Garden Mission. The rescue mission's labors expanded over the next 20 years, and many hundreds were converted to Christ through its evangelistic teams and gospel wagon ministries. Among PGM's most famous converts was Billy Sunday, the major-league-baseball-player-turned-revivalist.

The mission moved to its present location along State Street after its 1922 purchase of a former brothel known as the "White House." It later acquired three additional buildings to the north and south of this site. During World War II, under the leadership of Harry Saunier, the Pacific Garden Mission initiated a number of urban ministries, including a shelter for women and the homeless, and worship services and Bible-study meetings for men in the armed services. Following the war, the mission added a radio broadcast and film ministry, as well as a medical and dental clinic, to its list of services.

PGM's forays into radio broadcasting provided a successful means for the mission to enhance its image both locally and nationally. *Unshackled*, the Pacific Garden Mission's premier radio program, dramatized the true-life stories of lost souls who had found redemption as a result of PGM's ministries. The popular program aired intermittently throughout the late 1940s, the 1950s, and the 1960s and received an award from the National Religious Broadcasters. It was later syndicated in the 1970s as a regular half-hour program. *Unshackled* aired once more in the 1980s for a brief period over WGN, Chicago, as part of WGN's Saturday night religious lineup.

The Pacific Garden Mission continues its evangelistic and social-service ministry from its historic facilities in the heart of urban Chicago.

See also *Unshackled*

SOURCES

Erickson, Hal. *Religious Radio and Television in the United States, 1921–1991*. Jefferson, NC: McFarland, 1992.

Melton, J. Gordon. *Directory of Religious Organizations in the United States*. 3d ed. Detroit: Gale Research, 1993.

Reid, Daniel G., Robert D. Linder, Bruce L. Shelley, and Harry S. Stout, eds. *Dictionary of Christianity in America*. Downers Grove, IL: InterVarsity Press, 1990.

LUIS PALAU
born: 1934, Buenos Aires, Argentina

Evangelist Luis Palau is perhaps the best known Christian preacher ever to have emerged from South America. Palau has spoken to an esti-

Courtesy: National Religious Broadcasters

mated 11 million people in 62 nations during his large-scale evangelistic crusades. In addition, he has preached to many millions of persons in 95 countries through television and radio broadcasts. The charismatic preacher is fluent in both Spanish and English.

Luis Palau preached sermons as a teenager in Argentina but did not hold his first crusade until 1966 in Bogotá, Colombia. As he recalls in his autobiography, *Calling America and the Nations to Christ* (1994): "Sometimes it seems I have been preaching all my life. Actually, . . . it really wasn't until I was in my thirties that God opened the door for me to pursue full-time mass evangelism."

Palau graduated from Multnomah School of the Bible (now Multnomah Biblical Seminary) in Portland, Oregon, in 1961, and was ordained in Palo Alto, California, in 1963. By the 1970s, the Palau evangelistic team was conducting huge crusades and rallies throughout Central and South America. In the 1980s, Palau brought his crusades to Great Britain and continental Europe. During the 1990s, Palau has packed concert halls, stadiums, and arenas in such diverse venues as Denmark, Hong Kong, India, Indonesia, New Zealand, Russia, Romania, the Philippines, and Thailand. In the United States, Palau has held crusades in Des Moines, Iowa; Phoenix, Arizona; Fort Worth and San Anto-

nio, Texas; and throughout California's San Fernando Valley. The ministry, which is headquartered in Portland, Oregon, estimates that over 500,000 people have been converted to Christ during these events.

Palau's broadcasting ministries include two Spanish-language radio programs, *Luis Palau Responde* ("Luis Palau Responds"), a five-minute daily program in which Palau answers questions from listeners, and *Cruzada con Luis Palau* ("Crusade with Luis Palau"), a 15-minute daily devotional show for Christians. These programs are aired on over 380 stations throughout Latin America and the United States. A live, half-hour counseling telecast, *Night Talk with Luis Palau*, airs during his crusades on two national cable networks.

Palau is also the popular author of over 35 books and articles in both Spanish and English. The articles have appeared in such periodicals as *Charisma*, *Christian Parenting Today*, *Christianity Today*, and *Christian Herald*.

See also Premier Radio

SOURCES

"Casting Call for NRB 95." *Religious Broadcasting*, February, 1995.

EVERETT C. PARKER
born: January 17, 1913, Chicago, Illinois

One of the more distinguished and persuasive spokespersons for mainstream religious broadcasting over the past 50 years has been Everett C. Parker. Beginning with his groundbreaking studies of religious radio ministries between 1930 and 1940, Parker went on to become a major figure in the Broadcasting and Film Commission of the Federal Council of Churches (FCC) in the postwar era. He also appeared on such FCC-sponsored programs as *All Aboard for Adventure* and *Stained Glass Windows*.

Everett Parker is the son of Harry Everett Parker and Lillian Stern. After earning his bachelor of divinity degree (magna cum laude) from Chicago Theological Seminary in 1943, Parker began a pastorship at the Waveland Avenue Congregational Christian Church in Chicago. Between 1943 and 1945, he served as the assistant public service and war program manager at NBC. Parker was also the founder of the Protestant Radio Commission and its director from 1945 to 1950.

Between 1946 and 1958, Parker served as a lecturer in communications at Yale Divinity School. During this period he was the director of a communications research project that resulted in the 1955 study, *The Television-Radio Audience and Religion*. The book, which was coauthored with David W. Barry and Dallas W. Smythe, gave a critical assessment of popular religious programs in the New Haven, Connecticut, area, as well as the viewership of these broadcasts. Parker's central thesis was that the ecumenical "sustaining time" broadcasts of the religious mainstream offered a more balanced and thoughtful religious perspective than did the simplistic paid-time programming of such televangelists as Oral Roberts. ("Sustaining time" was the term used to describe the free-time slots networks allotted for public-interest programming, including religious programs.) Parker regarded independent religious broadcasting as irresponsible and mercenary. He was fighting a losing battle, however, with market forces. During the 1960s and 1970s, paid-time syndicated religious programs garnered larger and larger audiences and surpassed traditional sustaining time programming in creativity, innovation, and technological expertise.

During the early 1980s, Parker joined Father Ellwood Kieser (host of the popular Catholic program *Insight*) in an effort to force the Federal Communications Commission (FCC) to give equal broadcasting time to sustaining time programming. The deregulated state of the FCC doomed this initiative to failure, however, and paid-time programming has dominated the radio and television airwaves ever since.

In addition to his work in broadcasting, Parker served as the director of the Office of Communications for the United Church of Christ between 1954 and 1983; founded a citizen movement to protect minority rights in media in 1963; chaired the Broadcasting and Film Com-

mission of the National Council of Churches between 1969 and 1972; chaired the Study Commission on Theology, Education, and Electronic Media between 1985 and 1987; and was a member of the advisory committee on advanced television services of the FCC's Consumer Advocacy Group.

During his career, Parker was the producer and director of such national television programs as *Off to Adventure* (1956) and *Tangled World* (1965). He was also the originator of the PBS series, *Six American Families* (1977). Parker's latest scholarly work is entitled *Fiber Optics to the Home: The Changing Future of Cable, TV, and the Telephone* (1989).

For his work in communications, Parker was awarded the Public Service award by Black Citizens for a Fair Media in 1979, and the Pioneer award by the World Association for Christian Communications in 1988.

SOURCES

Erickson, Hal. *Religious Radio and Television in the United States, 1921–1991.* Jefferson, NC: McFarland, 1992.

Parker, Everett C., David W. Barry, and Dallas W. Smythe. *The Television-Radio Audience and Religion.* New York: Harper & Row, 1955.

ROD PARSLEY
born: June 13, 1957, Eastern Kentucky

Televangelist Rodney Parsley is the cofounder and pastor of World Harvest Church in Columbus, Ohio. His daily television program, *Breakthrough*, is broadcast over 600 stations covering a third of the United States. The popular program is also one of the mainstays of Trinity Broadcasting Network's weekly lineup, and can be seen on the Black Entertainment Network and Chicago superstation WGN-TV.

Parsley was born in eastern Kentucky and grew up in central Ohio. His father was a carpenter, and his mother ran her own real estate company. Parsley graduated from Columbus's Pickerington High School in 1975. He was a forward on the basketball team and wrote as

his yearbook epigram, "Be patient, God isn't finished with me yet." In 1977, Parsley incorporated the Sunrise Chapel with the support of his father and uncle, giving his parents' home as the ministry's address. His first sermon took place in his family's backyard and drew about 17 people. Parsley also enrolled in Circleville Bible College during this period but left the school in 1979 before completing his degree. Sunrise Chapel became Word of Life Church the same year and moved into a new building in Fairfield County.

In the early 1980s, Parsley began taping *Breakthrough*, a 30-minute program of preaching and music, at a Newark, Ohio, television studio. The Word of Life congregation grew rapidly, and new ground was broken for a $9.7 million complex in southeast Columbus in the late 1980s. The complex, which was renamed World Harvest Church in 1989, has a 5,200-seat worship center that regularly seats crowds of around 4,000 for Parsley's Sunday-morning services. *Breakthrough* now reaches an audience of millions and showcases segments from Parsley's weekly sermons, a prayer phone line, fundraising appeals, and a lively music ministry.

Parsley is a handsome, powerful, and charismatic pulpit presence who enjoys roaming through his congregation while he preaches. His sermons are filled with dramatic rhetorical flourishes, shouting, pleading, Bible verses, jokes, and homespun stories. He pulls no punches in his constant warnings that Satan is stalking the children of earth and that an eternity in the "smoky-black pit of hell" awaits those who have not accepted Christ as their personal Savior. Parsley makes no apologies for his dire "fire and brimstone" message, commenting "I'd rather be too hard now than have you stand in the Judgment with your blood dripping through my hands and you point your finger at me and say, 'You never told me.'"

The typical Sunday service at World Harvest Church includes the clapping, shouting, dancing, praising, singing, speaking in tongues, and healings found in most Pentecostal congregations. The size of the worship center and scale of the performance, however, makes the service

a spectacle of light, sound, and fervent emotion. Participants come from across Ohio and from such neighboring states as Michigan, West Virginia, Indiana, Pennsylvania, and Tennessee. The service gets underway when a huge maroon curtain rises on the stage and a 12-piece band and 66-member choir begin the first of many foot-stomping, joyful gospel songs. The congregation leaps up and begins to clap and sway and sing along to the rousing lyrics composed by the church's music director, Clint Brown. Brown leads the singing, and two 15-foot television monitors flash the lyrics to the audience. The service is committed to video tape by one hand-held and two stationary television cameras. Live clips from the service are sometimes flashed on the huge monitors that flank the stage.

After a long period of singing and praise, Parsley mounts the carpeted stage, slaps his Bible onto the clear plastic lectern, and joins in more singing. The services have an air of spontaneity, which Parsley claims is a result of his obedience to the movement of the Holy Spirit. On some days the music can go on for hours, while on others Parsley immediately launches into his sermon.

On certain Sundays, Parsley becomes a conduit for the faith healing of diseased or troubled church members. As those requesting aid pour toward the stage, Parsley moves among them, laying hands on some and speaking to others. Those who have been ministered to will sometimes drop to the stage floor and be quickly covered with a blanket by an assistant. After particularly dramatic individual instances of healing, Parsley will hop and jump around the stage, his legs and elbows jerking with residual spiritual energy. At the end of these healing services Parsley often prays over hundreds of healing cards spread over a table near the stage. On several occasions, he has leapt upon the table and crawled along its length in order to touch more cards. After a short homily, Parsley asks for donations to support the church and fund *Breakthrough*.

In 1993, Parsley claimed that his ministry spent over $10,000 each day to broadcast his television program over 600 stations nationwide. In addition, 5,000 people used the telephone prayer line daily at a cost to the church of 72 cents per call, and study guides costing over $20,000 per month were sent out to regular contributors. Listener contributions usually cover the costs of the ministry, but when donations from a Philadelphia station's viewing area did not match the cost of airtime, the program was pulled from the station's lineup.

World Harvest Church markets audiotapes of Parsley's sermons, and the church bookstore sells Parsley's seven books, his 27 video and audiotapes, and numerous other religious tapes and publications. Parsley has begun to imitate other religious television programs by taking short breaks from his preaching to solicit "love offerings" from "*Breakthrough* partners" and to pitch various books and tapes. Parsley is unapologetic about his increasingly insistent fundraising appeals. He contends that the Bible commands believers to donate at least 10 percent of their incomes to the church. If they do so faithfully, he promises they will be blessed with wealth and prosperity.

Parsley's ministry has been reticent to share its financial statements with the public, claiming that it does not need to provide a public accounting since God directs church leaders on how to spend the ministry's money. World Harvest Church does not belong to the Evangelical Council of Financial Accountability, the watchdog council that accredits television and humanitarian ministries. As of 1993, Parsley was also refusing to grant interviews to the media. According to World Harvest's administrator, Dean Radke, the rationale for this policy was that "the interviews do not result in accurate reporting or in showcasing the tremendous ministry work accomplished in the lives of people as the requests are initially postured. Rather, the reporting attempts to make an unfavorable association with situations encountered in a few other ministries."

In his book, *God's Answer to Insufficient Funds*, Parsley defended his opulent lifestyle and personal wealth by observing, "I don't care whether the world likes it or not. I am serving a God that said he will supply all my needs. . . .

Everybody believed in prosperity until the secular press got upset about it."

This decision for prosperity is reflected in Parsley's $857,000 five-bedroom home in Fairfax County, where he lives with his wife, Joni, and their two children. His parents live in a beautiful home within the same compound. An electronic gate, stables, and a corral are also part of the estate. Parsley travels to his frequent preaching appearances in a $500,000 Hawker Siddeley jet that seats seven passengers.

Parsley's ministry has had two minor scandals over the past two years. Parsley's aunt, Naomil Endicott, filed suit claiming that she had been sexually harassed by Parsley's father, her brother-in-law James Parsley. A second suit filed by Lewis Bungard, a former church member, alleged that Parsley and his father assaulted him during a dispute over a painting job. This civil suit also alleged that Bungard's $7,000 church donation to support a home for unwed mothers and a senior care facility was instead used "for the enrichment of Rodney Parsley, his parents and others so as to achieve an opulent lifestyle for themselves."

Parsley continues to be a rising star of Pentecostal-based televangelism. In August 1992, officials of World Harvest amended the church's incorporation papers. Parsley himself retains the ultimate authority over the ministry, according to the newly filed papers: "In the event of a conflict of opinion between the Board of Trustees and any auxiliary organization, the Pastor shall have the power to overrule and take precedence over any such organization." The ministry plans to expand its outreach to include the ordination of ministers, the ownership of television and radio stations, the operation of the World Harvest Christian Academy and World Harvest Bible College, and the establishment of an adoption agency, a home for unwed mothers, a rest home for the elderly, and a retreat center for ministers.

SOURCES

"An Empire of Souls." *Columbus Monthly*, May 1993.

JANET PARSHALL

see: Janet Parshall's America

EARL PAULK

born: May 30, 1927, Baxley, Georgia

Earl Pearly Paulk, Jr., is a popular televangelist and founder of the Gospel Harvesters Church. During the 1980s, Paulk's church became one of the fastest growing charismatic churches in the South. In 1992, the congregation changed its name to the Cathedral of the Holy Spirit and moved into a new 7,000-seat sanctuary located on a 100-acre campus in Decatur, Georgia. Since that time, Paulk's ministry has been embroiled in a costly sex scandal which has caused thousands of members to quit.

Like many other evangelists, Paulk came from a family of preachers. His father was Earl P. Paulk, Sr., a minister with the Church of God, Cleveland, Tennessee, who later became the denomination's assistant general overseer. Paulk, Jr., traveled throughout the country with his family during his father's years of itinerant preaching.

After finishing high school, Paulk entered Furman University in Greenville, South Carolina, and became a track stand-out. While in college, Paulk decided to follow in his father's footsteps and served as the Church of God's state youth director before graduating from Furman with his bachelor of arts degree in 1947. Paulk taught at Lee College in Cleveland, Tennessee, before enrolling at Emory University's Candler School of Theology in Atlanta, Georgia. While at Emory, Paulk was ordained to the ministry of the Church of God and pastored churches in Moultrie and Buford, Georgia.

Following his graduation with a bachelor of divinity degree from Candler in 1952, Paulk was called to pastor at Hemphill Church of God in Atlanta. During his tenure at Hemphill, Paulk began preaching on television and became known for his championing of civil rights. This controversial advocacy and his continual conflicts with standard practices of the Church of

God led to his resignation from the denomination in 1960.

Paulk then decided to inaugurate an independent evangelical ministry, which he dubbed the Harvesters, with his brother-in-law, Harry Mushegan. The ministry led to the formation of two new congregations in the Atlanta area, one of which moved with Paulk to suburban Decatur in 1973. The Chapel Hill Gospel Harvesters Church, as the new congregation was named, increased rapidly in size. By the late 1970s, the church counted over 6,000 members and had become renowned for its multifaceted programs of social outreach. Paulk began televising taped versions of the church's Sunday worship services in 1978. This initiative developed into the popular *Harvester Hour* broadcasting ministry.

Paulk continued to expand his ministry and its outreach during the 1980s. He began a fellowship with Archbishop Benson Idahosa of the Miracle Center in Benin City, Nigeria, and Bishop Robert McAlister of the New Life Pentecostal Church in Rio de Janeiro. After these two bishops came together to form the International Communion of Charismatic Churches in 1982, Paulk received consecration as a bishop in the communion from McAlister. In 1986, the ministry opened a liberal arts school, Earl Paulk College, which focused on biblical studies, music, art, drama, and business enterprise.

By the late 1980s, the Gospel Harvester Church had grown to a 10,000-member congregation served by a full-time pastoral staff of 21. The church's ministrations to unwed mothers, homosexual Christians, alcoholics, drug abusers, and prisoners earned it praise in 1991 as one of President George Bush's "thousand points of light." *Harvester Hour*, a weekly national telecast, continued to grow in popularity. The show aired on 18 stations, most of which were affiliated with the Trinity Broadcasting Network.

In December 1992, a former church staff member publicly accused Paulk of coaxing her into a sexual liaison that lasted more than a year. Other ex-congregants spoke out at a press conference and accused Paulk's brother and two other pastors of sexual misconduct during counseling sessions. Despite Paulk's denials of his own culpability, the scandal prompted almost 5,000 of the church's 12,000 members to defect. Weekly donations dropped from about $170,000 to $70,000, forcing the church to reschedule its debt payments. The allegations aroused so much protest in Georgia that the state legislature began to consider a bill making clergy sex abuse a crime requiring a prison term. The bill was modeled after an existing law that applied to psychotherapists. These controversies don't seem to have negatively affected Paulk's weekly television program. As of this writing, the *Harvester Hour* continues to air on the Trinity Broadcasting Network.

In addition to Paulk's broadcast ministry, he is the popular author of such books as *Your Pentecostal Neighbor* (1958), *Forward in Faith*, *The Divine Runner*, *Satan Unmasked* (1984), *The Wounded Body of Christ*, and *Sex Is God's Idea*. He was made a trustee and regent of Oral Roberts University in 1986 and was given an honorary doctorate by the school in 1987.

See also *Harvester Hour*

SOURCES

Burgess, Stanley M., Gary B. McGee, and Patrick H. Alexander, eds. *Dictionary of Pentecostal and Charismatic Movements*. Grand Rapids, MI: Regency Reference Library, Zondervan, 1988.

Niebuhr, Gustav. "An Instance of Wolves in Shepherd's Clothing?" *The Washington Post*, February 5, 1993.

Paulk, Earl, Jr. *Satan Unmasked*. Atlanta: K Dimension Publishers, 1984.

———. *20/20 Vision: A Clear View of the Kingdom of God*. Atlanta: Kingdom Publishers, 1988.

———. *Ultimate Kingdom*. Atlanta: K Dimension Publishers, 1984.

———. *Your Pentecostal Neighbor*. Cleveland: Pathway Press, 1958.

"Paulk's Accusers Lobby for Sex Bill." *Charisma*, October, 1993.

Weeks, Tricia. *The Provoker*. Atlanta: K Dimension Publishers, 1986.

NORMAN VINCENT PEALE

born: May 31, 1898, Bowersville, Ohio
died: December 24, 1993, New York City

Courtesy: National Religious Broadcasters

The American ethos has always included the utilitarian pursuit of self-fulfillment, self-empowerment, and material success. No one person more consistently spoke to this pursuit than the minister, teacher, author, and broadcasting personality, Norman Vincent Peale. Peale's simple gospel of "positive thinking," Christian faith, and this-worldly success, though roundly criticized by neo-conservative Protestants in the wake of the Holocaust and World War II, has come to dominate the televangelism of the 1980s and 1990s.

Born in a small Ohio town just before the turn of the century, Peale was reared by his devoutly Methodist father and mother. In his autobiographical work, *The True Joy of Positive Living* (1984), Peale recounted that his small-town upbringing had taught him "love of God and love of country and Christian morality." In many ways, Peale never deviated from those bedrock nineteenth-century rural America values. Peale's father, Charles Clifford Peale, had been trained as a doctor but decided to enter the Methodist ministry when he miraculously recovered from a serious illness. His mother, the former Anna Delaney, was an intelligent and vivacious woman who would, in time, become a strong proponent of international mission work. The Peale family moved from town to town in Ohio during Norman's youth, following Charles Peale's itinerant ministry. Eventually, Charles was elevated to district superintendent and served the Methodist bishop from his pastorate at First Methodist Church of Columbus.

Upon graduation from Bellefontaine High School, Norman Peale attended Ohio Wesleyan College. While there, he eagerly served on the debate team and became the president of the student body. He also had a memorable religious experience that was precipitated by a public scolding he had received from an economics professor while stuttering his way through an oral presentation. Both ashamed and challenged, Peale went to the college chapel and rededicated his life to Christ. After receiving his diploma in 1920, he worked as a journalist in Findlay, Ohio, and Detroit, Michigan. The Detroit paper's editor, Grove Patterson, taught Peale what, in hindsight, he claimed to be one of life's most important lessons: an idea is useful and important only if it can be communicated to ordinary people in plain, simple language. In time, Peale followed what he took to be his true calling and entered the school of theology at Methodist-sponsored Boston University.

Peale's personal ambition showed upon graduation, when he visited the Methodist bishop of New York with no prior appointment and requested a ministerial assignment. The bishop responded to the young man's positive self-presentation and made him pastor of a small Brooklyn congregation that had been gathering in a dilapidated building in the Flatlands district. Peale immediately set about expanding the church's outreach and membership rolls. He took advantage of a contact at the gas company and obtained the addresses of thousands of new families who were moving into a nearby housing development. He personally visited each of these families and invited them to attend his church services. He also employed a

tried-and-true marketing strategy by mailing out postcards with the message, "Why have our congregations increased until the church is crowded to capacity? . . . Come around and your questions will be answered." By 1927, his congregation, Kings Highway Methodist Church, had grown to 3,000 members and built a permanent church facility.

Peale used a similar sales strategy to increase membership at his next assignment, the old University Church in Syracuse, New York. He also jazzed up the services with a professional-sounding choir and invited nationally known guest speakers and singers. During his pastorate at University Church, Peale met and married Ruth Stafford and also was befriended by the head of Syracuse University's speech department, Hugh M. Tilroe. It was Tilroe who advised Peale to preach the gospel in a simple, relaxed manner and to eschew intellectual pretensions. Peale also began a radio ministry at this time and made guest speaking appearances throughout the country.

One of these engagements led to an offer of the senior minister's position at Marble Collegiate Church in lower Manhattan. The church had historic Dutch Reformed roots in New York City and was in need of a fresh and enthusiastic pastor to bring it to life again. After years of struggles during the Depression, Peale's refurbished church became a thriving congregation that drew thousands of people to its three Sunday services. Peale's ebullient, optimistic preaching style seemed to appeal to the masses who were struggling to keep their families afloat during times of economic adversity. His sermons were in such great demand that Peale was able to create a publications and mailing service, the Foundation for Christian Living, to distribute printed copies. The foundation was run by his wife, Ruth Peale.

Peale's broadcasting star began to rise in 1933 when the Federal Council of Churches invited him to inaugurate a new radio program. Peale eagerly accepted the invitation and began regular Saturday broadcasts of *The Art of Living*. The program would run for the next 40 years and make Peale one of the best-loved radio preachers of his era. Peale would later add *The American Character*, a 90-second feature, and broadcasts of his Sunday sermons to his radio repertoire. Like other pioneering radio preachers, Peale recognized the tremendous potential that radio held for reaching the masses with his message. He believed that the medium gave him the opportunity to touch people in an intimate way using the simple power of the human voice.

Television was another matter, however. Peale was never entirely comfortable with the medium, partly because he didn't enjoy seeing his image on the screen and partly because of the tremendous costs involved in television production. In spite of these misgivings, Peale decided to take advantage of the huge success of his national bestseller, *The Power of Positive Thinking* (1952), by taping a new television program, *What's Your Trouble?* in 1952. The show was distributed by Guild Films under the auspices of the National Council of Churches. It featured Peale sitting comfortably in a family den, expounding his positive-thinking philosophy. Each broadcast began with the relaxed-appearing Peale greeting his audience with, "Hello, there, how are you?" Ruth Peale often joined her husband during these 15-minute programs, asking questions that set up the segment's main theme. *What's Your Trouble?* and his other television show *Positive Thinking with Norman Vincent Peale* reached their widest coverage and peak of popularity during the "can-do" Eisenhower era of the 1950s. When the country began to fragment during the violent upheavals of the 1960s, Peale's message began to sound naive and outdated. Nevertheless, his television programs remained in syndication until 1978, when he was still being heard in almost 55 markets.

Peale also began a successful periodical, *Guideposts*, during the mid-1940s. The publication began as a newsletter intended for families, business executives, and churches. It contained inspirational stories, anecdotes, and quotations from persons who had overcome adversity by dint of hard work, self-confidence, and faith in God. Peale had been encouraged to start the newsletter by radio announcer Lowell Thomas and *Readers' Digest* publisher DeWitt

Wallace. Although *Guideposts* struggled to survive in its early years of publication, it would gradually build a circulation of over a million readers.

Another important dimension of Peale's work grew out of his cooperation with psychiatrist Smiley Blanton. Both men were convinced that many purportedly physical ailments were curable by a simple change in a person's mental attitude. Peale and Blanton set up clinics in the New York City area to treat patients, and this initiative eventually led to the establishment of the Blanton-Peale Institutes of Religion and Health. These institutes trained pastoral counselors in mental therapeutics and enjoyed a large degree of success. Peale and Blanton copublished *Faith Is the Answer* (1940) and *The Art of Real Happiness* (1950).

Peale's publishing career also included his authorship of a series of successful books on personal empowerment and success. These included, among many others, *The Art of Living* (1937), *You Can Win* (1938), *A Guide to Confident Living* (1948), *The Power of Positive Thinking for Young People* (1954), *The Tough-Minded Optimist* (1961), *Enthusiasm Makes the Difference* (1967), and *Dynamic Imaging: The Powerful Way to Change Your Life* (1982).

Peale essentially reduced human life to a struggle between good and evil: evil is those inner doubts and negative feelings that hold us back from achieving our highest potential; good is those positive thoughts and feelings that lead us to success, happiness, and self-fulfillment. Those who are "saved" are those who have mastered their mental powers and changed negative thoughts and emotions into positive ones. Overcoming one's defects and personal failures is always possible for those who call on God in faith and hope. Everett Parker, in a 1955 study, gave the following synopsis of a typical Peale broadcast, articulating these themes:

There is an infinite perfectibility about human nature. If you get firmly fixed in your mind the dynamic of change and will apply faith to your mental attitude, whatever your defect is, it can be corrected. Many of us have defects of the emotions of personality. Another type of defect is a moral defect. This, too, can be corrected. It is a fact that there is no change that cannot take place in a human being, none whatsoever, provided that individual wants to change and provided he will believe.

Peale's message of personal mastery, right thinking, and self-culture (i.e., cultivating one's virtues, talents, and personality) follows in a long tradition of American religious thought, including not only nineteenth-century mainstream Protestant writings concerning moral uplift and rational living, but also the mental hygienics and positive individualism of such figures as Ralph Waldo Emerson, Phineas Quimby, Mary Baker Eddy, Warren Felt Evans, Ralph Waldo Trine, and Emma Curtis Hopkins. Peale once told an audience at Hope College, "I've always felt that Christianity itself may be described as a science." He added, "I think that Jesus lays down certain simple formulas that if you follow them precisely, you will get an equivalent result."

Peale was particularly effective in communicating this message because he had the gift of storytelling, often using tales from the ordinary lives of family members, school teachers, and business executives. Some of his better-known stories included such figures as Branch Rickey, Jesse Owens, Eddie Rickenbacker, and J. L. Kraft. The pragmatism implicit in Peale's message appealed to the "striver" post-war generations who were working to raise themselves into the great American middle- and upper-middle classes.

Peale's fame was somewhat eclipsed in the early 1960s after it became known that he had emceed a dinner sponsored by opponents of John F. Kennedy's presidential candidacy—opponents whose anti-Catholicism was barely camouflaged beneath a rhetoric expressing concern of Papal power extending into the White House. Although Peale attempted to distance himself from the event, his reputation suffered. His association with conservative politicians such as Richard Nixon, Dwight Eisenhower, Ferdinand Marcos, and Richard Daley, and with the wealthy and powerful in the business world also lent itself to criticism during a decade of awareness of the rights of oppressed minori-ties, opposition to the war in Vietnam, and the war on poverty.

These criticisms notwithstanding, Peale endured as a powerful purveyor of American optimism and mental hygienics on radio and television well into his 90s. In 1969, he was elected president of the Reformed Church in America by colleagues who respected his attempts to steer clear of the liberal-conservative controversy that was splitting the denomination apart. The Reverend Arthur Caliandro, his successor at Marble Collegiate Church, declared on the occasion of Peale's death in 1993, "That man believed in me. Everybody felt that he believed in them. So many times I would sit here and be lifted so far beyond any place I ever thought I could be lifted, by him saying, 'Believe! Think big!'"

Peale's successor in television, Robert Schuller, often had Peale as a guest on his *Hour of Power* broadcast. Perhaps the most eloquent testimony to the enduring power of Peale's message is the fact that Schuller's program has been the top-rated religious television program throughout the late 1980s and early 1990s.

SOURCES

Bruce, Steve. *Pray TV: Televangelism in America*. London: Routledge, 1990.

Detrich, Richard Lewis. *Norman Vincent Peale*. Milwaukee: Ideals, 1969.

Gordon, Arthur. *Norman Vincent Peale: Minister to Millions*. Englewood Cliffs, NJ: Prentice-Hall, 1958.

Parker, E. C., D. W. Barry, and D. W. Smythe. *The Television-Radio Audience and Religion*. New York: Harper & Row, 1955.

Peale, Norman Vincent. *The Amazing Results of Positive Thinking*. Englewood Cliffs, NJ: Prentice-Hall, 1959.

———. *Faith Made Them Champions*. Carmel, CA: Guideposts Associates, 1954.

———. *Norman Vincent Peale's Treasury of Courage and Confidence*. Garden City, NJ: Doubleday, 1970.

———. *The Power of Positive Thinking*. New York: Prentice-Hall, 1952.

———. *Power of the Plus Factor*. Old Tappan, NJ: Fleming H. Revell, 1987.

———. *The True Joy of Positive Living: An Autobiography.* Pawling, NY: Foundation for Christian Living, 1984.

"Peale's Successor Pays Tribute to Life of Inspiration." *Daytona Beach News-Journal*, December 27, 1993.

BOB PIERCE

born: October 8, 1914, Fort Dodge, Iowa
died: September 6, 1978, Los Angeles, California

Though known primarily as an evangelist, humanitarian, and documentary film maker, Robert "Bob" Pierce hosted several religious radio programs between 1940 and 1964 as part of his broader mission of raising the social consciousness of evangelical Christians.

One of seven children, Pierce grew up in Iowa, Colorado, and Southern California. His father was Fred Asa Pierce, a carpenter who served as a lay preacher in both the Methodist and Nazarene Churches. During his teen years in Redondo Beach, California, Pierce attended Sunday School and worship services at the Church of the Nazarene and began to consider seriously a ministerial career. Although he attended Pasadena Nazarene College and became student body president during his junior year, Pierce never finished his degree. Instead he chose to marry Lorraine Johnson and become an evangelist. He would later receive an honorary doctor of laws degree from Northwestern College in Minneapolis.

During 1936 and 1937, Pierce traveled up and down the West Coast, preaching in different congregations and supplementing his education by taking theology and public speaking courses. He was given ministerial credentials in 1940 by a Baptist church in Wilmington, California. Pierce's first assistant pastorship was at the independent Los Angeles Evangelistic Center, a ministry that had been founded by Lorraine Pierce's parents. It was at the Evangelistic Center that Pierce met the pastor of Toronto's Peoples Church, Oswald J. Smith. This meeting was to impress upon the young evangelist the vital importance of international Christian missions.

Pierce next turned to auditorium evangelism, touring the country with the Jubilee Singers in early 1944. The young preacher was reasonably well received as he addressed the large crowds that came out to hear the singers. Following a series of inner struggles during which he dropped out of the ministry for a few months, Pierce helped found Youth for Christ International with Billy Graham and Torrey M. Johnson in late 1944. Pierce then took a job in Seattle with the new organization. Over the next five years he rose to the post of vice-president-at-large and preached to over 500,000 people in churches, auditoriums, and tents across the United States.

In 1947, Pierce made his first foreign evangelistic crusade, touring China and the Philippines. Moved by the overwhelming needs of the missionaries he encountered, Pierce began to produce professional-quality films of his trips that graphically depicted the struggles of missions in foreign countries. One of the most important films from this period was *The 38th Parallel* (1950), a wrenching depiction of the suffering Korean nation during the Korean War. Pierce showed these films to audiences around the United States and was able to raise funds for subsequent evangelistic tours to East Asia.

In 1950, building on a idea that had first come to him during his trips to China, Pierce and his colleague Dr. Frank Phillips organized World Vision in Portland, Oregon. The nonprofit ministry's primary goal was to help Christian missionaries in East Asia meet their emergency physical needs. As Pierce argued, "we must first treat people's physical needs so we can then minister to their real (spiritual) needs." Other aims of the organization included alerting Christians to the needs of international missions, conducting cooperative evangelistic crusades with indigenous churches, developing Christian leaders through international conferences, assisting the sick and the poor with basic medical and humanitarian assistance, and extending financial assistance to Christian missionaries to help them expand their operations.

World Vision expanded rapidly during the 1950s as it added new geographical regions to its sphere of nurture. By 1961, a World Vision children's program had established 156 orphanages that served 14,000 children in nine countries. World Vision also helped build hospitals and provide special care for victims of leprosy. By 1965, thanks to Pierce's tireless fundraising efforts, World Vision's hospitals and orphanages had expanded and were serving 65,000 children in 20 countries. For his labors on behalf of the Korean people, Pierce was honored by the Korean government in 1958 with a scroll commemorating his humanitarian statesmanship. The next year he received the South Korean Medal for Public Welfare Service.

Between 1956 and 1963, Pierce also hosted a weekly radio program, during which he preached from the Bible and interviewed guests such as Roy Rogers and Dale Evans. In 1964, he was forced by declining health to take a medical leave from the broadcast. Three years later Pierce relinquished control of World Vision to its board of directors. After a year of hospital rest, the evangelist took over Food for the World, a small humanitarian ministry, which he reorganized as Samaritan's Purse (now headed by Franklin Graham), with the help of World Vision. This new ministry's mission was to fund evangelism and relief in Asia.

Under Graham, Samaritan's Purse has grown from a two-person operation to a 60-person ministry with an annual budget of $22 million. In addition to providing humanitarian relief for victims of war and poverty, Samaritan's Purse builds hospitals and churches, and digs wells in such countries as India, Rwanda, Russia, and Romania. Like World Vision, Samaritan's Purse airs regular fundraising appeals on religious television networks, which feature the many facets of the ministry's outreach.

After a long bout with leukemia, Pierce died in 1978. He is remembered as a powerful advocate of compassionate Christian evangelism.

SOURCES

"Bob Pierce." *Current Biography*, 1961.

Dunker, Marilee P. *Days of Glory, Seasons of Night.* Grand Rapids, MI: Zondervan, 1984.

Graham, Franklin, and Jeannette Lockerbee. *Bob Pierce: This One Thing I Do.* Waco, TX: Word Books, 1983.

Reid, Daniel G., et al., eds. *Dictionary of Christianity in America.* Downers Grove, IL: InterVarsity Press, 1990.

JAMES A. PIKE

born: February 14, 1913, Oklahoma City, Oklahoma
died: September, 1969, Israel

Bishop James A. Pike was an Episcopalian churchman whose controversial theological insights and ability to use various popular communications media made him one of the most influential religious figures of his day. Pike hosted two of the nation's earliest religious television programs for six years on ABC-TV and established a reputation for addressing difficult social and theological questions in a popular, accessible format.

The future Episcopalian bishop was reared in a Roman Catholic family in Oklahoma City. Pike's father died when he was two, and his mother took him to live in Hollywood, California. By all accounts Pike was a devout Catholic who clearly intended to enter the priesthood when he enrolled at the Jesuit University of Santa Clara. During his sophomore year, however, he began to question Catholic teachings on papal infallibility and birth control. Before the year was finished, Pike had dropped out of school and left Roman Catholicism altogether. This critical approach to traditional Christian doctrine and governance would be an ongoing feature of Pike's thinking throughout his career.

During several years of radical disaffection from his Christian roots, Pike earned degrees in arts and in law from the University of Southern California. He passed the California bar exam in 1936 and enrolled at Yale, where he earned a doctorate in law. Pike then moved to Washington, DC, and worked as an attorney for the Securities and Exchange Commission. At this time, he also married and set up a law partnership.

During World War II, Pike taught on the faculty of George Washington University Law School, served in the US Maritime Commission and War Shipping Administration, and joined the Episcopal church. After the breakup of his marriage, he remarried, to a student at the university, and, having become once again interested in a religious vocation, decided to enter training for the Episcopal priesthood.

Pike was ordained to the Episcopalian diaconate in 1944 and enrolled at Virginia Theological Seminary. While studying at the seminary he served as a chaplain at Georgetown University. Wishing to complete his degree in theology at Union Theological Seminary (UTS), Pike moved with his wife to New York City. While at UTS, he came under the influence of the highly respected Protestant theologians Reinhold Niebuhr and Paul Tillich. After his ordination, Pike held brief chaplaincies at Vassar College and Columbia University. At Columbia, he was also given the opportunity to revamp the department of religion. Pike hired distinguished faculty, crafted a new curriculum, and drew outstanding graduate students. During his academic tenure at Columbia, Pike also coauthored *The Faith of the Church* (1953) with Norman Pittenger. This volume was used for many years by the Episcopal church for lay instruction.

Pike began to gain a national reputation in 1952 when he was elevated to dean of the Cathedral of Saint John the Divine in New York City. His eloquent sermons on controversial topics such as capital punishment, civil rights, birth control, and social reform drew large crowds and established the newly named Cathedral of New York as an influential voice in American Protestantism. During this period, Pike published articles in popular national periodicals and was himself the subject of a *Reader's Digest* feature, "The Joyful Dean." He also gained a reputation as a political and social liberal and at one point turned down an honorary doctorate from the University of the South (Sewanee, Tennessee) because the school was segregated.

Pike's national stature increased even more in 1954, when he began hosting a television program on the ABC-TV network, *American Religious Town Hall*. This weekly show provided a needed public forum for respected religious commentators to debate current issues in theology and society. Pike inaugurated an interview and documentary program, *The Dean Pike Show*, in 1957. This half-hour telecast was aired every Sunday afternoon on ABC-TV and later in syndication. During the late 1950s, the program allowed for a frank and open exchange of differing opinions on social and cultural issues—something that was unusual at the time. This sustaining time telecast lasted until 1960, when ABC-TV switched the show's structure to an ecumenical format with multiple principal speakers and renamed it *Directions*.

Pike was elected Bishop Coadjutor of California in 1958. By 1959, he had replaced the incumbent and become Bishop of California. During a tenure that lasted until 1966, Bishop Pike raised enough funds to complete Grace Cathedral in San Francisco, increased church membership, organized a variety of social service programs, and helped found the Consultation on Church Union, an important ecumenical organization.

Pike, like his UTS professors Niebuhr and Tillich, was a tireless proponent of the view that traditional Christianity needed to refashion itself to meet the challenges of the modern world. In books and articles, he questioned orthodox doctrines such as the Trinity and the virgin birth and warned of the dangers of limiting God in philosophical and theological concepts. He also commissioned stained-glass windows with representations of such "secular saints" as Albert Einstein and Thurgood Marshall for Grace Cathedral and invited Martin Luther King, Jr., to preach in his church's pulpit. In another break with tradition, he ordained the first Episcopalian woman minister.

These actions both shocked and scandalized Pike's conservative colleagues. Between 1960 and 1966, he was officially charged with heresy by a group of Georgia clergy, a coalition of

Arizona churchmen, and by Henry I. Louttit, a conservative Florida bishop. Bishop Pike responded to these charges in three substantial theological books, *A Time for Christian Candor* (1964), *What Is This Treasure?* (1966), and *If This Be Heresy* (1967). These works reflected Pike's modernizing tendencies and created the same tenor of controversy as that generated by Pike supporter John T. Robinson's *Honest to God.*

The mid-1960s were also a time of personal trial and trauma for Pike. The bishop struggled with alcoholism, had a disastrous affair with a woman who committed suicide, and endured the suicide of his son, Jim. In the aftermath of these tragedies, Pike turned to mysticism and psychic investigation in an attempt to contact his dead son. He consulted mediums and even appeared on a televised seance with the famous psychic Arthur Ford. Pike's book on these investigations, *The Other Side* (1968), detailed his discoveries and attempted to reinterpret Christian doctrines such as the Resurrection. The controversial bishop suffered professionally during this period, enduring censure by the House of Bishops for his irresponsible conduct. He gained a measure of vindication, however, when, after demanding a heresy trial, the Episcopal Church publicly endorsed an ethic of theological openness.

The final years of Pike's life were a study in unfulfilled religious searching. He was banned by his Episcopal peers from priestly functioning and decided with great sadness to leave the church. He also joined the staff of the Center for the Study of Democratic Institutions at the University of California at Santa Barbara. While conducting research on the Essene community in the Judean desert in 1969, he and his new wife Diane Kennedy were stranded because of car trouble. His wife managed to walk for help but Pike himself died of dehydration and exposure.

The former bishop and pioneer of religious television never found a complete answer to his religious questions, but, in the end, affirmed more traditional Christian teaching than he denied. Like other theological liberals, Pike made his greatest mark in adapting the "deposit" of the Christian tradition to modern values and concerns. Although his stands on civil rights, women in the priesthood, and theological tolerance have become widely accepted within the Episcopal denomination, Pike's theological writings are largely ignored and his influence has declined significantly since his death.

SOURCES

Day, Beth. "The Joyful Dean." *Reader's Digest* 72 (February 1958): 140–45.

Erickson, Hal. *Religious Radio and Television in the United States, 1921–1991.* Jefferson, NC: McFarland, 1992.

Hazelton, Roger. "The Bothersome Bishop." *New Republic* 157 (October 1961).

Holzer, Hans W. *The Psychic World of Bishop Pike.* New York: Crown, 1970.

Lippy, Charles H., ed. *Twentieth-Century Shapers of American Popular Religion.* Westport, CT: Greenwood Press, 1989.

Montgomery, John Warwick. "The Bishop, the Spirits, and the Word." *Christianity Today* 12 (February 16, 1968).

Pike, James A. *Beyond Anxiety: The Christian Answer to Fear, Frustration, Guilt, Indecision, Inhibition, Loneliness, Despair.* New York: Scribner's, 1953.

———. *Doing the Truth: A Summary of Christian Ethics.* Garden City, NJ: Doubleday, 1955.

———. *If This Be Heresy.* New York: Harper & Row, 1964.

———. *A Time for Christian Candor.* New York: Harper & Row, 1964.

———. *What Is This Treasure?* New York: Harper & Row, 1966.

———. *You and the New Morality: 74 Cases.* New York: Harper & Row, 1967.

Pike, James. A., and Diane Kennedy. *Search: The Personal Story of a Wilderness Journey.* Garden City, NJ: Doubleday, 1970.

Pike, James A., with Norman Pittinger. *The Faith of the Church.* Vol. 3 in *The Church's Teaching.* Greenwich, CT: Seabury, 1953.

Stringfellow, William, and Anthony Towne. *The Bishop Pike Affair: Scandals of Conscience and Heresy, Relevance and Solemnity in the Contemporary Church.* New York: Harper & Row, 1967.

Wren, Christopher S. "An American Bishop's Search for a Space-Age God." *Look* 30 (February 1966): 25–29.

PILGRIM'S HOUR
see: Charles Fuller

POINT OF VIEW
first aired: 1975

A production of Marlin Maddoux's International Christian Media Ministry, *Point of View* is a daily Christian radio talk show that features news commentary geared toward politically-active evangelicals. Hosted by Maddoux since its inception in 1975, *Point of View* was broadcast, in its early days, from Maddoux's broadcast studio in Dallas, Texas. The program gained national access via the Satellite Radio Network in 1983.

Somewhat after the style of Larry King, Maddoux, who still hosts *Point of View*, invites dozens of guest stars each week. One of his recurring guests in the early 1990s was Iran-Contra defendant and onetime candidate for the US Senate, Colonel Oliver North. Maddoux also gives his audiences an opportunity to call in their opinions and responses to current issues.

At present, *Point of View* airs over more than 300 stations via the USA Radio Network, a Christian network founded by Maddoux in 1985 and supported solely by commercial advertisement. *Point of View* earned the Talk Show of the Year award in 1996 from the National Religious Broadcasters.

See also Marlin Maddoux

SOURCES

Ward, Mark, Sr. *Air of Salvation: The Story of Christian Broadcasting*. Grand Rapids, MI: Baker Book House, 1994.

POINTS OF VIEW
see: William Temple

PRAISE REPORT
first aired: 1995

A recent addition to Pentecostal television programming is *Praise Report*, hosted by John and Mary Jane D'Alesio. The D'Alesios are senior ministers of Heartland Christian Center family churches, which are located throughout North and Central Florida. The couple's ministry, which began in 1989, places a strong emphasis on prophecy and healing, the traditional foci of charismatic churches. *Praise Report*'s format includes joyful singing and John D'Alesio's dramatic sermons and healings at Heartland Christian Center churches. The television program began airing in 1995 on WACX Channel 55, an independent UHF religious station broadcasting from Leesburg, Florida. The show was soon being broadcast nationwide via satellite on Lester Sumrall's LeSea Broadcasting Network.

PREMIER RADIO
established: 1994

In 1990, the British parliament passed the Broadcasting Act, a law that effectively opened the radio airwaves in Great Britain to independent religious broadcasting. In response to this deregulation, several Christian evangelicals, led by Peter Meadows, applied to the British Radio Authority for the right to broadcast in London. After four years of work, two application submissions, and the gathering of 90,000 petition signatures, an AM license was granted to London Christian Radio (whose on-the-air identification is Premier Radio) in October of 1994. Meadows's proposal essentially made the case that a local London station whose programming was based on Christian values and beliefs would increase the listening choices for London's 10 million adults.

Meadows, who became the station's chief executive officer, and Mark Seaman, who became its program director, set Premier Radio up as a nonprofit charitable trust, the chairperson of which is a British viscount. By the time the station went on the air June 10, 1995, it had raised $2.24 million to be spent on pre-publicity, the purchase of studio equipment, and operating expenses. The trust estimates it will take about $3 million annually to operate the station.

The station uses five transmitters with 2,500 to 5,000 watts, which enable it to reach one out of every five adults in the United Kingdom. Although the core audience of the station is committed Christians, its programming is crafted to express Christian values and beliefs in such a way as not to alienate nonbelievers who enjoy quality radio options.

Premier Radio was inspired by evangelist Luis Palau, who came to London for a crusade in 1981 and asked Meadows (the crusade's executive director), "When am I on radio?" When Palau learned that British law would not allow such broadcasts, he said, "Change the law." Meadows took up this challenge and has made Premier Radio a powerful force on the United Kingdom's airwaves. On the station's inaugural date, a large party was held in a London park by supporters of the outreach. Those in attendance included major Christian personalities in sports, entertainment, and the secular media.

SOURCES

"Premier Radio's Premiere." *Religious Broadcasting*, June 1995.

FREDERICK PRICE
born: January 3, 1932, Santa Monica, California

One of the most successful African American radio and television ministers in broadcast history, Frederick K. C. Price is the eldest of three children born to Fred and Winifred Price. Although raised as a Jehovah's Witness, Price did not attend Kingdom Hall services after he reached his teens.

Price was educated in the Los Angeles public school system, graduating from Dorsey High School in 1950. After graduation, he enrolled

Courtesy: *Ever Increasing Faith*

at Los Angeles City College and studied there until 1952. During this period, Price occasionally attended church with friend Betty Sue Stout. He and Stout would later marry. It was while attending a Pentecostal tent meeting with Stout in 1953 that Price converted to Christianity. After hearing a voice commanding him to preach the gospel, Price decided to pursue a ministerial career.

In 1966, after working for a number of different denominations, Price became minister of the West Washington Community Church in Los Angeles, a Christian and Missionary Alliance congregation. He remained its minister until 1973, when he gathered a congregation of 300 people and founded the Crenshaw Christian Center in Inglewood, California. Not long afterwards, he began to broadcast his sermons over local radio.

In April 1978, with the help of Paul Crouch, Price began to broadcast a televised version of his weekly church services over UHF station KTBN, Los Angeles. Within a month, Price moved his program, *Ever Increasing Faith*, to VHF station KTTV, Los Angeles. This change gave Price a greater African American broadcast market. Price's audiences have grown dramatically over his nearly 20 years of broadcast ministry. At present, his program airs over 125 television and 40 radio stations throughout the

United States, the Caribbean, and Nigeria. The show is broadcast Friday evenings over the Trinity Broadcasting Network.

Price's ministry with the Crenshaw Christian Center has also grown. In 1981, he moved his church to the old Pepperdine campus in downtown Los Angeles, erecting a huge worship center with a 10,000-seat broadcast sanctuary. In 1984, Price again moved his congregation, this time to 79th and Vermont in South Central Los Angeles. Growth continued unabated. In 1989, Price saw the completion of a new worship center, the geodesic Faithdome, at a cost of over $10 million. With a congregation totaling 15,000 members, Price's ministry and its outreach to the Los Angeles community continues to expand.

The magic of Price's message is its positive, ecumenical, and redemptive character. It is not unusual for Price to smile, laugh, shake people's hands, give encouragement, tell humorous personal anecdotes, and even jest with the congregation during his sermon. Although his program is available in only 32 percent of American homes, it is consistently among the 10 most-watched Christian devotional broadcasts in the country.

Price sees himself more as a teacher providing knowledge than as a preacher giving inspiration. He once observed, "When you get the right information, inspiration will automatically follow." At the beginning of each broadcast, the trim minister looks into the camera and urges his television audience to send in monetary support. He then moves among his congregation, delivering his message in a staccato style. Near the end of his sermon, he again looks into the television camera requesting financial assistance. By this time, however, his voice is indistinguishable from the clapping and shouting of his congregation.

See also *Ever Increasing Faith*

SOURCES

Burgess, Stanley M., and Gary B. McGee, eds. *Dictionary of Pentecostal and Charismatic Movements.* Grand Rapids, MI: Zondervan, 1988.

Hill, George H. *Airwaves to the Soul: The Influence and Growth of Religious Broadcasting in America.* Saratoga, NY: R & E, 1983.

"Increasing Faith: The Price Is Right." *Christianity Today*, October 2, 1995.

Murphy, Larry G., J. Gordon Melton, and Gary L. Ward. *Encyclopedia of African American Religion.* New York: Garland, 1993.

Price, Frederick K. C. *How to Obtain Strong Faith.* Tulsa, OK: Harrison House, 1977.

DEREK PRINCE
born: August 14, 1915, Bangalore, India

Pentecostal author and educator, Peter Derek Prince, was born in Bangalore, India, while his father was serving in the British army. Prince studied at Eton and earned bachelor's and master's degrees from Cambridge in 1937 and 1941. During this period, Prince also studied at Hebrew University in Jerusalem.

Prince served in the medical corps during World War II and converted to Christianity while stationed in North Africa. He reported receiving the baptism of the Holy Spirit a few days after his conversion. Upon discharge from the British army in Jerusalem in 1946, Prince married Lydia Christensen, the founder of a children's home in Jerusalem, whom he had met while stationed there. He remained in Jerusalem until the establishment of the new State of Israel in 1948.

After returning to London, Prince began a Pentecostal church. He served as its pastor until 1956, when he traveled to Kenya to become principal of the African Teacher Training College, a position he held from 1957 to 1961. Prince spent 1962 touring Canada and speaking on behalf of mission work for the Pentecostal Assemblies of Canada. In 1964, he moved his family to the United States, taking pastorates in Minnesota, Seattle, and Chicago.

During the 1960s, Prince's interest in demonology led him to focus more and more on a ministry of deliverance from demonic power. Prince taught that demons could possess Christians as well as non-Christians and held exorcisms during his tent and radio revivals. In 1968, he moved to Ft. Lauderdale, Florida, and founded Derek Prince Publications. The company published many of his books and tracts in support of the charismatic movement in America. In 1974, Prince helped found the Good News Church in Ft. Lauderdale with Don Basham and Bob Mumford. However, disagreement over discipling methods ended Prince's association with the church in 1984.

In 1979, Prince began his international radio ministry, *Today with Derek Prince*. The show features a Bible-teaching format and concludes with a call for prayer and deliverance. The radio outreach airs throughout the United States and, in translation, around the world.

During the 1980s, Prince established the Global Outreach program, a missionary initiative that sends Christian literature without cost to Third World countries. The ministry has offices in Ft. Lauderdale and Jerusalem. Prince is probably best known for his teachings on physical healing, demon possession, and the Last Days.

SOURCES

Burgess, Stanley M., and Gary B. McGee, eds. *Dictionary of Pentecostal and Charismatic Movements*. Grand Rapids, MI: Zondervan, 1988.

Melton, J. Gordon. *Religious Leaders of America*. Detroit: Gale Research, 1991.

Prince, Derek. *Derek Prince: The Man and His Ministry*. Ft. Lauderdale, FL: Derek Prince Ministries, 1984.

———. *The Last Word on the Middle East*. Lincoln, NE: Chosen Books, 1982.

PRISONERS BIBLE BROADCAST
see: Christ Truth Ministries; Dan Gilbert

PRO-LIFE PERSPECTIVE
first aired: 1985

Supporters of the pro-life movement in America have had their own radio broadcast, *Pro-Life Perspective*, since January of 1985. The program is the official radio outreach of the Na-

tional Right to Life Committee (NRLC), the largest pro-life group in the United States. *Pro-Life Perspective* is hosted by Dr. Wanda Franz, the NRLC's president, and features prominent pro-life guest speakers. Since its inception, the show has generated a growing audience that is estimated to be in the hundreds of thousands. The show offers personal and professional discussions of issues that are of concern to the pro-life movement. It also keeps its supporters informed about pending legislation that might affect, if passed, the pro-life agenda.

ELIZABETH CLARE PROPHET
born: April 8, 1939, Red Bank, New Jersey

Courtesy: Church Universal and Triumphant

Elizabeth Clare Prophet is the leader of the Church Universal and Triumphant, a New Age religious community headquartered at a 28,000-acre ranch in Montana that borders Yellowstone National Park. Since the 1980s, Prophet has made use of local community cable channels to broadcast a wide array of her lectures, dictations, and conferences. As of the winter of 1994, her programs were being aired on 203 cable stations in 37 states. Her church estimates that these programs are viewed by an audience in the millions.

Born Elizabeth Clare Wulf to a German father and a Swiss mother, Prophet grew up as an only child. She and her mother visited many of the churches in her hometown, and dinner-table conversation revolved around world politics and history. Her father, a retired ship's captain, was accused of anti-American activities during World War II and briefly imprisoned. According to Prophet, her father was released when several prominent Jews came to the prison facility and testified to his character and loyalty.

While still a young woman, Prophet became disillusioned with the religious teachings of her childhood. As she recalled, "I would hear the voice of Jesus speaking to me in my heart, speaking the truth as I heard error building upon error from the pulpit." She began exploring the writings of Mohandas Gandhi, Albert Schweitzer, Mary Baker Eddy, and Norman Vincent Peale. When she was 18, Prophet accidentally opened a book published by the I Am Movement. This group was a revelatory community derived from the Theosophical tradition and led by Edna and Donald Ballard. The group's founder, Guy Warren Ballard, had claimed to be the spokesperson for the "Ascended Masters," a group of advanced initiates believed to be guiding the spiritual evolution of humanity. On one of the book's pages, Prophet found a picture of Saint Germain, a purported Ascended Master. She experienced a revelatory moment of recognition and began an earnest search for this teacher.

After high school, Prophet studied French in Switzerland and later enrolled at Antioch College in Yellow Springs, Ohio. Before graduating from Antioch, Prophet decided to transfer to Boston University, where she pursued a degree in political science. It was during her studies in Boston, on April 22, 1961, that she attended a lecture by Mark L. Prophet, the founder and leader of The Summit Lighthouse. This small group was an offshoot of the I Am Movement and its derivatives, the Bridge to Freedom and the Lighthouse of Freedom. Mark Prophet had left these groups and organized The Summit Lighthouse in Washington, DC, in 1958. Like its predecessor groups, The Summit Light-

house claimed to be a vessel for revelations from the Ascended Masters.

Six weeks after this first meeting, Elizabeth Prophet was reportedly visited by El Morya, another Ascended Master, on her way to class. The master informed her that she must move to Washington DC, where she would be trained by Mark Prophet. The young woman obeyed this guidance and relocated to the nation's capital. Her first husband, a Norwegian law student whom she married in 1960, disagreed with this plan, and the couple were eventually divorced. On March 16, 1963, Mark and Elizabeth acknowledged their strong personal affinity by getting married. In 1964, Elizabeth Prophet reportedly received an anointing from Saint Germain to serve as a messenger of the Ascended Masters. She began, along with Mark Prophet, delivering "dictations" (oral messages from the masters) from this time onward. These messages were usually delivered in the context of a Summit Lighthouse public worship service. The couple also began to build their organization by traveling around the country, giving lectures and publishing the messages of the Ascended Masters. The best-known books coauthored by the Prophets included *Prayer and Meditation* (1978), *Corona Class Lessons* (1986) and *Climb the Highest Mountain* (1972).

In 1966, the Prophets moved their growing staff and one-year-old son to a new international headquarters in Colorado Springs, Colorado. Their retreat center in the Broadmoor area became a magnet for the young counterculture seekers of the late 1960s and early 1970s. Between 1966 and 1973, the Prophet's three daughters were born, and Elizabeth helped establish the Montessori International School, which trained children using the educational methods of Maria Montessori.

The Summit Lighthouse underwent a period of turbulence and disunity following the death of Mark Prophet from a stroke in February 1973. Elizabeth Prophet assumed control of the movement and became the sole messenger for the Ascended Masters. She moved the movement's headquarters first to a leased campus in Pasadena, California, and then to the 218-

acre Gillette estate in the Santa Monica Mountains behind Malibu. This estate became "Camelot," which the movement billed as a "New Age Mystery School." The facility offered a number of extended educational programs and attracted students from around the country.

Prophet changed the group's name to the Church Universal and Triumphant in 1974 and retained Summit Lighthouse as the appellation of the movement's educational division. During the mid-1970s, Prophet began to promote her teachings around the world. She traveled and lectured in Canada, Mexico, West Africa, Europe, Australia, India, and the Philippines. She gained national attention when she appeared on an episode of *In Search Of* that explored the mysterious Comte Saint Germain.

A long-standing part of the Church Universal and Triumphant's ideology has been its predictions of a coming apocalypse. For the most part, these predictions have centered around the outbreak of nuclear war between the United States and the (former) Soviet Union, catastrophic natural disasters, and a world economic collapse.

It was likely the expectation of these events that convinced Prophet and other church leaders to purchase the 13,000-acre Forbes ranch in Paradise Valley, Montana, in 1981. Within five years, the group had moved its headquarters to what was now called the Royal Teton Ranch and sold its Malibu property. The facility has been expanded to 28,000 acres and has become a self-sufficient spiritual community with about 600 permanent residents. In addition to being the national headquarters for the church, the Royal Teton Ranch also houses The Summit Lighthouse, Summit University, and Summit University Press. The compound holds international conferences and festivals throughout the year.

The Church Universal and Triumphant sees as its chief mission the publication and distribution of the teachings of the Ascended Masters. Students and members receive a weekly publication, *Pearls of Wisdom*, which contain Prophet's latest messages. More advanced students can join the Keepers of the Flame Fraternity and dedicate themselves to planetary enlightenment. For the privilege of membership and of receiving monthly lessons on spiritual development, devotees pledge a tithe of their income.

The teachings of the Ascended Masters include the usual elements of the Western Esoteric tradition, among which are a gnostic conception of Christ, belief in the law of karma and reincarnation, spiritual alchemy, astrology, and various devotional exercises and liturgies. Prophet's signature teachings emphasize the "science of the spoken word," also called "decreeing" (during which members verbally affirm their inner "I Am Presence"), and the invoking of "the violet flame," a kind of "sacred fire" that "transmutes the cause, effect, record, and memory of negative karma and misqualified energy that result in discord, disease, and death." According to Prophet, those who daily invoke this flame will experience spiritual transformation and soul liberation.

Prophet's entry into religious broadcasting began during the 1980s. Her students around the country were encouraged to purchase specially taped programs from the church and to show them on local cable access channels. By the summer of 1993, the organization's video supplement contained hundreds of Prophet's taped classes, conferences, lectures, and series covering every aspect of her church's activities. A sample of these programs includes the Mystical Paths of the World's Religions, the Coming Revolution in Higher Consciousness, Achieving Personal Success, Alchemy and Saint Germain, the Lost Years and Lost Teachings of Jesus, Prophecy and Astrology for the 1990s, the AIDS Conspiracy, the UFO Connection, and Summit University forums and seminars on the natural healing arts, the spiritual ramifications of abortion, and Montessori education. These programs are shown weekly on over 200 cable stations throughout the country. Along with Prophet's prolific output of books, these cable programs have given her eclectic spiritual teachings a broad dissemination throughout the country. The church owns sophisticated television and videotaping technology, and records each of her lectures and dictations for future distribution and broadcast.

During the 1980s and early 1990s, Prophet and her movement have come under increasing criticism from the national media, anticult groups, disgruntled ex-members, and local residents of Paradise Valley. The targets of criticism range from the group's development of its ranch compound to Prophet's constant warnings of impending apocalypse. Prophet's third husband, Randall King, left the group in the 1970s and sued his ex-wife for various damages during the 1980s. This costly trial brought to public attention a number of embarrassing allegations against Prophet, including Prophet's lavish lifestyle, unsuccessful commodities trading, and misuse of church funds. A second public relations fiasco occurred when Prophet's fourth husband, Edward Francis, was convicted of illegal firearms purchases during the late 1980s. After the Waco disaster in April 1993, the Church Universal and Triumphant was singled out by the media as the group most similar to the Branch Davidians and most likely to precipitate a crisis with law enforcement officials. The church has taken steps to refurbish its public image since that time and regularly invites university researchers and law enforcement officials to visit its ranch and hold discussions with church members. In spite of, if not because of these controversies, its membership continues to increase.

Elizabeth Clare Prophet continues to maintain a high national profile, conducting lecture tours around the world and appearing as a guest on such popular television programs as *Larry King Live*, *Nightline*, *48 Hours*, *The Oprah Winfrey Show*, and *Donahue*. She has been a strong and articulate defender of her church and its teachings in these forums. In addition, during February 1994, Prophet and other church officials appeared on an NBC-TV program entitled *Ancient Prophecies*. This prime-time special examined the apocalyptic prophecies of such figures as Nostradamus, Edgar Cayce, and Prophet.

Moreover, Summit University Press continues to publish Prophet's books and compilations of her dictations. Some of the press's most successful titles include *The Great White Brotherhood in the Culture, History, and Destiny of America* (1976); *The Chela and the Path* (1976); *Cosmic Consciousness* (1976); *Vials of the Seven Last Plagues: Prophecies for the 1980s by the Seven Archangels* (1983); *Mysteries of the Holy Grail* (1984); *Saint Germain on Prophecy: Coming World Changes* (1986); and *The Astrology of the Four Horsemen: How You Can Heal Yourself and Planet Earth* (1991).

SOURCES

Harris, Ron. "Offbeat Church Stirs Fears in Montana." *Los Angeles Times*, December 27, 1989.

Profile: Elizabeth Clare Prophet. Pamphlet. Livingston, MT: Summit University Press, 1992.

Prophet, Elizabeth Clare. [El Morya] *The Chela and the Path*. Colorado Springs: Summit University Press, 1976.

———. *The Great White Brotherhood in the Culture, History and Religion of America*. Los Angeles: Summit University Press, 1976.

———. *The Lost Teachings of Jesus*. 2 vols. Livingston, MT: Summit University Press, 1986, 1988.

———. *The Lost Years of Jesus*. Livingston, MT: Summit University Press, 1984.

———. *Saint Germain on Prophecy: Coming World Changes*. Livingston, MT: Summit University Press, 1986.

———. *Vials of the Seven Last Plagues*. Los Angeles: Summit University Press, 1983.

Prophet, Mark L., and Elizabeth Clare Prophet. *Climb the Highest Mountain*. Colorado Springs: Summit Lighthouse, 1972.

Rubenstein, Sara. "Trouble in Paradise." *The Sunday Oregonian*, October 4, 1987.

The Video Supplement: Elizabeth Clare Prophet. Pamphlet. Livingston, MT: Summit University Press, 1993.

THE PROTESTANT HOUR

see: The Lutheran Church in America

PSYCHOLOGY FOR LIVING

The first ever Christian psychology program, *Psychology for Living*, hosted by Clyde Narramore, began airing in the early 1950s. Originating in Pasadena, California, and featuring a question-and-answer format drawn from the letters of faithful listeners, the radio ministry has aired almost continually since that time, making it perhaps the longest running Christian program of its kind. The ministry's warm and empathetic approach is captured in the motto of the Narramore Christian Foundation, which sponsors *Psychology for Living*: "Every person is worth understanding."

With the appearance of rival, more up-to-date Christian psychology programs in the 1970s and 1980s, the popularity of *Psychology for Living* has begun to wane. Regardless of declining program audience and listener contributions, Narramore hopes to continue the radio ministry after his retirement through his son, Kevin Narramore.

See also Clyde M. Narramore

SOURCES

The Directory of Religious Organizations in the United States. 2d ed. Falls Church, VA: McGrath, 1982.

Erickson, Hal. *Religious Radio and Television in the United States, 1921–1991*. Jefferson, NC: McFarland, 1992.

Melton, J. Gordon. *Directory of Religious Organizations in the United States*. 3d ed. Detroit: Gale Research, 1993.

THE PTL CLUB
see: Jim Bakker

R

PAUL RADER

born: August 26, 1879, Denver, Colorado
died: July 19, 1938, Glendale, California

Courtesy: Billy Graham Center Museum

Paul Rader was an early pioneer of radio evangelism who had a significant influence upon the first generation of religious broadcasters.

Rader received his early religious training from his father, a Denver-based Methodist minister and revivalist. While attending the Universities of Denver and Colorado, the younger Rader boxed and played football. His first job after college was as the athletic director of Hamline University in Saint Paul, Minnesota. After making a decision to enter the ministry in 1906, Rader pastored Congregational churches in Boston, Massachusetts, and Portland, Oregon. He soon became discouraged with his work, however, and left the ministry altogether in 1908.

A couple of years later, while living in New York City, Rader came under the influence of E. D. "Daddy" Whiteside, one of the leaders of the Christian and Missionary Alliance (CMA). He experienced a renewal of his Christian commitment in 1911 and decided to work as an assistant minister under Whiteside at the Pittsburgh, Pennsylvania, CMA Tabernacle. Rader quickly established a reputation as an orator and evangelist and in 1915 was invited to take over the pastorship of Moody Memorial Church in Chicago. Following the death of CMA president Albert Benjamin Simpson in 1919, Rader, who had been serving as the alliance's vice president, was elected chief executive. He found that the demands of both jobs were too much, so he resigned from Moody Memorial in 1921 and moved to the CMA headquarters in New York.

It was at this time that Rader began working closely with Oswald J. Smith, a promising young alliance minister. The two men developed a vision dubbed "tabernacalism," which promoted the construction of evangelical tabernacles in large urban areas. The tabernacles would seat 3,000 worshippers and provide daily evangelistic services to those oppressed by the tumult of urban life. Although the CMA never fully supported the plan, Rader was able to build a prototype, the Chicago Gospel Tabernacle, in 1922. He decided to leave his post with the

CMA and become the tabernacle's full-time pastor.

In the summer of 1922, Rader was asked by Chicago mayor William Hale Thompson to preach over the local radio station WHT, which Thompson owned. Rader accepted the invitation and brought a brass quartet to the mayor's makeshift studio atop city hall. As quartet member Clarence Jones recounted,

> On that first broadcast, we had no studio—the mayor's men had set up a crude shack on the roof of the City Hall. So, out in the open air, we unpacked our instruments and, at the signal of the operator, pointed our trumpets and trombones at what he called a "microphone." It was literally an old telephone mouthpiece with a fearful array of wires, tubes, and gadgets behind it called a "transmitter."

The response to this cameo appearance was overwhelmingly positive. Buoyed by this success, Rader decided to use the airwaves as a means of spreading his fundamentalist gospel. After negotiations with other Chicago stations, Rader reached an agreement with radio station WBBM to use its studios for 14 hours every Sunday. He called his once-a-week-station WJBT ("Where Jesus Blesses Thousands") and included in his programming the Sunday evening worship services at Gospel Tabernacle, orchestra and organ concerts, choral performances, and such shows as the *Healing Hour*, the *Bible Drama Hour*, and *The Back Home Hour*. As a result of the broadcasts, many thousands of people began attending the live worship services at Gospel Tabernacle. Having heard the charismatic preacher in their own homes, many people were eager to see him live.

Rader enlisted the Gospel Tabernacle's music ministry when he began broadcasting his first daily program of radio evangelism, *The Breakfast Brigade*, on station WHT. The show was picked up as a weekly offering on the CBS radio network in 1931.

Due to his relaxed and persuasive style, many fellow evangelical preachers began to consider radio ministries. Among them was Charles E. Fuller, whose *Old Fashioned Revival Hour* would become one of America's most beloved

religious radio ministries. Another associate of Rader's who entered the field of religious broadcasting was Clarence Jones, one of the founders of HCJB in Quito, Ecuador. As Jones remembered of his mentor,

> I found in him a spiritual father, a wise and experienced counselor, but above all, a leader of challenging courage and vision. Among the many incidents of Mr. Rader's ministry that inspired my heart to greater personal faith was his ready comprehension and acceptance of radio as a means of getting the gospel to the unchurched masses.

Rader, however, never lost sight of the difference between a radio ministry and a church. He maintained that

> The church revealed to us in the Bible is made up of Christians who gather for worship, baptism, communion, marriage, funerals, Bible teaching, prayer, faith testimony, song and Christian fellowship, bearing of sorrows, joys and burdens. None of this can be done well by radio.

For Rader, broadcast technology was an effective means to spread the gospel to unbelievers. In answer to critics who considered radio ministries to be "tools of the devil," Rader claimed, "There's nothing in the Bible that tells the world to come to the church, but there's everything in the Bible that tells the church to go to the world. Radio takes the gospel to the unchurched. That's why I'm using it!"

After leaving the Christian Missionary Alliance movement in 1925, Rader established Christian World Couriers, a missionary organization. He was the organization's leader until his death in 1938.

SOURCES

Armstrong, Ben. *The Electric Church*. Nashville: Thomas Nelson, 1979.

"Jazz Age Evangelism: Paul Rader and the Chicago Gospel Tabernacle 1922–1933." Pamphlet produced for an Exhibit of the Archives of the Billy Graham Center, March 16 to October 27, 1984.

Jones, Clarence. "Paul Rader—Pioneer of Gospel Broadcasting," included in a letter to Lyell Rader (July 23, 1960), located in the Archives of the Billy Graham Center, Wheaton, Illinois.

Rader, Paul. *The Fight for Light and Other Sermons.* New York: The Book Stall, 1916.

———. *The Midnight Cry.* Chicago: Chicago Gospel Tabernacle, 1938.

———. *Round the World.* New York: Fleming H. Revell, 1922.

Reid, Daniel G., Robert D. Linder, Bruce L. Sheely, and Harry S. Stout. *Dictionary of Christianity in America.* Downers Grove, IL: InterVarsity Press, 1990.

Tucker, Leon W. *Rader's Redemption.* New York: The Book Stall, 1918.

Voskuil, Dennis. "The Power of the Air: Evangelicals and the Rise of Religious Broadcasting." In *American Evangelicals and the Mass Media*, edited by Quentin J. Schultze. Grand Rapids: Academie Books, 1990.

Ward, Mark, Sr. *Air of Salvation: The Story of Christian Broadcasting.* Manassas, VA: National Religious Broadcasters, 1994.

"What About a Radio Church?" *World-Wide Christian Courier*, July, 1926.

RADIO AR INTERCONTINENTAL, ARMENIA
established: 1989

After the breakup of the Soviet Union in the late 1980s, an Armenian superstation located in the mountains of Ararat opened its airtime to Radio AR Intercontinental (RARI), a gospel ministry spearheaded by Jacob Jambazian. The ministry uses more than 5 million watts of broadcasting power to reach Armenians living in China, the Middle East, Southeast Asia, South and Central America, and North Africa. Jambazian hosts a daily 30-minute program over a medium-wave transmitter of 1 million watts. He plans to broadcast the Christian gospel until the year 2001, when Armenia will celebrate 1700 years as a Christian enclave.

Jambazian is an ethnic Armenian who began his radio career in 1960 as a broadcaster of Armenian language programs over Trans World Radio (TRW). This powerful international religious network began broadcasting with Paul Freed and his Voice of Tangiers radio ministry in 1954. In 1959, Freed was forced to move his ministry from Tangiers, Morocco, to the principality of Monaco. When Jambazian began airing his Armenian broadcasts, TRW had just set up its new 100,000-watt short-wave transmitter on Mount Agel in Monaco.

Jambazian later brought humanitarian supplies to Armenia after the devastating earthquake of 1988, which killed 50,000 and left 500,000 homeless. Smuggled into the truckloads of blankets, food, and medical supplies were 200,000 New Testaments. These humanitarian efforts brought Jambazian into contact with Armenia's minister of media, who controlled all radio and television coverage. The minister offered to let Jambazian build a gospel station next to the government's own radio station. These mountain transmitters allow RARI's signal to overcome the blocking capacities of the Ural and Caucasus Mountains and reach Armenians around the world.

SOURCES

"Armenia—The New Superpower." *Religious Broadcasting*, June, 1995.

RADIO BIBLE CLASS MINISTRIES
established: 1938

Radio Bible Class Ministries (RBC) stems from the work of M. R. DeHaan, a former physician and pastor who started RBC in 1938. At that time, the ministry featured a format of Bible discussions, choral interludes, and the application of scriptural principles to everyday life. Following DeHaan's death in 1965, his son Richard took over the ministry and expanded its outreach with the help of Larry Langhorn. This expansion included the development of a youth-oriented series, *On the Move*, and a television ministry.

As of 1995, RBC Ministries was busy on a number of fronts. It continued to produce *Day of Discovery*, a nationally syndicated television show that has aired weekly for the past 25 years. This half-hour program has featured such teachers as M. R. DeHaan, Dave Burnham, Jimmy De Young, and Billy Strachan, who often deliver their Bible lessons from settings in the Middle East.

The ministry also produces *Radio Bible Class Daily*, a 15-minute discussion program, hosted by Haddon Robinson, that tries to relate the Christian Scriptures to everyday living. Other radio outreaches include *Radio Bible Class Weekend*, the original DeHaan half-hour program; *Sounds of the Times*, a daily 5-minute discussion of contemporary views on spiritual issues which is geared to young adults; and *Our Daily Bread Radio*, which provides daily devotional meditations.

RBC Ministries also publishes several periodicals, including *Our Daily Bread*, a bimonthly devotional guide; *Campus Journal*, which provides daily devotions for students; and *Discovery Series*, a Bible-study publication devoted to crucial contemporary issues.

In its promotional literature, the ministry states that it is a nondenominational organization dedicated to providing Bible-study resources to churches and individuals around the world. RBC's purpose is "to lead people of all nations to personal faith in Christ, to growth in Christlikeness, and to active involvement in a local church by teaching the Word of God through audio, video, print, and correspondence media."

The ministry, which is headquartered in Grand Rapids, Michigan, has branch offices in Canada, Australia, England, Singapore, the Philippines, India, Jamaica, Nigeria, Kenya, and Ghana.

See also M. R. DeHaan; *Day of Discovery*

SOURCES

Erickson, Hal. *Religious Radio and Television in the United States, 1921–1991*. Jefferson, NC: McFarland, 1992.

Radio Bible Class Ministries. Various promotional brochures, 1995.

RADIO BIBLE HOUR
first aired: December, 1935

Hosted by fundamentalist Baptist Minister J. Harold Smith since its founding, *Radio Bible Hour* has emanated from a number of locations during its stormy broadcast history. Not many years after its first airing over a local station in Greenville, South Carolina, the program gained a faithful following whose financial contributions helped keep Smith on the air during the Depression years. In the late 1930s, Smith expanded his operation and began to broadcast his Bible-teaching program over radio superstation WNOX, Knoxville, Tennessee. During this period, the broadcast grew in popularity within fundamentalist Baptist circles.

In the 1940s, however, Smith's fiery brand of Fundamentalism ran counter to the sensibilities of the Federal Council of Churches (FCC), which spent its energies trying to regulate religious broadcast programs. During one of his Bible-study programs, Smith characterized the FCC as a "mad dog of Hell" and a "hydra-headed Frankenstein." Smith was eventually forced off the air, but not without a fight. In protest, he, as well as a number of other fundamentalist preachers, poured their resources into buying broadcast time on the powerful 100,000-watt radio station XERF in Ciudad Acuna, Mexico, just across the border from Del Rio, Texas. In 1947, Smith also built radio station WBIK, Knoxville, over which he exercised a measure of independent control.

Recurring problems with the Federal Communications Commission led Smith to relocate his broadcast ministry headquarters to XERF in Mexico in 1953. With each move, Smith not only gained larger audiences but increased his unfavorable notoriety among liberals. Indeed, Smith's popular program remained on the air well into the 1980s, ending about the same time that the Mexican government decided to ban the broadcast of all English-language religious programming.

See also J. Harold Smith

SOURCES

Fowler, Gene, and Bill Crawford. *Border Radio.*
Austin: Texas Monthly Press, 1987.

Hill, George H. *Airwaves to the Soul: The Influence
and Growth of Religious Broadcasting in
America.* Saratoga, CA: R & E, 1983.

Roy, Ralph L. *Apostles of Discord.* Boston: Beacon
Press, 1953.

Ward, Mark, Sr. *Air of Salvation: The Story of
Christian Broadcasting.* Grand Rapids, MI: Baker
Book House, 1994.

RADIO CHAPEL SERVICE
first aired: April 1923

Radio Chapel Service, hosted by R. R. Brown,
was perhaps the first program that sought to in-
volve its audiences as though they were members of a nondenominational congregation of
the air. Brown accomplished this by inviting listeners to join the World Radio Congregation,
which issued official membership cards. First
broadcast from radio station WOW, in Omaha,
Nebraska, *Radio Chapel Service* spawned a
number of similar congregational concept programs. The Sunday radio show counted 100,000
listeners by 1925 and over half a million by
1935.

Not long before the broadcast ministry passed
to Brown's son, Robert Brown, it expanded its
programming into television. When the show
finally went off the air in 1977, *Radio Chapel
Service* had been the longest running radio program in religious broadcast history. Brown died
in 1964.

See also R. R. Brown

SOURCES

Hadden, Jeffrey K., and Charles E. Swann. *Prime Time
Preachers: The Rising Power of Televangelism.*
Reading, MA: Addison-Wesley, 1981.

Ward, Mark, Sr. *Air of Salvation: The Story of
Christian Broadcasting.* Grand Rapids, MI: Baker
Book House, 1994.

RADIO CHURCH OF GOD
see: Lightfoot Solomon Michaux

RADIO CORDAC
established: 1963

Radio Cordac began as a central African radio
ministry cosponsored by the Kansas Yearly
Meeting of Friends, the Free Methodists, and
the World Gospel Mission. The station started
its broadcasts in Burundi in 1963. The ministry
ran into difficulties due to internal political strife
in Burundi, and, after a temporary hiatus, was
shut down permanently in 1977.

SOURCES

Armstrong, Ben. *The Electric Church.* Nashville:
Thomas Nelson, 1979.

THE RADIO ENSEMBLE
established: 1933

The New England Fellowship (NEF) Radio
Ministry began in 1933 when a number of fellowship staff members began singing and playing music for various radio programs. The
Radio Ensemble, as the music group came to
be called, broadcast 150 programs over 16 radio stations throughout the region their first year.

In 1934, the ensemble played weekdays during the month of October over religious station
WHEB, Portsmouth, New Hampshire, then
launched its own morning program, *Tune Up
Your Heart*, on WHDH. They performed weekday mornings and on *Young People's Radio
Rally* on WCOP, Boston; and Monday and Tuesday afternoons on WBZ and WBSO respectively. By 1935, the ensemble was heard on 420
radio programs over 49 stations throughout New
England.

In June 1935, the ensemble toured the Midwest, broadcasting over a number of regional
stations, including WMBI, the radio station of

the Moody Bible Institute in Chicago, and other stations in metropolitan Chicago and Cleveland. The following year, the Radio Ensemble performed over WORL and again over WCOP and WBZ. Interestingly, the NEF staff were able to produce its programs at no cost to the Fellowship, since broadcasters were eager to provide their listeners with a variety of programming.

In 1937 and 1938, the Radio Ensemble made a coast-to-coast tour of the United States with J. Elwin Wright, NEF's director. In 1939, the ensemble broadcast some 218 programs over 18 stations; the following year, however, the number of performances dropped to only 108 programs over 16 stations. In 1944, the ensemble reorganized itself and began to broadcast a new program, *The Victory Hour,* over WHEB.

While the ensemble's original purpose had been to broaden the impact of NEF by promoting the fellowship's various summer conferences and evangelistic crusades, its impact expanded throughout the country, bringing together evangelicals of all varieties.

Although the NEF's popular Radio Ensemble was heard throughout the United States, the fellowship's main program, *The Fellowship Hour*, remained on WMEX, Boston, throughout the 1930s and 1940s.

SOURCES

Evans, Elizabeth. *The Wright Vision: The Story of the New England Fellowship*. Lanham, MD: United Press of America, 1991.

RADIO MANANTIAL
established: 1994

Since September 1994, the Hispanic community around the world has listened to the broadcasts of Radio Manantial, the Spanish program service of the World Radio Network. The service offers a nondenominational 24-hour format of Christ-centered music and teaching programs and is available via satellite. World Radio Network is a ministry of HCJB World Radio Fellowship. Radio Manantial is headquartered in San Juan, Texas.

See also HCJB, Ecuador

RADIO VOICE OF THE GOSPEL
established: 1963

Radio Voice of the Gospel (RVOG) was created by the Lutheran World Federation in 1963 as a missionary outreach to Africa, the Middle East, India, China, and Hong Kong. The ministry, which cost nearly 2 million dollars to build, was located in Addis Ababa, Ethiopia, and included 12 feeder studios around the world. Programming was broadcast in over 16 languages.

In 1974, a Marxist revolution toppled the pro-Western government of Ethiopian emperor Haile Selassie and, by 1977, the new government had confiscated the 200,000-watt RVOG facility in Addis Ababa. The government changed the station's name to Radio Voice of Revolutionary Ethiopia and used the facility to broadcast its Marxist-oriented propaganda.

SOURCES

Armstrong, Ben. *The Electric Church*. Nashville: Thomas Nelson, 1979.

Gilbert, W. Kent. *Commitment to Unity: A History of the Lutheran Church in America*. Philadelphia: Fortress Press, 1988.

RANGER BILL

Ranger Bill, a children's radio program sponsored by the Moody Bible Institute in Chicago, combined the do-good spirit of radio's *Lone Ranger* and *Sergeant Preston* with the environmental concerns of Smokey the Bear. Airing in the 1970s and 1980s, the basic plotline of the adventure program featured a skillful and ecologically-conscious forest ranger whose strong faith in God helped him tackle a host of daunting problems.

Although its characterizations of Ranger Bill's faithful Festusesque and Tonto-like companions were less than sensitive throwbacks to Hollywood B-movie stereotypes, the *Ranger Bill* program remained relatively popular with children throughout its decade-long run.

SOURCES

Hill, George H. *Airwaves to the Soul: The Influence and Growth of Religious Broadcasting in America.* Saratoga, CA: R & E, 1983.

RELIGIOUS NEWS SERVICE
established: 1933

The Religious News Service is an interfaith news organization that provides news reports, interest stories, and file photo services for religious publications, news agencies, and radio and television stations of all denominations and faiths. The service claims over 900 correspondents and is headquartered in New York City.

SOURCES

Melton, J. Gordon. *Directory of Religious Organizations in the United States.* 3d ed. Detroit: Gale Research, 1993.

RENEWING YOUR MIND
first aired: 1994

Renewing Your Mind is a daily radio broadcast hosted by R. C. Sproul, the founder and director of Ligonier Ministries, an Orlando-based producer of Christian educational materials. The program was being heard on over 70 stations nationwide by September 1995.

Sproul was born February 13, 1939, in Pittsburgh, Pennsylvania. He earned his doctorate in theology from the Free University of Amsterdam when he was just 25 years of age. Since that time he has taught theology and philosophy at colleges and seminaries, including the Reformed Theological Seminary in Orlando, Florida. Sproul is the author of over 30 books on Christian teaching and has recorded hundreds of messages on video and audiocassette.

The radio evangelist's deep concern for lay education stems from his vision of believers applying Christian teaching to every sphere of life:

> I dream of a new reformation, a reformation that is not simply a renewal of life but a new vision of life: a vision that yields new forms and structures in society and culture. As long as Christians restrict their Christianity to a religion, a faith that is compartmentalized and isolated from life, they can have revival but never, ever reformation.

Among the topics that have been discussed on *Renewing Your Mind* are anger, the drama of redemption, justification by faith alone, the life of David, the names of God, worldviews in conflict, and the words and writings of the Apostles, Jesus, and the Prophets. The radio ministry hoped to expand to 100 broadcast outlets by 1996.

Sproul had an earlier radio ministry, *Ask R. C.*, during the late 1980s. The show's format had Sproul answering questions from a small studio audience. The five-minute program was recorded live for later broadcast.

SOURCES

"Renewing Your Mind Online with R. C. Sproul." World Wide Web site http://www.gospelcom.net/ligonier/ (1995).

REVEREND IKE
born: June 1, 1935, Ridgeland, South Carolina

Frederick J. Eikerenkoetter II, known to his followers as "Reverend Ike," was one of the first African American ministers to appropriate the doctrines and practices of New Thought, a late nineteenth century religious movement that sought to harness the powers of the human mind for material and spiritual progress. He promoted his gospel of personal empowerment and prosperity in sermons on radio and television, in lectures around the United States, and through his United Church and Science of Living Institute.

Eikerenkoetter grew up in South Carolina where his fundamentalist Baptist father was the pastor of the Bible Way Church in Ridgeland. The future evangelist decided early in life to pursue a preaching ministry and became the assistant pastor of his father's church at age 14. After earning his bachelor of theology degree from the American Bible College in Chicago in 1956, Eikerenkoetter served two years as a chaplain in the Air Force. He then returned to South Carolina where he worked as a storefront preacher and founded the United Church of Jesus Christ for All People. It was not until Eikerenkoetter's subsequent relocations to Boston and New York City during the 1960s, however, that his ministry began to blossom.

While in Boston, Eikerenkoetter created the Miracle Temple and began a radio program. By 1969, he had relocated to New York, refurbished an abandoned theater, and organized both the United Christian Evangelistic Association and the United Church and Science of Living Institute. Within a short time, his radio broadcasts were being aired in 56 markets and he was beginning plans for a television program.

Joy of Living, his popular television show, premiered in 1973 and ultimately would be broadcast over 25 stations. At this time, the flamboyant preacher also became the object of a great deal of national media attention, appearing on popular talk shows and in newspaper and magazine articles.

Reverend Ike's message was a significant departure from the Baptist fundamentalism of his early youth. Influenced by the New Thought doctrines of mental healing and prosperity consciousness, he told his listeners that they should be more concerned with earthly rewards in their present lives than with heavenly rewards in the "sweet by and by." Eikerenkoetter offered his followers the opportunity to live in prosperity by signing on to his "blessing plan." This plan was essentially a stripped-down version of conventional prosperity-consciousness teachings. It emphasized affirmation of one's own abundance, giving to the church as a sign of faith, and manifesting the riches one desired. Eikerenkoetter also advocated the use of creative visualization to project what one desired onto the plane of causation. He transformed the traditional biblical teaching that "Money is the root of all evil" into "Lack of money is the root of all evil."

Eikerenkoetter also emphasized the importance of reconfiguring one's own self-image as the prerequisite condition for experiencing prosperity. Specifically, this entailed thinking of God as the core of one's true self and consequently feeling oneself to be worthy of God's abundant blessings.

At the peak of his popularity, Reverend Ike's boisterous worship services at the United Church Center Palace Auditorium in New York City had an average attendance of 5,000 people and his radio program was being heard on over 89 stations. His movement magazine, *Action!*, had a subscriber list of over one million. Eikerenkoetter also developed a sophisticated mail-order business that peddled "miracle prayer cloths," a magical money-generating powder that was to be sprinkled on one's empty wallet, healing ointments, and various pamphlets detailing "fantastic ideas" for how to get rich. Even though his star faded in the 1980s, his mail-order business continued to generate significant income for the ministry.

Reverend Ike's flamboyant lifestyle—he reportedly spent $1,000 per week on new clothing—and questionable fundraising methods inevitably drew criticism from both white and African American church leaders. For instance, Eikerenkoetter declared that his prayers for miracles for individual congregants had failed on occasion because these congregants had not given him a large enough contribution. This alienated him from other ministers who saw such tactics as blatant hucksterism. African American leaders who were active in the Civil Rights struggle also criticized Eikerenkoetter for shifting his followers' focus from social reform to their own private transformation of consciousness.

Although Reverend Ike was largely repudiated by mainstream Christian churches in the

1980s, he seemed to find a niche within the New Thought community. This community awarded him a doctorate in 1969 and a doctorate of science in 1971 and invited his movement to join the International New Thought Alliance. Eikerenkoetter is now a popular speaker at New Thought functions around the country. His huge popularity can be seen as rooted in his ability to inspire hope for a better life in his mostly poor, African American following.

SOURCES

Dupree, Sherry Sherrod. *Biographical Dictionary of African-American, Holiness-Pentecostals, 1880–1990.* Washington, DC: Middle Atlantic Regional Press, 1990.

Eikerenkoetter, Frederick J. II. *Health, Happiness and Prosperity for You!* New York: Science of Living Publications, 1982.

Erickson, Hal. *Religious Radio and Television in the United States, 1921–1991.* Jefferson, NC: McFarland, 1992.

Martin, William C. "This Man Says He's the Divine Sweetheart of the Universe." *Esquire* (June 1974): 76–78, 140–143.

Morris, James. *The Preachers.* New York: St. Martin's Press, 1973.

REVIVAL IN AMERICA
see: Leroy Jenkins

REVIVALTIME
first aired: 1949

Revivaltime grew out of the Assemblies of God's first foray into national religious broadcasting, *Sermons in Song*, hosted by Thomas Zimmerman. This popular sermon and music program, which was first broadcast in 1946, changed its name to *Revivaltime* and began airing over the ABC radio network on Christmas Day, 1949. The broadcast was heard on over 140 stations nationwide. Soon it was airing over 600 stations in the United States, plus 100 stations overseas. After ABC began divesting itself of religious programming in the early

Courtesy: National Religious Broadcasters

C. M. WARD

1960s, *Revivaltime* reentered the syndication market.

The program's speaker between 1953 and 1978 was the popular radio pioneer C. M. Ward. Ward ended each of his broadcasts with an invitation to accept Christ as one's personal Savior. He delivered 1,306 radio sermons during his long tenure on the show.

This revivalist format has been continued by Ward's successor, Dan Betzer, an experienced director and producer in both radio and television. As Betzer once explained,

From the beginning, *Revivaltime* was more than a radio broadcast. It's a 30-minute evangelistic service, not a worship service. It aims for the young adult audience and consists of good contemporary music, an evangelistic message, and an invitation to receive Christ as Savior. We're terribly concerned about interpersonal outreach, and radio forms a one-to-one relationship between the speaker and the listener. But we don't stop there. We train pastors and lay leaders to extend the personal touch and bring people into the fellowship of the local church. It's a team effort with local parishes paying for local airtime. The national office pays for time on stations in growth areas of this country and for stations overseas. In addition to sponsoring *Revivaltime*, one out of four Assembly of God churches sponsors its own local radio program.

The pentecostalist Assemblies of God, one of the fastest-growing denominations in the United

States, furnishes a prime example of the power of electronic broadcasting to reach mass audiences and to prepare local areas for more intensive person-to-person evangelism. The Assemblies of God even encourages their member denominations to design new facilities that are "television friendly." By 1979, over 200 local churches were producing their own national programs.

Currently, the Assemblies of God also produces a national television program entitled *Turning Point.* This popular show highlights the crucial spirtual turning points in the lives of its guests. In the words of its Director of Communications Lee Shultz,

> With guests ranging from celebrities, such as gospel singer Andrae Crouch and pro-football stars, to airline pilots and young mothers, the program has everything the man or woman outside the church can respond to and the church member can find uplifting.

Under Betzer's direction, *Revivaltime* has managed to retain its popularity. During the late 1980s, the program was rated fourth among weekly religious radio ministries.

See also Thomas Zimmerman

SOURCES

Armstrong, Ben. *The Electric Church*. Nashville: Thomas Nelson, 1979.

Erickson, Hal. *Religious Radio and Television in the United States. 1921–1991*. Jefferson, NC: McFarland and Co., 1992.

JOHN RICE

born: December 11, 1895, Cook County, Texas
died: December 29, 1980, Murfreesboro, Tennessee

An independent Baptist minister, revivalist, radio preacher, and longtime editor, John R. Rice was raised in the pious Southern Baptist home of William Rice and Sallie La Prade. He joined the Baptist Church after a conversion experience at age 12. At age 16, Rice received a teacher's certificate and taught in rural schools

from 1911 to 1916, when he entered Decatur Baptist College near Fort Worth, Texas.

In 1918, Rice was drafted into the US Army and served during World War I. He received an honorable discharge in 1919. Upon returning to Texas, Rice attended Baylor University, graduating in 1920. After enrolling for graduate study at the University of Chicago, Rice suddenly felt called to a ministerial career. He withdrew from the University of Chicago and returned to Texas to preach.

In 1923, Rice was called as assistant pastor by the Baptist Church in Plainview, Texas. The following year, he assumed the senior pastorate position at a church in Shamrock, Texas. After leaving this pastorate in 1926 to become an independent evangelist, Rice began broadcasting his own radio program. The program was carried over a Fort Worth, Texas, station run by the fundamentalist J. Frank Norris. Tensions within the Southern Baptist Convention during the fundamentalist-modernist controversies of the 1920s eventually led to Rice's break with the convention in 1927. In 1932, Rice became pastor of the Fundamentalist Baptist Church of Oak Cliff in Dallas.

In 1934, Rice began his own weekly news magazine, *The Sword of the Lord*, through which he promoted Fundamentalism and attacked all things liberal, whether religious or political. By 1939, Rice had resigned his pastorate at Oak Cliff, moved his operation to Wheaton, Illinois, and returned to a career as a full-time evangelist. He moved again in 1963, this time to Murfreesboro, Tennessee.

During the 1940s and 1950s, Rice organized national evangelism conferences. The first of these was held at the popular Winona Lake camping ground in Indiana, where a number of famous religious meetings had been held, including the historic summer Prophecy Conferences. As Rice's work spread, however, controversy spread with it. Never blessed with the gift of diplomacy, Rice attacked even the staunchest fundamentalists for what he interpreted as compromise.

A tireless "soul-winner," popular conference speaker, and prolific writer, Rice authored books and pamphlets numbering in the hundreds. Over 40 million copies of his pamphlet, *What Must I Do to Be Saved*, have been printed. Rice's last days were spent conducting evangelistic crusades and promoting the Fundamentalist cause, whether in person or over the 60 radio stations that carried his broadcasts. He died in 1980, less than a month after his eighty-fifth birthday.

SOURCES

Barlow, Fred M. *John R. Rice: Giant of Evangelism.* Murfreesboro, TN: Sword of the Lord, 1983.

Billy Graham Center Archives, Wheaton College, Wheaton, Illinois.

Dollar, George W. *A History of Fundamentalism in America.* Greenville, SC: Bob Jones University Press, 1973.

Rice, John R. *Revival Appeals.* Wheaton, IL: Sword of the Lord, 1945.

Stone, Jon R. *A Guide to the End of the World: Popular Eschatology in America.* New York: Garland, 1993.

RIO GRANDE BIBLE INSTITUTE
established: 1946

Since its founding, the Rio Grande Bible Institute (RGBI) has been sending missionaries, missionary support teams, and supplies to Mexico. In addition to missionary training and Christian education, the institute produces programs for broadcast in Mexico. RGBI is located in Edinburg, Texas, just across the border from Rio Bravo, Mexico.

SOURCES

Melton, J. Gordon. *Directory of Religious Organizations in the United States.* 3d ed. Detroit: Gale Research, 1993.

RIZZO, RITA ANTOINETTE
see: Mother Angelica

ORAL ROBERTS
born: January 24, 1918, Pontotoc County, Oklahoma

Courtesy: National Religious Broadcasters

Granville Oral Roberts, one of the pioneers of television evangelism, has continued to attract a large national audience during the 1990s.

Roberts's early life gave no indication of future fame. He was reared in abject poverty, struggled with a stutter throughout his youth, and had several bouts of serious illness in his teens, including tuberculosis. His father, an independent Pentecostal evangelist, encouraged his son's ministerial aspirations despite these obstacles. However, it wasn't until a revival meeting in 1935, led by George Moncey, that Roberts's future trajectory was set. His tuberculosis was miraculously healed as Moncey prayed over him, and shortly thereafter the young Roberts delivered his first homily, without stuttering.

Roberts's father helped him gain ministerial credentials from the Pentecostal Holiness church and, after studying a brief time at Phillips Baptist College, Oklahoma, Roberts decided to travel the United States as a faith healer and evangelist. In 1938, Roberts married Evelyn Lutman, whom he had met at a camp meeting and corresponded with for two years. He completed his first book, *Salvation by the Blood*, the same year.

By 1941, Roberts had decided to pursue a more pastoral ministry. He accepted an invitation to minister at a small independent church in Fuquay Springs, North Carolina, but resigned the following year after failing to convince the congregation to join the Pentecostal Holiness Church. The next few years saw Roberts pastoring small churches in Toccoa, Georgia, and in Shawnee and Enid, Oklahoma.

While serving as a minister in Enid, Roberts reportedly heard the voice of God calling him to a healing ministry. Soon after, he organized a successful Sunday afternoon healing service in a large hall in Enid. He began to gain notoriety as a faith healer after an angry bystander shot at him and barely missed during a Steve Pringle tent meeting in Tulsa. Several healing miracles were also reported at the meeting, and the story was picked up by the Associated Press. Within a short time, Roberts had decided to leave his pastoral position and devote his energies full-time to a healing ministry. He moved to Tulsa where he started a magazine, *Healing Waters* (later called *Abundant Life*), and wrote a best-selling book, *If You Need Healing—Do These Things* (1947).

Most of Roberts's early healing revivals took place in local churches and auditoriums. By 1948, however, he had purchased his first tent and begun holding miracle crusades throughout the region. These events regularly drew crowds of as many as 20,000 people and made Roberts one of the nation's foremost healing evangelists. Roberts officially incorporated his ministry in 1948.

Also during the late 1940s, Roberts hired advertising professionals to assist in marketing his ministry and began a radio program. It was through the program that he met Lee Braxton, a banker and former mayor of Miami, Florida, who would become Roberts's mentor in financial administration and right-hand man over the next 40 years.

In 1952, Roberts produced the film *Venture into Faith*. The film was distributed internationally and greatly increased the visibility and suc-

cess of his ministry. Moreover, Roberts's radio outreach thrived throughout the 1950s, successfully fending off a challenge by the Federal Communications Commission (FCC), which was uncomfortable with the program's undocumented "miracles." Roberts turned the tables on the FCC and virtually dared the commission to legally evaluate each of his miracles. Since such an action would have constituted a clear violation of Roberts's First Amendment rights, the commission backed off.

It was during the early 1950s that Roberts began to investigate the feasibility of a television program. The fruit of this investigation was a studio-produced telecast, *Your Faith Is Power,* that first aired over 16 stations on January 10, 1954. Roberts was unhappy with the program's "canned" atmosphere and asked a major television network whether he might be able to televise his tent meetings over live television. The network claimed that such a project was impracticable, but Roberts continued to pursue the idea and received encouragement from the successful television evangelist Rex Humbard.

Within a short time, a production company was found that was willing to film a healing crusade. The only problem was the rather stiff cost of the venture—$42,000. Roberts dealt with this problem by initiating the Blessing Pact, a fundraising scheme that sought out 420 people willing to donate $100 each. The evangelist promised these supporters that God would return their gift with interest within a year—or Roberts would personally refund their contributions. The financial appeal was a success, and Roberts's new healing program was first broadcast in February 1955. By 1958, the show was being aired over 136 channels nationwide. Roberts pioneered the use of high-speed film in these programs, which allowed him to be filmed in action under the low light of his tent, shouting, praying, strutting, and healing.

The new program's dramatic and emotional healing events caused a great deal of controversy in both mainline churches and network television board rooms. Eventually, the new program was prohibited from appearing on network television, and Roberts was forced to find non-network stations to carry his healing exhibitions. These shows would typically feature men and women who would share with the audience their illness or condition. Roberts, who was seated on a chair which was situated on a stage, would then pray over the person. After the prayer, he would ask the person to testify to what he or she had experienced. The evangelist always made it clear that he, himself, was merely a channel of God's healing grace. "Only God can heal," he repeated. Nevertheless, Roberts boldly declared his belief that God had called him "to bring healing to this generation."

The television healing ministry continued to grow in the 1950s. Roberts also found time, during this period, to author a number of new books, including his popular autobiography, *Oral Roberts' Life Story*. Then, in 1960, the evangelist announced his intention to build a new university in Tulsa, Oklahoma. In order to accomplish this goal, he had to curtail his demanding schedule of healing crusades around the world. He would also have to change the format of his weekly television program, which was heavily dependent on live testimonies and sermons from these tent meetings. Roberts decided, therefore, to make his radio show the centerpiece of his evangelistic association's outreach and to divide his time between getting the university off the ground and developing an entirely new television program. The $22 million Oral Roberts University was officially founded in 1967, and the healing crusades were discontinued the following year. In a controversial step, Roberts also decided, in the late-1960s, to leave the Pentecostal Holiness Church and to receive ordination into the United Methodist Church.

Roberts's new television program debuted in 1969. At its heart was a Bible-centered message from the evangelist. Surrounding that message was a glamorous, fast-paced variety show featuring contemporary music, state-of-the-art technology, and bright-faced young people. By 1976, the new show, *Oral Roberts and You*, was attracting a weekly audience of nearly 2.5 million households. When translated into individual viewers (7 million), this audience made the telecast the most watched syndicated religious program in the United States. The show was carried over 349 local and satellite stations, 13 of which were in Canada and nine overseas.

Roberts also began producing four hour-long television specials each year that featured such guest stars as Minnie Pearl and Mahalia Jackson. The prime-time national audiences for these programs numbered almost 50 million people. The popularity of the shows was evidenced by the nearly 100,000 letters received each day after the specials were aired. Roberts defended the specials against critics who accused him of selling out the gospel to "showbiz religion" and "soft-shoe salvation." He claimed that entertainment was used to capture people's attention and to make them feel comfortable and receptive. After these goals had been achieved, he presented his 20-minute gospel message. Roberts would look directly into the camera and talk about the mighty acts of God in the contemporary world. He finished his messages by calling his audience to "claim God's blessing" for their own lives.

These new programs were originally taped, edited, and distributed from the Burbank, California, studios of NBC-TV. By January 1974, however, Oral Roberts University had developed the necessary broadcasting and taping facilities to produce the shows completely from Tulsa. Most of the programs were initially taped at the large Mabee Center Fieldhouse on the University's campus. When the fieldhouse became overbooked with other events, a separate television production facility was built adjacent to the Mabee Center. Roberts described the new structure in the June 1977 issue of *Abundant Life*:

> The structure will be four stories high, 185 feet long, 130 feet wide. It will be the same design as the Mabee Center and will connect to the Center on the east with a walk-way between. Seating for 700, 1,000, or 1,500 is being provided as well as the largest single videotaping stage of its kind in the world. Video, audio and lighting equipment in the new structure will be computer controlled for the exacting demands and control of the highest level television programs. Here ORU students will work in the telecommunications department, learning all the new techniques of this great program.

Beginning in 1970, Roberts started to add a new dimension to his message of God's healing power. As articulated in his book, *The Miracle of Seed Faith* (1970), God's plan for believers was now said to include not only healing but material prosperity. This new gospel of prosperity cost Roberts some of his established audience, but his total number of viewers continued to grow.

Roberts supported his new television programs with low-key financial appeals that were only indirectly tied to his free offerings of books and other merchandise. He and his executive vice president for business and finance, Ron Smith, were adamant about not allowing direct solicitation of funds during the television broadcasts. For those who expressed a sincere interest in his ministry, Roberts offered by-invitation-only seminars at Oral Roberts University where the business of financial contributions could be conducted in a private setting. In addition, Roberts's youngest son, Robert, traveled around the country and solicited contributions in what were called Partner Meetings. Finally, Roberts used direct-mail campaigns that proved to be highly successful during the 1970s and 1980s.

The substantial amount of cash these ventures brought into the Roberts ministry inevitably drew public criticism. In response to this criticism, Roberts's biographer Wayne Robinson countered

> First, Oral's operating premise is that if his ministry meets the needs of people, then the ministry's needs will be taken care of also. The vast apparatus of the Association is geared to that end. The mail, magazines, television, radio, and books are all designed to solve or resolve the problems for which people ask help. It's a service-oriented approach.
>
> Secondly, Oral gives to people before they give to him. He risks receiving no return at all when he sends people books, mementos, and recordings free of charge (though reams of statistics on past giveaways insure that the return will be many times more than the cost). Every radio broadcast or television program concludes with Oral's offer to give the listener something free. Just write and ask for it. Not only is there never a charge; there's no mention made of the cost to the Association. Skeptics have discovered

that every offer is, indeed, free.

> Third, and this is vital: he never asks directly for gifts for himself or his ministry. Rather he puts it this way: If you need help give to him. He never asks you to help him by giving to him, but help yourself by giving to him.

During the late 1970s and 1980s, Roberts's ministry was buffeted by tragedy and controversy. In 1977, his daughter, Rebecca, died, and in 1982 his eldest son, Ronald, committed suicide. After his heir-apparent, Richard Roberts, was divorced in 1979, Richard's former wife authored a devastating exposé of the ministry, *Ashes to God.* Moreover, City of Faith Hospital, a key component of Oral Roberts University's medical complex, was forced to curtail its operations because of chronic underuse. Roberts was criticized for erecting the facility in the face of Tulsa's already existing glut of hospitals. Roberts also was widely criticized following his 1980 report of a personal encounter with a 900-foot-tall Jesus, and after claiming God would "call him home" if a certain amount of money was not donated for the financially strapped hospital.

Although Roberts's television program no longer attracts the largest national audiences, it has remained popular through the vicissitudes of the televangelism scandals of the 1980s. Roberts himself has become a kind of patriarch among Pentecostal evangelists, even though he is a Methodist, and appears regularly on such shows as *Praise the Lord.* In an interview, he spoke frankly about the challenges and blessings of televangelism:

> It's a struggle for me to get this message across to people. It's hard for them to see, as it was for me, that Jesus is really part of our lives, here and now. Through our spirit we see Jesus. When I speak to the TV audience the Spirit of Jesus in me lets me look right at the camera lens and see another human being. Every time we make a TV program I feel closer to the person watching me. I feel we are one in our spirits. The other person feels it too, for he or she writes to me and says, "Oral Roberts, you were talking only to me." It is Jesus in me who reaches out to this person.

Perhaps it is his ability to create this intimate sense of personal communication with his television audience that best explains Roberts's enduring popularity.

Oral Roberts has also become involved in charitable outreach during the 1980s, establishing retirement homes and finding work for unemployed Mexican Americans, African Americans, and Native Americans. The televangelist is well established as a civic leader in Tulsa, serving as a bank director, Rotarian, and member of the chamber of commerce. Roberts's son, Richard, developed his own television ministry during the 1980s, hosting a show called *Richard Roberts Live*.

SOURCES

Armstrong, Ben. *The Electric Church*. Nashville: Thomas Nelson, 1979.

Erickson, Hal. *Religious Radio and Television in the United States, 1921–1991*. Jefferson, NC: McFarland, 1992.

Harrell, David E. *Oral Roberts: An American Life*. Bloomington, IN: Indiana University Press, 1985.

Hutchinson, Warner. *The Oral Roberts Scrapbook*. New York: Grosset & Dunlap, 1978.

Lippy, Charles H. *Twentieth-Century Shapers of American Popular Religion*. New York: Greenwood Press, 1989.

Lloyd, Mark. *Pioneers of Prime Time Religion: Jerry Falwell, Rex Humbard, Oral Roberts*. Dubuque, IA: Kendall/Hunt, 1988.

"Lost the Tent, Gained the University." *The Asheville (North Carolina) Times*, December 7, 1977.

"A New Television Production Center under Construction." *Abundant Life*, June 1977.

Roberts, Evelyn. *His Darling Wife, Evelyn*. New York: Dell, 1976.

Roberts, Oral. *The Call*. New York: Doubleday, 1972.

———. *If You Need Healing—Do These Things*. Tulsa, OK: Standard, 1947.

———. *The Miracle of Seed Faith*. Charlotte, NC: Commission Press, 1970.

———. *My Twenty Years of Miracle Ministry*. Tulsa, OK: 1967.

———. *Oral Roberts' Life Story*. Tulsa, OK: 1952.

Robinson, Wayne A. *Oral: The Warm, Intimate Portrait of a Man of God*. Los Angeles: Acton House, 1976.

Smith, Ron (Producer and Executive Vice-President for Business and Finance of the Oral Roberts Association, Tulsa, Oklahoma). Private interview in Tulsa. January 14, 1977.

Woodin, George (Director of Purchasing at Oral Roberts University, Tulsa, Oklahoma). Private interview in Tulsa. January 5, 1977.

RICHARD ROBERTS
born: November 12, 1948, Tulsa, Oklahoma

Courtesy: National Religious Broadcasters

Son of famed televangelist Oral Roberts and current president of Oral Roberts University, Richard Roberts began his evangelistic career while still a boy, singing at a number of his father's tent revival meetings during the 1950s. Roberts's youth was not without conflict, however, as the constant disruption of his father's crusades began to manifest itself in teenage rebellion. Against his father's hopes, Roberts shunned the idea of the ministry and enrolled for study at Kansas University in 1966. Failing in his classes, he transferred to Oral Roberts University (ORU) in the fall of 1967 and, under his father's guidance, began to pursue a career as a gospel singer and televangelist.

By the end of his first year of study at ORU, Roberts had fallen in love with Patti Holcombe, a junior music major from Oregon. In defiance of her father's wishes, Holcombe had enrolled at ORU in 1965, becoming a member of ORU's first freshman class. After a sometimes stormy courtship that lasted a year, Roberts and Holcombe were married in November 1968.

In the summer of 1968, Roberts began working at the ORU campus radio station. In 1968, Roberts also recorded his first album, which was titled *My Father's Favorites*. The young singer began his television career in 1969 when he became the featured soloist with the ORU World Action Singers. The group debuted on Oral Roberts's first television special, *Oral Roberts and You*, in January 1969. The show also featured a special guest appearance by famed gospel singer Mahalia Jackson.

Throughout the 1960s, the question of succession to Oral Roberts's vast evangelistic enterprise became a pressing issue. Oral Roberts's older and more studious son, Ronald, had rebelled against his father and, though remaining devoted to his parents, announced his lack of interest in pursuing a ministry career. Oral Roberts's hopes next turned to his younger son Richard, who, though less intellectually gifted than Ronald, was much more charming in manner and handsome in appearance. Believing that Richard could lead the ministry in his absence, Oral Roberts took steps to secure his son's succession. First, although he was barely 20 years old, Richard was appointed by his father to the ORU board of directors. Then, in 1972, Oral named Richard as head of the Oral Roberts Evangelistic Association (OREA). The younger Roberts later became the director of his father's television broadcast ministry, periodically appearing on camera as Roberts's cohost.

During the 1970s, Richard Roberts and his wife, Patti, became a regular part of the Oral Roberts television ministry. During the musical portions of the program, they were usually linked arm-in-arm while singing traditional and contemporary spirituals. In addition, they traveled together as representatives of ORU and Oral Roberts Evangelistic Association, touring throughout the United States with the ORU World Action Singers.

Problems in Richard's marriage began to surface in the mid-1970s, creating tensions on the set. Patti finally ended her broadcast appearances in 1977. The Robertses separated amicably in late 1978 and divorced in January 1979.

In her biography, *Ashes to Gold* (1983), Patti Roberts painted a fairly sympathetic picture of Roberts and their troubled 10-year marriage, although it is considered an exposé of the family's ministry. Both Richard and Patti remarried within several years of their divorce. Though their marital breakup created a stir among Oral Roberts's most faithful supporters, Richard remained in his position as head of the OREA.

Since the 1970s, Richard Roberts has sought to establish himself as a worthy successor to his father. In addition to preaching regularly on television, Roberts has traveled to such countries as Nigeria in 1984 to hold his own healing crusades. In January 1993, Roberts succeeded his father as president of Oral Roberts University. As president, his first task was to reduce the school's budget short-fall of $42 million. This deficit had resulted from a number of embarrassing crises in the ministry during the 1980s. Through budget cutting and the sale of assets, Roberts was able to reduce the ORU deficit by 50 percent within two years.

With respect to the OREA, Roberts continues to maintain a central presence both on and off the television set, becoming a fitting successor to the vast Roberts evangelistic empire.

See also Oral Roberts

SOURCES

Harrell, David Edwin, Jr. *Oral Roberts: An American Life*. Bloomington: Indiana University Press, 1985.

Reid, Daniel G., Robert D. Linder, Bruce L. Shelley, and Harry S. Stout, eds. *Dictionary of Christianity in America*. Downers Grove, IL: InterVarsity Press, 1990.

Roberts, Evelyn. *His Darling Wife, Evelyn*. New York: Dell, 1976.

Roberts, Patti (with Sherry Andrews). *Ashes to Gold*. Waco: Word Books, 1983.

Sholes, Jerry. *Give Me That Prime-Time Religion*. New York: Hawthorn Books, 1979.

Stone, Jon R. *A Guide to the End of the World: Popular Eschatology in America*. New York: Garland, 1993.

PAT ROBERTSON
born: March 22, 1930, Lexington, Virginia

Courtesy: National Religious Broadcasters

Marion Gordon Robertson, better known as "Pat," is one of the giants of religious broadcasting. In 30 years he has built a multimedia conglomerate worth over $1 billion. The linchpin of this media colossus is the Christian Broadcasting Network (CBN), which sends out *The 700 Club* to 7 million viewers weekly and distributes Christian programming in over 75 countries worldwide. CBN owns US Media Corporation and its subsidiary, Broadcast Equities, Inc. These companies operate Standard News, a radio news network with 272 stations under contract, Zapnews, a fax news service to 315 broadcasting stations, and NorthStar Entertainment, which produces and distributes family-oriented television and films. Robertson is also the founder and chairman of International Family Entertainment, Inc., which began broadcasting the popular Family Channel in 1977 as an alternative to the alleged violence and immorality of network television. The Family Channel now reaches an estimated 58 million cable households and is traded on the New York Stock Exchange by a firm controlled by Robertson. This for-profit firm recently ac-

quired MTM Enterprises and its two popular syndication series *Mary Tyler Moore* and *Hill Street Blues*.

The last facet of Robertson's empire is his humanitarian and educational outreach, which includes Operation Blessing, the American Center for Law and Justice (ACLJ), the Christian Coalition, and Regent University. Operation Blessing manages mission initiatives worldwide and humanitarian relief to the needy. Robertson designed ACLJ to serve as a counterforce to the American Civil Liberties Union. Lawyers, most of whom are trained at Regents University, have a budget of $9 million to argue the conservative Christian viewpoint in Supreme Court cases. The Christian Coalition is a political lobbying group for right-wing causes. The coalition currently supports 850 chapters and claims over 450,000 contributing members. Its subscribers work at the local and regional levels to influence state legislatures, school boards, and county government. Regent University was founded in 1975 as CBN University. Located in Virginia Beach, Virginia, the university offers professional training for born-again Christians in law, business, communications, and public policy. The school is supported by a $200 million endowment made up primarily of Robertson's corporate stock.

Pat Robertson was born in Lexington, Virginia, to Gladys Churchill Willis and her husband, United States Senator A. Willis Robertson. After attending the exclusive McCallie prep school in Chattanooga, Tennessee, the young Robertson entered Washington and Lee University. There he distinguished himself as a scholar and graduated cum laude in 1950. He also became a Golden Gloves middleweight boxer. Robertson completed post-graduate work at the University of London School of Economics and served a two-year hitch in the Marine Corps during the Korean War. When he was discharged from the Marines, Robertson decided to pursue a law degree at Yale University. He married Adelia Elme in 1954 and graduated with a doctor of jurisprudence degree the following year. By this time, however, Robertson had become disillusioned with the legal profession. He subsequently failed the New York bar exam and decided to pursue a career in the electronics industry.

In 1956, Robertson met the Baptist minister Cornelius Vanderbeggen. Through Vanderbeggen's efforts, Robertson was "born again" and entered the Biblical Seminary of New York (which changed its name to New York Theological Seminary that same year) to gain ministerial credentials. During his time at the seminary, Robertson worked as an associate minister at the First Reformed Church in Mount Vernon. While assisting at First Reformed, the young student came under the influence of Harald Bredesen, the church's minister. Bredesen had undergone the Pentecostal experience of speaking in tongues and soon led Robertson to have such an experience. Robertson became a lifelong believer in Pentecostal "gifts of the spirit" and subsequently helped spread the Pentecostal message in traditional evangelical churches.

Following his graduation from seminary, Robertson moved back to his native Virginia. In 1959, he purchased a dilapidated, bankrupt UHF television station in Portsmouth for $37,000 and subsequently founded the Christian Broadcasting Network (CBN). During the first four years of the station's operation, Robertson worked as a Southern Baptist associate minister to help support the ministry. The Full Gospel Businessman's Fellowship also helped fund the station. CBN's first broadcast didn't air until October 1961, the same year that Robertson gained ministerial credentials in the Southern Baptist Convention. The station was the first UHF broadcaster to dedicate over half of its programming to religious topics.

The station's flagship program, *The 700 Club*, received its name from a 1963 fundraising campaign. Robertson told his audience that 700 people contributing $10 per month would allow the station to meet its monthly budget. The fundraising campaign provided the necessary operating funds for CBN and led to the first successful *700 Club Telethon* in 1965. Robertson quickly discovered that people would watch telethons even when no regular programming was aired because they enjoyed the reli-

gious testimonials of fellow viewers. The event was important for another reason. It was at this first telethon that new employees Jim and Tammy Faye Bakker became active participants in the CBN ministry.

After a successful 1966 follow-up telethon, *The 700 Club* evolved into a daily 90-minute broadcast. The program was presented in a talk-show format that featured Robertson discussing contemporary issues with various evangelical authors and musical performers. The show's first cohosts were the Bakkers. During the program, Robertson and his guests would pray for those calling into the show and allegedly cast out demons from those afflicted with various diseases. This talk-show and prayer format proved popular with both radio and television audiences and was as successful on secular stations as on religious networks. As Robertson recalled later,

> The blessing of God had come on CBN as we ministered as a team. I realized the program should be a team ministry of prayer and praise. The host and cohost sat at a desk, and behind us were the telephone volunteers, praying and counseling with people who called in. Hundreds were finding Jesus as Savior, and there were many dramatic answers to prayer. The program went on the air at 10:15 each night, and it sometimes ran as late as two or three in the morning. We knew that God had given us the answer to help reach the needs of mankind. . . . When you pray for people you make friends. It makes no difference who they are—Protestants, Catholics, Jews, Buddhists, even atheists—they all are grateful that you care enough to pray. We feel we introduced "two-way television."

By 1972, *The 700 Club* was syndicated nationally and restructured within a more predictable format and length. Within two years, CBN had earned the National Religious Broadcasters Award of Merit for Excellence in Station Operation. By this time, the network operated television stations in Dallas, Atlanta, and Portsmouth; and FM radio stations in Norfolk, Virginia, and in Albany, Syracuse, Ithaca-Elmira, Rochester, and Buffalo, New York.

Over the next three years, CBN became the first Christian television network to operate its own satellite earth stations. The network made uplinks to the Westar and RCA Satcom satellites, joining Ted Turner's Atlanta Superstation and Home Box Office, and built a chain of 60 earth stations nationwide. By 1979, *The 700 Club* had 7,000 volunteer prayer counselors working 24-hours-a-day around the country. The 100-plus telephone centers created a referral system that helped new converts find churches in their local areas. The ministry reported it received over 1 million prayer requests in 1977. CBN's operating budget for 1978 was nearly $40 million.

After consulting market research in 1980, Robertson retooled *The 700 Club* into its present talk-show and news-magazine format. This format mimics such morning network programs as *Good Morning America* and the *Today Show*. As Kenneth Clark observed, the show "competes with network morning news shows for many of the same guest political figures, movie stars, athletes, and authors; but whether they represent secular or religious interests, Christian testimony is threaded through every discussion."

In 1981, Robertson decided to rename his channel CBN Cable Network and began airing family programs like *Gentle Ben* and *Father Knows Best* in addition to his religious shows. Soon religious programming had been reduced to only 25 percent of the network's offerings. It was this network that in 1988 was renamed the Family Channel. Robertson's strategy was to attract a larger national audience by reducing overtly "Christian" programming. CBN also subsidized advertising costs and offered the Family Channel without charge to cable operators.

During the mid-1980s, Robertson sold many of CBN's broadcast holdings so that he could concentrate his investments in the development of programming and the operation of his satellite channel. In 1985, the network raised $233 million, most of it from donors' clubs and sympathetic corporations, to develop programming and expand and operate CBN's satellite channel. By 1987, CBN's signal was reaching over 190 different stations worldwide and the network's annual budget had grown to $200 million.

Robertson began to take an active interest in national politics following the successful presidential campaign of Ronald Reagan in 1980. He felt he had played an important role in the campaign by spearheading the Washington for Jesus rally in 1980. The rally demonstrated to the evangelist that Christians could play a decisive part in America's political future. Robertson honed his diagnosis of America's social and moral ills and published several books during the 1980s articulating these views. The most significant of these was *America's Date with Destiny*, which appeared in 1986. In its essentials, Robertson's message argued that America's problems stemmed from the rise of secular humanism. In his view, this godless philosophy and worldview had overcome the traditional Judeo-Christian values upon which America had been built.

Robertson held a news conference on September 17, 1986, to announce his candidacy for the US presidency. However, the bid was contingent upon whether 3 million voters would sign a pledge to support his campaign with work, prayers, and funding. Within a year, the 3 million pledges had been obtained, and Robertson announced that he would indeed run for the presidency. To avoid accusations that his candidacy was a bid for religious as well as political supremacy, Robertson resigned from the ministry and declared that he was simply a religious broadcaster. After several surprising showings in the early primaries, Robertson began to fade, eventually withdrawing from the race before the summer Republican convention.

During Robertson's absence from *The 700 Club*, the show's Nielsen rating dropped 30 percent and contributions fell from $60 million to $50 million. Upon his return, the program adopted a new theme song, more mainstream sets and graphics, and a new cohost, the Scottish contemporary Christian vocalist Sheila Walsh. Although at first viewers complained that Walsh's accent was difficult to understand, she later came to be seen as a sincere and caring presence on the program.

CBN ran afoul of IRS regulators when the IRS discovered that revenues from the Family Channel had been used to shore up Robertson's flagging television ministry during his failed presidential campaign of 1987–1988. Under pressure from the IRS, the Family Channel was legally separated from CBN's television ministry in December 1989 and recapitalized as a holding company of International Family Entertainment (IFE). The recapitalization of $250 million came from junk bonds and from Telecommunications Corporation International (TCI) of Denver, Colorado, which paid $40 million for a 13 percent share of IFE. By restructuring his media empire in this manner, Robertson was able to protect *The 700 Club* from the vagaries of television donors and to ensure a place for the show on what has become the nation's fifth largest cable channel. In 1992, the Family Channel was being viewed in 48.5 million homes.

During the early 1990s, the Family Channel expanded its programming to include vintage comedy and drama series, popular westerns, and original series of its own such as *Zorro*, *Bordertown*, and *The Adventures of the Black Stallion*. The channel now has a prime-time line-up seven days a week and produces original children's programming, including a 30-minute children's talk show. As the channel's president, Tim Robertson observed, "the trend of the '90s is a new search for values and a new quest for the meaning of life." For those dissatisfied with the violence and commercialism of network television, the Family Channel tries to "provide the very finest in alternative programming, shows that are positive, of high quality, that stress pro-family, Judeo-Christian values."

Robertson has tried to distance himself from the flamboyant and scandal-ridden world of television evangelism. On one occasion he stated, "We consider ourselves professional broadcasters. . . . I've never been an evangelist as such. It turned out that the Lord wanted me to buy a television station, but I never was an evangelist." Making this distinction was especially important during Robertson's 1988 presidential bid. As his director of communications

put it, "Pat has been labeled a TV evangelist, but he's not. He hasn't been a pulpit preacher for 25 years. He's a religious broadcaster, a businessman, a newscaster. There is a subtle difference."

See also Christian Broadcasting Network; *The 700 Club*

SOURCES

Armstrong, Ben. *The Electric Church*. Nashville: Thomas Nelson, 1979.

Clark, Kenneth R. "The $70 Miracle Named CBN." *Chicago Tribune*, July 26, 1985.

Fineman, Howard. "God and the Grass Roots." *Newsweek*, November 8, 1993.

Gerbner, George, et al. *Religion and Television*. Philadelphia: Annenberg School of Communications, April 1984.

Graham, Lamar. "700 Club." *Norfolk Virginian-Pilot*, August 2, 1988.

Harrell, David Edwin, Jr. *Pat Robertson: A Personal, Religious, and Political Portrait*. San Francisco: Harper & Row, 1987.

Hoover, Stewart. *Mass Media Religion*. Newbury Park, CA: Sage, 1986.

Horsfield, Peter. *Religious Television*. New York: Longman, 1984.

Lippy, Charles H. *Twentieth-Century Shapers of American Popular Religion*. New York: Greenwood Press, 1989.

Mayfield, Marjorie. "For CBN, the Worst May Be Over." *Norfolk Virginian-Pilot*, March 5, 1989.

Morken, Hubert. *Pat Robertson: Religion and Politics in Simple Terms*. Old Tappan, NJ: Fleming H. Revell, 1987.

Peck, Janice. *The Gods of Televangelism: The Crisis of Meaning and the Appeal of Religious Television*. Cresskill, NJ: Hampton Press, 1993.

Rice, P. M. "Interview with Pat Robertson." *Your Church*, May/June 1979.

Robertson, Pat. *America's Date with Destiny*. Nashville: Thomas Nelson, 1986.

———. *Answers to 200 of Life's Most Probing Questions*. Nashville: Thomas Nelson, 1984.

———. *Beyond Reason*. New York: William Morrow, 1984.

———. *My Prayer for You*. Old Tappan, NJ: Fleming H. Revell, 1977.

———. *The Secret Kingdom.* Nashville: Thomas Nelson, 1983

———. *Shout It from the Housetops.* South Plainfield, TX: Logos International, 1972.

Toulouse, M. G. "Pat Robertson: Apocalyptic Theology and American Foreign Policy." *Journal of Church and State* 31 (Winter 1989).

Witt, April. "Robertson Likely to Rejoin CBN." *Norfolk Virginian-Pilot,* May 11, 1988.

Wood, Daniel B. "Family Channel Focuses on the Inoffensive." *Christian Science Monitor,* February 9, 1990.

JAMES ROBISON
born: 1943, Houston, Texas

Courtesy: National Religious Broadcasters

Religious broadcaster James Robison is the founder and president of LIFE Outreach International, an evangelistic and humanitarian organization that ministers to needy children and adults around the world. LIFE Outreach also produces *LIFE TODAY*, a daily television program that is aired on over 120 stations in the United States and Canada.

Robison was born in the charity ward of a Houston hospital, the first son of the unmarried Myra Wattinger and her alcoholic lover, Joe Robison. Knowing she was unable to rear her son, Wattinger placed an advertisement in a local newspaper offering to give the infant to whomever would agree to provide him a home.

Herbert and Katie Hale responded to the ad and raised Robison as their foster son. Herbert Hale was the pastor at Memorial Baptist Church in Pasadena, Texas.

After a troubled and rebellious youth, Robison received Christ at the age of 15 in his father's Pasadena church. In response to a call to preach, the future evangelist enrolled at East Texas Baptist College in Marshall in 1961. Two years later he married Betty Freeman.

While pursuing his ministerial studies, Robison began to preach in large Baptist churches throughout the South. By the age of 19, he had become such a popular revivalist that he was asked to preach at W. A. Criswell's First Baptist Church in Dallas. Robison's heavy schedule of guest preaching forced him to drop out of Bible college in 1964. In 1967, he moved his ministry to Dallas-Fort Worth and established the James Robison Evangelistic Association. Robison's reputation as a revivalist continued to grow, and his citywide crusades drew record crowds in stadiums across the United States.

Evangelist Billy Graham was so impressed with Robison that he encouraged the young preacher to take his message to television. By 1973, Robison was a respected radio and television preacher who exhibited, according to LIFE Outreach International's promotional literature, "a tremendous anointing of boldness and a remarkable ability to communicate the gospel." Robison's television ministry went national in 1979 with a prime-time series of 15 weekly programs that were aired in 200 large cities. Robison's regular show, *James Robison, Man with a Message*, ranked eleventh on the Arbitron ratings in February 1980.

It was during the late 1970s that Robison became a controversial figure in religious broadcasting. Robison would often angrily condemn the feminist movement, homosexuality, secular humanism, and evolution during his programs. These condemnations got him into hot water when, in February 1979, he issued a blistering attack on local Dallas-Fort Worth gay-rights organizations. Citing a feature in the *National Enquirer* that claimed gays preyed on each other, he declared the murders of San Francisco City Supervisor Harvey Milk and Mayor George Moscone to be a manifestation of God's judgment on the homosexual community. Robison asserted that homosexuality was "perversion of the highest order" and quoted a police chief who asserted that gays both recruited and murdered little boys.

Robison's charges outraged Dallas's gay community. They organized a protest and cited the Personal Attack and Controversial Public Issues provisions of the Federal Communications Commission's Fairness Doctrine in their petition to television station WFAA for equal airtime to respond to Robison. WFAA not only provided the free airtime but also decided to cancel Robison's weekly program because of its controversial content. Robison had caused earlier invocations of the Fairness Doctrine by his denunciations of Mormons, Christian Scientists, and Garner Ted Armstrong's Church of God.

Robison responded to the cancellation of his program by hiring the flamboyant lawyer Richard "Racehorse" Haynes to represent him before the Federal Communications Commission (FCC). Haynes asked the FCC to investigate into whether WFAA-TV had infringed upon Robison's right to freedom of speech. Robison organized a "freedom rally" in Dallas that drew nearly 11,000 supporters. Throughout the controversy, Robison complained that he was being persecuted for preaching a simple biblical message. At one point he stated, "I did not attack an individual or any group, but rather a lifestyle condemned by the Bible."

After two years of nationwide headlines on the controversy, WFFA-TV relented and began airing Robison's program again. To his credit, Robison did allow that gays have a right to express their views and agreed to appear on a Dallas talk show with a local gay opponent. The same opponent was later invited to express his views in the pages of Robison's monthly periodical, *Life's Answers*.

Robison's controversial attacks on prominent religious leaders whom he considered to be too liberal led to other cancellations of his show in the early 1980s. The offended stations included

WSOC-TV in Charlotte, North Carolina, and a New York City station. The New York station was particularly displeased with Robison's relentless attacks on the National Council of Churches and his combative stance against abortion. In the wake of Robison's and televangelist Charles Sustar's uncompromising condemnations of gays, WSOC-TV decided to cancel all paid-time religious broadcasts.

Robison became a powerful player in the rise of the Christian Right throughout the early 1980s. During the presidential campaign of 1980, Robison broadcast a television special, "Wake Up, America: We're All Hostages!" According to Robison, the American government had become corrupted by ungodly people and upstanding, moral Americans were being held hostage by the purveyors of secular humanism and immorality. A number of ultra-right politicians appeared on the program to help detail the many forces that were working to bring down God's righteous judgment on America. The gist of Robison's warnings were well summarized in his book, *Save America*:

> America's star is sinking fast. If Christians don't begin immediately to assert their influence, it may be too late to save America from the destruction toward which it is plunging. And, since America now stands as the key base camp for missions around the globe, to fail to save America now would almost certainly be to miss its last opportunity to save the world.

Ed McAteer, an executive with the conservative Christian Freedom Foundation, recruited Robison to be the vice president of the Religious Roundtable in 1980. The Roundtable was a conservative Christian political caucus whose mission was to promote right-wing political causes and candidates and to stem the rising tide of secular humanism in America.

The Roundtable's first national event, the National Affairs Briefing, was held in Robison's home base of Dallas. During the two-day event, Robison was given enthusiastic ovations from the audience for his fiery, forceful rhetoric. The briefing's climactic moment came when, with Ronald Reagan seated nearby on the stage, Robison commanded his audience, "Don't you commit yourself to some political party or politician. You commit yourself to the principles of God and demand those parties and politicians align themselves with the eternal values in this word [the Bible]!" Both the crowd and Reagan rose to their feet in a fervent ovation. Reagan was able to take advantage of the occasion in his subsequent speech, stating, "I know this is a nonpartisan gathering and so I know you can't endorse me, but I . . . want you to know that I endorse you and what you are doing." Fifteen thousand conservative Christians rose to their feet and shouted "Amen!" and Reagan knew he had the support of a powerful voting bloc for the upcoming presidential election.

Robison joined other conservative Christian leaders in extolling the virtues of voting during the presidential campaign. He told his audiences "I'm a preacher, but I'm no longer just going to be talking about going to heaven." Robison also offered a "Vote" lapel pin on his television program that had the letter "t" enlarged and shaped as a cross. The same word was also printed as a bumper sticker and distributed to anyone who called or wrote the Robison ministry. Robison, along with such evangelical luminaries as Ben Armstrong, Bill Bright, Kenneth Copeland, Paul Crouch, James T. Draper, Jerry Falwell, Rex Humbard, D. James Kennedy, Adrian Rogers, Charles Stanley, Jimmy Swaggart, Robert Tilton, and Jack Van Impe became a board member of Tim LaHaye's conservative American Coalition for Traditional Values during this period.

In 1981, the millionaire industrialist Cullen Davis went on trial for the attempted murder of his wife and a judge. Davis was one of Robison's most famous converts and a personal friend. The two had gained local notoriety by claiming to have smashed $1 million worth of expensive Oriental art in Lake Worth. The reason given for this act of destruction was that the art objects were pagan idols. The Davis scandal touched Robison because the judge who was one of Davis's alleged murder targets was also the judge in Robison's never-completed divorce trial.

During this time of personal tribulation, Robison prayed with a prominent Baptist lay-man, Milton Green. Robison experienced what he reported to be a personal deliverance from demonic bondage that had plagued him for many years. The result of this deliverance was a healing of various bodily ailments and a renewed zeal to serve Christ. Within a short time, Robison's wife and three children had also been healed of their physical problems. Although Robison consented to giving an invocation at the Dallas Republican party nominating convention in 1984, he gradually removed himself from the political arena after these charismatic healings.

Robison's ministry began to emphasize Christian love and unity, the healing of the sick, exorcism, and the charismatic gifts of the Holy Spirit. Despite his refusal to label himself a "charismatic," Robison's new emphasis brought him into conflict with his staid Southern Baptist brethren. Amidst growing controversy, Robison broke off fellowship with his Euless, Texas, Baptist church. His daily television show and his weekly program, *Restoration with James Robison*, changed to a charismatic format and continued to be as popular as ever.

During the televangelism scandals of the late 1980s, Robison was mentioned as a candidate to take over Jim Bakker's PTL ministry. Robison's increasingly erratic charismatic activities, however, made other ministers uncomfortable and compelled Jerry Falwell to veto Robison's candidacy.

Robison was one of the few televangelists of the period, however, who was willing to discuss openly the latent sexuality in the evangelist's role. Robison admitted that women in his audiences found him sexually attractive and that he had come close to succumbing to temptation on a number of occasions. Unlike many of his peers, Robison also showed a willingness to seek professional counseling for his psychological problems.

During the early 1990s, Robison became touched with compassion during a series of missionary travels around the world. He increasingly experienced a desire to meet the physical needs of hurting people in addition to their spiritual needs. As Robison expressed it in the ministry's promotional literature, "We can no longer merely tell the story of Jesus. We must live it. We must show the world that Jesus is alive." In his increased identification with suffering people, Robison was following in the steps of such humanitarian evangelists as Bob Pierce and W. Stanley Mooneyham, the founders and leaders of World Vision International and Samaritan's Purse.

This change in emphasis was reflected in his ministry's change of name: the James Robison Evangelistic Association became LIFE Outreach International (LOI) in 1992. The new ministry supports missionary efforts already in operation and works to build orphanages and other aid programs in such crisis areas as Romania, China, the former Yugoslavia, Africa, and the former Soviet Union. LOI also supports relief efforts, street ministries, and orphanages in North America. A major focus of the ministry's outreach is children and families.

By the mid-1990s, LOI was involved in humanitarian outreach to 22 countries and had a staff of nearly 100 employees at its Euless, Texas, headquarters. The ministry's total income for 1993 was about $19.5 million. LOI became a member of the Evangelical Council for Financial Accountability in 1993.

As of 1995, Robison's hour-long program, *LIFE TODAY*, was being aired on over 120 stations in 35 states and provinces across the United States and Canada. The show was also being transmitted via satellite daily on the Inspirational Network, Vision TV (Canada), and the Keystone Network, and weekly on the Family Channel, Trinity Broadcasting Network, and Black Entertainment Television.

Life Outreach International markets a complete line of audio- and videotapes of Robison's sermons and seminars, books on personal growth, devotionals, and music. Among Robison's most popular books are *A New Beginning*, *The Right Mate*, *Winning the RealWar*, *The Spirit World*, and *Living in Holy Spirit Power*.

SOURCES

Bruce, Steve. *Pray TV: Televangelism in America*. New York: Routledge, 1990.

Hadden, Jeffrey K., and Anson Shupe. *Televangelism: Power and Politics on God's Frontier*. New York: Henry Holt, 1988.

Hadden, Jeffrey K., and Charles E. Swann. *Prime Time Preachers: The Rising Power of Televangelism*. Menlo Park, CA: Addison-Wesley, 1981.

Life Outreach International. Promotional literature, 1995.

Quebedeaux, Richard. *By What Authority: The Rise of Personality Cults in American Christianity*. San Francisco: Harper & Row, 1982.

Robison, James. *Thank God, I'm Free: The James Robison Story*. 1988.

ROCK CHURCH
see: Anne Giminez

ROCK THE WORLD
first aired: 1995

Rock the World is a recent addition to USA Radio Network's lineup of weekly talk shows. The family-oriented live talk program is designed to challenge and empower young people to take up a life of Christian discipleship. The show provides an opportunity for young Christians to discuss such contemporary issues as gangs, drugs, premarital sex, and AIDS. *Rock the World* is hosted by Jerry Huson.

ADRIAN ROGERS
born: September 12, 1931, West Palm Beach, Florida

Adrian Rogers is the highly respected pastor of the 23,000-member Bellevue Baptist Church in Memphis, Tennessee. His *Love Worth Finding* television show is aired internationally on over 350 stations, 1,600 cable systems, and two satellite networks, including Trinity Broadcasting Network. The show's daily 26-minute radio version is broadcast on more than 350 stations nationwide and in 50 countries around the world. In the United States, Rogers's potential viewership is estimated to be nearly 93 million households. In 1989, *Love Worth Finding* was given the National Religious Broadcasters Television Program Producer of the Year award.

Rogers is the son of Arden Rogers and Rose Purcell. He married the former Joyce Gentry on September 2, 1951, and was ordained as a Baptist minister the same year. His first pastorate, at First Baptist Church in Fellsmere, Florida, lasted from 1951 to 1954. After finishing his bachelor of arts degree at Stetson University in 1954, Rogers earned a master of theology degree from New Orleans Baptist Theological Seminary in 1958.

Between 1955 and 1975, Rogers served pastorates at Baptist churches in Waveland, Mississippi, and Fort Pierce and Merritt Island, Florida. Rogers's tenure at Bellevue Baptist began in 1975. Since that time, he has risen to prominence as the three-term president of the Southern Baptist Convention (1980, 1987, 1988). Rogers's terms coincided with the convention's decisive moves into the fundamentalist camp.

Rogers has long been an articulate and persuasive spokesperson for the doctrine of biblical inerrancy. Billy Graham once said of him, "We need ministers of the gospel to defend the Bible as the infallible Word of God. . . . I believe in my heart that Adrian Rogers is such a man."

In addition to his championing of conservative Christianity, Rogers has been a popular keynote speaker at the national conventions of such evangelical organizations as the National Religious Broadcasters, the Southern Baptist Convention, and the National Association of Evangelicals. He was also the honored keynote speaker at the 1992 National Day of Prayer and the 1980 Washington for Jesus rally. Former president George Bush is an admirer of Rogers and once commented, "There are many who presume to speak for the evangelical movement in America, but surely Dr. Rogers is one of a handful who truly represents [it]."

Rogers also is an accomplished author and teacher. Among his numerous publications are *The Secret of Supernatural Living, God's Way to Health, Wealth, and Wisdom,* and *Mastering Your Emotions.* The evangelist has accompa-

nied Billy Graham on crusades in Taiwan, South Korea, Russia, Romania, Brazil, and the United States. He has also taught at the Billy Graham School of Evangelism. Rogers has been granted honorary doctorates from Trinity College of Clearwater, Florida, and from California Graduate School of Theology in Glendale, California.

SOURCES

"Casting Call for NRB 95." *Religious Broadcasting,* February, 1995.

Who's Who in Religion. 4th ed. Wilmette, IL: Marquis, 1993.

LESTER ROLOFF

born: June 28, 1914, Dawson, Texas
died: November 2, 1982

Lester Roloff was the long-time host of *The Family Altar,* a radio ministry that is currently heard daily over more than 180 radio stations nationwide.

Roloff was born in Dawson, Texas, and raised on a cotton farm. At the age of 12 he joined the local Baptist church and, at age 18, decided to pursue a career in the Christian ministry. While attending Baylor University and Southwestern Seminary, Roloff pastored two churches on a part-time basis. After completing three years of study at Southwestern, Roloff served several additional pastorates before beginning a radio ministry in 1944. *The Family Altar* started as an effort by Roloff to reach as many people as possible with the Christian gospel. By the 1950s, the radio preacher had resigned his church ministry to devote his full energies to radio evangelism. In 1951, "Brother Roloff," as he came to be called, founded his umbrella organization, Roloff Evangelistic Enterprises.

Beginning in 1956, Roloff established a number of social service homes for orphans and for troubled men and women. The first of these was his City of Refuge, an alcohol and drug rehabilitation center for men. Shortly thereafter, Roloff founded the Jubilee Home for women,

The Lighthouse for young men, Anchor Home for teenage boys, Rebekah Home for young women, Bethesda Home for teenage girls, and Peaceful Valley Home for retirees. Roloff also helped found Regeneration Reservation, a mission ministry to Native Americans.

Though Roloff died in an airplane crash in 1982, he still hosts his radio program through the miracle of taped recordings. *The Family Altar Program*, as it is now known, originates from the headquarters of Roloff Evangelistic Enterprises in Corpus Christi, Texas. It has aired continuously with and without Roloff for over 50 years. In 1993, Lester Roloff was inducted, posthumously, into the National Religious Broadcasters Hall of Fame.

SOURCES

Melton, J. Gordon. *Directory of Religious Organizations in the United States.* 3d ed. Detroit: Gale Research, 1993.

Ward, Mark, Sr. *Air of Salvation: The Story of Christian Broadcasting.* Grand Rapids, MI: Baker Book House, 1994.

"ROME ETERNAL"

aired: four-part special, 1958

"Rome Eternal" was an acclaimed television series of four half-hour programs that aired on *The Catholic Hour* in 1958. The series was filmed in cooperation with NBC-TV and represented one of the more ambitious programs the long-running *The Catholic Hour* had ever attempted.

The first segment of "Rome Eternal" chronicled the early history of the church against a background of Roman triumphal arches, viaducts, catacombs, and columns. The next segment highlighted the era of Constantine, when Christianity finally gained legal sanction in the Roman Empire. The third program focused on the blossoming of Christian humanism during the High Renaissance. And in its final episode, "Rome Eternal" examined the late 1950s Vatican of Pope Pius XII.

Richard J. Walsh, the director of the electronic media division of the National Council of Catholic Men, conceived the project in 1956 and enlisted the help of NBC-TV's veteran news cameraman, Joe Vadala. Walsh also called in a veteran advisor to other *Catholic Hour* productions, the Reverend John J. Dougherty of the Immaculate Conception Seminary in Darlington, New Jersey. Dougherty brought to the project a thorough knowledge of Rome and its environs. This expertise, gained during nine years of study in the Eternal City, helped Walsh shape the scenario for the series. Walsh employed Pulitzer Prize-winning scriptwriter Paul Horgan to produce a script that dramatized the continuity of Christianity through 2,000 years of history. The series aired on Sunday afternoons at 1:30 PM on NBC-TV.

See also *The Catholic Hour*

SOURCES

"A Sense of the Sacred." *Newsweek*, January 13, 1958, 83.

MOISHE ROSEN

born: April 12, 1932, Kansas City, Missouri

Founder of the Christian evangelical organization, Jews for Jesus, Moishe Rosen was born Martin Rosen in Kansas City, Missouri, to Ben and Rose Rosen. Raised in a Reform Jewish home in Denver, Colorado, Rosen came to question the Jewish faith while still in his teens. After high school, Rosen attended Colorado College but dropped out before completing his degree. While still in college, he married Ceil Starr. Shortly thereafter, the couple had an encounter with Orville Freeman, an evangelical Christian, who spurred them on a spiritual quest. The Rosens were converted to Christianity in 1953.

After his conversion, Rosen moved to New York City with the idea of becoming a missionary among the Jews. He also became associated with the American Board of Missions to the Jews (ABMJ), an organization dedicated to converting Jews to Christ. In order to strengthen his knowledge of Christian doctrine, Rosen enrolled at Northeastern Bible College and, upon graduation in 1957, was ordained a Baptist minister. Later that same year he and his wife moved to Los Angeles, where they ministered to a number of Hebrew Christian fellowships.

Upon his return to New York City in 1967, Rosen became director of recruitment and training for ABMJ. After failing in his efforts to apply the evangelizing methods that were so successful in Southern California, he returned to California a few years later to minister among the "hippies" on the streets of San Francisco. Rosen specifically targeted Jews who had become part of the city's counterculture.

Seeking to expand his evangelistic work among Jews, Rosen founded Jews for Jesus and Hineni Ministries in 1974. These evangelistic ministries included sponsorship of a weekly television and radio program and the distribution of religious "broadsides," tracts that were simple, humorous invitations to consider Jesus. Rosen continues to air an annual television program during Passover that explains the feast and its fulfillment in the life and death of Christ.

In spite of his tireless evangelistic initiatives, Rosen had attracted only 100 or so followers by the late 1970s. In order to reach a larger audience with his message, Rosen began to rely more and more on publicity and aggressive street evangelism. Indeed, his tactics were so successful that, much to the aggravation of Jews and many Hebrew Christian groups, Jews for Jesus became nearly synonymous with Jewish evangelism by the 1980s.

Much of the controversy Rosen has created comes from his support of the assimilation of Jews into non-Jewish Protestant churches. Although he has emphasized the Jewishness of Jesus and the Christian faith—and even changed his name to Moishe (or Moses) to reflect this—the main focus of his ministry has been to bring Jews into conservative evangelical and fundamentalist churches.

In May 1996, Rosen announced his retirement as executive director of Jews for Jesus. How-ever, the evangelist remains involved with the organization in an unofficial capacity. Jews for Jesus currently supports mission stations in Canada, Argentina, South Africa, France, the United Kingdom, Russia, the Ukraine, and Israel.

SOURCES

The Directory of Religious Organizations in the United States. 2d ed. Falls Church, VA: McGrath, 1982.

Melton, J. Gordon. *Religious Leaders of America.* Detroit: Gale Research, 1991.

Rausch, David A. *Messianic Judaism: Its History, Theology, and Polity.* New York: Edwin Mellen Press, 1982.

Rosen, Moishe (with William Proctor). *Jews for Jesus.* Old Tappan, NJ: Fleming H. Revell, 1974.

ROUNDTABLE
see: John Ankerberg

LESLIE RUMBLE
born: 1892
died: November 9, 1975, Sydney, Australia

Dr. Leslie Rumble was one of the pioneers of religious radio in Australia and a symbol of Australian Catholicism between 1930 and 1968.

Rumble had tried different forms of Protestantism before converting to Catholicism as a young man. He eventually became a priest of the Missionaries of the Sacred Heart and a seminary lecturer. In 1928, Rumble was asked by the organizer of the Sydney Eucharistic Congress, Father James Meany, to give a series of lectures on the Catholic Eucharist over a commercial radio station. When the lectures garnered a favorable listener response, Meany set up Catholic station 2SM (after Meany's Sydney St. Mark's Church) to transmit Catholic teachings to a mass audience. Rumble's *A Question Box* became one of the station's most popular programs and would continue as a regular feature on 2SM until 1968, when Rumble retired.

A *Question Box*'s format was simple. Every Sunday evening Rumble would read questions from interested listeners and answer them with reasoned responses in his trademark sandpaper voice. During his first broadcast he admonished his audience, "I will take it for granted that it is your own personal difficulty [that motivated your questions], the result of much thought, perhaps the voice of years of distress and doubt."

Rumble, an avid student of the Bible from the age of 10, answered his interlocutors with a battery of Bible verses and an even, scholastic temper. On one occasion, this temper was sorely tried. Rumble read a letter from a woman who predicted that "Rumble would end his days starving in a monastery, his imagination wracked by the secret sins of women he had heard in the confessional, until he plunged into gloom or mental torment." Rumble handled such statements with theological rationality and an unsentimental vocabulary that was precise if not generous.

Father Meany was so impressed with Rumble's radio program that he helped the priest publish, in book form, nearly 8,000 questions and answers from *A Question Box* in 1934. The book, dubbed *Radio Replies*, had a remarkable publishing history. The first edition sold 50,000 copies, and subsequent editions did even better. These volumes, which appeared in Canada, the United Kingdom, South Africa, and the United States, had sold over 7 million copies by 1968. Rumble also published 50 booklets on various facets of Catholic faith and doctrine. Radio programs based on his publications were inaugurated in Shanghai, Paris, Poland, and Trinidad.

During the latter decades of the twentieth century, Rumble became a darling of conservative Catholics who adhere to a form of Catholicism that is capable of articulating its position on any topic in confident, concise questions and answers. He retired from broadcasting in 1968; the show ended at the same time.

SOURCES

Campion, Edmund. *Australian Catholics*. Ringwood, Victoria: Viking/Penguin, 1987.

O'Farrell, Patrick. *The Catholic Church and Community: An Australian History*. Kensington, NSW: University of New South Wales Press, 1992.

RUSSIA FOR CHRIST MINISTRIES
established: 1958

Founded by evangelist David Benson, Russia for Christ Ministries produces Russian-language radio broadcasts aimed at evangelizing Slavic-speaking peoples in the former Soviet Union and its Cold War satellites. Benson, a Slavic languages major at UCLA and graduate of Fuller Theological Seminary, first began broadcast production during the mid-1950s while teaching Bible classes at Hollywood Presbyterian Church. Since 1958, Benson has recorded *Christ's Warrior*, a 30-minute program that features Bible reading and stories, for broadcast over radio stations in a number of overseas outlets.

In addition to producing *Christ's Warrior*, Russia for Christ also distributes Bibles and other religious literature. Though his headquarters are in Santa Barbara, California, Benson has made regular trips to Russia and its neighboring countries in order to hand out Bibles and give encouragement to local churches.

See also David Benson

SOURCES

Benson, David V. *Christianity, Communism and Survival!* Glendale, CA: Regal Books, 1967.

———. *Miracle in Moscow*. Santa Barbara, CA: Miracle Publications, 1973.

Melton, J. Gordon. *Directory of Religious Organizations in the United States*. 3d ed. Detroit: Gale Research, 1993.

RUSSIAN GOSPEL MINISTRIES INTERNATIONAL
established: 1980

A fundamentalist Baptist missionary organization founded in 1980 by Georgi Vins, Russian Gospel Ministries International seeks to evangelize the peoples of the former Soviet Union and support members of the Russian Evangelical Baptist Churches, which was founded in 1867.

Vins came to the attention of Soviet authorities while leading an underground Baptist church in Russia during the height of the Cold War. He was arrested, tortured, and imprisoned on a number of occasions during the 1960s and 1970s. Repatriated during the Carter administration, Vins has been actively broadcasting the gospel to Russia ever since.

Much to the annoyance of the Russian Orthodox Church, Vins also is busy organizing new churches, distributing Bibles, and spreading the anti-clerical, Bible-based, and born-again message of the Evangelical Baptist Churches to the Russian, Ukrainian, and Georgian Republics.

SOURCES

Melton, J. Gordon. *Directory of Religious Organizations in the United States.* 3d ed. Detroit: Gale Research, 1993.

RUTHERFORD, JUDGE
see: Judge Rutherford

S

SACRED HEART
first aired: 1939

Sacred Heart was originally produced as a radio lecture program by the Society of Jesus (the Jesuits). Having no permanent host, *Sacred Heart* featured a 15-minute message by guest lecturers from across the nation. In 1957, the program was produced for television. By the late 1960s, *Sacred Heart* was being carried by 115 stations nationwide, maintaining a modest viewership for over three decades.

In the late 1980s, the Jesuits began experimenting with a television magazine show, patterned somewhat after *60 Minutes*, called the *Jesuit Journal*. The radio work of *Sacred Heart* continued during this time, with nine programs airing daily or weekly over 1,800 stations throughout the world.

SOURCES

Bluem, A. William. *Religious Television Programs: A Study of Relevance*. New York: Hastings House, 1969.

Erickson, Hal. *Religious Radio and Television in the United States, 1921–1991*. Jefferson, NC: McFarland, 1992.

SAMARITAN'S PURSE
established: 1970

Samaritan's Purse is a nonprofit Christian relief organization that specializes in meeting the physical needs of victims of war, natural disaster, disease, and poverty. The ministry was begun in 1970 by Bob Pierce, the founder of World Vision, another Christian humanitarian aid organization. Samaritan's Purse is currently under the leadership of Franklin Graham, the son of evangelist Billy Graham.

Like World Vision, Samaritan's Purse airs regular television fundraising specials that feature the many forms of outreach the ministry supports. The organization has provided, among other outreaches, Bibles for the people of Lebanon, airplanes for missionaries in New Guinea, Christmas gift boxes for the children of Bosnia, fresh water wells for famine victims in Ethiopia, hospitals and medicines for the people of Kenya, bicycles for pastors in Uganda, and shelters for orphans in Madagascar.

The goal of the ministry is to provide resources for Christian missionaries so that by demonstrating concern for people's immediate needs, missionaries can "earn a hearing for the message of salvation." The headquarters of the organization is in Boone, North Carolina.

See also Bob Pierce

SOURCES

Samaritan's Purse. Promotional brochures, 1995.

SATURDAY NIGHT ALIVE

Ron Hutchcraft Ministries is the Chicago-based producer of *Saturday Night Alive*, a program geared toward young Christians throughout

North America. The program features a live studio audience of young people who participate with Hutchcraft in creating each week's program. This participation often includes taking roles in dramatic skits and discussing questions on a weekly topic. *Saturday Night Alive* is now broadcast to international audiences on Trans World Radio.

MICHAEL SCANLAN

born: December 1, 1931, Far Rockaway, New York

Father Michael Scanlan is the president of the Franciscan University of Steubenville, Ohio, and the host of two broadcasting ministries produced by the university and aired on the Eternal Word Television Network and its radio affiliate, WEWN.

The television program, *Franciscan University Focus*, is a monthly panel discussion of important documents and events in the Roman Catholic Church. In addition to Father Scanlan, the panel consists of Father Giles Dimock, chairman of the Franciscan University's theology department; Dr. Scott Hahn, professor of biblical theology; Dr. Regis Martin, professor of dogmatic and systematic theology; and Dr. Ronda Chervin, professor of theology and philosophy. A guest panelist appears each month to bring special expertise to the subject under discussion. The radio ministry, *Franciscan University Connections*, is a "dynamic, faith-centered" radio program that features Father Scanlan and other noted Catholic speakers. The show airs three times a week on the short-wave broadcasting service, WEWN.

Father Scanlan is the son of Vincent Michael Scanlan and Marjorie O'Keefe. After earning his bachelor's degree from Williams College, Williamstown, Massachusetts, in 1953, Scanlan received a law degree from Harvard Law School in 1956. He then did graduate studies in political science and higher educational administration at Boston University and Catholic University of America. Scanlan entered the Franciscan Third Order Regular in 1957, studied at Saint Francis College in Loretto, Pennsylvania, and was ordained to the Catholic priesthood in 1964.

Following a two-year stint as acting dean of the College of Steubenville between 1964 and 1966, Scanlan served as dean of the General Honors Program between 1966 and 1969. He accepted the job of president of the College of Steubenville in 1974 after working as rector-president of St. Francis Major Seminary from 1969 to 1974. Scanlan earned a master of divinity degree from St. Francis in 1975 and has received honorary doctorates from the College of Steubenville (doctor of letters, 1972), Williams College (doctor of laws, 1978), and St. Francis College (doctor of philosophy, 1987).

Father Scanlan is also active in a number of national organizations, including the Catholic Alliance for Faith, Intercession, Repentance, and Evangelism (president), the Christian Film and Television Commission (board member), the Institute on Religious Life (member of advisory board), and Renewal Ministries (board member). He has published over 16 books and booklets, including *The Power in Penance* (1972), *Inner Healing* (1974), *A Portion of My Spirit* (1979), *Let the Fire Fall* (1986), *Appointment with God* (1987), and *The Truth about Trouble* (1989).

In addition to his broadcasting duties, Scanlan is a respected speaker at national and international conferences and a popular pilgrimage guide with Franciscan University Journeys. He has summed up his attitude toward his career as follows: "If you are going to change something, you've got to live on vision, before you live on reality. You have to be so inspired by the vision, that you keep telling everybody until it gets in them and they start living it with you."

See also *Franciscan University Focus*

SOURCES

"Franciscan University Focus." World Wide Web site. http://esoptron.umd.edu/fusfolder/focus.html (December, 1995).

ROBERT SCHAMBACH
born: 1926

Courtesy: Gary Monroe

Robert W. Schambach is a prominent Pentecostal healing evangelist who entered the field of religious broadcasting in the early 1970s with his radio program, *Voice of Power*. The flamboyant, forceful preacher later expanded into television with several television series, including *It's Time for Revival* and *Voice of Power*. Since 1991, Schambach has had a weekly half-hour broadcast on Paul Crouch's Trinity Broadcasting Network.

Schambach was reared in a nonreligious household and underwent a religious conversion at the age of 16 while listening to an Assemblies of God street preacher. Along with his family, Schambach joined the denomination. During World War II, Schambach enlisted in the Navy and gained some informal preaching experience onboard a Navy ship in the South Pacific. Following his discharge from the Navy, Schambach enrolled in Central Bible Institute, the Assemblies of God Bible college in Springfield, Missouri.

Schambach's first pastorship was in a small Philadelphia congregation that was too poor to pay him a proper salary. To support himself, he found a job at a local oil refinery. After gaining ministerial credentials from the Assemblies in 1951, Schambach pastored a church in Pittsburgh.

A major turning point in Schambach's life occurred in 1955, when he decided to join the revival ministry of A. A. Allen, the well-known Assemblies preacher. Allen was charged with drunken driving soon after and was subsequently asked by the Assemblies to withdraw himself temporarily from his public ministry. Although he maintained his innocence, Allen finally left the denomination and began an independent revival ministry, Miracle Revival Fellowship, in 1956. Schambach decided to remain with Allen and the other ministers and congregations who supported him. He turned in his ministerial credentials to the Assemblies of God and soon after became Allen's associate minister. Allen moved to Miracle Valley, Arizona, in 1959, where he founded a Bible school and the national headquarters for his revival ministry. Schambach followed his mentor to Arizona before breaking away in 1960 to found his own independent evangelical enterprise, Schambach Miracle Revivals, Inc.

Schambach continued to hold tent revival services in the emotional, charismatic style of Allen. With loud music, dramatic preaching, and regular instances of exorcism and miraculous physical healing, he became a popular revivalist during the 1960s and early 1970s, building an especially strong base of support among African Americans.

Schambach has always appealed to the poor and destitute, whom he exhorts in a positive way to rise above hopelessness and take constructive action to better themselves. In Newark, New Jersey, where he held his first revival, the crowds were so receptive that Schambach founded a new church in the city. He then spent the next few years buying abandoned theaters in cities such as Brooklyn, Chicago, and Philadelphia and establishing congregations. These "Miracle Temples," as they were called, were pastored by ministers who had trained with Schambach during his traveling revivals.

Schambach moved his headquarters from Ellwood City, Pennsylvania, to Tyler, Texas. The ministry now supports a Bible college, a publishing enterprise, an orphanage in Indonesia, and a continuing series of Schambach revivals around the world. One of the periodicals the ministry puts out is *Power*, which Schambach started in the 1970s. A. A. Allen's widow, Lexie, now serves as the publication's chief editor.

Schambach's radio series, *Voice of Power*, began in 1970. Within five years, the show was being aired in over 50 cities around the United States. With his foray into television in the 1980s, Schambach found a perfect medium for his inspirational, enthusiastic preaching. Schambach's style includes his lurching back and forth across the stage, evoking a loud, emotional response from his audience, and sometimes stopping and pointing straight into a handheld mini-camera, at which he shouts, "Don't follow me! Follow God!"

Since 1991, Schambach has broadcast his television programming around the world on the hugely successful Trinity Broadcasting Network. As of 1996, his show is still going strong.

See also A. A. Allen

SOURCES

Burgess, Stanley M., Gary B. McGee, and Patrick H. Alexander, eds. *Dictionary of Pentecostal and Charismatic Movements*. Grand Rapids, MI: Zondervan, 1988.

Erickson, Hal. *Religious Radio and Television in the United States, 1921–1991*. Jefferson, NC: McFarland, 1992.

Sims, Patsy. *Can Somebody Shout Amen!* New York: St. Martin's Press, 1988.

PAUL SCHERER

born: June 22, 1892, Mt. Holly Springs, Pennsylvania
died: March 26, 1969, Ohio

Paul Ehrman Scherer was a respected Lutheran homiletician and pastor who gained national fame as the alternate preacher on *Sunday Vespers*, Harry Emerson Fosdick's popular network radio broadcast. Along with such pioneers as Ralph Sockman and S. Parkes Cadman, Scherer helped make radio preaching an important influence on America's national religious life.

Scherer was born in Pennsylvania, the son of a prominent Lutheran minister, Melancthon Gideon G. Scherer. The elder Scherer, himself the son of a Lutheran churchman, pastored churches in Pennsylvania and North Carolina. He also served as president of North Carolina Lutheran College and as secretary of the United Lutheran Church.

Scherer's early education was directed by his pious mother, who encouraged him to recite Shakespeare from memory and to read the great works of American and English literature. Scherer attended a series of primary and secondary schools as the family moved where Melancthon Scherer's work took him. In spite of his somewhat reserved temperament, Scherer was an excellent student, graduating from the College of Charleston with high academic honors. After teaching rhetoric and English at Charleston and taking a position as a high school assistant principal, he earned a master's degree from his alma mater in 1913.

Scherer, who experienced a strong calling to the Christian ministry after graduating from college, began theological studies at Mt. Airy Lutheran Theological Seminary in Pennsylvania. The deep conviction of his calling and the gravity with which he approached the ministerial profession would cause him to later write

> We should . . . clear out of the road all the nonsense we have picked up if any in the matter of the call to the Christian ministry. There is such a call; and when it comes, it comes straight from God. I believe with all my heart that a man must hear it and feel its imperious constraint before he can ever give himself with any wholehearted devotion and abiding wonder to this stewardship of the gospel.

Scherer was strongly influenced during his student years by the social gospel movement, which was in its heyday during the early twentieth century. As a young pastor, he became a strong advocate of social reform and a firm believer in human progress. This optimism would later be tempered by the neo-orthodoxy that dominated theological reflection in the mid-twentieth century.

After earning a bachelor of divinity degree from Mt. Airy in 1916, Scherer took his first pastoral post at Holy Trinity Lutheran Church in Buffalo, New York. After 18 months of service as an assistant pastor, he returned to Mt. Airy where he taught history and ecclesiastical Latin. Scherer married Lilli Fry Benbow in 1919. Scherer's wife would bear him two daughters and become a trusted critic of his sermons.

In 1920, Scherer moved to Central Park West in New York City to pastor Holy Trinity Lutheran Church. The church was near the city's Hell's Kitchen neighborhood, and the young pastor saw firsthand the depredations of slum life. Scherer's sermons during his 25-year pastorate at Holy Trinity would reflect a genuine social concern for the poor. They would also reflect Scherer's strong pacifism and support for conscientious objectors during World War II. Out of similar moral convictions, Scherer joined in a collective ministerial protest against the development of hydrogen bombs and spoke out against such "preventive wars" as the Korean conflict during the post-World War II era.

Scherer took his preaching duties very seriously and requested as part of his pastoral contract at Holy Trinity that he have mornings free to prepare his weekly homilies. He regularly spent 30 hours on his Sunday sermon and developed a weekly pattern of preparation. On Monday he would select a topic and biblical text and begin to outline the sermon's main themes. Over the next two days he would carefully examine the biblical text and decide whether his sermon would have a doctrinal, ethical, pastoral, expository, or evangelistic style. He then wrote out the homily's outline, introduction, and conclusion. By Thursday, Scherer was working on a complete draft. He believed that a preacher must discipline himself to write frequently and carefully. Over the next two days Scherer would complete the rough draft and begin extensive revisions. On Sunday morning he would read the sermon once again before his morning meal and then preach it with few, if any notes. The manuscript he had written was placed in a sermon notebook for future reference or publication.

Scherer got a chance to showcase his homiletic skills when, in 1932, he was asked to be the vacation replacement preacher on *Sunday Vespers*, Harry Emerson Fosdick's national radio broadcast. Scherer continued in this replacement role for the next 13 years, developing a loyal following of listeners who often sent him over 1,500 letters a week. Along with Fosdick, S. Parkes Cadman, Ralph Sockman, Walter A. Maier, and Charles E. Fuller, Scherer helped make religious broadcasting a powerful evangelistic tool of the American Protestant community.

Scherer's philosophy of preaching was shaped by two convictions. First, he believed that the Word of God was eternally relevant and need only be articulated in a way that spoke to the real dilemmas of contemporary humanity. Second, he asserted that the preaching of the Word was the bedrock of Christian worship and liturgy. Nothing else could sufficiently take its place. The goal of preaching, in Scherer's view, was to bring about a confrontation between God and humanity and to mediate the Word of God to a suffering world. Preaching was a radical transaction that ushered believers into the presence of Christ and forced them to discuss matters of the soul.

In addition to his homiletic duties, Scherer committed himself to pastoral care. He claimed that effective preaching grew out of effective pastoring. Holy Trinity grew during his 25-year tenure from 350 to 1,000 members.

Scherer left his pastoral duties to assume the Brown Professorship of Homiletics at Union Theological Seminary in 1945. He gained a formidable reputation among his students as both mentor and homiletic genius. As former student John R. Fry recounted,

> He knew the sound of greatness. He would not settle for less from his students. In his preaching classes a student would occasionally present a pretty good sermon. When that happened Scherer might respond with real salty tears of exaltation. That was seldom. Mostly he was muttering and making nervous little asides and laughing in a nonfunny way as a student sermon was

being presented. Scherer's creativity was, you see, reconstructing the whole bulk of what he was hearing into a first-class sermon. . . . He would resay the student's words into great words, which, off the cuff, were suitable for binding into any book of great sermons.

When he was not preaching, Scherer was a popular lecturer at conventions, seminaries, and universities. His most significant series of talks were the Lyman Beecher Lectures on Preaching delivered in 1943 at Yale University. This event was especially significant because Scherer was the first Lutheran ever asked to deliver these lectures.

Scherer disclosed four principles of homiletic style in his Yale lectures. These were the use of truthful, measured words; the use of simple, short words; the use of words that bring clarity and elevation to the mind; and the use of picturesque words. About commonplace phrases he once wrote,

> [Exchange them] leaving those that lie down on the page with their four legs in the air, panting out their life, for others that gird their loins to run. . . . Never use the word "thing," or that other word "great." Be specific. Say what thing you mean and say how great it is. . . . [Careful word selection] is hardly writing; it is painting. . . . It is the attempt to make men see, to turn their ears into eyes.

Scherer also devoted time to the writing and publishing of devotional materials and homiletic books and worked as part of the editorial board for the Interpreter's Bible. In 1960, Scherer retired from his post at Union and began a series of visiting professorships. Two of the more memorable of these professorships were at Union Seminary in Richmond, Virginia, and Princeton Theological Seminary. At the latter seminary, Scherer served as the Francis Lauder Patton Visiting Professor of Homiletics. This post was to be his last. He died in 1969 and his ashes were interred at Princeton.

Throughout a long and illustrious career, Scherer devoted his homiletic skills to a profound examination of the human condition, the inspiration of his listeners to a more heartfelt devotion, and the proclamation of divine love. Though finely crafted and carefully reasoned, Scherer's sermons managed to convey a deep sense of reverential awe.

See also Harry Emerson Fosdick

SOURCES

Fant, Clyde E., Jr., and William M. Pinson, Jr. *20 Centuries of Great Preaching.* Vol. 10. Waco, TX: Word Books, 1971.

Reid, Daniel G., et al., eds. *Dictionary of Christianity in America.* Downers Grove, IL: InterVarsity Press, 1990.

ROBERT SCHULLER
born: September 16, 1926, Alton, Iowa

Courtesy: National Religious Broadcasters

Robert Harold Schuller is an unparalleled success story in religious television. By 1990, his *Hour of Power* weekly broadcast was watched by 2.7 million Americans, and fully 2.5 percent of the country's households with a television. His 10,000-member Crystal Cathedral of the Reformed Church in America boasted a wide range of service programs and a magnificent $20 million glass-roofed-and-walled worship facility. While the television ministries of Jimmy Swaggart, Jim Bakker, and Robert Tilton were falling apart because of various scandals,

Schuller maintained his position as one of the country's most respected and most watched televangelists.

Robert Schuller was reared on a farm in northwest Iowa, where his nineteenth-century ancestors had helped establish a thriving rural enclave for Dutch Reformed immigrants. In the household of his parents, Anthony and Jenny Schuller, Robert learned the doctrine and practice of orthodox Calvinism as well as the traditional agrarian virtues of industry, perseverance, and self-reliance.

Upon his graduation from high school in 1943, Schuller attended Hope College, a small liberal arts university in Holland, Michigan, associated with the Dutch Reformed Church. At Hope, Schuller prepared for the ministry by taking preseminary coursework. When he had completed his bachelor's degree, he immediately enrolled in Western Theological Seminary, a Reformed institution also located in Holland. Schuller distinguished himself as a confident and persuasive speaker during this period of professional training and won a preaching award at the end of his senior year. In June 1950, Schuller gained ordination in the Reformed Church and married Arvella DeHaan, a woman from his hometown of Newkirk. The Schullers would eventually have five children, each of whom would become involved in their parents' religious empire.

Schuller's first ministerial job was at the Ivanhoe Reformed Church of Riverdale, Illinois. Using his gifts as a speaker and community-builder, he increased the church's membership from 40 to 400 in four years. His success in Riverdale caught the attention of Reformed leaders, who asked Schuller to establish a new church in Garden Grove, California. The young minister accepted the assignment with characteristic enthusiasm and arrived in California in 1955 with $400, an electric organ, and an old Chevrolet. The mid-1950s were a boom time in the Southern California property market and the only place Schuller could gain permission to hold Sunday services was a drive-in theater. His plan was to gather a congregation there and raise enough money to build a worship facility.

Schuller advertised his new "church" in local papers and proclaimed, "Come as you are in the family car." This innovative pitch was perfectly geared to the many unchurched families in the area who had grown wary of conventional religious worship. The weekly services began with Arvella playing the organ and leading the congregation in song. Her husband then mounted the tar-paper roof of the refreshment stand and delivered his sermon. People remained in their cars, dressed in casual attire, and listened through the drive-in speakers.

Following a guest appearance by Norman Vincent Peale, people began flocking to the "drive-in church" and enough funds were raised to build the nation's first combined drive-in, walk-in church. Schuller built his audience into a congregation by offering a range of programming designed to meet people's practical and spiritual needs. His Garden Grove Community Church offered an around-the-clock telephone suicide counseling service, a daycare center, a ministry for single adults, Bible-study groups, and a school. As Schuller once remarked, "a church has to be willing to put the spiritual needs of the non-religious people just a slight notch above the spiritual needs of its communicant Christian membership, or it will not grow."

As his membership mushroomed into the thousands, Schuller built a multistory, multiuse facility in 1968 called the Tower of Power. At the top of this building he erected a huge 90-foot cross that could be seen at night throughout Orange County. The church sanctuary was outgrown by the mid-1970s and Schuller hired Phillip Johnson, a nationally acclaimed architect, to design the Crystal Cathedral, a spectacular church sanctuary built completely of steel wrapped in over 10,611 window panes. It was shaped in the form of a five-pointed star and contained a huge pipe organ and main floor, and balconies with seating for 3,000 worshipers. In commemoration of the church's origins, large glass doors were installed at one end of the cathedral that could be opened to allow congregants to plug in their headphones and worship from their cars. Schuller christened the new facility in September 1980 after a colorful procession with the entire congregation from the old church sanctuary to the Crystal Cathedral.

The total cost of the project was estimated to be around $20 million. Much of the money was raised from 10,000 supporters who gave $500 each to have their names engraved on one of the structure's window panes. In defense of such a huge allocation of resources, Schuller proclaimed the cathedral to be a monument to God similar in conception to Europe's Gothic cathedrals. He also contended that the facility would attract the money to fund important service programs. Upon viewing the imposing structure for the first time, Norman Cousins, a longtime friend of Schuller's, is reported to have remarked: "This is the kind of church God would build; if he could afford it." Regardless of one's personal view, the Crystal Cathedral is a modern architectural marvel that arguably recreates the grandeur and sense of transcendence of Europe's great cathedrals.

The phenomenal success of Schuller's congregation-building efforts led him to create the Robert H. Schuller Institute for Successful Church Leadership in 1969. The institute holds four-day conferences for ministers and their spouses from around the world. To date many thousands have attended the conferences. In addition to the workshops and seminars offered, participants listen to five presentations by Schuller himself. In these low-key, humorous talks, Schuller shares what he believes are the essential features of a successful church: a ministry that serves people's practical, psychological, and spiritual needs; preaching that avoids controversy and speaks to a large audience; strong pastoral leadership; and a focus on positive thinking.

Schuller's television ministry emerged from his desire "to communicate the gospel of Christ to people who are nonbelievers." After encouragement from Fred Dienert (a producer of Billy Graham's crusades), who recognized the minister's charismatic "star quality," Schuller began broadcasting *Hour of Power* to West Coast audiences in January 1970. Like all independent televangelists, Schuller had to pay for airtime with private funds generated by the program itself. The Reformed Church in America did not sponsor the broadcasts.

The new program was a telecast of Garden Grove's Sunday worship services and was designed to give the audience an enjoyable, uplifting, therapeutic, and "redemptive" experience. As Schuller expressed it,

> During the 1960s, nonreligious people had a negative impression of churches in general. I felt that the Garden Grove Community Church presented a positive experience. . . . If that image could be put before the American people, then maybe week after week, year after year, the institutional church could get a different reputation.

Hour of Power typically begins with professional-quality classical church music, guest soloists, and congregational hymns. Views of flowing fountains, lush gardens, and blue skies then fade into the smiling face of Robert Schuller, dressed in the gray-blue ministerial robes of a Reformed minister. Schuller stretches out his arms and exclaims, "This is the day the Lord has made! Let us rejoice and be glad in it!" The order of the service does not vary from that of most Reformed churches, except that Schuller usually includes a dialogue with a famous celebrity. This innovation came about when the evangelist discovered the positive impact that special guests had on weekly ratings. The guests—who have included, among others, former Black Panther Eldridge Cleaver, Mickey Rooney, ex-Nixon administration official Chuck Colson, singer B. J. Thomas, baseball stars Bert Blyleven and Steve Garvey, Billy Graham, Oral Roberts, and boxing champion George Foreman—usually discuss how God has helped them in their lives. To avoid an impression of political partisanship, Schuller invites both conservatives and liberals to appear on the podium.

The broadcast also includes regular fundraising appeals for new service programs. Schuller has been one of the most creative of the televangelists in devising new methods to overcome his audience's resistance to sending money. He regularly offers "free" premiums, e.g., jewelry with religious significance, as an incentive for donations. *Hour of Power*'s director of administration, Carl Wallace, has defended these methods, contending: "You can't just preach the gospel and wait for the money to come in. . . . It doesn't happen that way. You've got to offer some incentive for people to communicate with you. The minute we stop offering gifts, our revenues go down dramatically."

Hour of Power's centerpiece is Schuller's sermon. These sermons are variations on the evangelist's basic ideology, which he calls "possibility thinking." The creed of this positive thinking ideology is: "When faced with a mountain, I will never quit, I will keep on striving, until I climb over, find a pass through, travel underneath, or simply stay and turn the mountain into a goldmine! With God's help."

Schuller's homilies avoid complex theological discourse and focus instead on the practical resolution of the problems of ordinary people. When he speaks of the life in Christ, Schuller emphasize the benefits to be gained by the believer rather than God's judgment of sinners. He defends this "user-friendly" theology by noting its effectiveness in attracting unbelievers. Once a person has expressed interest in joining his church, he or she is given a traditional Reformed catechesis that identifies Jesus as "the only begotten Son of God" who "gave His life as the perfect sacrifice for the sins of the world."

A good example of Schuller's method can be seen in his conclusion to a sermon broadcast in 1978:

> At a deep level I am enthusiastic because the problem of my guilt is handled. Jesus died and rose again. We don't understand it. I can't explain it, but I know that if we dial "C" for courage, He is listening. And He always gets our message. He gives us what we need. And we get it all together through Him.
>
> I invite you to meet Him—to accept Him. It's not an argument: it's a choice. That's important. You've probably been making it a mental debate; that's not where it's at. It's not an argument; it's a choice. God came into the world to tell us that He wants to forgive us, and He wants to save us. That's what Jesus Christ can do for you! Choose Him today!

Schuller's sermons often use mnemonic devices to drive home his main points. To take one example, he organized a sermon on personal transformation around five rhymed verbs: fantasize, analyze, verbalize, organize, and concretize. Although this method has been criticized as tending to oversimplify and even trivialize complex issues, it is a logical extension of Schuller's stated desire to communicate the gospel in simple, clear language that is accessible to the widest possible audience.

Hour of Power quickly gained a nationwide audience and by 1980 was being watched by over 2 million people on 149 stations. It was also the only religious broadcast to be aired regularly on the Armed Services Network, a telling index of its noncontroversial, nondogmatic tenor. To assist listeners with spiritual and psychological problems, a nationwide telephone counseling ministry was added to the program. Unlike most other television ministries, *Hour of Power*'s counselors included callers on the contributions mailing list only if they were explicitly requested to do so by the callers themselves.

Over the past 14 years, Arbitron and Nielsen have consistently ranked *Hour of Power* as one of the two most watched religious television programs in North America; the other is *The World Tomorrow*. The show tends to draw more viewers from the Midwest and urban Northeast than any of its competitors. The reason for this probably lies in the fact that Schuller is not a fundamentalist, does not deliver a Southern-style Pentecostal sermon, and attempts to communicate a broad, middle-of-the-road message. In addition, the program's message of positive self-esteem, optimism, and human potential makes a strong appeal to the pragmatic individualism of the American ethos. In the last few years, *Hour of Power* has begun airing in Europe over Norwegian charismatic Hans Bratterud's European Broadcasting Network.

A bimonthly periodical, *Possibilities*, which offers articles and editorials that promote Schuller's "possibility thinking" gospel, is now sent out to over 800,000 readers for a nominal subscription fee of $5. Schuller's message has also been articulated in a number of successful books. These include *Move Ahead with Possibility Thinking* (1967), *Peace of Mind through Possibility Thinking* (1977), *You Can Become the Person You Want to Be* (1980), *The Peak to Peak Principle* (1980), *Self-Esteem: The New Reformation* (1982), and *The Power of Being Debt Free* (1985).

According to these books, sin is not so much a rebellion of the will against God as it is a lack of self-esteem. Salvation, for Schuller, is liberation from an unhealthy self-image: "To be saved is to know that Christ forgives me, and now I dare to believe that I am somebody and I can do something for God and my fellow human beings." The saving power of Christ, in this view, is that he restores our God-created sense of human dignity.

Schuller suggests three simple practices to help condition the mind in a positive, life-affirming direction: 1) "imagineering," or focusing the mind on what one desires; 2) auto-suggestion, or repeating positive affirmations; and 3) possibility thinking meditation, or relaxing the mind and allowing it to block negative thinking. All of these techniques place Schuller in a direct line of American mental hygienists which includes Phineas Quimby, Mary Baker Eddy, Warren Felt Evans, Emma Curtis Hopkins, Ralph Waldo Trine, Ernest Holmes, Charles and Myrtle Fillmore, Dale Carnegie, and Norman Vincent Peale.

In spite of his many critics among orthodox Christian theologians, Schuller continues to exert a generally positive influence on American televangelism. His financial dealings have been given a clean bill of health by investigators, and he continues to receive accolades and support from his congregation and television audience. In the wake of the televangelism scandals of the 1980s, Schuller's viewership, like that of his competitors, dropped sharply. However, recent research indicates that he has managed to persuade his remaining supporters to increase their per capita contributions. Thus, his income has actually increased since the 1980s scandals.

In recent years, Schuller has begun to use his *Hour of Power* broadcasts to promote a new alliance of mega-church pastors, Churches United in Global Mission (CUGM). Contending that historic denominations and ecumenical organizations like the National Council of Churches and the National Association of Evangelicals have lost their usefulness in effectively spreading the Christian gospel, the 80-church alliance seeks to create "an expanding network of Christian churches, from many denominations, uniting to share positively the message of Jesus Christ and his love for the world . . . [and] seeking to address the needs of humanity and our environment." During his sermons Schuller encourages new believers to join local churches that are affiliated with CUGM. Schuller was elected the new alliance's first president in November 1991.

SOURCES

Armstrong, Ben. *The Electric Church*. Nashville: Thomas Nelson, 1979.

Board, Stephen. "Moving the World with Magazines: A Survey of Evangelical Periodicals." In *American Evangelicals and the Mass Media*, edited by Quentin J. Schultze. Grand Rapids, MI: Academie Books, 1990.

Bruce, Steve. *Pray TV: Televangelism in America*. New York: Routledge, 1990.

Coleman, Sheila Schuller. *Robert Schuller, My Father and My Friend*. Milwaukee: Ideals, 1980.

Hadden, Jeffrey K., and Charles E. Swann. *Prime Time Preachers: The Rising Power of Televangelism*. Menlo Park, CA: Addison-Wesley, 1981.

Nason, Michael, and Donna Nason. *Robert Schuller: The Inside Story*. Waco, TX: Word Press, 1983.

Schuller, Robert. *The Be Happy Attitudes*. Waco, TX: Word Books, 1985.

———. *The Greatest Possibility Thinker That Ever Lived*. Old Tappan, NJ: Fleming H. Revell, 1973.

———. *Move Ahead with Possibility Thinking*. Old Tappan, NJ: Spire Books, 1967.

———. *Peace of Mind through Possibility Thinking*. Garden City, NJ: Doubleday, 1977.

———. *The Peak to Peak Principle*. Garden City, NJ: Doubleday, 1980.

———. *The Power of Being Debt Free*. With Paul Dunn. Nashville: Thomas Nelson, 1985.

———. *Self-Esteem: The New Reformation*. Waco, TX: Word Books, 1982.

————. *You Can Become the Person You Want to Be.* Old Tappan, NJ: Spire Books, 1980.

————. *Your Church Has a Fantastic Future.* Ventura, CA: Regal Books, 1987.

Schultze, Quentin J. *Televangelism and American Culture: The Business of Popular Religion.* Grand Rapids, MI: Baker Book House, 1991.

Springer, Kevin. "Schuller Engineers Megachurch Network." *Christianity Today,* April 6, 1992, 88–90.

Stumbo, Bella. "Schuller: The Gospel of Success." *Los Angeles Times,* May 29, 1983, 1, 3, 22–24.

Voskuil, Dennis N. *Mountains into Goldmines: Robert Schuller and the Gospel of Success.* Grand Rapids, MI: Eerdmans, 1983.

Yates, Ronald. "From Outdoor Theater to Cathedral— A Religious Success Story." *Chicago Tribune Magazine,* July 27, 1980, 10–11, 23–24, 26.

QUENTIN J. SCHULTZE

born: 1952, Chicago, Illinois

Quentin James Schultze is one of the leading scholars and interpreters of American religious broadcasting. He has been interviewed on the topic of religious broadcasting by such radio and television networks and programs as ABC Talk Radio, CNN, CBS, NBC (*Today*), and Mutual, and by such national print media as the *Los Angeles Times,* the *Chicago Tribune, USA Today, Newsweek, The Wall Street Journal,* and *U. S. News and World Report.*

Schultze earned his doctorate in communications from the University of Illinois and has taught at Drake University (where he chaired a graduate program in mass communications), Hope College, and Regent College in Vancouver, British Columbia. Since 1992, he has been professor of communication arts and sciences at Calvin College in Grand Rapids, Michigan. Schultze is a popular lecturer to collegiate audiences, churches, youth groups, and professional conventions. In February 1996, he was a featured speaker at the National Religious Broadcasters annual convention in Indianapolis, Indiana.

Schultze is also a respected author in the field of religion and popular culture. His books include *Dancing in the Dark: Youth, Popular Culture, and the Electronic Media* (1991), *Televangelism and American Culture: The Business of Popular Religion* (1991), *Redeeming Television* (1992), *Winning Your Kids Back from the Media* (1994), *The Best Family Videos* (1995), and *Internet for Christians* (1995).

Schultze's well-received *Televangelism and American Culture* delineates his views on the religious broadcasting industry and the ways this industry has distorted the "historic Judeo-Christian tradition." Schultze examines the cultural correlates of American televangelism, especially the American faith in technology and quest for personalized, mythic heroes. He also offers a theological indictment of televangelism that includes three charges.

First, televangelism exploits well-intentioned but biblically-illiterate viewers by delivering a shallow "health and wealth" gospel in return for monetary support. Second, television preachers, rather than converting the world to Christ, "de-Christianize" America by promoting a secular gospel of personal success. Finally, television ministries turn congregations into passive, unreflective audiences and the gospel into popular entertainment. The book's final chapter, however, offers suggestions as to how Christianity can successfully use modern communications technologies once it has confronted their considerable dangers.

SOURCES

Schultze, Quentin J. *Televangelism and American Culture: The Business of Popular Religion.* Grand Rapids, MI: Baker Book House, 1991.

EUGENE SCOTT

born: 1929, Buell, Idaho

Eugene V. Scott is one of the more unique personalities in religious broadcasting. His rambling sermons, parodies of other preachers, musical guest stars, and bizarre fundraising segments during the 1970s and 1980s allowed him to carve out a loyal, if limited, national audience. During the 1990s, Scott has expanded his broadcasting ministry into 24-hour-a-day radio programming around the world. He has also been the featured cover story for the *Stanford Alumni Magazine* and for the *Los Angeles Times Sunday Magazine*.

Scott grew up in rural Idaho, the son of an Assemblies of God minister. He regularly attended camp meetings and imbibed his parents' fundamentalist religious orientation.

Following his marriage to Betty Ann Frazer in the early 1950s, Scott earned a doctorate in education from Stanford University. Under the tutelage of his advisor, Scott's dissertation created a taxonomy for the analysis of social institutions. This development led to his employment as a consultant for the Sunset Mausoleum Association of Berkeley, California, and Reborn Foundation of São Paulo, Brazil. During this time he attempted to apply philosophy to Christian teachings and subsequently lapsed into a period of agnosticism.

By the early 1960s, Scott had regained his Christian faith and was working with Oral Roberts. He served briefly on the faculty of Evangel College (1964–1965) and later assisted the Assemblies of God with its reorganization process. In 1969, Scott signed on as the pastor of Faith Center, a 45-year-old congregation in Glendale, California. During that same year, Scott was responsible for inaugurating the nation's first 24-hour religious television station, KHOF-TV. This small UHF station was soon providing religious programming for national syndication under the name Faith Broadcasting Network. Scott himself hosted the station's flagship program *Festival of Faith*. KHOF's head of production during this founding period was a young Pentecostal minister named Paul Crouch, who later would use what he learned at KHOF to establish the Trinity Broadcasting Network.

Festival of Faith featured both singing and Bible preaching. Scott discussed the role of the church in the modern world and criticized any institution that encroached on his church's constitutional rights. However, KHOF's struggle to survive taught Scott that it was necessary to offer more than pat sermons and songs if one wanted to maintain a loyal audience. He de-

cided that his best asset was his own flamboyant, eccentric personality. *Festival of Faith* soon became a showcase for that personality. Scott often appeared on stage seated in a chair, smoking a cigar, and wearing different costumes. His trademark props were hats, and during the show's long run his headware ranged from western cowboy styles to leather motorcycle chic. Scott also wore an assortment of sunglasses and reading glasses. The programs were videotaped in extended sequences and then rebroadcast overnight on stations around the country.

At times Scott delivered conventional Christian sermons to his live auditorium audiences. On other occasions he would spend hours criticizing labor unions, the federal government, the Internal Revenue Service, and competing televangelists. Jerry Falwell seemed to draw particular ire from Scott, and he referred to the Virginia-based preacher as "Jerry the Fat." Scott regularly punctuated his telecasts with musical performances by special guests and by his various in-house bands. This music was often accompanied by video of trotting horses, street scenes, and the audience. Throughout the segment a telephone number for contributions was prominently displayed on the screen.

Scott spent hours of program time threatening to close down his ministry if viewers did not immediately phone in with pledges of financial support. In one memorable sequence, he admitted that he wanted to buy a Tennessee trotting horse for his birthday and that he would gauge how much his listeners cared about him by the amount of pledges he received toward that end. Such honesty proved costly, however. In May 1983, the Federal Communications Commission (FCC) terminated KHOF's broadcasting license, justifying its action on a number of grounds. Scott used the last moments of his station's broadcasting time to condemn the federal agency for its "ignorance and censorship." As the program dissolved into electronic snow, Scott pointed to three wind-up toy monkeys, his representation of the FCC's commissioners.

Scott managed to resuscitate his television ministry in the late 1980s, when he began broadcasting his Sunday church services and nightly talk show 24-hours-a-day via satellite to Mexico, the Caribbean, and North America. In Southern California, Scott's television ministry was now seen on Channels 31, 38, 24, 56, 63, and on the Century and Charter cable services.

In 1990, Scott inaugurated a new role for himself as the international voice of the World University Network. This new outreach beams radio broadcasts 24-hours-a-day to 180 countries around the world on medium- and short-wave stations. The network's programming is aired live over Radio Moscow via two Russian satellites and transmitters in Krasnodar, Samara, and Novosibirsk, Russia. The network also is broadcast from Mt. Hermon in Israel; Anguilla in the Caribbean; Dallas, Nashville, and Simi Valley, California, in the United States; and from Palau in the Pacific.

Scott is also a prolific author, having written and published over 20 books. Unlike many televangelists, he can claim to be a philosopher, philatelist, equestrian, bibliophile, and artist in addition to his work as a pastor and philanthropist. Scott's collection of milestone editions of the English Bible is on display at his flagship church, the Los Angeles University Cathedral. Scott's ministry with this church attempts to follow in the tradition of Christ and Paul the Apostle by welcoming sinners of all stripes. His congregation in downtown Los Angeles boasts over 15,000 members.

SOURCES

Burgess, Stanley M., Gary B. McGee, and Patrick H. Alexander, eds. *Dictionary of Pentecostal and Charismatic Movements*. Grand Rapids, MI: Zondervan, 1988.

Erickson, Hal. *Religious Radio and Television in the United States, 1921–1991*. Jefferson, NC: McFarland, 1992.

JAY SEKULOW

see: Case in Controversy

SEMAE (SOCIEDAD EVANGÉLICA MISIONERA DE ADIB EDEN)

see: Adib Eden Evangelistic Missionary Society

SET FREE

first aired: 1995

Set Free, hosted by Molly D'Andrea, is a recent addition to the Christian Television Network's lineup. The program is based in Clearwater, Florida, and purports to answer such controversial questions as "Can a homosexual be set free?" "Can he stay free?" "Is he ashamed to talk about it publicly?" How does the Body of Christ deal with his testimony?" and "Do pastors want them in the church?"

THE 700 CLUB

established: 1966

The flagship program of Pat Robertson's Christian Broadcasting Network (CBN) is *The 700 Club*, a one hour live television show that features a blend of news, interviews, commentary, feature stories, and spiritual healing. The program has been on the air since 1966, making it one of the most enduring television ministries in broadcast history.

The name for the show can be traced back to a 1963 CBN telethon during which Robertson asked 700 viewers to pledge $10 a month to help the fledgling network meet its first budget. A subsequent telethon in 1965 was accompanied by what the ministry described as "a remarkable outpouring of spiritual revival among its viewers and a burst of contributions to a program with a format of prayer and ministry coupled with telephone response." Robertson named the new program *The 700 Club* in hopes of capitalizing on the charismatic fame of past telethons.

The program is now carried over 271 television stations throughout the United States and on Robertson's Family Channel cable network. The estimated daily audience for the show is 1 million television households. Ben Kinchlow, Robertson's current cohost (along with Terry Meeuwsen), hosts an international edition of *The 700 Club* that is seen in 60 foreign countries.

In a mid-1980s study conducted by the Annenberg and Gallup organizations, a profile of Robertson's audience was created. One quarter of his viewership had at least some college education and 10 percent were college graduates. In addition, fully 40 percent were from the Midwest and 47 percent were between 30 and 50 years old. In all age groups the majority of viewers were women, and in the over-50 age group this number was 70 percent. A subsequent Nielsen survey found that *The 700 Club* attracted only 22 percent male viewers. Of this 22 percent, 61 percent were between 25 and 54. These numbers appeared to indicate that *The 700 Club* was attracting a younger, more educated audience than that of other televangelists.

The 700 Club, which for most of its history was 90 minutes long, now airs for one hour and is followed each morning by *Heart to Heart*, a 30-minute interview program hosted by former *700 Club* cohost Sheila Walsh. Both programs air every weekday morning and evening on the Family Channel. Each broadcast of *The 700 Club* offers a series of short independent features that may or may not be tied together by a larger theme. Robertson is usually joined by his standing cast, cohosts Ben Kinchlow and Terry Meeuwsen. The cohosts engage Robertson in on-set banter and discussions and conduct interviews. They also provide continuity from program to program.

Many of *The 700 Club's* features are pretaped human interest and personal salvation stories. Celebrities from the worlds of sports and entertainment often appear on the program to testify to the role of Christian faith in their lives. On every show Robertson holds forth with social and political analyses of contemporary issues. Each of these analyses is designed to educate Robertson's followers on the agenda of the conservative Christian Right. The program is shot in a professional studio in Virginia Beach

before a live audience and later distributed to smaller markets on tape.

Some recent highlights on the program include specials on the aftermath of the Los Angeles riots, the life of Malcolm X, and appearances by Senators Bob Dole, Phil Gramm, and Kit Bond, and sports celebrities David Robinson and Evander Holyfield. A recent series called "What My Parents Did Right" showed well-known personalities discussing their childhood years.

See also Pat Robertson

SOURCES

"Christian Broadcasting Company." World Wide Web site. http://www.cbn.org/ (August, 1996).

FULTON J. SHEEN
born: May 8, 1895, El Paso, Illinois
died: December 9, 1979, New York City

Courtesy: National Religious Broadcasters

Bishop Fulton J. Sheen is considered one of the pioneers of religious radio and television broadcasting in the United States. Along with Father Charles Coughlin, Sheen was one of the most visible Roman Catholics of his generation and an effective spokesperson for the church's views. Having communicated for many years with a radio audience, the refined and articulate clergyman made an immediate impact on religious television when his half-hour weekly telecast began airing in 1952. Throughout the 1950s, Sheen's television program introduced a large national audience to the essential teachings of historic Catholicism. The popular cleric also reflected the larger culture's staunch anti-Communism, its optimistic view of the future, and its concern for the religious and psychological plight of humanity in the modern world.

Born Peter Fulton Sheen, the future cleric was reared in a second-generation Irish family in central Illinois. His parents, Newton Morris Sheen, a farmer and merchant, and Delia Fulton, sent him to parochial schools throughout his early years. When he was confirmed, the young boy decided to adopt John as his given name. He later took his mother's maiden name, Fulton, as his given name and kept John as a middle name.

Showing an early flair for scholarship, Sheen enrolled at St. Viator College in Bourbonnais, Illinois, upon graduation from high school. He earned both a bachelor's and master's degree there before entering St. Paul's Seminary in St. Paul, Minnesota. Sheen received holy orders in the Catholic priesthood in 1919.

Like many gifted priests of his generation, Sheen was given the opportunity to pursue advanced degrees in the finest Catholic universities in the United States and Europe. He took doctor of sacred theology and bachelor of canon law degrees in 1920 after studying philosophy at Catholic University of America and was awarded a doctorate in 1923 from the Catholic University of Louvain, Belgium. His doctoral thesis, *God and Intelligence*, earned him the Cardinal Mercer International Prize in Philosophy. This distinction was especially notable because Sheen was the first American to have received the award. During this period the young priest also studied at the Collegio Angelico in Rome (from which he earned his doctor of divinity degree) and the Sorbonne in Paris. His first formal teaching experience came at St. Edmund's College in Ware, England.

Upon his return from Europe, Sheen was sent by his bishop to Peoria, Illinois, to pastor a run-down parish. The young priest apparently acquitted himself well during this "test of obedience," for he soon was given the chair of apologetics at Catholic University of America. Sheen would serve as a faculty member there until 1950. After transferring to the philosophy department, Sheen gained a name for himself as a neo-Thomist scholar. He published his first book of Thomistic studies, *God and Intelligence in Modern Philosophy: A Critical Study in the Light of the Philosophy of Saint Thomas*, in 1925.

Over the next 50 years Sheen produced a prodigious number of popular books on philosophy and religious life, including *The Life of All Living* (1929), *Way of the Cross* (1932), *The Mystical Body of Christ* (1935), *Freedom under God* (1940), *Communism and the Conscience of the West* (1948), *Children and Parents* (1970), and *Those Mysterious Priests* (1974). Sheen's complete bibliography amounts to over 60 books, several of which were bestsellers and went through multiple revisions.

Because of his gifts as a speaker and teacher, Sheen was frequently asked to deliver sermons around the world. He was a regular preacher at St. Patrick's Cathedral in New York. Sheen was also called upon to teach introductory classes in Catholicism for large groups of inquirers and for private individuals. He gave individual instruction to many prominent figures, including Clare Booth Luce, Henry Ford II, and Fritz Kreisler. Sheen's tireless service to the church did not go unrecognized. He was made a papal chamberlain in 1934 and assumed the title Monsignor. A year later he was given the rank of Domestic Prelate and designated Right Reverend Monsignor.

Sheen's national stature outside Catholic circles was greatly increased when he began *The Catholic Hour* radio program in 1930. This half-hour sustaining time presentation of NBC radio and the National Council of Catholic Men was an immediate success. Sheen soon was giving the annual pre-Lenten and Lenten broadcasts and attracting a listening audience estimated in the millions. His career in television began on a memorable Easter Sunday in 1940, when he stood before cameras for the first time during an historic Roman Catholic Easter telecast.

It was not until February 12, 1952, however, when his program *Life Is Worth Living* was first telecast, that Sheen became a household fixture. The newly ordained auxiliary bishop (1951) was the hands-down choice for the assignment because of his mediagenic personality and his finely-honed skills as a spokesperson for the Catholic faith. Sheen enthusiastically embraced the new medium, once going so far as to compare it to the difference between the Old Testament (radio) and the New Testament (television). In television, he declared, "the Word is seen as it becomes flesh and dwells among us."

Sheen's personal charisma and dramatic delivery offered compelling viewing during *Life Is Worth Living*'s six-year run. The program was taped before a live audience in New York's Adelphi Theater and broadcast initially over the old DuMont Television Network to 17 stations. When favorable mail began pouring in, and Milton Berle's competing broadcast dropped 10 rating points, the show's sponsor, Admiral Corporation, recognized it had a hit on its hands. It sold the program to ABC-TV (after both CBS and NBC rejected it), and Sheen was soon being watched by an estimated 20 million viewers on 123 stations nationwide. On February 24, 1953, Sheen delivered a sermon entitled the "Death of Stalin." When Stalin actually died two weeks later on March 5, Sheen's reputation as an ardent anti-Communist and prophetic Christian voice increased greatly. The bishop won an Emmy award for the show later that year.

From 1955 to 1957, *Life Is Worth Living* appeared at 8 PM on Tuesdays. The program became a fixture of many people's weekly viewing and more than held its own against secular prime-time shows starring Berle and Frank Sinatra. As one commentator recounted, "many bars tuned their television sets to his program; taxi drivers would stop work for a half-hour in order to watch. A blind couple in Minneapolis

bought an Admiral television set in express gratitude to the sponsor of his program."

Eschewing the trappings of entertainment programming that other religious television shows employed—musical flourishes, pastoral backgrounds, and shifting camera angles—Sheen kept to his simple, spare, and highly effective format. He began each program with a courtly bow and thanked his audience for letting him come into their homes again. Sitting in a chair, surrounded by only a blackboard, a table, and a Bible, Sheen discussed Catholic teachings in a manner accessible to people of all religious backgrounds. He focused upon such universal themes as personal responsibility, sin, guilt, redemption, motherhood, and the value of the worshipping community. His black cassock, red skullcap, and floor-length red cape lent an air of drama and elegance to each broadcast. At times Sheen would pace the floor or spread out his arms, allowing the sleeves of his clerical clothing to fall gracefully into wing-like patterns. His trademark features were his deep-set, penetrating eyes and arching dark eyebrows. It is said that the bishop's eyes were underlighted to intensify his piercing gaze.

Sheen would speak directly into the camera and give the impression of communicating personally with each viewer. His monologues were peppered with humorous stories, witticisms, and personal anecdotes. He would often joke about the "angel" who cleaned his blackboard during shifts in camera angle and quip that he owed his success to his writers Matthew, Mark, Luke, and John. He was in every way the embodiment of the stern, paternal, and caring parish priest. At the close of each broadcast, Sheen would offer the benediction, "God love you." The huge volume of mail the bishop received daily—nearly 6,000 pieces—attested to the show's popularity. Following a two-year hiatus between 1957 and 1959, Sheen returned to television and produced two more series. The second of these, *The Bishop Sheen Program*, ran successfully between 1961 and 1968.

Sheen remained an active Catholic churchman throughout his broadcasting career. In addition to his work as the auxiliary bishop of the

New York Archdiocese between 1951 and 1966, he served as the national director of the Society for the Propagation of the Faith from 1950 to 1966. He dedicated himself to this latter office with characteristic zeal, writing books, editing news magazines, coordinating fundraising, and donating the proceeds from his broadcasting and publishing ventures to Catholic missions worldwide. He also wrote a popular newspaper column on missionary work, "God Love You," during this period.

Sheen, however, never mastered the finer points of church politics and became engaged, from 1951 to 1966, in a feud with Francis Cardinal Spellman of New York. After allegedly discovering that the imperious Cardinal had dissembled during a dispute being adjudicated by the Vatican, Sheen was given the unglamorous post of bishop of Rochester, New York, in 1966. There, Sheen attempted to carry out the post-Vatican II commission of making the church more relevant to contemporary Catholic laypersons. He also changed the age of confirmation from the traditional 10 or 12 to 17 or 18 and became involved in a racial conflict involving Eastman-Kodak. Sheen ultimately found diocesan administration to be beyond his training and talents and successfully petitioned the Vatican for retirement in 1969.

After receiving the honorary title of Archbishop of Newport, Wales, Sheen spent the rest of his life in quiet seclusion in New York City. He wrote several more books and made occasional guest appearances around the world. In recognition of his outstanding accomplishments as a pioneer television personality, Sheen was asked to appear before the 1977 convention of the National Religious Broadcasters. Although he had never been inducted into the organization's Hall of Fame and never been awarded its Award of Merit, he received a thunderous welcome. No doubt the assembled broadcasters were expressing their appreciation of Sheen's many years of scandal-free, learned, and dignified religious programming. Sheen's autobiography, *Treasure in Clay*, was published after his death in 1979.

See also *The Catholic Hour*

SOURCES

Armstrong, Ben. *The Electric Church*. Nashville: Thomas Nelson, 1979.

Bruce, Steve. *Pray TV: Televangelism in America*. New York: Routledge, 1990.

Hadden, Jeffrey K. *Prime Time Preachers: The Rising Power of Televangelism*. Menlo Park, CA: Addison-Wesley, 1981.

Horsfield, P. G. *Religious Television: The American Experience*. New York: Longman, 1984.

Sheen, Fulton J. *Children and Parents*. New York: Simon & Schuster, 1970.

———. *Communism and the Conscience of the West*. Indianapolis: Bobbs-Merrill, 1948.

———. *The Eternal Galilean*. New York: D. Appleton-Century, 1934.

———. *Freedom under God*. Milwaukee: Bruce, 1940.

———. *God and Intelligence in Modern Philosophy: A Critical Study in the Light of the Philosophy of Saint Thomas*. New York: Longman, 1925.

———. *Life Is Worth Living*. 5 vols. New York: McGraw-Hill, 1953–57.

———. *The Life of All Living*. London: Century, 1929.

———. *The Mystical Body of Christ*. New York: Sheed and Ward, 1935.

———. *Peace of Soul*. New York: Whittlesey, 1949.

———. *Philosophies at War*. New York: Scribner's, 1943.

———. *The Seven Virtues*. New York: P. J. Kenedy and Sons, 1940.

———. *These Are the Sacraments*. New York: Hawthorn, 1962.

———. *Those Mysterious Priests*. Garden City, NJ: Doubleday, 1974.

———. *Treasure in Clay*. Garden City, NJ: Doubleday, 1980.

———. *Walk with God*. New York: Maco, 1965.

———. *Way of the Cross*. Garden City, NJ: Garden City Books, 1932.

DICK SHEPPARD

born: September 2, 1880, Windsor, England
died: October 31, 1937, Glasgow, Scotland

Hugh R. L. Sheppard, or "Dick" as he was known to the public, was a much-loved pioneer of English religious radio. He was also an innovative ecclesiastical reformer who opened his

Anglican churches to common people and tried to awaken Christian faith and charity in the lives of millions of British citizens.

Sheppard grew up in Windsor, England, the son of a subdean of the Chapels Royal. His early studies took him to Marlborough College and Cambridge University, where he showed more talent for making friends and having fun than for academic achievement.

Sheppard's first job after graduation was as lay secretary to a local bishop. This position brought Sheppard into intimate contact with the poor. During this time, he developed a deep concern for the lot of the downtrodden and organized a number of programs for their aid. After a period of intense thought and prayer, Sheppard decided to enter the ranks of the Anglican priesthood, where he believed he could best serve to alleviate human suffering. He studied theology at Cuddesdon College and served as chaplain at Oxford House in London following his ordination in 1907. By 1909, Sheppard had become the head of the Oxford House ministry and begun a lifelong series of innovative service outreaches to the poor.

In 1911, Sheppard suffered a physical breakdown and was forced to step down from his Oxford House pastorate. Upon his recovery, he held increasingly prestigious appointments, culminating in a vicarship at St. Martin-in-the-Fields in central London. This position gave Sheppard national, even international, prominence in Anglican circles and provided him with a powerful pulpit from which to articulate his increasingly vocal criticisms of the church. He was particularly impatient with those church professionals who tolerated the earthly suffering of parishioners so long as they had the proper faith and were heaven-bound. The church failed, he claimed, when it loved people's souls more than people themselves.

Sheppard was determined to make St. Martin's a place of warmth and succor, where all who entered experienced the love of Christ in tangible ways. This did not mean that he wished to turn the church into a social service agency; rather, he believed the church must be vitally concerned with both the physical and spiritual needs of believers, while remaining

vigilant lest it become overly accommodated to worldly values.

To this end, Sheppard introduced a number of innovations at St. Martin's. He rid the church of overt class distinctions by allowing parishioners to sit wherever they chose. He organized a homeless shelter within church precincts and served hot meals to local workers. The church also instituted a visitation program that blanketed the district with volunteers who shared the good tidings of St. Martin's caring ministry. To bring a spirit of laughter and gaiety back into the community the church also held parties and Saturday matinee music concerts.

Sheppard also was innovative in the area of religious worship, introducing afternoon services for soldiers during World War I and a Sunday afternoon service dubbed the "people's service." According to one observer,

> Every Sunday afternoon the church was packed with all sorts and kinds of people, mostly "tired bits of humanity coming to learn something of the love of Jesus Christ." When all the pews were filled, they sat wherever they could find room— on the floor, on the pulpit steps, on the step of the Communion rail, and those who found nowhere to sit just stood. The music was provided by a Guards band in the Chancel, and the service consisted of hymns, prayers, a lesson, and a very simple talk, in which Christianity was related to everyday life. About 50 per cent [*sic*] of the Confirmation candidates every year were people who had first learnt through the Peoples' Service what the love of God meant and that it was concerned with daily life, and they came to attend the ordinary services of the church because of what they found on Sunday afternoons.

Sheppard was also an innovator in the use of communications media and drama. He experimented with newspapers, plays, and radio broadcasts to reach the masses with his message of Christian love. Sheppard's first broadcast was given over BBC radio in July 1923. After this experimental program, he began to formulate a special radio church service that would appeal to people who had fallen away from Christianity, yet who were receptive to sincere prayer and worship in a nonsectarian atmosphere. The BBC's Sunday Committee, which was charged with developing religious broadcasting, helped Sheppard rehearse his St. Martin's congregation for the first broadcast of its Sunday 8:15 PM service. On the evening of the broadcast's premiere, January 6, 1924, queues lined up outside the church. Sheppard began the service with the words, "Tonight we begin the happy, if difficult, task of making contact with a great multitude of unseen people which no man can number. It is our ambition that one day this may ripen in a friendship." This first broadcast received overwhelming support across social, educational, and ecclesiastical boundaries. By 1927, the BBC was airing St. Martin's broadcast on the second Sunday of each month over its 20 stations and Sheppard had become a national celebrity.

Sheppard's sermons over radio communicated his warmth and kindly spirit and made him England's first popular radio preacher. Before each broadcast, Sheppard tried to imagine himself talking to a lonely person next to a warm fireplace. Listeners felt as though Sheppard were reaching out to them personally with sympathetic understanding. His sermons generally contained a mixture of humorous stories, simple illustrations from daily life, and the practical application of gospel teachings. He appealed to the emotions of his listeners and was always most effective when he spoke from his deep inner passion for social justice and his incisive critique of the Anglican Church.

In many ways Sheppard was at his best in venues where he could be close to his listeners and use his talent for sensitively attuning his message to the spirit of the group. He was not a "great" preacher in the traditional sense, yet, as Ernest Jeffs once remarked, "There is no preacher today who does with greater effectiveness two of the primary things for which preaching exists: first, to comfort and strengthen, second, to pierce home to conscience." In Sheppard's own view, a preacher

need not, thank God, be an orator. . . . It would be much better to let any tendency to slang, elaborated humor or shouting be vigorously repressed. . . . His words are for those who are hard pressed in the difficult business of Christian living.

Sheppard avidly defended the use of radio for religious instruction and for preaching against those who contended that attendance at church was necessary for spiritual growth. He wrote: "A lack of interest in churches and church affairs may be perfectly compatible with a genuine and sincere enthusiasm for Christianity. It is here that religious broadcasting has an opportunity which probably none of us even yet recognizes."

In 1926, Sheppard was forced by another bout of poor health to resign his post at St. Martin's. During his convalescence, he continued his radio broadcasts and wrote a controversial book, *The Impatience of a Parson*, that took the Anglican Church to task on a number of fronts. Over the next 11 years, continued poor health followed by recovery led him to accept posts at Canterbury (deanery) and St. Paul's Cathedral (canon). His last major commission came when he defeated several distinguished rivals (including Winston Churchill) for the post of lord rector of Glasgow University. Sheppard's victory was to be short-lived, however. After a period of ill health and marital difficulties, Sheppard died in 1937.

The highly regarded Anglican reformer, innovator, and broadcaster was perhaps best eulogized by Jeffs:

In him, more than in any other preacher of our time, the new glory of the pulpit is illustrated—not the glory of sublime oratory or profound thought, but the greater glory of the man who stands in the midst of the people, a friend and brother, pouring out his soul in the passion of service.

SOURCES

Fant, Clyde E., Jr., and William M. Pinson, Jr. *20 Centuries of Great Preaching.* Vol. 9. Waco, TX: Word Books, 1971.

Dick Sheppard and His Friends. London: Hodder & Stronghton, 1938.

Jeffs, Ernest H. *Princes of the Modern Pulpit in England.* Nashville: Cokesbury Press, n.d.

Sheppard, H. R. L. *The Human Parson.* Milwaukee, WI: Morehouse, 1929.

Wolfe, Kenneth M. *The Churches and the British Broadcasting Corporation: The Politics of Broadcast Religion.* London: SCM Press, 1984.

T. T. SHIELDS

born: November 1, 1873, Bristol, England
died: April 4, 1955, Toronto, Canada

The Canadian independent Baptist minister Thomas Todhunter "T. T." Shields was the son of a nonconformist Methodist minister. In 1888, the Shields family immigrated to Ontario, Canada, where the elder Shields was reordained as a Baptist minister.

Though lacking in formal education, Shields used the Bible training he was given at home to become ordained as a Baptist minister in 1894; he accepted an assignment to the Baptist Church in Florence, Ontario, later that same year. During the following decade, he served a number of pastorates in Ontario, including a six-year ministry at the Adelaide Street Baptist Church in London, Ontario, before becoming the pastor of the Jarvis Street Baptist Church in Toronto, the largest Baptist church in Canada. He served as head minister of this congregation from 1910 until his death 45 years later.

During the period from 1915 to 1920, Shields became progressively more active in fundamentalist concerns, e.g., attacking what he saw as creeping liberalism at McMaster University, a leading Baptist institution. In 1921, his church suffered a split over Shields's fundamentalist activities. He survived the schism, however, and quickly rebuilt the church's membership. In 1922, Shields launched his newsletter, *The Gospel Witness*, subscriptions for which would eventually grow to over 30,000 in some 60 countries worldwide. In 1923, Shields helped organize the Baptist Bible Union (BBU), whose mission was to purge modern elements from the Northern Baptist Convention. He served as the union's first president. In 1932, the BBU became the General Association of Regular Baptist Churches.

Shields's continued attacks against McMaster University led to his censure by the Baptist Convention in 1926. He withdrew from the convention in 1927 to form his own denomination, the Union of Regular Baptist Churches of Ontario and Québec, which split again to form the Association of Regular Baptist Churches of Canada.

In 1927, the BBU took control of the now defunct Des Moines University (DMU), a Baptist college in Des Moines, Iowa, with the aim of converting it into a fundamentalist college. This experiment was short-lived, however, as Shields's less than diplomatic handling of the affairs of DMU resulted in catastrophe. Resentment by the faculty, accusations of sexual improprieties, and a revolt against Shields by the student body led to the complete collapse of the college in 1929.

After returning to Canada, Shields turned his attention to the expansion of his influence in fundamentalist circles. In 1936, Shields added a radio ministry to his growing empire. The program broadcast the Sunday morning services from his church to Toronto and the surrounding areas. In response to the founding of the liberal World Council of Churches in 1948, Shields helped organize the International Council of Christian Churches with Carl McIntire.

Shields died in Toronto, Canada, in 1955, at the age of 81.

SOURCES

Furniss, Norman F. *The Fundamentalist Controversy, 1918–1931.* New Haven, CT: Yale University Press, 1954.

Marsden, George M. *Fundamentalism and American Culture.* New York: Oxford University Press, 1980.

Reid, Daniel G., Robert D. Linder, Bruce L. Shelley, and Harry S. Stout, eds. *Dictionary of Christianity in America.* Downers Grove, IL: InterVarsity Press, 1990.

SAMUEL SHOEMAKER

born: December 27, 1893, Baltimore, Maryland
died: October 31, 1963, Burnside, Maryland

Samuel Moor Shoemaker had already attained national eminence as the pastor of Calvary Episcopal Church in Manhattan and as the spiritual counselor for the organizers of Alcoholics

Anonymous when he began his career as a radio preacher.

Shoemaker was the son of Samuel Moor Shoemaker and Nellie Whitridge. He entered an Episcopal boarding school in Rhode Island at the age of 14 and enrolled at Princeton University in 1912. After actively participating in Princeton's religious and intellectual life for five years, he moved to China in 1917 to teach at Princeton's extension program in Beijing. Following a meeting with Frank N. Buchman, the Lutheran founder of the Oxford Movement (later renamed Moral ReArmament), Shoemaker began a lifelong commitment to personal evangelism.

Shoemaker was ordained as an Episcopal deacon in 1920 and was ordained a priest the following year. He joined the staff of Grace Episcopal Church in New York City and, in 1925, became the pastor of Calvary Episcopal Church. Shoemaker inaugurated a number of innovative programs in urban evangelism and opened Calvary Mission in the gaslight district of Manhattan in 1926. During the early 1930s, Shoemaker's Calvary House, an expanded mission to down-and-outers and alcoholics, became the center of the Oxford Movement's work in the United States. It was during this period that Shoemaker met Bill W., the founder of Alcoholics Anonymous (AA). Shoemaker was instrumental in developing AA's small-group model.

In 1945, Shoemaker began broadcasting a weekly program, *Faith in Our Time*, over radio station WJZ in New York City. This show and a subsequent daily program, *Gems for Thought*, promoted Shoemaker's conservative interpretation of Scripture and dynamic evangelicalism. Both broadcasts aired over 120 ABC radio stations between 1945 and 1946.

Before long, Shoemaker had become the main speaker on two national broadcast outreaches of the Federal Council of Churches, *The Episcopal Hour* and the *Art of Living*. In 1952, he accepted the pastorate at Pittsburgh's Calvary Episcopal Church, where he continued his radio ministry with *Faith that Works*. This show was broadcast over KDKA, the country's first radio station. KDKA was also the first station to broadcast a program of religious worship, on January 2, 1921, from Calvary Episcopal Church. Faith that Works, Inc., is still going strong and has been responsible for a number of popular religious broadcasting ministries over the past 50 years.

Shoemaker is a respected author of such popular books on the religious life as *Twice Born Men*, *The Church Can Save the World*, *The Experiment of Faith*, and *Revive Thy Church*. He also pioneered the Pittsburgh Experiment, a program that reached out to wealthy business leaders.

SOURCES

Armstrong, Ben. *The Electric Church*. Nashville: Thomas Nelson, 1979.

Shoemaker, Helen Smith. *I Stand by the Door: The Life of Samuel Shoemaker*. Waco, TX: Word Books, 1978.

Shoemaker, Samuel Moor. *Calvary Church Yesterday and Today*. New York: Fleming H. Revell, 1936.

ROBERT SHULER

born: Aug. 4, 1880, Grayson County, Virginia
died: Sept. 11, 1965, Los Angeles, California

Robert "Fighting Bob" Pierce Shuler (not to be confused with Robert Schuller of the *Hour of Power* television program) was one of the more controversial and colorful characters of early religious radio.

The son of John William Webster Shuler and Rosa Elvira Cornett, the future evangelist grew up in Virginia, where he graduated in 1903 from Emory and Henry College. Shuler was subsequently ordained within the Holston Conference of the Methodist Episcopal Church, South, and moved with his new wife, Nelle Reeves, to Texas in 1906. While there, he pastored several churches and gained a name for himself in Austin for his outspoken attacks on corrupt local officials. When his attacks on corruption began to include some of Austin's leading citizens, Shuler was forced to leave town. In 1920, the combative minister was appointed as pastor of

Trinity Methodist Church in Los Angeles. It was there that he would serve for the next 33 years and gain his national reputation.

Shuler was an unrepentant fundamentalist who vehemently opposed Christian "modernism," the social gospel, the teaching of evolution, the proposed union between the Methodist Episcopal Church's northern and southern factions, and the ordination of women. In time he emerged as the leading spokesperson for the fundamentalist viewpoint within his denomination and was elected head of the conservative Church Federation of Los Angeles. Shuler promoted his fundamentalist views in the pulpit, in print (he published three magazines during his career, *Bob Shuler's Magazine*, *The Fundamentalist*, and *The Methodist Challenge*) and over radio station KGEF, Los Angeles. He also used these forums to denounce corrupt officials in the Los Angeles city government—at one point succeeding in having the city's chief of police removed from office.

In 1926, Shuler used his new radio program to attack his main broadcasting competitor in the Los Angeles area, Aimee Semple McPherson. Not only was McPherson a woman preaching in the church, Shuler charged, but she had also engaged in suspicious business practices. When McPherson returned from her famous pseudo-kidnapping escapade, Shuler took great delight in poking holes in the popular evangelist's story. After numerous court appearances and a spirited self-defense, McPherson was cleared of any intent to defraud the public. In the end, Shuler's relentless and mean-spirited attacks on McPherson came to be perceived as the grandstanding of a publicity monger and ended up costing him listeners and financial supporters.

Undeterred, Shuler threw himself into local affairs, condemning the lax morals of Hollywood's movie industry, supporting the Ku Klux Klan, and accusing Catholics of plotting to murder Protestants in their beds during Al Smith's 1928 presidential campaign. In 1932, Shuler himself was nominated as a candidate for the United States Senate by the reform-minded Prohibition Party. Although he received over 500,000 votes, Shuler lost the election and subsequently pronounced a curse on the State of California for spurning him. For years, popular legend held that the Long Beach earthquake of 1933 was the result of this curse.

Throughout the rest of the 1930s, Shuler steadily lost influence and support. His radio license was revoked in 1931 by the Federal Radio Commission, which accused the fiery evangelist of using the airwaves to disseminate "public gossip." During this time, Shuler changed his mind and supported the national merger of the Methodist Episcopal Church, South, the Methodist Episcopal Church, and the Methodist Protestant Church in 1939.

Though he continued to have supporters who applauded his efforts to root out civil corruption, Shuler was never quite at home in the new Methodist Church. As the denomination moved in a more liberal and tolerant direction during the 1940s and 1950s, Shuler represented a distinct minority among his ministerial peers. In 1953, isolated and forgotten, he retired from the pastorate of Trinity Methodist Church.

It is thought that the character of Father Jerry (played by Pat O'Brien) in the 1938 gangster film, *Angels with Dirty Faces*, was inspired by Fighting Bob Shuler.

See also Aimee Semple McPherson

SOURCES

Clark, David L. "Miracles for a Dime: From Chautauqua Tent to Radio Station with Sister Aimee." *California History* 57 (1978–1979).

Harmon, Nolan B. *The Encyclopedia of World Methodism.* 2 vols. Nashville: United Methodist Publishing House, 1974.

Howell, Clinton H., ed. *Prominent Personalities in Methodism.* Birmingham, AL: Lowrey Press, 1945.

SILENT WITNESS
see: Ricky Skaggs

SILHOUETTE

During the mid-1960s, the American Lutheran Church tried to reach the youth culture with a radio program called *Silhouette*. The show aired Sunday mornings on AM radio stations around the United States and featured such "soft" rock-and-roll hits as "Turn, Turn, Turn" and "The Man from Galilee." Interwoven with the music was commentary on the meaning of life and the Christian way of living for contemporary teens.

SIM INTERNATIONAL
established: 1893

The Society for International Ministries (or SIM International) is an independent missionary organization that supports mission work in a number of countries throughout Asia, Africa, and South America. The ministry's main efforts center on evangelism, church planting, medical relief, and Christian education. SIM International also supports a broadcast ministry that beams programs over both radio and television.

The organization's philosophy of missions emphasizes training and equipping indigenous leaders to guide the work of its local missions. Its present organizational structure is a result of mergers with the Andes Evangelical Mission in 1982 and the International Christian Fellowship in 1989. The ministry's headquarters are in Charlotte, North Carolina.

SOURCES

Melton, J. Gordon. *Directory of Religious Organizations in the United States.* 3d ed. Detroit: Gale Research, 1993.

RICKY SKAGGS
born: July 18, 1954, Cordell, Kentucky

Ricky Skaggs is a highly successful country and bluegrass artist who has become a featured per-former on the Trinity Broadcasting Network (TBN). Skaggs hosts his own television show, *Silent Witness*, Saturday evenings on TBN.

Skaggs began his career as a musician at an early age. When he was three, he sang gospel harmonies with his mother at family gatherings and church services, and performed with family members at fairs and social gatherings. By the age of five, Skaggs had taught himself mandolin. Within five years he had also begun to learn the guitar and fiddle. When he was only six, Skaggs was brought on stage at a Bill Monroe concert in Martha, Kentucky, to play the mandolin. His performance of "Ruby" on Monroe's mandolin brought him thunderous applause from the audience. The following year Skaggs secured his first paid performance on the *Lester Flatt and Earl Scruggs* television program.

Later, as a teen, Skaggs was asked to play mandolin for Ralph Stanley's Clinch Mountain Boys. After a successful stint with this group, he founded his own band, Boone Creek. The group was at the cutting edge of a musical movement that was attempting to meld together such diverse musical genres as jazz, rock, folk, bluegrass, and country. Skaggs's new band lasted from 1975 to 1977, when Emmy Lou Harris asked him to join her Hot Band. Harris's much praised 1980 record, *Roses in the Snow*, features several of Skaggs's arrangements.

Skaggs has been a featured guest on such television specials and programs as *Academy of Country Music Awards*, *Grand Ole Opry 60th* and *65th Anniversary*, *Entertainment Tonight*, *Good Morning America*, and *The Today Show*. The Grand Ole Opry inducted Skaggs as its youngest member in June 1982. Skaggs has recorded 12 albums and won such awards as the Gospel Voice Diamond Award (1993), Christian Country Artist of the Year (1993), Best Country Vocal Collaboration (1992), and a Grammy in 1992. He is a gifted musician, having mastered the guitar, banjo, mandolin, fiddle, mandocaster, and telecaster.

In addition to his music ministry on TBN, Skaggs and his wife, Sharon White, are active in Teens in Trouble, a nonprofit ministry they founded in 1991. The organization distributes money to groups that help teenagers cope with drug and alcohol abuse, sexual abuse, pregnancy, illnesses, and other crisis situations. Skaggs was a featured performer at the 1995 National Religious Broadcasters annual convention in Nashville, Tennessee. His show, *Silent Witness,* features a musical variety format and is a good example of the increasing popularity of contemporary Christian musical programming.

SOURCES

"Casting Call for NRB 95." *Religious Broadcasting,* February, 1995.

TOM SKINNER
born: June 6, 1942, New York City

The radio evangelist Tom Skinner is the son of a Baptist minister who moved north with thousands of other southern blacks during the Great Depression. Though raised in the church, and a leader in his youth group, Skinner became alienated from religion and drifted into gang activity in Harlem. By the age of 14, Skinner was a leader in the Harlem Lords gang, all the while remaining active in church and high school. After two years of gang leadership, he was converted to Christ after hearing a radio preacher. He quit the Lords and, as a street evangelist, began preaching about his newfound faith. Skinner converted a number of people, including members of his former gang.

In 1958, Skinner enrolled at the Manhattan Bible Institute, graduating in 1962. In 1959, at the age of 16, he was ordained a minister in the United Missionary Baptist Association of the National Baptist Convention. He encountered opposition from established ministers in Harlem, as well as resistance from black militants, who criticized him for his espousal of "white" religion.

While still a student at Manhattan Bible Institute in 1961, Skinner cooperated with a number of other Harlem ministers in forming the Harlem Evangelistic Association. This organization held its first crusade at the Apollo The-

ater in Harlem the following year. This success was followed by crusades in Brooklyn, Barbados, Bermuda, British Guiana (now Guyana), and elsewhere.

In 1964, Skinner expanded his outreach by adding a radio ministry and formally establishing Tom Skinner Crusades (becoming Tom Skinner Associates in 1966). Using this organization as a foundation, Skinner cultivated a national radio audience and developed an urban ministry. His evangelistic sermons aimed at converting African Americans and provided social as well as spiritual services. In time, Skinner became one of the most influential voices in the black evangelical community. His autobiography, *Black and Free* (1968), was well-received within both the black and white communities.

In the 1970s, Skinner turned his attention more and more toward global outreach among blacks in the Caribbean and Africa. He began to develop a black theology, which emphasized evangelism and social work among the urban poor. His books, *How Black Is the Gospel?* (1970) and *Words of Revolution* (1970), document his evolution toward black urban ministry.

SOURCES

Melton, J. Gordon. *Religious Leaders of America.* Detroit: Gale Research, 1991.

Murphy, Larry G., J. Gordon Melton, and Gary L. Ward. *Encyclopedia of African American Religion.* New York: Garland, 1993.

Skinner, Tom. *Black and Free.* Grand Rapids, MI: Zondervan, 1968.

SLAVIC MISSIONARY SERVICE
established: 1945

Slavic Missionary Service, Inc., is a religious radio outreach offering script translation, program production, and a cassette ministry for Russian-speaking people. The service is run by Alex Leonovich and Tim Semenchuk. Leonovich has been broadcasting his gospel message into the former Soviet Union and around the world since 1945. The ministry's radio program, *Slavic Missionary Service*, has been broadcast since the 1970s. Leonovich is a board member of the National Religious Broadcasters. Slavic Missionary Service is headquartered in South River, New Jersey.

J. HAROLD SMITH
born: 1910, Woodruff, South Carolina

The staunchly fundamentalist Baptist minister J. Harold Smith was the longtime host of the *Radio Bible Hour*, a program that featured Smith's Sunday sermons.

He began his controversial career in religious broadcasting in 1935 when he bought daily air time on a local station in Greenville, South Carolina. Smith routinely excoriated liberal ministers during his broadcasts and spoke against worldly activities and unbelievers. Within several years, Smith had moved his program to radio station WNOX in Knoxville, Tennessee, and garnered a much larger and more fiercely loyal audience. During the 1940s, Smith's stridently anti-liberal positions gained him enemies in the Federal Council of Churches. When the council moved to ban him from the airwaves, Smith fought back, calling it "a demoniac vulture sitting upon the pinnacles of our churches" and vowing to destroy it. In 1947, he built his own radio broadcast station in Knoxville, WBIK.

After being forced off the air by the Federal Communications Commission in 1953, Smith relocated his ministry to Ciudad Acuna, just across the Texas-Mexico border, and bought broadcast time on XERF, a powerful 100,000-watt superstation which reached two-thirds of the United States. Throughout the years, Smith's popularity with fundamentalist audiences never waned. He remained on the air until the 1980s, when the Mexican government banned all English-language religious broadcasts from within its borders.

See also *Radio Bible Hour*

SOURCES

Fowler, Gene, and Bill Crawford. *Border Radio.* Austin: Texas Monthly Press, 1987.

Hill, George H. *Airwaves to the Soul: The Influence and Growth of Religious Broadcasting in America.* Saratoga, NY: R & E, 1983.

Roy, Ralph L. *Apostles of Discord.* Boston: Beacon Press, 1953.

Ward, Mark, Sr. *Air of Salvation: The Story of Christian Broadcasting.* Grand Rapids, MI: Baker Book House, 1994.

OSWALD SMITH
born: November 8, 1889, Odessa, Ontario, Canada
died: January 25, 1986, Toronto, Ontario, Canada

Courtesy: Billy Graham Center Museum

The Canadian fundamentalist radio preacher and promoter of missions, Oswald J. Smith, was born to Benjamin and Alice Smith and raised in rural Ontario, Canada. He attended a local Presbyterian church and, after hearing Reuben A. Torrey preach in Toronto in 1906, was converted to Christianity at the age of 16. Smith returned home from Toronto and started a Sunday school and preaching ministry shortly thereafter.

Zeal for evangelism led Smith to pursue a career in the missions field. Because of health problems and poor academic qualifications, however, he was rejected by the Foreign Missions Board of the Canadian Presbyterian Church in 1908. Dauntless in his enthusiasm for evangelism, Smith went to preach the gospel in rural Canadian churches. During this time, Smith also served as a Bible salesman for the Upper Canada Bible Society.

From 1909 to 1910, Smith attended Manitoba College. He continued his studies from 1910 to 1912 at Toronto Bible Training School (later Toronto Bible College, still later Ontario Bible College). Following his graduation, Smith attended McCormick Theological Seminary and earned his graduate degree in 1915. During the same year, he was ordained by the Presbyterian Church of Canada and began an associate pastorate with Dale Presbyterian Church in Toronto. A short time later, Smith became the church's interim pastor, a position he retained throughout the remainder of World War I.

Smith's relations with his Presbyterian congregation became strained when he found that his zeal for evangelism was not well-received. He later resigned his ordination, but remained on good terms with the Presbyterian denomination. In 1920, Smith began holding services at the Gospel Tabernacle, an independent church which shared Smith's enthusiasm for evangelism. The following year Smith merged his church with the Parkdale Christian and Missionary Alliance congregation to form the Parkdale Tabernacle. The mixed congregation grew quickly, forcing the construction of a new church building in 1922. The facility was dedicated by evangelist Paul Rader.

For a number of years, in addition to his pastorate, Smith traveled abroad, promoting missions. He periodically returned home to raise money and recruit missionaries. These activities led him to found the Cosmopolitan Tabernacle in Toronto in 1928, a large independent missions-oriented church. Smith would serve as the congregation's minister until 1959.

Smith began his radio ministry in 1930, the same year the Cosmopolitan Tabernacle moved and was renamed the Toronto Gospel Tabernacle (it would later move again and be renamed the People's Temple). Smith's radio program, *Back Home Hour*, was a worship-style broadcast that aired in the Toronto area on Sunday nights after the evening service.

As his work prospered, Smith expanded his church's ministry to include a publishing house, a periodical, and a Bible institute. The church's media ministry also expanded, adding film, audiocassette, and television programming. Smith also appeared as a featured speaker over WKBW, Buffalo, the broadcast station of the Churchill Tabernacle, during the 1930s and 1940s.

Although Smith's primary interests lay in supporting foreign missions, he took time to write over 30 books. These works have been translated into 130 languages. Smith also composed over 1,000 poems and 200 church hymns. He died in Toronto, Canada, in 1986, at the age of 96.

SOURCES

Billy Graham Center Archives, Wheaton College, Wheaton, Illinois.

Melton, J. Gordon. *Religious Leaders of America*. Detroit: Gale Research, 1991.

Smith, Oswald J. *The Peoples Church and Its Founder*. Toronto: Peoples Press, 1961.

———. *The Story of My Life*. London: Marshall, Morgan, & Scott, 1962.

Stone, Jon R. *A Guide to the End of the World: Popular Eschatology in America*. New York: Garland, 1993.

SOCIETY FOR EUROPE'S EVANGELIZATION
established: 1956

The Society for Europe's Evangelization (SEE) is a Baptist missionary organization with a special emphasis on French missions. Headquartered in Bradenton, Florida, SEE distributes Bibles, plants new churches, and offers Bible classes. It also produces radio programs that help extend its ministry of gospel outreach.

SOURCES

Melton, J. Gordon. *Directory of Religious Organizations in the United States.* 3d ed. Detroit: Gale Research, 1993.

RALPH SOCKMAN

born: October 1, 1889, Mount Vernon, Ohio
died: August 29, 1970, New York, New York

Ralph Washington Sockman was one of the early giants of religious radio. His weekly sermons on NBC's *National Radio Pulpit* were heard by millions of listeners for 33 years. The Methodist clergyman was once referred to by RCA's David Sarnoff as "broadcasting's most durable celebrity." Sockman provided a steady and respected voice for American religious liberalism during the middle years of the twentieth century. Yet, in spite of the considerable fame and influence he garnered during his lifetime, Sockman has been largely ignored by contemporary preachers and religious scholars.

Sockman grew up in rural Knox County, Ohio, the son of Rigdon Potter Sockman and Harriet O. Ash. He attended primary and secondary schools in Mount Vernon and Fredericktown. The academically-gifted teen graduated as class valedictorian from Fredericktown High School in 1906. He then spent a year teaching in local primary schools and working on the family farm before enrolling at Ohio Wesleyan University in 1907. Sockman distinguished himself in scholarship during his college years and was elected to Phi Beta Kappa in 1911. He remained close to his family, returning home during vacations to work in his father's new construction business. He also earned the designation "Octopus" because of his active participation in numerous extracurricular activities.

Upon graduation in 1911, Sockman decided to study political science and law at Columbia University in New York City. He worked under the tutelage of the noted historian Charles Beard and for a time entertained the idea of becoming a history professor. The hardworking midwesterner supported himself by serving as an intercollegiate secretary for the YMCA and by working at the Physician and Surgeons Club of New York. Through his acquaintance with resident students at the club, Sockman began attending Madison Avenue Methodist Episcopal Church.

After taking his master's degree in political science in 1913, Sockman decided to change vocational directions and enroll in Union Theological Seminary (UTS) in New York City. He also was hired as an assistant pastor at Madison Avenue Church. While studying at UTS, Sockman took a course with the renowned homiletician, Harry Emerson Fosdick. As Fosdick recounted in his autobiography, Sockman "exhibited such mature ability and skill that I told the class he acted as though he had twenty years of experience behind him . . . and I doubted whether even a homiletical professor could spoil him." After earning his bachelor of divinity degree and marrying Zellah Widmer Endly, a childhood friend, in 1916, Sockman went on to complete a doctorate at Columbia University in 1917.

The rest of Sockman's career was spent as the highly-respected pastor of Madison Avenue Methodist Church. His longevity at the church became something of a legend in Methodist circles, for the standard ministerial stay in the denomination was no more than four to five years. Sockman took a declining church of 450 members, located in a rundown neighborhood, and slowly built it into a thriving congregation. He did this in part by convincing his congregation to open its doors to members of other denominations in a spirit of ecumenical reconciliation.

The church merged with the East Sixty-First Street Methodist Episcopal Church to form the Christ Church and began construction of a new worship facility in April 1929. Although the stock market crashed in October, Sockman went ahead with his ambitious building plans. He hired the noted architect Ralph Adams Cram, who created a magnificent edifice that incorporated early Byzantine, Italian, and Russian architectural and iconographic styles. The church became a focus of controversy during the Depression, and many deplored the large expenditures required to import building materials from Europe during a time of widespread economic suffering. The ornate church, which was finally completed in 1949, was justified by Bishop Francis J. McConnell in his inaugural sermon. The bishop observed "that the beauty of the building would go on feeding the souls of men down the decades long after people would have forgotten the food which could have been bought with the money spent on the building."

Sockman's career as a religious radio personality began in the summer of 1928. Because of his reputation as a preacher, he was asked to take over NBC's *National Radio Pulpit* during host S. Parkes Cadman's annual summer vacation. Sockman became Cadman's regular replacement for the next eight years and was asked to take over the program when Cadman retired in 1936. Sockman's weekly sermons became a much-loved fixture in millions of American homes over the next 24 years. The show was aired via short-wave in Europe and on AM stations throughout the United States and Canada. Sockman's fame as a radio preacher brought many thousands to Christ Church on Park Avenue for his Sunday sermons. Like Charles Fuller, Sockman gained his greatest fame not for his many books and church activities, but because of his radio ministry. The popularity of his program was attested by the 30,000 letters he received every year from listeners asking for advice and religious guidance. Toward the end of his career, Sockman added a television ministry to his busy schedule.

Throughout his career as a radio personality, Sockman kept up a busy schedule of guest speaking around the world. During religious seasons such as Lent and Christmas he would often travel from Monday to Friday, delivering sermons and lectures in different cities each evening. He prepared his weekly radio sermons every weekend between mid-afternoon on Saturday and early Sunday morning. In composing these homilies he used personal reflections, ideas from his extensive reading, and short notes accumulated during the previous week. After a quick perusal of the manuscript on Sunday morning, Sockman mounted the pulpit and usually delivered his sermon without notes.

Sockman spoke directly to the dilemmas of ordinary people living in the conditions of modernity. His sermons used scriptural references to set a theme, but they were always topical rather than expository. The messages frequently contained a prophetic critique of contemporary social and economic practices. Racism and consumerism were two of his favorite targets. In each sermon, Sockman appealed to the "moral intelligence" of his audience and tried to guide them to proper ethical judgments. Unlike other preachers, however, he did not speak out against people who were not part of his own congregation. By all accounts, the radio preacher was also an effective and successful pastor. He counted among his congregation the powerful and famous yet was able to mingle socially with people of all classes. Between 1917 and 1942, Christ Church membership increased from 450 to 2,000.

Sockman's career as an author began in 1924 with the publication of his first book, *The Suburbs of Christianity*. This volume, which was essentially a collection of sermons, articulated what were to be the main themes of Sockman's long ministry: 1) The need to extend "the boundaries of Christ's rule" into the broader social landscape; 2) The need to speak to the inquisitiveness of young people concerning religious truth; 3) "The sharpening hunger for human brotherhood in industrial and international relations"; 4) The need for international reconciliation between nations; and, 5) The need for Christians to transcend narrow doctrinal disputes and to open their hearts to those on the periphery of religious faith. In these areas of concern Sockman followed closely in the footsteps of his mentor, Fosdick. His first book was followed by many others, including the much-read *The Higher Happiness* (1950), *How to Believe* (1953), *The Whole Armor of God* (1955), and *Man's First Love* (1958). These four volumes were chosen as either Religious Book Club or Pulpit Book Club selections. In the course of his illustrious career, Sockman wrote 20 books, numerous magazine and journal articles, and a weekly newspaper column.

In his larger social ministry, Sockman was a tireless worker for international peace. He was elected to the chairmanship of the World Peace Commission of the Methodist Episcopal Church, a post he held from 1928 until 1960, and served as president of the Carnegie Foundation's Church Peace Union. During World War II, Sockman spearheaded efforts to prepare churches for the eventual rebuilding of Europe. The famed preacher was also elected president of the Federal Council of Churches and served as a board-of-trustee member for Ohio Wesleyan, Drew, New York, and Syracuse universities. He held numerous academic posts, including visiting professor in homiletics at Yale University and Harry Emerson Fosdick Visiting Professor at UTS. Preferring teaching and preaching to administration, he refused to be nominated as a Methodist bishop.

Sockman's pacifism underwent severe tests during World War II and the Korean conflict. In each case, he accommodated himself to the prevailing national mood of patriotism and heroic sacrifice. On one occasion during this period, Sockman even observed that "beatitudes cannot stop a blitzkrieg." The churchman's anti-Communist rhetoric was not sufficient enough to satisfy committed cold warriors in the late 1940s, however, and he had to endure a brief period during which he was labeled as a Communist sympathizer. In the end, Sockman's cordial relations with FBI director J. Edgar Hoover provided him the political cover needed to quiet such accusations.

When Sockman finally resigned from his pastorate at Christ Church in 1961, he was honored with a gala dinner at the Waldorf Astoria. In his farewell speech, he appealed for less concern about the spread of Communism and more concern for the spread of Christian godliness. Sockman spent the remaining years of his life writing, preaching, and traveling. The last position he held was as director of the Hall of Fame for Great Americans at New York University. Sockman embraced an optimistic view of humanity throughout his life and succeeded, in no small measure, in helping the urban church to become socially responsible and intellectually alive.

SOURCES

Abbey, Merrill R. *The Epic of United Methodist Preaching: A Profile in American Social History.* Lanham, MD: University Press of America, 1984.

Harmon, Nolan B. *The Encyclopedia of World Methodism.* 2 Vols. Nashville: United Methodist Publishing House, 1974.

Haselden, Kyle. "An Honor Roll of American Preachers." *Pulpit* 35 (1964): 3.

Hibbard, Robert B. "The Life and Ministry of Ralph Washington Sockman." Ph. D. diss., Boston University, 1957.

Lawrence, William B. "Ralph Sockman: The Compleat Methodist." *Quarterly Review* 5 (1985): 27.

Lippy, Charles H., ed. *Twentieth-Century Shapers of American Popular Religion.* Westport, CT: Greenwood Press, 1989.

Sockman, Ralph Washington. *Date with Destiny: A Preamble to Christian Culture.* Nashville: Abingdon-Cokesbury, 1944.

———. *The Higher Happiness.* New York: Abingdon-Cokesbury, 1950.

———. *The Highway of God.* New York: Macmillan, 1942.

———. *How to Believe: The Questions That Challenge Man's Faith Answered in the Light of the Apostles' Creed.* Garden City: Doubleday, 1953.

———. *Live for Tomorrow.* New York: Macmillan, 1939.

———. *Man's First Love: The Great Commandment.* Garden City: Doubleday, 1958

———. *The Meaning of Suffering.* New York: Abingdon, 1961.

———. *The Morals of Tomorrow.* New York: Harper, 1931.

———. *The Paradoxes of Jesus.* New York: Abingdon, 1936.

———. *The Suburbs of Christianity.* New York: Abingdon, 1924.

———. *The Unemployed Carpenter.* New York: Harper, 1933.

———. *The Whole Armor of God.* New York: Abingdon, 1955.

DANUTA SODERMAN

Danuta Rylko Soderman served as the ebullient cohost of Pat Robertson's *The 700 Club* from March 1983 until June 1987, when she was reassigned to another ministry. Her partners included regulars Robertson and Ben Kinchlow, and guest cohost Terry Meeuwsen, who became the program's permanent cohost in June 1993. Soderman studied communications at the University of Colorado before moving to Phoenix, Arizona, where she worked as a camera operator. After a two-year stint as a ski reporter for a San Francisco radio station, she worked as a newsreporter in San Diego and finally as the cohost of *Sun-Up San Diego*, a morning television talk show. Soderman was an earnest spiritual seeker during these years, studying Zen Buddhism, Western occultism, macrobiotics, and transcendental meditation. While participating in a philosophy Bible-discussion group, she experienced a conversion to evangelical Christianity.

Soderman's forte on *The 700 Club* was interviewing. Not only did she interview such prominent figures as Jeanne Kirkpatrick, Bob Dole, and George Bush, but she also interviewed Robertson on the air. It is openly acknowledged that Soderman's 20 hours of recording-studio interviews with Robertson gave him the material for his book, *Answers to 200 of Life's Most Probing Questions*. Soderman was also skillful at lightening the mood on the program. On one occasion she brought her pet sheep to the studio, and the animal wet on the director's shoes. In addition, Soderman participated in the show's healing segment, during which she, Robertson, and Kinchlow closed their eyes, clasped hands, and announced healings taking place around the world through the "word of knowledge" revealed by the Holy Spirit. Soderman is an active outdoorsperson, enjoying sky diving, scuba diving, white-water rafting, and motor sports.

After Soderman's reassignment, actress Susan Howard (from the secular program *Dallas*) served as *The 700 Club*'s cohost from July 1987 to November 1987. Howard was succeeded by Sheila Walsh Miller, who was Robertson's cohost from 1988 until September 1992. Miller left the show due to physical and emotional problems and went on to pursue a degree in counselling. The show's current cohosts are Kinchlow and Meeuwsen.

See also *The 700 Club*

SOURCES

Peterson, Richard G. "Electric Sisters." In *The God Pumpers*, edited by Marshall Fishwick and Ray B. Browne. Bowling Green, KY: Bowling Green State University Popular Press, 1987.

SOLID GOSPEL

Solid Gospel is a radio music service that reflects the growing national popularity of Southern-flavored gospel music during the mid-1990s. The service provides 24-hours-a-day, seven-days-a-week programming that features the best-known Southern gospel artists in the country. Since its inception, the service has been picked up by over 75 stations nationwide. Solid Gospel is distributed through the Reach Satellite Network.

SONGTIME
see: John DeBrine

SOUTHERN BAPTIST CONVENTION, RADIO AND TELEVISION COMMISSION
established: 1938

The Southern Baptist Convention's involvement in broadcast ministries began in 1938 when Samuel Franklin Lowe petitioned the convention to consider the radio as a tool to extend its evangelistic efforts. Lowe, then pastor of Euclid Avenue Baptist Church in Atlanta, Georgia, was placed in charge of a Radio Committee that guided the convention into its first media effort. *The Baptist Hour* was inaugurated on January 5, 1941. It was originally given a three-month probationary period to test its effectiveness, but the show was such a success that it has continued without a break into the mid-1990s. The following year, 1942, Lowe was employed as the committee's full-time director, and a building was purchased in Atlanta to house its operation. Lowe headed the committee until his death in 1952, when he was succeeded by Paul Morris Stevens.

The committee soon absorbed other radio work that had been inaugurated independently by the Home Mission Board in 1946. In 1954, Stevens recommended that the committee change its name to the Radio and Television Commission. The following year the ministry was moved to Fort Worth, Texas, where it began a steady expansion. *The Answer*, a television drama series, first appeared in April 1956. The commission was assigned the task of developing programs for the United States and urged to cooperate with the Foreign Missions Board in developing programs to disseminate overseas.

With *The Baptist Hour* and *The Answer* solidly in place for American audiences, the commission began efforts to reach the overseas mission field. *The Baptist Hour* was translated into Spanish, and *La Hora Bautista* began to be heard in the Caribbean and South America. *Buona Novella* ("Good News") was also begun as a Italian-language radio program with a worship-service format. Dubbing segments of *The Answer* into Japanese, Portuguese, and Spanish began in 1961.

The commission also began to expand its offerings to English-speaking audiences and developed a series of innovative radio programs. These programs included *Master Control,* a music and variety program containing interviews of celebrities and other personalities of interest; *The International Sunday School Lesson*, a weekly church-school lesson; *Chapel Upstairs,* a devotional program; and a shortened version of *Master Control,* which was prepared for broadcast to England by short-wave. By the end of the 1960s, the commission was responsible for over 100,000 separate broadcasts around the world annually.

The Southern Baptist Convention has made the largest commitment to broadcast ministries (in both domestic and foreign fields) of any of the major denominations. The convention's budget expanded steadily as the denomination grew through the 1970s and 1980s. In October 1978, the convention debuted *At Home with the Bible*, a radio and television Bible-teaching program that featured Frank Pollard. During the 1980s, the Radio and Television Commission became an important part of the convention's major program emphasis, termed the Bold Mission Thrust. Through this initiative, the convention has committed itself to enable every person on earth to hear the Christian message by the end of the century. In addition, prominent Southern Baptist ministers such as Charles Stanley have developed popular broadcast ministries which supplement the work of the commission.

By the late 1980s, the commission's radio programs, which are offered free of charge to local stations, were some of the most popular religious broadcasts in the nation. *The Baptist Hour* was being heard on 465 stations, *Master Control* on 863 stations, *On Track* on 569 stations, *Streams in the Desert* on 701 outlets, *Powerline* on 1,498 stations, and *Country Crossroads* on 1,395 outlets.

During the 1990s, the Southern Baptists have created their own cable service, the ACTS Network. The acronym symbolizes both the biblical Book of Acts and American Christian Television Systems.

See also *The Baptist Hour*

SOURCES

Baker, Robert A. *The Southern Baptist Convention and Its People, 1607–1972*. Nashville: Broadman Press, 1972.

Baptist Advance. Forest Park, IL: Roger Williams Press, 1964.

Erickson, Hal. *Religious Radio and Television in the United States, 1921–1991*. Jefferson, NC: McFarland, 1992.

McBeth, H. Leon. *The Baptist Heritage*. Nashville: Broadman Press, 1987.

THE SOWER

see: Guido Evangelistic Association

SPANISH WORLD GOSPEL MISSION
established: 1959

The Spanish World Gospel Mission (SWGM), founded in 1959 as Spanish World Gospel Broadcasting, is an independent evangelical Protestant organization with headquarters in Winona Lake, Indiana. The mission seeks to evangelize Latin America through the distribution of Spanish-language Bibles and religious tracts, the establishment of churches, and the education and training of lay leaders. One of the primary elements of the mission is SWGM's radio ministry, which sends its signal over 125 stations to 26 Central and South American countries. SWGM's directors estimate that their radio program *El Camino de la Vida* ("The Way of Life"), reaches over 35 million people.

SOURCES

Melton, J. Gordon. *Directory of Religious Organizations in the United States.* 3d ed. Detroit: Gale Research, 1993.

R. C. SPROUL
see: Ligonier Ministries; Renewing Your Mind

STAINED GLASS WINDOW
see: Everett C. Parker

CHARLES STANLEY
born: September 25, 1932, Dry Fork, Virginia

Charles Frazier Stanley, Jr., was born in rural Virginia in 1932 to Charles and Rebecca Stanley. Raised in a Baptist home, he dedicated his life to Christian service while still a teenager.

Stanley received a bachelor of arts degree from the University of Richmond in 1954, a master of theology degree from Southwestern Baptist Theological Seminary in 1957, and a

Courtesy: National Religious Broadcasters

doctor of theology degree from Luther Rice Seminary in 1970. During his seminary years, Stanley served pastorates in a number of small Baptist churches in North Carolina (1957–1958), Ohio (1959–1962), and Florida (1962–1969). In 1969, Stanley accepted a call to pastor the First Baptist Church of Atlanta, Georgia. The church quickly prospered, and Stanley sought out an array of new avenues of ministry, including a radio and television outreach.

Stanley's radio program, *In Touch with Charles Stanley*, featured Stanley's Sunday morning sermon. The show has been in production for over 20 years and currently airs over more than 500 radio stations nationwide. The televised version of the program is seen over more than 100 broadcast stations. In 1990, the show was rated sixth in the nation among comparable sermon-format programs. In 1988, Stanley was inducted into the National Religious Broadcasters Hall of Fame.

During Stanley's 20-year tenure as its pastor, the First Baptist Church has grown to more than 8,000 members. In 1988, Stanley established a satellite church in suburban Atlanta which now boasts a membership of 4,000. From 1984 to 1986, Stanley served two terms as president of the Southern Baptist Convention.

In recent years Stanley's ministry has been plagued by rumors of marital conflict. He and his wife of 40 years separated in 1992, creating tension within Stanley's $35-million-a-year In Touch Ministries organization. As of this writing, Stanley has indicated his intention to remain at the helm of In Touch Ministries and its broadcasts. However, steps have been taken for him to relinquish his pulpit in the event of a final divorce from his wife. Such a course of action would be in accord with long-standing Southern Baptist custom regarding the issue of divorced ministers.

SOURCES

Bird, Warren. "Stanley Dilemma Underscores Troubled Clergy Marriages." *Christianity Today* (October 23, 1995), 82–83.

Ward, Mark, Sr. *Air of Salvation: The Story of Christian Broadcasting*. Grand Rapids, MI: Baker Book House, 1994.

AUGUSTA STETSON

born: October 12, 1842, Waldoboro, Maine
died: October 12, 1928, Rochester, New York

Augusta Emma Stetson was an important Christian Science leader of the early twentieth century who ventured into religious broadcasting after her excommunication by church leaders. Stetson's daily radio show promoted her independent views on mental healing and her anti-Catholic "Americanism." The program was largely unsuccessful, however, and was unable to rebuild her dwindling following during the mid-1920s.

Stetson was born Augusta Emma Simmons in Maine, the descendant of a proud New England clan with Pilgrim roots. Her family attended a Methodist fellowship, and Stetson's talent for music landed her the position of church organist during her teens. Stetson enrolled at Lincoln Academy in New Castle, Maine, and majored in public speaking. Upon graduation, she married a businessman, Frederick J. Stetson, whose shipbuilding company sent the couple to live in such exotic lo-

cales as India and Burma. These overseas assignments were cut short, however, due to her husband's poor health. Frederick Stetson had been a prisoner of the Confederacy during the Civil War and never fully recovered from the privations of that period.

Following the couple's return to Boston, Augusta Stetson decided to continue her training in public speaking. In November 1884, she enrolled in a class at Mary Baker Eddy's Massachusetts Metaphysical College. Upon completing the class, she moved to Maine and began a successful career as a Christian Science practitioner.

When Mrs. Eddy heard of her accomplishments, she called Stetson to serve as one of five preachers at the mother church's Boston pulpit. In November 1886, Eddy sent Stetson to organize a loose group of Christian Scientists in New York City. Within 15 months, Stetson had gathered enough students to incorporate the First Church of Christ, Scientist. She was elected as the church's pastor and formally ordained in October 1890. The church grew steadily under her charismatic leadership and a new training facility for Christian Science practitioners, the New York City Christian Science Institute, opened under her direction in 1891. Within the church and the institute, Stetson maintained a loyal inner circle of dedicated members.

By the turn of the century, the New York City church was attracting upper-class women and men and beginning to outgrow its rented facilities. Using donated funds, Stetson built a million-dollar granite church on Central Park West that included an adjoining home for herself. The new facility was dedicated in November 1903. The erection of this opulent church complex, coupled with Stetson's rhetorical skills and growing cadre of loyal followers, became a cause for concern within the Christian Science mother church in Boston. Many feared that Stetson's power and influence in the movement were beginning to rival that of Eddy herself. Although it is not certain that the action was related to these fears, Eddy decided in 1902 to limit the terms of church leaders to three years. Stetson stepped down at her appointed time but retained her dominant influence within the New York City Christian Science community. Her relationship with Eddy took a turn for the worse when Eddy expressly forbade Stetson to build another proposed branch church in the New York City area.

In 1909, Eddy decided to investigate allegations that Stetson had participated in false teaching and the building of a private following. The Boston mother church's board of directors completed the inquiry and decided to revoke Stetson's license to teach and practice healing as a Christian Scientist. During a subsequent private hearing in Boston, Stetson was excommunicated, with Eddy's approval, on the grounds of heresy and attempting to injure and control others "by mental means."

Stetson responded to this humiliation by remaining loyal to Eddy and stoically maintaining her innocence. She confided to close associates that she was merely being tested by Eddy and would soon be reinstated to her former position. When Eddy died the following year without attempting to reverse the mother church's decision, Stetson decided to forge ahead as an independent Christian Science teacher. She retained control of the Christian Science Institute and turned her residence into the organization's headquarters. Stetson would spend the remaining years of her life teaching her dwindling number of loyal followers.

The tenor of Stetson's teachings began to change in 1910. She came to interpret her expulsion from the mother church as an ordeal of purification that had freed her from an organization mired in material concerns and spiritual decline. Liberated from the material church's grasp, she was now empowered to serve as the independent spokesperson of the "Church Triumphant," Eddy's true church of Christian Science. Stetson began to publish books and pamphlets which defended her new teachings and criticized Christian Science leaders for accommodating themselves to state medical laws. It was in the midst of a major print campaign to stimulate interest in her ministry that she inaugurated a daily radio show in New York City.

The show gave her a forum for presenting her independent Christian Science teachings and for promoting the "Protestant" principle against the rising danger of Roman Catholicism. Stetson's nativist convictions also led her to support, over the air, the *American Standard*, a periodical that espoused the supremacy of the Nordic peoples. Stetson's media campaign was largely unsuccessful.

While visiting a nephew in Rochester, New York, in 1928, Stetson was stricken with edema and died within a few days. Her cremated remains were interred near her childhood home in Damariscotta, Maine. She, along with Alma White of the Pillar of Fire Church, was one of the first women to air her religious teachings over the radio airwaves. She was also one of the few early radio preachers who did not espouse a conventional form of Christian doctrine and practice.

SOURCES

Braden, Charles. *Christian Science Today: Power, Policy, Practice*. Dallas: Southern Methodist University Press, 1958.

Melton, J. Gordon. *Biographical Dictionary of American Cult and Sect Leaders*. New York: Garland, 1986.

Reid, Daniel G., et al., eds. *Dictionary of Christianity in America*. Downers Grove, IL: InterVarsity Press, 1990.

Report of the Board of Trustees of First Church of Christ, Scientist of New York City. New York: 1909.

Stetson, Augusta E. *Augusta E. Stetson Refutes the Statement that She Is Not a Christian Scientist*. New York: 1911.

———. *Reminiscences, Sermons, and Correspondence Proving Adherence to the Principle of Christian Science as Taught by Mary Baker Eddy*. New York: G. P. Putnam's Sons, 1913.

———. *Sermons Which Spiritually Interpret the Scriptures and Other Writings on Christian Science*. New York: G. P. Putnam's Sons, 1926.

Swihart, Altman K. *Since Mrs. Eddy*. New York: H. Holt, 1931.

JOHN R. STRATON
born: April 6, 1875, Evansville, Indiana
died: October 29, 1929, Clifton Springs, New York

The fundamentalist preacher John Roach Straton was a pioneer of religious radio during the great fundamentalist-modernist debates of the 1920s. Straton spent his childhood in Alabama and Georgia where his father, Henry Dundas Straton, served as a Baptist minister. John Straton enrolled at Mercer University in 1895 and quickly won accolades for his talent as a public orator. When his father died, the younger Straton was forced by economic circumstances to postpone work on his degree. Based on his achievement during three years of study, however, he was appointed to a lectureship in oratory in 1899.

Straton experienced his conversion to Christianity through the influence of the Southern Baptist evangelist James Boardman Hawthorne. In response to a call to the ministry, Straton enrolled at Southern Baptist Theological Seminary in Louisville, Kentucky. His first ministerial post was at the Baptist Mission Church of Highland Park, Kentucky, which ordained him in 1900. Straton was again unable to complete his degree and, in 1903, moved with his new wife Georgia Hillyer to Waco, Texas. There he taught classes in oratory and literary interpretation at Baylor University and pastored a church in nearby Hubbard. Between 1905 and 1918, Straton served urban pastorates at Second Baptist Church in Chicago, Seventh Baptist Church in Baltimore, and First Baptist Church in Norfolk, Virginia. Between the latter two ministerial posts, Straton worked as the executive secretary of the Interchurch Federation of Baltimore.

In 1918, Straton began his outspoken 11-year ministry at New York City's Calvary Baptist Church. While there, he switched from the Southern Baptist Convention to the Northern Baptist Convention and plunged headlong into the growing controversies between fundamentalists and modernists in the nation's largest city.

Straton was an outspoken advocate of the fundamentals of Christian belief and a fierce opponent of what he believed were the destructive forces of modernism. His superb oratorical skills and fearless willingness to combat the moral and political corruption in his midst drew him to the center of several controversial events during his tenure at Calvary Baptist and made him a regular subject of press coverage. His first great crusade came in 1922 when he condemned the corruption of New York City's theaters and suggested they be censored. Two years later he entered into a famous debate with the Unitarian minister Charles F. Potter over the issues of biblical inerrancy and natural evolution. During this period of public debate, Straton became adept at the use of the mass media. The fledgling medium of religious radio, in particular, provided him with a perfect platform for his gifts as a speaker.

Straton's radio ministry began on October 25, 1922, when members of Calvary Baptist voted to appropriate $1,000 to install radio broadcasting equipment in the church. In March of 1923, Calvary's own 250-watt WQAQ aired the church's evening service, and Straton delivered his first sermon. At installation ceremonies a few weeks earlier Straton had proclaimed, "I shall try to continue to do my part . . . in tearing down the strongholds of Satan, and I hope that our radio system will prove so efficient that when I twist the Devil's tail in New York, his squawk will be heard across the continent." Straton's program could be heard over a wide area during the mid-1920s, because so few stations were broadcasting at that time. Soon, all three of Calvary Baptist's Sunday services and the church's Wednesday evening prayer meetings were being aired on WQAQ. The station merged with the more powerful New York station WHN in 1927, increasing Straton's radio outreach.

Because of his stridently anti-denominational stands, Straton came into conflict with the Baptist World Alliance. In 1926, these tensions came to a head and he decided to withdraw from the National Baptist Convention. Straton's final fundamentalist campaign came against the

Roman Catholic presidential candidate, Al Smith. The Protestant conservative, who condemned Smith as a corrupt foe of moral progress, traveled extensively through the American South campaigning against him. Straton's exhausting schedule took its toll on his health. He died of a stroke on the day of the New York Stock Market crash, October 29, 1929. Straton's untimely death (he was only 54) left his church deeply in debt and unable to continue his legacy in any effective manner for a number of years. Calvary Baptist no longer owns and operates a radio station, but it continues to broadcast its religious programs throughout the United States and overseas on radio stations such as Trans World Radio, ELWA, and HCJB.

During his career, Straton was a strong proponent of social activism and the just treatment of minorities. His vision of God's millennial kingdom on earth, however, emphasized spiritual regeneration over social reform and classical Christian salvation over sociological progressivism. His dedication to doctrinal purity and biblically-based social justice earned him the epithets "prophet of social righteousness" and "Pope of Fundamentalism."

SOURCES

Dollar, George W. *A History of Fundamentalism in America*. Greenville, SC: Bob Jones University Press, 1973.

Hill, George H. *Airwaves to the Soul: The Influence and Growth of Religious Broadcasting in America*. Saratoga, CA: R & E, 1983.

Reid, Daniel G., et al., eds. *Dictionary of Christianity in America*. Downers Grove, IL: InterVarsity Press, 1990.

Russell, C. Allyn. *Voices of American Fundamentalism: Seven Biographical Studies*. Philadelphia: Westminister Press, 1976.

Straton, John Roach. *The Battle Over the Bible*. New York: George H. Doran, 1924.

———. *The Famous New York Fundamentalist-Modernist Debates*. New York: George H. Doran, 1925.

———. *Fighting the Devil in Modern Babylon*. Boston: Stratford, 1929.

———. *God's Prophetic Calendar*. Neptune, NJ: Loizeaux Brothers, 1987.

LESTER SUMRALL
born: February 15, 1913, New Orleans, Louisiana
died: April 28, 1996

Courtesy: National Religious Broadcasters

Lester Frank Sumrall was a successful radio and television evangelist between the late 1960s and the mid-1990s. He served as the chairman of the Lester Sumrall Evangelistic Association (LeSea, Inc.) and broadcasted his weekly television show, *LeSEA Alive*, over the Inspirational Network. Sumrall managed to maintain a reputation for financial and moral integrity during the 1980s and 1990s in the face of well-publicized scandals in other religious broadcasting ministries.

Sumrall grew up in Louisiana with an irreligious father and a fervent Pentecostal mother. His mother became the dominant influence during his early life, and Sumrall accompanied her regularly to church. After experiencing a complete recovery from a life-threatening case of tuberculosis in his late teens, Sumrall decided to leave his Florida home and begin a ministry as a traveling evangelist. Upon receiving ministerial credentials at the age of 19 from the Assemblies of God, Sumrall founded the first of his many churches worldwide in Green Forest, Arkansas.

During this period, the young preacher experienced a powerful vision of the future destiny of unredeemed humanity. About 18 months later, Sumrall met the Pentecostal leader Howard Carter, who had recently experienced a vision of his own of an evangelist who would come to work with him. Sumrall accepted Carter's invitation to join his missionary labors, and the two traveled together around the world. Sumrall preached and started churches in Australia, Asia, and Eastern Europe during this period.

In time, he established his own missionary ministry. During a trip to South America in 1943, Sumrall met a Pentecostal Assemblies of Canada missionary named Louise Layman, and the couple was married on September 30, 1944. Their ministry lasted until 1947, when Sumrall accepted a call to pastor the Calvary Assemblies of God church in South Bend, Indiana.

A few years later, in 1952, Sumrall accepted a call to missionary work in the Philippines. During his two-and-a-half-year stay in Manila, he gained an international reputation as an evangelist and a church planter. This mission resulted in the building of a successful Pentecostal mega-church in Manila, the Bethel Temple. Today the church has over 13,000 members. Sumrall would later use this mission as a model for future church planting around the globe. After returning to South Bend in the mid-1950s to reinvigorate his congregation, Sumrall decided to establish a new mission in the British colony of Hong Kong. Using the experience and contacts gained during his stay in Manila, Sumrall built another successful church, the New Life Temple. A literature ministry, which distributes religious publications throughout Southern Asia, was also inaugurated at this time.

Sumrall decided to leave the Assemblies of God denomination and establish his own evangelistic association upon his return to South Bend in 1959. The Lester Sumrall Evangelistic Association, or LeSea, Inc., soon began planning church-planting missions in Brazil and Israel. Sumrall was also asked to pastor a new, independent Pentecostal congregation in South Bend. Bethel Temple, as the church was first named, evolved into a multifaceted evangelistic ministry, now called the Christian Center Cathedral of Praise. In addition to establishing the World Harvest Home for Orphans, the World Harvest Bible College in 1975, and *World Harvest Magazine*, Sumrall's ministry began a religious radio program in 1968 and a religious television ministry in 1972. By 1989, Sumrall's weekly, hour-long show, *LeSEA Alive*, was appearing on six LeSea-owned television stations (including one in Indianapolis and one in Honolulu) and on the Inspirational Network.

Sumrall believed that religious television should avoid constant fundraising—and especially crisis appeals—on the air. His ministry holds periodic week-long telethons during which the audience is informed of the ministry's outreach and instructed on how they might help support these activities. Aside from this, the ministry does no on-the-air fundraising.

Sumrall also avoided the lavish lifestyles of other televangelists, explaining,

> As missionaries most of our adult lives, my wife and I lived frugally; we raised our boys frugally. I have never received a salary from the church, television—anything. Twice a year my church gives me a love offering. I've had opportunities to be a millionaire, and I've turned them down. . . . When a man begins to love the things of this world—big homes, expensive cars, lots of gold—the world opens the door to the flesh, and the Devil latches on.

Sumrall firmly believed that moral lapses are not an inevitable result of television ministries, claiming, "There are far more good examples than bad examples of Christian gentlemen who've not tried to lay their hands on the money that comes in."

Sumrall whole-heartedly believed in the power of religious broadcasting to bring souls to Christ: "I've met countless people who've said they were saved because of Christian television." Like Rex Humbard, Sumrall conceived of his television audience as an "electronic congregation." While conducting communion services on his weekly show, he invited viewers to participate at home. At times he even encouraged viewers to run to their refrigerators to get the food and drink necessary for the ritual.

Sumrall was a prolific author and publisher. His many books addressed such Pentecostal themes as demon exorcism and the "gifts of the spirit." Sumrall's autobiography, *Run with the Vision* (1977), was revised in 1983 as *My Story to His Glory*. Sumrall was also the recipient of numerous awards, including the Congressional Award of the United States House of Representatives (1980), the Honor Citation from National Religious Broadcasters (NRB) (1982), NRB's Award of Merit (1983), and the Meritorious Achievement award from the International Association of Christian Clinical Counselors (1983). Sumrall held a doctor of divinity degree from Berea Bible College (1964) in Berea, Kentucky, a doctor of letters degree from Indiana Christian University (1974) in Indianapolis, Indiana, and a doctorate in religious studies from Golden State University (1983) in San Francisco, California. Oral Roberts University conferred an honorary doctor of divinity degree on the televangelist in 1983.

See also LeSea Broadcasting

SOURCES

Burgess, Stanley M., Gary B. McGee, and Patrick H. Alexander, eds. *Dictionary of Pentecostal and Charismatic Movements*. Grand Rapids, MI: Zondervan, 1988.

Hadden, Jeffrey K., and Charles E. Swann. *Prime Time Preachers: The Rising Power of Televangelism*. Menlo Park, CA: Addison-Wesley, 1981.

Lilly, Fred. "Lester Sumrall: Cathedral of Praise." *Charisma*. November, 1985, 48–52.

"No Glitter for Lester." *Christianity Today,* February 3, 1989, 36.

Sumrall, Lester. *The Gifts and Ministries of the Holy Spirit*. Tulsa, OK: Harrison House, 1982.

———. *Living Free*. Nashville: Sceptre, 1979.

———. *Miracles Don't Just Happen*. Plainfield, TX: Logos International, 1979.

———. *My Story to His Glory*. Nashville: Thomas Nelson, 1983.

———. *Run with the Vision*. Plainfield, TX: Logos International, 1977.

———. *Supernatural Principalities and Powers*. Nashville: Thomas Nelson, 1983.

BILLY SUNDAY
born: November 18, 1862, Ames, Iowa
died: November 6, 1935, Chicago, Illinois

Courtesy: Billy Graham Center Museum

The famed "Baseball Evangelist" and radio preacher, William Ashley "Billy" Sunday, was the son of William Sunday and Mary Jane Corey. Sunday's father, a soldier in the Union Army, died of pneumonia within a month of Sunday's birth. Though his widowed mother remarried, Sunday and his older brother H. Edward were sent away in 1874 to live first at the Soldiers' Orphan Home in Glenwood, Iowa, and then at an orphanage in Davenport, Iowa. Two years later they went to live with their maternal grandparents in central Iowa. After an argument with his grandfather, Sunday moved to Nevada, Iowa, in 1879, where he held odd jobs and attended high school for a short time. He never graduated.

Sunday, who began playing amateur baseball in Marshalltown, Iowa, started his professional career in 1883 with the Chicago White Stockings. The team drafted him because of his ability as a fielder and quickness around the bases. While playing for the White Stockings, Sunday attended Chicago's Pacific Garden Mission and, in the autumn of 1886, was converted to Christianity. In 1888, Sunday married Helen

"Nell" Thompson, whom he had met at a Christian Endeavor social sponsored by the Jefferson Park Presbyterian Church.

After his conversion, Sunday began to preach in the cities where his team was playing. In his spare time, he also worked for the Chicago YMCA. Though sophisticates thought him crude and his sermons crass and shallow, his baseball résumé gave him cachet among blue-collar workers in urban areas, and soon Sunday was convinced that he should pursue a ministerial career. He left baseball in 1891 to become a full-time Christian worker for the local YMCA. While in this position he taught Bible-study techniques and evangelism. In 1893, Sunday began work with evangelists J. Wilbur Chapman and Milan B. Williams. In 1896 he was invited to conduct his own revival campaign in Garner, Iowa, thus launching his career as an independent evangelist. He was licensed to preach by the Presbyterian Church in 1898 and received full ordination in 1903.

At first, most of Sunday's campaigns were restricted to small Midwestern towns. As his fame began to spread, however, he was invited to preach in larger urban centers, bringing with him the flavor of rural revival. Sunday's flamboyant style of preaching, including dramatic antics and theatrical poses, gained him extensive newspaper coverage, more often as a curiosity than as serious copy. His sermons, punctuated with slang terms bordering on crudeness, delighted those attending his campaigns. His gestures were demonstrative, if not comical, and his movements on the platform bordered on the burlesque.

In 1911, he and his wife settled in Winona Lake, Indiana, where they built a home to raise their four children. In 1917, Sunday held an extended campaign in New York City, and another in Chicago the following year. These campaigns cemented Sunday's fame as a renowned evangelist, and he became a popular speaker on New York's Chautauqua lecture circuit.

Though his major concern was mass evangelism, Sunday took on the demons of modern urban life, including moral laxity, modernist thought, honky-tonk music, and "booze." Sunday's wife, Helen, proved to be a superb organizer for his campaigns. She selected the venues, arranged the precampaign publicity, and ran the events once they were underway.

During World War I, Sunday vigorously crusaded for the American war effort, holding "Hang the Kaiser" and other types of patriotic rallies. Through his sermons against liquor interests, he was also instrumental in the passage of Prohibition in 1919. And during the Red Scare of the early 1920s, the rural evangelist helped fan hysteria among fundamentalists by demanding that Communist sympathizers be deported. Although Sunday was progressive compared to other fundamentalists on issues such as women's rights and racial harmony, his views were still offensive to liberals. For instance, he believed blacks were spiritual but not racial equals to whites, and women should be allowed to preach but not receive ordination.

Although he distanced himself from the Scopes Trial and even further from the Ku Klux Klan, Sunday's long ministry was not without its scandals. He was sued for plagiarism by Hugh A. Weir over the authorship of his book, *Great Love Stories in the Bible and Their Lessons for Today* (1917), and was also accused of financial improprieties, charges that haunted him for the remainder of his career.

After the war, and partly because of these scandals, Sunday's popularity began to drop precipitously. He was forced to return to mostly small-town revivals. His last large-scale crusade was against the Catholic Democratic presidential candidate, Alfred E. Smith, in 1928. It was during this presidential campaign that the evangelist was heard over numerous radio stations verbally attacking Smith.

Although Sunday's popularity was rapidly fading, he began his own radio preaching ministry in 1929. His program, *Back Home Hour* (not to be confused with Oswald Smith's radio program of the same name), was aired over the Columbia Broadcasting System (CBS) until 1935. In one memorable radio sermon, the fiery preacher vowed to "bite" the demon of drink into submission until his teeth gave out. After that, he would "gum it to death!" In recognition of his evangelistic work, Sunday received an honorary doctorate in 1935 from Bob Jones University in South Carolina.

Sunday suffered a heart attack while on a preaching tour and died in Chicago in November 1935, just 12 days short of his seventy-third birthday.

SOURCES

Billy Graham Center Archives, Wheaton College, Wheaton, Illinois.

Dorsett, Lyle W. *Billy Sunday and the Redemption of Urban America*. Grand Rapids, MI: Eerdmans, 1991.

Marsden, George M. *Fundamentalism and American Culture*. New York: Oxford University Press, 1980.

McLoughlin, William. *Billy Sunday Was His Real Name*. Chicago: University of Chicago Press, 1955.

Stone, Jon R. *A Guide to the End of the World: Popular Eschatology in America*. New York: Garland, 1993.

Sunday, Billy. *Great Love Stories from the Bible and Their Lesson for Today*. New York: G. P. Putnam's Sons, 1917.

———. *Life and Labors of Rev. Wm. A. (Billy) Sunday*. Decatur, IL: Herman, Poole & Co., 1908.

SUNDAY TO SUNDAY
first aired: 1977

Sunday to Sunday is a broadcast production of the Paulist National Catholic Evangelization Association (PNCEA). The program airs weekly over regional television in Washington, DC. Founded in 1977, the PNCEA is a Catholic organization that seeks to evangelize the "lost" or unaffiliated and to bring nonpracticing Catholics back into the Roman Catholic fold.

SOURCES

Melton, J. Gordon. *Directory of Religious Organizations in the United States*. 3d ed. Detroit: Gale Research, 1993.

JIMMY SWAGGART
born: March 15, 1935, Ferriday, Louisiana

Jimmy Lee Swaggart is one of the most flamboyant and impassioned television evangelists in the history of religious broadcasting. He is also one of the most maligned and ridiculed because of the sensational sex scandals that have plagued his ministry since 1988.

Swaggart was reared in rural Louisiana by Willie Leon Swaggart and Minnie Bell Huron. His extended family included rocker Jerry Lee Lewis and country-western star Mickey Gilley. The future evangelist began preaching at six and experienced the baptism of the Holy Spirit at eight. This "second birth" experience occurred within the "dirt-poor, circuit-riding tradition of Pentecostal evangelism" and included speaking in tongues. Swaggart developed his musical skills with his cousin, Jerry Lee Lewis, but the pair parted ways when Swaggart received a call to full-time evangelism in his teens. Swaggart dropped out of high school and committed himself to a preaching ministry on January 1, 1958. Soon he was preaching on street corners and in Assemblies of God revivals throughout the southern United States.

Swaggart's first radio show, *Camp Meeting Hour*, began in 1969 and was soon being broadcast on hundreds of stations. By 1972, Swaggart felt compelled by the "Great Commission" to use the television airwaves to extend his evangelistic outreach. His new show, *The Jimmy Swaggart Telecast*, which first aired in 1973, had all the markings of a religious revival service. In the style of an old-fashioned camp-meeting preacher, Swaggart strode back and forth across the speaking platform and employed a wide range of emotions to articulate his message of good and evil, sin and redemption, and the glory of the Holy Spirit. This range often shifted from impassioned shouting and exhortation to pleading, tearful whispers in a matter of seconds. Originally, *The Jimmy Swaggart Telecast* was 30 minutes long and filmed in the Nashville studio used for *Hee Haw*. It included a gospel music segment, a Bible lesson, and promotion for Swaggart's crusades and albums. By 1981, the telecast had expanded to an hour-long format and was being syndicated on 222 television stations as well as a number of cable systems.

This longer program opened with the inspirational hymn, "There Is a River," during which an announcer related the different activities of the Swaggart ministry. The next segment of the show was a plea for funds by either Swaggart, his wife Frances, or his son Donnie. The fundraising segment was usually followed by a one-minute announcement of upcoming events such as revivalist crusades and Bible conferences. The show then moved into a musical segment during which Swaggart and his Nashville-style band played everything from slow, sentimental ballads about Christ's sacrificial love to good-time, hand-clapping gospel songs. About 20 minutes into the show, an abbreviated 20-minute version of a live Swaggart sermon was aired. Although Swaggart never spoke in tongues during these sermons, he regularly defended the practice and claimed that those churches who criticized it were in a state of spiritual decline. The program concluded with a traditional altar call and another short promotional spot. This format was designed to create a visually appealing and emotionally compelling experience for viewers and to highlight the figure of Swaggart as a fiery, prophet-like evangelist.

At the height of his popularity in early 1988, Swaggart was reaching an estimated monthly US audience of 9.3 million and drawing 80,000 to his Latin American crusades. In addition, he had become a successful musician and singer, recording over 50 gospel albums and selling over 15 million copies by 1985. The records and cassettes were pitched during his television program and accounted for a good percentage of his ministry's income. Swaggart's enterprises employed 1,500 people and included a 7,500-seat Family Worship Center, a wide array of foreign missions, The Jimmy Swaggart Bible College, and two programs aired from a state-of-the-art teleproduction center. One of these programs was a 30-minute panel discussion show, *Teachings in the Word*, that aired on weekdays. The other was an hour-long broadcast of his worldwide evangelistic crusades or an airing of the Sunday worship services at his local Baton Rouge church. These shows were translated into 13 languages and aired in 145 countries. Jimmy Swaggart Ministries was taking in over $141 million in annual income by this time, and the ministry's monthly magazine, *The Evangelist*, claimed a circulation of 800,000.

During a nationally televised show on February 21, 1988, Swaggart tearfully confessed to voyeuristic engagements with a prostitute. This stunning announcement had an immediate and devastating impact on his ministry. By 1989, the Arbitron ratings for his Sunday television program had fallen from 1.96 million to 851,000 homes. Donations to the ministry decreased 50 percent during the same one-year period. These losses in income and viewership stemmed from both viewer disillusionment and the broadcast industry's response to the Swaggart scandal. The national Assemblies of God Executive Presbytery suspended Swaggart for one year from his ministerial duties, extending the three-month suspension that had earlier been imposed by the Assemblies of God Louisiana District Presbytery. When Swaggart balked at this more severe penalty, he was summarily dismissed from the denomination.

The news of his official dismissal, coupled with the animosity felt by other religious broadcasters toward Swaggart for his harsh condemnation in 1987 of Jim Bakker's sexual misconduct, resulted in a series of industry reprisals against his programs. Pat Robertson's Christian Broadcasting Network cancelled both the Sunday and the weekday Swaggart shows, and PTL and the Black Entertainment Network soon followed suit. These cancellations deprived Swaggart's broadcasts of weekly access to over 70 million homes. Ted Turner's Atlanta superstation WTBS followed the lead of Robertson and dropped the Sunday crusade program. These developments, coupled with layoffs, defections by ministers and students, cancellations by independent stations, and a dwindling local congregation, forced Swaggart's ministry to the brink of extinction.

Swaggart refused to give up, however. He drastically reduced the size and outreach of his evangelistic empire and funneled all his remaining resources into national preaching tours and television. This return to his roots on the sawdust trail was seen as the best possible way to revive his struggling ministry. Swaggart was able to use his personal disgrace as a parable for the evangelical gospel of sin, contrition, confession, and redemption. As Swaggart wrote in his magazine *The Evangelist,*

> God cannot receive glory out of sin, but He can receive glory out of a crucified life. And when you see Jimmy Swaggart stand behind the pulpit and over television, you will see a man who has crucified the flesh. It has come at a terrible price, but better that price than no price at all.

Many of Swaggart's followers reported that they could more easily identify with him now, since, like them, he had sinned, suffered, and sought forgiveness from a merciful Savior.

Unfortunately, Swaggart's personal renewal was short-lived. In October of 1991, he was pulled over in Southern California for a minor traffic violation. Seated next to him was a prostitute. This second scandal reached the national airwaves and Swaggart soon announced that his weekly telecasts would be discontinued for the foreseeable future. This announcement was followed by the resignation of Swaggart and his wife Frances from his ministry board and the handing over of his authority to a trio of executives, one of whom was his son Donnie. Added to these misfortunes was the decision of a New Orleans jury to award $10 million to Louisiana evangelist Marvin Gorman in his defamation suit against Swaggart. Swaggart had charged Gorman with sexual misconduct in 1988 and helped ruin Gorman's Louisiana television ministry. In an attempt to salvage his local church and Bible college, Swaggart sold off most of his ministry's broadcasting equipment and real estate holdings. Through this desperate move, he managed to maintain a few telecasts on cable networks. These cable shows consisted primarily of reruns of earlier crusades.

By the summer of 1995, Swaggart was back on the air with *Sunday Night Live with Jimmy Swaggart*, a one-hour television program of music featuring Ted Garrett, Debra Wilemon, Darrell Winn, the Family Worship Center Resurrection Choir, and Swaggart. The program was being aired live at 7 PM EST Sunday evenings and on a delayed basis in such large city markets as WGN-TV in Chicago. Swaggart's renamed educational outreach, World Evangelism Bible College and Seminary, in Baton Rouge, Louisiana, continues to train Pentecostal missionaries, ministers, and students under its president, Larry D. Hunt. *Sunday Night Live*, like its predecessors, is a showcase for Swaggart's impassioned preaching. It appears Swaggart has lost none of his Pentecostal zeal or taste for taking controversial stands on various social and religious issues.

See also Jim Bakker

SOURCES

Applebome, Peter. "Swaggart's Troubles Show Tension of Passion and Power in TV Evangelism." *New York Times*, February 28, 1988.

Dunne, Mike. "Swaggart TV Rating Nose-Dive." *Baton Rouge Morning Advocate*, June 28, 1988.

Finch, Susan. "Swaggart Ministries Going off the Air." (New Orleans) *Times-Picayune*, October 26, 1991.

Hadden, Jeffrey K., and Charles E. Swann. *Prime Time Preachers: The Rising Power of Televangelism.* Menlo Park, CA: Addison-Wesley, 1981.

Niebuhr, Gustav. "TV Evangelists Rebound from Viewer Erosion." *Atlanta Journal*, May 1, 1989.

Peck, Janice. *The Gods of Televangelism: The Crisis of Meaning and the Appeal of Religious Television.* Cresskill, NJ: Hampton Press, 1993.

Swaggart, Jimmy, with Robert Paul Lamb. *To Cross a River.* Plainfield, TX: Logos International, 1977.

CHUCK SWINDOLL
born: October 18, 1934, El Campo, Texas

Host of the daily half-hour radio program *Insight for Living* and current president of Dallas Theological Seminary, Charles "Chuck" Rozell Swindoll was the third child of Earl Langston Swindoll and Lovell Lucille Lundy. The elder Swindoll worked as a mechanical engineer, and his son decided to follow in his footsteps. After

Courtesy: National Religious Broadcasters

high school, Swindoll attended the University of Houston Trade School. In June 1955, he married Cynthia Ann Parker. Following his graduation in 1957 as a journeyman machinist, Swindoll joined the US Marine Corps and served in Okinawa for 18 months.

Though not a regular churchgoer as a youth, Swindoll studied the Bible with The Navigators, an international evangelistic association, during his two-year tour of duty and decided to pursue a ministerial career when he returned home. In 1959, Swindoll enrolled for study at Dallas Theological Seminary. He graduated magna cum laude in 1963 and began serving as assistant pastor of Grace Bible Church in Dallas, Texas, under the Reverend J. Dwight Pentecost. In 1965, Swindoll left Grace Bible to become pastor of the Evangelical Free Church in Waltham, Massachusetts. Two years later, he returned to suburban Dallas as pastor of Irving Bible Church. In 1971, Swindoll accepted a ministerial call from the First Evangelical Church of Fullerton, California, where he served as senior minister for 23 years. Under Swindoll's leadership, First Evangelical Free Church grew to nearly 5,000 members.

Swindoll's radio ministry began in 1977 when First Evangelical Free Church began producing broadcast programs featuring half-hour segments of Swindoll's Sunday sermons. The program, entitled *Insight for Living*, was initially broadcast over 27 stations throughout the United States. It now airs over more than 1,000 stations around the globe and is heard in English, Spanish, Portuguese, Hindi, and Norwegian. Swindoll's preaching blends the learned expository sermon style of mainline Protestantism with the personal-concern style of the evangelical pastor. In every sermon he preaches, Swindoll offers his listeners practical advice for daily Christian living.

Swindoll was appointed president of Dallas Theological Seminary in 1994, filling the void left in 1986 by the retirement of well-known prophecy scholar John F. Walvoord. In recent years, Swindoll has also been a featured speaker at several Promise Keepers conferences. A prolific author, he has written a variety of books on themes ranging from marriage and family life to personal spiritual development. Some of Swindoll's more popular titles include *Dropping Your Guard*; *Hand Me Another Brick*; *Improving Your Serving*; *The Quest for Character*; *Strengthening Your Grip*; *Strike the Original Match*; and *Three Steps Forward, Two Steps Back*.

See also *Insight for Living*

SOURCES

Ward, Mark, Sr. *Air of Salvation: The Story of Christian Broadcasting*. Grand Rapids, MI: Baker Book House, 1994.

THE SWORD OF THE LORD
see: John Rice

T

TAKE HEED MINISTRIES

see: Exposing the Lie

TAKE KERR

first aired: 1975

Take Kerr ("Kerr" rhymes with "care") was a daily, five-minute program of cooking tips that first appeared in 1975. The program was the brainchild of Graham and Treena Kerr, two born-again Christians who had successfully produced and starred in the popular syndicated television program *The Galloping Gourmet* between 1969 and 1971. Following a serious auto accident, the Kerrs changed their materialistic lifestyle and came up with the idea of *Take Kerr*, a shortened version of *The Galloping Gourmet*.

The syndication company for *Take Kerr*, Fremantle Company, quickly became unhappy with the religious messages and scriptural verses that the Kerrs were slipping into their new broadcast. Within a year, the Kerrs cancelled their program and devoted their energies to charitable works, the authoring of inspirational cookbooks, and a marriage-counseling ministry. Graham Kerr would become a popular guest during the late 1970s on such religious talkshows as *The 700 Club*. Following Treena Kerr's near-fatal heart attack in 1986, Graham Kerr began a new syndicated cooking show in 1990 dedicated to battling high cholesterol diets.

SOURCES

Erickson, Hal. *Religious Radio and Television in the United States, 1921–1991*. Jefferson, NC: McFarland, 1992.

LOUIS TALBOT

born: October 19, 1889, Sydney, Australia
died: January 27, 1976, Los Angeles, California

Louis Thompson Talbot, an evangelical minister and longtime president of the Bible Institute of Los Angeles (Biola), was born in Sydney, Australia, to John and Elizabeth Talbot. As a boy, he attended the local Congregational church with his family. Talbot immigrated to the United States in 1911 and took up studies at the Moody Bible Institute in Chicago, Illinois. He graduated from Moody in 1913.

After serving as a pastor at the First Congregational Church in Paris, Texas (1913–1915), marrying the former Audrey Hogue (1914), and receiving ordination in the Congregational Church (1915), Talbot returned to Chicago to seek an advanced degree from McCormick Theological Seminary. While still a seminarian, Talbot began the Madison Street Church in Oak Park, Illinois. He would later serve in Presbyterian churches in Keokuk, Iowa (1921–1925) and Minneapolis, Minnesota (1925–1929). It was while in Minneapolis that Talbot started a radio ministry which briefly aired over station WRHM.

In 1929, Talbot assumed the ministerial leadership of the Philpott Tabernacle in Hamilton, Ontario, Canada, during the absence of its popular pastor, Peter W. Philpott, who accepted a call to the Church of the Open Door in Los Angeles where he served from 1929 to 1934.

Talbot left Canada and joined Philpott's Los Angeles ministry in 1932 as a pastor. At the time, the congregation's membership exceeded 1,000 people. During his long tenure as minister of the Church of the Open Door, Talbot saw the membership increase from 1,000 to nearly 3,500. Talbot held this position until 1948, during which time he began a broadcast ministry that aired over local radio stations from the church auditorium every Sunday afternoon.

In 1931, Talbot was elected president of the Bible Institute of Los Angeles (Biola), which is located on the same downtown corner as the Church of the Open Door. He held the position until 1935. As president and board member of Biola, Talbot helped bring fiscal solvency to the institute through several successful fundraising drives over the radio.

Upon retirement from his ministry at the Church of the Open Door in 1948, Talbot returned as president of Biola, presiding over the creation of both a college and a seminary, the latter being named after him. At Talbot's urging, both Biola College and Talbot Seminary moved to the Los Angeles suburb of La Mirada in 1957. In his later years, Talbot traveled to Asia, Africa, and Latin America to help promote foreign missions.

SOURCES

Billy Graham Center Archives, Wheaton College, Wheaton, Illinois.

Melton, J. Gordon. *Religious Leaders of America*. Detroit: Gale Research, 1991.

Stone, Jon R. *A Guide to the End of the World: Popular Eschatology in America*. New York: Garland, 1993.

Talbot, Louis T. *For This I Was Born: The Captivating Story of Louis T. Talbot*. Chicago: Moody Press, 1977.

TALK-BACK

see: Bob Larson

CLYDE TAYLOR

born: 1904, Fort Smith, Arkansas
died: 1988

Clyde Taylor, nicknamed "Mr. NAE," was the longtime director of the National Association of Evangelicals (NAE) and executive secretary of the Evangelical Foreign Missions Association (EFMA).

Called to missions work while still in his teens, Taylor attended Nyack Missionary Institute, Nyack, New York, in 1924 and then served from 1925 to 1927 as a missionary to Peru for the Christian and Missionary Alliance. Following this missionary stint, he enrolled for study at Gordon College in Boston, graduating in 1931 with a bachelor of theology degree. He earned a master of arts from Boston University in 1942.

From 1931 to 1941, Taylor worked as a missionary to Colombia. After returning to Boston in 1941, he served as minister to the Central Baptist Church in Quincy, Massachusetts, until 1944. Taylor then moved to Washington, DC, to help coordinate the efforts of the newly formed National Association of Evangelicals. NAE had been created by conservative Protestants who were seeking a national forum for inter-church cooperation that would not compromise their doctrinal convictions. The NAE was to serve as a counterforce to the liberal-leaning Federal Council of Churches (FCC), an ecumenical body of mainstream Christian denominations.

After serving as the nascent organization's secretary from 1944 to 1963, Taylor became the NAE's general director, a position he retained until his retirement in 1974. During his long ministry of administrative service, Taylor aided foreign mission agencies and was instrumental in founding the Evangelical Foreign Missions Association in 1944. He served as the executive director of the association from 1944 until 1974. From 1970 to 1974, Taylor also served as general secretary of the World Evangelical Fellowship, an organization that sought international unity among evangelical Protestants.

As NAE secretary in its Office of Public Affairs in Washington, DC, Taylor successfully fought off attempts by the Federal Council of Churches to gain a monopoly on free religious radio time. He also helped gain greater access to paid radio broadcast time for evangelicals not affiliated with the FCC.

After a lifetime of service to interdenominational evangelical associations, Taylor died in retirement in 1988.

SOURCES

Murch, James DeForest. *Cooperation without Compromise: A History of the National Association of Evangelicals*. Grand Rapids, MI: Eerdmans, 1956.

Reid, Daniel G., Robert D. Linder, Bruce L. Shelley, and Harry S. Stout, eds. *Dictionary of Christianity in America*. Downers Grove, IL: InterVarsity Press, 1990.

Shelley, Bruce L. *Evangelicalism in America*. Grand Rapids, MI: Eerdmans, 1967.

HERBERT J. TAYLOR
born: 1893, Pickford, Michigan
died: 1978, Chicago, Illinois

Herbert J. Taylor was a Chicago civic leader and Christian philanthropist who played a central role in the development of key evangelistic organizations. Taylor was a particularly important figure in the expansion of the evangelical use of radio and television. He was among the church leaders who chartered the National Association of Evangelicals (NAE), which supported the founding of the National Religious Broadcasters (NRB) the following year. He bankrolled many broadcasters that came and went, though his unflagging support went to Charles Fuller's radio ministry, the *Old Fashioned Revival Hour*. For many years the president of Club Aluminum Products Company, Taylor became involved in organizations to which his personal and financial support almost always guaranteed success.

In 1940, Taylor became chairman of InterVarsity Fellowship. Under his leadership it became an international campus outreach organization. Taylor was instrumental in the founding of the NAE, becoming one of 147 charter signatories in 1941 and 1942. In 1947, Taylor, a close friend and supporter of Charles Fuller, was appointed to the board of trustees of the Fuller Theological Seminary. He donated substantial amounts of money to help the school through rough times during the 1950s and 1960s.

Taylor later established the Christian Workers Foundation, through which he financed evangelistic rallies and a number of other Chicago-area evangelical activities, including Young Life. He was also among the planners of Key '73, an ecumenical evangelistic push aimed at bringing about a Christian revival in America. The philanthropist also served as president of the Rotary Club, International.

SOURCES

Billy Graham Center Archives, Wheaton College, Wheaton, Illinois.

Gasper, Louis. *The Fundamentalist Movement: 1930–1956*. Grand Rapids, MI: Baker Book House, 1981 [1963].

Marsden, George M. *Reforming Fundamentalism: Fuller Seminary and the New Evangelicalism*. Grand Rapids, MI: Eerdmans, 1987.

Reid, Daniel S., Robert D. Linder, Bruce L. Shelley, and Harry S. Stout, eds. *Dictionary of Christianity in America*. Downers Grove, IL: InterVarsity Press, 1990.

TEEN QUEST

Teen Quest (formerly *Teen Scene*) was one of two new programs launched in the 1980s by the Back to the Bible (BTTB) ministry service of Lincoln, Nebraska. BTTB is an evangelical organization that seeks to help Christians mature in their faith by applying biblical principles to their everyday lives. Hosted by Steve Sheppard, *Teen Quest* is a 15-minute radio show for adolescents that addresses contemporary teen issues and emphasizes proper Christian living.

SOURCES

Melton, J. Gordon. *Directory of Religious Organizations in the United States*. 3d ed. Detroit: Gale Research, 1993.

TELE-MISSIONS INTERNATIONAL
established: 1954

Headquartered just outside metropolitan New York City in Valley Cottage, Tele-Missions International is an independent interdenominational missionary organization with contacts in Ecuador and in African countries such as Kenya, Sierra Leone, Zaire, and others. In its efforts to spread the Christian Gospel, Tele-Missions makes use of indigenous radio broadcasting as well as literature distribution and church planting.

SOURCES

Melton, J. Gordon. *Directory of Religious Organizations in the United States*. 3d ed. Detroit: Gale Research, 1993.

WILLIAM TEMPLE
born: October 15, 1881, Exeter, England
died: October 26, 1944, Canterbury, England

Archbishop William Temple was a renaissance man of early twentieth-century Anglicanism. He was known and respected as a churchman and administrator, gifted writer and philosopher, social reformer, early advocate of Christian ecumenism, and popular radio preacher. Temple's career culminated in his accession to the post of archbishop of Canterbury, the highest ecclesiastical post in the Anglican Church.

Temple's early life and ancestral heritage foreshadowed his ecclesiastical career. His father was a prominent Anglican churchman who held posts as a bishop in Exeter, London, and finally Canterbury. Temple spent his boyhood in London's Fulham Palace and attended Rugby School, where he distinguished himself more in gaining friends than in athletic ability.

Temple next enrolled at Oxford, where he gained recognition as a scholar. Following his election as a fellow of Queen's College in 1904, he lectured in philosophy and began developing a strong interest in social reform.

Despite questions concerning credal formulas, Temple felt a call to the Anglican priesthood and was ordained in 1909. The following year, he was appointed chaplain to the archbishop of Canterbury and headmaster of Repton School. In June 1916, he married Frances Anson, a vivacious and socially concerned secretary for the Westminster branch of the Christian Social Union. The couple never had children.

As Temple's reputation as a preacher and Christian apologist began to grow, he moved quickly up the Church of England's ecclesiastical ladder. Following a rectorship at St. James, Piccadilly, London, Temple served as canon of Westminster, bishop of Manchester and, beginning in 1929, archbishop of York. Temple was elected archbishop of Canterbury in 1942 but was destined to serve only two years in that post. He died in 1944.

During his career, Temple demonstrated an abiding concern for the needs of the poor and suffering. He worked tirelessly to provide better educational opportunities for the working classes, better wages and working conditions for laborers, and improved treatment of children. He also made it clear that he felt the Anglican church should take a leading role in England's crusade for social justice and welfare. In his popular book, *Christianity and the Social Order*, he observed

> The claim of the Christian Church to make its voice heard in matters of politics and economics is very widely resented, even by those who are Christian in personal belief and in devotional practice. It is commonly assumed that Religion is one department of life, like Art or Science, and that it is playing the part of a busybody when it lays down principles for the guidance of other departments, whether Art and Science or Business and Politics.

He concluded

> There is no hope of establishing a more Christian social order except through the labor and sacri-

fice of those in whom the Spirit of Christ is active. . . . The first necessity for progress is more and better Christians taking full responsibility as citizens for the political, social and economic system under which they and their fellows live.

Temple worked to engage the church and its lay people in the challenges of social reform through his writings, sermons, and activities as a church administrator. He believed that, due to contemporary conditions and needs, social action was a kind of "pre-evangelism." Put simply, the church needed to demonstrate Christian love in social reform to spark the interest of non-believers. Once this interest had been drawn, the church could tend to individual spiritual needs. The work of evangelism in the modern age, he contended, needed an active cooperation among preachers, church officials, and lay persons.

Temple was also a passionate advocate of Christian ecumenism. He was largely responsible for the formation of the British Council of Churches and an early supporter of the World Council of Churches. As a prominent church spokesperson at ecumenical meetings, Temple ably represented the Anglican position. He also prodded his colleagues in the Church of England to open themselves to progressive ideas about expanding cooperation with other Christians.

Temple has been called "the ablest preacher that has ever filled either of the provincial thrones." A square-headed, stocky figure, Temple was a popular speaker to business groups, bankers, and workers because of his unassuming manner and his gift for articulating profound ideas in a plainspoken, direct manner. Though more rational than emotional in his approach, he communicated the Anglican position on the great issues of the day with an intellectual fervor that compelled his listeners' attention.

Temple had a gift for extemporaneous preaching and often delivered homilies with no more than a few notes scribbled on a half-sheet of paper. A biographer summed up Temple's homiletic skills by observing that "he possessed to an unusual degree those qualities by which an audience is moved and held—obvious authority, intense conviction, and a mastery of words which placed him among the most lucid teachers in Christendom."

Temple's skills as a communicator translated well into the new medium of radio. In the series of chatty talks that he gave on his BBC program *Points of View* during the late 1920s, he changed his homiletic style somewhat, using informal illustrations and stories to speak to more personal issues, rather than to larger social concerns. During World War II, Temple gave BBC radio talks that explained religion's crucial role in understanding the challenges that faced the British nation. The broadcasts were designed to place the war in a larger historical and ideological context. For Temple, the purpose of the war was to defend Christian civilization against those who would destroy it altogether. As he once proclaimed, "We should make no terms with Herr Hitler or his Government."

Temple also gave a series of talks over the BBC in Spring 1942 entitled "How Christians Worship." The program's stated objective was to answer the simple question: Why do people go to church? Its deeper agenda, however, was to break down the parochial denominational barriers among Christian believers and to enable Christians of all traditions to understand each other better.

Temple's radio talks were well-received by the English masses and made him one of the most highly respected and beloved churchmen of his time. Those who had extensive exposure to both his formal and informal addresses agreed that Temple was at his best when speaking to a radio audience and explaining profound Christian truths in his friendly, personal style.

SOURCES

Fant, Clyde E., Jr., and William M. Pinson, Jr. *20 Centuries of Great Preaching, Vol. 9*. Waco, TX: Word Books, 1971.

Wolfe, Kenneth M. *The Churches and the British Broadcasting Corporation: The Politics of Broadcast Religion*. London: SCM Press, 1984.

THERE'S HOPE

see: Richard Lee

THINGS TO COME MISSION

established: 1955

Headquartered in Cope, Colorado, Things to Come Mission is an independent evangelical organization that supports work in Brazil, Britain, India, Indonesia, Kenya, Nigeria, and the Philippines. Most of its activities center around evangelism, church planting, literature distribution, and theological training of indigenous mission leaders. Things to Come Mission also produces evangelistic radio broadcast programs for distribution to a number of these foreign missions.

SOURCES

Melton, J. Gordon. *Directory of Religious Organizations in the United States.* 3d ed. Detroit: Gale Research, 1993.

THIS IS THE LIFE

first aired: 1952

This Is the Life was the brainchild of Herman Gockel and his colleagues in the communications department of the Lutheran Church, Missouri Synod. Having successfully produced *The Lutheran Hour* on radio, the communications team sought to create a religious drama series for the nascent medium of television. The series would target the unchurched and dramatize true-to-life stories about human relationships and the individual's relationship to God. The Missouri Synod's national agency decided to support Gockel's vision and allocated $750,000 in 1950 to develop a television ministry. Over the ensuing decades, the agency would continue to underwrite the ministry's production costs and distribute series episodes to over 200 stations free of charge.

Tommy Thompson of the Lutheran Laymen's League once explained the Missouri Synod's rationale for underwriting *This Is the Life*:

> Television can make contact where we wouldn't otherwise reach at all. . . . Over the years we have invested ten dollars per one thousand people reached with *This Is the Life*. There's no other way to reach that many people so economically and so effectively.

The first episode of *This Is the Life* aired on ABC-TV in September of 1952. A month later the program was picked up by the DuMont network. Since it ran like other network shows, *This Is the Life* was constrained by the Federal Communications Commission to maintain a nondenominational tone. The show became an instant hit and went on to win Emmy awards and the National Religious Broadcasters Award of Merit. The series was produced by Family Films, Inc., and photographed in part at Hal Roach Studios. Each episode featured respected Hollywood and Broadway directors, actors, and writers. The script was written to direct the viewer to a living faith in Christ.

Throughout its run, the program typically ended with an invitation: "If you have a spiritual problem and no one to advise you, *This Is the Life* will be happy to give you the counsel of God's Word." Each week, nearly 2,000 viewers took advantage of this offer and received a personalized letter from Gockel with suggested nearby churches they could attend. They also received a small booklet entitled "God's Invitation to You." When Gockel read the letter of a person with urgent problems, he quickly notified a local pastor who would then minister to the person in whatever way was appropriate.

The problems confronted on the program during the 1950s included juvenile delinquency, Communism, greed, and cold-heartedness. During the 1960s and 1970s, the show shifted its emphasis to such issues as racial prejudice, illegitimacy, the Vietnam War, and drug addiction. Such character actors as James Flavin, Willis Bouchey, Ann Doran, and Anthony Caruso continued the show's long tradition of first-rate acting. The series went to full-color during the late 1960s, although it had experimented with color as far back as 1957.

This Is the Life peaked in popularity in the 1970s, when it claimed 1.5 million viewers. Throughout the 1980s and early 1990s, the show has continued to maintain a respected presence on an estimated 300 stations nationwide.

See also *The Lutheran Hour*

SOURCES

Armstrong, Ben. *The Electric Church*. Nashville: Thomas Nelson, 1979.

Bluem, A. William. *Religious Television Programs: A Study of Relevance*. New York: Hastings House, 1969.

Hadden, Jeffrey K., and Anson Shupe. *Televangelism: Power and Politics on God's Frontier*. New York: Henry Holt, 1988.

Hadden, Jeffrey K., and Charles E. Swann. *Prime Time Preachers: The Rising Power of Televangelism*. Reading, MA: Addison-Wesley, 1981.

Ward, Mark, Sr. *Air of Salvation: The Story of Christian Broadcasting*. Grand Rapids, MI: Baker Book House, 1994.

THIS IS YOUR DAY
see: Benny Hinn

THIS WEEK IN BIBLE PROPHECY
first aired: December 18, 1994

This Week in Bible Prophecy (TWBP) is a conservative Christian television program that seeks to examine current events and issues in the light of biblical texts. Produced by Paul and Peter LaLonde, the show features such guests as Ian Taylor, Dave Breese, Don Patton, Eric Penrose, Howard Katz, and David Harris. It appears three times a week on the Trinity Broadcasting Network, twice weekly on Vision TV of Canada, and once a week on Cornerstone TV of Pittsburgh and Altoona, Pennsylvania, and United Christian Broadcasting of San Jose and Concord, California. The topics covered on the program and in its complementary publication, *This Week in Bible Prophecy Magazine*, include, among others, the Antichrist, droughts in Southern Africa, the Israeli-Palestinian peace negotiations, British Columbia's multipurpose government identification card, microchip management for livestock, the coming world government, and Creationism.

TWBP's statement of faith confirms the program's belief in the infallibility and inerrancy of Scripture, the Trinity, the virgin birth of Christ, the Vicarious Atonement, the Rapture of the church at Christ's Second Coming, the eternal blessedness of the redeemed in Heaven, and the eternal damnation of the unregenerate in Hell.

SOURCES

"This Week in Bible Prophecy." World Wide Web site. http://www.niagra.com/%7etwibp/ (December 1995).

THRU THE BIBLE
see: J. Vernon McGee

ROBERT TILTON
born: 1946, McKinney, Texas

Courtesy: National Religious Broadcasters

At the height of their popularity in 1991, Robert Tilton's prosperity gospel programs were being broadcast in all 235 United States television markets. During that time, Tilton's ministry was also purchasing 5,000 hours of television time each month, making it the largest buyer of television time among all broadcasting ministries. By October 1993, however, Tilton had ended his career in religious broadcasting and was preparing to fight several lawsuits brought against him and his Word of Faith Ministry.

Following his graduation from high school, Tilton attended Cook County Junior College and Texas Technological University. His conversion to Christianity, which came during a period of drug abuse and marital difficulties, occurred after a group of young people came to his home and shared the gospel with him. Soon after, Tilton founded his Word of Faith Outreach Center in the Dallas suburb of Farmers Branch. By 1985, the church had grown to 8,000 members and had built a 4,000-seat auditorium. During this period, Tilton decided to take his health and wealth message to the masses and started broadcasting a weekly television program, *Word of Faith*, from the Word of Faith Center. Tilton also created a closed-circuit satellite network that carried his monthly seminars to over 2,000 churches nationwide as well as a televised Bible school that claimed over 6,000 students in 600 locations.

Tilton's essential message was that personal spiritual growth and financial prosperity could be gained through faith in Jesus Christ. Tilton's self-representation on his second syndicated series, *Success 'N' Life,* bore witness to his own prosperity. He was always impeccably dressed and flashing a smile as he invoked "Jesus's inheritance." *Success 'N' Life* featured cutting-edge graphics and camera angles and a staff of telephone volunteers who never tired of praising Tilton's messages. In many ways, the program mimicked the late-night infomercials that became common fare on cable channels during the late 1980s.

Tilton's rising star met with catastrophe after ABC-TV's news program *PrimeTime Live* pro-

filed his ministry on November 21, 1991. The program, which used hidden cameras to penetrate the ministry, gained the second highest Nielsen rating for *PrimeTime Live* since its debut in August 1989. In the broadcast, *PrimeTime Live* alleged that Tilton spent more money on Dallas-area billboards than he spent on the international missions he claimed to support. The program also suggested that Tilton was not sending money to an orphanage in Haiti, as he claimed, and that he was buying vials of "holy water" from Taiwan instead of Israel. In the meantime, Tilton's staff members were allegedly buying lavish homes and paying Tilton a large salary. Most damning of all, however, was *PrimeTime Live*'s claim that Tilton's bank in Tulsa, Oklahoma, was opening the ministry's mail, removing monetary contributions, and dumping prayer requests into the trash. A Tulsa recycling center later corroborated the story, saying it had found thousands of prayer requests addressed to Tilton mixed with other recyclable scrap paper.

Tilton and his lawyer, J. C. Joyce, quickly disavowed the program's allegations. Joyce commented, "Everything the show did was a lie. Why did they do it? Ratings, greed. There are a lot of people who want to believe this. Robert Tilton will tell you it's the devil coming out." Joyce also produced a number of photocopied checks that he claimed had been sent monthly to the Haitian orphanage. Tilton himself declared on his national television program, "Go ahead and listen to all that negativism. The devil would not be making a play for God's servants over the last couple, three, four, five years if there wasn't something God's trying to do."

PrimeTime Live's allegations galvanized both state and federal law enforcement agencies into action. The postal inspector's office in Tulsa began an investigation into allegations of mail fraud, and the Dallas County district attorney initiated his own inquiry into Tilton's Word of Faith World Outreach Center. Within a short time, the Internal Revenue Service and the Federal Bureau of Investigation had also opened investigations of the Tilton empire. On January 22, 1992, Texas Attorney General Dan Morales initiated yet another inquiry. In a letter to Tilton, Morales said his office had reason to believe that his ministry was engaged in trade practices and charitable solicitations that may have violated provisions of the Texas Consumer Protection and Deceptive Trade Practices Act. Morales would later begin a criminal investigation in addition to his civil inquiry.

As if these concurrent investigations were not enough, several widows filed suit against Tilton over the next few months, alleging that they had received letters from his ministry promising healing miracles for their husbands—who had already died. The suits contended that Tilton had committed fraud and malicious infliction of emotional distress. Each suit sought $40 million in punitive damages. Other fraud suits followed, including one from a woman who had not sought early treatment for rectal cancer, believing she would be healed through Tilton's prayers. She donated over $1,000 after receiving letters indicating she would be healed and prosper financially if she offered money to Tilton's ministry. Medical officials claimed that the woman could have been successfully treated for the cancer had it been treated earlier.

Although contributions to his Word of Faith Ministry had begun to fall off, Tilton plunged ahead, signing a lease agreement with Texas Channel 55, KDLT-TV, in May of 1992. The agreement allowed him to air his church-related programming 24-hours-a-day. The negative publicity stemming from the lawsuits, investigations, and television exposés, however, began taking its toll. Tilton gradually lost 85 percent of his national audience—from 235 United States television markets in 1991 to 26 in 1993. He also filed for divorce from his wife of 25 years in 1993 and saw church membership in Dallas drop from 8,000 to 2,000. The Word of Faith Ministry suffered a drop in annual donations from $80 million to $25 million during this time—despite the fact that pleas for financial assistance were taking up 86 percent of Tilton's airtime. In September of 1993, Tilton's lawyer announced that Tilton's last broadcast would be October 29. Moreover, the staff at the Word of Faith Ministry would be reduced from its 1991 high of 800 to 32. Later in 1993, Tilton

filed for a preliminary injunction to prevent any rebroadcast of the *PrimeTime Live* segment on his ministry. The injunction was thought to be a precursor to a possible libel suit. As of this writing, none of the lawsuits brought against Tilton have been successfully prosecuted, although several remain pending.

SOURCES

Brown, Rich. "Trouble in Paradise." *Broadcasting,* December 2, 1991.

"Evangelist Tilton Will Make Last Broadcast Next Month." *The Orlando Sentinel,* September 30, 1993.

"FBI, IRS Also Watch Dallas TV Preacher." *San Antonio Light*, December 7, 1991.

Kennedy, John W. "End of the Line for Tilton?" *Christianity Today,* August, 1993.

"Robert Tilton Wants You to Be a Success in Life." *Charisma*, July, 1985.

St. Pierre, Nancy. "Another Widow Sues Evangelist." *The Seattle Times*, March 18, 1992.

"Texas Attorney General Starts Investigation of Evangelist." *Los Angeles Daily Journal*, January 23, 1992.

"TV Show Spurs Local Probe of Televangelist's Donations." *San Antonio Express-News*, November 24, 1991.

"2 Dallas Women Sue Tilton, Alleging Fraud." *Austin American-Statesman*, April 4, 1992.

TODAY WITH DEREK PRINCE

see: Derek Prince

TODAY'S FATHER

In the mid-1990s, a national religious movement that encourages men to be better fathers and husbands began to take shape.

Promise Keepers, an outreach started by former University of Colorado football coach Bill McCartney, is one manifestation of this movement. The ministry sponsors huge rallies in stadiums around the country where Christian men spend over 13 hours praying, singing hymns, and exhorting each other to be responsible, "godly" men. The Million-Man March of African American men to Washington, DC, sponsored by Nation of Islam leader Louis Farrakhan in October 1995, is another manifestation of the movement. A third manifestation is *Today's Father*, a 3-minute radio program that seeks to provide practical spiritual direction for America's fathers.

This radio ministry is the brainchild of Ken Canfield, the executive director of the National Center for Fathering. The center is a research organization dedicated to turning "the hearts of fathers to their children." Canfield is also a best-selling author, speaker, and spokesperson in Christian evangelical circles. *Today's Father* is cosponsored by Tyndale House Publishers of Carol Stream, Illinois.

TRANS WORLD MISSIONS
established: 1949

Headquartered in the Los Angeles suburb of Glendale, California, Trans World Missions (TWM) is an interdenominational missionary organization with ministries in Mexico, Central America, and Brazil. Among its many services, Trans World Missions engages in evangelism, church planting, and a variety of social services for children and the poor. Its philosophy of missions is to support indigenous church leaders. An important aspect of TWM's evangelistic ministry is the production and distribution of radio broadcast programs.

SOURCES

Melton, J. Gordon. *Directory of Religious Organizations in the United States.* 3d ed. Detroit: Gale Research, 1993.

TRANS WORLD RADIO
established: 1954

The powerful international religious network Trans World Radio (TWR) had its origins in the concern of Paul Freed, a Youth for Christ

director from Greensboro, South Carolina, for the evangelical churches of Spain. Freed had first heard of these churches' plight in 1948 while attending an international missions meeting in Beatenburg, Switzerland. On his way home, Freed stopped in Spain and discovered that evangelical Christians were being persecuted by the right-wing Catholic regime of Francisco Franco. He decided to publicize this situation in America and to raise funds for some form of missionary outreach. In 1952, Freed returned to Spain with Ben Armstrong. They set about documenting the situation of Spanish evangelicals on 16-millimeter color film. The plan was then to use the film in fundraising efforts in American evangelical churches.

The fruit of these efforts, a feature film entitled *Banderilla*, was voted evangelical film of the year in 1952. The film also helped Freed raise the $100,000 that was needed to build a religious radio station in Tangiers, Morocco. The "Voice of Tangiers" began broadcasting with a 2,500-watt transmitter on February 22, 1954. Freed's father, Ralph, a veteran Christian Missionary and Alliance representative in the Middle East, agreed to oversee the new station in Tangiers while Paul Freed continued to raise funds for equipment in the United States. The senior Freed would continue as the station's chief executive until his passing in 1973. Ben Armstrong joined the ministry in 1958 as director of home operations, which were headquartered in Chatham, New Jersey.

The station's outreach expanded quickly beyond Spain, reaching, in 1959, North Africa and the entire European continent with a new 50,000-watt transmitter. Among the many countries receiving the Voice of Tangiers' signal were the (former) Soviet Union, Poland, Czechoslovakia, Hungary, and Rumania. The station also organized a staff of announcers that broadcast programs in over 30 languages.

The year 1959 also marked the first major crisis in Voice of Tangiers's history. Tangiers lost its status as an international city and came under the authority of the newly formed Moroccan government. The government soon informed Voice of Tangiers that, as of December

31, 1959, it would no longer be permitted to operate in Morocco. This sudden news forced Ralph Freed and his corps of 33 missionaries to find a new broadcast site in Western Europe. After several rejections, the station was finally able to sign a long-term lease agreement with Radio Monte Carlo in the Principality of Monaco. Successful fundraising efforts in the United States enabled the ministry to purchase new equipment and to make its lease payments on time. Two of the new station's most prominent supporters were the popular American radio ministries *Back to the Bible* and *Hour of Decision*. During this period of negotiations, the station changed its name from Voice of Tangiers to Trans World Radio.

Charles Fuller's *Old Fashioned Revival Hour* was the first TWR program to hit the airwaves. The show was broadcast over the station's new 100,000-watt short-wave transmitter on October 16, 1960. The actual broadcast site was a large, bomb-proof building on Mount Agel that had been constructed by Adolf Hitler during World War II. Though the site never became operational, Hitler had planned to use it to broadcast Nazi propaganda throughout the world.

By the late 1970s, TWR's mountainside headquarters housed a battery of station antennas that were powered by 3.4 million watts of transmitting capacity. The battery included a 1,200 kW AM, a 2,000 kW long-wave, and two 100 kW short-wave transmitters. In addition, the station's programming had expanded into 40 languages and blanketed all of Europe, North Africa, and the Middle East.

The programs themselves were typically produced in the countries to which they would be broadcast. Local religious leaders, preachers, church musicians, and singers were employed to tape the shows, after which the tapes were flown to TWR for broadcast. Indigenous TWR organizations sprang up all over the world to coordinate local program production, fundraising, and staffing.

For example, the German TWR branch, Evangeliums Rundfunk (ER), became a highly sophisticated producer of German-language programming. Headquartered in Wetzlar, ER was producing nearly 2,000 hours of programs yearly and funding 1,000 hours of programming in other languages by 1979. Under the leadership of the Reverend Horst Marquardt, ER created shows that introduced Bible stories for children, provided popular music for teens, and pioneered advanced Bible study courses for adults. ER also sponsored major conferences and invited hundreds of local pastors to preach on its shows.

By the late 1970s, programming for listeners behind the Iron Curtain and in mainland China also was being produced in Monaco by recent émigrés from those countries. These religious broadcasts were heard by the many millions of local citizens who owned short-wave radios. Although Communist officials took great pains to jam foreign political broadcasts, they tended to ignore religious broadcasts in the belief that their citizens had evolved beyond the need for religion. A large body of evidence, including the reports of émigrés, letters, and firsthand accounts by visitors, attested to the fallacy of this belief. Following the fall of Communism in Eastern Europe, a resurgence of public interest in religion and spirituality has made it clear that the religious aspirations of these peoples never completely disappeared.

TWR also sought to expand its outreach into Latin America, western Africa, and the Caribbean. However, when Paul Freed filed a license application with the FCC to operate from a site near San Juan, Puerto Rico, the commission announced they had decided to freeze international licenses for at least 10 years. Newton Minow, the chairman of the FCC at the time, was apparently ambivalent about granting licenses for private international broadcasting. Freed was undeterred by this ruling and found another site outside US jurisdiction on which to build TWR's new facility. The site was on the Netherlands's Antilles island of Bonaire, located some 60 miles off the Venezuelan coast. By 1979, the facility featured a huge tower, a 500,000-watt AM station that broadcast at 800 kHz, and a 250,000-watt short-wave transmitter. The Bonaire transmitters are situated near salt flats that naturally amplify the already powerful radio signals. As a result, these signals blanket large regions of the western hemisphere and can be heard at night across the southeast United States.

TWR's international outreach has not been limited to Europe and Latin America, however. The network has also leased time on a 600 kW AM station in Cyprus, for example. This station broadcasts religious programming throughout the Middle East in such languages as Arabic, Armenian, Farsi, French, and Russian. To evangelize the southern hemisphere in Africa, a powerful short-wave transmitter was installed in Swaziland. This station sends out programming in over 20 languages. The Indian subcontinent began to receive TWR's programming in 1978 from a newly constructed 400,000-watt AM station in Sri Lanka. Moreover, the Far East has become the target of TWR's two 100,000-watt short-wave transmitters on the US territory of Guam. This station reaches over 1 billion people in every major Far East language and is especially effective in reaching the citizenry of Communist China, many of whom own inexpensive short-wave radios.

TWR's continually expanding worldwide ministry was employing over 400 radio evangelists and utilizing over 5 million watts of broadcast power by the late 1970s. Its shows were being sent out in over 70 languages. Today, TWR's station on Mount Agel airs its gospel programming over five transmitters with a combined power of 2.7 million watts. The Monaco ministry is complemented by seven other stations located in strategic sites throughout the world. These stations are believed able to reach almost 80 percent of the world's population with gospel-based programming.

See also Paul Freed

SOURCES

Armstrong, Ben. *The Electric Church*. Nashville: Thomas Nelson, 1979.

Ward, Mark, Sr. *Air Of Salvation: The Story of Christian Broadcasting*. Manassas., VA: National Religious Broadcasters, 1994.

TRINITY BROADCASTING NETWORK
established: 1973

Since its humble beginnings in 1973, Trinity Broadcasting Network (TBN) has built itself into a worldwide television network that provides state-of-the-art Christian programming 24-hours-a-day. As of 1995, the network was being carried to over 28 million American households over thousands of local cable systems and to over 500 television stations around the world. The ministry's international programming is translated into numerous foreign languages with the help of its International Production Center in Irving, Texas. TBN proudly promotes the charismatic Christianity and "traditional American values" of its founders, Paul and Jan Crouch, and bills itself as a "safe, friendly place" in a "world that seems hostile to family values."

Paul Crouch, the son of the first Assemblies of God missionaries to Egypt, met Jan Bethany, the daughter of Assemblies of God evangelist Edgar Bethany, while the two were attending a Bethany camp meeting. Following their marriage in 1958, the Crouches pastored several small churches before moving to Southern California. In Burbank, Paul Crouch parlayed the skills he had gained at a radio station in South Dakota into a managerial job at an Assemblies of God film studio.

TBN got off the ground when Crouch received a "word of prophecy" at an evening church service that "a new television ministry is coming to birth." After garnering the support of a group of local Christian businessmen, Crouch leased the facilities of a failing UHF station for $250,000. The new station ironed out some early transmission difficulties and began live broadcasting on May 28, 1973. Although its first year of operation saw the station regularly on the verge of bankruptcy, TBN managed to survive thanks to the generous donations of listeners and the entertainment charisma of the young Jim Bakker. By the late 1970s, TBN had emerged as America's first 24-hour Christian television network.

TBN expanded during the 1980s by buying television stations in large cities and turning them into full-time Christian broadcasting centers. The network also began to send its programming out to over 200 independent cable systems around the country, a venture made possible by new RCA satellite services, which cost the ministry as little as $34,000 per month. Crouch claimed that shortly before buying space on RCA's new transponder, he had a prophetic vision:

> The lights went out, and it was as though I was several thousand miles in outer space, looking down on the earth. Then, a great light came into being right over the center of the United States, and I could see beams of light going out and hitting the major metropolitan areas of America. Then, as those secondary lights lit up, I could see little pencil threads of light emanating from them, and forming little dots of light until the whole country became like a blaze, a network of light all over. I was fascinated, enthralled, enraptured by it! I asked the Lord, "What is it?" And I heard one word: "S A T E L L I T E."

By the end of the 1980s, TBN had bought more than 100 stations nationwide and exercised control over 12 other stations through financial arrangement with the network or Crouch family members. The stations owned by TBN included its home-base channel 40, KTBN-TV in Santa Ana, California, and stations in Tustin, California; Phoenix, Arizona; Oklahoma City, Oklahoma; Miami, Fort Pierce, and Jacksonville, Florida; Richmond and Greenwood, Indiana; Fishkill, New York; Federal Way, Washington; Westminster, Colorado; Louisville, Irving, Harlingen, Orange, and Houston, Texas; Decatur, Georgia; Portland, Oregon; Nevis, West Indies; Castries, Saint Lucia; Milan, Italy; Athens, Greece; Bisho, Ciskei, and Umata, Transkei (South Africa); San José, Costa Rica; and Nueva San Salvador, El Salvador. TBN also broadcasts over a super-power short-wave radio frequency on station KTBN, two noncommercial radio stations in the US, and Radio Paradise, a 50,000-watt non-directional AM radio station located in St. Kitts, West Indies.

In the early 1980s, TBN purchased a mobile satellite transmitter housed on an 18-wheel truck. "The Holy Beamer," as the unit was dubbed, was built by a firm that hoped to market the mobile units around the world. Trinity used this transmitter to cover such live events as Billy Graham crusades and Full Gospel Business Men's conventions.

By the mid-1990s, TBN was the most-watched religious network in America, according to Nielsen. It claimed 3,500 cable affiliates, 28 million cable subscribers, and 500 full-power and low-power television broadcast stations worldwide. The network's programming is nondenominational and its guests and program hosts represent a diverse cross section of Christian churches. This inclusive programming is designed to broaden TBN's appeal to the greatest possible number of viewers. TBN is noncommercial and refuses to air off-network reruns, infomercials, game shows, or old movies.

A demographic profile of TBN's audience compiled in July 1994 showed that TBN's appeal is indeed far-reaching. Of all the network's viewers, 55 percent are male, 60 percent have incomes over $25,000 per year, 67 percent have only a high school diploma or less, 63 percent are married, 53 percent have no children, 76 percent are white, and the largest age cohort—38 percent—are in the 29- to 48-year-old category.

TBN's weekly programming includes a lineup of syndicated evangelists such as Charles Stanley, John Osteen, D. James Kennedy, E. V. Hill, Ray McCauley, Kenneth Copeland, Robert Schuller, and Greg Laurie. In addition, the network televises German evangelist Reinhard Bonnke's massive African crusades and the popular rallies of such major Christian teachers as Billy Graham, Benny Hinn, Adrian Rodgers, and Frederick Price. Prominent prophecy teachers such as Hal Lindsey, Jack Van Impe, and Peter LaLonde host programs that attempt to explain the biblical significance of current events.

No viewing day would be complete without live telecasts and reruns of the Crouches' popular *Praise the Lord* show. This program features both talk-show and variety-show formats and includes interviews with prominent Christians and musical performances by such popular entertainers as Charlie Daniels, Glen Campbell, Ricky Van Shelton, and black gospel stars Bebe and Cece Winans.

Other programs carried on the network include the fast-paced magazine program *The Carol Lawrence Show*; three popular weekly series hosted by medical doctors, including *Calling Dr. Whitaker*, a half-hour show that relates the latest in medical science to Christian values, *Doctor to Doctor*, an interview show that features medical doctors, nutrition counselors, and medical experts, and *Doctor and the Word*, a weekly show that explains biblical concepts concerning nutrition and healthy lifestyles; *Seniors*, a long-running TBN weekly variety show hosted by Dale Evans; *Treasures Out of Darkness*, featuring the inner-city ministries of ex-drug addict Sonny Arguinzoni; *Night Light*, an entertainment show hosted by Todd and Donna Fisher; *The Bible Bowl*, a quiz game show for Bible scholars; *One Way Game*, a Bible-based quiz program for high schoolers; *Joy*, a daily song-and-sermon series; the preview program *Behind the Scenes*; the news program *TBN Today*; and *Get in Shape*, a morning exercise show.

Other shows that have been added to TBN's lineup include *Charisma*, a magazine program sponsored by *Charisma Magazine* that highlights new recording artists, best-selling books, and major Christian events around the world; *Back on Course*, a marriage enrichment show hosted by Gavin and Patti MacLeod; the music shows *Time 2* (with CARMAN), *Silent Witness* (with Ricky Skaggs), *Gospel America* (with Pat Boone), and *Homeland Harmony*; the teen programs *John Jacobs and the Power Team*, *Real Videos*, *Fire by Nite* (a fast-paced variety program designed to help youth deal with peer pressure through interviews, discussions of relevant issues, and humorous skits), and *Leon Patillo and Friends*; and the children's programs *Gospel Bill Show*, *Kids Against Crime* (hosted by Rosey Grier), *Becky's Barn*, *Kids Like You*, *Superbook*, and *TBN's Kids Club*.

TBN raises its funds through twice-yearly telethons and special gift offers and projects the rest of the year. By 1989, the network's market value stood at $500 million, and the ministry was virtually free of debt. Trinity also supports a volunteer prayer counselor ministry that provides over 100 phone counselors each evening. Moreover, TBN works to assist the growth of local churches through its referral program. When individuals who use TBN's round-the-clock counseling lines give their lives to Christ, they are encouraged by TBN counselors to attend a local referral church for further spiritual guidance.

Trinity became the subject of an investigation by the National Religious Broadcasters (NRB) Ethics Committee in 1989. Under investigation were charges of age and sex discrimination at a Trinity station in Tacoma, Washington; unfair labor practices against unionized employees at Trinity's flagship station KTBN, Channel 40 in Tustin, California; and a hostile takeover of a Buffalo, New York, station. On December 22, the NRB's executive committee decided that there was insufficient documentation of Crouch's alleged violations to warrant a termination of TBN's membership. In January 1990, Crouch announced that TBN was withdrawing from NRB and "every earthly man-made organization" because "lying, trumped-up charges were aimed at the very heart" of TBN. He concluded, "It was not a good year to be a TV evangelist! Of course, it was Satan's strategy to tar all TV ministries with the same brush. . . . Media reports were merciless. Many bought the lie and gave credibility to the enemies of TBN."

Despite NRB's allegations and a 1992 FCC investigation of TBN, the network continued to flourish in the mid-1990s. TBN expanded its outreach into the Russia in 1992 and began broadcasting its shows on Russian State television a few hours per week. The network is currently finishing a Channel 40 studio in Saint Petersburg that will be the first privately-owned television station in the former Soviet Union. Channel 40 will carry TBN's full complement of Christian programming.

See also Paul Crouch

SOURCES

Armstrong, Ben. *The Electric Church*. Nashville: Thomas Nelson, 1979.

"Broadcaster Quits Christian Group." *Los Angeles Times*, January, 1990.

Erickson, Hal. *Religious Radio and Television in the United States, 1921–1991*. Jefferson, NC: McFarland, 1992.

Mark I. Pinsky. "Head of Religious Network Answers Allegations." *Los Angeles Times*, February 14, 1989.

Newsweek. "The T Stands for Troubled." March 30, 1992, 60.

Praise the Lord. August, 1992. Vol. 19, no. 8.

Roberts, Dennis. "Trinity Broadcasting Network: The Dream Almost Didn't Happen." *Charisma*, June 1983, 18–25, 88–90.

TBN: The Heart and Soul of America. Promotional Packet, 1995.

TRUTHS THAT TRANSFORM

see: D. James Kennedy

TURNING POINT

first aired: 1979

The Assemblies of God (AOG), a fast-growing Pentecostalist denomination in the United States, encourages their member denominations to design new facilities that are "television friendly." By 1979, over 200 local churches were producing their own national television shows. The AOG also began producing a national radio program, entitled *Turning Point*, in the late 1970s. In the words of AOG's former director of communications, Lee Shultz,

> With guests ranging from celebrities, such as gospel singer Andrae Crouch and pro-football stars, to airline pilots and young mothers, the program has everything the man or woman outside the church can respond to and the church member can find uplifting.

The popular show, which ran through the 1980s, highlighted the crucial spiritual turning points in the lives of its guests.

Turning Point was also the name of a sermon-format radio show hosted by David Jeremiah of El Cajon, California, during the 1980s and early 1990s. Moreover, the Full Gospel Business Men's Fellowship used the title for a group of 60-minute specials it produced.

See also *Revivaltime*

SOURCES

Armstrong, Ben. The Electric Church. Nashville: Thomas Nelson, 1979.

Erickson, Hal. *Religious Radio and Television in the United States, 1921–1991*. Jefferson, NC: McFarland, 1992.

THE TWENTIETH CENTURY REFORMATION HOUR

see: Carl McIntire

U

UNDA

established: 1928

Roman Catholics have long recognized radio and television's potential for spreading their teachings around the world. In 1928, the Roman Catholic Church created the International Catholic Committee for Radio to explore how radio might be used as a medium for teaching and proselytizing. The first headquarters for the committee was in Cologne, Germany. This organization later changed its name to UNDA (from the Latin for "wave") and moved its headquarters to Brussels, Belgium. UNDA has become an international association of Catholic broadcasting professionals which includes national and continental member groups that share its overall objectives. UNDA-USA and UNDA-ASIA are prominent examples of these member groups.

UNDA's mission is to assist in the coordination of various Catholic-run apostolic and professional broadcasting ministries. UNDA accomplishes this mission by sponsoring conferences, research projects, and publications. The association is particularly interested in fostering broadcast ministries in the Third World and in finding ways to collaborate with non-Catholic broadcast ministries that have compatible goals. In Third World countries located in Africa, Latin America, Asia, and Oceania, UNDA plans and subsidizes development programs in religious broadcasting. These regional and local programs are then submitted to the Congregation for the Evangelization of People in Rome and to other international funding agencies for financial support.

In order to inform interested organizations and individuals on its activities, UNDA publishes a documentation quarterly and a monthly newsletter in both French and English.

SOURCES

"UNDA." *New Catholic Encyclopedia, Vol. 17*. New York: McGraw-Hill, 1979.

UNDA-USA

established: 1939

UNDA-USA is the American affiliate of UNDA, the international association of Catholic broadcasting professionals. The organization began in 1939 as the radio series, *Catholic Forum of the Air*. This outreach evolved into a national professional organization, the Catholic Broadcasters Association of America, in 1948. By 1972, the association had established a relationship with UNDA and changed its name to UNDA-USA. Since that time it has functioned under a board of directors that includes representatives from the Catholic Television Network, the Association of Catholic Radio and Television Syndicators, the United States Catholic Conference's (USCC) Department of Communication, USCC's twelve regional headquarters, and individuals from the media and government. The association's total membership numbers around 300 organizations and individuals.

UNDA-USA encourages cooperation among diocesan communications officials, instructional television personnel, religious program syndicators, and the USCC Department of Communication. The association also works to forge cooperative links with other religious broadcasters, to assess the societal impact of communications media both within the United States and abroad, to foster discerning audiences for media programming, and to help develop mutual understanding between various ethnic and cultural communities. UNDA-USA is particularly interested in preserving freedom of expression for religious communities and in monitoring media-government relations. The association, which moved its headquarters from Los Angeles to Akron, Ohio, during the 1980s, holds an annual general assembly and publishes a bimonthly newsletter.

By the late 1980s, UNDA-USA was responsible for a large percentage of the closed-circuit and cable television programs provided by Catholics for educational purposes. In addition, it was presenting annual Gabriel awards to both local and national television and radio shows that "best entertained, enriched, or informed with a vision of life reflecting basic religious principles." These awards were also presented to television and radio stations whose programming quality was judged to be of consistently high quality, and to individuals who had demonstrated exemplary leadership in professional broadcasting contexts. Mother Angelica, for example, was awarded a Gabriel award for her phenomenal success on the Eternal Word Broadcasting Network. The award was especially meaningful given her reputation in broadcasting circles as a maverick and independent.

See also UNDA

SOURCES

Erickson, Hal. *Religious Radio and Television in the United States, 1921–1991*. Jefferson, NC: McFarland, 1992.

"UNDA." *New Catholic Encyclopedia, Vol. 17*. New York: McGraw-Hill, 1979.

UNSHACKLED
first aired: 1940s

The signature radio program of the Pacific Garden Mission (PGM), *Unshackled* dramatizes the true-life stories of the spiritually lost who found salvation from sin as a result of the PGM ministries. Beginning in the 1940s, *Unshackled* aired over radio intermittently until the 1960s. In the 1970s, *Unshackled* became a regular half-hour syndicated program, with a midpoint break that highlighted the benefits of the mission's ministries. It aired briefly in the 1980s over WGN, Chicago, as part of their Saturday night religious broadcasts. For its popularity and consistently excellent production quality, *Unshackled* received the Radio Program Producer of the Year award from the National Religious Broadcasters in 1996.

See also Pacific Garden Mission

SOURCES

Erickson, Hal. *Religious Radio and Television in the United States, 1921–1991*. Jefferson, NC: McFarland,1992.

Reid, Daniel G., Robert D. Linder, Bruce L. Shelley, and Harry S. Stout, eds. *Dictionary of Christianity in America*. Downers Grove, IL: InterVarsity Press, 1990.

USA RADIO NETWORK
see: Marlin Maddoux

SARAH UTTERBACH
born: 1937

Sarah Utterbach, with her husband, Clinton Utterbach, is the copastor of Redeeming Love Christian Center (RLCC) in Nanuet, New York. The Utterbachs are also the cohosts of *Listen to Jesus*, an international radio program that first aired in 1981 as *The Word Alive*. Sarah Utterbach also recently debuted as host of *The*

Choice Is Yours, a live call-in program aired on WMCA-AM, New York. This show includes prayer partners who staff telephone lines at RLCC and in the radio station.

Utterbach was reared in a Christian family in a black ghetto of Norfolk, Virginia. According to Utterbach, she transcended ghetto life by deciding early that the ghetto was more a state of mind than a place. Even though she had pulled herself out of the ghetto and was enjoying the creature comforts that worldly success brought her, Utterbach was still dissatisfied with her life and found herself, one day, on the balcony of a high-rise apartment seriously considering suicide. This experience catalyzed a rededication of her life to Christ. Subsequently, Utterbach became a gifted minister and counselor to both non-Christians and Christians who were not wholly submitted to Christ. She and her husband began a home Bible study and later quit their managerial positions to enroll full-time at RHEMA Bible Training Center in Tulsa, Oklahoma.

The Utterbachs' RLCC ministry began in 1980 and today includes not only *Listen to Jesus* and *The Choice Is Yours*, but also *Horizons Unlimited*, the ministry's quarterly four-color magazine. Utterbach was a featured speaker at the National Religious Broadcasters 1995 national convention in Nashville, Tennessee. She is one of the few African American women in religious broadcasting.

SOURCES

"Casting Call for NRB 95." *Religious Broadcasting*, February, 1995.

V

ABE VAN DER PUY
born: 1919, Sheboygan, Wisconsin

Chairman of the board for World Radio Missionary Fellowship and host of the *Voice of Missions* radio broadcast, Abe C. Van der Puy has served in the missionary field for more than 50 years. While still a teenager, Van der Puy became a Christian and decided to pursue a ministerial career. He graduated from Wheaton College in 1941 and studied for a time at Calvin Seminary.

After his studies, Van der Puy joined HCJB World Radio as a missionary to Ecuador. He served in a number of capacities before being promoted, in 1950, to HCJB station manager. Van der Puy became HCJB's mission director in 1955 and president of World Radio Missionary Fellowship in 1962. He was elected board chairperson in 1982 and continues to direct the ministry's activities from its headquarters in Colorado Springs, Colorado.

Since 1979, Van der Puy has been host of the weekly broadcast, *Voice of Missions*, a radio program sponsored by the Back to the Bible Ministries. He was the presiding chairman of the National Religious Broadcasters between 1975 and 1978.

See also HCJB, Ecuador; National Religious Broadcasters

SOURCES

Ward, Mark, Sr. *Air of Salvation: The Story of Christian Broadcasting*. Grand Rapids, MI: Baker Book House, 1994.

JACK VAN IMPE
born: February 9, 1931, Freeport, Michigan

Courtesy: National Religious Broadcasters

Jack Leo Van Impe is one of America's premier apocalyptic televangelists. His half-hour weekly program of news analysis, *Jack Van Impe Presents!*, is now broadcast on over 700 stations around the world and on the Inspirational Network, the Trinity Broadcasting Network, VisionTV in Canada, and Black Entertainment Television. Van Impe is the son of two first-generation Belgian immigrants, Oscar and Louise Van Impe. Oscar Van Impe, a migrant farm laborer, had his son baptized in the Roman Catholic Church. After moving his family around the Midwest in search of seasonal work, the elder Van Impe settled in Detroit, where he found employment in the automobile industry. Jack Van Impe's musical ability was encouraged by his father, who augmented the family income by playing accordion in Belgian American beer gardens.

Within a year of his father's conversion to evangelical Christianity in 1943, Van Impe began attending a conservative Baptist church across the street from his home. He, too, underwent a born-again experience and was baptized. The entire Van Impe family soon became members of the Liberal Avenue Baptist Church. Van Impe again followed his father's example by enrolling in the independent Detroit Bible College. After his graduation in 1951, he received ordination into the independent Baptist movement. The young minister made his name initially by performing music at Youth for Christ meetings.

While at a Youth for Christ rally in Pontiac, Michigan, Van Impe met Rexella Shelton. The couple married in 1952 and created Ambassadors for Christ, a traveling evangelical music ministry. While Rexella sang, Van Impe accompanied her on accordion. The musical performances slowly changed into a more conventional preaching ministry, and the Van Impes began to build up an audience among the more conservative branches of the Baptist church.

In 1970, Van Impe organized Jack Van Impe Crusades, Inc., and chose the Detroit suburb of Royal Oak as the ministry's headquarters. By the 1990s, he had moved the headquarters to nearby Troy. Van Impe soon was able to expand his venues beyond single congregations and preach to coalitions of fundamentalist churches around the country. The evangelist's first venture into religious broadcasting occurred in 1971, when he began a radio ministry. In time, the radio ministry was being aired in five languages around the world. By the late 1970s, Van Impe had added a television show, *Jack Van Impe Presents!*, to his evangelistic enterprise. The show became an overnight success on religious television channels and by 1980 was being broadcast on 81 stations nationwide. His viewing audience had grown in this short time to an estimated 175,000 people.

Van Impe's telecast, at the time, opened with fast-moving canned film and a musical performance by Rexella. Van Impe came out next and was interviewed by Rexella on issues of contemporary interest and concern. The show ended with a Van Impe sermon on the menace of world Communism and the imminence of Christ's Second Coming. Today's *Jack Van Impe Presents!* usually offers a free book or gift to listeners and promotes the ministry's periodical, *Perhaps Today*. The show is aired in both the United States and abroad over the Inspirational Network, the 357 stations of the Trinity Broadcasting Network, Black Entertainment Television, Cornerstone TV, and Christian Channel Europe.

Of Van Impe's numerous books, his most famous, *Everything You Always Wanted to Know about Prophecy, but Didn't Know Who to Ask!*, is a kind of primer on his apocalyptic worldview. The book claims that time is running out on the human race and that cataclysmic events await the world. Prior to the end of the Cold War, Van Impe regularly called for a cleansing crusade against all Communist influences in America.

Van Impe's influence has been felt mainly in conservative Baptist circles. He has had a "chair of evangelism" established in his honor at the Baptist University of America in Decatur, Georgia, and has been in the forefront of the Bible memorization movement. Van Impe himself has committed to memory large segments of Scripture and is sometimes referred to as "The Walking Bible." The evangelist's greatest accomplishment has been to harness the interest generated by apocalyptic books such as Hal Lindsey's *The Late Great Planet Earth* and to create a professional quality broadcasting ministry based on eschatological speculation.

See also *Jack Van Impe Presents!*

SOURCES

Campbell, Roger F. *They Call Him the Walking Bible: The Story of Dr. Jack Van Impe*. Royal Oak, MI: Jack Van Impe Ministries, 1988.

Hadden, Jeffrey K., and Charles E. Swann. *Prime Time Preachers: The Rising Power of Televangelism.* Menlo Park, CA: Addison-Wesley, 1981.

Van Impe, Jack. *11:59 . . . and Counting!* Nashville: Thomas Nelson, 1987.

———. *Israel's Final Holocaust.* Nashville: Thomas Nelson, 1979.

REXELLA VAN IMPE
born: 1932, Pontiac, Michigan

Rexella Van Impe is the cohost of *Jack Van Impe Presents!*, a half-hour weekly news program that analyzes and interprets world events in the light of biblical prophecy. The show's other cohost is her husband Jack Van Impe, known as "The Walking Bible" for his claim to have memorized over 10,000 Bible verses.

Born Rexella Shelton, Van Impe grew up in a devout Christian home and was baptized at the age of 12 in the First Baptist Church of Pontiac, Michigan. She was active in her church music ministry as both a vocalist and a pianist, and won vocal honors at a University of Michigan solo and ensemble festival. Following high school, Van Impe attended Bob Jones University in Greenville, South Carolina, from 1950 to 1951, where she studied religious music. Shortly after recommitting her life to Christ as a young adult, she met Jack Van Impe at a Youth for Christ rally in Pontiac, Michigan. Two months later Rexella met Jack again on the set of *The America Back to God Hour*, where she was performing as a vocalist and he was playing accordion. The couple began dating in December 1951 and were married on August 21, 1952. The Van Impes pooled their musical talents and created Ambassadors for Christ, a traveling evangelical music ministry. Ambassadors for Christ crisscrossed the United States many times over the next 20 years and slowly changed into a more conventional preaching ministry.

In 1970, the Van Impes organized the Jack Van Impe Crusades, Inc., and set up headquarters in Royal Oak, Michigan. The couple's first venture into religious broadcasting occurred in 1971, when Jack Van Impe put the first of a series of 13 recorded sermons, entitled "The Coming War with Russia," on 100 stations. By Easter Sunday 1972, the Van Impes were hosting a regular weekly radio broadcast that was heard nationwide. On January 7, 1973, the Sunday broadcast began being transmitted around the world on Trans World Radio. The program's announcer was the Van Impes's longtime friend, Charles Ohman. Van Impe showcased her talents as musical soloist on the show and shared letters with her listeners. Her husband reported on the various crusades the ministry was sponsoring and preached a Bible message. These messages were frequently on the subject of biblical prophecy. The programs were translated into 83 languages, including Chinese, Spanish, Russian, Hebrew, and Arabic.

In 1980, the Van Impes added a half-hour weekly television show to their ministry, *Jack Van Impe Presents!* Within a short time the telecast was being aired on 81 stations nationwide, with an estimated audience of 175,000 people. The program opened with fast-moving images from such international settings as London and the Holy Land. After a musical performance by the "First Lady of Sacred Music," as Van Impe had come to be known, Jack Van Impe came out and was interviewed by his wife on contemporary issues of concern. The show finished up with a sermon by Jack that often highlighted the menace of world Communism and the imminence of the Second Coming of Christ.

In 1985, the Van Impes switched from a weekly telecast to a series of hour-long television specials that focused on such topics as New Age religion and the coming battle of Armageddon. Their 1987 special, "Jack Van Impe Presents the Occult World," earned them a Silver Angel award for "its outstanding contribution to prime-time TV programming." Van Impe continued to provide the musical entertainment for these specials and to conduct interviews with special guests.

Jack Van Impe Presents! came back on the air during the early 1990s and is now broadcast internationally over the Inspirational Network, the 357 stations of the Trinity Broadcasting Network, Black Entertainment Television, Chicago's WGN superstation, Cornerstone TV, and Christian Channel Europe. The ministry

estimates that the weekly program is carried to over 25,000 cities and towns in North America and to 160 nations via television and radio.

Rexella Van Impe is the global news telecast's cohost. She reports on international affairs and has interviewed over 200 influential world leaders, Christian writers, and Christian scholars. Van Impe also has been honored by the International Women in Leadership with its Outstanding Woman in Ministry award and by Religion in Media with its Gold Angel award. The Van Impe ministry team has received 17 Silver Angel awards for excellence in media.

See also Jack Van Impe

SOURCES

Campbell, Roger F. *They Call Him the Walking Bible: The Story of Dr. Jack Van Impe.* Royal Oak, MI: Jack Van Impe Ministries, 1988.

Hadden, Jeffrey K., and Charles E. Swann. *Prime Time Preachers: The Rising Power of Televangelism.* Menlo Park, CA: Addison-Wesley, 1981.

Peterson, Richard G. "Electric Sisters." In *The God Pumpers*, edited by Marshall Fishwick and Ray B. Browne. Bowling Green, KY: Bowling Green State University Popular Press, 1987.

VATICAN RADIO
established: 1931

The Roman Catholic Church was quick to recognize the potential of radio for propagating the faith to its global community. In 1925, the director of communications for Vatican City, Father Guiseppe Gianfranceschi, S. J., began drawing up plans for the inauguration of a radio station in the Vatican. Gianfranceschi asked the Italian scientist and inventor of wireless telegraphy, Guglielmo Marconi, to submit an initial plan of operation for the station and to organize meetings with the needed personnel for the project. Four days after the signing of the Lateran Treaty in 1929, Marconi received the final go-ahead to begin the station's construction. Pope Pius XI personally involved himself in every step and detail of Marconi's project. On September 21, 1930, Gianfranceschi was appointed as the first Director General of Vatican Radio.

On the afternoon of February 12, 1931, the station's new transmitters were given a final test. A short time later, trumpets sounded the arrival of the papal limousine. After being conducted into the generator room, Pius XI activated the transmitter's circuits. The station's first signals were sent out in Morse code. They typed out the words, "In nomine Domini, Amen, that is, In the Name of the Lord, amen!" After a brief introduction by Marconi, Pius XI stepped before the microphone at 4:49 PM and inaugurated the first international radio broadcast ever given by a pope. In Rome, wherever there was a radio, people crowded to listen to Pope Pius proclaim the universality of the gospel message. Loudspeakers in electric and appliance shops boomed out the message to assembled crowds. In London, 3,500 Catholics stood for hours in Westminster Cathedral to hear the pontiff's speech.

Vatican Radio soon became a sophisticated religious and political weapon in the papacy's struggle, during the 1930s, to reach its constituents under the fascist reign of Benito Mussolini. From its earliest days, the Society of Jesus (Jesuits) was given responsibility for operating Vatican Radio. By 1975, 27 Jesuits worked full-time in the station's language and regional sections, and broadcasts were being translated into 32 different languages. The duration of the daily transmissions was usually short by international standards, often lasting only 15 minutes or less. Beginning in 1957, the station augmented its religious broadcasts with a professional news service and sophisticated musical programs.

The broadcast service played a crucial role in sustaining Catholic populations in Eastern Europe during the Cold War and in communicating to Catholics in localities similarly cut off from the rest of the world. On the occasion of its 40th birthday, the station acknowledged this role:

> Today it is difficult to imagine how the Holy Father [i.e., the Pope] could fully accomplish his universal prophetic mission without it, so effectively does the radio fulfill the needs of the evangelical mandate. . . . Through the microphones

of Vatican Radio, every sector of the Church, in every part of the world, at whatsoever state of development, can communicate daily with all other sectors, edify them by its living example and inspired activity and, in time of trial, feel close by offering them consolation and hope.

Vatican Radio currently offers daily programming in 34 languages, including, among others, Armenian, Russian, Lithuanian, Latvian, Scandinavian, Latin, French, Polish, German, Byelorussian, Ukrainian, and Portuguese. The broadcasts are sent out on short and medium waves, satellites, and FM. The programming includes daily mass, news, live coverage of papal audiences, and the praying of the Angelus and Rosary with the pope. Father Pasquale Borgomeo, S.J., is the present Director General of the Station, which employs people from 60 nations.

SOURCES

Hale, Julian. *Radio Power: Propaganda and International Broadcasting.* Philadelphia: Temple University Press, 1975.

"Vatican Radio." World Wide Web site. http://www.wrn.org/vatican-radio/story.html (June 1996).

VERNON BROTHERS QUARTET
see: Christian Television Mission

VOICE OF CHRISTIAN YOUTH
see: Vic Eliason

THE VOICE OF HEALING
see: Gordon Lindsay

VOICE OF HOPE
first aired: 1973

A radio broadcast of High Adventure Ministries (HAM), *Voice of Hope* is heard in Latin America, the Middle East, and parts of Asia. HAM also sponsors medical care and various relief efforts to the poor and orphaned in its Asian and Middle Eastern broadcast zones. HAM's radio outreach is currently directed by George Otis from the ministry's headquarters in Simi Valley, California, located 30 miles northwest of Los Angeles. HAM was founded in 1973.

SOURCES

Melton, J. Gordon. *Directory of Religious Organizations in the United States.* 3d ed. Detroit: Gale Research, 1993.

VOICE OF MISSIONS
see: Abe Van Der Puy

VOICE OF POWER
see: Robert Schambach

VOICE OF PROPHECY

Courtesy: *Voice of Prophecy*

H. M. S. RICHARDS, SR.

Airing since the golden age of radio in the 1930s, *Voice of Prophecy* became the Seventh-Day Adventists' first successful radio broadcast ministry. Originally hosted by H. M. S. Richards, Sr., *Voice of Prophecy* was syndicated in 1942. It was one of a number of radio Bible-study programs that aired during this period. The show sought to promote a deeper under-standing of the Bible and evangelism and to help its Adventist listeners feel part of the greater Adventist movement.

In the 1960s, the Seventh-Day Adventists expanded into television broadcasting, with *Voice of Prophecy* appearing for a time in that medium. The Seventh-Day Adventists also began producing other television programs, including *It Is Written,* hosted by Mark Finley. *Voice of Prophecy*, which is now hosted by H. M. S. Richards, Jr., still airs daily over radio stations nationwide. The program has retained its Bible-study format and its Adventist end-time flavor.

SOURCES

Ward, Mark, Sr. *Air of Salvation: The Story of Christian Broadcasting*. Grand Rapids. MI: Baker Book House, 1994.

VOICE OF TANGIERS

see: Trans World Radio

VOICE OF THE ANDES

see: HCJB, Ecuador

W

C. M. WARD

see: Revivaltime

CLARA WARD

born: April 21, 1924, Philadelphia, Pennsylvania
died: January 16, 1973, Los Angeles, California

Clara Mae Ward, the first lady of gospel music, was the daughter of George Ward and Gertrude Mae Murphy. Gertrude had grown up in poor circumstances in South Carolina and had emerged as an accomplished mezzo-soprano soloist in her local church choir before moving to Philadelphia in the 1920s. The family Clara was born into was often penniless and on the verge of eviction from their place of residence. At times, her parents were even forced to stand on Philadelphia street corners waiting for day work offered by whites.

This changed in 1931, however, when Gertrude Ward experienced a spiritual vision in which she was commanded to go and sing. Within a few months, she and her two young daughters had begun a professional family gospel group, The Ward Trio. At first, Clara and her sister, Willa, played the piano as accompaniment to their mother's singing. Soon, however, Clara became the star, stroking the piano with her long fingers and belting out such gospel tunes as "On the Jericho Road There's Room for Just Two," and "I'm Gonna Work until the Day Is Done."

When Lightfoot Solomon Michaux, a popular black evangelist based in Washington, DC, began broadcasting *Radio Church of God* on radio station WJSV, he enlisted Clara Ward as a member of the program's 156-voice choir. When the CBS radio network bought WJSV, Michaux's program was picked up by 50 stations throughout the network. The estimated national radio audience of Michaux's Saturday evening show in 1934 was around 25 million, making him the most listened to African American of his time. His broadcasts were also carried on short-wave frequencies around the world. Clara Ward and Mahalia Jackson, the show's most prominent soloists, garnered national attention through their performances on *Radio Church of God*.

The Ward Trio became a headline attraction on the gospel circuit in 1943, following their much-applauded performance before the National Baptist Convention USA in Philadelphia. By 1948, the group had added two new members and recast itself as the Famous Ward Singers. Henrietta Waddy, one of the new singers, was a middle-aged Philadelphian whose voice bore an uncanny resemblance to blues singer Ma Rainey. The other newcomer was Marion Williams, a teenage soloist from Miami whose vocal range and power had caused a stir in her Florida home church. Williams's growling bottom notes and floating high soprano became the group's trademark sound. Over time, the Ward Singers would add such prominent female soloists as Martha Bass, Frances Steadman, and Kitty Parham to its ranks.

The Famous Ward Singers started recording in the late 1940s and scored a big hit with W. Herbert Brewster's "Surely God Is Able." Clara Ward accompanied the group on piano and brought live performances to their climax with her beautiful alto renditions of such Isaac Watts hymns as "The Day Is Past and Gone," "The Fountain," and "Amazing Grace." Ward's brilliant phrasing and delivery of these hymns on solo recordings during this period led to her selection as "best gospel singer" in a newspaper poll. Some reviewers dubbed her the "Queen of the Moaners."

In the early 1950s, the Famous Ward Singers toured the country with Cecil L. Franklin, a renowned evangelist-singer and the father of Aretha Franklin. The younger Franklin became Ward's escort and would later copy Ward's style. Franklin openly acknowledges Ward as a major source of inspiration for her subsequent career.

As the 1950s progressed, the Famous Ward Singers became the hottest gospel group in the country. Their recordings for Savoy featured exceptional solo singing, Brewster's fine songwriting, and Ward's innovative arrangements. Over an 11-year period the group packed more venues and had more hits than any other gospel group before them. "Surely God Is Able" alone sold 1 million copies, which at the time was a record for a gospel recording. Ward's annual income is reported to have been close to $250,000.

In the late 1950s, Ward began to exercise more artistic control over her group. She got rid of the homespun choir robes of the 1930s and 1940s and introduced flamboyant wigs and gowns and bare-backed slippers for stage performances. These innovations helped make gospel music popular in nightclubs and theaters.

After a 1955 show at the Apollo Theater in Harlem, the group was asked to join the Big Gospel Cavalcade of 1957, a one-month, nonstop touring show featuring the Ward Singers and other well-known gospel groups. The year was capped by an appearance on an all-gospel afternoon program at the Newport (Rhode Island) Jazz Festival in 1957. This performance was significant because it was the group's first appearance before a predominantly white audience. Around this time Ward and her mother established Ward's House of Music, a music publishing business that included the Brewster catalogue. The business also produced souvenir books that featured restored photos of both group and family.

A new phase in Ward's career began when Marion Williams and the other singers in the group quit en masse. The main grievances were probably economic: Ward and her mother kept a large share of the group's earnings for themselves and required the other singers to pay part of their substandard salaries back to them in rent. A succession of talented singers, including Thelma Jackson, Jessie Tucker, and Carrie Williams would sing with the group over the next few years. Except for a successful Scandinavian tour in 1959, however, the group's popularity declined rapidly.

Following her mother's retirement in 1961, Ward decided to market the Ward Singers as a nightclub act. The group played the Village Vanguard in New York City and then signed a lucrative Las Vegas contract that guaranteed them $5,000 weekly over a 40-week schedule. The contract was said to be the longest consecutive booking by a performing troupe in the history of Las Vegas. Ward's fame as a nightclub artist grew during the 1960s. Her group changed its name to the Clara Ward Singers and played such prominent venues as Radio City Music Hall in New York City. Ward also starred in Langston Hughes's ill-fated Broadway play, *Tambourines to Glory*, and worked for Disneyland. A more successful stint on Broadway took place with Hughes's *God's Trombones*, in which Ward costarred with Louis Gossett, Jr.

Ward's shift of venue from churches to nightclubs and theaters opened her to persistent criticism from gospel purists. She defended herself, however, and insisted that black dresses and sad faces were not the hallmark of all authentic religious expression. She also pointed out that alcoholic beverages were never served during her group's club and theater performances. Ward drew more criticism by adding such popular "message" tunes as "Born Free" and "Zippety Doo-Dah" to her performing repertoire.

Ward was an important entertainer in early religious radio and went on to bring gospel music to an international audience. In her later years she made triumphant tours of Europe and Japan. Her Clara Ward Singers were honored in 1967 by becoming the first gospel group to perform at the Philadelphia Academy of Music.

Ward suffered the first of several debilitating strokes in the late 1960s. After returning to her nightclub act for a brief period, she died of a stroke in 1973. Ward was only 48 years of age.

See also Lightfoot Solomon Michaux

SOURCES

"Clara Ward." *Newsweek*, January 29, 1973.

"Glamour Girl of Gospel Singers." *Ebony*, October, 1957.

Heilbut, Tony. *The Gospel Sound: Good News and Bad Times.* New York: Simon & Schuster, 1971.

"Singing for Sinners." *Newsweek*, September 2, 1957.

THE WESLEYAN HOUR
established: 1975

The Wesleyan Hour, a radio Bible-study program hosted by Norman G. Wilson, began as an outreach of the Methodist Church. The program is heard in English, Russian, and Spanish around the world and is represented by Walter Bennett Communications. Wilson celebrated his radio ministry's twentieth anniversary of national syndication in 1995. The show is taped in Indianapolis, Indiana.

WEWN, VANDIVER, ALABAMA
established: 1992

Worldwide Catholic Radio WEWN is the radio apostolate of the Eternal Word Network, an educational and inspirational broadcasting ministry for Roman Catholics. The radio ministry operates the largest privately owned short-wave radio station in the world. Located in Vandiver, Alabama, WEWN has been covering 90 percent of the world with 24-hour Catholic programming since 1992. Among the programs transmitted by the station are Mother Angelica's *Holy Hour, Mother Angelica Live, Stations of the Cross, Sunday Mass from Our Lady of the Angels Monastery, St. Joseph's Radio Presents, Life Issues*, and Father Ken Roberts's *The Family*.

The station has plans to expand its broadcasting range to include both AM and FM radio frequencies. Specifically, it intends to transmit its short-wave programs, formatted for rebroadcast on AM or FM radio, from its studio in Vandiver to the satellite uplink facility in Irondale, Alabama. It also plans to transmit its signal on both the Galaxy 1R (for North America) and Intelsat 601 (for South America, Africa, and Europe) satellites by the end of 1995. The station is managed by Richard W. Jones.

See also Eternal Word Television Network

SOURCES

"WEWN." World Wide Web site. http://www.crnet.org/wewn.html (December, 1995).

WHAT MAKES YOU TICK?

A production of Paraclete Press, *What Makes You Tick?* is a Christian talk show telecast throughout the United States. Paraclete Press is an ecumenical Christian publisher that produces and distributes music, religious literature, and video tapes. The company is headquartered in Orleans, Cape Cod, Massachusetts.

SOURCES

Melton, J. Gordon. *Directory of Religious Organizations in the United States.* 3d ed. Detroit: Gale Research, 1993.

ALMA WHITE

born: June 16, 1862, Lewis County, Kentucky
died: June 26, 1946, Zarephath, New Jersey

Alma Bridwell White was the founder of the Pillar of Fire Church and an early pioneer of religious radio. During the 1920s, she purchased radio stations KPOF in Denver and WAWZ in Zarephath, New Jersey, and began a broadcasting ministry that aired her conservative theological and political views. Her church later purchased a third station, WAKW, in Cincinnati. All three stations were still on the air into the mid-1990s.

White was born into a poor Kentucky family during the Civil War. She and her 10 siblings worked in their father's tannery as children. White escaped this life of drudgery by enrolling in Vanceberg Seminary and earning a teacher's certificate. After working at a mountain school where classes were held only three months of the year, she earned a bachelor of arts degree at Millersburg Female College in 1881. This degree subsequently enabled her to take teaching positions in Paris, Kentucky, and on the Montana frontier.

White received her early religious training from her mother, who was a devout Methodist. At a revival meeting led by William Godbey in 1878, White gave her life to Christ and professed a call to the ministry. With the encouragement of her pastor, she sought to marry a minister and fulfill her calling by working as a minister's wife. She met and married Kent White, a ministerial student, in Montana in December 1887. A short time later, the couple moved to Denver, where Kent attended the University of Denver. For the next few years, White supported her husband's ministry and took a leadership role in his congregation's worship.

A new phase in White's life began in 1893, when she experienced the baptism of the Holy Spirit. This sanctifying "second work of grace" emboldened White to overcome her "man-fearing spirit" and begin preaching to her husband's Methodist Episcopal congregation. Methodist church officials opposed this more active ministerial role for White and criticized the emotional outbursts that occurred in her meetings.

With her husband's support, White withdrew from the Methodist Church and began conducting revivals at independent holiness association camp meetings. In addition to preaching at these meetings, White and her husband organized urban missions in Colorado, Montana, and Wyoming. These missions were modeled after the early Methodist societies that had sprung up within the Anglican Church. After a brief period of affiliation with the Metropolitan Church Association, White incorporated her missions in 1901 as the Methodist Pentecostal Union. In an unprecedented step, White became the church's first bishop in 1910. The name of the ministry's periodical, *Pillar of Fire*, was taken as the church's new appellation in 1917.

Kent White assisted in his wife's new ministry until 1909, when he embraced Pentecostalism. Because of his wife's refusal to accept the doctrine of speaking in tongues, he withdrew from her church and moved to England. There he gained a legal separation from his wife and joined a British Pentecostal congregation, the Apostolic Faith Church. Alma White's church continued to flourish during this period. She toured the United States and England, conducting evangelistic revivals, establishing branch congregations, and publishing books. A tract of donated land in Zarephath, New Jersey, became the Pillar of Fire's international headquarters in 1907. It was there that White founded Alma White College in 1921, the first of eight church-sponsored schools. At both this institution and a college in Denver, White purchased radio stations and started a pioneering broadcasting ministry. The ministry's programming promoted White's millennial holiness religious views, as well as her ideas concerning moral renewal, spiritual healing, and women's roles in Christian ministry.

The doctrine of White's church was essentially Wesleyan holiness, with an acceptance of the Methodist Twenty-five Articles of Religion. Pillar of Fire embraced spiritual healing, premillennialism, vegetarianism, and pacifism, as well as the right of women to participate in the ministry. White was an early advocate of women's rights, and she actively encouraged women to join the ministry. Moreover, her church published the periodical *Women's Chains* for a number of years.

White gained notoriety during the 1920s when she became a strong advocate of the Ku Klux Klan. In her book, *Guardians of Liberty*, she praised the Klan as a divinely appointed agent of social order. She was first introduced to the Klan when it appeared at her church in Bound Brook, New Jersey, and helped prevent an attack by an alleged "Roman Catholic mob." White embraced the Klan's virulent anti-Catholicism throughout the decade of the 1920s, a stance from which her church was eventually forced to dissociate itself.

During her lifetime, White edited several magazines and authored over 35 books, including several volumes of poetry. At her death in 1946, she had established the Pillar of Fire as a national church with over 4,000 members.

White's two sons, Ray B. White and Arthur K. White, ran the Pillar of Fire between 1946 and 1976. The present bishop and general superintendent is Dr. Donald J. Wolfram. The church operates Belleview Junior College and Bible Seminary in Westminster, Colorado, and Pillar of Fire Bible Seminary in Zarephath. Other schools have been established in Cincinnati, Ohio, Jacksonville, Florida, Los Angeles, California, and London, England. The church's 56 foreign congregations are located in Great Britain, Yugoslavia, Malawi, Liberia, Nigeria, Spain, and the Philippines. There are 20 functioning congregations in the United States.

WAWZ-FM, Zarephath, celebrated its 65th year of continuous ministry in 1996. The station, which serves the tri-state region of New Jersey, New York, and Pennsylvania, is currently under the leadership of Allen Lewis Lewicki. National Religious Broadcasters awarded WAWZ-FM its Radio Station of the Year award in 1996.

SOURCES

Melton, J. Gordon. *Biographical Dictionary of American Cult and Sect Leaders*. New York: Garland, 1986.

Reid, Daniel G., et al., eds. *Dictionary of Christianity in America*. Downers Grove, IL: InterVarsity Press, 1990.

White, Alma. *Guardians of Liberty.* 2 vols. Zarephath, NJ: Pillar of Fire, 1943.

———. *Hymns and Poems*. Zarephath, NJ: Pillar of Fire, 1946.

———. *The New Testament Church*. Zarephath, NJ: Pillar of Fire, 1929.

———. *The Story of My Life*. 5 vols. Zarephath, NJ: Pillar of Fire, 1919–34.

———. *Why I Do Not Eat Meat*. Zarephath, NJ: Pillar of Fire, 1938.

White, Arthur Kent. *Some White Family History*. Denver: Pillar of Fire, 1948.

THE WHOLE TRUTH
see: Sherrod Johnson

DAVID WILKERSON
born: May 19, 1931, Hammond, Indiana

The popular Pentecostal evangelist David Wilkerson was raised in a religious home—both his parents, Kenneth and Ann Wilkerson, were Pentecostal ministers. After attending Central Bible Institute in Springfield, Missouri, from 1951 to 1952, Wilkerson pastored a small Assemblies of God church in Philipsburg, Pennsylvania. During his tenure, he produced a religious television program that aired regionally.

In early 1958, Wilkerson read an article in *Time* magazine about the murder trial of seven New York City teen gang members. After prayerful reflection, he decided to go to New York to build an evangelical ministry for street gangs. Though thwarted from speaking at the trial of the gang members by a local judge—who ejected him from the courtroom—Wilkerson gained instant notoriety, appearing on the front page of the *New York Daily News*. Wilkerson's rejection by civil authorities led to his acceptance among gang members, and he soon began witnessing on the streets of New York. Shortly thereafter, he founded Teen Challenge, an organization which focused exclusively on evangelizing urban street gangs.

In 1963, Wilkerson published *The Cross and the Switchblade*, a best-selling book that documented his work among gang members. In 1972, the book would become a hit movie, starring Pat Boone as Wilkerson. Since a great many of his converts were drug and alcohol addicts, Wilkerson founded a home to help these teens and young adults make the transition to a sober life off the streets. By 1966, this home had expanded to include the Teen Challenge Bible Institute, which aimed at training reformed gang members for Christian ministry. In 1972, Wilkerson founded World Challenge to assist in ministering to gang members nationally.

Throughout the late 1970s and 1980s, Wilkerson was a popular guest on Christian radio and television programs such as *The 700 Club* and *Praise the Lord*. In 1987, Wilkerson resigned his ordination from the Assemblies of God, founding his own non-denominational ministry, Times Square Church in New York City. Although Wilkerson is not currently involved in radio or television broadcasting, his sermons at Times Square Church are recorded and played on occasion on Christian radio stations. The congregation now includes models, actors, heiresses, and corporate executives among its membership, as well as prostitutes, street people, and substance abusers.

In addition to *The Cross and the Switchblade*, Wilkerson has written over 20 books, including *Hey, Preach, You're Coming Through!* (1968), *The Untapped Generation* (1971), and *The Vision* (1974). The latter publication recounts a dramatic angelic visitation during which Wilkerson reportedly received a vision of the endtimes.

See also Pat Boone

SOURCES

Billy Graham Center Archives, Wheaton College, Wheaton, Illinois.

Burgess, Stanley M., and Gary B. McGee, eds. *Dictionary of Pentecostal and Charismatic Movements*. Grand Rapids, MI: Zondervan, 1988.

Melton, J. Gordon. *Religious Leaders of America*. Detroit: Gale Research, 1991.

Stone, Jon R. *A Guide to the End of the World: Popular Eschatology in America*. New York: Garland, 1993.

JOHN WILLKE
born: April 5, 1925, Maria Stein, Ohio

Over the past 10 years, John Charles Willke has established himself throughout the United States as an expert on Pro-Life issues through his Christian radio ministries. He began his broadcasting career in 1984 as the featured speaker on the National Right to Life Committee's radio outreach, *Pro-Life Perspective*. Willke now broadcasts a daily five-minute program called *Life Issues*. This program is produced by Life Issues Institute, Inc., whose mission is to serve the educational needs of the Pro-Life movement. The institute is headquartered in Cincinnati, Ohio.

Willke is the son of Gerard Thomas Willke and Marie Wuennemann. He was married to the former Barbara Hiltz in 1948, the same year he earned his doctor of medicine degree from the University of Cincinnati. Following two years as a medical resident at Good Samaritan Hospital in Cincinnati, he began a private practice that lasted until 1988. Willke served as cochair of Cincinnati Right to Life between 1970 and 1987 and as president of Ohio Right to Life between 1975 and 1980. He was a member of the National Right to Life Committee between 1980 and 1991 and participated in the International Right to Life Federation between 1985 and 1991.

Willke has been a significant spokesperson for Right to Life issues on such national television forums as *The Phil Donahue Show, 60*

Minutes, *Good Morning America*, the *Today Show*, *Crossfire*, *Larry King Live*, *The 700 Club*, and *Geraldo Rivera*. His written works include *The Wonder of Sex* (1964), *Marriage* (1971), *Handbook on Abortion* (1971), *Abortion and Slavery* (1984), and *Sex and Love* (1991).

See also *Pro-Life Perspective*

SOURCES

Who's Who in Religion. Chicago: Marquis Who's Who, 1976.

NORMAN G. WILSON
see: The Wesleyan Hour

WMBI, CHICAGO
established: 1925

In 1925, the Moody Bible Institute—founded in 1889 in Chicago, Illinois, by the influential fundamentalist Dwight L. Moody—began broadcasting over radio station WMBI. The institute was in its third decade of operation when its leaders decided to utilize radio as part of their evangelistic enterprise. The institute began to raise funds for this purpose in 1925 and gained its entry onto the airwaves when two of its students volunteered to offer musical entertainment for a local Chicago broadcast. This offering led to a regular Sunday evening gospel music program produced by the institute and eventually to a two-hour evening program combining Bible lectures and music that was broadcast six days a week.

In July 1925, the institute received its federal license to broadcast over its own transmitters as station WMBI. Unfortunately, a competing station began broadcasting over the same frequency during this time and WMBI's signal was disrupted. The station's manager, Henry C. Crowell, who had an engineering degree from Yale, lobbied strongly with the Federal Communications Commission (FCC) in Washington, DC, to remedy this situation. Although he was not altogether successful, Crowell did learn about the forthcoming technical requirements the FCC was planning to institute in 1927 and was able to prepare WMBI's technical facilities so that they met the new standards.

Wendel Loveless, a composer of religious songs, became WMBI's first program director, announcer, pianist, and vocalist. He was largely responsible for the station's excellent educational programming. One of the first of these programs was a Bible-study series taught by James Gray, the institute's president. This broadcast class began with 75 students listening at home for their instruction. This program was the precursor to other programs of daily religious instruction such as *Radio School of the Bible* and *Bible College of the Air*. *Stories of Great Christians* was another pioneering effort from this period. This popular series would become the longest running dramatic series on radio.

Moody Bible Institute slowly expanded its electronic broadcasting outreach. By 1979, the institute owned and operated eight radio stations and was continuing to distribute its programs to other Christian broadcasters. The range of this programming included music, drama, children's shows, programs for women, Bible studies geared to different age groups, and reviews of current books. The institute's most respected radio show (and the ninth rated religious weekly program during the late 1980s) continues to be *Moody Presents*, a half-hour program of inspirational talks and religious music. The show is aired on hundreds of religious and secular radio stations worldwide.

WMBI has spawned a number of religious radio stations around the country. The first of these was WCRF-FM in Cleveland, Ohio. Others stations on the Moody Radio Network, established officially in 1958, include WMBI-FM, in Chicago, WDLM in East Moline, Illinois, WMBW in Chattanooga, Tennessee, KMBI-AM and FM in Spokane, Washington, and WGNB and WKES in St. Petersburg, Florida. The network's costs are met through individual listener contributions.

An attempt to limit the use of FM's educational band by religious broadcasters occurred in 1974, when Jeremy Lansman and Lorenzo Milan, two secular broadcasters, filed a petition with the FCC following their unsuccessful bid for a station license in Spokane. Their petition attacked the programming of WMBI as

a single, long diatribe for the Moody world view— a full-time, ongoing, nonstop, endless, open-ended 24-hours, seven-days-a-week, 52-week-year, year-after-year commercial for the Moody Bible Institute, their pin-hole view of humanity, and their dank view of the Divine."

Following a massive mail campaign opposing the petition that amounted to over 700,000 letters by August 1975, the FCC ruled in favor of continuing FM educational religious broadcasting. Amazingly, the letters kept coming, even after an organized effort was made to inform the public that FM religious broadcasting was no longer in danger. Finally, in 1978, the volume of mail dropped off, but not before 9 million letters had been received by the FCC.

WMBI has kept at least 20 programs in national syndication since 1945. In addition to those programs mentioned above, the station produces the five-minute news commentary *Christian Perspective on the News;* the children's program *Ranger Bill;* and the musical show *Songs in the Night.*

SOURCES

Armstrong, Ben. *The Electric Church.* Nashville: Thomas Nelson, 1979.

Erickson, Hal. *Religious Radio and Television in the United States, 1921–1991.* Jefferson, NC: McFarland, 1992.

WOMAN TO WOMAN
first aired: March 1995

Woman to Woman is a recent addition to religious radio that aspires to broadcast "a message of Christian encouragement on life's daily challenges." The weekly 30-minute program is sponsored by Lutheran Hour Ministries and focuses on pressing women's issues. Since its first airing in March of 1995, the program has been picked up by radio stations in 16 states across the country. Phyllis Wallace is the show's host.

See also *The Lutheran Hour*

WORD OF FAITH
see: Robert Tilton

WORD OF LIFE HOUR
first aired: 1940

Word of Life Hour, an evangelistic radio program geared toward youth, was created in the early 1940s and hosted by fundamentalist Jack Wyrtzen. Wyrtzen was a well-known youth evangelist who held massive rallies in New York City and other urban centers during and after World War II. It was Wyrtzen who voiced the strongest opposition to Billy Graham's successful 1955 New York City crusade, which had sought to be ecumenically sponsored. *Word of Life Hour* is produced by the Word of Life Association, headquartered in Schroon Lake, New York.

On the air into the 1990s, *Word of Life Hour* emphasizes youth spirituality and encourages teens to adhere to traditional Christian morals. Wyrtzen continues to host the program and still devotes much of his energies to worldwide evangelism.

SOURCES

Marsden, George M. *Reforming Fundamentalism: Fuller Seminary and the New Evangelicalism.* Grand Rapids, MI: Eerdmans, 1987.

Ward, Mark, Sr. *Air of Salvation: The Story of Christian Broadcasting.* Grand Rapids, MI: Baker Book House, 1994.

WORD TO RUSSIA
established: 1972

Word to Russia is an independent evangelical Protestant organization that beams short-wave radio programs to areas within the former Soviet Union. Founded in 1972, Word to Russia augments its evangelistic efforts through the distribution of religious literature and the direct support of indigenous Protestant churches. The ministry's headquarters are located in Sacramento, California.

SOURCES

Melton, J. Gordon. *Directory of Religious Organizations in the United States.* 3d ed. Detroit: Gale Research,1993.

WORLD CHANGERS RADIO
first aired: 1995

World Changers Radio is a daily 15-minute program whose mission is to teach Christians how to lead nonbelievers to Christ. The show's content is based on the principles developed by evangelist Bill Bright during his 40 years of successful ministry. Bright is the founder and president of Campus Crusade for Christ, an international evangelistic ministry. The ministry has trained millions of people through the use of Bright's booklet "Have You Heard of the Four Spiritual Laws" and his film *Jesus*. Along with Steve Douglass, Campus Crusade's executive vice president, Bright cohosts the show and provides "solid Bible training and guidance" designed to help listeners make a positive difference in their neighborhoods, cities, and homes. In late 1995, the program could be heard Monday through Friday on 51 stations around the country.

See also Bill Bright

SOURCES

"Campus Crusade for Christ: World Changers." World Wide Web site. http://www.mdalink.com/worldchangers/index.html (1995).

WORLD EVANGELISM
see: Morris Cerullo

WORLD MISSIONS FAR CORNERS
established: 1958

Founded as World Missions, World Missions Far Corners is an independent evangelical organization that sends missionaries to various parts of Asia (Hong Kong, India, the Philippines, South Korea), Africa (Ghana, South Africa), Latin America (Bolivia, Ecuador, Mexico, Peru), the United Kingdom, and Jamaica. The organization engages in evangelism, church planting, support of lay leaders, and radio broadcasting. The ministry's headquarters are located in Long Beach, California,

SOURCES

Melton, J. Gordon. *Directory of Religious Organizations in the United States.* 3d ed. Detroit: Gale Research, 1993.

WORLD OUTREACH
established: 1932

An independent Protestant missionary support organization, World Outreach provides a variety of services to evangelical missions around the world. These services include correspondence courses, literature distribution, religious educational programs, and a radio broadcast service. World Outreach's offices are in McGregor, Texas, near Waco.

SOURCES

Melton, J. Gordon. *Directory of Religious Organizations in the United States.* 3d ed. Detroit: Gale Research, 1993.

WORLD RADIO MISSIONARY FELLOWSHIP
see: Abe Van der Puy

THE WORLD, THE WORD AND YOU BROADCAST
see: Dennis Finnan

THE WORLD TOMORROW
see: Herbert W. Armstrong

WORLD VISION
see: W. Stanley Mooneyham

J. ELWIN WRIGHT
born: 1890, West Corinth, Vermont
died: 1972, Rumney, New Hampshire

An independent evangelist and executive director of the New England Fellowship, James Elwin Wright grew up in Vermont, the son of Freewill Baptist minister Joel Wright and his wife, Mary Goodwin. Though fairly well established as a Baptist minister, the elder Wright became increasingly interested in the holiness teachings of John Wesley. By 1892, Joel Wright had withdrawn from membership in the Freewill Baptists and become a minister in the Free Methodist Church.

In 1896, Joel Wright moved his family to New Hampshire and began to hold tent meetings. He founded the First Fruit Harvesters Association in 1897 and the Christian community "Har-vestville," near Rumney, New Hampshire, in 1900. The aim of the community was to unite evangelicals throughout the region for common service work. At age 15, Elwin Wright went into partnership with his father and traveled throughout the region.

Distressed by the plight of abused and neglected children he saw during his travels with his father, Elwin Wright helped established a home for distressed children in 1909. This mission, known as Bethesda Home, continued until 1935. After founding Bethesda Home, Wright became increasingly active in the concerns of children, chairing the legislative committee of the New Hampshire State Conference of Social Work and helping to pass the Mother's Aid bill in 1915.

In 1924, Wright became leader of the First Fruit Harvesters Association, pledging to return the association to its original mandate, i.e., the uniting of evangelicals. Over the next several years, Wright expanded the association's summer conference to include groups from Canada and a dozen states. In 1929, the first annual summer Conference for Pastors and Christian Workers, sponsored by First Fruit Harvesters, was held at Rumney. By 1932, this conference had become known as the New England Fellowship. The conference's official motto came from St. Augustine: "In essentials, unity; in non-essentials, liberty; in all things, charity."

In 1942, Wright, his associates at the New England Fellowship, and a number of evangelical leaders and popular radio preachers throughout the United States founded the interdenominational National Association of Evangelicals (NAE), an alternative organization for evangelicals dissatisfied with the liberal-leaning Federal Council of Churches.

In February 1931, while wintering in Miami, Florida, Wright began working in radio at the invitation of station WQAM. He recorded a number of musical and inspirational spots, which aired in Miami, with Homer Grimes, "Daddy" Hall, and Kathryn and Elizabeth Evans. Elizabeth Evans would later become a missionary with the World Radio Missionary

Fellowship. In 1933, the New England Fellowship launched its own radio ministry, forming a polished music group that became known as the Radio Ensemble. Wright toured throughout the country with the ensemble in 1937 and 1938.

Wright's involvement with radio broadcasting deepened when the Mutual network, at the urging of the Federal Council of Churches (FCC), announced in 1943 that it would restrict the sale of radio airtime for religious programs. In response, the National Association of Evangelicals appointed a committee on religious broadcasting with the purpose of representing the concerns of conservative evangelical radio ministers.

Later that year, Wright spoke before the annual conference of the Institute of Education by Radio (IER), which supported the proposed changes because of the fiscal abuses of some radio evangelists. Wright soundly defended the ethics of the majority of religious broadcasters. In spite of his efforts to persuade the delegates otherwise, however, the IER pressed forward its ban on paid religious broadcasts.

When it appeared that independent action would be of little effect, a special session of the 1944 NAE annual meeting was convened by William Ayer with the express purpose of forming a national religious broadcasting association to set down professional and ethical standards for religious broadcasters. More than 100 broadcasters attended the meeting and approved a set of strict broadcasting guidelines. These guidelines laid the foundation for National Religious Broadcasters, which drew up its charter in September 1944. Due to these and other efforts, the FCC's attempt to monopolize air-time for religious broadcasts was eventually thwarted, and independent evangelicals were able to continue and expand their broadcasting ministries.

Throughout the remainder of his long life, Wright continued to lead the New England Fellowship, resigning as its president in 1950. He also continued to participate in the summer conferences at Rumney and kept close ties with the NAE.

SOURCES

Evans, Elizabeth. *The Wright Vision: The Story of the New England Fellowship*. Lanham, MD: United Press of America, 1991.

Ward, Mark, Sr. *Air of Salvation: The Story of Christian Broadcasting*. Grand Rapids, MI: Baker Book House, 1994.

Y

YOUNG PEOPLE'S CHURCH
OF THE AIR
first aired: 1931

Beginning in the early 1930s, Percy Crawford, a respected evangelical youth minister, educator, and preacher began broadcasting a religious music and variety show from Flourtown, Pennsylvania. The program, *Young People's Church of the Air*, featured a glee club and was one of the earliest evangelical radio ministries to reach a national radio audience. In time, the show would be heard on over 600 stations nationwide, 450 of which belonged to the Mutual and ABC radio networks.

Crawford, who had been drawn to a youth ministry early in his career, inaugurated Saturday night evangelical rallies in 1930 that would later develop into the Youth for Christ movement. In 1950, Percy renamed his radio program *Youth on the March* and moved into Sunday evening television. This live show aired on the ABC-TV network until May 1952 and on the DuMont television network from October 1952 until April 1953. *Youth on the March*, which featured lively young musicians and speakers in an entertainment format, would become the launching pad for a number of top executives in religious broadcasting. At the height of its popularity in 1951, the program's national audience was estimated to number in the millions.

See also Percy Crawford

SOURCES

Armstrong, Ben. *The Electric Church*. Nashville: Thomas Nelson, 1979.

Reid, Daniel G., et al., eds. *Dictionary of Christianity in America*. Downers Grove, IL: InterVarsity Press, 1990.

Ward, Mark, Sr. *Air of Salvation: The Story of Christian Broadcasting*. Manassas: National Religious Broadcasters, 1994.

YOUR STORY HOUR
first aired: 1949

Your Story Hour is a nondenominational broadcasting ministry for children. Since its founding in 1949, *Your Story Hour* has been producing children's stories in English and Spanish based on biblical and nonbiblical character-building themes for radio broadcast throughout the world. *Your Story Hour* also offers Bible correspondence courses, a children's magazine, and video and audiocassettes of stories. *Your Story Hour* is headquartered in Berrien Springs, Michigan.

SOURCES

Melton, J. Gordon. *Directory of Religious Organizations in the United States*. 3d ed. Detroit: Gale Research, 1993.

YOUTH FOR CHRIST
see: Billy Graham; Jay Kesler; Torrey Johnson

Z

Z MUSIC TELEVISION
established: 1993

Z Music Television is a rapidly growing Christian alternative to MTV, a music-video cable television station. It features the same musical styles as its secular counterpart, including pop, rock, rap, and heavy metal. However, the content of the lyrics of Z Music Television's videos are unabashedly Christian. The Nashville-based network got off the ground in 1993. Within two years it was being offered in 17 million cable households. The network reaches another 13 million households at least part of the day on regular broadcast stations. By the year 2000, the network hopes to be available to 30 million cable households.

Pitched as the alternative to MTV for the approximately 50 million adults who listen to Christian music, the network features such hit Christian artists and groups as Amy Grant, Sandi Patti, Margaret Becker, Gary Chapman, Petra, DC Talk, Steve Green, Michael Card, Susan Ashton, Christine Dent, Kim Boyce, Bob Carlisle, Seneca, Ken Hollaway, Kathy Troccoli, CeCe Winans, and Steven Curtis Chapman.

The network's president, Ken Yates, believes that music and television are powerful influences on youth. His advice to concerned parents is to not give the network too great a seal of approval. "What the parents ought to do is to take a good look at it, realize its content, and then just keep quiet." Graham Barnard is the network's programming manager and the host of *Z Buzz*, a program segment that features interviews with artists and news from the Christian music business. He maintains that the network will not air any videos with excessive sex or violence. "Any illicit activity, if it's too libertine, we don't put it on the air. . . . The videos that we play on Z have a very high standard, both the visual and lyrical content." Barnard believes that if young people are exposed to hip Christian music that is not parent-approved, many will gravitate to contemporary Christian artists and groups.

One of the network's more popular shows is called *The Brimstone Chronicles*. The program features a long-haired host who introduces Christian heavy metal and grunge groups from an industrial club set.

SOURCES

"Christian Z Music Offers All the Sound and Fury of MTV." *Daytona Beach News-Journal*, August 26, 1995.

ZERO 1960
first aired: 1957

Zero 1960 was a pro-American, Catholic religious television program that aired from 1957 to the end of 1960. Blending Cold War politics and apocalyptic prediction, *Zero 1960* gave vent to the fear of Communist world domination. It argued that unless halted by vigilant Christian action, a cataclysmic event brought on by godless Communism would occur sometime during 1960. The program's run in syndication lasted until January 1, 1961.

SOURCES

Erickson, Hal. *Religious Radio and Television in the United States, 1921–1991*. Jefferson, NC: McFarland, 1992.

THOMAS ZIMMERMAN

born: March 26, 1912, Indianapolis, Indiana
died: January 2, 1991, Springfield, Missouri

Courtesy: National Religious Broadcasters

The general superintendent of the Assemblies of God from 1959 to 1985, Thomas Fletcher Zimmerman was born into a Methodist home. After his mother, Carrie Kenagy Zimmerman, experienced healing from tuberculosis in 1919 through a Pentecostal minister, the Zimmermans affiliated with a local Pentecostal church. It was about this same time that the young Thomas Zimmerman experienced a conversion to Christ. He received the baptism of the Holy Spirit four years later at the age of 11 and became a leader of his Sunday school class. While still a teenager, Zimmerman decided to pursue a ministerial vocation with the intention of becoming a missionary to China.

After high school, Zimmerman attended Indiana University for a year. Financial pressures, however, forced him to quit school and find gainful employment. In 1928, Zimmerman became assistant pastor of an Assemblies of God church in Indianapolis. He married Elizabeth Price, the head pastor's daughter, in 1933. In 1936, following his ordination to the Christian ministry of the Assemblies of God, Zimmerman served a number of pastorates throughout the Midwest, including Kokomo, Indiana (1933), Harrodsburg, Indiana (1934), South Bend, Indiana (1935–1939), Granite City, Illinois (1939–1942), Springfield, Missouri (1943–1947), and Cleveland, Ohio (1951–1952).

In 1945, Zimmerman helped launch the radio department of the Assemblies of God, which he directed for a brief time. From 1946 to 1949, Zimmerman became the narrator of the weekly radio program *Sermons in Song* (later renamed *Revivaltime*). This long-running program was hosted by C. M. Ward from 1953 until Ward's retirement in 1978. It was the earliest regular radio broadcast of the Assemblies of God. Zimmerman's ministry with *Sermons in Song* earned him the distinguished Churchill award of the National Religious Broadcasters for outstanding achievement in 1947. He shared the honor with Myron Boyd of the *Light and Life Hour*.

Zimmerman also was among those who founded the National Religious Broadcasters in September 1944, serving on its first board of directors and later as chairman, from 1954 to 1956. It is Zimmerman who is credited with having pointed out the limitations of "sustaining-time" broadcasts in achieving the evangelistic aims of independent religious broadcasters and with having encouraged evangelicals to pursue paid-time broadcasting as an alternative.

From 1952 to 1959, Zimmerman served as assistant general superintendent for the Assemblies of God. He was appointed superintendent in 1959, a position he retained until 1985. Throughout his long and successful tenure, Zimmerman worked to bring the Assemblies of God into the evangelical mainstream. During this same period, Zimmerman served on the executive board of the National Association of Evangelicals (NAE) and was later elected the association's president, becoming the first Pentecostal ever to hold that position. In this capacity he helped maintain the strong affiliation the Assemblies of God enjoyed with the NAE since joining it as a charter member in 1942.

In 1987, Zimmerman was inducted into the National Religious Broadcasters Hall of Fame. He died in Springfield, Missouri, just two months before his seventy-ninth birthday.

See also *Revivaltime*; National Religious Broadcasters

SOURCES

Melton, J. Gordon. *Religious Leaders of America.* Detroit, MI: Gale Research, 1991.

Murch, James DeForest. *Cooperation Without Compromise: A History of the National Association of Evangelicals.* Grand Rapids, MI: Eerdmans, 1956.

Ward, Mark, Sr. *Air of Salvation: The Story of Christian Broadcasting.* Grand Rapids, MI: Baker Book House, 1994.

JOHN ZOLLER

born: 1888
died: 1979, Belmont, Michigan

Courtesy: National Religious Broadcasters

John Zoller's greatest contributions to religious radio were his long-running program *Christ for Everyone* and his work in establishing the National Religious Broadcasters (NRB) in April 1944.

Zoller began his radio career in 1922, when his religious program, *Christ for Everyone*, aired for the first time over WWJ, Detroit, Michigan. The broadcast took place during a violent thunderstorm that should have blocked its reception by crystal receivers. In spite of the storm, one listener wrote in to testify that Zoller's broadcast homily signaled a turning point in his life. This inspired Zoller to fully pursue a broadcasting ministry. As the evangelist recounted later, "At once I asked God to open the door so I could broadcast the gospel."

By 1935, Zoller was hosting daily programs on Detroit stations WEXI and WMBC, as well as on stations in Baltimore, New York City, and Chicago. In 1938, he inaugurated a new radio ministry, *America Back to God Hour*, which was geared toward America's servicemen. During World War II, the show was aired around the world over the War Department stations, the Mutual network, and on independent stations. Most of these radio ministries folded in 1946, signalling the end of Zoller's radio broadcasting career. After 1946, Zoller became active in tract and literature distribution.

Zoller was honored by the NRB at a special Pioneers Night in 1975. Along with Clarence Jones, Charles Fuller, and Walter Maier, Zoller was inducted into NRB's Hall of Fame for his lifelong contributions to radio broadcasting.

See also National Religious Broadcasters

SOURCES

Armstrong, Ben. *The Electric Church.* Nashville: Thomas Nelson, 1979.

Hill, George H. *Airwaves to the Soul: The Influence and Growth of Religious Broadcasting in America.* Saratoga, CA: R & E, 1983.

Appendix A
National Religious Broadcasters Founders

The National Religious Broadcasters (NRB) was founded on April 12, 1944, in Columbus, Ohio, at a special session of the annual convention of the National Association of Evangelicals (NAE). The broadcast advocacy group incorporated on December 18, 1944. The concept of an organization of religious broadcasters was first envisioned by William Ward Ayer, the first president of the NRB. Ayer's vision was tirelessly championed in the NAE by James DeForest Murch. Dale Crowley, Sr., host of *Right Start for the Day*, served as the NRB's first secretary.

The 12 founders of the NRB include

William Ward Ayer
Calvary Baptist Church, New York City

Myron Boyd
Light and Life Hour, Seattle, Washington

Dale Crowley, Sr.
Right Start for the Day, Washington, DC

Howard Ferrin
President, Barrington College,
Rhode Island

Torrey Johnson
President, Youth for Christ International,
Wheaton, Illinois

Bob Jones, Sr.
President, Bob Jones University,
Greenville, South Carolina

Charles Leaming
Faith Gospel Broadcast,
St. Petersburg, Florida

Paul Myers
Haven of Rest, Los Angeles, California

James DeForest Murch
The Christian's Hour, Ohio

Glenn Tingley
Radio Revival Hour, Toccoa Falls, Georgia

Thomas Zimmerman
Assemblies of God, Springfield, Missouri

John Zoller
Christ for Everyone, Detroit, Michigan

Appendix B
National Religious Broadcasters
Presiding Chairmen

William Ward Ayer
Calvary Baptist Church, New York City
(1944–1945)

Clinton Churchill
Whose broadcasts were heard over
WKBW Radio, Buffalo, New York
(1945–1947)

Theodore Elsner
Gospel Tabernacle, Philadelphia
(1948–1952)

Myron Boyd
Light and Life Hour, Seattle, Washington
(1952–1953)

Thomas Zimmerman
Director of radio programming for and
later president of the Assemblies of
God, Springfield, Missouri
(1954–1956)

James DeForest Murch
Editor of *United Evangelical Action* and
host of *The Christian's Hour*, Cincinnati, Ohio (1956–1957)

Eugene Bertermann
Lutheran Laymen's League, St. Louis,
Missouri (1957–1975)

Abe Van der Puy
World Radio Missionary Fellowship,
Colorado Springs, Colorado
(1975–1978)

David Hofer
Whose broadcasts were heard over
KRDU-AM, Dinuba, California
(1979–1982)

E. Brandt Gustavson
Moody Broadcasting Network, Chicago
(1982–1985)

Robert Cook
The King's Hour, Briarcliff Manor,
New York (1985–1988)

Jerry Rose
Whose television program was broadcast
over WCFC, Channel 38, Chicago
(1988–1991)

David Clark
KMC Media, Dallas, Texas (1991–1994)

Robert Straton
Walter Bennett Communications,
Philadelphia (1994–)

Appendix C
National Religious Broadcasters
Broadcasting Hall of Fame

William Ward Ayer
Founding president of NRB, 1978

Donald Grey Barnhouse
Bible Study Hour, 1978

Eugene Bertermann
Lutheran Laymen's League, 1984

Myron Boyd
Light and Life Hour, 1980

R. R. Brown
World Radio Congregation, 1976

Lois Crawford
KFGQ Radio, Boone, Iowa, 1977

Percy Crawford
Youth on the March, 1982

Richard DeHaan
Radio Bible Class, 1983

James Dobson
Focus on the Family, 1991

Bruce Dunn
Grace Worship Hour, 1994

Theodore Epp
Back to the Bible, 1986

Jerry Falwell
Old-Time Gospel Hour, 1985

Charles Fuller
Old Fashioned Revival Hour, 1975

Herman Gockel
This Is the Life, 1979

Billy Graham
Hour of Decision, 1981

Rex Humbard
Rex Humbard Ministry, 1991

Clarence Jones
HCJB World Radio, 1975

Walter Maier
The Lutheran Hour, 1975

J. Vernon McGee
Thru the Bible, 1989

Paul Myers
Haven of Rest, 1977

George Palmer
Morning Cheer, 1976

Bill Pearce
Nightsounds, 1992

Paul Rader
The Breakfast Brigade, 1976

Pat Robertson
Christian Broadcasting Network,
Family Channel, 1986

Lester Roloff
The Family Altar, 1993

Carl Smith
Consulting radio engineer, 1994

Charles Stanley
In Touch Ministry, 1988

C. M. Ward
Revivaltime, 1993

Thomas Zimmerman
General superintendent of the Assemblies
of God and narrator of *Sermons in
Song*, 1987

John Zoller
Christ for Everyone, 1975

Appendix D

Blease Amendment to the Dill Radio Control Bill of 1926

In mid-1926, the United States Senate debated a bill authored by Senator C. C. Dill of Washington State to establish a commission, later called the Federal Communications Commission, to oversee domestic commercial use of radio. The commission was to be given the power to censor broadcasting. On July 2, 1926, Senator Cole Blease of South Carolina offered an amendment to the Dill Radio Control Bill, as it was known, that would further empower the radio commission "to make and enforce regulations to censor and prohibit all discourses broadcast from stations under its control regarding the subject of evolution." Senator Blease believed that as long as the US Senate was intending to establish a commission that was empowered to censor "almost everything in the world except the question of religion," it should at least express its view on proper religious content.

Although Blease showed little concern for the passage of his amendment in Senate transcripts, he did intend to go on record against belief in evolution. As he put it, "It does not make any difference to me whether the Senate adopts the amendment or not, but I am willing for the world to know that on this proposition I am on the side of Jesus Christ." After brief discussion, the amendment was defeated.

While the Blease Amendment represented no serious effort by fundamentalists to censor evolution, its introduction and brief debate in the Senate marked the closest point fundamentalists and other conservative Christians came to imposing their antievolutionist agenda on national radio broadcast standards.

Appendix E
Sustaining Time

"Sustaining time" is the free airtime that secular radio and television networks gave to religious broadcasters after the passage of the Communications Act of 1934.

Between 1927, when the Federal Radio Commission (FRC) was established, and 1934, when the Federal Communications Commission (FCC) replaced it, strong support grew for a plan to reserve specific sections of the radio broadcast spectrum for public interest programming. Included in this category were educational, nonprofit, and religious programs. In order to make room for the new public interest stations, however, a number of successful commercial stations would be forced off the air. When the Wagner-Hatfield Amendment, a congressional amendment to the Communications Act that would have made such spectrum allocation public policy, failed in a close vote, a compromise was reached. The FCC agreed to forgo allocations of certain frequencies to noncommercial programming provided it was convinced that such action was unnecessary. In other words, secular radio network broadcasters, such as NBC and CBS, would need to allocate a certain amount of weekly airtime to public interest programming themselves, or risk unwanted federal regulation and possible denial of license renewals. These airtime allocations became known as "sustaining time."

After 1934, a large number of religious groups sought to gain their share of these allocations proposed by the major networks. It soon became apparent, however, that there was not enough airtime for everyone who wanted it, and the networks were not willing to allocate more than they had already offered. To address this problem in a rational and fair manner, an agreement was reached among the networks and such national ecumenical bodies as the Federal Council of Churches, the Southern Baptist Convention, the Jewish Seminary of America, and the National Council of Catholic Men. These large bodies agreed to sort out the competing demands of their constituents and decide which programs would be allocated the available sustaining time.

By having these mainstream ecumenical bodies act as the final allocators of sustaining-time broadcasts, independent nondenominational evangelicals and fundamentalists, who were not part of these national groups, found themselves locked out of the sustaining-time system. During this period, only the programs of member denominations, Catholics, and large evangelical churches were heard on network sustaining time. Mainline denominational officials defended this system by claiming that their programs enjoyed a large national constituency, whereas the constituency of evangelical and fundamentalist programming was limited to the Bible Belt. The great liberal churchman Harry Emerson Fosdick even went so far as to proclaim: "It is sure that we have opportunity in religion-on-the-air to make an incalculable contribution that will outflank, overpass, and undercut sectarians in religion."

Some sustaining-time programs were produced by individual denominations and some were produced cooperatively by parachurch organizations and broadcasting networks. The content of the programming included the broadcast of local church services, discussions of religious issues by prominent preachers and scholars, instructional documentaries and dramas, and conventional sermons and lectures.

With the beginning of regular television broadcasting in 1939 and 1940, the networks and local ecumenical groups provided the facilities and equipment to create religious television programs that were then used by local affiliates for broadcast on sustaining-time slots—usually early Sunday morning. In an effort to be as inoffensive as possible, much of this early television programming was bland and lifeless.

The de facto segregation of sustaining time religious broadcasting by theological origin had unforeseen consequences. First, it catalyzed evangelicals to form the National Association of Evangelicals, a parachurch group that fought against the Federal Council of Church's monopoly of Protestant noncommercial radio broadcasting. This new association was able to coax some free time for its members from the Mutual Broadcasting System and from what would become the American Broadcasting Company (ABC). Second, the Council's monopoly led to the formation of the National Religious Broadcasters, an evangelical pressure group that would have a significant impact on the future course of religious broadcasting in America.

A third unforeseen consequence was that mainline churches concentrated their broadcasting outreach on the limited sustaining-time opportunities available to them. Because they did not have to purchase this time, there was little incentive to improve programming quality or to experiment with creative innovations. In time, the sustaining-time broadcasts of the mainline churches would diminish in popularity and be outperformed by the more bold and exciting paid broadcasts of independent evangelicals.

Fourth, independent evangelicals and sectarians became adept at the economic and production aspects of paid-time broadcasting. Early

on, CBS had experimented with selling commercial time to religious programs but had decided to provide only sustaining time when the commercial broadcasts of Father Charles E. Coughlin had become an embarrassment. The only other major network to offer unrestricted commercial time to independent religious broadcasters, Mutual, was pressured to place strict conditions on this programming in 1944 by mainline denominations who were critical of its quality and content. According to these new conditions, independent broadcasters had to limit their shows to 30 minutes on Sunday mornings and refrain from on-air solicitations. In spite of these restrictions, commercial religious programs such as *The Lutheran Hour* and the *Old Fashioned Revival Hour* became hugely popular throughout the country, drawing audiences of more than 20 million.

By 1960, when the FCC decided that commercial stations could meet their public service obligations with either paid- or sustaining-time programming, as they saw fit, independent evangelical and fundamentalist broadcasters, because of their long experience with commercial broadcasting, were poised to dominate religious television and radio. In the wake of the FCC's decision, profit-conscious station managers began substituting paid independent religious programs for the sustaining-time shows produced by the networks and local church councils.

Combined with a general relaxing of governmental and industry policies with regard to paid religious programming and the emergence of new technologies such as cable and satellites, the FCC's ruling helped make conditions ripe for the explosion of independent evangelical religious broadcasting that took place during the 1970s and 1980s. Between 1970 and 1978 alone, the number of syndicated evangelical programs purchasing airtime from local stations increased from 38 to 72. Moreover, commercial religious programming increased from 58 percent to 92 percent of all religious broadcasting between 1959 and 1977. Religion had suddenly become a profit-making dimension of commercial broadcasting.

The successor to the Federal Council of Churches, the National Council of Churches, decided in 1977 to adapt to market realities and allow for the purchase of airtime for its religious programming. In 1980, CBS canceled two of its longest-running sustaining-time television series because only a few local affiliates were airing the show. In 1988, CBS canceled *For Our Times*, the last sustaining-time show available on a major network.

Appendix F

Christian Colleges and Universities
Broadcasting Programs

Conservative Christian colleges and universities throughout the United States offer state-of-the-art education in radio and television broadcasting. Many of these academic programs provide on-the-job training at campus radio and television stations. Graduates from these programs often find jobs at commercial stations and at Christian broadcast ministries.

The following Christian institutions of higher learning are among those that provide programs in broadcasting. Some of these programs include such subareas as journalism, film studies, management, performance, production, public relations, media arts, telecommunications, speech communications, computer graphics, and video production.

Anderson University, Anderson, Indiana
Ashbury College, Wilmore, Kentucky
Bethel College, St. Paul, Minnesota
Biola University, La Mirada, California
Bob Jones University, Greenville, South Carolina
Bryan College, Dayton, Tennessee
Calvin College, Grand Rapids, Michigan
Campbellsville College, Campbellsville, Kentucky
Cedarville College, Cedarville, Ohio
Cornerstone College, Grand Rapids, Michigan
Dordt College, Sioux Center, Iowa
Eastern Nazarene College, Quincy, Massachusetts
Evangel College, Springfield, Missouri
George Fox College, Newberg, Oregon
Grace University, Omaha, Nebraska
Greenville College, Greenville, Illinois
Houghton College, Houghton, New York
Huntingdon College, Huntingdon, Indiana
Johnson Bible College, Knoxville, Tennessee
Lee College, Cleveland, Tennessee
Liberty University, Lynchburg, Virginia
Malone College, Canton, Ohio
Mississippi College, Clinton, Mississippi

Mount Vernon Nazarene College, Mount Vernon, Ohio
Northwestern College, Orange City, Iowa
Northwestern College, St. Paul, Minnesota
Nyack College, Nyack, New York
Olivet Nazarene University, Kankakee, Illinois
Oral Roberts University, Tulsa, Oklahoma
Reformed Bible College, Grand Rapids, Michigan
Regents University, Virginia Beach, Virginia
Southern California College, Costa Mesa, California
Southern Nazarene University, Bethany, Oklahoma
Spring Arbor College, Spring Arbor, Michigan
Taylor University, Upland, Indiana
Toccoa Falls College, Toccoa Falls, Georgia
Trevecca Nazarene College, Nashville, Tennessee
Warner Southern College, Lake Wales, Florida
Wheaton College, Wheaton, Illinois.

Appendix G
Selected Historic Highlights of Religious Broadcasting

Some historical figures, stations, and programs mentioned in the historic highlights are not represented by entries in this book due to the incomplete nature of the information available.

1921

The first religious broadcast is aired in January over radio station KDKA, Pittsburgh, consisting of the Sunday vesper services of the Calvary Episcopal Church.

Radio Church of America is broadcast in November in New York City, becoming the first regularly scheduled religious program to air over radio.

1922

Paul Rader begins his radio broadcast ministry, becoming America's first radio evangelist.

Harry Emerson Fosdick's program, *National Vespers*, begins airing in New York City.

Aimee Semple McPherson becomes the first woman to preach over radio, delivering an evangelistic sermon in San Francisco, California.

J. C. Massee begins weekly broadcasts of his Sunday services over radio station WNAC, Boston.

1923

R. R. Brown begins his broadcast ministry in April as host of the *Radio Chapel Service*.

Aimee Semple McPherson expands her evangelistic ministry by founding radio station KFSG, Los Angeles. Broadcast begins the following February with a reading from St. John's Gospel.

1924

Dick Sheppard becomes Britain's first British religious radio personality after he begins regular broadcasts over the BBC in January.

Walter Maier founds KFUO, St. Louis, in December and begins his successful career as a radio evangelist. By 1930, his program is broadcast nationally.

1925

The Moody Bible Institute, directed by James M. Gray, receives a license to begin broadcasting from its own radio station, WMBI, Chicago. By the following summer, full operation of its hugely successful radio broadcast venture begins.

1927

The Federal Radio Commission is created to regulate the booming radio industry. Licensing requirements and broadcasting stations are introduced.

Lois Crawford becomes the first woman religious broadcaster when she is awarded a license to broadcast over radio station KFGQ, Boone, Iowa.

Donald Grey Barnhouse, minister of Philadelphia's Tenth Presbyterian Church, begins his broadcast ministry. In 1928, he become the first evangelist to buy airtime from a major network.

1928

Samuel Parkes Cadman hosts the Federal Council of Churches's *National Radio Pulpit*, the first religious program broadcast from a studio.

Convinced that religious broadcasting is a form of public service, the National Broadcasting Company (NBC) agrees to offer free or "sustaining time" to recognized religious organizations.

1930

Walter Maier's popular radio program, *The Lutheran Hour*, begins airing nationally over network radio.

The Catholic Hour, hosted by Bishop Fulton Sheen, begins radio broadcasts as part of NBC's "sustaining time" programming.

1931

The Roman Catholic Church begins radio broadcasts throughout Western Europe over Vatican Radio, Vatican City.

Percy Crawford begins broadcast of *Young People's Church of the Air*, which becomes the first religious radio program aimed at reaching America's youth.

HCJB, Ecuador, founded by Clarence Jones and Reuben Larson, begins operation in December. Known as "The Voice of the Andes," HCJB becomes the first Christian missionary radio station in the world.

1933

The Religious News Service is founded.

The Radio Ensemble of J. Elwyn Wright's New England Fellowship forms, becoming the first touring religious music group.

1934

The newly formed Mutual Broadcasting System begins selling radio time to independent evangelists, opening the airwaves to conservative Protestants.

"First Mate Bob" Paul Myers begins his long-running *Haven of Rest* program.

1937

Evangelist Charles Fuller, host of the *Old Fashioned Revival Hour*, buys national airtime from the Mutual Broadcasting System. His program draws a national audience of some 10 million listeners weekly.

1940

The first religious television broadcast airs over station W2XBS, New York.

1941

Radio Bible Class, hosted by M. R. DeHaan and originally begun with mixed success in 1938, begins daily broadcasts. DeHaan becomes one of the first religious broadcasters to send copies of his lessons to listeners upon request.

1943

Under pressure from the Federal Council of Churches to ban the sale of airtime to independent churches and religious organizations, the Mutual Broadcasting System decides to limit such sales by the end of 1944.

1944

During the annual meeting of the National Association of Evangelicals, the National Religious Broadcasters is chartered by prominent radio evangelists with the purpose of setting guidelines to raise the standards of religious broadcasting.

Faced with severe reduction in airtime for his programs, Charles Fuller forms a network of independent radio stations. Later, other religious broadcasters follow suit.

The Eternal Light, the first national Jewish radio program, airs. In 1951, it evolves into an ecumenical television program broadcast over NBC.

1946

KRDU, Dinuba, California, founded by David and Egon Hofer, becomes the first commercial Christian radio station.

1947

Faith healer Kathryn Kuhlman begins her radio ministry, becoming the most popular woman evangelist of her time.

1948

The Lutheran Hour airs New Year's Day over KSD-TV, St. Louis, becoming the first regularly scheduled television broadcast of a religious program.

The Far East Broadcasting Company begins radio transmissions from Manila, the Philippines.

1949

The American Broadcasting Company (ABC) lifts its ban on the sale of airtime to religious broadcasters.

The first prison broadcasts begin with the airing of *Prisoners Bible Broadcast*, hosted by radio revivalist Dan Gilbert.

1950

Youth on the March, hosted by evangelist Percy Crawford, becomes the first independent religious program to air over network television.

Evangelist Billy Graham enters the broadcast arena with the airing of his Atlanta crusade over local radio stations. Graham entitles his program *Hour of Decision*.

1952

Bishop Fulton Sheen begins telecast of his popular television program *Life is Worth Living*.

Norman Vincent Peale and his wife, Ruth, cohost their positive thinking television program *What's Your Trouble?*, initiating one of the first husband and wife program formats.

1953

With the airing of his Sunday services, Rex Humbard launches his successful television career. His program later evolves into the popular *Cathedral of Tomorrow*.

Controversial fundamentalist evangelist J. Harold Smith of the *Radio Bible Hour* moves his broadcasting headquarters across the border into Mexico to escape federal regulation.

1954

Tent revivalist Oral Roberts expands his healing ministry to include television. Regular broadcasts of Roberts' program begin the following year.

Paul Freed establishes "The Voice of Tangiers" radio station in Tangiers, Morocco

Bishop James A. Pike hosts *American Religious Town Hall*, the first public forum on religious issues aired over television.

Singer Mahalia Jackson becomes the first African American woman to host a radio program. Her show, *Mahalia*, airs until February 1955.

1955

Robert Schuller establishes the first drive-in church in a Southern California theater.

1956

Baptist minister Jerry Falwell begins his lifelong radio and television ministry broadcasting Sunday services from the Thomas Road Baptist Church in Lynchburg, Virginia.

1957

NBC and the Columbia Broadcasting Company (CBS) lift their bans completely on the sale of radio airtime to independent religious broadcasters.

Billy Graham's New York crusade is televised, becoming the first nationally broadcast religious revival over that medium.

1958

Clyde Narramore begins America's first Christian psychology radio program, *Psychology for Living*.

1959

Harold Camping launches Family Radio, San Francisco, the first independent religious radio station supported solely by listener contributions.

1960

Percy Crawford buys WPCA-TV, Philadelphia, becoming the first independent evangelist to own his own television station.

Trans World Radio (formerly "The Voice of Tangiers") begins broadcasting from its newly built station in Monte Carlo, Monaco.

1961

Evangelist Pat Robertson forms the Christian Broadcasting Network in Portsmouth, Virginia, airing over television under the call letters WYAH-TV.

1964

Creation of the UHF television band opens inexpensive local television airwaves to aspiring independent televangelists throughout the United States and Canada.

1966

Pat Robertson initiates the first television talkshow program, entitled *The 700 Club*.

1968

LeSea Broadcasting, headed by Lester Sumrall, initiates family-oriented radio and, later, television, featuring wholesome religious and non-religious programs as an alternative to regular network television.

1969

Eugene Scott, minister of Faith Center, Glendale, California, establishes KHOF-TV, the first all-religious television station.

1970

Robert Schuller's *Hour of Power* first airs.

1973

Jimmy Swaggart launches his televangelism career with the revival-style program *The Jimmy Swaggart Telecast*.

1977

The Christian Broadcasting Network receives a federal license to operate via satellite, opening international television broadcasting to a number of televangelists.

The Trinity Broadcasting Network, founded in Santa Ana, California, in 1973 by Paul and Jan Crouch, becomes the first television station to broadcast religious programming 24 hours-a-day.

Focus on the Family, hosted by child psychologist James Dobson, premieres in Los Angeles, California, over local radio.

1978

Radio station WYIS, Philadelphia, begins broadcasts, becoming the very first African-American owned religious radio station.

Zola Levitt begins airing his popular Jewish Christian variety programs aimed at acquainting Christian viewers with Jewish culture and religious customs.

1979

The Moral Majority, directed by Jerry Falwell, and the Freedom Forum, headed by Pat Robertson, are formed, launching religious broadcasters into national politics.

1981

The Hispanic National Religious Broadcasters organization is established.

Mother Angelica, a Franciscan nun, founds the Eternal Word Television Network, airing her homespun program *Mother Angelica Live*.

1983

Rex Humbard retires after 30 years of television broadcast ministry.

1987

Oral Roberts relates to his viewers a message he received from God telling him that unless he raises some 8 million dollars, he will be taken to heaven. Later, Roberts announces that the devil had tried to kill him while he was in bed and that he had also died and been resurrected. Though the money is raised, Roberts is ridiculed by the press as mentally unstable, becoming an embarrassment to the religious broadcasting industry.

Jim Bakker, host of *The PTL Club*, resigns over allegations of sexual misconduct. He is later tried and imprisoned for defrauding his supporters and for misappropriation of funds.

1988

During a broadcast, televangelist Jimmy Swaggart, who had condemned Jim Bakker's marital infidelity, confesses to his viewers that he is guilty of sexual perversion. Despite this, and despite being defrocked by the Assemblies of God for refusing to abide by its sanctions, Swaggart retains his broadcast ministry.

Televangelist Pat Robertson runs for the GOP nomination for President of the United States. He wins delegates only from Washington State.

1991

ABC-TV's *PrimeTime Live* uncovers financial abuses by televangelist Robert Tilton, resulting in a series of federal investigations and the eventual end of Tilton's television ministry in 1993.

1996

Radio and television ministries, such as Greater Love and Chosen People ministries, begin establishing websites on the Internet. Many abandon traditional broadcasting media in favor of the Internet.

Appendix H
Select Bibliography

Ahlstrom, Sydney E. *A Religious History of the American People*. Vol. 2. Garden City, NY: Image Books, 1975.

Alexander, Thomas G. *Mormonism in Transition: A History of the Latter-day Saints, 1890–1930*. Urbana, IL: University of Illinois Press, 1986.

Ammerman, N. T. *Bible Believers: Fundamentalists in the Modern World*. New Brunswick, NJ: Rutgers University Press, 1987.

Armstrong, Ben. *The Electric Church*. Nashville: Thomas Nelson, 1979.

Barnouw, Erik. *The Golden Web: A History of Broadcasting in the United States, 1933–1953*. New York: Oxford University Press, 1968.

Benson, Dennis C. *Electric Evangelism*. Nashville: Abingdon Press, 1973.

Beversluis, John. *C. S. Lewis and the Search for Rational Religion*. Grand Rapids. MI: Eerdmans, 1985.

Billy Graham Center Archives, Wheaton College, Wheaton, IL.

Bluem, A. William. *Religious Television Programs: A Study of Relevance*. New York: Hastings House, 1969.

Bowden, Henry Warner. *Dictionary of American Religious Biography*. Westport, CT: Greenwood Press, 1977.

Bruce, Steve. *Pray TV: Televangelism in America*. New York: Routledge, 1990.

Burgess, Stanley M., and Gary B. McGee (eds.). *Dictionary of Pentecostal and Charismatic Movements*. Grand Rapids, MI: Zondervan, 1988.

Cardwell, J. D. *Mass Media Christianity*. Lanham, MD: University Press of America, 1984.

Clabaugh, Gary K. *Thunder on the Right: The Protestant Fundamentalists*. Chicago: Nelson-Hall, 1974.

Dick, Donald. "Religious Broadcasting 1920–1965: A Bibliography." *Journal of Broadcasting* 9 (1965); 10 (1976).

Dinwiddie, M. *Religion by Radio: Its Place in British Broadcasting*. London: George Allen & Unwin, 1968.

Dollar, George W. *A History of Fundamentalism in America*. Greenville, SC: Bob Jones University Press, 1973.

Dorgan, Howard. *The Airwaves of Zion: Radio and Religion in Appalachia*. Knoxville, TN: University of Tennessee Press, 1993.

Dorsett, Lyle W. *Billy Sunday and the Redemption of Urban America*. Grand Rapids, MI: Eerdmans, 1991.

Duke, Judith S. *Religious Publishing and Communications*. White Plains, NY: Knowledge Industry Publications, 1981.

Dunning, John. *Tune in Yesterday: The Ultimate Encyclopedia of Old Time Radio, 1925–1976*. Englewood Cliffs, NJ: Prentice-Hall, 1976.

Ellens, J. H. *Models of Religious Broadcasting*. Grand Rapids, MI: Eerdmans, 1974.

Ellis, W. T. *Billy Sunday: The Man and His Message*. Philadelphia: John C. Winston, 1917.

Elvy, P. *Buying Time: The Foundations of the Electronic Church*. Great Wakering, Essex, England: McCrimmons, 1986.

Elwell, Walter A. (ed.). *Evangelical Dictionary of Theology*. Grand Rapids, MI: Baker Book House, 1984.

Erickson, Hal. *Religious Radio and Television in the United States, 1921–1991: The Programs and Personalities*. Jefferson, NC: McFarland, 1992.

Evans, Elizabeth. *The Wright Vision: The Story of the New England Fellowship*. Lanham, MD: United Press of America, 1991.

Fishwick, Marshall, and Ray B. Browne (eds.). *The God Pumpers: Religion in the Electronic Age.* Bowling Green, OH: Bowling Green State University Popular Press, 1987.

Fore, W. F. *Television and Religion: The Shaping of Faith, Values and Culture.* Minneapolis: Augsburg Publishing House, 1987.

Fowler, Gene, and Bill Crawford. *Border Radio.* Austin, TX: Texas Monthly Press, 1987.

Frankl, Razelle. *Televangelism: The Marketing of Popular Religion.* Carbondale, IL: Southern Illinois University Press, 1987.

Freed, Paul. *Towers to Eternity: Reaching the Unreached.* Chatham, NJ: Transworld Radio, 1979.

Furniss, Norman F. *The Fundamentalist Controversy, 1918–1931.* New Haven, CT: Yale University Press, 1954.

Gartenhaus, Jacob. *Famous Hebrew Christians.* Grand Rapids, MI: Baker Book House, 1979.

Gasper, Louis. *The Fundamentalist Movement: 1930–1956.* Grand Rapids, MI: Baker Book House, 1981 [1963].

Gatewood, Willard B., Jr., ed. *Controversy in the Twenties.* Nashville: Vanderbilt University Press, 1969.

Green, Roger Lancelyn and Walter Hooper. *C. S. Lewis: A Biography.* London: Souvenir Press, 1988 [1974].

Hadden, Jeffrey K., and Anson Shupe. *Televangelism: Power and Politics on God's Frontier.* New York: Henry Holt & Co., 1988.

Hadden, Jeffrey K., and Charles E. Swann. *Prime Time Preachers: The Rising Power of Televangelism.* Reading, MA: Addison-Wesley, 1981.

Hale, Julian. *Radio Power: Propaganda and International Broadcasting.* Philadelphia: Temple University Press, 1975.

Hammack, Mary L. *A Dictionary of Women in Church History.* Chicago: Moody Press, 1984.

Harrell, David Edwin, Jr. *All Things Are Possible.* Bloomington, IN: Indiana University Press, 1975.

———. *Oral Roberts: An American Life.* San Francisco: Harper & Row, 1985.

———. *Pat Robertson: A Personal, Religious, and Political Portrait.* San Francisco: Harper & Row, 1987.

Heilbut, Tony. *The Gospel Sound: Good News and Bad Times.* New York: Simon & Schuster, 1971.

Hill, George H. *Airwaves to the Soul: The Influence and Growth of Religious Broadcasting in America.* Saratoga, CA: R & E, 1983.

Hoover, Stewart M. *Mass Media Religion: The Social Sources of the Electronic Church.* Newbury Park, CA: Sage, 1988.

Horsfield, Peter G. *Religious Television: The American Experience.* New York: Longman, 1984.

Hutchison, William R. *The Modernist Impulse in American Protestantism.* New York: Oxford University Press, 1976.

Jorstad, Erling. *The Politics of Doomsday: Fundamentalists of the Far Right.* Nashville: Abingdon Press, 1970.

Kuhns, William. *The Electronic Gospel.* New York: Herder and Herder, 1969.

Liebman, R. C., and R. Wuthnow, (eds.). *The New Christian Right: Mobilization and Legitimation.* New York: Aldine, 1983.

Lippy, Charles H. (ed.). *Twentieth-Century Shapers of American Popular Religion.* Westport, CT: Greenwood Press, 1989.

Marcus, Sheldon. *Father Coughlin: The Tumultuous Life of the Priest of the Little Flower.* Boston: Little, Brown, 1973.

Marsden, George M. *Fundamentalism and American Culture.* New York: Oxford University Press, 1980.

———. *Reforming Fundamentalism: Fuller Seminary and the New Evangelicalism.* Grand Rapids, MI: Eerdmans, 1987.

Marty, Martin E. *Modern American Religion* (vol. 2: *The Noise of Conflict, 1919–1941*). Chicago: The University of Chicago Press, 1991.

Matelski, Marilyn J. *Vatican Radio: Propagation by the Airwaves.* Westport, CT: Praeger, 1995.

McLoughlin, W. G., Jr. *Billy Sunday Was His Real Name.* Chicago: University of Chicago Press, 1955.

McNeil, Alex. *Total Television: A Comprehensive Guide to Programming from 1948 to the Present.* 2d ed. New York: Penguin, 1984.

McNulty, Edward N. *Television, A Guide for Christians.* Nashville: Abingdon Press, 1976.

Meggs, Peter A. H., Everett C. Parker, and John M. Culkin. *Television-Radio-Film for Churchmen.* Nashville: Abingdon Press, 1969.

Melton, J. Gordon. *Religious Leaders of America.* Detroit: Gale Research, 1991.

Morris, James. *The Preachers.* New York: St. Martin's Press, 1973.

Murch, James DeForest. *Cooperation without Compromise: A History of the National Association of Evangelicals.* Grand Rapids, MI: Eerdmans, 1956.

Murphy, Larry G., J. Gordon Melton, and Gary L. Ward. *Encyclopedia of African American Religion*. New York: Garland, 1993.

Noll, Mark A., Nathan O. Hatch, George M. Marsden, David F. Wells, and John D. Woodbridge (eds.). *Eerdman's Handbook to Christianity in America*. Grand Rapids, MI: Eerdmans, 1983.

O'Neill, Dan. *Mother Angelica: Her Life Story*. New York: Crossroads, 1986.

Owens, Virginia S. *The Total Image, Or Selling Jesus in the Modern Age*. Grand Rapids, MI: Eerdmans, 1980.

Parker, Everett C., David W. Barry, and Dallas W. Smythe. *The Television-Radio Audience and Religion*. New York: Harper & Row, 1955.

Peck, Janice. *The Gods of Televangelism: The Crisis of Meaning and the Appeal of Religious Television*. Cresskill: Hampton Press, 1993.

Quebedeaux, Richard. *By What Authority: The Rise of Personality Cults in American Christianity*. New York: Harper & Row, 1982.

———. *I Found It! The Story of Bill Bright and Campus Crusade*. New York: Harper & Row, 1979.

———. *The Worldly Evangelicals*. New York: Harper & Row, 1978.

Randi, James. *The Faith Healers*. Buffalo, NY: Prometheus, 1987.

Rausch, David A. *Messianic Judaism: Its History, Theology, and Polity*. New York: Edwin Mellen Press, 1982.

Reid, Daniel G., Robert D. Linder, Bruce L. Shelley, and Harry S. Stout (eds.). *Dictionary of Christianity in America*. Downers Grove, IL: InterVarsity Press, 1990.

Roy, Ralph L. *Apostles of Discord*. Boston: Beacon Press, 1953.

Russell, C. Allyn. *Voices of American Fundamentalism*. Philadelphia: Westminster Press, 1976.

Ruthven, Malise. *The Divine Supermarket: Shopping for God in America*. New York: William Morrow, 1989.

Shelley, Bruce L. *Evangelicalism in America*. Grand Rapids, MI: Eerdmans, 1967.

Shephard, Charles E. *Forgiven: The Rise and Fall of Jim Bakker and the PTL Ministry*. New York: Atlantic Monthly Press, 1989.

Sholes, J. *Give Me That Prime-Time Religion*. Oklahoma: Oklahoma Book Publishing, 1979.

Stone, Jon R. *A Guide to the End of the World: Popular Eschatology in America*. New York: Garland, 1993.

Straub, Gerard T. *Salvation for Sale: An Insider's View of Pat Robertson's Ministry*. Buffalo, NY: Prometheus, 1986.

Synan, Vinson. *Twentieth Century Pentecostal Explosion*. Altamonte Springs, FL: Strang Communications, 1987.

Walsh, Chad. *C. S. Lewis: Apostle to the Skeptics*. New York: Macmillan, 1949.

Ward, Mark, Sr. *Air of Salvation: The Story of Christian Broadcasting*. Grand Rapids, MI: Baker Book House, 1994.

Wolfe, Kenneth M. *The Churches and the British Broadcasting Corporation: The Politics of Broadcast Religion*. London: SCM Press, 1984.

Wolseley, Roland E. *Interpreting the Church through Press and Radio*. Philadelphia: Muhlenberg Press, 1951.

Index

by Phillip Charles Lucas